Entrepreneurship

Canadian Edition

William D. Bygrave
Babson College

Andrew Zacharakis
Babson College

Sean Wise
Ryerson University

Contributors
Madelon Crothers, Ryerson University
Phillip Raffi, Ryerson University
Dana Abou Shackra, Ryerson University

WILEY

Production Credits

Vice President & Publisher:	Veronica Visentin
Acquisitions Editor:	Darren Lalonde
Marketing Manager:	Anita Osborne
Editorial Manager:	Karen Staudinger
Media Editor:	Luisa Begani
Production and Media Specialist:	Meaghan MacDonald
Developmental Editor:	Gail Brown
Editorial Assistant:	Maureen Lau
Cover Design:	Joanna Vieira
Cover Photo:	Image Source/Getty Images
Typesetting:	Aptara
Printing and Binding:	LSC Communications

Library and Archives Canada Cataloguing in Publication

Bygrave, William D., 1937-, author
    Entrepreneurship / William D. Bygrave, Babson College, Andrew Zacharakis, Babson College, Sean Wise, Ryerson University. —Canadian edition.
ISBN 978-1-118-90685-9 (pbk.)
1. New business enterprises. 2. Entrepreneurship. 3. Small business—Management. I. Zacharakis, Andrew, author II. Wise, Sean, 1970-, author III. Title.
    HD62.5.B94 2014   658.4'21   C2014-906820-4

Printed and Bound in the United States of America
2 3 4 5 CC 18 17

WILEY

John Wiley & Sons Canada, Ltd.
5353 Dundas Street West, Suite 400
Toronto, Ontario, M9B 6H8, Canada
Visit our website at www.wiley.ca

PREFACE

Entrepreneurship gives an economy its vitality. It gives rise to new products and services, fresh applications for existing products and services, and new ways of doing business. Entrepreneurship stirs up the existing economic order and prunes out the dead wood. Established companies that fail to adapt to the changes cease to be competitive in the marketplace and go out of business.

Within the broadest definition, entrepreneurs are found throughout the world of business because any firm, big or small, must have its share of entrepreneurial drive if it is to survive and prosper. Bygrave, *Entrepreneurship*, Canadian Edition focuses on starting and growing independent new ventures. It is based on entrepreneurship courses taught at Babson College in Massachusetts, Ryerson University in Toronto, and at universities around the world. Babson College is ranked as the top school for entrepreneurship in the world and Ryerson University is ranked as the top entrepreneurship school in Canada. This provides an excellent foundation and creates a more relevant resource for Canadian students. The Canadian edition of Bygrave, *Entrepreneurship*, has been thoroughly revised and enhanced throughout and includes cases and examples from a Canadian perspective.

Since the dawn of the twenty-first century entrepreneurial paradigms have been crystalized and startup pedagogy has evolved. One of the most common questions that entrepreneurship educators are asked is, Can entrepreneurship be taught? Our response is that anyone with a desire to become an entrepreneur will be more successful if he or she has taken a course on how to start and grow a new venture. About 30% of the students who have taken the new-venture course at Babson College since 1985 have gone on to start full-time businesses at some time in their careers. Many have started more than one.

While this textbook empowers would-be entrepreneurs to start and grow their new ventures, it's not only for them. Any student who reads this book will learn about the entrepreneurial process and the role of entrepreneurship in the economy. We believe that all business students, regardless of whether they start a new business, will benefit from learning about entrepreneurship. After all, entrepreneurship and small business create most of the jobs in the U.S. and Canadian economies. They are ubiquitous and so integral to the economy that almost every student will work in one way or another with entrepreneurs and small businesses after graduation. This textbook will stand students in good stead—not only for starting their own firms, but also for dealing with startups as investors, bankers, accountants, lawyers, customers, vendors, employees, landlords, and in any other capacity.

Information technology and the Internet have profoundly changed the way companies do business, none more so than startup companies. Today's students were born after the personal computer came into common use, and they came of age in the era of the Web. We believe they need an entrepreneurship text in which information technology is completely integrated all the way through.

This book combines concepts and cases to present the latest theory about entrepreneurship and relate actual experiences. The concepts cover what would-be entrepreneurs need to know to start and grow their businesses, and the cases illustrate how real entrepreneurs have gone out and done it. They cover all stages of the entrepreneurial process, from searching for an opportunity to shaping it into a commercially attractive product or service, launching the new venture, building it into a viable business, and eventually harvesting it. We have also included concepts such as the lean startup methodology, agile development, and customer development—all concepts that are less than a decade old.

Chapter 1 discusses the role of entrepreneurship in the economy and looks at the entrepreneurial competitiveness of nations throughout the world. Chapter 2 is an overview of the factors critical for starting a new enterprise and building it into a successful business.

Chapters 3 through 9 look in detail at what budding entrepreneurs need to do before they open their doors for business. The section starts with searching for opportunities and evaluating them. It explains how to build a workable business model and covers marketing, selling, strategy, team building, financial projections, and business planning. At the end of this section students will know how to write a business plan and how much startup capital they will need to start their ventures.

The next section, chapters 10 through 12, deals with financing businesses. Chapter 10 reviews the sources of financing for starting and growing businesses. Chapter 11 discusses the nuts and bolts of raising money, particularly equity, to start and grow a business. Chapter 12 examines debt and other sources of financing.

Entrepreneurs need to understand the legal and tax issues associated with organizing a new business. They also need to know how to protect their intellectual capital. Chapter 13 explores these topics.

Anyone can start a new venture, but very few new businesses grow into substantial enterprises. Chapter 14 discusses what it takes to grow a business into a healthy company that provides financial rewards for the entrepreneur and good jobs for employees.

Finally, Chapter 15 looks at social entrepreneurship. Today, many students are looking at business ideas that may not only earn a profit, but also address a social concern.

Each chapter is accompanied by a case study of entrepreneurs in action. We chose the cases carefully, using these criteria:

- The entrepreneurs and their companies represent a spectrum of situations and industries that is as broad as we could make it.
- The judgment point in most cases occurs in the twenty-first century.
- All stages of the entrepreneurial process are covered, from pre-startup through harvest.

There's no substitute for the experience gained from actually starting a business, but we believe that the case studies provided at the end of each chapter will enable students to gain wisdom that would take years to pick up by trial and error as entrepreneurs starting and building businesses from scratch. In Chapter 2, the end-of-chapter case features iconic Canadian entrepreneur John Sleeman and his family's legacy—Sleeman Breweries. The Chapter 4 case looks at Zumba and how three South American entrepreneurs created a new exercise craze. It explores the entrepreneurs as they try to determine the best business model for their venture. In Chapter 5 we examine Eu Yang Sang and how this highly successful Singaporean company works to grow into new global markets—specifically China and the United States. The company has to consider how customers in these markets are different and also what kinds of channels might be appropriate to reach these customers. The Chapter 7 case featuring Zeo, Inc. looks at how three college-age founders build their team. They recruit and form a scientific advisory board, and they seek and hire a CEO to help the company penetrate and build its market. Chapter 11 features Derek Szeto, founder of Red Flag Deals as he started, grew, and finally exited his successful venture. Finally,

Chapter 15 features Bruce Poon Tip founder of G Adventures, a social entrepreneurship that successfully harmonizes a profitable bottom line with environmental quality and social justice. With these and other cases and examples throughout the textbook, we are confident that the Canadian edition of Bygrave, *Entrepreneurship*, fulfills our mission of empowering and enabling young entrepreneurs.

Each chapter ends with a unique Opportunity Journal. Here students can reflect on the lessons learned and think about how to apply them to their own entrepreneurial ventures or to managing their careers. Finally, a Web exercise builds upon key concepts covered in each chapter.

Teaching Supplements

The following teaching supplements to accompany Bygrave, *Entrepreneurship*, Canadian Edition are available on the instructor's companion website at www.wiley.com/go/bygravecanada.

Instructor's Manual. The instructor's manual has been designed to facilitate convenient lesson planning and includes the following:

- *General Chapter Outline.* The main headers provide a quick snapshot of all of the chapter content.
- *Case Teaching Notes.* Detailed teaching notes go into depth on the material covered in each chapter's accompanying case. They include discussion questions, classroom activities, and additional information on the businesses and entrepreneurs from the cases.

PowerPoint Slides. A robust set of PowerPoint slides gives you the ability to completely integrate your classroom lecture with a powerful visual statement of chapter material.

Test Bank. With 60 questions per chapter, the test bank consists of multiple choice, true/false, and short answer questions of varying difficulty. A computerized version of this test bank is also available so that you can customize your quizzes and exams.

Additional Cases. In addition to the 15 cases included in the book, additional cases, available on the book's companion site, give instructors more choices and give students more real-life examples.

Videos. A hallmark of the Canadian edition is the video content integrated throughout. These videos feature author Sean Wise's series *The Naked Entrepreneur Show* (www.NakedEntrepreneur.tv). The show features interviews with prominent entrepreneurs and innovators sharing their experience, knowledge, and insight into what it takes to be a successful entrepreneur. Icons throughout the textbook indicate where related video content is available.

As well, an additional set of videos on the book's website provide students with first-hand accounts from entrepreneurs with in-depth, detailed analysis of their venture. These videos feature entrepreneurs in a question-and-answer session with students—an invaluable opportunity for students to gain first-hand knowledge.

These videos are ideal lecture launchers and a great way to grab a class's attention.

Entrepreneurship Simulation. Available with the textbook is *Traction*, a strategic entrepreneurship simulation game that allows students to develop a startup company in both pre- and post-revenue stages—focusing on the team, funding, product development, business models, internal processes, and so on. This simulation combines academic concepts and practical experience. Students learn to manage in an information-uncertain environment with an evolving business model, complete with Web access, live agent support, topical social media, grading metrics, syllabus support, and presentations of concepts. Traction provides students with an opportunity to put entrepreneurship concepts into practice. Ask your local Wiley representative for more information.

Acknowledgments

We are forever indebted to everyone involved in the entrepreneurial process who has shared their experience and wisdom with us. They include entrepreneurs from novices to old hands, informal investors, business angels, venture capitalists, bankers, lawyers, and landlords—indeed, anyone involved with entrepreneurs. We have learned so much from them. We're especially thankful for all the students and alumni we have worked with over the years. Their feedback has helped us shape what we teach and how we teach it.

We would also like to thank our student research assistants, Ryerson University graduates Madelon Crothers and Phillip Raffi. Video content was produced by Ryerson's Radio & Television faculty and managed by Dana Abou Shackra.

Many reviewers offered thoughtful suggestions that have improved this book. We are indebted to every one of them:

Richard Benedetto, *Merrimack College*

Lowell Busenitz, *University of Oklahoma*

Luella Chiasson, *Nova Scotia Community College*

Pat H. Dickson, *Georgia Institute of Technology*

Hung-bin Ding, *Loyola University*

Angelo Dossou-Yovo, *Dalhousie University*

William Gartner, *Clemson University*

Todd A. Finkle, *University of Akron*

Vance H. Fried, *Oklahoma State University*

Jeffrey June, *Miami University of Ohio*

Steve Karpenko, *Bishop's University*

Mohammad Keyhani, *University of Calgary*

Jay Krysler, *The Northern Albert Institute of Technology (NAIT)*

Nicola Lacertera, *University of Toronto*

Mark Lieberman, *USC Marshall School of Business*

Peter Miller, *Seneca College*

Heidi Neck, *Babson College*

William R. Sandberg, *University of South Carolina*

P.K. Shukla, *Chapman University*

We are indebted to our families, our patient and supportive spouses, and our beautiful and talented children. Thank you for being so understanding when we were pushing hard to meet our deadlines. Finally, much love is sent to our latest entrepreneur, born during the writing of this text, Edison Atlas Wise.

CONTENTS

Fred Lum/The Globe and Mail/The Canadian Press

Jim Balsillie, businessman, philanthropist, and co-founder and former co-CEO of BlackBerry (formerly Research In Motion).

THE POWER OF ENTREPRENEURSHIP

CHAPTER OUTLINE

Entrepreneurship and Small Business in Canada

Learning Objective 1.1 Describe entrepreneurship and small business in Canada.

Causes of the Entrepreneurial Revolution

Learning Objective 1.2 Outline the causes of the entrepreneurial revolution.

Global Entrepreneurship Monitor (GEM)

Learning Objective 1.3 Describe what the Global Entrepreneurship Monitor (GEM) is and outline the principal findings from GEM.

Twenty-First-Century Economies: Anglo-Saxon or Social Models?

Learning Objective 1.4 Compare the Anglo-Saxon economic system and the social model.

THIS IS THE entrepreneurial age. More than 500 million people worldwide either were actively involved in trying to start a new venture or were owner-managers of a new business in 2012.[1]

More than 99,000 new businesses are born each year in Canada.[2] Entrepreneurs are driving a revolution that is transforming and renewing economies worldwide. Entrepreneurship is the essence of free enterprise because the birth of new businesses gives a market economy its vitality. New and emerging businesses create a large proportion of the innovative products and services that transform the way we work and live, such as personal computers (PCs), computer software, the Internet and the World Wide Web (WWW or the Web), social media, biotechnology drugs, overnight package deliveries, and big-box stores. They also generate most new jobs; from 2001 through 2011, companies with 100 or fewer employees created 43% of all new jobs in Canada.[3]

There has never been a better time to practise the art and science of entrepreneurship. But what is entrepreneurship? Early in the twentieth century, Joseph Schumpeter, the Moravian-born economist writing in Vienna, gave us the modern definition of an entrepreneur: a person who destroys the existing economic order by introducing new products and services, by introducing new methods of production, by creating new forms of organization, or by exploiting new raw materials. According to Schumpeter, that person is most likely to accomplish this destruction by founding a new business, but may also do it within an existing one.

Schumpeter explained how entrepreneurs had suddenly increased the standard of living of a few industrialized nations.[4] When the Industrial Revolution began in England around 1760, no nation had enjoyed a standard of living equal to that of Imperial Rome 2,000 years earlier. However, from 1870 to 1979, the standard of living of 16 nations jumped sevenfold, on average.[5]

Very few new businesses have the potential to initiate a Schumpeterian "gale" of creative destruction, as Apple Computer did in the computer industry. The vast majority of startups enter existing markets. So, in this textbook, we adopt a broader definition of entrepreneurship than Schumpeter's. Ours encompasses everyone who starts a new business. Our entrepreneur

The Changing Economy

General Motors was founded in 1908 as a holding company for Buick. On December 31, 1955, General Motors became the first American corporation to make over $1 billion in a single year. At one point, it was the largest corporation in the United States in terms of its revenues as a percentage of gross domestic product (GDP). In 1979, its employment in the United States peaked at 600,000. In 2008, General Motors reported a loss of $30.9 billion and burned through $19.2 billion in cash. In a desperate attempt to save the company in February 2009, GM announced plans to reduce its total U.S. workforce from 96,537 people in 2008 to between 65,000 and 75,000 in 2012. By March 2009, GM, which had already received $13.4 billion of bailout money from the U.S. government, was asking for an additional $16.6 billion. The Obama administration forced GM's CEO, Rick Wagoner, to resign; his replacement, Fritz Henderson, said that bankruptcy was a real possibility. It became a reality when GM filed for bankruptcy in June and emerged a shrunken company 40 days later. In 2012, its U.S. workforce was 77,000.

Walmart, the world's largest corporation, was founded by Sam Walton in 1962. As of 2014, Walmart had 2.2 million employees and 11,119 stores in 27 countries worldwide. Walmart recorded sales of $476.29 billion and earnings of $15.88 billion.

"We're all working together; that's the secret. And we'll lower the cost of living for everyone, not just in America, but we'll give the world an opportunity to see what it's like to save and have a better lifestyle, a better life for all. We're proud of what we've accomplished; we've just begun."

—Sam Walton (1918–1992)

is the person who perceives an opportunity and creates an organization to pursue it. Moreover, the entrepreneurial process includes all the functions, activities, and actions associated with perceiving opportunities and creating organizations to pursue them. Our entrepreneur's new business may, in a few rare instances, be the revolutionary sort that rearranges the global economic order, as Walmart, FedEx, Apple, Microsoft, Google, eBay, and Amazon have done and social networking companies such as Facebook and Twitter are now doing. But it is much more likely to be of the incremental kind that enters an existing market.

In this chapter, we will look at the importance of entrepreneurship and small business to Canada and the global economies, describe the entrepreneurial revolution, present a conceptual model for the entrepreneurial sector of the economy, and use it to explain major factors in the revolution; finally, we will compare and contrast entrepreneurial activity among nations within the context of the conceptual model.

Entrepreneurship and Small Business in Canada

In 2011, there were approximately 1.1 million employer-owned Canadian businesses, of which approximately 98% were small businesses.[6] In general, businesses with 100 or fewer employees are classified as small.[7] They employed approximately 5 million individuals in Canada, or 48% of the total labour force in the private sector.[8] Not only are small businesses the engine for job creation, but they are also a powerful force for innovation. Their share of Canadian research and development (R&D) accounted for 31% of the total R&D expenditure.[9]

Approximately 55% of the employer-owned small businesses in Canada have one to four employees.[10] About one-half of the full-time businesses in Canada are unincorporated, while the other half are incorporated.[11] Self-employment is more prevalent among men, white Canadians, and Asians; and it is more common in construction, services, and agriculture industries.[12]

At any one time, approximately 15% of Canadians in the labour force[13] deem themselves "a nascent entrepreneur" trying to create a new business; they have conceived an idea for a new venture and have taken at least one step toward implementing their idea. Many of them abandon their ventures during the gestation period and never actually open their businesses; nonetheless, an average of 100,000 new ventures are born in Canada each year.[14] Two in every three businesses are started in the owner's home. Most of these new ventures remain tiny because they are part-time businesses (e.g. SMEs). Approximately 55% of businesses in Canada have less than four employees.[15]

Survival rates for new businesses have been the focus of several different studies. One of the most thorough was done by the Analytical Studies branch of Statistics Canada, which calculated the five-year survival rates of business establishments. It found that 77% of new ventures survive for at least one year, but only 36% of new ventures survive their first five years.[16] Survival rates also varied somewhat by industry, but not as strongly as with age and size.

Referring to Figure 1.1, a **high-growth firm** is a firm whose business generates significant positive cash flows or earnings, which

A survey by the Bank of Montreal found the following:[17]

- Almost half of Canadian postsecondary students surveyed—46%—said they see themselves starting a business after graduation.

A survey by the Business Development Bank of Canada (BDC) found the following:[18]

- Almost 45% of Canadians who intend to start a new business say they are motivated by a desire to seize an opportunity.

- In fact, 44.4% of those who intend to start a business said that one of their main reasons was the desire to take advantage of a business opportunity. This compares to only 7.7% who said they wanted to start a business because they had no other choice.

Entrepreneurial Performance Indicator	2001	2002	2003	2004	2005	2006
Birth rate	9%	10%	9%	10%	10%	12%
Death rate		8%	9%	8%	9%	
1-year survival rate		87%	85%	86%	85%	85%
2-year survival rate			74%	73%	73%	70%
3-year survival rate				65%	63%	62%
4-year survival rate					58%	53%
5-year survival rate						51%
Proportion of high-growth firms (employment)				4%	4%	4%
Proportion of high-growth firms (sales)				7%	7%	8%
Proportion of gazelles (employment)						0.5%
Proportion of gazelles (sales)						1.1%

* Includes only firms with paid employees.

Source: Data from Industry Canada, *The State of Entrepreneurship in Canada, 2010,* Table 3, p. 9, www.ic.gc.ca/eic/site/061.nsf/vwapj/SEC-EEC_eng.pdf/$file/SEC-EEC_eng.pdf.

Figure 1.1

Canada's performance from 2001 to 2006 on key indicators of entrepreneurial performance

The World Bank estimates that Canada ranks well in measures such as the number of procedures, time, and cost of starting a business. For example, Canada ranks first with only one procedure required to start a business; third in terms of ease of starting a business; and 10th for total time spent starting a business (about five days). Also, based on the cost of starting a business Canada ranks fifth, at about 0.4% of income per capita, compared to 1.4% in the U.S., which ranks 20th. According to Statistics Canada, the costs of corporate registration requirements are on average $181 per business ($22 per employee) with over $67 million total per year.[i]

[i] Industry Canada, *Determinants of Entrepreneurship in Canada: State of Knowledge*, October 2014.

increases at significantly faster rates than the overall economy, whereas a **gazelle** is a company with an annual growth rate of 20% or more, as measured in sales revenue.[19] These companies typically sustain this growth for at least four years and begin with sales of at least $1 million.

Of course, survival does not necessarily spell success. In general, the median income of small business owners is almost the same as that of wage and salary earners. However, the income distribution is much broader for small business owners, which means that they are more likely to have significantly less income or significantly more income than wage and salaried workers.[20] But small business owners are also building equity in their companies as well as taking income from them, so it is possible that small business owners are better off overall than their wage-earning cohorts. However, a study of business owners disposing of their businesses through sale, closure, passing it on, and other methods found that comparatively few saw their standard of living changed by their business. Only 17% reported that their business had raised their standard of living, while 6% reported the opposite.[21]

Looking back at the new business formation index, we can see that it was stable through the 1950s and most of the 1960s; there was virtually no growth. By 1970, net new business formation was growing, and the growth continued through the 1970s and 1980s and into the 1990s.[22] No one noticed the change at the time. One of the first documented references to what was taking place was in a December 1976 article in *The Economist* called "The Coming Entrepreneurial Revolution."[23] In this article, Norman Macrae argued that the era of big business was drawing to an end and that future increases in employment would come mainly from either smaller firms or small units of big firms. In 1978, David Birch published his book *Job Creation in America: How Our Smallest Companies Put the Most People to Work*.[24] The title says it all. It captures the important finding from Birch's comprehensive study of business establishments.

No issue gets the attention of politicians more than job creation. Birch's findings and the stream of research that ensued forever changed the attitude of policymakers toward small business.[25] Until then, most of their focus had been on big business. After all, in 1953 Charles Erwin Wilson, then GM president, is reported to have said during the hearings before the Senate Armed Services Committee, "What's good for General Motors is good for the country." At the time, GM was one of the largest employers in the world—only Soviet state industries employed more people.[26]

Entrepreneurial Revolution

On November 1, 1999, Chevron, Goodyear Tire & Rubber Company, Sears Roebuck, and Union Carbide were removed from the Dow Jones Industrial Average (DJIA) and replaced by Intel, Microsoft, Home Depot, and SBC Communications. Intel and Microsoft became the first two companies traded on the NASDAQ exchange to be listed in the DJIA. This event symbolized what is now called the *entrepreneurship revolution* that transformed the North American economy in the last quarter of the twentieth century. Intel and Microsoft are the two major entrepreneurial driving forces in the information technology revolution that has fundamentally changed the way in which we live, work, and play. SBC (formerly Southwestern Bell Corporation) was one of the original "Baby Bells" formed after the U.S. Department of Justice antitrust action resulted in the breakup of AT&T. It is an excellent example of how breaking up a monopoly leads to entrepreneurial opportunities. And Home Depot exemplifies the big-box stores that have transformed much of the retail industry.

Intel was founded in Silicon Valley by Gordon Moore and Robert Noyce and funded by Arthur Rock, the legendary venture capitalist. Gordon Moore, the inventor of Moore's Law,[27] and Robert Noyce, one of the two inventors of the integrated circuit,[28] had been at the birth of Silicon Valley with William Shockley, the co-inventor of the transistor, when Shockley Semiconductor Laboratory was founded in Mountain View in 1956. They left Shockley in 1957 to found Fairchild Semiconductor, which in 1961 introduced the first commercial integrated circuit. In 1968, they left Fairchild to start Intel.

Ted Hoff, employee number 12 at Intel, invented the microprocessor in 1968. In 1971, Intel launched the first commercial microprocessor, heralding a new era in integrated electronics. Then, in 1974, it launched the first general-purpose microprocessor, the Intel 8080, which was the brain of the first personal computer,[29] the Altair 8800—a $439 hobbyist's kit—announced by MITS (Micro Instrumentation and Telemetry Systems of Albuquerque) on the front cover of the January 1, 1975, edition of *Popular Electronics*.

According to personal computer folklore, Paul Allen, then working at the minicomputer division of Honeywell in Massachusetts, hurried to his childhood friend and fellow computer enthusiast, Bill Gates, who was a Harvard sophomore, and waving *Popular Electronics* with a mock-up of the Altair 8800 on its front cover, exclaimed, "This is it! It's about to begin!" Within a month or so, Gates had a version of BASIC to run on the Altair. He and Allen joined together in an informal partnership called Micro-Soft and moved to Albuquerque.

> "When I was 19, I caught sight of the future and based my career on what I saw. I turned out to have been right."
>
> –Bill Gates

Microsoft grew steadily by developing software for personal computers. By 1979 it had moved to Bellevue, Washington, near Seattle, where Gates and Allen had grown up. It then had revenue of more than $2 million and 28 employees. It got its big break in 1980–1981 when, building on the core of a product acquired from Seattle Computer

Rob Kinmonth/Time & Life Pictures/Getty Images

Bernard Marcus and Arthur Blank, founders of Home Depot

Products, Microsoft introduced MS-DOS for IBM's first PC. Fourteen years later, when Microsoft released Windows 95 in 1995, it sold 4 million copies in four days. Its success helped to move the personal computer into 250 million homes, businesses, and schools worldwide. In the early 1990s, Microsoft committed itself to adding Internet capabilities to its products. When Microsoft joined the DJIA in 1999, there were more than 200 million Internet users, up from 3 million just five years earlier.

SBC came about in 1984 because of the breakup of AT&T. SBC's growth has come mainly through acquisitions, so we are not making the case that SBC itself is especially entrepreneurial. However, the breakup of AT&T did unleash a wave of entrepreneurship that produced the explosive growth of the telecommunications industry in the last 20 years. According to a recent survey, the top five innovations since 1980 are the Internet, cellphones, personal computers, fibre optics, and email.[30] Without a doubt the phenomenal growth of wireless communications and the Internet would not have happened if AT&T had been allowed to keep its pre-1983 stranglehold on the telecom industry. (AT&T floundered after it was broken up. In 2004 it was dropped from the DJIA, and in 2005 it was acquired by SBC, which then adopted AT&T, Inc. as its corporate name; as a result, AT&T's legendary "T" ticker symbol on the New York Stock Exchange returned to the DJIA.)

Home Depot was founded in 1979 by Bernie Marcus and Arthur Blank. The chain of hardware and do-it-yourself (DIY) stores holds the record for the fastest time for a retailer to pass the $30 billion, $40 billion, $50 billion, $60 billion, and $70 billion annual revenue milestones. It is the second largest retailer in the United States, surpassed only by Walmart. And it almost set the record for the fastest time from starting up to joining the DJIA when it was only 20 years old. By comparison, Walmart was 35 years old when it displaced F. W. Woolworth in the DJIA. Along with Walmart, Home Depot has set the pace for the retail industry in the last two decades. Together, the two account for more than 2% of U.S. GDP and 1.7 million jobs.

BlackBerry, formerly known as Research In Motion (RIM), is a global leader in wireless innovation and is headquartered in Waterloo, Ontario. Mike Lazaridis and Douglas Fregin, two Canadian entrepreneurs, founded the technology giant in 1984. The duo managed to raise $30 million in pre-IPO financing before the company went public on the Toronto Stock Exchange (TSX) in 1998.[31] As of December 1, 2012, BlackBerry had 79 million users globally[32] and continues to be a leader in wireless handheld devices.

The Toronto Stock Exchange (TSX), which was officially created in 1861, has gone through many transformations and iterations throughout the years.[33] The index originally listed 18 securities and was formally incorporated in 1878 by an act of the Ontario legislature. The TSE, an index that tracked the 300 most influential stocks listed on the TSX, was created in 1977 and is similar to the DJIA, which lists the top stocks on the New York Stock Exchange (NYSE).[34] In 2002, Standard & Poor's agreed to take over management of the TSE 300 Composite Index. It was renamed to its current name, S&P/TSX Composite Index.

In 1987, the TSE 35 composite index was created, which comprised Canada's 35 largest corporations. This was followed by Toronto 35 Index Participation units called TIPs and later Toronto 100 Index units called HIPs—now known as ETFs (exchange traded funds). In 2000, these products merged into the iUnits S&P/TSE 60 Index Participation Fund; and in 2006, the fund name was changed to the iShares CDN S&P/TSX 60 Index Fund, the name it uses today (see Figure 1.2).[35]

The companies listed on the TSE 35 to the now S&P/TSX 60 Index Fund have gone through many transformations throughout the years. The most obvious changes can be seen in

2006		2014	
Royal Bank of Canada	Nortel Networks Corp.	Royal Bank of Canada	First Quantum Minerals Ltd.
Manulife Financial Corp.	National Bank of Canada	Toronto Dominion	Teck Resources Ltd.
Bank of Nova Scotia	Canadian Pacific Railway Ltd.	Bank of Nova Scotia	Talisman Energy Inc.
Encana Corporation	Husky Energy Inc.	Suncor Energy Inc.	Catamaran Corp.
Toronto-Dominion Bank	Magna International Inc.	Canadian National Railway Company	Canadian Oil Sands Ltd.
Suncor Energy Inc.	Thomson Reuters Corporation	Bank of Montreal	Cameco Corp.
Bank of Montreal	Penn West Petroleum Ltd.	Valeant Pharmaceuticals International	Power Corp. of Canada
Canadian Natural Resources Limited	Tim Hortons Inc.	Canadian Natural Resources Limited	Silver Wheaton Corp.
Barrick Gold Corporation	Yellow Pages Income Fund	Enbridge Inc.	Shaw Communications Inc.
Canadian Imperial Bank of Commerce	Shaw Communications Inc.	Manulife Financial Corp.	Husky Energy Inc.
Canadian National Railway Company	Agnico-Eagle Mines Limited	Canadian Imperial Bank of Commerce	Arc Resources Ltd.
Sun Life Financial	Canadian Tire Corp. Ltd.	BCE Inc.	CGI Group Inc.
Petro-Canada	Bombardier Inc.	Transcanada Corporation	Tim Hortons Inc.
Research In Motion	Ipsco Inc.	Potash Corporation of Saskatchewan	Canadian Tire Corp. Ltd.
Goldcorp Inc.	Kinross Gold Corp.	Canadian Pacific Railway Ltd.	Yamana Gold Inc.
BCE Inc.	Transalta Corporation	Barrick Gold Corp.	SNC-Lavalin Group Inc.
Talisman Energy Inc.	Agrium Inc.	Brookfield Asset Management Inc.	Saputo Inc.
Alcan Inc.	Loblaw Cos. Ltd.	TELUS Corp.	Fortis Inc. (Canada)
TELUS Corp.	Cognos Inc.	Goldcorp Inc.	Agnico-Eagle Mines Limited
Transcanada Corporation	Lundin Mining Corp.	Magna International Inc.	Gildan Activewear Inc.
Rogers Communications Inc.	Fording Canadian Coal Trust	Sun Life Financial	Bombardier Inc.
Teck Resources Ltd.	Ace Aviation Holdings Inc.	Cenovus Energy Inc.	Kinross Gold Corp.
Brookfield Asset Management Inc.	George Weston Ltd.	Encana	Metro Inc.
Potash Corporation of Saskatchewan	Nordion Inc.	Rogers Communications Inc.	BlackBerry Ltd.
Nexen Inc.	Biovail Corp.	Crescent Point Energy Corp	Eldorado Gold Corporation
Cameco Corporation	Nova Chemicals Corporation	Agrium Inc.	Loblaw Cos. Ltd.
Enbridge Inc.	Novelis Inc.	National Bank of Canada	Penn West Petroleum Ltd.
Canadian Oil Sands Trust	Celestica Inc.	Thomson Reuters Corporation	Enerplus Corp.
Imperial Oil Ltd.	Domtar Inc.	Imperial Oil Ltd.	George Weston Ltd.
Shoppers Drug Mart Corp.	Cott Corporation	Shoppers Drug Mart Corp.	Transalta Corporation

Source: http://ca.ishares.com/product_info/fund/holdings/XIU.htm

Figure 1.2

iShares CDN S&P/TSX 60 Index Fund companies

the financial and energy sectors. In 2006, the financial sector held 33.05% of the fund while the energy sector held 30.02%. In 2014, both the financial and energy sector were still dominating the fund, but the financial sector had increased its holding to 37.05% while the energy sector had fallen to 22.9%.[36]

Perhaps one of the most revolutionary entrepreneurial ideas outside of high-tech industries was Fred Smith's notion to deliver packages overnight anywhere in the United States. Smith identified a need for shippers to have a system designed specifically for air freight that could accommodate time-sensitive shipments such as medicines, computer parts, and electronics in a term paper that he wrote as a Yale undergraduate. Smith's professor did not think much of the idea and gave it a 'C' grade. After tours of duty in Vietnam, Smith founded his company, Federal Express (FedEx) in 1971, and it began operating in 1973 out of Memphis International Airport. In the mid-1970s, Federal Express had taken a leading role in lobbying for air cargo deregulation, which finally came in 1977. These changes allowed Federal Express to use larger aircraft and spurred the company's rapid growth. Today FedEx has the world's largest all-cargo air fleet, including McDonnell Douglas MD-11s and Airbus A-300s and A-310s.[37]

In 1971, when Southwest Airlines began operations, *interstate* airline travel was highly regulated by the U.S. federal government, which had set up the Civil Aeronautics Board (CAB) in 1938 to regulate all domestic air transport as a public utility, setting fares, routes, and schedules. The CAB was required to ensure that the airlines had a reasonable rate of return. Most of the major airlines, whose profits were virtually guaranteed, favoured the system. Not surprisingly, competition was stifled, and almost no new airlines attempted to enter the market. However, *intrastate* passenger travel was not regulated by the CAB, so Southwest, following the pioneering path of Pacific Southwest Airline's (PSA's) service within California, initiated passenger service within Texas. The success of PSA and Southwest in providing cheap airline travel within California and Texas provided powerful ammunition for the deregulation of *interstate* travel, which came about in 1981 as a consequence of the Airline Deregulation Act of 1978.[38] Since deregulation, more than 100 startup airlines have inaugurated interstate scheduled passenger service with jet aircraft.[39] Herb Kelleher, the charismatic co-founder of Southwest Airlines, is often credited with triggering airline deregulation by persevering with his legal battle to get Southwest airborne in the face of fierce legal opposition from Braniff, Trans-Texas, and Continental Airlines. Two of those airlines took their legal battle all the way to the U.S. Supreme Court, which ruled in Southwest's favour at the end of 1970.[40]

Dennis "Chip" Wilson, born March 3, 1956, is a Canadian businessman and entrepreneur who founded several retail apparel companies. The most notable of them is the yoga-inspired athletic apparel company lululemon athletica, commonly referred to as lululemon.[41] Wilson attended his first yoga class in 1997 and was quickly inspired; by 1998 he had started lululemon, which he quickly built into a leading retailer of yoga apparel for men and women. lululemon reached revenues of $100 million in the mid-2000s and went public in 2007, raising $327.6 million through the public offering.[42] By 2011, the company had expanded rapidly and had generated revenues of $1 billion.[43]

WestJet, founded in 1996 by Clive Beddoe and four partners, is currently Canada's second-largest airline behind Air Canada. WestJet was created on the premise of offering patrons a lower-cost alternative to flying without sacrificing the quality of flight and service. Initially, the airline had three aircraft, 220 employees, and only flew to five Canadian destinations.[44] Incorporating a unique corporate culture, WestJet has established a solid footing within the airline industry. WestJet was inducted into the corporate hall of fame after being named one of Canada's most admired corporate cultures in 2005, 2006, 2007, and 2008. The company offers each of their 9,600 employees the opportunity to purchase company shares through an employee share purchase plan (ESPP).[45] Currently, WestJet has a fleet of 98 aircraft and is Canada's leading high-value low-fare airline and offers flights to 76 unique destinations in Canada, the United States, Mexico, and the Caribbean.[46]

Robert Swanson was 27 when he hit upon the idea that a company could be formed to commercialize biotechnology. At that time, he knew almost nothing about the field. By reading the scientific literature, Swanson identified the leading biotechnology scientists and contacted them. "Everybody said I was too early—it would take 10 years to turn out the first microorganism from a human hormone or maybe 20 years to have a commercial product—everybody except Herb Boyer."[47] Swanson was referring to Professor Herbert Boyer at the University of California at San Francisco, co-inventor of the patents that, according to some observers, now form the basis of the biotechnology industry. When Swanson and Boyer met in early 1976, they almost immediately agreed to become partners in an endeavour to explore the commercial possibilities of recombinant DNA. Boyer named their venture Genentech, an acronym for genetic engineering technology. Just seven months later, Genentech announced its first success, a genetically engineered human brain hormone, somatosin. According to Swanson, they accomplished 10 years of development in seven months. Most observers say it was Swanson's entrepreneurial vision that brought about the founding of the biotech industry. By 2012, there were about 1,850 U.S. biotech companies with combined revenues of more than $87 billion.[48]

At almost the same time that Swanson was starting Genentech in southern San Francisco, not many miles away Steve Jobs and Stephen Wozniak were starting Apple Computer in Silicon Valley. Their computer, the Apple I in kit form, was an instant hit with hobbyists. The Byte Shop—the first full-time computer store anywhere in the world, which opened in Silicon Valley in December 1975—ordered 25 of them in June 1976. The owner of The Byte Shop asked Jobs to put the Apple I computer board in a case because his customers were asking for complete units, not just kits. When they did so, both Apple and The Byte Shop had a hot product on their hands. The Byte Shop grew to a chain of 75 stores. "Without intending to do so, Wozniak and Jobs had launched the microcomputer by responding to consumer demand."[49]

Genentech's initial public offering (IPO) in October 1980, followed by Apple's IPO only two months later, signalled that something magical was stirring in the biotech and personal computer industries. It triggered a wave of venture capital investment and IPOs in both industries.

A tipping point in the infant personal computer industry was the introduction of the VisiCalc spreadsheet. Dan Bricklin conceived it when he was sitting in an MBA class at Harvard in 1978, daydreaming about how he could make it easier to do repetitive calculations. Bricklin designed the prototype software to run on an Apple II. Together with Bob Frankston he formed a company, Software Arts, to develop the VisiCalc spreadsheet. When they introduced their first version in May 1979, it turbocharged the sale of Apple computers. Subsequently, sales of IBM PCs were rocketed into the stratosphere by Mitch Kapor's Lotus 1-2-3 worksheet.

The late 1970s and early 1980s were miraculous years for entrepreneurial ventures in the computer industry. Miniaturization of hard-disk drives, a vital component in the information technology revolution, was pioneered by Al Shugart, first at Shugart Associates, then at Seagate Technology. Dick Eagan and Roger Marino started EMC Corporation in 1979, initially selling computer furniture, and with the seed money from that, they launched into selling Intel-compatible memory. From that beginning, Eagan and Marino built EMC into a company that during the 1990s achieved the highest single-decade performance of any listed stock in the history of the New York Stock Exchange. Today it is the dominant company in the data storage industry.

Robert Metcalfe, the inventor of Ethernet, founded 3Com in 1979 to manufacture computer network products. 3Com built its business around Ethernet plug-in cards for personal computers. Today Ethernet is so widely used that it is usually built into most PC motherboards.

Michael Dell, while still a student at the University of Texas, Austin, in 1984, began selling IBM-compatible computers built from stock components that he marketed directly to customers. By concentrating on direct sales of customized products, Dell became the largest manufacturer of personal computers in the world, and Michael Dell was CEO longer than any other executive in the PC hardware industry.

Geoffrey Ballard, a Canadian geophysicist and businessman, founded Ballard Research Inc. in 1979 to develop commercial applications in high-energy lithium batteries. In 1983, and operating under the name Ballard Power Systems, Ballard ventured into the development of proton exchange membrane fuel cells, which later evolved into full-scale prototype systems.[50] Ballard worked with automakers such as Daimler and Ford Motor Company to evolve

Household electricity (1873)	46 years
Telephone (1875)	35 years
Automobile (1885)	55 years
Airplane travel (1903)	54 years
Radio (1906)	22 years
Television (1925)	26 years
VCR (1952)	34 years
PC (1975)	15 years
Smart Phones (2002)	10 years
World Wide Web (1992)	5 years
Facebook (2009)	5 years
Tablet (2011)	3 years

Source: The Wall Street Journal, June 1997; http://en.wikipedia.org/wiki/Advanced_Mobile_Phone_Service; www.netbanker.com/2000/04/internet_usage_web_users_world.html; http://blogs.hbr.org/2013/11/the-pace-of-technology-adoption-is-speeding-up/ (smartphones); www.imagingnotes.com/go/article_free.php?mp_id=186 (Facebook); www.technologyreview.com/news/427787/are-smart-phones-spreading-faster-than-any-technology-in-human-history/ (tablet).

■ Figure 1.3

Time for new technologies to penetrate 25% of U.S. population

their use of lithium batteries in motor vehicles.[51] In 1999, Ballard was named "Hero of the Planet" by *Time* magazine[52] because his technology continues to help companies incorporate high-efficiency technologies that do not negatively impact the environment.

Entrepreneurs were at the conception and birth of new products and services that have transformed the global economy in the last 35 years. However, what is turning out to be the biggest of them all began in 1989 when Tim (now Sir Timothy) Berners-Lee conceived the World Wide Web. We are in the midst of a revolution that is changing our lives more profoundly and faster than anyone could have imagined before the Web became operational in 1992. No major new product has been adopted as quickly by such a large percentage of the population as the Web.

The Web: Three Revolutions Converge

In 1989, when Tim Berners-Lee wrote a proposal to develop software that resulted in the World Wide Web, he was not the first to conceive the idea. As far back as 1945, Vannevar Bush proposed a "memex" machine with which users could create information "trails" linking related text and illustrations and store the trails for future reference.[53]

As it turned out, he was 50 years ahead of the technologies that were needed to implement his idea. After all, the first digital computer was then only a couple of years old. Fifteen years later Ted Nelson, inspired by Bush's "memex," was the first person to develop the modern version of hypertext. He wrote—prophetically, as it turned out—in 1960 that "the future of humanity is at the interactive computer screen . . . the new writing and movies will be interactive and interlinked . . . we need a world-wide network to deliver it."[54]

But Nelson, too, was far ahead of the technology. In 1962, there were fewer than 10,000 computers in the world. They cost hundreds of thousands of dollars, they were primitive machines with only a few thousand bytes of magnetic core memory, and programming them was complicated and tedious. AT&T had a monopoly over the phone lines that were used for data communication. And the ARPANET, which was the forerunner of the Internet, had not yet been conceived.[55]

Berners-Lee was a 25-year-old physics graduate of Oxford University working as a consultant at CERN, the European Particle Physics Laboratory in Geneva, Switzerland, in 1980

	Population (2011 estimate)	Internet Users Dec. 31, 2000	Internet Users Dec. 31, 2011	Penetration (% Population)	Growth 2000–2011
Africa	1,037,524,058	4,514,400	139,875,242	14%	2988%
Asia	3,879,740,877	114,304,000	1,016,799,076	26%	790%
Europe	816,426,346	105,096,093	500,723,686	61%	376%
Middle East	216,258,843	3,284,800	77,020,995	36%	2245%
North America	347,394,870	108,096,800	273,067,546	79%	153%
Latin America/Caribbean	597,283,165	18,068,919	235,819,740	40%	1205%
Oceania/Australia	35,426,995	7,620,480	23,927,457	68%	214%
WORLD TOTAL	6,930,055,154	360,985,492	2,267,233,742	33%	528%

Source: internetworldstats.com, http://www.internetworldstats.com/stats.htm.

■ **Figure 1.4**

World Internet usage and population statistics

when he wrote his own private program for storing information using the random associations the brain makes. His Enquire program, which was never published, formed the conceptual basis for his future development of the Web.[56] In 1980, the technology existed for implementing Berners-Lee's concept, but the power of the technology was low and the installed base of computers was tiny compared to what it would be 10 years later.

By 1989, when he revived his idea, three revolutions were ready for it. They were in *digital technology, information technology (IT)*, and *entrepreneurship*. The semiconductor revolution enabled the digital revolution, which in turn enabled the IT revolution. By 1992, when the Web was released by CERN, the Internet had 1 million hosts, computers were 1,000 million times faster, and network bandwidth was 20 million times greater than 20 years earlier. The entrepreneurship revolution meant that there was an army of entrepreneurs and would-be entrepreneurs, especially in the United States, with the vision and capacity to seize the commercial opportunities presented by the Web. In February 1993, the National Center for Supercomputing Applications (NCSA) released the first alpha version of Marc Andreessen's Mosaic. By December 1994, the Web was growing at approximately 1% a day—with a doubling period of less than 10 weeks.[57] In the next 10 years, Internet usage exploded.[58] By 2009, users numbered 1.7 billion, which was about 25% of the entire population of the world (see Figure 1.4).

Entrepreneurship Revolution Strikes Gold

Marc Andreessen moved to Silicon Valley in 1994, teamed up with veteran IT entrepreneur Jim Clark, and incorporated Mosaic Communications (later renamed Netscape Communications). Clark put $6 million of his own money into Mosaic, and venture capitalists added another $6 million.[59] Their intent was to create a browser that would surpass the original Mosaic. It was a classic Silicon Valley startup with programmers working 18-hour days, seven days a week, sometimes even working 48 hours at one stretch just coding. In October 1994, the Netscape browser was posted as a download on the Internet. In no time at all, it was the browser of choice for the majority of Web users; in December 1994, Netscape Communications began shipping Netscape Navigator, which started to produce income.

Netscape Navigator was an instant success, gaining 75% of the browser market within four months of its introduction. Netscape Communications was only 16 months old when it went public in August 1995. Its IPO was one of the most spectacular in history and made Jim Clark the first Internet billionaire. According to an article in *Fortune*, "It was the spark that touched off the Internet boom."[60]

A gold rush was under way. "Netscape mesmerized investors and captured America's imagination. More than any other company, it set the technological, social, and financial tone of the Internet age."[61] A generation of would-be entrepreneurs was inspired by Netscape's success. What's more, corporate executives from established businesses wanted to emulate Jim Barksdale, the former president of McCaw Communications, who joined Netscape's board in October 1994, became CEO in January 1995, and made a huge fortune in just eight months. Investors—both angels and venture capitalists—hustled to invest in Internet-related startups. It seemed as if everyone was panning for Internet gold, not only in Silicon Valley but throughout North America—and a couple of years later throughout the rest of the world.

Netscape is a superb example of American venture capital at its best, accelerating the commercialization of innovations, especially at the start of revolutionary new industries driven by technology. Venture capital was in at the start of the semiconductor and the minicomputer industries in the late 1950s and early 1960s and the biotech and personal computer industries in the late 1970s, and now it was eager to invest in what promised to be the biggest revolution of them all, the Internet and the Web.

Venture capital is not invested exclusively in technology companies. It was in at the beginning of the overnight package delivery industry with its investment in Federal Express, at the start of major big-box retailers such as Home Depot and Staples, and at the creation of new airlines, including JetBlue. No wonder Jiro Tokuyama, then dean of the Nomura School of Advanced Management in Japan and a highly influential economist, stated that entrepreneurial firms and venture capital are the great advantages that North Americans have.[62] Since the early 1970s, approximately $500 billion of venture capital has backed 32,000 U.S. companies. In 2010, those venture-backed companies employed more than 12 million people, or 11% of the private-sector employment, and generated revenues of $3.1 trillion, or 21% of the U.S. GDP.[63]

In Canada, venture capital has had a tremendous impact on the development of small and medium-sized enterprises. This can be best depicted by a report completed by Thompson Reuters, which stated the following:

> *Increased Canadian VC market activity in 2013 was reflected in most regions of the country. Ontario led trends in dollar terms, showing $676 million invested last year, or 35% of the domestic market total. Ontario-based disbursements were also up 3% from 2012. Year-over-year growth was greater in Québec, which saw $589 million invested in 2013, or 46% more than in 2012, giving it a 30% share of the Canada-wide number.*
>
> *British Columbia experienced the largest increase of any Canadian region in 2013, with VC invested totaling $478 million, or better than double the $198 million invested the year before. This gave the province an above-average 24% market share. Alberta-based VC activity also expanded last year, with $155 million invested in total, compared to $96 million invested in 2012.[64]*

During a 1999 news conference at the World Economic Forum in Davos, Switzerland, reporters pestered Bill Gates again and again with variations of the same question: "These Internet stocks, they're a bubble?" An irritated Bill Gates finally confronted the reporters: "Look, you bozos, of course they're a bubble, but you're all missing the point. This bubble is attracting so much new capital to the Internet industry; it is going to drive innovation faster and faster."[i]

[i] T. L. Friedman, *The World Is Flat* (New York, NY: Farrar, Straus, and Giroux, 2005), 72.

The Web presented numerous opportunities that were soon being exploited by entrepreneurs. It created a huge demand for more capacity on the Internet, which in turn presented opportunities for hardware and software entrepreneurs. They were fortunate to find venture capitalists eager to invest in their startups. The period from 1996 through 2000 was a golden era for classic venture capitalists and the entrepreneurial companies they invested in.[65] It was golden both metaphorically and literally, as more and more venture capitalists and entrepreneurs seemed to have acquired the Midas touch. Some of the financial gains from venture capital–backed companies were indeed of mythological proportions. For instance, Benchmark Capital's investment of $5 million in eBay multiplied 1,500-fold in just two years.[66]

True, Benchmark's investment in eBay set the all-time record for Silicon Valley, but there were plenty of instances when investments increased at least a hundredfold and in some cases a thousandfold. With investments such as those, overall returns on classic venture capital soared, with the one-year return peaking at 143% at the end of the third quarter in 2000, compared with average annual returns in the mid-teens prior to the golden era.

However, in 2000, the Internet bubble burst; the gold rush had come to an end. Many companies failed, others were forced into fire-sale mergers, investors were hammered, many jobs were lost, and doom and gloom were pervasive. There was much hand wringing about the incredible wastefulness of the U.S. method of financing new industries. However, by August 9, 2005—the tenth anniversary of Netscape's IPO—some companies founded during the gold rush were thriving. The market capitalization of just four of them—Google, eBay, Yahoo, and Amazon—was about $200 billion, which handily exceeded all the venture capital invested in all the Internet-related companies through 2000; what's more, it even topped the combined amount raised from venture capital and IPOs. Granted, there were many more losers than winners, but five years after the bust it was clear that society as a whole had already benefited mightily and the best was yet to come—but not for everyone. As Schumpeter observed, revolutionary entrepreneurship creates new products, services, and business methods that undermine and sometimes destroy old ones.

Creative Destruction

The Web is blowing gales of creative destruction through many old industries, none more so than that of print newspapers, whose publishers were slow to recognize that their business models were endangered—perhaps fatally—by the Web. Some long-established U.S. newspapers, such as the *Rocky Mountain News* and the *Tucson Citizen*, shut down completely; others have drastically reduced their operations; and a few, including the *Christian Science Monitor* and the *Seattle-Post Intelligencer*, now publish only on the Web and no longer produce print editions. *Newsweek's* final print edition was published on December 31, 2012, ending almost 80 years in print. Several prominent newspaper chains, including the Tribune Company, the Minneapolis Star Tribune, Philadelphia Newspapers, and the Sun-Times Media Group, have filed for bankruptcy. The 2009 demise of *Editor and Publisher*, the 125-year-old trade magazine for the newspaper industry, seemed to symbolize the plight of the industry.

Newspapers had not only withstood potential competition from the introduction of other forms of news broadcasting, such as radio in the 1920s and 1930s, television in the 1950s, and 24-hour cable news channels in the 1980s and 1990s, but had actually prospered more and more. Why, then, should they have foreseen in the early 1990s the havoc that the fledgling Web was about to wreak on their industry? What most print publishers did not foresee was that the Web would undermine the two basic sources of newspaper revenues: advertising and paid circulation. Annual ad revenue, for example, plunged from its peak of more than $60 billion in 2000 to $20 billion in 2012.[67] The underlying cause is the changes in society brought about by the Internet, which was used by about 80% of the U.S. population in 2012 compared with less than 3% in 1993.[68] Web portals such as Yahoo, social networking services such as Twitter, and individual bloggers give readers instant access to breaking news stories and often break news ahead of the old media; Google and other search engines make it easy to find stories from anywhere in the world at lightning speed; and perhaps best of all, most web content is free. For advertisers, the allure of the Web over print newspapers and magazines is that it allows them to target ads to individuals—every Web user is now a market segment of just one individual—and it provides much better metrics for tracking the effectiveness of ads.

The Internet has devastated the North American print media's business model, and publishers are groping for a new one. Some think it will be a hybrid of print and the Web; others believe that print will continue to lose ground to the Web and more papers will publish only

Web editions. And what else in this age of government bailouts? Some in the U.S. Congress have even proposed a "Newspaper Revitalization Act" to help ailing newspapers.[69] Similar trends regarding the use of the traditional newspaper have also risen in Canada. Recent data released by Statistics Canada shows that the majority of Canadians (63.7%) went online in 2007 to read about news or sports.[70] This is primarily because of the ease of access, vast resource of information, and the ability to participate in community interaction. In 2007, 29.2% of Canadians went online to read comments by other community members regarding trending media topics.[71]

For non-Internet-related companies or sectors, there are other determinants in creatively destroying a business or even an entire industry. Those determinants are related to the 10x rule, which states that you must be 10x cheaper, smaller, faster, and more efficient compared to current market trends to overcome and creatively destroy the incumbents.[72] A classic example of this concept is email, which destroyed snail mail because email is 10x faster.

Causes of the Entrepreneurial Revolution

Canada has always been a nation of entrepreneurs. But why has it become more and more entrepreneurial since the end of the 1960s—creating what is now called the entrepreneurial revolution?

First, we need to step back and look at the U.S. economy (which has had, and continues to have, the biggest impact on the Canadian economy) in the decades before the 1970s. The Great Depression, which followed the stock market collapse of October 1929, had an enormous effect on society. By 1932, when Franklin Roosevelt was elected president, over 13 million Americans had lost their jobs, and the gross national product had fallen 31%. The Roosevelt administration implemented many policies to try to bring the nation out of the Depression, but it was not until World War II that the nation once again started to become prosperous. The end of the war in 1945 heralded an era of economic growth and opportunity. But the memories left by the Depression meant that workers wanted secure jobs with good wages and benefits that medium and big companies offered. And big business was booming.

The period from the late 1940s to the 1960s was the era of the corporate employee. The era was immortalized by William Whyte in *The Organization Man*,[73] in which he "argued in 1956 that American business life had abandoned the old virtues of self-reliance and entrepreneurship in favor of a bureaucratic 'social ethic' of loyalty, security and 'belongingness.' With the rise of the postwar corporation, American individualism had disappeared from the mainstream of middle-class life."[74] The key to a successful career was this: "Be loyal to the company and the company will be loyal to you." Whyte's writing assumed the change was permanent and it favoured the large corporation.

Big American businesses were seen as the way of the future, not just in North America but worldwide. John Kenneth Galbraith's seminal book *The New Industrial State*[75] and Jean-Jacques Servan-Schreiber's *Le Défi Américain* (The American Challenge)[76] both "became the bible to advocates of industrial policies"[77] supporting big business. Both books were instant best sellers. *Le Défi Américain* sold 600,000 copies in France alone and was translated into 15 languages. Galbraith wrote in 1967, "By all but the pathologically romantic, it is now recognized that this is not the age of the small man." He believed that the best economic size for corporations was "very, very large."

The works of Whyte, Galbraith, and Servan-Schreiber were required reading in universities through the 1970s. Schumpeter's work was hardly ever mentioned,[78] and when it was, it was his book *Capitalism, Socialism, and Democracy*, published in 1942,[79] in which he was very pessimistic that capitalism would survive. Unlike Karl Marx, who believed the proletariat would bring about the downfall of capitalism, Schumpeter reasoned that the very success of free enterprise would create a class of elites who would favour central control of the economy and thereby curb free enterprise. His first book, *The Theory of Economic Development*,[80] originally published in German in 1911, in which he endorsed entrepreneurship, was hardly ever mentioned. What's more, in the 1970s there was an abundance of university courses dealing with Karl Marx and almost none dealing with entrepreneurship. It's not surprising that the world was first alerted to the entrepreneurial revolution by a journalist, Norman Macrae, rather than by an academic scholar. About a decade later, researchers confirmed retrospectively that entrepreneurial activity had indeed been on the increase in the United States in the 1970s.[81]

Entrepreneurship did not disappear in the 1930s, 1940s, 1950s, and 1960s; it simply did not grow very much. What brought about the change in the economy that stirred up entrepreneurship around 1970? To try to understand what changes were taking place, we need to look at the social, cultural, and political context of an economy. A framework for this perspective is presented in Figure 1.5, the Global Entrepreneurship Monitor (GEM) model for the economy.[82]

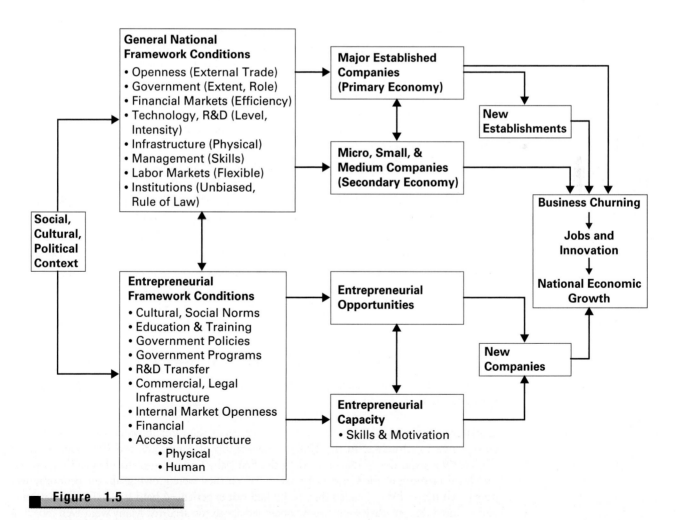

Figure 1.5

GEM model of economic growth

The central argument[83] of the GEM model is that national economic growth is a function of two sets of interrelated activities: those associated with established firms and those related directly to the entrepreneurial process. Activity among established firms explains only part of the story behind variations in economic growth. The entrepreneurial process may also account for a significant proportion of the differences in economic prosperity among countries and among regions within countries.

Regardless of the country, looking at the nature of the relationship between entrepreneurship and economic growth, it is important to distinguish between entrepreneurial opportunities and entrepreneurial capacity. What drives entrepreneurial activity is that people perceive opportunities and have the skills and motivation to exploit them. The outcome is the creation of new firms and, inevitably, the destruction of inefficient or outmoded existing firms. Schumpeter's process of creative destruction is captured in the model by business churning. Despite its negative connotation, creative destruction actually has a positive impact on economic growth—declining businesses are phased out as startups manoeuvre their way into the market. These dynamic transactions occur within a particular context, which the GEM model calls *entrepreneurial framework conditions* and which includes factors such as availability of finance, government policies, and programs designed to support startups, R&D transfer, physical and human infrastructure, education in general, education and training for entrepreneurship, cultural and social norms, and internal market openness.

Over the last four centuries, entrepreneurs have helped drive the Canadian economy forward. It started with Aboriginal peoples trading amongst themselves, and when the Europeans arrived they started a lucrative global fur trade. In the nineteenth century, the city of Toronto began to challenge Montreal's dominance over the Canadian economy.[84] Throughout this era, businesses arose that would dominate the Canadian business landscape, such as Timothy Eaton's department stores, Peter Larkin's Salada Tea Company, and George Cox's Canada Life Insurance.[85] We have seen signs of entrepreneurship in Canadians for many years, but in recent years more people are becoming or thinking of becoming entrepreneurial. What are the reasons for this sudden change or trend? Industry Canada has outlined three primary reasons:

- The implicit understanding between employers and employees has changed. In the past, people expected to be retained as employees as long as they did their jobs. Recent economic downturns, though, have been accompanied by downsizing, and people want to regain control over their paycheques by starting their own business.[86]

- People—especially younger people—increasingly prefer an independent lifestyle. They want to do work they like and have autonomy over their hours and working conditions.[87]

- Entrepreneurs have become influential. Canadian entrepreneurs are celebrated in their communities and in the media, and in an age where people are cynical about many public figures, they are becoming new role models.[88]

Changes in the Entrepreneurial Framework Conditions

Now let's look at some of the major changes in the framework conditions that have fuelled the entrepreneurial revolution.

Cultural and Social Norms. First, let's consider the most important components, the entrepreneurs themselves. In the 1960s, a generation of Americans and Canadians born in the late 1930s and the 1940s—including the first baby boomers—came of age. They had no first-hand memory of the Great Depression. When they were growing up, the economy was doing well most of the time, so they really had not experienced hard times like their parents had endured. Hence, they were not as concerned about job security. Many were even rebelling against large corporations, some of which were seen as members of the military–industrial complex that was supporting the unpopular war in Vietnam; some companies were trading with South Africa, where apartheid still prevailed; and others were under attack by consumer activists such as Ralph Nader.[89] It was a generation who were better educated than their parents, and for them starting a new business was a credible career.

The *Fortune* 500 employed 20% of the American workforce in the 1960s. That percentage began to decline in 1980 and continued to do so every year since then, down to about 10% by 2005. Hence, jobs in big companies became scarcer. Many companies downsized, and according to George Gendron, who was the publisher of *Inc.* magazine during the 1980s and 1990s, 20% of downsized executives started businesses. Gendron also suggested that some of the executives who were retained—often the "best and the brightest"—became disillusioned by their career prospects in stagnant companies, which led to a "second exodus" that produced more entrepreneurial activity.[90]

Other important social changes boosted entrepreneurship in the 1990s. More women became business owners, and the proportion of firms owned by visible minorities increased (especially among the Asian, Hispanic, and black populations). According to Gendron, for people with limited options in employment, entrepreneurship represents the "last meritocracy."

Another social boost to entrepreneurship came from people like Ian Portsmouth, publisher and editor of *Profit* magazine. *Profit* is Canada's most-read publication for entrepreneurs and small businesses. Portsmouth is a passionate believer in the power of entrepreneurship, which is illustrated in the various articles within *Profit* that focus on how to find and seize an opportunity within Canada. *Profit* is published six times per year and is Canada's most-read and best-targeted publication for entrepreneurs and small business executives.[91]

Government. The 1970s were the decade when the U.S. government bailed out companies such as Penn Central Railroad, Lockheed, and Chrysler. Washington seemed more concerned with big business than with small. But it did recognize the need to pay attention to startups with high potential, especially the ones funded by venture capitalists. There had been a burst of venture capital–backed startups in the last half of the 1960s. But in the early 1970s, venture capital dried up to a trickle. Looking back from the perspective of almost 50 years, when $26.7 billion of new money flowing into the venture capital industry seems routine, it is scarcely believable that only $10 million of new money was committed in 1975. The U.S. Congress took urgent steps in 1978 to stimulate the venture capital industry, including reducing the capital gains tax and easing the ERISA prudent man rule, which had inhibited pension funds from investing in venture capital funds. The pension floodgates opened, and the inflow of venture capital increased to $4.9 billion by 1987. Likewise, venture capital invested in portfolio companies increased from a low of $250 million in 1975 to $3.9 billion in 1987—a sixteen-fold increase.[92]

The U.S. government asserted its role of ensuring *market openness* by minimizing anti-competitive behaviour. We've already mentioned that legislation toward the end of the 1970s deregulated the airfreight and airline passenger industries. That was followed in the early 1980s by the U.S. Justice Department's move to break up AT&T's monopoly.

The U.S. government deserves immense credit for its funding of R&D in government, universities, and corporations, both directly and indirectly through purchases of products. Its support was vital in the development of the computer, communications, biotech, and many other industries.

Washington activated the Small Business Innovation Research (SBIR) program in 1983 to ensure that small businesses shared some of the federal R&D dollars for new technology-based developments. In 2009, around 5,800 awards, totalling $2.2 billion, went to small businesses as a result of the SBIR program. In general, funds awarded under the SBIR program go to develop new technologies that are high risk and high reward. Some might say it is pre-venture capital money. From that viewpoint, $2 billion is a significant amount when compared with

$1.7 billion that venture capitalists invested in 350 seed-stage companies in 2009. A total of $30 billion has been awarded over the 28 years of the SBIR program through to 2010.[93] Symantec, Qualcomm, DaVinci, and iRobot received R&D funding from this program.

The Canadian government has also implemented programs and various government subsidiaries that help businesses with financing, growth, and international import/export guidelines.

In September 1944, the Canadian Parliament proclaimed the creation of the Industrial Development Bank (IDB).[94] With an eye to the future, the government recognized that it would need to stimulate economic growth and help create new jobs for Canadians once the war ended. On July 13, 1995, the Business Development Bank of Canada Act was adopted.[95] This statute gave the BDC a broadened and dynamic public interest mandate under which the bank pays special attention to exporting businesses and to businesses in the technology sector.

Export Development Canada (EDC) is Canada's export credit agency. It supports the development of Canada's export trade by helping Canadian companies respond to international business opportunities.[96] It also provides insurance, financial services, and small business solutions to Canadian exporters and investors.

The Canadian government also recognized the importance of supporting young entrepreneurs and their business ideas. The Canadian Business Youth Foundation (CYBF), which is now called Futurepreneur Canada, was established in 1996 and has invested in more than 5,600 young Canadian entrepreneurs.[97] Futurepreneur offers entrepreneurs four fully integrated services that are built around the life cycle of a young entrepreneur, helping to ensure the development and success of every new startup or small business. The services include prelaunch expertise, online business resources, financing opportunities, and expert mentoring. So far, Futurepreneur has created 23,000 new Canadian jobs and $163.6 million in tax revenue.[98]

Research and Development. Commercial development of intellectual property resulting from federally funded research is a major benefit to the Canadian economy. The Canadian government offers two incentive programs to businesses conducting research and innovative projects: the Scientific Research and Experimental Development (SR&ED) program and the Industrial Research Assistance Program (IRAP).

The SR&ED program is a federal tax incentive program administered by the Canada Revenue Agency (CRA) that encourages Canadian businesses of all sizes and in all sectors to conduct research and development (R&D) in Canada. The SR&ED program gives claimants cash refunds or tax credits for their expenditures on eligible R&D work done in Canada. The purpose of the program is to incentivize companies to further their R&D, thereby leading to new, improved, or technologically advanced products or processes. The SR&ED program is the largest single source of federal government support for industrial R&D.[99] Thus far, Canadian-controlled private corporations (CCPC) reap the largest SR&ED benefits. They can earn SR&ED tax credits for 35% of eligible expenditures up to the first $2 million.[100] Any expenditure above the $2 million threshold is eligible for tax credits of 20%. Additionally, other Canadian corporations, such as public companies, partnerships, and trusts, can earn tax credits equivalent to 20% of eligible R&D expenditures.[101]

IRAP is headed by the National Research Council (NRC) and has been providing developing enterprises with funding for over 60 years. IRAP provides financial support to qualified small and medium-sized companies in Canada to help them undertake innovative technology initiatives. To be eligible for IRAP, a company must have 500 or fewer full-time employees. IRAP aims to stimulate Canada's technology innovation by investing in projects that strengthen the national technology industry. The program typically offers nonrepayable grants ranging from $10,000 to $250,000. Furthermore, IRAP goes beyond financial assistance by providing companies with strategic support by connecting enterprises with established industry professionals.

Physical Infrastructure. The biggest change in entrepreneurship in the last 10 years is due to the Web, the great equalizer. Small businesses now have at their fingertips a tool so powerful that it is levelling the playing field. Big businesses no longer enjoy as many scale economies as they did before the Internet. Information that could have been gathered only by a multitude of market researchers can now be found with a search engine and a couple of clicks of a mouse. Entrepreneurs don't have to spend a fortune to reach customers with print, radio, and television advertising; they can target their potential customers anywhere in the world via the Web. When they want to find a vendor, the Web is there to help them—as it is when they are seeking employees, bankers, and investors. Furthermore, the cost of communications of all kinds (except snail mail) has plummeted since AT&T was broken up. A long-distance telephone call that cost 40 cents a minute in 1980 now can be made for as little as 1 cent. And if these entrepreneurs need to travel by air, they can shop the Web to find the cheapest plane ticket, automobile rental, and hotel room.

The worldwide distribution of goods and services is now open to everyone. Just consider what eBay has already done to change the entrepreneurial landscape. According to a 2005 study by ACNielsen International Research, 724,000 Americans report that selling on eBay is their primary or secondary source of income.[103] A similar study conducted in 2006 found that more than 33,000 Canadian sellers use eBay as a primary or secondary source of income.[104] An entrepreneur can sell merchandise to a customer anywhere in the world; PayPal (founded in 1998 and now part of eBay) can ensure that the entrepreneur receives payment speedily and securely online, the merchandise can be delivered to the buyer within a day or so via FedEx, and the buyer and seller can track the shipment online at each step of its journey.

Andrew Burton/Getty Images

Twitter co-founders (left to right) Jack Dorsey, Biz Stone, and Evan Williams on the floor of the New York Stock Exchange (NYSE) on November 7, 2013 after Twitter's initial public offering.

Outsourcing services and goods makes companies more efficient and effective. Entrepreneurs can now focus on their company's core competency and let vendors take care of noncore items such as payroll, Web hosting, telemarketing, manufacturing, and distribution. There are even companies that will help entrepreneurs find outsource partners. Outsourcing enables small businesses to act like big ones, and some small companies are even called *virtual companies* because they outsource so much of their work.

For some entrepreneurs, business incubators combine many of the advantages of outsourcing. Incubators provide not only physical space but also shared services. Many incubators also provide ready access to human infrastructure. In 1980, there were only 12 business incubators in the United States; over the period between 1985 and 1995, the number of U.S. incubators grew fifteenfold, from 40 to nearly 600[105]—and by 2006, there were some 1,115 incubators.[106] The National Business Incubation Association (NBIA) estimated that in 2005 alone, North American incubators assisted more than 27,000 startup companies that provided full-time employment for more than 100,000 workers and generated annual revenue of more than $17 billion.[107]

According to the Canadian Association of Business Incubation (CABI), there are approximately 130 startup incubators in Canada. These include both physical locations as well as virtual incubators that help startups with funding and early-stage growth.[108] A few noteworthy incubators include Vancouver's GrowLab and Version One Ventures, and Toronto's Extreme Startups and Digital Media Zone.

Human Infrastructure. Access to human infrastructure is as important as access to physical infrastructure—maybe more so. The human infrastructure for entrepreneurs grew rapidly in the last 20 years or so, and gaining access to it has never been easier. Thirty years ago starting a new venture was a lonely pursuit fraught with pitfalls that would have been avoided by someone with prior entrepreneurial experience. Today numerous entrepreneurship experts gladly help people who are starting or growing companies. There are support networks, both informal and formal, of professionals who know a lot about the entrepreneurial process. Just search the Web for "entrepreneur AND assistance AND *your town*," and you might be astonished by the number of hits.

Education, Training, and Professionalization. Entrepreneurship education and training is now readily available, which is part of the professionalization of entrepreneurship that has taken place over the last 20 years.[109] According to Gendron, a body of knowledge and skills has developed over the last 20 years to enhance the chances of entrepreneurial success. A good illustration is the widely dispensed advice that would-be entrepreneurs should write a business plan before they launch their new ventures. The world of entrepreneurship is awash with information about business plans. The field has come a long way since the pioneers of entrepreneurship training put writing a business plan at the core of their programs in the 1970s.[110]

When Babson College and the University of Texas started their internal business plan competitions in 1985, only a few schools had entrepreneurship courses. Now more than 60% of four-year colleges and universities have at least one entrepreneurship course, and many have entrepreneurship centres. Today entrepreneurship training courses are readily available to all sectors of the population.

In Canada, Ryerson University has aggressively focused on promoting entrepreneurial courses within the business curriculum. Ryerson has one of the largest entrepreneurship departments in Canada, with both major and minor degree programs. Ryerson also hosts a yearly business plan competition, providing students with first-hand experience while obtaining valuable feedback and ideas for improving their business plan from industry experts. The two winning participants are each given a $25,000 cash prize to help them successfully launch their business.

The Accidental Entrepreneur

Like many other scientists and engineers who have ended up founding companies, I didn't leave Caltech as an entrepreneur. I had no training in business; after my sophomore year of college I didn't take any courses outside of chemistry, math, and physics. My career as an entrepreneur happened quite by accident.

There is such a thing as a natural-born entrepreneur . . . But the accidental entrepreneur like me has to fall into the opportunity or be pushed into it. Most of what I learned as an entrepreneur was by trial and error, but I think a lot of this really could have been learned more efficiently.

—Gordon Moore (co-founder of Fairchild Semiconductor in 1957 and Intel in 1968).

Source: G. E. Moore, The Accidental Entrepreneur, Engineering & Science 57 (Summer 1994): 23–30; http://nobelprize.org/physics/articles/moore.

Financial. Raising money for a new business is seldom easy, but the process of raising startup and expansion capital has become more efficient in the last 20 years or so. In 1982, for instance, an economist at the National Science Foundation stated that venture capital was shrouded in empirical secrecy and an aura of beliefs.[111] The same held true for angel investing. In contrast, today there is an abundance of help. The amount of venture capital under management has grown from $3.7 billion in 1980 to $199 billion in 2012.[112] We do not have reliable numbers for business angel investors, but we do know that informal investors—everyone from parents to external business angels—now invest more than $100 billion annually in startup and baby businesses. Furthermore, informal investors are ubiquitous. Five percent of American adults report that they "invested" in someone else's venture in the last three years.[113] It is impossible to claim that the availability of financing has driven the entrepreneurial revolution, but it does appear that sufficient financing has been available to fuel it.

Canada's Venture Capital and Private Equity Association (CVCA) is dedicated to pursuing growth opportunities for the Canadian venture capital and private equity industry. Currently, Canada's venture capital and private equity industry represents over $105 billion in capital under management.[114] Deal-making activity showed moderate growth in 2013 with $12.3 billion in funding, a 5% increase from 2012, which transacted $11.8 billion in funding.[115]

Angel investing in Canada also plays a significant role in startup and small-business funding. The Ontario Securities Commission estimates that there are up to 500,000 accredited investors in Canada.[116] The Organisation for Economic Co-operation and Development (OECD) estimates that angel investors invest between $500 million and $1 billion annually in Canada's growth-oriented companies.[117] Angel investors typically invest within sectors they are familiar with and play an active role in mentoring the company's founder while assuming a position on the company's board.

Churning and Economic Growth

Technological change, deregulation, competition, and globalization presented countless opportunities that entrepreneurs seized and commercialized. It caused a lot of **churning**, or Schumpeter's creative destruction. But 11 new businesses with employees were started for every 10 that died over the decade 1990–2000.[118] It is this churning that gives the economy its vitality. Only a society that willingly adapts to change can have a dynamic economy.

We can find examples of churning in every industry that is not a monopoly or a regulated oligopoly. Who can recall VisiCalc or for that matter Lotus 1-2-3? At the height of their fame they were two of the most widely used software packages for PCs. Today Excel is the spreadsheet of choice. In one week alone in May 1982, when Digital Equipment Corporation (DEC) introduced its ill-fated Rainbow PC, four other companies introduced PCs.[119] At the peak of the PC industry frenzy in the early 1980s, more than 200 companies either had introduced PCs or were planning to do so. Only a handful of PC manufacturers exists today. DEC, which in 1982 was the second-largest computer manufacturer in the world, was eventually bought by Compaq, which in turn merged with Hewlett-Packard. In 2004, IBM sold its PC division to Lenovo, a company founded in 1984 by a group of academics at the government-backed Chinese Academy of Sciences in Beijing.

Entrepreneurial competition, according to Schumpeter, "strikes not at the margins of the profits . . . of the existing firms but at their foundations and very lives." Established companies that stick with their old ways of doing business self-destruct as their customers turn to new competitors with better business models.

Not only did the advent of the PC churn up the entire computer industry, but it also virtually wiped out the typewriter industry. And it changed the way office work is organized. Secretaries had to learn computer skills or they were out of work.

And who knows what the future holds for the PC itself? In February 2013, one of the giants of the PC industry, Dell Inc., is likely to be bought out by a group of investors headed by Michael Dell, its founder; Dell is hoping to revive the company, whose sales are dropping as laptop PCs face increasing competition from tablet computers like the iPad and smartphones. Indeed, in 2013 Schumpeterian disruptions abound throughout the information technology space: The PC industry is being upset by mobile technologies, and servers and data storage are being challenged by the cloud.

More examples abound of churning: Southwest Airlines is now the most successful U.S. airline; two of its giant rivals in 1971 no longer exist, and the third, Continental, has been bankrupt twice, in 1983 and 1990. United Airlines, US Airways, Hawaiian Airlines, ATA Airlines (also known as American Trans Air), Delta, Northwest, Aloha Airlines, and American Airlines have all been in Chapter 11 bankruptcy, and only a handful of the 100 or so passenger airlines started up since deregulation are still around. Skyservice, a Canadian charter airline that employed approximately 2,000 people filed for bankruptcy in March 2010.[120] Increased competition from WestJet, Porter, and Air Canada coupled with an increase in fuel costs forced the Toronto-based airline to wind up operations. And who goes to a travel agent to get a regular airline ticket or book a hotel room today? Where is the fax machine headed? Likewise for video stores and CD retailers? Why are newspapers laying off workers? Who is buying a film camera? And even entrepreneurship academics had to watch out. Donald Trump, building on his TV success with *The Apprentice*, started Trump University in 2005 to teach—what else?—entrepreneurship; but so far success has eluded Trump in the education field.

> *"The power of Walmart is such, it's reversed a 100-year history in which the manufacturer was powerful and the retailer was sort of the vassal . . . It turned that around entirely."*
> —Nelson Lichtenstein,
> University of California,
> Santa Barbara

Granted, churning causes a lot of disruption—and nowhere more than in the lives of those who lose their jobs as a result. But overall society is the beneficiary. Entrepreneurship produces new products and services, it increases productivity, it generates employment, and in some cases it keeps inflation in check. Economists estimate that Walmart alone knocked 20%—perhaps as much as 25%—off the rate of inflation in the 1990s.[121] According to Alfred Kahn, the father of airline deregulation, airline passengers are now saving $20 billion a year.[122] And with Skype and the Internet, you can "talk to anyone, anywhere in the world for free. Forever."[123]

Next we will look at how various nations are faring with entrepreneurship.

Global Entrepreneurship Monitor (GEM)

The Global Entrepreneurship Monitor (GEM) was conceived in 1997[124] to study the economic impact and the determinants of national-level entrepreneurial activity. GEM is the largest coordinated research effort ever undertaken to study population-level entrepreneurial activity. Since its inception, a total of 99 economies accounting for approximately 95% of the world's GDP and 85% of its population have participated in GEM's annual study. Because of its worldwide reach and rigorous scientific method, GEM has become the world's most influential and authoritative source of empirical data and expertise on the entrepreneurial potential of nations.[125]

The main objectives of GEM are to gather data that measure the entrepreneurial activity of nations and other data related to entrepreneurial activity; to examine what national characteristics are related to levels of entrepreneurial activity; and to explain how differences in entrepreneurial activity are related to different levels of economic growth among nations. GEM distinguishes between two types of entrepreneurial activity:[126]

◉ *Nascent entrepreneurs* are individuals who are actively trying to start a new business but who have not yet done so.

◉ *Baby business managers* are owner-managers of a new business that is no more than 42 months old.

There are three main measures of entrepreneurial activity:

◉ **TEA (total entrepreneurial activity)** is the percentage of the adult population that is either nascent entrepreneurs or baby business owner-managers or both. It measures the overall entrepreneurial activity of a nation.

- ▣ **TEA (opportunity)** is the percentage of the adult population that is trying to start or has started a baby business to exploit a perceived opportunity. They are classified as improvement-driven opportunity motivated if they additionally seek to improve their income or independence through entrepreneurship.
- ▣ **TEA (necessity)** is the percentage of the adult population that is trying to start or has started a baby business because all other options for work are either absent or unsatisfactory.

Principal Findings from GEM

In 2012, more than 198,000 people in 69 economies participated in the annual GEM study, collectively representing all regions of the world and a broad range of economic development levels.[127] The World Economic Forum's (WEF) *Global Competitiveness Report* identifies three phases of economic development based on GDP per capita and the share of exports comprising primary goods. According to the WEF classification, the *factor-driven* phase is dominated by subsistence agriculture and extraction businesses, with a heavy reliance on (unskilled) labour and natural resources. The focus of development efforts tends toward building a sufficient foundation of basic requirements. In the *efficiency-driven* phase, an economy has become more competitive with further development accompanied by industrialization and an increased reliance on economies of scale, with capital-intensive large organizations more dominant. This phase is generally accompanied by improved (and improving) basic requirements, and attention is then directed toward developing the efficiency enhancers. As development advances into the *innovation-driven* phase, businesses are more knowledge intensive and the service sector expands.

Activity

Total entrepreneurial activity (TEA) is a key indicator of GEM. It measures the percentage of adults (aged 18–64) in an economy who are nascent and new entrepreneurs. In economies with low GDP per capita, TEA rates tend to be high, with a correspondingly higher proportion of necessity-motivated entrepreneurship. Conversely, high-GDP economies show lower levels of entrepreneurship, but a higher proportion of those with opportunity motivations. To at least some extent, then, development levels are associated with particular patterns in the level and type of entrepreneurial activity.

The highest average TEA rates (Table 1.1) were found in sub-Saharan Africa and Latin America/Caribbean. Zambia (41%) and Ecuador (27%) reported the highest rates in these regions. The Asia Pacific/South Asia region showed a mix of TEA levels with Thailand (19%) and China (13%) recording the highest rates.

While TEA rates were typically higher than established business rates in factor-driven economies, the gap narrows in the innovation-driven economies, with some showing more established business owners than entrepreneurs. For example, Greece, Spain, Switzerland, Ireland, and Finland in the EU and Japan, Republic of Korea, and Taiwan in Asia show at least one-third more established business owners than entrepreneurs. When viewed geographically, non-EU and Middle East and North Africa (MENA) regions have low rates of both TEA and established business ownership while sub-Saharan Africa has high rates of both, although TEA rates are much higher—twice as high on average compared with established business ownership.

Differences across regions can also be seen in the reasons for business discontinuance. For example, financing was identified as the key issue in business discontinuance in sub-Saharan Africa, but was less an issue in Asia. In North America and the European Union, individuals cited other jobs or business opportunities more often than those in other regions as a reason for business discontinuance—these are generally considered more positive causes.

TABLE 1.1	Entrepreneurial activity in the 69 GEM countries in 2012, by geographic region

(Rate in columns 3–6 is the percent of adults 18–64 engaged in the specified activity.)

Country	Economy Classification F=factor, E=efficiency, I=Innovation	Nascent entrepreneurship rate	New business ownership rate	Early-stage entrepreneurial activity (TEA) rate	Established business ownership rate	Discontinuation of businesses rate	Necessity-driven (% of TEA)	Improvement-driven opportunity (% of TEA)
LATIN AMERICA & CARRIBEAN								
Argentina	E	12	7	19	10	5	35	47
Barbados	E	10	7	17	12	3	12	63
Brazil	E	4	11	15	15	5	30	59
Chile	E	15	8	23	8	5	17	69
Colombia	E	14	7	20	7	7	12	48
Costa Rica	E	10	5	15	3	3	20	48
Ecuador	E	17	12	27	19	8	36	30
El Salvador	E	8	8	15	9	8	35	39
Mexico	E	8	4	12	5	4	13	52
Panama	E	7	3	9	2	2	19	57
Peru	E	15	6	20	5	7	23	53
Trinidad & Tobago	E	9	7	15	7	5	15	60
Uruguay	E	1	5	15	5	5	18	40
Average		11	7	17	8	5	22	51
MIDDLE EAST & NORTH AFRICA								
Algeria	F	2	7	9	3	7	30	47
Egypt	F	3	5	8	4	5	34	23
Iran	F	4	6	11	10	5	42	36
Israel	I	3	3	7	4	4	19	46
Palestine	F	6	4	10	3	8	42	27
Tunisia	E	2	2	5	4	4	35	42
Average		4	5	8	5	6	34	37
SUB-SAHARAN AFRICA								
Angola	F	15	19	32	9	26	24	38
Botswana	F	17	12	28	6	16	33	48
Ethiopia	F	6	9	15	10	3	20	69
Ghana	F	15	23	37	38	16	28	51
Malawi	F	18	20	36	11	29	42	43
Namibia	E	11	7	18	3	12	37	37
Nigeria	F	22	14	35	16	8	35	53
South Africa	E	4	3	7	2	5	32	40
Uganda	F	10	28	36	31	26	46	42
Zambia	F	27	15	41	4	20	32	46
Average		15	15	28	13	16	33	47

Continued

TABLE 1.1 (*Continued*)

ASIA PACIFIC & SOUTH ASIA								
China	E	5	7	13	12	4	37	39
Japan	I	2	2	4	6	1	21	66
Republic of Korea	I	3	4	7	10	3	35	46
Malaysia	E	3	4	7	7	2	13	61
Pakistan	F	8	3	12	4	3	53	24
Singapore	I	8	4	12	3	4	15	54
Taiwan	I	3	4	8	10	6	18	43
Thailand	E	9	11	19	30	3	17	67
Average		5	5	10	10	3	26	50
EUROPEAN UNION								
Austria	I	7	3	10	8	4	11	38
Belgium	I	3	2	5	5	2	18	62
Denmark	I	3	2	5	3	1	8	71
Estonia	E	9	5	14	7	4	18	49
Finland	I	3	3	6	8	2	17	60
France	I	4	2	5	3	2	18	59
Germany	I	4	2	5	5	2	22	51
Greece	I	4	3	7	12	4	30	32
Hungary	E	6	4	9	8	4	31	35
Ireland	I	4	2	6	8	2	28	41
Italy	I	2	2	4	3	2	16	22
Latvia	E	9	5	13	8	3	25	46
Lithuania	E	3	4	7	8	2	25	51
Netherlands	I	4	6	10	9	2	8	66
Poland	E	5	5	9	6	4	41	30
Portugal	I	4	4	8	6	3	18	53
Romania	E	6	4	9	4	4	24	38
Slovakia	I	7	4	10	6	5	36	43
Slovenia	I	3	3	5	6	2	7	64
Spain	I	3	2	6	9	2	26	33
Sweden	I	5	2	6	5	2	7	49
UK	I	5	4	9	6	2	18	43
Average		5	3	8	7	3	21	47
NON-EUROPEAN UNION								
Bosnia and Herzegovina	E	5	3	8	6	7	58	20
Croatia	E	6	2	8	3	4	34	36
Macedonia	E	4	3	7	7	4	52	29
Norway	I	4	3	7	6	1	7	70
Russia	E	3	2	4	2	1	36	31
Switzerland	I	3	3	6	8	2	18	57
Turkey	E	7	5	12	9	5	31	55
Average		4	3	7	6	4	34	43
CANADA & THE UNITED STATES								
Canada	I	8	5	12	8	-	2	10
USA	I	9	4	13	9	4	21	59

Source: *GEM 2012 Global Report*, http://www.gemconsortium.org/docs/download/2645; 2013 GEM Canada National Report, http://www.thecis.ca/cms3/userfiles/Image/GEM%20Canada%20Report%202013.pdf.

Necessity- and Opportunity-Driven Entrepreneurs

GEM defines necessity-driven entrepreneurs as those who are pushed into starting businesses because they have no other work options and need a source of income. Opportunity-motivated entrepreneurs, on the other hand, are those entering this activity primarily to pursue an opportunity. The latter are further distinguished as improvement-driven opportunity motivated if they additionally seek to improve their income or independence through entrepreneurship.

Necessity-driven motives tend to be highest in the factor-driven economies. With greater economic development levels, the proportion of entrepreneurs with necessity motives generally declines, while improvement-driven opportunity increasingly accounts for a great proportion of motives. Geographic differences exist, however, even at the same economic development level. For instance, the Latin America/Caribbean region, generally containing efficiency-driven economies, reported twice as many entrepreneurs with improvement-driven opportunity motives than those with necessity motivations. In contrast, the non-EU region, also with mainly efficiency-driven economies, reported almost equal levels of either motive.

Age Distribution

Economies in all geographic regions showed bell-shaped age distributions with the highest entrepreneurship rates generally occurring among 25- to 34-year-olds (Figure 1.6). High participation levels also occurred in the next oldest age group: 35–44 years. Together, these two age categories made up close to 50% or more of all entrepreneurs. In Chile, Republic of Korea, Singapore, Netherlands, the United Kingdom, and the United States, the 35- to 44-year-olds had the highest level of participation in entrepreneurship among the age groups.

Entrepreneurship was prevalent among youth in the non-EU economies, where half of the entrepreneurs were between 18–34 years of age. China was also distinct in having a high

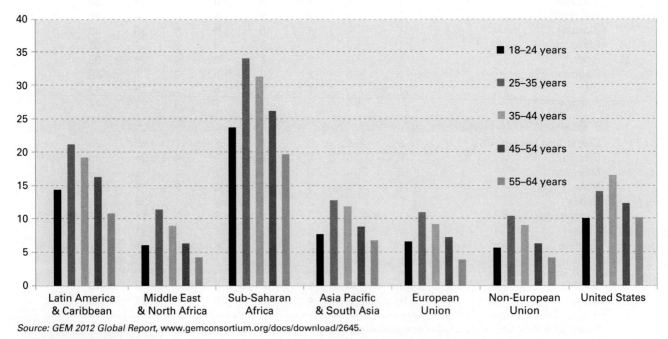

Source: GEM 2012 Global Report, www.gemconsortium.org/docs/download/2645.

Figure 1.6

TEA by age for geographic regions

proportion of young entrepreneurs, with 57% between 18 and 34 years of age, and less than one-quarter falling into the older age groups (45–64 years). In certain economies, there was a flattening out of the bell-shaped curve, where similar participation levels were reported across all or most of the age ranges. Examples of this pattern include Palestine, Japan, Pakistan, Hungary, and Bosnia/Herzegovina.

Gender Differences

GEM findings have consistently reported greater involvement in entrepreneurship among men than women in most economies. The ratio of male to female participation in early-stage entrepreneurial activity varied considerably across the sample (Figure 1.7). Participation among men and women was almost equal in most sub-Saharan Africa economies, while men were 2.8 times more likely than women to start a business in the MENA region. In Egypt, Palestine, and Republic of Korea, less than one-fifth of all entrepreneurs were women. More notably, only 5% of the entrepreneurs in Pakistan were women. The only economies where female TEA rates were higher than male rates were in Ecuador and Panama in Latin America, Ghana and Nigeria in sub-Saharan Africa, and Thailand in Asia.

An analysis of opportunity and necessity motives shows that men in Latin America and sub-Saharan Africa are more likely to be opportunity motivated, while women have higher necessity motives. This is interesting, given that these regions have fewer differences between the sexes in TEA rates. In other words, although relatively more women participate in entrepreneurship in these regions, they are more likely necessity motivated. In contrast, women in Asia are proportionately more likely to be opportunity motivated, with men showing comparatively greater necessity motivations. But with low entrepreneurship rates among women in this region, there are still fewer opportunity-motivated women than male entrepreneurs in the population; yet there are even fewer with necessity motives. It indicates that necessity drives more men than women to enter this activity in Asia. Two regions where men and women have comparable entrepreneurial motives are MENA and the EU; both also show among the highest regional-level gender disparities. While it appears that women are pushed into entrepreneurship out of necessity more often than men in Latin America and sub-Saharan Africa, a lower sense of necessity may help account for the lower levels of female participation in Asia, MENA, and the EU.

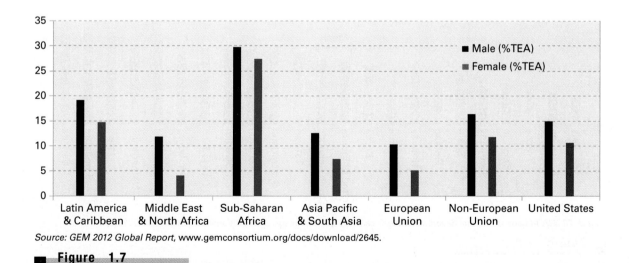

Source: GEM 2012 Global Report, www.gemconsortium.org/docs/download/2645.

Figure 1.7

TEA by gender for geographic regions

Growth Expectations and Job Creation

While TEA rates indicate how many entrepreneurs there are in each economy, growth expectations represent a quality measure of this activity. Entrepreneurs differ in their growth ambitions, and this can have significant potential impact on the employment growth and competitive advantage of their economies.

The non-EU, despite its low TEA rate, showed nearly a fifth of its entrepreneurs with projected growth of 20 or more employees. The United States exhibited a high proportion of 20+ growth projections in addition to the highest TEA rate among the innovation-driven economies, demonstrating both the prevalence of entrepreneurship and its impact on the U.S. economy. Turkey, Latvia, Singapore, China, and Colombia also displayed both high TEA and high proportions of 20+ growth entrepreneurs relative to other economies in their regions. Canada did not participate in the 2009 GEM report but had a separate report completed in 2013, which indicated a Canadian TEA score of 12.2%, just behind the United States, which had a TEA score of 12.7%,[128] as indicated in Figure 1.8.

We now look at the prevalence of high-growth expectations among both nascent entrepreneurs and owner-managers of baby businesses, as identified in GEM's adult population surveys from the years 2004 to 2009.[129]

The GEM method enables the categorization of early-stage startup attempts according to their growth expectations. GEM asks all identified early-stage entrepreneurs how many employees they expect to have (other than the owners themselves) within five years' time. Out of every 10 early-stage entrepreneurs, seven expected some job creation. However, expectations of high growth are rare among nascent and new entrepreneurs. Only 14% of all those involved in startup attempts expected to create 20 or more jobs, while 44% expected to create five or more jobs.

High-growth entrepreneurs, also known as *gazelles*, receive heightened attention from policymakers because their firms contribute a disproportionate share of all new jobs created by new firms.[130, 131] Figure 1.9 shows the prevalence rates of high-expectation entrepreneurial activity (HEA) in the working-age population.

Among high-income countries, the United Arab Emirates, Iceland, the United States, Canada, Singapore, Ireland, and Australia had the highest levels of HEA over the 2004–2009

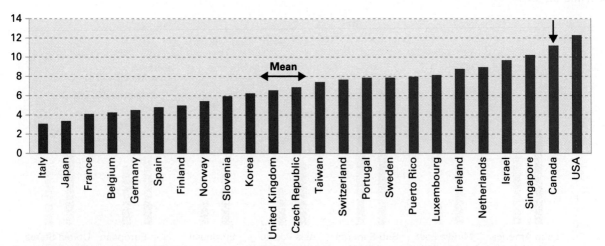

Source: 2013 GEM Canada National Report, www.thecis.ca/cms3/userfiles/Image/GEM%20Canada%20Report%202013.pdf.

Figure 1.8

TEA values for innovation-driven economies

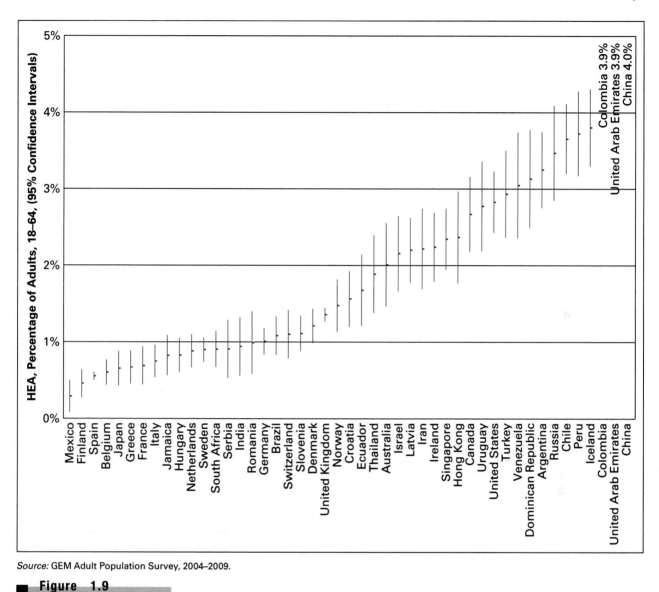

Source: GEM Adult Population Survey, 2004–2009.

■ **Figure 1.9**

Early-stage HEA rates in 2004–2009

period. The HEA rate for these countries is well over 1%. The lowest levels of HEA, at under 0.5%, occur in Spain, Belgium, Japan, and France. HEA rates can vary even among broadly similar high-income countries. Among the large European Union economies, the United Kingdom and Germany exhibit higher HEA rates than do France and Spain. In the Benelux countries, the Netherlands's rate is higher than Belgium's. In Scandinavia, Iceland was at the top on this measure, while Finland was at the bottom and Sweden, Denmark, and Norway were in the middle.

Although GEM data are for expected job creation, they are consistent with empirical studies of actual job creation. For instance, one study found that 4% of new firms in the United Kingdom created 50% of all jobs created by all new firms.[132] And another study reported that more than 70% of the employment growth in the United States came from only 3% of all firms.[133]

SMEs versus Startups

In recent years there has been much deliberation when comparing a small to medium-sized enterprise (SME) to a startup. Steve Blank, author of *The Lean Startup*, states the largest differentiating factor between an SME and a startup is in their top financial objectives. Small businesses are driven by profitability and stable long-term value, while startups are focused on growth potential and scalable profitability.[134] According to Blank, a startup is "a temporary organization that is searching for a sustainable, repeatable, scalable business model." Typically, an SME will consist of businesses such as laundromats, restaurants, retail stores, etc., whereas a startup is a scalable business and is most often in the technology or software sector. Most startups consist of software companies, mobile applications companies, and Web-based businesses.

Twenty-First-Century Economies: Anglo-Saxon or Social Models?

It is interesting that a group of nations with so-called **Anglo-Saxon economic systems** (the United States, Canada, Ireland, and Australia) has higher HEA rates—which translate into more job creation—than does a group of European nations with strong **social models** (Denmark, Sweden, Finland, the Netherlands, Germany, and France).

Figure 1.10 shows that the stricter a country's employment security, the lower its early-stage HEA rate.[135] Stricter employment protection inhibits HEA in two ways: First, it makes would-be HEA entrepreneurs more reluctant to give up a secure job to start their own company; second, if they do start one, it makes them more hesitant to hire employees because firing them is costly. Of course, the optimal balance depends on a nation's norms and social values. However, the results in Figure 1.10 suggest that lowering employment protection may benefit employees in the longer term because of the possibility that more jobs will be created by these early-stage HEA entrepreneurs.

Here is former UK Prime Minister Tony Blair's challenge for Europe in his address to the European Parliament in June 2005:[136]

> *What would a different policy agenda for Europe look like? First, it would modernize our social model. Again some have suggested I want to abandon Europe's social model. But tell me: What type of social model is it that has 20 million unemployed in Europe, productivity rates falling behind those of the USA; that is allowing more science graduates to be produced by India than by Europe; and that, on any relative index of a modern economy—skills, R&D, patents, IT—is going down, not up. India will expand its biotechnology sector fivefold in the next five years. China has trebled its spending on R&D in the last five.*
>
> *Of the top 20 universities in the world today, only two are now in Europe.[137] The purpose of our social model should be to enhance our ability to compete, to help our people cope with globalization, to let them embrace its opportunities and avoid its dangers. Of course we need a social Europe. But it must be a social Europe that works.*
>
> *And we've been told how to do it. The Kok report[138] in 2004 shows the way. Investment in knowledge, in skills, in active labour market policies, in science parks and innovation, in higher education, in urban regeneration, and in help for small businesses. This is modern social policy, not regulation and job protection that may save some jobs for a time at the expense of many jobs in the future.*

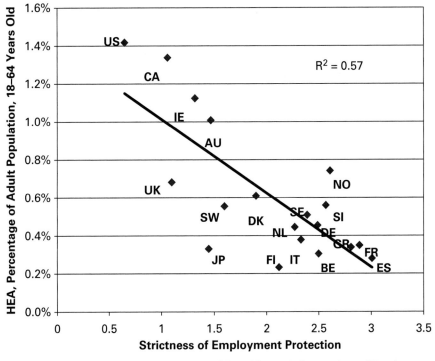

Source: GEM Adult Population Survey, 2004–2009; Office of Economic Cooperation and Development, Employment Strictness Data, 2004.

■ Figure 1.10

Strictness of employment protection and early-stage HEA rates in 2004–2009

Early in 2006, Dominique de Villepin, France's prime minister, proposed legislation aimed at cutting chronic youth unemployment by easing rigid labour laws that make it difficult to fire employees. Students rose up all over France to protest the proposed changes and shut down classes at half of France's 84 state-run universities in the biggest student uprising since 1968 (when student riots forced the de Gaulle government to hold an election). The students' attitude in 2006 was summed up by these comments:[139]

> *Elodie, 21, a sociology student, said: "The issues are different from those our parents were protesting about. We are marching for the right to proper jobs."*
> *Romain, 20, a communications student, said: "We don't want the Anglo-Saxon economic model here."*

One survey discovered that the top career goal of three-quarters of young French people was to be a civil servant.[140] This is in stark contrast to the United States, where the majority of young people want to be an entrepreneur at some time during their career.[141] A survey by the Bank of Montreal found that almost half of Canadian postsecondary students surveyed—46%—said they see themselves starting a business after graduation.[142]

But it does not follow that young people in France and other European countries with social models are more likely than their North American counterparts to become engaged in entrepreneurial activities with a social goal. On the contrary, when GEM made its first comprehensive study of social entrepreneurship in 2009, European nations had a lower level of early-stage social entrepreneurial activity (SEA) than did the United States (see Figure 1.11).

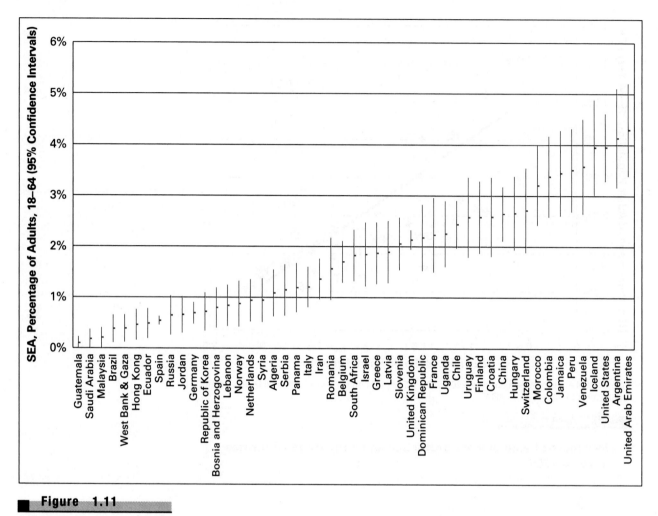

Figure 1.11

Early-stage SEA rates by country, 2009

CONCLUSION

Entrepreneurial activity in North America now accounts for much of the region's prosperity and competitiveness in the global economy. The disappearance of "old" jobs, particularly in mature manufacturing industries, and their replacement by "new" jobs, especially in service and knowledge-based industries, is disconcerting to workers whose jobs are threatened. But society has to accept *churning*—the creation of new enterprises and the destruction of obsolete ones—because it gives the Canadian and American economies their vitality.

The entrepreneurial framework includes factors such as availability of finance, government policies and programs designed to support startups, R&D transfer, physical and human infrastructure, general education, specific education and training for entrepreneurship, social and cultural norms, and internal market openness. All of these factors combined determine the degree of entrepreneurial activity in a nation, or for that matter in a region within a nation. What's more, the so-called Anglo-Saxon economic systems seem to engender more entrepreneurial activity than systems dominated by the social model, which is the prevalent system in much of continental Europe. The question remains: How do both Anglo-Saxon and social economies find an entrepreneurial path that leads them out of the economic crisis?

In this chapter we have looked at the importance of entrepreneurship to national economies. In the following chapters, we will look at the specifics of how entrepreneurs start and grow their new ventures.

YOUR OPPORTUNITY JOURNAL

We are excited that you are exploring an entrepreneurial journey, one that may lead you to launch a business while in university, after graduation, or at some future point in your life. We know that all great entrepreneurs are avid readers and thinkers, and as such, we encourage you to capture some of your thoughts as you read this book. These thoughts may focus on a new venture that you are interested in creating, or they may focus more on your entrepreneurial career plan. In either event, we will close each chapter with space for you to reflect on what it means to you and your potential venture.

Reflection Point	Your Thoughts. . .
1. What world-changing industries or opportunities do you see developing over the next 5 to 10 years?	
2. What innovations or new technologies will drive these world-changing opportunities?	
3. Which regions of the world have the greatest potential for developing these opportunities? Which are you most interested in?	
4. What skills do you need to develop to take advantage of these opportunities?	

WEB EXERCISE

What do you think will be the next major innovation (e.g., the Internet) that changes the way we live, work, and play? Search the Web to identify trends, statistics, and other evidence to support your insight. (*Hint:* Venture capitalists have a knack for spotting emergent industries.)

Alison Barnard

Having spent her Saturday morning redesigning window displays, folding inventory, and following up with a supplier who seemed disinclined to take back an entire shipment she felt was unacceptable, Alison Barnard, 27, was finally settled at her desk in the corner—fully intending to make some progress on her growing management task list. Chief among those neglected missions was getting up to speed on her software system for monitoring sales and inventory.

In-jean-ius, her upscale "jeans and T-shirt" boutique in Boston's North End, was attracting professional and wealthy women from Maine to Rhode Island. As one of many satisfied customers wrote, "Alison has an uncanny ability to match up the right person with the perfect pair of jeans. If you have ever gone 'jean shopping' you know that that is not an easy thing to do! Experience In-jean-ius for yourself. You won't shop for jeans anywhere else again."

Alison looked up from her work with a weary smile.

Open just over six months, and actuals are tracking nearly twice my projections . . .

As it had from the very beginning, running her hit venture continued to consume nearly every waking hour. The creative, high-energy founder was far less concerned with burning out than with having the day-to-day concerns usurp her ability to plan and manage for growth. And with only one full-time employee—not yet fully trained—Alison couldn't expect much relief anytime soon.

Her attention was suddenly drawn to an exchange between her salesperson and a well-dressed, middle-aged woman who was favouring a sleek pair of low rises. From where she sat, Alison could see that the woman was built for something a bit less daring. When the associate began fishing for the correct size in that style, Alison left her desk (and her task list) to steer the sale toward a more conservative brand that would ultimately prove to offer the best fit. Another satisfied customer . . .

Alison Barnard: Shopper

Like many rural-suburban American teens, young Alison Barnard had been an avid shopper. But there was something more. The daughter of a serial entrepreneur and an enterprising mother, she had developed an eye for opportunity and value-add that she ceaselessly trained on the business of creating a unique upscale shopping experience: trends, service, selection, presentation, decor. Despite her keen interest in retailing, she headed off for college with a more conservative career track in mind:

> *I really thought I wanted to be in brand management, marketing, or retail consulting. I figured that someday I would have a store but thought it might be something I'd do when I retired, like you kind of hung out in your store.*
>
> *But I had all of these ideas. I like clothing, I like the shopping experience, and I like dealing with people. One idea was to have an all-black store because black apparel is such a staple for any woman's wardrobe.*

In May 2002, Alison received her undergraduate degree in business from the University of Richmond. Back in the Boston area, her first job was with a dot-com startup. She left there for an interesting opportunity with another high-potential venture. While the work environment there was most definitely not for her, that "mistake" would have a major impact on her career trajectory.

Catalysts

Hired as part of the seminar development team at a medical device company in Cambridge, Massachusetts, Alison quickly discovered that her talents weren't exactly appreciated:

> They were part of this old boy network that really looked down on females. They told me, for example, that I needed to cover on Thursdays for the receptionist when she went to lunch. Swell. I hated that place, and I immediately began interviewing for something better.
>
> At one point, I went on a job interview, and since my boss approved of higher education, I told her I had gone to Babson College to investigate their MBA program. When I checked into it in order to support my little lie, I found out that Babson had a one-year program that looked really interesting; you're there, you're focused and doing it, and then you're out.

Alison began the one-year MBA at Babson in the spring of 2003. Since she was still brainstorming retail store concepts with anyone who would engage, her mom's hairdresser suggested that as a next step she ought to get some floor time in the real world. That summer Alison started work as a part-timer at an upscale boutique near Boston. Although she still had no immediate plans to develop a new venture, her MBA studies melded well with her exposure to retailing:

> I quickly realized that my first concept about an all-black store was a bad idea. Women buy black, but they don't shop for it. They'll even go into a store and say they want anything but black—because they have too much black in their wardrobe. But then in the end, they'll buy something black.
>
> At that time, I was really getting into jeans myself. At Babson, I wore jeans and a T-shirt every day. My first pair was Sevens, one of the early entrants into what I would call the premium denim revolution. Jeans are no longer just weekend wear; they are worn in the workplace and for going out. Premium denim has become a fashion staple, and women now have an average of about eight pairs of jeans in their wardrobe.
>
> So an all-jeans store became sort of my fun idea—something I thought would be just another idea that would be passed by. Still, my concept was interesting enough to attract a team in class to do the business plan.

Realizations

Nothing Alison and her team members discovered in their research surprised her in the least (see Exhibit 1.1). When asked what pain point she expected her store to relieve, she didn't hesitate a moment:

> Women's point of pain is themselves. The reality is that every female hates herself in some sort of way. And if she doesn't like something about her body, jeans can bring out the worst qualities. But they can also make you look great if they fit right.
>
> There are some decent stores in the area that sell premium jeans (see Exhibit 1.2), but they all forget to mention the fact that fit is by far a woman's number one concern when searching for jeans. Women are not brand loyal; they are fit loyal.

When she graduated in the spring of 2004, Alison was offered an opportunity to learn even more:

> The woman who was managing the boutique was going on maternity leave starting in the fall. The partners knew I wanted to open a store someday and they said that they would train me and help me out until she returned in the spring of 2005.

EXHIBIT 1.1 | **Research Findings**

What Women Want: Survey Results

We conducted primary research through a survey of 90 women in the Boston area to find out their jean-buying habits, including number of jeans owned, where they purchase their jeans, brands they are loyal to, and what they would like to see in a jean store. The complete results can be found in Exhibit 1.2.

The survey conducted to extract the jean-purchasing behaviours of 90 females aged 21–35 reveals the following:

◘ Women are willing to spend money for jeans

    ◘ 28% $25–$50
    ◘ 16% $51–$75
    ◘ 14% $76–$85
    ◘ 17% $86–$100
    ◘ 16% $101–$130
    ◘ 9% $130+

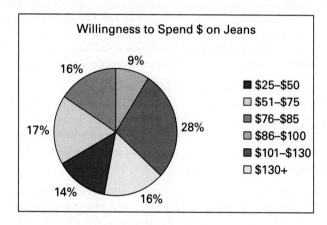

◘ Fit matters and influences where and which brands women purchase

    ◘ 86.7% of woman said their one reason for shopping at certain stores was that these stores carried jeans that fit them

    ◘ Brand preference is based on fit

◘ 82% of women say they are not loyal to one brand of jean. Woman need . . . .

    ◘ More selection → 49.4% want more options

    ◘ More information → so many jean brands and styles and so little time

    ◘ More help → make the process less time consuming, less of a hassle

In addition, open-ended questions regarding what they dislike about the jean-buying process and what they would like to see in a new jean store environment revealed the following:

◘ Overall, women dislike the jean-buying process, even though they enjoy buying a new pair of jeans.

◘ Disorganization of the store and inconsistency of jean sizes by brands made woman want to see more sales help, which was lacking in the stores they currently frequent for jean buying.

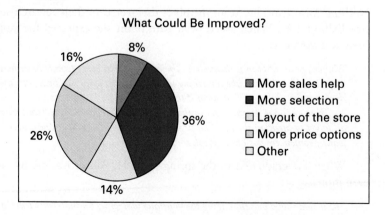

EXHIBIT 1.2   Premium Jean Stores in Eastern Massachusetts

Store	Private Label	Trendy Jean Brands	Jean Expertise	Knowledgeable Customer Service	Welcome Atmosphere	Large Selection of Brands
Jean Therapy		X	X	X		
The National Jean Co.		X		X		X
Banana Republic	X					
Express	X					
Riccardi		X				X
Diesel	X		X	X		
Intermix		X			X	
Gap	X					
Mudo		X	X	X		
Lucky Brand	X					
Jasmine Sola*		X			X	X
Jeans Addiction		X		X		X

*Luciano Manganella, who founded this upscale boutique in Harvard Square in 1970, four years after emigrating from Italy, sold Jasmine Sola in the summer of 2005 to the nearly national 500-store New York & Co. This move, Manganella said, was the only way he could expand beyond his present 15 stores to an expected 25 stores—all on the East Coast—by the end of 2006. The undisclosed amount of the sale was estimated to be in excess of $20 million.

Alison accepted their offer. She soon discovered, however, that they would be delivering far less than they promised:

I never got anything we had agreed to, including health insurance or training of any kind. I did learn how to handle receivables, pricing, dating, and ordering, but I figured out that stuff on my own by examining the invoices and checking in the orders.

It wasn't long before Alison was certain that she could run a shop of her own. She was still drawn to the $6.3 billion women's denim market, a highly fragmented space with hundreds of manufacturers and inconsistent retail offerings, from boutiques, chain stores, and department stores. Still, she felt that she "would have to jump on it right away before anyone else did"—it was now or never:

I had been keeping my idea secret from the store owners because I didn't trust them at all. Sure, they liked me, but they also had money and resources. That summer, I was attending a fashion show with one of the owners. He said that he had always wanted to open a jeans and T-shirt store but that his business partner—a woman—wasn't interested in the concept. At that point, I told him about my idea, and before you know it, we were talking about going into business together.

He called a few times after the trip to talk it over. We never touched on details like money or ownership breakdown, but we did go to look at a spot in Wellesley [Massachusetts]. But then he just dropped it; never talked about it again. It was as if we had never had a conversation about it! That's the sort of thing you get from a lot of people in this industry.

But how was I going to do it alone? Where was I going to get the money?

Commitments

Based on her projections (see Exhibit 1.3), Alison expected her retail store would have first-year sales of just over $375,000. She had also calculated that startup costs, including build-out and

EXHIBIT 1.3	Five-Year Projections, Income Statement				
Sales	**Year 1**	**Year 2**	**Year 3**	**Year 4**	**Year 5**
Jeans					
Unit Sales	1,635	1,962	2,315	2,547	2,801
Average Price	135	142	149	156	164
	220,725	278,604	344,935	397,332	459,364
Tops					
Unit Sales	2,453	3,434	4,120	4,862	5,737
Average Price	54	40	42	45	48
	132,462	137,360	173,040	218,790	275,376
Accessories					
Unit Sales	550	633	791	988	1,235
Average Price	45	45	50	50	55
	24,750	28,485	39,550	49,400	67,925
Total Sales	**377,937**	**444,449**	**557,525**	**665,522**	**802,665**
Cost of Sales					
Jeans	94,912	119,589	148,171	171,137	197,663
Tops	58,860	61,803	79,108	97,237	126,313
Accessories	11,550	13,283	12,452	15,565	19,457
Total Cost of Sales	165,322	194,675	239,731	283,939	343,433
Sales Expenses					
Credit Card Commissions	10,222	12,000	14,737	17,482	21,186
Discounts & Promos	2,759	3,476	4,307	4,975	5,746
Returns	14,031	16,470	20,228	23,995	29,078
Damage & Theft	12,026	14,117	17,338	20,567	24,924
Total Sales Expenses	39,038	46,063	56,610	67,019	80,934
Gross Margin	**173,577**	**203,711**	**261,184**	**314,564**	**378,298**
Buying Expenses Incl. Travel	2,400	3,600	4,000	4,200	4,400
Administration					
Rent	17,500	31,200	32,400	33,600	34,800
Staff Salaries & Benefits	24,960	31,200	33,600	33,600	33,600
Staff Payroll Taxes	7,488	9,360	10,080	10,080	10,080
Management Salaries	51,996	52,800	55,000	60,000	65,000
Management Payroll Taxes	15,439	15,840	15,840	15,840	15,840
Health Insurance	3,000	3,000	3,000	3,000	3,000
Interest	900	1,200	1,040	880	720
Communications & Media	3,300	3,300	3,300	3,300	3,300
Professional Fees	4,308	4,308	4,308	4,308	4,308
Depreciation	12,266	13,381	13,381	13,381	13,381
Insurance	2,880	2,880	2,880	2,880	2,880
Utilities (Electric & Gas)	4,200	4,200	4,200	4,200	4,200
	148,237	172,669	179,029	185,069	191,109
Total Expenses	**150,637**	**176,269**	**183,029**	**189,269**	**195,509**
Pretax Profit	22,940	27,442	78,155	125,295	182,789
Net Profit	**14,844**	**17,425**	**47,914**	**76,265**	**110,825**

EXHIBIT 1.3	(Continued)				
Sales	**Year 1**	**Year 2**	**Year 3**	**Year 4**	**Year 5**
Beginning Cash	125,000	19,077	47,883	125,561	235,571
Inflows					
Sales	377,937	444,449	557,525	665,522	802,665
Depreciations	12,233	13,381	13,381	13,381	13,381
Outflows					
Cost of Sales	(165,322)	(194,675)	(239,731)	(283,939)	(343,333)
Sales Expenses	(39,038)	(46,063)	(56,610)	(67,018)	(80,934)
Marketing Expenses	(2,400)	(3,600)	(4,000)	(4,200)	(4,200)
Admin. Expenses	(148,237)	(172,669)	(179,029)	(185,069)	(191,109)
Note Payment	(20)	(2,000)	(2,000)	(2,000)	(2,000)
Taxes	(8,096)	(10,017)	(30,798)	(49,030)	(71,964)
Pre-opening & Build-Out	(58,000)				
Opening Inventory	(75,000)				
Increase in A/P			18,940	22,364	26,990
Net (Outflow) Inflow	(105,923)	28,806	77,678	110,010	149,296
Ending Cash Balance	19,077	47,883	125,561	235,571	384,867

inventory, would be in the range of $125,000. She was confident that she could attract investors, but first she wanted to secure a location that would be acceptable to what she was sure would be her toughest constituency:

> Fashion denim manufacturers are represented by showrooms in New York City and in LA [Los Angeles]. They are very committed to their brands—and very particular about whom they will sell to. To avoid saturation, they won't sell to a store that is too close to another client, and they will even shut off an established shop that locates a new store too close to another buyer. Territory protection is a great asset for existing stores, but it makes it very hard to find locations that have the right customer traffic and are not in conflict with existing vendors.

Alison's boyfriend, Bryan, was active in the Boston real estate market. On weekends, Alison often accompanied him as he made the rounds to various properties he was managing. One icy morning in early 2005, Alison fell for a corner location in the North End:

> This place was a bit removed from the busiest section of Hanover Street, but the outside was SO nice; all dark wood, newly redone. I had Bryan call the number because as a real estate agent, I knew they would take him seriously. He set up a meeting with the landlord—a top neurosurgeon who owned the building as an investment. He had already denied seven previous proposals, but said he liked mine a lot.

Soon, they were talking hard numbers:

> I learned a lot in negotiating with him because he had a huge ego—just like a lot of good surgeons do. I had to figure out how to make him feel he was still getting something out of it. He was also getting stuck on little details. For example, he wanted to control my window displays and be able to go to arbitration over it.
>
> And the space may have been beautiful on the outside, but the inside was unbelievably awful. It was scary. It needed new floors, new ceilings, new walls, and a new heating system.

In late February, Alison signed a three-year lease that included a few months of free rent—she now had until September. All along, her father had felt strongly that she should have lined up the capital first:

> *My dad was saying, "What are you thinking?" He totally disagreed with what I was doing, but I told him I'd find the money. He loaned me the deposit on the location, and he called up my uncle, who is an accountant. The three of us sat down and came up with an investment offering.*

Finding the Money

Before she went the equity route, Alison wanted to investigate other avenues. The news was not good:

> *My dad referred me to some people he knew at Boston Private Bank—very conservative. Talks went fine until they became insistent that, if they were going to do anything, they would have to have a guarantor for the loan—a co-signer. Well, I wasn't going to do that; I wanted this to be my responsibility.*
> *I tried to get an SBA loan through a small bank on the North Shore, but I had no collateral, and I was paying off student loans. They said no way because, even though the SBA would be backing it, a bad loan would give them a worse rating through the SBA. I looked into grants, but the process was too long. I also tried to get startup funding through the Hatchery Program at Babson. They said no as well; that really surprised me.*

With the clock ticking on her lease, Alison went ahead with the investor plan she had crafted with her closest advisors:

> *We were not going to give people the option of deciding how much money they could invest. Instead, we said this is the deal: There are six slots of $25,000 each, and your options are full equity, debt/equity, or full debt.[143]*
> *I sent an email to all my contacts saying that this is where I am and that I was looking for investors. A lot of people responded to me; I was shocked.*
> *A former classmate at Babson (who had started a men's skincare line) emailed to say that he was very upset with me because he thought I was giving up way too much equity. But I didn't look at it that way at all. It was a different business model; he was going to the masses, and I was very local.*

Her father was in for one share; all equity. Her uncle let her choose, so she set him up as a debt/equity investor. She had a Babson woman (who had always liked her idea) in for all equity and a private investor in Denver for all debt. The final two shares were to be all equity:

> *A guy I used to work with told me he wanted to do $50,000, but he wanted to do it for 15% equity instead of 12.5%. I quickly said no. I had deals in place with other people; those are the terms. He said that's fine, he'd still like to do it.*

Armed with a bit of cash and some solid commitments, Alison charged forward to make her vision a bricks-and-mortar reality.

Building Momentum (and Shelving)

Having initially envisioned a space in the range of 1,800 square feet, Alison found the 600 square foot shell to be a significant creative challenge—so much so that she hired an expert:

> *I needed to accommodate a starting inventory of around 600 pairs of jeans and a selection of tops (see Exhibit 1.4). My biggest concern was we had to have wide enough aisles to walk around.*

EXHIBIT 1.4	Opening Inventory: Brand Selection
Denim Vendors	**T-Shirt/Tops Vendors**
ABS	ABS
AG	C & C California
Bella Dahl	Central Park West
Big Star	Custo
Blu Jeanious	Ella Moss
Cambio	Hale Bob
Chip and Pepper	Jakes
Christopher Blue	James Perse
Citizens of Humanity	Juicy Couture
Habitual	Lilla P.
Hudson	Michael Stars
IT Jeans	Mimi & Coco
James Jeans	Muchacha
Juicy Couture	Notice
Kasil	Rebecca Beeson
Notify	Splendid
Paper Denim & Cloth	Susana Monaco
Parasuco	Three Dots
Red Engine	Troo
Rock & Republic	Velvet
Sacred Blue	
Saddelite	
Salt Works	
Seven for All Mankind	
Tacto	
True Religion	
Tylerskye	
Womyn	
Yanuk	

I thought I could do it myself, but against my better judgment, I hired an interior designer. I worked with him and came up with a compact shelving system that started almost at the floor and went up only as high as I could reach. I am 5'5", and that is about the average. If someone was shorter, I could get it for them. I really wanted my store to feel very comfortable and warm—like you're in a good friend's closet. But the designer never quite got the need to maximize the space.

She added with a smile that she had been able to attract effective talent to the task of building out her vision:

Bryan built all of the shelving with his father, an engineer. I showed them my drawings, gave them the measurements, and they did it. He actually project managed the build-out, and we did a lot of the work together. I saved so much money because of him. We painted it ourselves, and did other little things here and there. The contractors knew him well, and since he gives them so much business, they were willing to cut us breaks here and there. I went around and found furniture pieces for practical use that would make it feel more homey, like an armoire, a big dining room table, and a couple of benches. The furniture is all white, so the store has a shabby-chic feeling to it.

To monitor her sales and margins, Alison invested in a high-end software inventory system. The trouble was that the salesperson had yet to train her, and he wasn't returning her calls. But that challenge would have to wait; it was time to buy.

Learning Curves

With investors in place and the build-out moving along, Alison flew to Los Angeles and New York to haggle (and sashay) for "permission" to play:

I had a list of brands that I wanted, based on my experience at the boutique. I was very concerned about fit and consistency. I was constantly looking at other girls' butts, so I knew that there was a core group of "in fashion" trendy jeans that I needed to have and that people liked. I also had to have some Mom jeans: higher-waisted, not young, but still sophisticated and nice looking.

From there, it was about attending big trade shows in New York to touch the material and examine the styles. That doesn't tell you much about fit, and unfortunately you can't try on the floor samples.

Buying is always stressful. There are times when my head is pounding and everything looks the same. The sellers are really snobby, and I had to dress totally trendified so they could look me up and down and say, "Okay, you can buy from us." Great, thanks. If I'm a good businessperson, does the way I'm dressed matter at all? No, of course not; but that's what it's like.

Although I had a pretty good idea of what I needed for my opening inventory, I did make some mistakes. I also bought some jeans that I would not have normally, but I couldn't get some of the brands that I wanted to start with—they wouldn't sell to a new store.

The denim reps that did sell to her demanded full payment up front. Using bank cards secured with her mother's credit, Alison pulled together a $75,000 inventory of jeans, tops, and accessories like trendy shoes and jewellery. That's when she was given a bit of a scare:

A month before I opened, my last investor calls to say he's going to knock his investment down because he didn't want to be an aggressive shareholder. I panicked; I was in the final phases of my build-out, I had done all my buying, and here he was telling me I was going to be $25,000 short!

Despite her angst, Alison decided to sit tight. Things were moving along nicely, and it wasn't long before she realized that she'd be able to open her store without the additional capital.

In-jean-ius

A week before her opening in July 2005, Alison hired a friend of a friend as her first employee. Her mom was there to help out, along with her 17-year-old sister. The plan was to be open from around lunchtime to just past dinnertime, six days a week, and stay open a bit later on Sundays. Alison explained that it was soon evident that the location required a flexible approach:

The North End is interesting because in the summer they have a variety of feasts and festivals. I was often staying open until nearly midnight. I was working all the time—anything that would make a sale. I immediately surpassed my business plan estimates, and it kept building.

As a new retailer in town, she attracted a few of the usual suspects who thought they might be able to take advantage of the young proprietor. They thought wrong:

The area is safe, but like any city neighbourhood, it has its share of drug addicts. The first week I was open, two junkies came in. The guy was distracting me while the girl was stealing. I knew what was going on, but I didn't see her take anything. The general idea is that unless you see them do it, you can't do anything.

When they left, a girl walks in and says, "Excuse me, those two just walked out with a pair of jeans." Well, I am not a very tough person—I grew up in the suburbs—and I don't know what I was thinking or what came over me, but I ran after them. I took the jeans out of the guy's hand and the bag off of her shoulder. I told her that I knew she had jewellery of mine, and I found it in there. I walked away from them to call the police. They ran away and my neighbours got in their car to go find them. They took my younger sister with them because she knew what they looked like.

They found them and brought them back to the store so I could positively ID them. They were arrested and taken away. From then on, everyone in the North End thought hey, she's tough—and the druggies, who all talk, stayed away.

Soon after that, Alison was in hot pursuit again:

I chased another girl down the street, and when I wouldn't let her get in her car, she tried to punch me. Bryan tells me all the time I have to stop doing that; someday I could get hurt.

Of course, I tell my employees not to do anything like that; just call the police. But I take it so personally; that's mine, you're stealing from me! How can you do that? Don't you know I'm a new business?

Over the next few months, Alison's total loss to theft was a single pair of shoes and a pair of earrings. The other good news was that sales continued to track far ahead of her estimates. In the first six months, the store had generated a net income of $20,307 on sales of $294,061. Alison explained that, although word of mouth was an important factor in her early success, attracting the imagination of the local press had been key:

I'm not the only one who has had this idea, and other trendy jeans stores have definitely gotten their share of press, but people are really taking to my message: "You're going to get help, and we're going to work with you to find jeans that fit. We have jeans for everybody." Nobody else is saying that this is all about fit, and that's the message that I relay in every piece of PR that I send out. And they keep coming to talk to me.

While the young entrepreneur was thrilled with how things were going, she was ready to start spending less time on the sales floor and more time with strategic and management challenges. Easier said than done.

Fold or Finance?

Since the local press always seemed to focus on *her* skills and *her* story, Alison wondered how that might impact her ability to replicate her concept:

How do you grow when the store is about you? People come here because they like dealing with me. How do I duplicate myself? That's not to say that someone can't do what I'm doing and do it well, but employees are never going to treat people exactly the way you do. I have a lot of learning to do in terms of managing my employees, delegating, and sharing my knowledge.

One of her many priorities was to develop a training manual that, in addition to describing the particular fit characteristics of various brands, would clearly articulate her vision for customer service. She thought of contacting the Ritz-Carlton in Boston—to her mind a master of customer service—to see if they might let her review their training materials. Until she did have some documentation in place though, she'd have to communicate her philosophy on the fly:

I sort of torture my employees when they're hired. They have to come in and spend a few hours trying on everything in the store—like a restaurant that requires their servers to try everything on the menu so they can talk about it.

I am also pretty strict about keeping the store neat and organized. I think that is so important in a small space like this. Whenever I come into the store, I can immediately see items that are unfolded or out of place.

My office is a desk in the corner, so I'm right there to offer help or teach them the little tricks I've learned. I also try to stay at my desk and let them take care of whoever comes in, but I can't just keep quiet if they are not saying the right thing. I always have to get my two cents in.

Now that she had a full-time employee nearly up to speed and a sharp former classmate from Babson working on weekends as a fun job, Alison had begun to carve out some time each week to recharge:

I have had to give up spending much time with Bryan, and that has been a huge problem. My taking Sundays has become so important because we get to spend time together. Despite the fact that he is also an entrepreneur, he has had a really big struggle with the idea that he is number two to this business. That's been hard and it's something we're working on.

Her other challenging relationship was with the numbers:

Nailing down the actuals is a big issue for me, and I am in the process of doing that. I'm not bad with financials, but they are a bit intimidating; I am really just much more into customer service and marketing. There are so many other things that I could be doing to bring in sales, so I'd rather do those things first.

It's true; I would rather have my store neat and folded than work on my financials. That is always my first priority. If the store looks good, then I can do other things. The problem is that I am constantly rearranging the store, and that is my way of being creative: putting different things together, doing the windows over every week.

My uncle does my accounting, and I am paying close enough attention to know I'm doing much better than my projections, but I need to focus on it more. And I need to find a training course for that inventory software so I can run those reports and coordinate things the right way.

Down by One

It had been one of the best-selling days to date. Alison closed her shop at 8:30 that night and returned to her desk with the absurd idea that she might have some energy left for paperwork. It wasn't just that she was tired; she now had a brand-new challenge on her plate: That day her one full-time employee had given her two-week notice.

Discussion Questions

1. Is this business scalable? Discuss the limitations and challenges.
2. What tasks and goals should Alison be focusing on at this stage of her venture?
3. Discuss the signing of a lease prior to having the money. What was the risk?
4. Discuss her fundraising and valuation. If you were an equity investor, what return expectations would you have?
5. If women are coming to Alison's store from all over, how important is location? Discuss the implications for growth.

NOTES

1 Estimate based on GEM Adult Population Surveys; www.gemconsortium.org.

2 Industry Canada, "Key Small Business Statistics, July 2012: How Many Businesses Appear and Disappear Each Year?" www.ic.gc.ca/eic/site/061.nsf/eng/02716.html.

3 Industry Canada, "Key Small Business Statistics, July 2012," www.ic.gc.ca/eic/site/061.nsf/vwapj/KSBS-PSRPE_July-Juillet2012_eng.pdf/$FILE/KSBS-PSRPE_July-Juillet2012_eng.pdf.

4 J. A. Schumpeter, *The Theory of Economic Development* (Cambridge, MA: Harvard University Press, 1934). (This book was originally published in German in 1911.)

5 A. Maddison, *Phases of Capitalist Development* (New York, NY: Oxford University Press, 1989); W. J. Baumol, "Entrepreneurship and a Century of Growth," *Journal of Business Venturing* 1, no. 2 (1986): 141–145.

6 Industry Canada, "Key Small Business Statistics, August 2013: How Many Businesses Are There in Canada?" www.ic.gc.ca/eic/site/061.nsf/eng/02804.html.

[7] Industry Canada, "Key Small Business Statistics, July 2012," www.ic.gc.ca/eic/site/061.nsf/vwapj/KSBS-PSRPE_July-Juillet2012_eng.pdf/$FILE/KSBS-PSRPE_July-Juillet2012_eng.pdf.

[8] Ibid.

[9] Industry Canada, "Key Small Business Statistics, August 2013: How Much Do Small Businesses Innovate?" www.ic.gc.ca/eic/site/061.nsf/eng/02810.html.

[10] Industry Canada, "Key Small Business Statistics, August 2013: How Many Businesses Are There in Canada?" www.ic.gc.ca/eic/site/061.nsf/eng/02804.html.

[11] Industry Canada, "Key Small Business Statistics, July 2012: How Many People Are Self-Employed?" https://www.ic.gc.ca/eic/site/061.nsf/eng/02724.html.

[12] Steven H. Hipple, "Self-Employment in the United States," *Monthly Labor Review* (September 2010): 17.

[13] Canadian Press, "Record Number of Canadians Starting Own Businesses," *CBC News,* September 25, 2012, www.cbc.ca/news/business/record-number-of-canadians-starting-own-businesses-1.1256453.

[14] Industry Canada, "Key Small Business Statistics, July 2012: How Many Businesses Appear and Disappear Each Year?" www.ic.gc.ca/eic/site/061.nsf/eng/02716.html.

[15] Industry Canada, "Key Small Business Statistics, August 2013: How Many Businesses Are There in Canada?" www.ic.gc.ca/eic/site/061.nsf/eng/02804.html.

[16] J. R. Baldwin and Statistics Canada, *Determinants of Innovative Activity in Canadian Manufacturing Firms: The Role of Intellectual Property Rights* Ottawa, ON: Analytical Studies Branch, Statistics Canada, 2000).

[17] BMO Financial Group, "Half of Canadian Students Aspire to Start Their Own Business after Graduation: BMO Survey," news release, September 6, 2013, http://newsroom.bmo.com/press-releases/half-of-canadian-students-aspire-to-start-their-ow-tsx-bmo-201309060896440001.

[18] BDC, "Survey Finds Post-Recession Entrepreneurship Surge," October 13, 2010, www.bdc.ca/en/advice_centre/manage_your_assets/financial/Pages/RelatedArticles.aspx?PATH=/EN/advice_centre/articles/Pages/2010_survey_post_recession_entrepreneurship_surge.aspx.

[19] BusinessDictionary.com, "Gazelle Company," www.businessdictionary.com/definition/gazelle-company.html.

[20] National Federation of Independent Business (NFIB), *The Shape of Small Business,* www.nfib.com/object/PolicyGuide2.html.

[21] W. J. Dennis, Jr., and L. W. Fernald, Jr., "The Chances of Financial Success (and Loss) from Small Business Ownership," *Entrepreneurship Theory and Practice* 1 (2002): 75–83.

[22] NFIB, *The Shape of Small Business.* The net business formation index was discontinued in 1995 when one of its two components was no longer available.

[23] N. Macrae, "The Coming Entrepreneurial Revolution," *The Economist,* December 15, 1976.

[24] David L. Birch, *Job Creation in America: How Our Smallest Companies Put the Most People to Work* (New York, NY: Free Press, 1978).

[25] For example, Z. Acs, *The New American Evolution* (Washington, DC: U.S. Small Business Administration, Office of Economic Research, June 1998); and Kirchhoff, *Entrepreneurship and Dynamic Capitalism.*

[26] At one point, General Motors was the largest corporation ever to exist in the United States in terms of its revenues as a percentage of GDP. In 1953, Charles Erwin Wilson, then GM's president, was named by President Eisenhower as secretary of defense. When he was asked, during the hearings before the Senate Armed Services Committee, if as secretary of defense he could make a decision adverse to the interests of General Motors, Wilson answered affirmatively but added that he could not conceive of such a situation "because for years I thought what was good for the country was good for General Motors and vice versa." Later this statement was often garbled when quoted, suggesting that Wilson had said simply, "What's good for General Motors is good for the country." At the

time, GM was one of the largest employers in the world—only Soviet state industries employed more people. "Charles Erwin Wilson," Wikipedia, http://en.wikipedia.org/wiki/Charles_Erwin_Wilson.

27 Definition of Moore's Law: "The observation made in 1965 by Gordon Moore, co-founder of Intel, that the number of transistors per square inch on integrated circuits had doubled every year since the integrated circuit was invented. Moore predicted that this trend would continue for the foreseeable future. In subsequent years, the pace slowed down a bit, but density has doubled approximately every 18 months, and this is the current definition of Moore's Law. Most experts, including Moore himself, expect Moore's Law to hold for at least another two decades." "Moore's Law," Webopedia, www.webopedia.com/TERM/M/Moores_Law.html.

28 Working independently and unaware of each other's activity, Jack Kilby at Texas Instruments and Robert Noyce at Fairchild Semiconductor Corporation invented almost identical integrated circuits at the same time. "In 1959 both parties applied for patents. Jack Kilby and Texas Instruments received U.S. patent #3,138,743 for miniaturized electronic circuits. Robert Noyce and the Fairchild Semiconductor Corporation received U.S. patent #2,981,877 for a silicon-based integrated circuit. The two companies wisely decided to cross license their technologies after several years of legal battles, creating a global market now worth about $1 trillion a year." Mary Bellis, "The History of the Integrated Circuit, aka Microchip," About.com, http://inventors.about.com/library/weekly/aa080498.htm.

29 The first personal computers were actually called microcomputers. The phrase "personal computer" was common currency before 1981 and was used as early as 1972 to characterize Xerox PARC's Alto. However, due to the success of the IBM PC, what had been a generic term came to mean specifically a microcomputer compatible with IBM's specification. "IBM Personal Computer," Wikipedia, http://en.wikipedia.org/wiki/Ibm 5150.

30 The top 25, in descending order, are the Internet, cellphone, personal computer, fibre optics, email, commercialized GPS, portable computers, memory storage disks, consumer-level digital cameras, radio frequency ID tags, MEMS, DNA fingerprinting, air bags, ATMs, advanced batteries, hybrid cars, OLEDs, display panels, HDTVs, space shuttles, nanotechnology, flash memory, voice mail, modern hearing aids, and short-range high-frequency radio. CNN, "To 25: Innovations," June 19, 2005, www.cnn.com/2005/TECH/01/03/cnn25.top25.innovations.

31 "Financing the BlackBerry," Blackberrynationbook.com.

32 "Research In Motion Reports Third Quarter Fiscal 2013 Results," Marketwire, December 20, 2012, www.marketwired.com/press-release/research-in-motion-reports-third-quarter-fiscal-2013-results-nasdaq-rimm-1740316.htm.

33 TMX, "TMX Group History at a Glance," www.tmx.com/en/pdf/TMXHistory.pdf.

34 Ibid.

35 TMX, "TSX First in the World to List an ETF in 1990," news release, April 22, 2010, www.tmx.com/en/news_events/news/news_releases/2010/4-22-2010_TMX-Group-ETF20years.html.

36 http://ca.ishares.com/product_info/fund/overview/XIU.htm.

37 FedEx, "About FedEx," www.fedex.com/us/about/today/history.

38 "Airline Deregulation Act," Wikipedia, http://en.wikipedia.org/wiki/Airline_Deregulation_Act.

39 W. A. Jordan, "Airline Entry Following U.S. Deregulation: The Definitive List of Startup Passenger Airlines, 1979–2003," Transportation Research Forum, www.trforum.org/forum/getpaper.php?id=22&PHPSESSID=119446d6d13ce93d6c6aea3df05010ce.

40 www.tsha.utexas.edu/handbook/online/articles/SS/eps1_print.html.

41 "The World's Billionaires: #950 Chip Wilson," *Forbes,* www.forbes.com/profile/chip-wilson/.

42 "LuLulemon's IPO Prices at $18/shr—Underwriter," Reuters, July 26, 2007, www.reuters.com/article/2007/07/26/lululemon-ipo-idUSWEN980820070726.

43 Michael Mink, "Chip Wilson's Design Made Lululemon a Winner," *Investor's Business Daily,* June 8, 2012, http://news.investors.com/management-leaders-in-success/060812-614215-chip-wilson-designed-lululemon-with-sweat-equity.htm.

44 J. Wynbrandt, *Flying High: How JetBlue Founder and CEO David Neeleman Beats the Competition ... Even in the World's Most Turbulent Industry* (Hoboken, NJ: John Wiley & Sons, 2010).

45 WestJet Fact Sheet, www.westjet.com/pdf/investorMedia/factSheet.pdf.

46 WestJet Backgrounder, www.westjet.com/pdf/investorMedia/westjetBackgrounder.pdf.

47 W. D. Bygrave and J. A. Timmons, *Venture Capital at the Crossroads* (Boston, MA: Harvard Business School Press, 1992).

48 "Biotechnology in the USA: Market Research Report," NAICS NN001, August 2012, www.ibisworld.com/industry/default.aspx?indid=2001.

49 E. M. Rogers and J. K. Larsen, *Silicon Valley Fever: Growth of High-Technology Culture* (New York, NY: Basic Books, 1984).

50 Canadian Press, "Geoffrey Ballard, Founder of Fuel-Cell Firm Ballard Power Systems, Dies," *CBC News,* August 6, 2008, www.cbc.ca/news/canada/geoffrey-ballard-founder-of-fuel-cell-firm-ballard-power-systems-dies-1.730304.

51 Jeremy Pearce, "Geoffrey Ballard, 75, Fuel-Cell Pioneer Who Created Bus Powered by Hydrogen, Dies," *New York Times,* August 11, 2008, www.nytimes.com/2008/08/12/business/12ballard.html?_r=0.

52 Margot Hornblower, "Geoffrey Ballard: In a Hurry to Prove the 'Pistonheads' Wrong," *Time,* March 8, 1999.

53 Vannevar Bush, "As We May Think," *The Atlantic Monthly,* July 1, 1945.

54 Ted Nelson, "The Story So Far," *Ted Nelson Newsletter*, no. 3, October 1994.

55 Computer History Museum, "Internet History," www.computerhistory.org/internet_history/.

56 World Wide Web Consortium, "Tim Berners-Lee, Inventor of the World Wide Web, Knighted by Her Majesty Queen Elizabeth II," July 16, 2004, www.w3.org/2004/07/timbl_knighted.

57 *New Scientist Magazine*, December 17, 1994.

58 The Internet and the World Wide Web (now usually called the Web) are two separate but related entities. However, most people use the terms interchangeably. The Internet is a vast network of networks, a networking infrastructure. The Web is a way of accessing information over the Internet. It is an information-sharing model that is built on top of the Internet.

59 www.smartcomputing.com/editorial/dictionary/detail.asp?DicID=17855.

60 Adam Lashinsky, "Remembering Netscape: The Birth of the Web," *Fortune,* www.fortune.com/fortune/print/0,15935,1081456,00.html.

61 Ibid.

62 D. Gevirtz, *The Entrepreneurs: Innovation in American Business* (New York, NY: Penguin Books, 1985), 30.

63 National Venture Capital Association, *Impact: The Economic Importance of Venture Capital-Backed Companies to the U.S. Economy,* 2010.

64 Thomson Reuters, *Canada's Venture Capital Market in 2013,* https://www.cvca.ca/files/Downloads/VC_Data_Deck_2013_English.pdf.

65 Classic venture capital is money invested privately in seed, startup, expansion, and late-stage companies. The term *classic* is used to distinguish it from money invested privately in acquisitions, buyouts, mergers, and reorganizations.

66 M. Bernhard, "Failing Companies Tarnish Benchmark," *Forbes*, February 6, 2001, www.forbes.com/2001/02/06/0207VC.html.

67 Mark Fitzgerald, "How Did Newspapers Get in This Pickle?" *Editor & Publisher,* March 18, 2009, http://editorandpublisher.

com/PrintArticle/How-Did-Newspapers-Get-in-This-Pickle-.

68 World Bank, *World Development Indicators*, http://data.worldbank.org/data-catalog/world-development-indicators.

69 M. O'Brien, "Obama Open to Newspaper Bailout Bill," *The Hill* (blog), September 20, 2009, http://thehill.com/blogs/blog-briefing-room/news/59523-obama-open-to-newspaper-bailout-bill.

70 B. Veenhof, B. Wellman, C. Quell, and B. Hogan, "How Canadians' Use of the Internet Affects Social Life and Civic Participation," Research Paper, Statistics Canada, December 2008, www.statcan.gc.ca/pub/56f0004m/56f0004m2008016-eng.pdf.

71 Ibid.

72 "In Conversation: Sean Wise," *Toronto Business Times*, April 30, 2012, www.insidetoronto.com/news-story/77179-in-conversation-sean-wise.

73 W. Whyte, *The Organization Man* (New York, NY: Simon & Schuster, 1956).

74 V. Postrel, "How Has 'The Organization Man' changed?" *New York Times, January 17, 1999*.

75 J. K. Galbraith, *The New Industrial State* (Boston, MA: Houghton Mifflin, 1967).

76 J. J. Servan-Schreiber, *The American Challenge* (New York, NY: Scribner, 1968).

77 Norman Macrae, "We're All Intrapreneurial Now," April 17, 1982, www.normanmacrae.com/intrapreneur.html.

78 For example, a mid-1980s study by Calvin Kent of the content of popular principles of economics "revealed that entrepreneurship was either neglected, improperly presented, or only partially covered." C. A. Kent and F. W. Rushing, "Coverage of Entrepreneurship in Principles of Economics Textbooks: An Update," *Journal of Economics Education* 20 (Spring 1999): 184–189.

79 J. A. Schumpeter, *Capitalism, Socialism, and Democracy*, 3rd ed. (New York, NY: Harper Torchbooks, 1950). (Originally published in 1942.)

80 J. A. Schumpeter, *The Theory of Economic Development* (Cambridge, MA: Harvard University Press, 1934).

81 D. M. Blau, "A Time-Series Analysis of Self-Employment in the United States," *Journal of Political Economy* 95 (1987): 445–467; D. Evans and L. S. Leighton, "The Determinants of Changes in U.S. Self-Employment," *Small Business Economics* 1, no. 2 (1987): 111–120.

82 Z. J. Acs, P. Arenius, M. Hay, and M. Minniti, *The Global Entrepreneurship Monitor: 2004 Executive Report*, www.gemconsortium.org.

83 This is excerpted from P. D. Reynolds, M. Hay, W. D. Bygrave, S. M. Camp, and E. Autio, *Global Entrepreneurship Monitor: 2000 Executive Report*, www.gemconsortium.org.

84 Sile Cleary, "Canada's First Entrepreneurs," *Toronto Standard*, January 26, 2012, http://torontostandard.com/industry/canadas-first-entrepreneurs.

85 Ibid.

86 E. Fisher and R. Reuber, "The State of Entrepreneurship in Canada, February 2010," Industry Canada, https://www.ic.gc.ca/eic/site/061.nsf/vwapj/SEC-EEC_eng.pdf/$file/SEC-EEC_eng.pdf.

87 Ibid.

88 Ibid.

89 Ralph Nader's best-selling book *Unsafe at Any Speed: The Designed-In Dangers of the American Automobile*, published in 1965, claimed that automobile manufacturers were ignoring safety features like seat belts and were reluctant to spend money on improving safety.

90 "George Gendron on the State of Entrepreneurship," December 2002, www.pioneer-entrepreneurs.net/bigidea_gen dron.php.

91 "Ian Portsmouth," *PROFIT Magazine*, www.profitguide.com/experts/ian-portsmouth.

92 Bygrave and Timmons, *Venture Capital at the Crossroads*.

93 Statement of Edsel M. Brown, Jr., Assistant Director Office of Technology, U.S. Small Business Administration, before the House Committee on Small Business United States House of Representatives, April 22, 2009, www.house.gov/smbiz/hearings/hearing-4-22-09-technology-economic-recovery/Brown.pdf.

94 Bank of Development Canada, "BDC's History," www.bdc.ca/EN/about/overview/ history/Pages/default.aspx.

95 Ibid.

96 Export Development Canada, "About Us," www.edc.ca/EN/About-Us/Pages/default. aspx.

97 Futurepreneur Canada, "About," www. futurpreneur.ca/en/about/.

98 Ibid.

99 "About the SR&ED Program," Canada Revenue Agency, www.cra-arc.gc.ca/tx-crdt/sred-rsde/bts-eng.html.

100 "About the SR&ED Program," SR&ED Experts, www.scientificresearch.ca/index. php?sred=about&t661=sred.

101 Ibid.

102 "Comparing SR&ED and IRAP for Research & Innovation Funding," Enhanced Capital Recovery, www.enhancedcapital-recovery.com/sred-vs-irap.

103 M. Singletary, "How to Get the Most Bang from eBay," *Maine Sunday Telegram,* August 7, 2005.

104 Canada Newswire, "eBay Names Andrew Sloss Country Manager for Canada," April 22, 2008, www.newswire.ca/fr/ story/320379/ebay-names-andrew-sloss-country-manager-for-canada.

105 J. Wiggins and D. V. Gibson, "Overview of US Incubators and the Case of the Austin Technology Incubator," *International Journal of Entrepreneurship and Innovation Management* 3, nos. 1/2 (2003): 56–66.

106 National Business Incubation Association, "Business Incubation Frequently Asked Questions," www.nbia.org/re-source_library/faq/index.php#3.

107 Ibid.

108 "Looking for a Business or a Technology Incubator?" Canadian Association of Business Incubation, www.cabi.ca/incu-bator-listing.php.

109 "George Gendron on the State of Entrepreneurship."

110 J. Lange, A. Mollov, M. Pearlmuttter, S. Singh, and W. Bygrave, "Pre-Startup Formal Business Plans and Post-Startup Performance: A Study of 116 New Ventures," Paper Presented at the Babson Kauffman Entrepreneurship Research Conference, Babson College. June 2005.

111 M. Boylan, "What We Know and Don't Know about Venture Capital," American Economic Association Meeting, December 28, 1981, and National Economist Club, January 19, 1982.

112 *National Venture Capital Association Yearbook, 2013.*

113 W. D. Bygrave (with Mark Quill), *Global Entrepreneurship Monitor: 2006 Financing Report,* www.gemconsortium.org.

114 Canada's Venture Capital and Private Equity Association, www.cvca.ca.

115 "Canada's Buyout Market in 2013: Moderate Growth, Record Breaking Fundraising," CVCA, March 4, 2014, www. cvca.ca/files/News/CVCA_MEDIA_ RELEASE_PE_Q4_2013_FINAL.pdf.

116 National Angel Capital Organization, "Who We Are," http://nacocanada.com/ about/who-we-are.

117 Ibid.

118 U.S. Small Business Administration, www. sba.gov/advo/research/dyn_b_d8 902.pdf.

119 G. Rifkin and G. Harrar, *The Ultimate Entrepreneur: The Story of Ken Olsen and Digital Equipment Corporation* (Chicago, IL: Contemporary Books, 1998).

120 "Canada's Airlines: Risky Business," *CBC News,* June 17, 2008, www.cbc.ca/ news/business/canada-s-airlines-risky-business-1.709662.

121 N. Lichtenstein, "Is Walmart Good for America?" *PBS Frontline,* June 9, 2004, www.pbs.org/wgbh/pages/frontline/shows/ walmart/interviews/lichtenstein.html.

122 *Cornell Chronicle,* www.news.cornell.edu/ stories/April05/HEC.05.cover.html.

123 Skype, www.skype.com.

124 GEM in itself is an example of not-for-profit (social) entrepreneurship. It was conceived in 1997 by Babson College and London Business School professors. It was prototyped with bootstrap funding and volunteers and was officially launched in 1998 with research teams from 10 nations and supported with funding raised by each

THERE ARE MULTIPLE DEFINITIONS of what makes someone an entrepreneur. French economist Jean Baptist defined an entrepreneur as someone who shifts economic resources out of an area of lower productivity into an area of higher productivity. Joseph Schumpeter defined an entrepreneur as an "agent of change." He views the agent of change as one who exploits an opportunity to create new innovations and ways of doing business (which he called *creative destruction*). Basically, an **entrepreneur** is someone who perceives an opportunity and creates an organization to pursue it. The **entrepreneurial process** includes all the functions, activities, and actions that are part of perceiving opportunities and creating organizations to pursue them.

> An entrepreneur is someone who perceives an opportunity and creates an organization to pursue it.

> The entrepreneurial process includes all the functions, activities, and actions that are part of perceiving opportunities and creating organizations to pursue them.

But is the birth of a new enterprise just happenstance and its subsequent success or failure a chance process? Or can the art and science of entrepreneurship be taught? Clearly, professors and their students believe that it can be taught and learned because entrepreneurship is one of the fastest growing new fields of study in higher education. A study by the Kauffman Foundation found that 61% of U.S. colleges and universities have at least one course in entrepreneurship.[1] It is possible to study entrepreneurship in certificate, associate's, bachelor's, master's, and PhD programs.

In Canada, the same trend can be found. A study by the Ontario Council of Ontario Universities in 2013 determined that universities are nurturing entrepreneurship more and more. There are over a dozen programs and hundreds of courses available to students across Canada. A study conducted by CIBC indicated that Canadians across the nation are expected to start their own companies (and become their own bosses) at an accelerated pace in the years leading up to 2024.[2] Each year universities are offering more courses that focus on building students' knowledge and skills in entrepreneurship.

That transformation in higher education—itself a wonderful example of entrepreneurial change—has come about because a whole body of knowledge about entrepreneurship has developed during the past two decades or so. The process of creating a new business is well understood. Yes, entrepreneurship can be taught. No one is guaranteed to become a Bill Gates or a Mark Zuckerberg, any more than a physics professor can guarantee to produce an Albert Einstein or a tennis coach can guarantee a Eugenie Bouchard. But students with the aptitude to start a business can become better entrepreneurs.

Critical Factors for Starting a New Enterprise

We will begin by examining the entrepreneurial process (see Figure 2.1). These are the factors—personal, sociological, organizational, and environmental—that give birth to a new enterprise and influence how it develops from an idea to a viable enterprise. A person gets an idea for a new business through either a deliberate search or a chance encounter. Whether he or she decides to pursue that idea depends on factors such as alternative career prospects, family, friends, role models, the state of the economy, and the availability of resources.

There is almost always a *triggering event* that gives birth to a new organization. Perhaps the entrepreneur has no better career prospects. For example, Melanie Stevens was a high school dropout who, after working a number of minor jobs, had run out of career options. She decided that making canvas bags in her own tiny business was better than earning low wages working for someone else. Within a few years, she had built a chain of retail stores throughout Canada.

Sometimes the person has been passed over for a promotion or even laid off or fired. Howard Rose had been laid off four times as a result of mergers and consolidations in the pharmaceutical industry, and he had had enough of it. So he started his own drug packaging business, Waverly Pharmaceutical. Tim Waterstone founded Waterstone's bookstores after W. H. Smith fired him. Ann Gloag quit her nursing job and used her bus-driver father's $40,000 severance pay to set up Stagecoach Bus Company with her brother, exploiting legislation deregulating the United Kingdom's bus industry. Jordan Rubin was debilitated by Crohn's disease when he

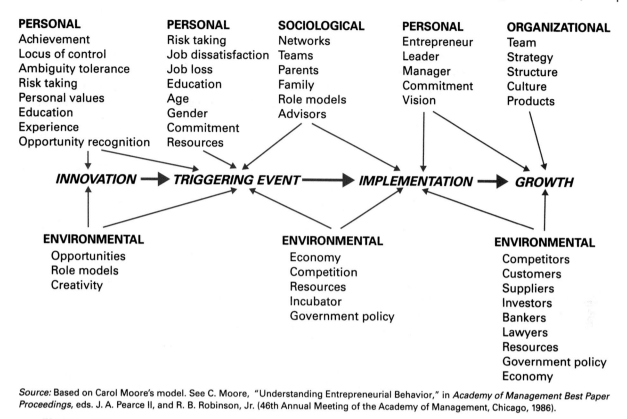

PERSONAL	PERSONAL	SOCIOLOGICAL	PERSONAL	ORGANIZATIONAL
Achievement	Risk taking	Networks	Entrepreneur	Team
Locus of control	Job dissatisfaction	Teams	Leader	Strategy
Ambiguity tolerance	Job loss	Parents	Manager	Structure
Risk taking	Education	Family	Commitment	Culture
Personal values	Age	Role models	Vision	Products
Education	Gender	Advisors		
Experience	Commitment			
Opportunity recognition	Resources			

INNOVATION → TRIGGERING EVENT → IMPLEMENTATION → GROWTH

ENVIRONMENTAL	ENVIRONMENTAL	ENVIRONMENTAL
Opportunities	Economy	Competitors
Role models	Competition	Customers
Creativity	Resources	Suppliers
	Incubator	Investors
	Government policy	Bankers
		Lawyers
		Resources
		Government policy
		Economy

Source: Based on Carol Moore's model. See C. Moore, "Understanding Entrepreneurial Behavior," in *Academy of Management Best Paper Proceedings,* eds. J. A. Pearce II, and R. B. Robinson, Jr. (46th Annual Meeting of the Academy of Management, Chicago, 1986).

Figure 2.1

A model of the entrepreneurial process

invented a diet supplement that restored his health; he founded a company, Garden of Life, to sell that supplement. Noreen Kenny was working for a semiconductor company and could not find a supplier to do precision mechanical work, so she launched her own company, Evolve Manufacturing Technologies, to fill the void. The Baby Einstein Company was started by Julie Aigner-Clark when she discovered that there were no age-appropriate products available to help her share her love of art, classical music, language, and poetry with her newborn daughter.

Origins of Home Depot

Bernie Marcus was president of the now-defunct Handy Dan home improvement chain, based in California, when he and Arthur Blank were abruptly fired by new management. That day and the months that followed were the most pivotal period in his career, he says. "I was 49 years old at the time and I was pretty devastated by being fired. Still, I think it's a question of believing in yourself. Soon after, we [Blank and Marcus] started to realize that this was our opportunity to start over," says Marcus.

Marcus and Blank then happened upon a 120,000-square-foot store called Homeco, operating in Long Beach, California. The two instantly realized that the concept—an oversized store packed with merchandise tagged with low prices—had a magical quality. They wanted to buy the business, but it was essentially bankrupt. Marcus and Blank talked Homeco owner Pat Farah into joining them in Atlanta, and the trio, along with Ron Brill, began sketching the blueprint for Home Depot.[i]

[i] *Stores Magazine,* www.stores.org/archives/jan99cover.asp.

Jim Poss, while walking down a Boston street, observed a trash vehicle idling at a pick-up point, blocking traffic, with smoke pouring out of its exhaust, while litter was still prevalent on the street. Poss was struck by the thought that there had to be a better way; it led to his invention of the BigBelly solar-powered trash compactor.

Canadian entrepreneur Michael Petrov was born into a family that welcomed and embraced change. This taught him the value of adapting to different environments while at the same time developing a talent for spotting entrepreneurial opportunities. At the young age of 11, Petrov enjoyed playing computer games more than any other hobby or activity. Realizing that his son was exceptionally talented and interested in using technology, Petrov's father encouraged him to do more with his time than simply play games—Petrov started taking programming courses, developing his computer and technological skills, and making friends with other children who enjoyed learning similar skills. It wasn't long before he became an expert in software development, which at the time was a rare skill within the general market. Noticing that such skills were needed in the business world, Petrov recognized this as an opportunity to start up his own freelance software consulting company.

Petrov studied at Waterloo University where he created a team of five Canadians to develop the iPhone app Couple (previously known as Pair). The team travelled to California to take part in the Y Combinator, a unique accelerator that provides candidates with mentorship, funding, and support from some of the leading Silicon Valley entrepreneurs. The idea for the app came from three of the co-founders who had to leave their significant others in Canada when they moved down to California. Finding it difficult to stay connected with their loved ones, Petrov and his team created the "social network for lovebirds." With over 220,000 users and $4.2 million in funding from investors (including Ashton Kutcher's company A-Grade Investments), the application has become highly successful within North America.[3]

For some people, entrepreneurship is a deliberate career choice. Sandra Kurtzig was a software engineer with General Electric who wanted to start a family and work at home. She started ASK Computer Systems Inc., which became a $400-million-a-year business.

Where do would-be entrepreneurs get their ideas? More often than not it is through their present line of employment or experience. In addition, entrepreneurs often identify an opportunity by either observing trends (demographics, economic forces, fashions, new technologies, political changes, etc.), solving a problem (often from a personal experience), or finding gaps in the marketplace (e.g., Curves).[4] Observing or studying trends in the marketplace includes monitoring economic factors (changes in gross domestic product, exchange rates, interest rates, etc.), social factors (social influences, changes in demographics, activities, etc.), technological advances (the Internet, abilities of mobile devices, new technologies on the market), and political action or regulatory statutes (changes in political parties in power, new or changing laws, etc.). In order to solve a problem, an entrepreneur must observe consumer challenges, seek problems that they have themselves or have observed, listen to peoples' complaints, or think about their everyday lives and problems they encounter along the way.

Others start businesses over and over again in related industries. In 1981, James Clark, then a Stanford University computer science professor, founded Silicon Graphics, a computer manufacturer with 1996 sales of $3 billion. In April 1994, he teamed up with Marc Andreessen to found Netscape Communications. Within 12 months, its browser software, Netscape Navigator, dominated the Internet's World Wide Web (WWW or the Web). When Netscape went public in August 1995, Clark became the first Internet billionaire. Then in June 1996, Clark launched another company, Healtheon (subsequently merged with WebMD), to enable doctors, insurers, and patients to exchange data and do business over the Internet with software incorporating Netscape Navigator.

Much rarer is the serial entrepreneur such as Wayne Huizenga, who ventures into unrelated industries: first in garbage disposal with Waste Management, next in entertainment with Blockbuster Video, then in automobile sales with AutoNation. Along the way he was the original owner of the Florida Marlins baseball team, which won the World Series in 1997.

Most of these examples have been from the United States, but entrepreneurship is quite prevalent in Canada, too. In fact, Canada has twice the percentage of self-employed individuals compared to the United States (20% versus 10%), making Canada's entrepreneurial community proportionately double the size.[5] The major driving force behind the creation of new companies and jobs by Canadian entrepreneurs are first-generation entrepreneurial success stories. For instance, many tech-oriented entrepreneurs chose to base their businesses out of Waterloo, Ontario, because of Research In Motion's (RIM) success story. Canadians are also known to be innovators; they are early adopters who are eager to get popular, new technologies in the marketplace.[6] Finally, Canadian innovators and entrepreneurs are known to have the ability to see an idea through the initial stages, constantly thinking to themselves, "Where is this project going to be in 15 years?" or "Where is this market going to be in 15 years?"[7]

What factors influence someone to embark on an entrepreneurial career? Like most human behaviour, entrepreneurial traits are shaped by *personal attributes* and *environment*.

Personal Attributes

In the entrepreneurial 1980s, there was a spate of magazine and newspaper articles that were entitled "Do you have the right stuff to be an entrepreneur?" or words to that effect. The articles described the most important characteristics of entrepreneurs and, more often than not, included a self-evaluation exercise to enable readers to determine if they had the right stuff. Those articles were based on flimsy behavioural research into the differences between entrepreneurs and non-entrepreneurs. The basis for those exercises was the belief, first developed by David McClelland in his book *The Achieving Society*, that entrepreneurs had *a higher need for achievement* than non-entrepreneurs and that they were moderate risk takers. One engineer almost abandoned his entrepreneurial ambitions after completing one of those exercises. He asked his professor at the start of an MBA entrepreneurship course if he should take the class because he had scored very low on an entrepreneurship test in a magazine. He took the course, however, and wrote an award-winning plan for a business that was a success from the very beginning.

There is no neat set of behavioural attributes that allows us to separate entrepreneurs from non-entrepreneurs. A person who rises to the top of any occupation, whether an entrepreneur or an administrator, is an achiever. Granted, any would-be entrepreneur must have a need to achieve, but so must anyone else with ambitions to be successful.

It does appear that entrepreneurs have a higher internal locus of control than non-entrepreneurs, which means that they have a stronger desire to be in control of their own fate (i.e., how much people believe they have the ability to control events that affect them; if a project succeeds they will take credit, and if it is unsuccessful they blame themselves).[8] This has been confirmed by many surveys in which entrepreneurs said independence was an important reason for starting their business. The main reasons they gave were independence, financial success, self-realization, recognition, innovation, and roles (to continue a family tradition, to follow the example of an admired person, to be respected by friends). Men rated financial success and innovation higher than women did. Interestingly, the reasons that nascent entrepreneurs gave for starting a business were similar to the reasons given by non-entrepreneurs for choosing jobs.[9]

The most important characteristics of successful entrepreneurs are shown in Figure 2.2.

Environmental Factors

Perhaps as important as personal attributes are the external influences on a would-be entrepreneur. It's no accident that some parts of the world are more entrepreneurial than others. The most famous region of high-tech entrepreneurship is Silicon Valley. Because everyone in Silicon Valley knows someone who has made it big as an entrepreneur, role models abound. This situation produces what Stanford University sociologist Everett Rogers called "Silicon Valley fever."[10] It seems as if everyone in the valley catches that bug sooner or later and wants

Dream	Entrepreneurs have a vision of what the future could be like for them and their businesses. And, more important, they have the ability to implement their dreams.
Decisiveness	They don't procrastinate. They make decisions swiftly. Their swiftness is a key factor in their success.
Doers	Once they decide on a course of action, they implement it as quickly as possible.
Determination	They implement their ventures with total commitment. They seldom give up, even when confronted by obstacles that seem insurmountable.
Dedication	They are totally dedicated to their businesses, sometimes at considerable cost to their relationships with friends and families. They work tirelessly. Twelve-hour days and seven-day workweeks are not uncommon when an entrepreneur is striving to get a business off the ground.
Devotion	Entrepreneurs love what they do. It is that love that sustains them when the going gets tough. And it is love of their product or service that makes them so effective at selling it.
Details	It is said that the devil resides in the details. That is especially true when starting and growing a business. The entrepreneur must be on top of the critical details.
Destiny	They want to be in charge of their own destiny rather than be dependent on an employer.
Dollars	Getting rich is not the prime motivator of entrepreneurs; money is more a measure of success. Entrepreneurs assume that if they are successful they will be rewarded.
Distribute	Entrepreneurs distribute the ownership of their businesses with key employees who are critical to the success of the business.

■ **Figure 2.2**

The 10 Ds—The most important characteristics of a successful entrepreneur

to start a business. To facilitate the process, there are venture capitalists who understand how to select and nurture high-tech entrepreneurs, bankers who specialize in lending to them, lawyers who understand the importance of intellectual property and how to protect it, landlords who are experienced in renting real estate to fledgling companies, suppliers who are willing to sell goods on credit to companies with no credit history, and even politicians who are supportive.

Many of Canada's larger cities have been labelled as great environments for startups and entrepreneurs alike. Among the top are Toronto, Vancouver, and Montreal. Toronto has become a popular creatively driven city for entrepreneurs and startups alike. Many incubator programs have developed in downtown Toronto, making it the go-to city for budding entrepreneurs. For example, Ryerson University's Digital Media Zone (DMZ) is one of Canada's largest incubators. It is a multidisciplinary working space infused with innovative energy and resources, making it the hub for digital media innovation, collaboration, and commercialization.[11]

In addition to ranking high for overall quality of life, Vancouver offers a unique mixture of schools in technology and arts that produce pools of people who are innovative, creative, and educated in entrepreneurship. The close proximity to Silicon Valley is another draw for entrepreneurs as it gives them better access to the programs, entrepreneurs, and innovation in the area.[12] In fact, technology is growing faster in British Columbia than the forestry, mining, or energy industries that the region is known for.[13] HootSuite is a well-known Vancouver-based startup that was able to raise US$165 million in funding from the same venture capitalists who also backed Facebook and Twitter.[14]

Montreal is also considered one of the best places for startups due to its strong, diverse, and friendly startup scene.[15] The city is home to a diverse population with innovative community members, not to mention it has been labelled the second happiest city in the world with a very low cost of living.[16] Montreal has put efforts into becoming a go-to community for entrepreneurs by launching FounderFuel, an accelerator program that hosts the Montreal International Startup Festival each summer. The city also boasts entrepreneurial success stories like the social media company Wajam.[17]

Knowing successful entrepreneurs at work or in your personal life makes becoming one yourself seem much more achievable. Indeed, if a close relative is an entrepreneur, you are more likely to want to become an entrepreneur yourself, especially if that relative is your mother or father. Half of the Inc. 500 entrepreneurs in 2012 had a parent who was an entrepreneur.[18] But you don't have to be from a business-owning family to become an entrepreneur. Bill Gates, for example, was following the family tradition of becoming a lawyer when he dropped out of Harvard and founded Microsoft. He was in the fledgling microcomputer industry, which was being built by entrepreneurs, so he had plenty of role models among his friends and acquaintances. Canada has a growing list of highly successful entrepreneurs whose companies have expanded throughout North American and even globally, including Brian Scudamore (1-800-GOT-JUNK), Sir Terry Matthews (Nortel Networks), John Sleeman (Sleeman Breweries), Michael Cowpland (Corel Corporation), Ron Joyce (Tim Hortons), Guy Laliberté (Cirque du Soleil), and Rebecca MacDonald (Just Energy Group). Some universities are hotbeds of entrepreneurship. For example, Ryerson University and the Massachusetts Institute of Technology (MIT) have produced numerous entrepreneurs among its faculty and alumni. Companies with an MIT connection transformed the Massachusetts economy from one based on decaying shoe and textile industries into one based on high technology:

> According to [a 2009 MIT] study, "Entrepreneurial Impact: The Role of MIT," which analyzes the economic effect of MIT alumni–founded companies and its entrepreneurial ecosystem, if the active companies founded by MIT graduates formed an independent nation, their revenues would make that nation at least the 17th-largest economy in the world…
>
> The overall MIT entrepreneurial environment, consisting of multiple education, research and social network institutions, contributes to this outstanding and growing entrepreneurial output. Highlights of the findings include:
>
> > An estimated 6,900 MIT alumni companies with worldwide sales of approximately $164 billion are located in Massachusetts alone and represent 26 percent of the sales of all Massachusetts companies.
> >
> > 4,100 MIT alumni–founded firms are based in California and generate an estimated $134 billion in worldwide sales.
> >
> > States currently benefiting most from jobs created by MIT alumni companies are Massachusetts (estimated at just under 1 million jobs), California (estimated at 526,000 jobs), New York (estimated at 231,000 jobs), Texas (estimated at 184,000 jobs) and Virginia (estimated at 136,000 jobs).[19]

It is not only in high tech that we see role models. Consider these examples:

- It has been estimated that half of all the convenience stores in New York City are owned by Koreans.
- It was the visibility of successful role models that spread catfish farming in the Mississippi Delta as a more profitable alternative to cotton.
- Portland, Oregon, has 40 microbreweries within its city boundaries, which according to the Oregon Brewers Guild is more than any other city in the world.
- Hay-on-Wye—a tiny town in Wales with 1,500 inhabitants—has 39 secondhand bookstores. It claims to be the "largest used and antiquarian bookshop in the world." It all began in 1961 when Richard Booth, an Oxford graduate, opened his first bookstore.

Role models are so important that a lack of them can stifle entrepreneurial action among certain sectors of the population. For example, black Americans make up 12% of the U.S. population but owned only 4% of the nation's businesses in 1997.[20] A similar problem exists among Aboriginal peoples in both Canada and the United States. Fortunately, this situation is rapidly improving. Between the 1992 and 1997 U.S. censuses, the number of minority-owned businesses grew more than four times as fast as U.S. firms overall, increasing from 2.1 million to about 2.8 million firms.[21] According to the 2007 census, Hispanics/Latinos owned 8.5% of the nation's businesses, black Americans owned 7.0%, Asian Americans owned 5.9%, and American Indians and Alaskan Natives owned 1.1%.[22]

Other Sociological Factors

Besides role models, entrepreneurs are influenced by other sociological factors. Family responsibilities play an important role in the decision to start a company. It is a relatively easy career decision to start a business when you are 25 years old, single, and without many personal assets and dependents; it is a much harder decision when you are 45 and married with teenage children preparing to go to university, a hefty mortgage, car payments, and a secure, well-paying job. A survey of European high-potential entrepreneurs, for instance, found that on average they had 50% of their net worth at risk because it was tied up in their businesses. And when you are over the age of 45, if you fail as an entrepreneur, it will not be easy to rebuild a career working for another company. But despite the risks, plenty of 45-year-olds are taking the plunge; in fact, the median age of the CEOs of the 500 fastest-growing small companies—the Inc. 500—in 2009 was 41 and the median age of their companies was six years.[23] According to *Profit* magazine, the average age of CEOs running Canada's fastest-growing startups is 39. On average they clock in 61-hour workweeks (compared to the average 40 hours), and 66% of the CEOs are serial entrepreneurs, meaning their latest company is their second, third, or even fourth startup.[24] For example, Yona Shtern launched four startups prior to his highly successful recent company Beyond the Rack.

Another factor that determines the age at which entrepreneurs start businesses is the trade-off between the *experience* that comes with age and the *optimism* and *energy* of youth. As you grow older you gain experience, but sometimes when you have been in an industry a long time, you know so many pitfalls that you are pessimistic about the chance of succeeding if you decide to go out on your own. Someone who has just enough experience to feel confident as a manager is more likely to feel optimistic about an entrepreneurial career. The best performing businesses tend to be started when the entrepreneurs had 10 years management experience after graduation.

Perhaps the ideal combination is a beginner's mind—someone who looks at a situation from a new perspective with a can-do spirit—matched with the experience of an industry veteran. For example, 27-year-old Robert Swanson was a complete novice at biotechnology but was convinced that it had great commercial potential. His enthusiasm complemented Professor Herbert Boyer's unsurpassed knowledge about the use of recombinant DNA to produce human protein. The two just assumed that Boyer's laboratory work could be scaled up to industrial levels. Looking back, Boyer said, "I think we were so naïve, we never thought it couldn't be done." Together they succeeded and started a new industry.

Likewise, Marc Andreessen had a beginner's mind in 1993 when, as a student and part-time assistant at the National Center for Supercomputing Applications at the University of Illinois, he developed the Mosaic browser and produced a vision for the Internet that until then had eluded many computer industry veterans, including Bill Gates. When Andreessen's youthful creativity was joined with James Clark's entrepreneurial wisdom, which had been earned over a dozen years as founder and chair of Silicon Graphics, it turned out to be an awesome combination. Their company, Netscape Navigator, distributed 38 million copies of Navigator in just two years, making it the most successful new software introduction ever.

We cannot specify how much managerial expertise it takes to become a skilled entrepreneur. However, we do know that venture capitalists recognize that neophyte high-tech entrepreneurs, especially very young ones, do not have enough experience, so they often recruit seasoned entrepreneurial managers to guide them. An example is Google, where Eric Schmidt was hired as CEO to guide Larry Page and Sergey Brin. (It is also an excellent example of what venture capitalists call *value-added*.) Then after 10 years at the helm, Schmidt announced he would step aside to allow Page to take over the reins as CEO in 2011.

When entrepreneurs are building their team for their startup, they need to join forces with other people who have complementary skills and expertise, fulfilling all three components of what is known as the *talent triangle*. The talent triangle refers to the attributes of successful management teams and includes three elements: business acumen (skills and expertise in the development of strategy and the execution of business planning), operational experience (prior know-how about building and delivering the solution; e.g., if a startup was producing apps for the iPhone, previous operational experience in mobile software would be desired), and domain knowledge (understanding the customers and the industry within the business domain).[25]

Before leaving secure, well-paying, satisfying jobs, would-be entrepreneurs should make a careful estimate of how much sales revenue their new businesses must generate before they will be able to match the income they presently earn. It usually comes as quite a shock when they realize that, if they are opening a retail establishment, they will need annual sales revenue of at least $750,000 to pay themselves a salary of $70,000 plus fringe benefits such as healthcare coverage, retirement pension benefits, and long-term disability insurance. To make $750,000 a year requires about $15,000 per week, or about $2,500 per day, or about $250 per hour, or about $4 per minute if they are open six days a week, 10 hours a day. Also, they will be working much longer hours and bearing much more responsibility if they become self-employed. A sure way to test the strength of a marriage is to start a company that is the sole means of support for your family. For example, 22.5% of the CEOs of the Inc. 500 got divorced while growing their businesses. On a brighter note, 59.2% got married, and 18.3% of divorced CEOs remarried.[26]

When they actually start a business, entrepreneurs need both social capital and a social network, including customers, suppliers, investors, bankers, accountants, and lawyers. So it is important to understand where to find help before embarking on a new venture. A network of friends and business associates can be of immeasurable help in building the contacts an entrepreneur will need. They can also provide human contact, which is important because opening a business can be a lonely experience for anyone who has worked in an organization with many fellow employees.

Fortunately, today there are more organizations than ever before to help fledgling entrepreneurs. Often that help is free or costs very little. The Small Business Association of Canada (SBA Canada) and Startup Canada provide free or minimal-cost assistance to entrepreneurs and startups across the country. Startup Canada is one of the country's most followed national entrepreneurship organizations.[27] More than 55,000 entrepreneurs and over 400 partner organizations support other Canadian entrepreneurs through education, mentorship, tools, networks, workshops, conferences, and so on, helping to foster and strengthen Canada's entrepreneurship ecosystem.[28] Many colleges and universities also provide help. Some are particularly good at writing business plans, usually at no charge to the entrepreneur. In addition, there are dozens of incubators and accelerators in Canada where fledgling businesses can rent space, usually at a very reasonable price, and spread some of their overhead by sharing facilities such as copying machines, secretarial help, answering services, and so on. Incubators are often associated with universities, such as Ryerson University's incubator the Digital Media Zone and its accelerator Ryerson Futures Incorporated. Accelerators and incubators often provide free or inexpensive counselling. Notable accelerators and incubators across the country include Extreme Venture Partners (Toronto), The Next 36 (Toronto), MaRS Discovery District and Jolt (Toronto), UW Velocity (University of Waterloo), FounderFuel (Montreal), Executive Labs (Montreal), Flightpath Ventures (Edmonton), GrowLab (Vancouver), Innovate Calgary (Calgary), Innovate Niagara (Niagara), and Communitech HyperDrive (Waterloo).[29] Figure 2.3 shows a sample of accelerators across Canada, including their location, pitch, and requirements. For full details, see www.cmf-fmc.ca/documents/files/programs/2013-14/apps/exp/2013-14_a3p_accelerators.pdf.

	FounderFuel	Execution Labs	Ryerson Futures	Communitech HYPERDRIVE
Location	Montreal	Montreal	Toronto	Waterloo region
Pitch	A top-tier, mentor-driven accelerator that helps early stage Web, mobile, and SaaS startups raise seed capital.	Helps independent game developers produce games and bring them to market.	Ryerson Futures and DMZ helps emerging leaders fast-track their product launches and grow their companies by connecting with mentors, customers, and each other.	A tech startup seed-accelerator program with a global focus to seed, fund, and grow new businesses.
Focus	Web, mobile, and SaaS	Mobile games	Technology at large	Any technological startup
Value Proposition for A3P Applicants	Provides selected applicants with a $50,000 investment in exchange of 9% equity. The CMF will provide an additional non-refundable contribution of $30,000 to the selected applicants, free of equity. Selected applicants can be eligible to a $150,000 convertible note from the BDC.	The CMF will contribute a non-refundable $30,000 to selected applicants. Execution Labs will provide the balance of the investment, up to $70,000 (for a total standard investment of $100,000) for a standard 15% equity rate (calculated on $100,000) in the companies, to be retained by Execution Labs.	The CMF will contribute a non-refundable $30,000 to be paid directly to selected applicants, in exchange for a standard investment rate of 5% in equity, to be retained by Ryerson Futures Inc. In addition, upon acceptance in the program selected applicants will receive a 4-month free stay in the DMZ and could qualify for an additional $50,000 in financing directly from Ryerson Futures Inc.	The CMF will contribute a non-refundable $30,000 to selected applicants for the program in replacement of the usual amount invested by Communitech HYPERDRIVE. Nonetheless, a standard 4% in equity will be retained by Communitech HYPERDRIVE in exchange for all other services related for the acceleration program.
Program Format	Selected applicants will participate in a 12-week intensive program involving mentors and experts coaching, networking, and a Demo Day.	Flexible 9-month program in residence; the first 6 months focus on getting games ready for launch, the next 3 months focus on building market traction and making tweaks based on live metrics; also included a Demo day, global mentors, and marketing opportunities.	Incubation program: Semi-structured 4-month program with an optional additional 8 months (fees may apply). Acceleration program: 4 to 8 months with ability to extend for a fee.	Three-month sprint with focus on customer and market validation, followed by hands-on guidance from mentors for up to 24 months; one-week in New York to meet funders, partners, and potential customers, additional soft landing opportunities in foreign markets, demo days, and chances to pitch to top tech investors.
Best Fit Candidate	Startups with big ambitions who want to refine their business, scale it fast, and raise follow-on capital.	Small teams of 2 to 5 seasoned people with industry experience and an early stage idea.	Best fit candidates range from early-stage unfunded projects to companies looking to refine or accelerate their growth.	Early-stage technology startups.
Requirements	Open to teams of 2 or more people, with at least one co-founder with technical skills.		Welcomes multidisciplinary teams of passionate entrepreneurs who have an idea that involves some aspect of technology.	Open to teams of 2 or more people.
Link	www.founderfuel.com	http://executionlabs.com	http://digitalmediazone.ryerson.ca	http://hyperdrive.communitech.ca

Source: Canada Media Fund, "CMF Accelerators Partnership Pilot Program," www.cmf-fmc.ca/documents/files/programs/2013-14/apps/exp/2013-14_a3p_accelerators.pdf. Accessed November 24, 2014. For more details and for the ongoing updated list, visit www.cmf-fmc.ca/funding-programs/experimental-stream/accelerator-partnership-pilot-program.

■ **Figure 2.3**

Examples of accelerators across Canada

Evaluating Opportunities for New Businesses

Let's assume you believe that you have found a great opportunity for starting a new business. How should you evaluate its prospects? Or, perhaps more important, how will an independent person such as a potential investor or a banker rate your chances of success? The odds of succeeding appear to be stacked against you because, according to small business folklore, only 1 business in 10 will ever reach its 10th birthday. Even though the Canadian government declared 2011 the "Year of the Entrepreneur," not all new ventures succeed. The five-year survival rate of new ventures in Canada is, on average, less than 50%, and fast forward to 10 years later and you'll find that only 10% of the startup ventures successfully remain in business. A new startup firm has a 77% chance of surviving its first year in Canada, but only a 36% chance of surviving the first five years. This lack of success can be attributed to many factors, including (but not limited to) market entry in unfavourable conditions, a lack of financial literacy and financial management skills, and inadequate business acumen.

But survival may not spell success. Too many entrepreneurs find that they can neither earn a satisfactory living in their businesses nor get out of them easily because they have too much of their personal assets tied up in them. The happiest day in an entrepreneur's life is the day doors are opened for business. For unsuccessful entrepreneurs, an even happier day may be the day the business is sold—especially if most personal assets remain intact. What George Bernard Shaw said about a love affair is also apt for a business: Any fool can start one, but it takes a genius to end one successfully.

How can you stack the odds in your favour so that your new business is a success? Professional investors, such as venture capitalists, have a talent for picking winners. True, they also pick losers, but a startup company funded by venture capital has, on average, a four-in-five chance of surviving five years—better odds than for the population of startup companies as a whole. Very few businesses—perhaps no more than one in a thousand—will ever be suitable candidates for investments from professional venture capitalists. But would-be entrepreneurs can learn a lot by following the evaluation process used by professional investors.

There are three crucial components for a successful new business: the opportunity, the entrepreneur (and the management team, if it's a high-potential venture), and the resources needed to start the company and make it grow. These are shown schematically in Figure 2.4. At the centre of the framework is a business plan, the result of integrating the three basic ingredients into a complete strategic plan for the new business. The parts must fit together well. It's no good having a first-rate idea for a new business if you have a second-rate management team. Nor are ideas and management any good without the appropriate resources.

Roger Martin, past dean at the University of Toronto's Rotman School of Management, believes that to have a successful new business there are three factors involved: an unmet need, a 10X solution, and the proper entrepreneur(s).[30] Identifying an unmet need in the marketplace means that there is an inefficient, unsatisfactory, or suboptimal problem within the industry. The entrepreneur(s) are attracted to the suboptimal situation and want to provide a solution that is 10 times (10X) better than what is currently available. Building the optimal entrepreneurship team is the final component of a successful new business.

The crucial driving force of any new venture is the lead entrepreneur and the founding management team. Georges Doriot, the founder

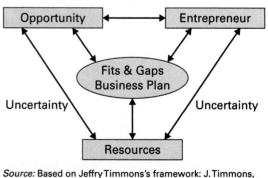

Source: Based on Jeffry Timmons's framework: J. Timmons, *New Venture Creation* (Homewood, IL: Richard D. Irwin, 2001).

Figure 2.4

Three driving forces

> The crucial ingredients for entrepreneurial success are a superb entrepreneur with a first-rate management team and an excellent market opportunity.

of modern venture capital, used to say something like this: "Always consider investing in a grade-A man with a grade-B idea. Never invest in a grade-B man with a grade-A idea." He knew what he was talking about. Over the years he invested in about 150 companies, including Digital Equipment Corporation (DEC), and watched over them as they struggled to grow. But Doriot made his statement about business in the 1950s and 1960s. During that period, there were far fewer startups than there are today; U.S. firms dominated the marketplace, markets were growing quickly, there was almost no competition from overseas, and most entrepreneurs were male. Today, in the global marketplace, with ever-shortening product life cycles and low growth or even no growth for some of the world's leading industrial nations, the crucial ingredients for entrepreneurial success are a superb entrepreneur with a first-rate management team and an excellent market opportunity.

> In entrepreneurship, as in any other profession, luck is where preparation and opportunity meet.

It's often said that entrepreneurship is largely a matter of luck. That's not so. We do not say that becoming a great quarterback, a great scientist, or a great musician is a matter of luck. There is no more luck in becoming successful at entrepreneurship than in becoming successful at anything else. In entrepreneurship, it is a question of recognizing a good opportunity when you see one and having the skills to convert that opportunity into a thriving business. To do that, you must be prepared. In entrepreneurship, as in any other profession, *luck is where preparation and opportunity meet.*

In 1982, when Rod Canion proposed to start Compaq to make personal computers, there were already formidable established competitors, including IBM and Apple, and literally hundreds of companies that were considering entering the market or had already done so. Despite the competition, Ben Rosen of the venture capital firm Sevin Rosen Management Company invested in Compaq. Started initially to make transportable PCs, Compaq quickly added a complete range of high-performance PCs and grew so fast that it soon broke Apple's record for the fastest time from founding to listing on the *Fortune* 500.

What did Ben Rosen see in the Compaq proposal that made it stand out from all the other personal computer startups? The difference was Rod Canion and his team. Rod Canion had earned a reputation as an excellent manager at Texas Instruments. Furthermore, the market for personal computers topped $5 billion and was growing at a torrid pace. So Rosen had found a superb team with a product targeted at an undeveloped niche, transportable PCs, in a large market that was growing explosively. By 1994, Compaq was the leading PC manufacturer with 13% of the market.

The Opportunity

Perhaps the biggest misconception about an idea for a new business is that it must be unique. Too many would-be entrepreneurs are almost obsessed with finding a unique idea. Then, when they believe they have it, they are haunted by the thought that someone is just waiting to steal it from them. So they become super-secretive, reluctant to discuss it with anyone who doesn't sign a nondisclosure agreement. That makes it almost impossible to evaluate the idea, and many counsellors who provide free advice to entrepreneurs refuse to sign nondisclosure agreements. Generally speaking, these super-secret, unique ideas are big letdowns when the entrepreneurs reveal them. Some notable recent examples were drive-through pizza by the slice, a combination toothbrush and toothpaste gadget, and a Mexican restaurant in Boston. One computer programmer said he had a fantastic new piece of software for managing hairdressing salons. He was completely floored when he found that less than a month previously another entrepreneur had demonstrated a software package for exactly the same purpose. Another entrepreneur had an idea for fluoride-impregnated dental floss. Not three months later, the identical product turned out to be available in Boots—Britain's largest chain of drug stores and a major pharmaceutical manufacturer.

Almost any idea a would-be entrepreneur might have will also have occurred to others. In fact, some of the most revolutionary thoughts in the history of humankind occurred to more than one person almost simultaneously. Newton and Leibnitz independently invented calculus within a few years of each other; Darwin was almost preempted by Wallace in publishing his theory of evolution; Poincaré almost formulated a valid theory of special relativity about the same time Einstein did; and the integrated circuit was invented in 1959, first by Jack Kilby at Texas Instruments and then independently by Robert Noyce at Fairchild a few months later. And as we read in Chapter 1, Berners-Lee was not the first person to introduce the concept of hypertext. Nor was Google the first company to introduce a Web search engine.

The idea in itself is not what is important. In entrepreneurship, ideas really are a dime a dozen. Developing the idea, implementing it, and building a successful business are the important things. Alexander Fleming discovered penicillin by chance but never developed it as a useful drug. About 10 years later Ernst Chain and Howard Florey unearthed Fleming's mould and immediately saw its potential. They soon were treating patients in England with it, and before the end of World War II penicillin was saving countless lives. It was a most dramatic pharmaceutical advance and heralded a revolution in that industry.

According to the late Stanford Professor Rajeev Motwani, who mentored Sergey Brin and Larry Page, "At some point these guys said, we want to do a company. Everybody said you must be out of your minds. There are like 37 search engines out there and what are you guys going to do? And how are you going to raise money, how will you build a company, and these two guys said, we'll just do it and they went off and did it. And then they took over the world."[31]

> The idea in itself is not what is important. In entrepreneurship, ideas really are a dime a dozen. Developing the idea, implementing it, and building a success-ful business are the im-portant things.

The Customer

Many would-be entrepreneurs fail to think carefully enough about who makes up the market for their product or service. They should have a very specific answer to this question: "Can you give me the names of prospective customers?" If they have a consumer product—let's say it's a new shampoo—they should be able to name the buyers at different chains of drug stores in their area. If they are unable to name several customers immediately, they simply have an idea, not a market. There is no market unless customers have a real need for the product—a proven need rather than a hypothetical need in the mind of a would-be entrepreneur. A few rare cases may be revolutionary new products with markets waiting to be formed, but most entrepreneurial ideas are for existing products with improved performance, price, distribution, quality, or service. Simply put, customers must perceive that the new business will be giving them better value for their money than existing businesses.

> Would-be entrepre-neurs who are unable to name a customer are not ready to start a business. They have found an idea but have not yet identified a mar-ket need.

Even though finding investors to help start a new business is important, without custom-ers no business is viable. There are many reasons that customers trump investors (and why customers are so important):

1. Customers are nondilutive: The more customers a startup entrepreneur can speak to throughout the process, the more valuable information and feedback he or she will receive.

2. Customers are your market: You can never ask enough questions or talk too much to cus-tomers throughout the development process.

3. Customers provide a positive feedback loop: Having a positive feedback loop throughout the process allows startups to pivot or adjust throughout the development process, ensur-ing they are creating the best possible product or solution.

4. Customers provide proof of concept: Customer buy-in provides the most proof of concept for any startup.

The Timing

Time plays a crucial role in many potential opportunities. In some emerging industries, there is a definite window of opportunity that opens only once. For instance, about 35 years ago, when videocassette recorders (VCRs) were first coming into household use in North America, there was a need for video stores in convenient locations where viewers could pick up movies on the way home from work. Lots of video retail stores opened up on main streets and in shopping centres that were usually run by independent store owners. Then the distribution of videos changed. National chains of video stores emerged, and supermarket and drug store chains entered the market. Then the technology changed, and VCR cassettes were replaced by digital video discs (DVDs), which are much less bulky. You can get DVDs via postal mail or pick them up at vending machines that are found in convenient locations. And now even DVDs are being supplanted by digital downloads and streaming over the Internet. Today the window of opportunity for starting an independent video store is closed.

In other markets—high-quality restaurants, for example—there is a steady demand that does not change much from year to year, so the window of opportunity is always open. Nevertheless, timing can still be important because, when the economy turns for the worse, those kinds of restaurants are usually hit harder than lower-quality ones; thus, the time to open one is during a recovering or booming economy.

If the window of opportunity appears to be very brief, it may be that the idea is a consumer fad that will quickly pass away. It takes a skilled entrepreneur to make money out of a fad. When Lucy's Have a Heart Canvas of Faneuil Hall Marketplace in Boston introduced shoelaces with hearts on them, they flew off the shelves. Children and teenagers could not get enough of them for their sneakers, so the store ordered more and more of them. Then demand

Slimming Fad Fades Fast, Inventories Balloon

The late Dr. Robert C. Atkins built a business around the low-carbohydrate, high-protein diet that bears his name. The 1992 and 1999 editions of his book *Dr. Atkins' New Diet Revolution* sold more than 10 million copies worldwide. The book is among the top 50 bestselling books ever published and was on the *New York Times* bestseller list for five years. Atkins's company, Atkins Nutritionals, Inc., expanded into 250 food products (nutrition bars, shakes, bake mixes, breads) and nearly 100 nutritional supplements (antioxidants, essential oils) in more than 30,000 outlets. Sales ramped up rapidly at the beginning of the 2000s. Demand was boosted in 2003 by a widely publicized article in the May edition of the influential *New England Journal of Medicine*, reporting that subjects on a low-carb, high-protein diet not only lost weight but also—and perhaps more importantly—had an increase in good cholesterol levels and a decrease in triglycerides, which was contrary to expectations. In October 2003, Goldman Sachs & Company and Boston-based Parthenon Capital LLC bought a majority stake in the firm for an estimated $700 million.

At the peak of the low-carb "get-thin-quick" craze in January 2004, 9.1% of the U.S. population claimed to be on the diet. There were 16 national distributors of low-carb products. National supermarkets also introduced low-carb products, and food manufacturers rushed to promote low-carbohydrate products. The diet was so popular that it was partially blamed for the bankruptcy of Interstate Bakeries, the producer of Twinkies and Wonderbread. Then the fad faded fast. By 2005, only 2.2% of Americans were on low-carb diets. The fall was so precipitous that manufacturers were caught with bloated inventories. Surplus low-carb products were being shipped to food banks. For the year ending 2004, Atkins Nutritionals lost $341 million. In August 2005, it filed for bankruptcy with liabilities of $325 million. The number of its products was slimmed down to 40 from more than 300 at the peak of the low-carb fad, and Roark Capital bought the company in 2010.

suddenly dropped precipitously. The store and the manufacturer were left holding huge inventories that could not be sold. As a result, the store almost went under.

Most entrepreneurs should avoid fads or any window of opportunity they believe will be open for a very brief time because it inevitably means they will rush to open their business, sometimes before they have time to gather the resources they will need. That can lead to costly mistakes.

The Entrepreneur and the Management Team

Regardless of how right the opportunity may seem to be, it will not become a successful business unless it is developed by a person with strong entrepreneurial and management skills. What are the important skills? The three key skills are domain knowledge, business acumen, and operational experience, and they make up what is known as the talent triangle of a successful management team. (See Chapter 7 and Figure 7.1 for a more detailed discussion of the talent triangle.)

First and foremost, entrepreneurs should have experience in the same industry or a similar one (i.e., domain knowledge). Starting a business is a demanding undertaking indeed—it is no time for on-the-job training. If would-be entrepreneurs do not have the right experience, they should either get it before starting their new venture or find partners who have it.

Some investors say the ideal entrepreneur is one who has a track record as a successful entrepreneur in the same industry and who can attract a seasoned team. Half the CEOs of the *Inc.* 500 high-growth small companies had started at least one other business before they founded their present firms. When Joey Crugnale acquired his first ice cream shop in 1977, he already had almost 10 years experience in the food service industry. By 1991, when Bertucci's brick-oven pizzeria went public, he and his management team had a total of more than 100 years' experience in the food industry. They had built Bertucci's into a rapidly growing chain with sales of $30 million and net income of $2 million.

Without relevant experience, the odds are stacked against the neophyte in any industry. An electronics engineer thought he had a great idea for a chain of fast-food stores. When asked if he had ever worked in a fast-food restaurant, he replied, "Work in one? I wouldn't even eat in one. I can't stand fast food!" Clearly, he would have been as miscast as a fast-food entrepreneur as Crugnale would have been as an electronics engineer.

True, there are entrepreneurs who have succeeded spectacularly with no prior industry experience. Jeff Bezos of Amazon.com, Anita Roddick of The Body Shop, Ely Callaway of Callaway Golf, and Richard Branson of Virgin Airlines are four notable examples—but they are the exceptions.

Second to industry know-how is management experience (i.e., business acumen), preferably with responsibility for budgets or, better yet, accountability for profit and loss. It is even better if a would-be entrepreneur has a record of increasing sales and profits. Of course, we are talking about the ideal entrepreneur. Very few people measure up to the ideal, but that does not mean they should not start a new venture. It does mean they should be realistic about the size of the business they should start. Eighteen years ago, two 19-year-old students wanted to start a travel agency business in Boston. When asked what they knew about the industry, one replied, "I live in California. I love to travel." The other was silent. Neither of them had worked in the travel industry, nor had anyone in either of their families. They were advised to get experience. One joined a training program for airline ticket agents; the other took a course for travel agents. They became friends with the owner of a local Uniglobe travel agency who helped them with advice. Six months after they first had the idea, they opened a part-time campus travel agency. In the first six months, they had about $100,000 of revenue and made $6,000 of profit but were unable to pay themselves any salary. In that way, they acquired experience at no expense and at low risk. Upon graduation, one of them, Mario Ricciardelli, made it his full-time job and continued building the business and gaining experience at the same time. In 2012, after many bumps in the road, the business—now named Studentcity.com—is one of the largest student travel businesses in the world.

The third necessary know-how is operational experience. At least one person on the management team has to have prior experience and knowledge about how to build and deliver the solution that the business is working towards. For example, if the startup were centred on building application(s) for smartphones, having experience in the mobile industry would be beneficial to the whole team. When opening the first location of the popular Lebanese-style pita sandwich parlour Pita Pit, the founders, Nelson Lang and John Sotiriadis, fulfilled the business acumen and domain knowledge corners of the talent triangle but were lacking operational experience. The two founders made it a high priority to find people with experience in fast food and the restaurant industry to ensure they had someone with superior operational knowledge on their team. Within two years of opening their first location in Kingston, Ontario, Pita Pit franchise stores began opening across the country. Today there are more than 300 Pita Pit locations in Canada and the United States. A major milestone for Pita Pit occurred in 2009 when it was ranked number one within its category on the *Entrepreneur* Franchise 500 list.[32]

Resources

Entrepreneurial frugality requires

- Low overhead,
- High productivity, and
- Minimal ownership of capital assets.

It's hard to believe that Olsen and Anderson started DEC with only $70,000 of startup capital and built a company that at its peak ranked in the top 25 of the Fortune 500 companies. "The nice thing about $70,000 is that there are so few of them, you can watch every one," Olsen said. And watch them he did. Olsen and Anderson moved into a 100-year-old building that had been a nineteenth-century woolen mill. They furnished it with secondhand furniture, purchased tools from the Sears catalogue, and built much of their own equipment as cheaply as possible. They sold $94,000 worth of goods in their first year and made a profit at the same time—a rare feat indeed for a high-tech startup.

Successful entrepreneurs are frugal with their scarce resources. They keep overheads low, productivity high, and ownership of capital assets to a minimum. By so doing, they minimize the amount of capital they need to start their business and make it grow.

Determining Resource Needs and Acquiring Resources

Entrepreneurs often think that their idea is the perfect concept or product, but in reality that's rarely the case. Many first-time entrepreneurs discount their ability to pivot throughout the process. Pivoting refers to startups making the required course corrections during the development process to dramatically improve their odds for success. For example, Derek Szeto, founder of RedFlagDeals.com (a daily virtual destination for over 450,000 Canadian consumers who are seeking and sharing coupons, promotions, and deals with each other) learned the value of pivoting during his rise to the top of the Canadian coupon and consumer deals industry. He initially launched PriceCanada.com in November 2005, offering a space for Canadian shoppers to compare prices, products, and retailers. Knowing a similar business model had been successful in the United States, Szeto was keen to bring the concept to the Canadian market. Unfortunately there was not enough mass market and traffic within Canada, forcing him to shut down PriceCanada.com because it was only breaking even. Szeto and his team knew they had a potential opportunity at their fingertips, but they needed to pivot their focus toward developing RedFlagDeals.com. In February 2010 Szeto and the RedFlagDeals.com team collectively made the decision to sell to Yellow Pages Group Canada, where it continues to attract more than 2.5 million monthly readers with coupons and promotions across 14 different categories.[33]

In order to determine the amount of capital that a company needs to get started, an entrepreneur should first assess what resources are crucial for the company's success in the marketplace. Some resources are more critical than others. What does the company expect to do better than any of its competitors? That is where it should put a disproportionate share of its scarce resources. If the company is making a new high-tech product, technological know-how will be vital, and the most important resource will be engineers and the designs they produce. Therefore, the company must concentrate on recruiting and keeping excellent engineers and on safeguarding the intellectual property they produce, such as engineering designs and patents. If the company is doing retail selling, the critical factor will most likely be location. Choosing the wrong initial location for a retail store just because the rent is cheap can be a fatal mistake because it's unlikely there will be enough resources to relocate.

When Southwest Airlines started up in 1971, its strategy was to provide frequent, on-time service at a competitive price between Dallas, Houston, Austin, and San Antonio. To meet its objectives, Southwest needed planes that it could operate reliably at a low cost. It was able to purchase four brand-new Boeing 737s—very efficient planes for shorter routes—for only $4 million each because the recession had hit the airlines particularly hard and Boeing had an inventory of unsold 737s. From the outset, Southwest provided good, reliable service and had one of the lowest costs per mile in the industry.

Similarly in Canada, Robert Deluce launched Porter Airlines as a regional airline out of Billy Bishop Toronto City Airport (located on the Toronto Islands right next to downtown). Launched in 2006, Porter now offers numerous daily flights between Toronto and various other locations for consumers travelling in and out of the region. When it first started in the winter of 2006, the only flights available were between Toronto and Ottawa or Toronto and Montreal. Operating planes built by Canadian manufacturer Bombardier, the newly developed airline provided lots of jobs to Canadians as well as increased traffic at Toronto's island airport, which had been experiencing declines in revenues and the amount of traffic. Through proof of concept (providing safe, affordable, and convenient travel options to consumers) the airline has expanded to a fleet of 26 Q400 Bombardier aircrafts and Porter now serves 19 regional destinations. More than 2.5 million travellers flew Porter in 2012.[34]

Items that are not critical should be obtained as thriftily as possible. The founder of Burlington Coat Factory, Monroe Milstein, likes to tell the story of how he obtained estimates for gutting the building he had just leased for his second store. His lowest bid was several thousand dollars. One day he was at the building when a sudden thunderstorm sent a crew of labourers working at a nearby site to his building for shelter from the rain. Milstein asked the crew's foreman what they would charge for knocking down the internal structures that needed to be removed. The foreman said, "Five." Milstein asked, "Five what?" The foreman replied, "Cases of beer."

A complete set of resources includes everything the business will need, but a business does not have to do all of its work in-house with its own employees. It is often more effective to sub-contract the work. That way the business doesn't need to own or lease its own manufacturing plant and equipment or to worry about recruiting and training production workers. Often, it can keep overhead lower by using outside firms to do work such as payroll, accounting, advertising, mailing promotions, janitorial services, and so on.

Even startup companies can get amazingly good terms from outside suppliers. An entrepreneur should try to understand the potential suppliers' marginal costs. Marginal cost is the cost of producing one extra unit beyond what is presently produced. The marginal cost of the labourers who gutted Milstein's building while sheltering from the rain was virtually zero. They were being paid by another firm, and they didn't have to buy materials or tools. In another example, a small electronics company was acquired by a much larger competitor. The large company took over the manufacturing of the small company's products, and production costs shot up. An analysis revealed that much of the increase was due to a rise in the cost of purchased components. In one instance, the large company was paying 50% more than the small company had been paying for

GOOGLE founders Larry Page and Sergey Brin bought a terabyte of disks at bargain prices and built their own computer housings in Larry's dorm room, which became Google's first data centre. Unable to interest the major portal players of the day, Larry and Sergey decided to make a go of it on their own. All they needed was a little cash to move out of the dorm—and to pay off the credit cards they had maxed out buying a terabyte of memory. So they wrote up a business plan, put their PhD plans on hold, and went looking for an angel investor. Their first visit was with a friend of a faculty member.

Andy Bechtolsheim, one of the founders of Sun Microsystems, was used to taking the long view. One look at their demo and he knew Google had potential—a lot of potential. But although his interest had been piqued, he was pressed for time. As Sergey tells it, "We met him very early one morning on the porch of a Stanford faculty member's home in Palo Alto. We gave him a quick demo. He had to run off somewhere, so he said, 'Instead of us discussing all the details, why don't I just write you a check?' It was made out to Google Inc. and was for $100,000." The investment created a small dilemma. Since there was no legal entity known as "Google Inc.," there was no way to deposit the cheque. It sat in Larry's desk drawer for a couple of weeks while he and Sergey scrambled to set up a corporation and locate other funders among family, friends, and acquaintances. Ultimately, they brought in a total initial investment of almost $1 million.

On September 7, 1998, more than two years after they began work on their search engine, Google Inc. opened its door in Menlo Park, California. The door

Getty Images

Google founders Sergey Brin (left) and Larry Page (right) speak at a press conference announcing Google's launch of a transit mapping feature of Google Maps with the Metropolitan Transit Authority at Grand Central Station on September 23, 2008, in New York City.

came with a remote control, as it was attached to the garage of a friend who sublet space to the new corporation's staff of three. The office offered several big advantages, including a washer and dryer and a hot tub. It also provided a parking space for the first employee hired by the new company: Craig Silverstein, who became Google's director of technology.

Source: Google, "Our History in Depth," www.google.com/about/company/history.

the same item. It turned out that the supplier had priced the item for the small company on the basis of marginal costs and for the large company on the basis of total costs.

Smart entrepreneurs find ways of controlling critical resources without owning them. A startup business never has enough money, so it must be resourceful. It should not buy what it can lease. Except when the economy is red hot, there is almost always an excess of capacity of office and industrial space. Sometimes a landlord will be willing to offer a special deal to attract even a small startup company into a building. Such deals may include reduced rent, deferral of rent payments for a period of time, and building improvements made at low or even no cost. In some high-tech regions, landlords will exchange rent for equity in a high-potential startup.

When equipment is in excess supply, new businesses can lease it on favourable terms. A young database company was negotiating a lease with IBM for a new minicomputer when its chief engineer discovered that a leasing company had identical secondhand units sitting idle in its warehouse. The young company was able to lease one of the idle units for one-third of IBM's price. About 18 months later, the database company ran out of cash. Nevertheless, it was able to persuade the leasing company to defer payments because by then there were even more minicomputers standing idle in the warehouse, and it made little economic sense to repossess one and add it to the idle stock.

Startup Capital

You've developed your idea, you've carefully assessed what resources you will need to open your business and make it grow, you've pulled all your strategies together into a business plan, and now you know how much startup capital you need to get you to the point where your business will generate a positive cash flow. How are you going to raise that startup capital?

There are two types of startup capital: debt and equity. Simply put, with **debt** you don't have to give up any ownership of the business, but you do have to pay current interest and eventually repay the principal you borrow; with **equity** you have to give up some of the ownership of the business to get it, but you may never have to repay it or even pay a dividend. So you must choose between paying interest and giving up some of the ownership.

In practice, your choice usually depends on how much of each type of capital you can raise. Most startup entrepreneurs do not have much flexibility in their choice of financing. If it is a very risky business without any assets, it will be impossible to get any bank debt without putting up some collateral other than the business's assets—and most likely that collateral will be personal assets. Even if entrepreneurs are willing to guarantee the whole loan with their personal assets, the bank will expect entrepreneurs to put some equity into the business, probably equal to 25% of the amount of the loan. If your personal assets are less than the amount of the loan, the bank might recommend an SBA-guaranteed loan, in which case you would have to put in more equity.

The vast majority of entrepreneurs start their businesses by leveraging their own savings and labour. Consider how Apple, one of the most spectacular startups of all time, was funded. Steve Jobs and Stephen Wozniak had been friends since their school days in Silicon Valley. Wozniak was an authentic computer nerd. He had tinkered with computers from childhood, and he built a computer that won first prize in a science fair. His SAT math score was a perfect 800, but after stints at the University of Colorado, De Anza College, and Berkeley, he dropped out of school and went to work for Hewlett-Packard. His partner, Jobs, had an even briefer encounter with higher education: After one semester at Reed College, he left to look for a swami in India. When he and Wozniak began working on their microcomputer, Jobs was employed at Atari, the leading video game company.

Apple soon outgrew its manufacturing facility in the garage of Jobs's parents' house. Their company, financed initially with $1,300 raised by selling Jobs's Volkswagen and Wozniak's calculator, needed capital for expansion. They looked to their employers for help. Wozniak proposed to his supervisor that Hewlett-Packard produce what later became the Apple II. Perhaps not surprisingly, Hewlett-Packard declined. After all, Wozniak had no formal qualification in computer design; indeed, he did not even have a college degree. At Atari, Jobs tried to convince founder Nolan Bushnell to manufacture Apples. He too was rejected.

However, on the suggestion of Bushnell and Regis McKenna, a Silicon Valley marketing ace, the two partners contacted Don Valentine, a venture capitalist, in the fall of 1976. In those days, Jobs's appearance was a holdover from his swami days; he definitely did not project the image of Doriot's grade-A man, even by Silicon Valley's casual standards. Valentine did not invest, but he did put them in touch with Armas Markkula, Jr., who had recently retired from Intel a wealthy man. Markkula saw the potential in Apple, and he knew how to raise money. He personally invested $91,000, secured a line of credit from Bank of America, put together a business plan, and raised $600,000 of venture capital.

In 2000, Steve Jobs said, "I was very lucky to have grown up in this industry. I did everything coming up—shipping, supply chain, sweeping floors, buying chips, you name it. I put computers together with my own hands. As the industry grew up, I kept on doing it."[i]

"In November 2009, Steve Jobs was voted CEO of the decade by Fortune. In the first decade of the 21st century, he reordered three industries: music with the iPod, movies with Pixar, and mobile phones with the iPhone. And back in the 1970s he shook up the computer industry with the Apple. Reordering one market as Henry Ford did with automobiles, Fred Smith with package delivery, Conrad Hilton with hotels, and Jeff Bezos with book retailing is an extraordinary achievement for any one lifetime; reordering four as Steve Jobs did before he was 55 is a gigantic feat."[ii] But he was not yet done. A year or so before he died in 2011, he made that five industries when he introduced the iPad, the first tablet computer, which was an instant success; within a couple of years it was severely eroding the sales of PCs. According to Jobs, "The reason that Apple can come out with products like the iPad is that we've always tried to be at the intersection of technology and liberal arts."[iii] Some marketing gurus even claim that Steve Jobs's tally of five should really be six because his Apple store concept is a major innovation in retailing.

[i] "Steve Jobs' Magic Kingdom," *Businessweek*, February 6, 2006, 66.

[ii] Emma Barnett, "Steve Jobs Voted 'CEO of the Decade," *The Telegraph*, November 6, 2009, www.telegraph.co.uk/technology/apple/6513511/Steve-Jobs-voted-CEO-of-thedecade.html.

[iii] Walter Isaacson, *Steve Jobs* (New York, NY: Simon and Schuster, 2011), 494.

"[Mike Markkula] emphasized that you should never start a company with the goal of getting rich. Your goal should be making something you believe in and making a company that will last." Steve Jobs.[35]

The Apple II was formally introduced in April 1977. Sales took off almost at once. Apple's sales grew rapidly to $2.5 million in 1977 and $15 million in 1978. In 1978, Dan Bricklin, a Harvard business student and former programmer at DEC, introduced the first electronic spreadsheet, VisiCalc, designed for the Apple II. In minutes, it could do tasks that had previously taken days. The microcomputer now had the power to liberate managers from the data guardians in the computer departments. According to one source, "Armed with VisiCalc, the Apple II's sales took off, and the personal computer industry was created." Apple's sales jumped to $70 million in 1979 and $117 million in 1980.

Getty Images

Steve Jobs and his legacy at the launch of the iPad in 2010.

In 1980, Apple sold some of its stock to the public with an initial public offering (IPO) and raised more than $80 million. The paper value of their Apple stock made instant millionaires of Jobs ($165 million), Markkula ($154 million), Wozniak ($88 million), and Mike Scott ($62 million), who together owned 40% of Apple. Arthur Rock's venture capital investment of $57,000 in 1978 was suddenly worth $14 million, an astronomical compound return of more than 500% per year, or 17% per month.

By 1982, Apple IIs were selling at the rate of more than 33,000 units a month. With 1982 sales of $583 million, Apple hit the *Fortune* 500 list. It was a record. At five years of age, Apple was at that time the youngest company ever to join that exclusive list.

Success as spectacular as Apple's has never been equalled. Nonetheless, its financing is a typical example of how successful high-tech companies are funded. First, the entrepreneurs develop a prototype with personal savings and **sweat equity**, or ownership earned in lieu of wages. Then a wealthy investor—sometimes called an informal investor or business angel, who knows something about the entrepreneurs or the industry or both—invests some personal money in return for equity. When the company is selling product, it may be able to get a bank line of credit secured by its inventory and accounts receivable. If the company is growing quickly in a large market, it may be able to raise capital from a formal venture capital firm in return for equity. Further expansion capital may come from venture capital firms or from a public stock offering.

The vast majority of new firms will never be candidates for formal venture capital or a public stock offering. Nevertheless, they will have to find some equity capital. In most cases, after they have exhausted their personal savings, entrepreneurs will turn to family, friends, and acquaintances (see Figure 2.5). It can be a scary business. Entrepreneurs often find themselves with all their personal net worth tied up in the same business that provides all their income. That is double jeopardy because, if their business fails, they lose both their savings and their means of support. Risk of that sort can be justified only if the profit potential is high enough to yield a commensurate rate of return.

Would-be entrepreneurs sometimes say that they did not start their ventures because they could not raise sufficient money to get started. More often than not, they were unrealistic about the amount of money that they could reasonably have expected to raise for their startup businesses. The truth is that many of the best companies started with very little capital. Further, over the past decade the cost of financing a new venture has come down substantially because of improvements in technology, open source resources, and the new digital age. In 1997, it cost approximately $2 to $5 million to get from initial formation to success in the market. In 2005 the cost dropped to a range between $250,000 to $500,000. The lowest cost to finance a startup to date occurred in 2013, ranging between $25,000 and $30,000 depending on the size of the startup. Companies such as Shopify, Amazon, and other cloud-based servers, support, and ecommerce services make it possible for a startup to get up and running with considerably less funding than in the past. Technically speaking, this low startup cost makes almost anyone an angel investor to entrepreneurs.

	All Nations
Close family member	40%
Other relative	11%
Work colleague	10%
Friend/Neighbour	28%
Stranger	9%
Other	2%
	100%

Source: Global Entrepreneurship Monitor data set. Accessed at www.gemconsortium.org.

Figure 2.5

Relationship of investor to entrepreneur

Profit Potential

The level of profit that is reasonable depends on the type of business. On average, small and medium-sized businesses in Canada make about 12% net income.[36] Hence, on one dollar of revenue, the average company makes a 12-cent profit after paying all expenses and taxes. A company that consistently makes 10% is doing very well, and one that makes 15% is truly exceptional. Approximately 50% of the Inc. 500 companies make 5% or less; 13% of them make 16% or more. Profit margins in a wide variety of industries for companies both large and small are published by Robert Morris Associates, so entrepreneurs can compare their forecasts with the actual performance of similar-sized companies in the same industry.

Any business must make enough profit to recompense its investors (in most cases that is the entrepreneur) for their investment. This must be the profit after all normal business expenses have been accounted for, including a fair salary for the entrepreneur and any family members who are working in the business. A common error in assessing the profitability of a new venture is to ignore the owner's salary. Suppose someone leaves a secure job paying $70,000 per year plus fringe benefits and invests $100,000 of personal savings to start a new venture. That person should expect to take a $70,000 salary plus fringe benefits out of the new business. Perhaps in the first year or two, when the business is being built, it may not be possible to pay $70,000 in actual cash; in that case, the pay that is not actually received should be treated as deferred compensation to be paid in the future. In addition to an adequate salary, the entrepreneur must earn a reasonable return on the $100,000 investment. A professional investor putting money into a new, risky business would expect to earn an annual rate of return of at least 40%, which would be $40,000 annually on a $100,000 investment. That return may come as a capital gain when the business is sold, or as a dividend, or as a combination of the two. But remember that $100,000 compounding annually at 40% grows to almost $2.9 million in 10 years. When such large capital gains are needed to produce acceptable returns, big capital investments held for a long time do not make any sense unless substantial value can be created, as occasionally happens in the case of high-flying companies, especially high-tech ones. In most cases, instead of a capital gain, the investor's return will be a dividend, which must be paid out of the cash flow from the business.

The cash flow that a business generates is not to be confused with profit. It is possible, indeed very likely, that a rapidly growing business will have a negative cash flow from operations in its early years even though it may be profitable. That may happen because the business may not be able to generate enough cash flow internally to sustain its ever-growing needs for working capital and the purchase of long-term assets such as plant and equipment. Hence, it will have to borrow or raise new equity capital. So it is important that a high-potential business intending to grow rapidly make careful cash-flow projections so as to predict its needs for future outside investments. Future equity investments will dilute the percentage of ownership of the founders, and if the dilution becomes excessive, there may be little reward remaining for the entrepreneurs.

Biotechnology companies are examples of this problem: They have a seemingly insatiable need for cash infusions to sustain their research and development (R&D) costs in their early years. Their negative cash flow, or burn rate, sometimes runs at $1 million per month. A biotechnology company can easily burn up $50 million before it generates a meaningful profit, let alone a positive cash flow. The expected future capital gain from a public stock offering or sale to a large pharmaceutical company has to run into hundreds of millions of dollars, maybe into the billion-dollar range, for investors to realize an annual return of 50% or higher, which is what they expect to earn on money invested in a seed-stage biotechnology company. Not surprisingly, biotechnology entrepreneurs as a group have to give up most of the ownership to finance their ventures. A study of venture capital–backed biotechnology companies found that after they had gone public, the entrepreneurs and management were left with less than 18% of the equity, compared with 32% for a comparable group of computer software companies.[37]

> **For entrepreneurs, happiness is a positive cash flow.**

We've said that most businesses will never have the potential to go public. Nor will the owners ever intend to sell their business and thereby realize a capital gain. In that case, how can those owners get a satisfactory return on the money they have invested in their businesses? The two ingredients that determine return on investment are (1) the amount invested and (2) the annual amount earned on that investment. Entrepreneurs should invest as little as possible to start their businesses and make sure that their firms will be able to pay them a "dividend" big enough to yield an appropriate annual rate of return. For income tax purposes, that "dividend" may be in the form of a salary, bonus, or fringe benefits rather than an actual dividend paid out of retained earnings. Of course, the company must be generating cash from its own operations before that dividend can be paid. For entrepreneurs, happiness is a positive cash flow. And the day a company begins to generate **free cash**—that is, more cash than needed to sustain operations and purchase assets to keep the company on its growth trajectory—is a very happy day in the life of a successful entrepreneur.

Awash with Cash

Apple is an awesome money machine. Apple's stash of cash kept piling up so that by 2012 its cash and short-term investments stood at $114.2 billion. It was enough money to give each household in the United States $1,026, or put another way, it was enough to purchase an iPad for every American more than 5 years old.

In 2012, Apple generated $4.6 billion of cash flow from operations every month—almost $7,429 per second on the basis of a five-day working week, eight hours per day. No wonder Apple, with a market capitalization of more than $620 billion, was the most valuable company in history.

Source: Apple, "Apple Reports Third Quarter Results," Apple Press Info, July 24, 2012, www.apple.com/pr/library/2012/07/24Apple-Reports-Third-Quarter-Results.html.

Ingredients for a Successful New Business

The great day has arrived. You found an idea, wrote a business plan, and gathered your resources. Now you are opening the doors of your new business for the first time, and the really hard work is about to begin. What are the factors that distinguish winning entrepreneurial businesses from the also-rans? Rosabeth Moss Kanter prescribed Four Fs for a successful business,[38] a list that has been expanded into the Nine Fs for entrepreneurial success (see Figure 2.6).

First and foremost, the founding entrepreneur is the most important factor. Next comes the market. This is the "era of the other," in which, as Regis McKenna observed, the fastest-growing companies in an industry will be in a segment labelled "others" in a market-share pie chart. By and large, they will be newer entrepreneurial firms rather than large firms with household names; hence, specialization is the key. A successful business should focus on niche markets.

The rate of change in business gets ever faster. The advanced industrial economies are knowledge based. Product life cycles are getting shorter. Technological innovation progresses

Founders	Every startup company must have a first-class entrepreneur.
Focused	Entrepreneurial companies focus on niche markets. They specialize.
Fast	They make decisions quickly and implement them swiftly.
Flexible	They keep an open mind. They respond to change.
Forever innovating	They are tireless innovators.
Flat	Entrepreneurial organizations have as few layers of management as possible.
Frugal	By keeping overhead low and productivity high, entrepreneurial companies keep costs down.
Friendly	Entrepreneurial companies are friendly to their customers, suppliers, and employees.
Fun	It's fun to be associated with an entrepreneurial company.

Figure 2.6

The Nine Fs for entrepreneurial success

at a relentless pace. Government rules and regulations keep changing. Communications and travel around the globe keep getting easier and cheaper. And consumers are better informed about their choices. To survive, let alone succeed, a company has to be quick and nimble. It must be fast and flexible. It cannot allow inertia to build up. Look at retailing: The historical giants such as Kmart are on the ropes, while nimble competitors dance around them. Four of the biggest retailing successes are Les Wexner's The Limited, the late Sam Walton's Walmart, Bernie Marcus and Arthur Blank's Home Depot, and Anita Roddick's The Body Shop. Entrepreneurs such as these know that they can keep inertia low by keeping the layers of management as few as possible. Tom Peters, an authority on business strategy, liked to point out that Walmart had three layers of management, whereas Sears had 10 a few years back when Walmart displaced Sears as the nation's top chain of department stores. "A company with three layers of management can't lose against a company with ten. You could try, but you couldn't do it!" says Peters. So keep your organization flat. It will facilitate quick decisions and flexibility and will keep overhead low.

Small entrepreneurial firms are great innovators. Big firms are relying increasingly on strategic partnerships with entrepreneurial firms to get access to desirable R&D. The trend is well under way. Hoffmann-La Roche, hurting for new blockbuster prescription drugs, purchased a majority interest in Genentech and bought the highly regarded biotechnology called PCR (polymerase chain reaction) from Cetus for $300 million. Eli Lilly purchased Hybritech. In the 1980s, IBM spent $9 billion a year on research and development, but even that astronomical amount of money could not sustain Big Blue's commercial leadership. As its market share was remorselessly eaten away by thousands of upstarts, IBM entered into strategic agreements with Apple, Borland, Go, Lotus, Intel, Metaphor, Microsoft, Novell, Stratus, Thinking Machines, and other entrepreneurial firms for the purpose of gaining computer technologies.

When it comes to productivity, the best entrepreneurial companies leave the giant corporations behind in the dust. According to 2012 computer industry statistics, Dell's revenue per employee was $549,000 and Microsoft's was $788,000, while Hewlett-Packard's was $363,000 and IBM's was $250,000. Of course, Dell subcontracts more of its manufacturing, but this does not explain all the difference. Whether you hope to build a big company or a small one, the message is the same: Strive tirelessly to keep productivity high.

But no matter what you do, you probably won't be able to attain much success unless you have happy customers, happy workers, and happy suppliers. That means you must have a friendly company. It means that everyone must be friendly, especially anyone who deals with customers. "The most fun six-month period I've had since the start of Microsoft" is how Bill Gates described his astonishing accomplishment in reinventing his 20-year-old company to meet the threat posed by Internet upstarts in the mid-1990s. In not much more than six months of Herculean effort, Microsoft had developed an impressive array of new products to match those of Netscape. Having fun is one of the keys to keeping a company entrepreneurial. If Microsoft's product developers had not been having fun, they would not have put in 12-hour days and sometimes overnighters to catch up with Netscape. And big as it is, Microsoft still has the entrepreneurial spirit. In June 2009, Microsoft introduced its Bing search engine to compete with Google's; four months after its introduction,

When it introduced the first personal computer (PC) in 1981, IBM stood astride the computer industry like a big blue giant. Two suppliers of its personal computer division were Intel and Microsoft. Compared with IBM, Intel was small and Microsoft was a midget. By 2002, Intel's revenue was $26.8 billion and Microsoft's was $28.4 billion. Between 1998 and 2002, Microsoft's revenue increased 86%, while IBM's stood still. In 2002, IBM—the company that invented the PC—had only 6% of the worldwide market for PCs. In December 2004, IBM announced that it was selling its PC division to Lenovo, the leading Chinese manufacturer of PCs. By then it was Microsoft's Windows operating system and Intel's microprocessors—the so-called WINTEL—that were shaping the future of information technology. And in 2013, Microsoft's Windows is threatened by Google's Android, which has become the operating system of choice of handheld devices except those made by Apple.

Bing had already captured almost 10% of the lucrative search and advertising market.[39] By December 2012, that share had increased to 16.3% and Google's appeared to have plateaued at 66.7%.

Most new companies have the Nine Fs at the outset. Those that become successful and grow pay attention to keeping them and nurturing them. The key to sustaining success is to remain an entrepreneurial gazelle and never turn into a lumbering elephant and finally a dinosaur, doomed to extinction.

CONCLUSION

It is easy to start a business in Canada; anyone can do it. What distinguishes successful entrepreneurs from less successful ones is the ability to spot an opportunity for a high-potential venture and then to develop it into a thriving business. As the business grows, the successful entrepreneur is able to attract key management team members, motivate employees, find more and more customers and keep them coming back, and build increasingly sophisticated relationships with financiers.

YOUR OPPORTUNITY JOURNAL

Reflection Point	Your Thoughts...
1. What life events might trigger your entrepreneurial career?	
2. What ideas do you have for a new business?	
a. What ideas can you draw from your past work experience?	
b. What ideas can you draw from your family's work experience?	
3. Which of your personal attributes will most help you succeed as an entrepreneur?	
4. Which attributes do you think you need to further develop?	
5. Who are your entrepreneurial role models? Can you foster any of them into mentors?	
6. Is your idea an opportunity? Explain.	
7. Is the timing right to launch your venture?	
8. What are some cost-effective ways for you to get started?	

◩ *CASE* — John W. Sleeman—A Canadian Icon
John W. Sleeman—A Canadian Icon

In 2006, Sleeman Breweries, a family-owned business, had been in the hands of John W. Sleeman for 21 years. Sleeman Breweries was Sleeman's third business venture. He enjoyed building businesses and derived satisfaction from knowing his idea came to fruition while simultaneously proving naysayers wrong. Sleeman's objective was to build his brewery into a sustainable and profitable entity for future generations of Sleeman members. At this point, Sleeman Breweries was a public company, and through dilution John Sleeman had retained 22% of the company's shares.

One evening in 2006, Sleeman went for a late night walk, knowing that an extremely difficult decision awaited him. Sleeman's shares in the company, albeit a good amount, were not enough to keep the other shareholders from agreeing to sell the company. Sleeman Breweries had encountered financial hardship in recent years and a decision regarding the fate of the company was inevitable. Several large players in the beer brewing industry had expressed interest in purchasing Sleeman Breweries, which would typically be considered good news, but not for John Sleeman. Sleeman had never intended to sell his family business and even though a change in circumstance had him considering it, Sleeman did not want his beer being made in another facility by someone else's employees. Sleeman's decision would impact approximately 1,000 of the brewery's employees, not to mention his family legacy.

The Sleeman Family Legacy

In the 1600s, the Sleeman family, originally Slyman, was a family of pirates, running an illegal business venture in England.[40] For decades, business was good for the Slyman family. The Sleeman business was passed down from generation to generation. It was not until the 1800s that the Slymans felt compelled to legitimize their business, and in doing so, changed their name to Sleeman, opened a string of pubs (or inns, as they were referred to at that time), and began brewing beer to supply those pubs. Shortly thereafter, the Sleemans stopped running the pubs and focused solely on the brewery. In 1834, some of the Sleeman family left Cornwall, England, and started a business in St. Catharines, a small town outside of Toronto.[41] After a short stint in St. Catharine's where they encountered a polluted water supply—water is essential for brewing beer—the Sleemans moved their business yet again, this time to Guelph, Ontario.

The Sleemans found a home in Guelph and grew a successful brewery well into the twentieth century. It wasn't until 1933 that the Sleemans encountered a major obstacle in their family business.[42] The Industrial Revolution sprouted a new lifestyle among people, and alcohol was a major part of that lifestyle. In the early 1900s, alcohol became the main topic of legislators and election campaigns.[43] Under the Temperance Movement, the prohibition of alcohol arose at various times in certain provinces within Canada and within certain states in the United States. Prohibition was in effect in Ontario, where the Sleemans ran their business from 1919 to 1927. However, in Chicago, prohibition lasted until 1933.[44] Throughout the overlapping period, one of the Sleeman brothers decided to smuggle alcohol to organized crime kingpin Al Capone.[45] In 1933, the Sleemans were caught and reprimanded with a 50-year ban on brewing and distributing alcohol of any sort.[46] The Sleeman brewery and the family business was closed. However, Florian Sleeman, a member of the Sleeman family, kept one bottle of beer and the Sleeman recipe book in hopes that an unborn member of the family would one day continue in the family tradition of beer brewing.

John W. Sleeman

John W. Sleeman was born in Toronto in 1953 and was orphaned at birth. The Sleeman family, not being able to have children of their own, adopted John shortly after he turned 1-year-old and brought him to their home in Ottawa.[47] He had a modest upbringing and grew up in an alcohol-free household where his family's history of beer brewing was rarely discussed.

From an early age, John Sleeman began challenging and questioning authority. He strived for efficiency and did not accept at face value everything he was told. John also found school to be rather meaningless, and he continuously pondered what he could accomplish if school was not in the way. At the age of 16, after failing his junior year in high school and not faring very well afterwards, John finally convinced his parents to let him drop out of school to pursue his own unconventional means to an end. He began working at McDonald's and quickly questioned the methods he was taught by recommending more efficient practices. Needless to say, these types of recommendations, however insightful, were not received well from senior management, especially since they came from a 16-year-old teenage boy.

At the age of 19, John sought out to explore new beginnings and moved to England, where he was immediately drawn to the growing culture of the "pub lifestyle" London had to offer. Soon after moving to Nottingham, John married his first wife. Wanting to support his family, he started working for a telecommunications company. Shortly thereafter, John's desire to create something of his own became increasingly apparent. However, John encountered his first roadblock in discovering that entrepreneurship was not favourably looked upon in England, and being a Canadian citizen did not make things easier. So John decided to move back to Canada, but he did not leave England empty handed. He realized that Canada lacked the "pub lifestyle" he enjoyed in England, and since no one else was building English-style pubs in Canada, John decided this would be an area for him to explore. With the help of his wife, his wife's father, and some bank loans, John secured enough equity to build his first pub in Oakville, Ontario.

John's true passion was the pub. He loved the culture and the atmosphere associated with the classic English pub. However, despite the creation of his pub, John still felt that something was missing. He wanted authentic British draft beer to be served, which at the time was unavailable. John went back to England, knocked on the doors of Britain's largest breweries and asked, "How would you like an agent in Canada to import and distribute your draft beer?"[48] To John's surprise, they all said yes. John's philosophy of "if you don't ask, you don't get" is clearly illustrated by his continuous pursuit of making things happen. Even though John was successful in attaining agreements with the large British beer breweries, he did encounter setbacks in Canada; some provincial liquor boards stopped him, temporarily, from importing British beer. John's answer to the setback was simple: flexibility. John knew that when one door closes, another must open, so there was more than one path to reach a goal.

A Brewery Reborn

In 1979, two years after opening his Oakville pub, John Sleeman founded the Imported Beer Company.[49] His goal was to distribute imported beer across Canada. Business was good and John could not be happier.

In 1984, John had the most important meeting of his life with his Aunt Florian. To John's amazement she handed him the original Sleeman beer bottle and recipe book. Stored away for decades, in the hope of one day reemerging. John's initial reaction was to decline, and with good reason. John's beer-importing business consumed all his time, had a strong cash flow, and had minimal capital requirements. John did not want to give up his successful importing business to spend millions of dollars opening a beer brewery and be forced to compete with Molson and Labatt.

John's Aunt Florian, being as persistent and persuasive as John himself, would not relent. Eventually, John promised to look into the idea and mentioned that should he pursue the venture, he would want to reacquire the original company name, which was now owned by Standard Brands, a subsidiary of Nabisco.[50] Soon after his conversation with his Aunt Florian, John called Nabisco, told them he wanted to restart the family business and that he would like the company name back, which was inactive at the time. John hoped Nabisco would say no—that way he could tell his aunt that he failed and then he could get back to his successful business of importing beer. However, to John's amazement, Nabisco thought it was a great idea and offered to sell the company name back to John for one dollar. John now had the recipe book, the old bottle, the company name, the trademark, and few reasons left not to restart the old family business. John found a property on the outskirts of Guelph, Ontario, and in 1985 reincorporated the Sleeman Brewing and Malting Company.[51]

It took John three years to get the Sleeman Brewing and Malting Company ready to produce its first bottle of beer. This journey was not an easy one; it required John to exude an extremely high level of resiliency. Financing this venture was also not easy; being a beer brewery did not make things any easier, and having two large companies monopolizing the industry made it that much more difficult. John was forced to eventually use his house as collateral for the bank loans. Moving forward, John created the production process, bought the necessary machines and fermenters, built the brewery, and would soon be ready to open the doors when he realized that he did not have enough working capital to keep the company afloat until opening day. Before he could find a working solution to the lack of capital, the Canadian bank financing John's brewery, pulled their loans and foreclosed on the brewery, a mere 30 days before opening day. John lost his house in the process. The financial stress and extremely long workdays also strained John's marriage—they eventually parted ways. Not wanting to give up, John went to the United States and secured the loans he would need. He used the capital to satisfy the Canadian bank and got back to building a brand.

Building the Sleeman Brand

In 1988, after securing his financial needs from the United States, John officially opened Sleeman Brewing and Malting Company, which had now been dormant for 55 years. John began re-creating all-natural ales and lagers based on his family's recipes. By 1991, the Sleeman Brewing and Malting Company had attained a 1% market share in the Canadian beer market, which may sound insignificant but, at the time, represented sales of 60 million bottles per year.[52]

John Sleeman's family history of piracy and bootlegging is not one that most would want to publicize. However, John had a different take on his past and was proud of his family's history. Instead of hiding his past from the media and running the risk of media personnel uncovering these facts, which could then be presented with a negative connotation, John decided to embrace and promote his history with his customers. To turn his family's infamy into esteem, John produced and starred in a series of advertisements, thus turning a potential obstacle into an opportunity to build a strong Canadian brand.

Even though the commercials were a success, John's openness had some backlash. They made John Sleeman a recognizable face and showcased his growing wealth. This led to threats on his family from a variety of unsavoury characters.[53] Eventually, John's home needed heightened security measures and at times even needed 24-hour police surveillance. The Sleeman Brewing and Malting Company was also accused of promoting and condoning organized crime by several protesting community organizations. John did not let these obstacles stand in the way of continuing to air and create innovative commercials, which mainly portrayed his face and family heritage along with the Sleeman brand.

By the early 1990s, John Sleeman successfully retrieved the rights to his family business, built a brewery, and captured a slice of the Canadian beer market. John's next plan was to expand his empire and build breweries from coast to coast, and build them himself. However, after seven years in the business, John felt that doing this himself would take far too long and would be far too costly. John, being highly adaptable, pivoted and changed his plan. Instead of going it alone, John decided to amalgamate with other breweries to build his empire. This meant merging or purchasing other established breweries, which expanded his distribution rights. In 1996, John purchased Okanagan Spring in British Columbia, which was a public company owned by Allied Strategies Incorporated. The only way to successfully purchase the company was through a reverse takeover bid of Allied Strategies Incorporated. The deal turned Sleeman Brewing and Malting from a private company into a public company, and in the process John changed the company name from Sleeman Brewing and Malting to Sleeman Breweries.

Between the years of 1996 and 2004, Sleeman Breweries acquired six different Canadian breweries (Okanagan Spring, Upper Canada Brewing Company, Brasserie Seigneuriale, Shaftebury Brewing Company, Maritime Brewing Company, and Unibroue Inc.).[54] In addition to the acquisitions, Sleeman Breweries also signed the distribution rights of two other beer brands, Stroh brands in Canada and Sapporo Breweries in the United States. Throughout all of Sleeman's acquisitions, Sleeman Breweries gained more market traction and had now attained a 2% market share in the Canadian beer industry.[55] John Sleeman was pursuing his dream of building a beer brewing empire from coast to coast. John's dreams were coming to fruition; however, an unsuspecting John Sleeman would soon have to make the most difficult decision of his life.

The Takeover

In the early 2000s, Canadians started to develop a taste for foreign beer brands. Imported beer, such as Heineken, Corona, and Carlsberg, among others, started making headway in the Canadian beer market.[56] As some Canadians experimented with new premium-imported brands, discount beer brewers quietly lured in other Canadian drinkers. Lakeport Breweries, known for their "Buck a Beer" motto, gained traction in the craft beer industry. In 2006, Lakeport beers were among the top 10 selling beers in Ontario. In addition to the surge of foreign and discount beer, many Canadians started switching from beer to wine. In 2000, beer had a 53% market share while wine only commanded a 23% market share.[57] Fast forward to 2011, and beer's market share slumped to 45% while wine's market share rose to 30%.[58] Despite the various forms of competition, Sleeman Breweries was able to maintain itself as the third-largest Canadian beer brewer behind Molson Coors and Labatt, and was the only one of the three that was without foreign ownership. Notwithstanding, the rise in wine and foreign beer consumption led Sleeman Breweries into financial hardship. To salvage the company, John was forced to cut 20% of his staff and reduced a large amount of discretionary expenses.[59] John's efforts to keep the brewery alive, as difficult as they may have been, were not enough. He wanted to eliminate the company's debt and continue expanding the brand. However, John knew that the only way to accomplish his goals was to consider selling his beloved brewery. In May 2005, John decided to sell Sleeman Breweries. It had been 21 years since John Sleeman reopened his family business, and the decision to sell was not an easy one. Yet his main concern in selling the company was preserving the Sleeman brand and Sleeman's employees. He refused to accept any offer that would render his employees unemployed.

As word of the sale spread within the beer industry, a few potential buyers approached John. Both Molson Coors and Labatt were interested in acquiring Sleeman Breweries. John's initial reaction was not one of excitement or relief. His main concern and focus with both

Aaron Harris/The Canadian Press

John Sleeman, Chairman and CEO of Sleeman Breweries Ltd., speaks during a press conference in Toronto on October 18, 2006, in the wake of the company's successful takeover by Japan's Sapporo Breweries Ltd.

prospective buyers was with their intention after the completion of the sale. Regardless of the price being offered and the amount of wealth John would receive, he needed a guarantee that his brewery and employees would remain intact. He received no such confirmation from either candidate, and thus did not sell his company, despite the financial hardships of Sleeman Breweries. John Sleeman risked his own financial well-being for his employees and for the preservation of his family legacy. It was clear that Sleeman Breweries needed a white knight—a buyer whose plans and ambitions were directly in line with those of Sleeman Breweries.

In August 2006, nearly one and a half years since John Sleeman decided to sell his family business, Sapporo International approached him. Sleeman Breweries had been manufacturing and distributing the Sapporo brand in the United States since 2002,[60] and the two companies had established a good working relationship. Sapporo was the white knight Sleeman Breweries was looking for; their interests were directly aligned with those of John. Sapporo agreed not to close the brewery and also agreed to retain all of its employees. On August 11, 2006, Sapporo International acquired Sleeman Breweries for $400 million.[61] This purchase was Sapporo's first major investment outside of Japan. Even though Sleeman Breweries was the last of the top three Canadian beer breweries to be acquired by an international company, John Sleeman ensured that his family legacy would continue to thrive and saved the jobs of all his employees. It was not his intention to ever sell Sleeman Breweries, but he recognized that as times changed and unsuspected events occurred in the beer brewing industry, his goals and aspirations for Sleeman Breweries also had to change. Staring in the face of adversity and immense amounts of self-inflicted liability, John Sleeman kept his core beliefs and ethical values at the forefront of his decision. At the request of Sapporo International, John stayed on as CEO of Sleeman Breweries and continued leading the company into a prosperous state.

Sleeman Today

Presently, John Sleeman is over 60 years of age, is married to his second wife with whom he has two children, and is chair of Sleeman Breweries.[62] Sleeman Breweries now operates breweries across Canada and has approximately 1,000 employees. John recently stepped down as CEO but remains very much intertwined with the company's activities as chair. He now primarily deals with marketing, mergers and acquisitions, and maintaining a working relationship with the Canadian government.

John Sleeman attributes much of his success to his entrepreneurial character and personality. He believes that entrepreneurship is not something that can be learned but rather something that is engrained in one's character. John credits his entrepreneurial ways for his vision, perseverance, and appetite for risk. By having a "do-it-yourself" attitude, John learned a valuable lesson throughout his career. He realized that to scale a business and become truly successful, one must realize your weaknesses and surround yourself with people and employees who make up for those shortfalls. John Sleeman has no immediate plans on retiring, and when asked about the subject, simply answered, "I'd like to die doing what I love doing, sitting behind my desk, working."[63]

Discussion Questions

1. What are the potential advantages of "being the brand," as John Sleeman became? What are the potential disadvantages? What would you do?

2. Going it alone can be lucrative and it allows you to move quickly, but Sleeman decided the risk outweighed the rewards. Discuss both the risks and the rewards.

3. John Sleeman had multiple offers to buy his company. Other than price and personal gain, what factors would you examine in deciding amongst competing offers?

NOTES

1. According to the 2002 Kauffman study, 1992 two- and four-year colleges and universities offered at least one course in entrepreneurship, up from about 300 in the 1984–1985 academic year. Source: P. B. Gray, "Can Entrepreneurship Be Taught?" CNN Money, March 10, 2006, http://money.cnn.com/magazines/fsb/fsb_archive/2006/03/01/8370301/.

2. Council of Ontario Universities, "Fueling Success," October 1, 2013, www.cou.on.ca/publications/reports/pdfs/entrepreneurship-at-ontario-universities---fuellin.

3. N. Scallan, "Why Ashton Kutcher Is Attracted to a Monogamous Social Network for Lovers Developed by Waterloo U Grads," *Toronto Star*, May 4, 2012.

4. J. McElgunn, "Canadian Entrepreneurs Kick Ass," Profitguide.com, August 22, 2005, www.profitguide.com/opportunity/canadian-entrepreneurs-kick-ass-28680?print.

5. Ibid.

6. Ibid.

7. Ibid.

8. R. Brockhuas, "Risk-Taking Propensity of Entrepreneurs," *Academy of Management Journal* 23 (1980): 509–520.

9. N. M. Carter, W. B. Gartner, K. G. Shaver, and E. J. Gatewood, "The Career Reasons for Nascent Entrepreneurs," *Journal of Business Venturing* 19 (2003): 13–39.

10. E. M. Rogers and J. K. Larsen, *Silicon Valley Fever: Growth of High-Technology Culture* (New York, NY: Basic Books, 1984).

11. Digital Media Zone, "About DMZ," January 7, 2014, http://digitalmediazone.ryerson.ca/about/.

12. H. Rakotomalala, "Vancouver: Canada's Greatest Startup City?" Montreal Tech Watch, August 2007, http://montrealtechwatch.com/2007/08/07/vancouver-canadas-greatest-start-up-city.

13. B. Dudley, "Vancouver Steps Up as Next Tech Hot Spot," *Toronto Star*, October 10, 2013.

14. Ibid.

15. H. Rakotomalala, "Montreal Is the Best Startup City in the World," Montreal Tech Watch, August 1, 2010, http://montrealtechwatch.com/2010/08/01/montreal-is-the-best-startup-city-in-the-world.

16. Ibid.

17. A. Welsch, "Tech Startups Are Flourishing in Montreal," *Montreal Gazette*, November 9, 2013.

18. *Inc.*, "Top 500 Entrepreneurs of 2012," September 2012.

19. Excerpted from "Kauffman Foundation Study Finds MIT Alumni Companies Generate Billions for Regional Economies," *MIT News*, February 17, 2009, http://web.mit.edu/newsoffice/2009/kauffman-study-0217.html.

20. U.S. Census Bureau, www.census.gov/Press-Release/www/2001/cb01-54.html.

21. U.S. Census Bureau, www.census.gov/Press-Release/www/2001/cb01-115.html.

22. U.S. Census Bureau, www.census.gov/Press-Release/www/releases/archives/cb05_108_table.xls.

23. *Inc.*, "500," September 2009; *Inc.* "500 CEO Survey 2004," www.inc.com/multimedia/slideshows/content/crunching-numbers_pagen_3.html.

24 J. McElgunn, "Hot 50: Anatomy of a CEO," Profitguide.com, August 29, 2012, www.profitguide.com/news/profit-hot-50-anatomy-of-a-ceo-39748.

25 S. Wise, "The Talent Triangle," *Globe and Mail*, April 5, 2009, www.theglobeandmail.com/report-on-business/the-talent-triangle/article1099632/?page=all.

26 *Inc.*, "500," 2000.

27 Startup Canada, "About," www.startupcan.ca/about/.

28 Ibid.

29 MaRS Commons, "Accelerators and Incubators," January 15, 2014, http://marscommons.marsdd.com/startup-library/accelerators-and-incubators.

30 R. L. Martin and S. Osberg, "Social Entrepreneurship: The Case for Definition," *Stanford Social Innovation Review* (April 2007): 32–36.

31 "Obituary: Professor Rajeev Motwani," *The Telegraph,* June 9, 2009.

32 Pita Pit, "Corporate History," http://pitapit.ca/consumer/corporate/history.

33 RedFlagDeals.com, "About Us," www.redflagdeals.com/info/about.

34 Porter Airlines, "Porter Airlines Passes 10 Million Passengers," November 12, 2013, news release, www.flyporter.com.

35 W. Isaacson, *Steve Jobs* (New York, NY: Simon and Schuster, 2011), 78.

36 Industry Canada, "Canadian Industry Statistics (CIS): Financial Performance Data," https://www.ic.gc.ca/eic/site/cissic.nsf/eng/h_00032.html.

37 W. D. Bygrave and J. A. Timmons, *Venture Capital at the Crossroads* (Boston, MA: Harvard Business School Press, 1992).

38 R. M. Kanter, *Change Masters: Innovation and Entrepreneurship in the American Corporation* (New York, NY: Simon & Schuster, 1985).

39 AFP, "Bing Gains Search Market Share, Nears 10 Percent," November 17, 2009, http://www.thefreelibrary.com/Bing+gains+search+market+share,+nears+10+percent-a01612061763.

40 S. Wise, "John Sleeman: The Naked Entrepreneur," March 25, 2013, www.youtube.com/watch?v=kER-LSLC6gc.

41 Ibid.

42 Ibid.

43 "Prohibition Issues in the Industrial Revolution Sociology Essay," UK Essays, www.ukessays.com/essays/sociology/prohibition-issues-in-the-industrial-revolution-sociology-essay.php.

44 Ibid.

45 S. Wise, "John Sleeman."

46 Ibid.

47 Ibid.

48 J. Miers, "John Sleeman," *From the Top,* October 16, 2012, www.youtube.com/watch?v=vBIVr79OPes.

49 S. Wise, "John Sleeman."

50 J. Miers, "John Sleeman."

51 University of Guelph Archival and Special Collections, "The Sleeman Collection," www.lib.uoguelph.ca/sleeman-collection.

52 Ibid.

53 S. Wise, "John Sleeman."

54 University of Guelph Archival and Special Collections, "The Sleeman Collection."

55 W. Lilley, "Big Sales, Small Beer," *Financial Times of Canada*, April 1, 1991.

56 *CTV News,* "Is Wine Poised to Take over Beer's Reign in Canada?" March 26, 2012, www.ctvnews.ca/is-wine-poised-to-take-over-beer-s-reign-in-canada-1.787193.

57 Ibid.

58 Ibid.

59 P. Mitchell, "Sapporo to Buy Sleeman Brewery in $400 Million Deal," *Booze News,* August 2006, www.boozenews.ca/index.php?itemid=31.

60 University of Guelph Archival and Special Collections, "The Sleeman Collection."

61 *CBC News,* "Sapporo Acquisition of Sleeman on Tap," August 11, 2006, www.cbc.ca/news/business/sapporo-acquisition-of-sleeman-on-tap-1.578154.

62 G. Konotopetz, "Brewery CEO Is Chip off Sleeman Block," *Business Edge News Magazine*, July 2005, www.businessedge.ca/archives/article.cfm/brewery-ceo-is-chip-off-sleeman-block-10102.

63 S. Wise, "John Sleeman."

identifies their pain points.[10] For example, in an ABC *Nightline* segment about IDEO, the team went to a grocery store to better understand how customers shop and, more specifically, how they use a shopping basket. The team's mission was to observe, ask questions, and record information. They did not ask leading questions in hopes that the customer would validate a preconceived notion of what that shopping cart should be. Instead, the questions were open ended.

Beware the leading question. As an entrepreneur who is excited about your own concept, you may find it all too easy to ask, "Wouldn't your life be better if you had concept X?" or "Don't you think my product/service idea is better than what exists?" While this might be a direct way to validate your idea, it requires that people answer honestly and understand exactly what they need. Most people like to be nice, and they want to be supportive of new ideas— until they actually have to pay money for them. Also, many times people can't envision your product/service until it actually exists, so their feedback may be biased.

During the "gathering stimuli" phase, act as if you were Charles Darwin observing finches on the Galapagos Islands—just *observe*. Ideally, you'll gather stimuli as a team so that you have multiple interpretations of what you have learned.

Multiply Stimuli. The next phase in the IDEO process is to multiply stimuli. Here the team members report back on their findings and then start brainstorming on the concept and how to improve on the solution. One of our colleagues shared with us the trick of comedy improv for facilitating this process. A group of actors (usually three to four) poses a situation to the audience and then lets the audience shout out the next situation or reply that one actor is to give to another. From these audience suggestions, the actors build a hilarious skit. The key to success is to always say, "Yes, and . . ." Doing so allows the skit to build on itself and create a seamless and comical whole. Likewise, multiplying stimuli requires the team to take the input of others and build on it. Be a bit wild-eyed in this process. Let all ideas, no matter how far-fetched, be heard and built upon because, even if you don't incorporate them into the final concept, they might lead to new insights that are ultimately important to the product's competitive advantage.

Remember that "Yes, and . . ." means that you build on the input of your colleagues. All too often in a group setting it is easy to say, "That won't work because . . ." These kinds of devil's advocate debates, while important in the later phases of business development, can prematurely kill off creative extensions in this early phase. Also beware of "Yes, but . . ." statements, which are really just another way of saying "Your idea won't work and here's why . . ." The key to this phase of development is to generate as many diverse ideas as possible.

As you go through this multiplication stage, *brain writing* is a useful technique to avoid prematurely squashing interesting extensions. The process is like brainstorming, but the focus is on written rather than verbal communication. The biggest shortcoming of brainstorming is that it opens up the opportunity for the most vocal or opinionated members of the group to dominate the conversation and idea-generation process. In contrast, brain writing ensures that everyone has a chance to contribute ideas. To start, the team identifies a number of core alternative variations to the central idea (if you have a disparate team, as you might for an entrepreneurship class, use each member's favoured idea). Put the core ideas onto separate flip-chart sheets and attach them to the wall. Then the team and trusted friends, or classmates, go around and add "Yes, and . . ." enhancements to each idea. Keep circulating among the flip-chart sheets until everyone has had an opportunity to think about and add to each idea. At the end of that cycle, you'll have several interesting enhancements to consider. Instead of publicly discussing the ideas, have everybody vote on the three to five they like best by placing different-coloured sticky notes on the sheets. In essence, this is another "market test" in which your team and other interested parties are gauging the viability of the idea.[11]

Create Customer Concepts. Once you've narrowed the field to the idea and features you think have the most potential, the next step is to create customer concepts. In other words, build a simple mock-up of what the product will look like. This helps the team visualize the final product and see which features/attributes are appealing, which are detrimental, and which are nice to have but not necessary. Keep in mind that this mock-up doesn't need to be functional; it is just a tool to solidify what everybody is visualizing and to help the team think through how the product should be modified.

When your team is developing a service, your mock-up won't necessarily be a physical representation but rather some kind of abstract modelling of what you hope to achieve. For example, the initial mock-up for a restaurant is often just a menu. Entrepreneurs who want to take the research process even further will often test the product or service in a low-cost way. This process allows for rapid-fire prototyping of ideas, and it also provides the luxury of failing early and often before making substantial investments in a bricks-and-mortar establishment. This is also known as a **minimum viable product (MVP)**, which is the minimum feature set that a customer is willing to pay for. An MVP is a bare-bones version of the final product and does not contain all the bells and whistles that will aesthetically and functionally enhance the product when it officially goes to market.

Optimize Practicality. Quite often at this stage people "overdevelop" the product and incorporate every bell and whistle that the team has come up with during the brainstorming process. This is fine—the next and last step is to optimize practicality, when the team will identify those features that are unnecessary, impractical, or simply too expensive.

Rapid-Fire Prototyping

Kevin Plank, walk-on Maryland football player, found himself being slowed down by his 100% cotton undershirts. "I was short and slow—I was looking for every second I could spare," he says. "Even if it was raining outside, the sweat-soaked cottons gave me that slowed-down lethargic feeling."[i]

With a mission to develop a T-shirt using moisture-wicking fabric for athletic performance, Plank experimented with synthetic fabrics at a local tailor shop outside College Park, Maryland. Spending only $500, he ran through seven prototypes before deciding on the one he wanted to use. He asked his former teammates to try his prototypes: "My first goal was getting athletes to believe in the fact that they needed an alternative to a basic cotton T-shirt. The way you do that is with a great product, but you also do it with influencers."[ii] As Plank's friends moved on to play in the NFL, he would send them T-shirts, requesting that they pass them out to other players in their locker rooms. People started to take notice of the brand when the front page of USA Today featured Oakland Raiders quarterback Jeff George wearing an Under Armour mock turtleneck. Soon after, Under Armour apparel was featured in two popular football movies, Any Given Sunday and The Replacements. Gaining considerable media attention and positive reviews from players, word began to spread and orders began to increase.

In November 2005, Under Armour raised $157 million in its IPO, offering 12.1 million shares at $13/share.[iii] Since its IPO, it has grown revenues 27.9% annually, reaching over $2.3 billion in 2013 and stock prices have increased from $13 to $70.[iv] Under Armour now sponsors nine collegiate sports programs and some of the world's most famous athletes across multiple sports, including Tom Brady, Cam Newton, Bryce Harper, Ryan Howard, and Michael Phelps.[v]

[i] "From Rags to Microfiber: Inside the Rapid Rise of Under Armour," Sports Illustrated, April 9, 2009, www.si.com/more-sports/2009/04/09/under-armour.

[ii] Ibid.

[iii] MarketWatch, "Under Armour's IPO Doubles," November 18, 2005, http://www.marketwatch.com/story/under-armour-up-100-in-biggest-us-open-since-2000.

[iv] Under Armour, "2013 Annual Report," http://files.shareholder.com/downloads/UARM/3394600311x0x735952/1020FA20-6420-440E-8167-BCD7DB8D5422/2013_Annual_Report.pdf .

[v] Under Armour, "Our History," www.underarmour.jobs/our-history.asp.

This is the phase in which it is important to play devil's advocate. As the IDEO developers state, it is a time for the "grownups" to decide which features are the most important to optimize. If the previous steps have gone well, the team has learned a tremendous amount about what the customer may want, and that means they have a deeper understanding of the features/attributes that create the greatest value for the customer. Referring to the Jim Poss case[12] presented at the end of this chapter, Jim and his team found that the most important attributes of his solar-powered trash receptacles were (1) durability—the bins were in public places, and rough treatment or vandalism was a real threat; (2) size—the receptacle couldn't be overly large or it wouldn't fit in the public places intended, and the bags couldn't weigh too much when filled; and (3) price—the higher upfront purchase cost had to be offset by the reduced trips to collect trash so the receptacle would pay for itself within a year. Understanding these basic parameters helped Jim's team refine its original design. For durability, they found that sheet metal was a cost-effective casing, that a Lexan plastic cover on the solar panel prevented vandalism and accidental chipping, and so forth. They went through a similar process to determine the right size. These steps helped them design a product that the customer would want at a price the customer was willing to pay.

The entire idea-generation process is iterative. At each of the four steps we've presented, you learn, adjust, and refine. You start to understand the critical criteria that customers use in their purchasing decision and the pain points in building your product or delivering your service. This process allows you to identify and refine your idea with relatively little cost, compared to the costs you'd incur if you immediately opened your doors for business with what you believed to be the most important attributes. Nonetheless, up to this point you still don't know whether your idea, which is now quite robust and well thought out, is a viable opportunity.

Is Your Idea an Opportunity?

While the idea-generation process helps you shape your idea so that it is clearer and more robust, it is only part of the process. The difference between venture success and failure is a function of whether your idea is truly an opportunity. Before quitting your job and investing your own resources (as well as those of your family and friends), spend some time studying the viability of your idea and proving your concept will actually work. A viable opportunity contains a favourable set of circumstances that are attractive (financially), durable (long lasting), timely (the market is ready for it), and creates or adds value for the end user. There are five major areas you need to fully understand prior to your launch: (1) customers, (2) competitors, (3) suppliers and vendors, (4) the government, and (5) the broader global environment (see Figure 3.2). We'll discuss each of these areas in turn.

The Customer

Who is your customer? This broad question, the first you must answer, can be problematic. For instance, you might be tempted to think, if you're hoping to open a restaurant, that anyone who would want to eat in a restaurant is your customer—in other words, just about everyone in the world except for the few hundred hermits spread out across the country. But you need to narrow down your customer base so that you can optimize the features most important to your customer. So a better question is, "Who is your *core* customer?" Understanding who your primary customer is lets you better direct your efforts and resources to reach that customer. You can further refine your definition.

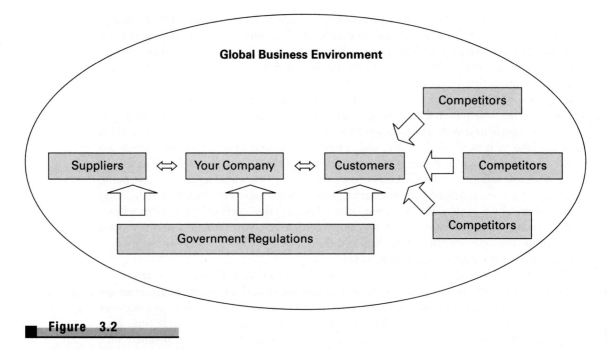

Figure 3.2

The opportunity space

Starting with your initial definition, break your customers down into three categories: (1) the core customer group or **primary target audience (PTA)**, (2) the **secondary target audience (STA)**, and (3) the **tertiary target audience (TTA)**. Most of your attention should focus on the PTA. These are the customers you believe are most likely to buy at a price that preserves your margins and with a frequency that reaches your target revenues. The larger the PTA, the larger the **total addressable market (TAM)** will be.[13] TAM can be calculated as the size of the customer's pain point multiplied by the quantity of customers experiencing that pain.

Let's consider our fast-casual Thai restaurant example. The sector is growing, even during an economic downturn, as consumers seek less-expensive food that does not sacrifice quality. Fast-casual restaurants usually have larger footprints (more square feet) than fast-food restaurants and food court outlets. Thus, you want a customer willing to pay a bit more than a fast-food customer for perceived higher quality. A wise location might be a destination mall with tenants like Indigo, Pottery Barn, and other stores that attract middle-income and higher-income shoppers. Your PTA, in this situation, might be soccer moms (30 to 45 years old with household incomes ranging from $50,000 to $150,000). These women tend to shop, watch what they eat, and enjoy ethnic food.

During the investigation stage, you would focus your attention on better understanding your PTA. How often do they shop? How often do they eat out? What meals are they more likely to eat outside the home? What other activities do they participate in besides shopping and dining out? What you are collecting is information about things like income and ethnicity (demographics) and about personality traits and values (psychographics).[14] Both categories help you design and market your product or service. During the launch phase, you would design the decor in a manner that most appeals to the PTA. You would create a menu that addresses their dietary concerns and appeals to their palate. During operations, you would market toward your PTA and train your employees to interact with them in an appropriate and effective manner. Note that the efforts across the three stages of your venture (investigation, launch, and operations) are different than they would be if you were launching a fast-food restaurant or a fancy sit-down French restaurant because your target audience would be different.

Fast-Casual Demographics

The most often-cited reason for the growth in the fast-casual segment is the generation of consumers who grew up on fast food and won't eat it anymore. Add the aging baby boomers who are looking for healthier alternatives and who can afford to pay a little more for better quality. The price of a meal in a moderately priced restaurant has dropped; it's now only 25% more than the price of a meal purchased in a grocery store and prepared at home, making dining out an economically viable alternative. Other fast-casual demographics include the following:

- The 18–34 age group is most likely to opt for fast-casual and makes up 37% of the traffic at such outlets.

- A newly emerging segment of fast-casual consumers is married, dual-income couples with no kids (known as "DINKs"). These DINKs range in age from 35 to 54, and 38% own a home worth $100,000 to $199,000. They make up 28% of the customer base.

- Fifteen percent of fast-casual customers were under the age of 18.

- Casual dining is too slow for kids, and parents don't want to eat fast food.

- Fast-casual restaurants offer teens on dates a destination their parents are comfortable with that does not serve alcohol.

- Casual dining companies are responding to the fast-casual trend by aggressively marketing take-out business.

- Casual dining has now become an event, not a spur-of-the-moment dining decision.

- The number of fast-casual dining units has grown from 11,013 in 2007 to 13,643 in 2011.

- Annual traffic at fast-casual restaurants has also increased from 4% to as much as 11% from 2007 to 2011. Conversely, traffic has been on the decline for fast-food, casual dining, and midscale establishments from 2009 to 2011.

- In 2011 fast-casual restaurants accounted for $27 billion in annual sales.

- In 2011 the fast-casual segment represented 14% of all quick-service restaurant sales, compared to 5% ten years ago. Moving forward, sales are forecasted to compound 8% annually over the next five years, according to Technomic.

Adapted from E-Business Trends (Food and Beverage), August 21, 2002, www.army.mil/cfsc/documents/business/trends/ _E-TRENDS-8-21-02.doc. Updated with facts from "Webinar: Fast-Casual Restaurant Trends Forecast 2009," Fast Casual.com, www.fastcasual.com/specialpub.php?i=97&s=4; F. Minnick, "Knowing Your Customer," FastCasual.com, May 30, 2006, www.fastcasual.com/article.php?id=5120& na=1&prc=43; V. Killifer, "NPD: Fast Casual Only Growth Segment during Down Economy," FastCasual.com, February 7, 2012, www.fastcasual.com/article/190159/NPD-Fast-Casual-only-growth-segment-during-down-economy; "2012 Fast Casual Top 100 Movers and Shakers: The Top Restaurant Chains, People, Trends and Technologies Shaping the Fast Casual Segment," http://global.networldalliance.com/downloads/white_papers/fc_top100_042012_v7.pdf

While you should focus most of your attention on your PTA, the STA group also deserves some attention. The PTA may be your most frequent, loyal customers, but to increase your revenues you'll want to bring in some of your STA as well. In the restaurant example, your STA may be men with similar demographics as your PTA, older couples who are active and near retirement age, and younger working professionals (see the box entitled "Fast-Casual Demographics"). These groups are likely to find your restaurant appealing but may not attend with the same frequency (possibly more on weekends or during the dinner hour versus the lunch hour). Your STA may also be part of your growth strategy. For instance, after you get past your first two to three restaurants, you may choose to expand your menu or your location profile (to urban centres, for instance). Understanding which STA is the most lucrative helps you make better growth decisions.

Demographics	Psychographics
Age	Social group (white collar, blue collar, etc.)
Gender	Lifestyle (mainstream, sexual orientation,
Household income	materialistic, active, athletic, etc.)
Family size/family life cycle	Personality traits (worriers, Type A's, shy,
Occupation	extroverted, etc.)
Education level	Values (liberal, conservative, open minded,
Religion	traditional, etc.)
Ethnicity/heritage	
Nationality	
Social class	
Marital status	

■ **Figure 3.3**

Common demographic and psychographic categories

Finally, your TTA requires a little attention, too. During the investigation and launch stage, you shouldn't spend much time on the TTA. However, once you begin operating, a TTA may emerge that has more potential than you originally realized. Keeping your eyes and ears open during operations helps you adjust and refine your opportunity to better capture the most lucrative customers. In our Thai restaurant example, you might find that soccer moms aren't your PTA but that some unforeseen group emerges, such as university students. If you segment your customer groups throughout the three stages as we have outlined, you'll be better prepared to adapt your business model if some of your preconceptions turn out to be incorrect.

We've said that it's important to understand your audience's demographics and psychographics. Part of your investigation phase should include creating customer profiles. Figure 3.3 provides a sampling of the types of demographics and psychographics that might be used in describing your customer.

Trends. Customers aren't static groups that remain the same over time. They evolve; they change; they move from one profile to another. To best capture customers, you need to spot trends that are currently influencing their buying behaviour and that might influence it in the future. When considering trends, look at broader macro trends and then funnel down to a more narrow focus on how those trends affect your customer groups. Trends might also occur within customer groups that don't affect the broader population.

One of the most influential trends in the macro environment within North America over the last 50 years has been the life cycle of the baby boomer generation. Born between 1946 and 1964, Canada's 9.6 million baby boomers are usually married, well educated, and make up 32.7% of the working population. Generation X , born between 1965 and 1984, represents only 18% of the workforce.[15] What links baby boomers as a generation is the experience of growing up in the post–World War II era, a time of tremendous growth and change.

Since they represent such a large percentage of the Canadian population, it is no wonder that baby boomers have created numerous new categories of products and services. For example, in the 1950s the disposable diaper industry emerged and then exploded to the point where today it has $4 billion in sales. In the late 1950s and through the 1960s, the rapidly growing population created a need for large numbers of new schools, which in turn led to a building frenzy. In the late 1960s and the 1970s, the rock-and-roll industry exploded. Then in the 1980s, as these baby boomers became parents, a new car category was created (the minivan), which saved Chrysler from bankruptcy. In the 1990s, the boomers were in their prime working years, and new investment categories emerged to help them plan for their retirement and their children's postsecondary educations. Today, as the boomers age, we see growth in pharmaceuticals and other industries related to the more mature segment. According to one market research firm, "boomers are expected to change America's concepts of aging, just as they have about every previous life stage they have passed through."[16] How does this macro trend influence your idea?

Numerous macro trends affect the potential demand for your product or service. Trends create new product and service categories, or emerging markets, that can be especially fruitful places to find strong entrepreneurial opportunities. For example, knowing that millennials are 42% more likely to use their smartphones to go online, as indicated in Figure 3.4, might affect the trend of a product or service. The convergence of multiple trends enhances the power of an opportunity like the Internet boom. First, the personal computer (PC) was common in the workplace, and as a result many people grew comfortable using it. That led to a proliferation of PCs in the home, especially for children and teenagers who used it for school, work, and video games. While the Internet had been available for decades, the development by Tim Berners-Lee of the World Wide Web (WWW or the Web) system of hyperlinks connecting remote computers, followed by the development of the Mosaic Web browser (the precursor to Netscape and Explorer) and the proliferation of Internet service providers like Prodigy and AOL, created huge opportunities for commerce online. From the very first domain name—symbolics.com—assigned in 1985, the Web has evolved into an integral component of the modern economy. Even though many dot-coms failed, others, such as eBay and Amazon, have established themselves as profitable household names. That many of these successful businesses have become multi*billion*-dollar companies in less than a decade speaks to the incredible power of convergent trends.

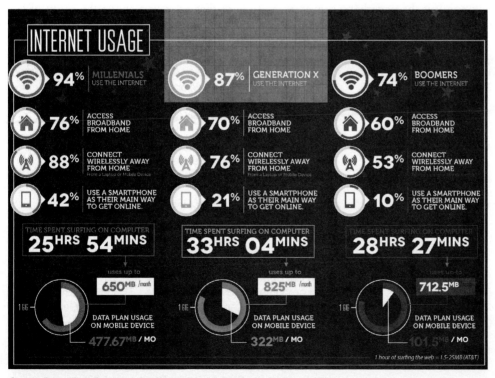

Source: From "Data Footprints by Generations" infographic. Courtesy of Wikibon. Available at http://wikibon.org/blog/infographics.

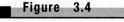
Figure 3.4

Demographic Internet usage

Trends also occur in smaller market segments and may be just as powerful as macro trends; in fact, they may be precursors to larger macro trends. For example, according to Packaged Facts, a market research consultancy, the market for religious products (including blockbuster movies, music, clothing, books, and even games and toys) reached $6 billion in annual sales in 2013, up from the $5.6 billion sold in 2004.[17] Indeed, major companies are capitalizing on this market. At the end of 2005, Starbucks announced it would be featuring a quotation on its coffee cups from Rick Warren, pastor and bestselling author of *The Purpose-Driven Life*, which includes the line, "You were made by God and for God, and until you understand that, life will never make sense."[18] While the quote is just one of many that the company featured on its coffee cups, you can rest assured that the decision to include it was a calculated move to make the company's products more appealing to the growing Christian market.

Another important trend is the widespread difference between the baby boomers and the millennials, also known as Generation Y. The millennial generation—those born after 1980—are accustomed to a digital life. According to Don Tapscott, author of *Growing Up Digital*:

> *For the first time in history, children are more comfortable, knowledgeable, and literate than their parents with an innovation central to society. And it is through the use of the digital media that the Millennial Generation will develop and superimpose its culture on the rest of society. Already these kids are learning, playing, communicating, working, and creating communities very differently than their parents. They are a force for social transformation.*[19]

The millennial generation's prolific use of the Internet coupled with a sense of digital mastery will be the driving force for social transformation.[20]

Trends often foretell emerging markets and suggest when the window of opportunity for an industry is about to open. Figure 3.5 lists some influential trends over the last 50 years. However, it is the underlying convergence of trends that helps us measure the power of our ideas and whether they are truly opportunities.

Trend	Impact
Baby boom generation	Pampers, rock 'n' roll, television, minivans, real estate, McMansions, etc.
Personal computing	Internet, electronic publishing, spreadsheets, electronic communication
Obesity	Drain on healthcare system, growth of diet industry, changes in food industry, health clubs, home gyms
Dual-income households	Childcare, home services—landscaping, housecleaning, prepared foods
Smartphones	Apps, location-based couponing, NFC (near field communication) and mobile payments, ecommerce retailers moving to mobile, voice-activated commands
High-speed Internet	Cloud computing, streaming media, free online education— Khan Academy, edX.org (free online courses from Harvard, MIT, Cal Berkeley, and University of Texas)
Touch computing	Tablet computers and eReaders—iPad, BlackBerry PlayBook, Window Surface, Amazon Kindle Fire, Samsung Galaxy, Motorola Xoom; touch-based operating systems— Windows 8 and Mac OS X Lion
Social media	Widespread popularity of Facebook, Twitter, LinkedIn, Pinterest, Google+; "frictionless sharing" through social media apps like Spotify, Social Reader, and Gilt

■ **Figure 3.5**

Important trends over the last 50 years

How Big Is the Market? Trends suggest increasing market demand. Thus, one of the questions that distinguish ideas from opportunities asks whether there is sufficient market demand to generate the level of revenues necessary to make this an exciting career option. Venture capitalists and other investors are typically interested in companies in industries that have a cumulative annual growth rate (CAGR) of at least 25%, which stems from the underlying premise that "a rising tide floats all boats."[21] As we pointed out in Chapter 2, an entrepreneur typically needs the new venture to generate a minimum of $750,000 per year in revenue to meet market rates on his or her forgone salary of $70,000 plus benefits. While this level might make a nice "mom and pop" store, many students are interested in creating something bigger. The larger your goals, the more important your market demand forecasts. To accurately gauge your demand, start at the larger macro market and funnel demand down to your segment and your geographic location. Granted, as you expand, you'll likely move beyond your segment and your geographic origins, but the most critical years for any venture are its first two. You need to be certain that you can survive the startup, and that means you need to be confident of your base demand.

Let's go back to our Thai fast-casual restaurant example to begin to understand how large our market demand might be. Figure 3.6 steps through the demand forecast. It is best to start with the overall market size—in this case, the size of the entire restaurant industry in the United States. Next, segment the industry into relevant categories. We are interested in both the relative size of the fast-casual segment and the size of the ethnic segment. It would be ideal

Restaurant Industry Sales Projections in 2012	**$632 Billion**
Size of Market Segments	
Eating Places	**$419.2 Billion**
Quick service restaurants including fast-casual	**$174 Billion**
Fast-casual restaurants	**$24.3 Billion**
Retail, vending, recreation, mobile	**$61.2 Billion**
Managed services	**$44.4 Billion**
Lodging place restaurants	**$31.4 Billion**
Bars and taverns	**$18.9 Billion**
Other	**$56.7 Billion**
Market share for ethnic restaurants	**$210.7 Billion***
Market share by state	
Massachusetts	
Overall restaurant sales	**$12.6 Billion**
Ethnic	**$4.2 Billion**
Natick (we are opening in Natick shopping district)	
Massachusetts population... 6.59M	
Natick population.. 33K	
Framingham population... 68K	
Wellesley population 28K	
Natick, Framingham, Wellesley population is 2% of total Massachusetts population	
Natick, Framingham, Wellesley ethnic restaurant sales	**$82 Million**
Soccer moms (women between 30 and 45)...................... 4K or 11% of Natick, Framingham, and Wellesley population	**$8.9 Million**

*Full-service Steams Ahead, *Restaurants USA*, October 2001, http://national restaurantassociation.org/tools/magazi nes/rusa/magArchive/year/article/?ArticleID=671. This article estimates that ethnic food accounts for one-third of total restaurant sales, so we multiplied the total industry size by one-third.

▪ Figure 3.6

Market size for Thai fast-casual restaurant

to find the size of the fast-casual-ethnic (or better yet, Thai) segment, but as you narrow down to your opportunity, there is likely to be less information because you may be riding new trends that suggest future demand that has yet to materialize. Finally, during your initial launch, you'll likely have some geographic focus. Extrapolate your overall market data to capture your geographic market. In this case, we took the population of the towns within a five-mile drive along the major thoroughfare on which our restaurant would be located and multiplied that percentage of the state population by the total spent in the state (Massachusetts). Basically, for this last step, you should try to assess the number of soccer moms in your geographic reach. The U.S. Census makes this very easy, as it breaks out demographics by town. Thus, it appears that there are roughly 14,000 soccer moms in this target market.

Market Size Today and into the Future. While it is important to size your market today, you'll also need to know how big it will be in the future. If you are taking advantage of trends, your market is likely growing. Attractive opportunities open up in growing markets because there is more demand than supply, and a new firm doesn't need to compete on price. In the early years, when the firm is going through a rapid learning curve, operational expenses will be proportionately higher than in later years, when the firm has established efficient procedures and systems. Furthermore, market growth means that your competitors are seeking all the new customers entering the market rather than trying to steal customers away from you.

Projecting growth is notoriously difficult, but you can make some educated guesses by looking at trends and determining overall market size as described earlier. Then make some estimates of what type of market penetration you might be able to achieve and how long it will take you to get there. If all else fails, the easiest thing to do is to verify past growth. As trend analysis tells us, past growth is usually correlated with future growth, which means you can make reasonable estimates based on historical numbers. The **S-curve** is a powerful concept that highlights the diffusion of product acceptance over time.[22] When a product or innovation is first introduced, few people are aware of it. Typically, the firm has to educate consumers about why they need this product and the value it offers. Hence, the firm concentrates its effort on early adopters. It is expensive to develop the right concept and educate the consumer, but the firm can offset this cost somewhat by charging a high price.

As customers react to the concept, the company and other new entrants learn and modify the original product to better meet customer needs. At a certain point (designated as point 1 in Figure 3.7), customer awareness and demand exceed supply and the market enters a fast-growth phase. During this time (the time between points 2 and 3 in Figure 3.7) a dominant design emerges and new competitors enter to capture the "emerging market." Typically, demand exceeds supply during this phase, meaning that competitors are primarily concerned with capturing new customers entering the market. After point 3, market demand and supply equalize, putting price pressure on the companies as they fight to capture market share from each other. Finally, innovations push the product toward obsolescence, and overall demand declines.

Frequency and Price. Market size and growth are important, but we also need to think about how often our average customer buys our product or service and how much he or she is willing to pay. Ideally, our product or service would have perfectly inelastic demand: The customer would pay any price to have it. For a product with elastic demand, the quantity demanded will go down if the price goes up, and vice versa. Inelasticity results in the opposite—whether prices increase or decrease, the demand for the product stays stable. Consider front row seats for your favourite baseball team or theatre production. Nearly everyone would like to sit in the front row, but

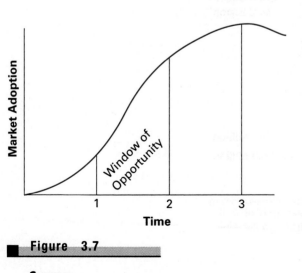

Figure 3.7

S-curve

most of us can't or don't because the price is too high. However, if the price were lowered by a certain amount, we might be more than happy to buy the tickets. This is an example of elastic demand: As price decreases, demand for that product increases.

In contrast, consider gasoline. People who rely on a car to get to work have little choice but to pay the prices charged at the pump. If prices go down, they are unlikely to buy more gas, and if prices go up, they will still need to buy enough gas to get to work and run errands. While not perfectly inelastic, the demand for gasoline is relatively inelastic. In reality, there will almost always be elasticity in customer demand, and our price will be a function of that elasticity. We need to determine the optimal price that encourages regular purchases, accounts for the value inherent in our product, and allows us to earn an attractive margin on the sale. These three variables are highly correlated, and an imbalance would hurt the profitability and even the viability of the firm.

In a classic mistake, some entrepreneurs use a penetration-pricing strategy. They reason that to pull customers from existing alternatives, the firm needs to price their product lower than the competition. Then, once the product is able to gain acceptance and market share, the company can raise prices to increase gross margins and better reflect underlying value. There are a number of flaws in this logic. First, as we've noted, attractive ventures are often launched in emerging markets where demand exceeds supply. This means that price is relatively inelastic—consumers want the product and are willing to pay a premium for it. Second, many new products are designed to be better than existing alternatives. These products offer greater value than competitive products, and the price should reflect this greater value, especially since it usually costs more to add the features that led to the increased value. Third, price sends a signal to the customer. If a product with greater value is priced lower than or the same as competing products, customers will interpret that signal to mean it isn't as good, despite claims that it has greater value. Fourth, even if customers flock to the low-priced product, this rapid increase in demand can sometimes cause serious problems for a startup. Demand at that price may exceed your ability to supply, resulting in stockouts. Consumers are notoriously fickle and are just as likely to go to a competitor as wait for your backlog to catch up.[23] Finally, these same customers may resist when you try to recapture value by raising prices in the future. They will have developed an internal sense of the value of your product, and they may take this opportunity to try other alternatives. The last thing you want is a business built around customers who are always searching for the lowest price. These will be the first people to leave you when a competitor finds a way to offer a lower price.

Furthermore, entrepreneurs should be accustomed to calculating several important accounting principles that help mathematically determine their ability to attain and retain customers. The first determining factor is the **cost of client acquisition (CoCA)**, which indicates the cost for a business to get a single revenue-generating customer. The second factor is the **average revenue per user (ARPU)**, which represents how much extra a company makes with the addition of each new customer. The third factor is the **cost of goods sold (COGS)**, which must be less than ARPU. In order for a company to be profitable, its ARPU must be much greater than its CoCA.[24]

The Internet boom and bust saw many poor pricing decisions. Internet firms entered the market at very low price points. Take Kozmo.com, for example. Many thought the company's revolutionary approach to delivering things like groceries and videos would change the way people shopped, but in the end the value proposition was too good to be true. The company was delivering goods at a cost higher than it was charging. The total ticket for a simple order of a few soft drinks, a bag of chips, and a candy bar might be only $7, but Kozmo.com was paying as much as $10 to the person who had to find those items and then deliver them. The venture capital–backed company burned through almost all its cash before it finally recognized the flaw of its pricing logic, but by then it was too late.[25]

In 2005, Amp'd Mobile, an edgy mobile phone service geared to 18- to 35-year-olds, was created as the first integrated mobile entertainment company for young people and early adopters. Sales exploded by 70% in the first quarter of 2007 to about 175,000 customers after running ads on MTV Networks that emphasized the carrier's mobile music and video services.[26] With the average revenue per subscriber being over $100, collecting payments from the youth proved to be a challenge. By May, the number of nonpaying customers reached 80,000, nearly half of Amp'd's customer base. On June 1, 2007, Amp'd Mobile filed for bankruptcy protection. According to the bankruptcy filing, "The debtor began to find a host of credit and collections problems (that) contributed ultimately to a liquidity crisis."[27]

The argument many unsuccessful Internet entrepreneurs made at the time was that the "number of eyeballs" looking at a site was more important than profitability, which firms figured would come later as they developed a critical mass of customers. These firms reasoned that they could charge lower prices than brick-and-mortar outlets (traditional stores that the customer had to physically visit) because they didn't have the overhead costs of renting or buying so many store locations. Furthermore, Internet companies could serve a larger volume of customers via a single website than a chain of stores could serve in thousands of physical locations. For the most part, these strategies failed for a number of reasons.

First, the Internet firms continued reducing prices to the point where they weren't generating a positive gross margin. The continued decrease in price was a function of competition. New online firms that were basically identical started to appear. For instance, a competitive online pet product marketplace and a difficult financing environment led to the demise of Pets.com and Petopia.com. Pets.com stock had fallen from over $11 per share in February 2000 to $0.19 per share in November 2000, resulting in liquidation. Similarly, Petopia.com was struggling with only $8.8 million in sales in 1999 and $48 million in losses. Only a month after Pets.com shut down, its strategic partner Petco acquired Petopia.com. Traditional retailers responded by adding websites as an additional channel of distribution. Toys "R" Us was able to enter and secure new customers at one-tenth the cost of Toys.com because of higher name recognition.

Finding the right price to charge is difficult. It requires understanding your cost structure. You cannot price under your cost of goods sold (COGS) for an extended period of time unless you have lots of financing (and are certain that access to financing will continue into the future). Thus, your minimum price should be above your COGS. For instance, Figure 3.8

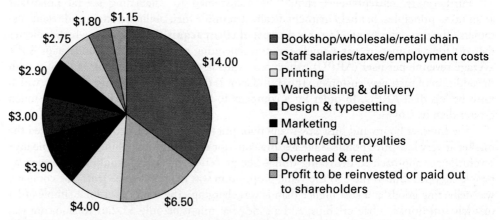

Source: Adapted from T. Grover, "Where Does the Money Go?" Channel View Publications, July 29, 2011. Accessed at http://channelviewpublications.wordpress.com/2011/07/29/where-does-the-money-go/.

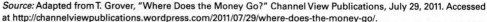

Figure 3.8

Cost of goods sold of a book

illustrates a sample COGS for a book. The total cost of goods sold in this case would be $40. The book publisher could then sell the book to a retailer for $50, leaving a $10 profit margin. At this point the retailer, who paid the supplier $50 for the book, could sell it to the public for $60, providing them with a $10 profit margin as well.

Some firms look at their cost to produce a unit of the product and then add a set percentage on top of that cost to arrive at the price. This is called **cost-plus pricing**, and the problem is that it may set your price lower or higher than the underlying value of your product or service. For example, if you price at 40% above marginal cost, that may result in your product being a great value (software usually has gross margins of 70% or better) or drastically overpriced (groceries often have gross margins in the 20% range).

A better approach is to assess market prices for competing products. For instance, consider GMAT test-preparation courses that help students strengthen their business school applications. At the time of this writing, a quick scan of Kaplan and Princeton Review reveals that prices for their classroom GMAT programs are both $1,599. Given the similarities of the content, structure, and results of these programs, it is no surprise that their prices are comparable. Over the years, Kaplan and Princeton Review have gained deep insight into what parents will pay. For an entrepreneur entering this marketplace, Kaplan and Princeton Review provide a starting point in deciding what price can be charged. The entrepreneur would adjust his or her price based on the perceived difference in value of the offering.

Many entrepreneurs claim that they have no direct competition so it is impossible to determine how much customers might pay. In such cases, which are very rare, it is essential to understand how customers are currently meeting the need that you propose to fill. Assess how much it costs them to fulfill this need and then determine a price that reflects the new process plus a premium for the added value your product delivers.

Margins. For new ventures, research suggests that gross margins of 40% are a good benchmark that distinguishes more attractive from less attractive opportunities. It is important to have higher gross margins early in the venture's life because operating costs during the early years are disproportionately high; this is often due to learning curve effects. For instance, no matter how experienced they are in the industry, your team will incur costs as you train yourselves and new hires. Over time, the team will become more efficient and the associated costs of operations will reach a stability point. Another reason for keeping margins high is that the new venture will incur costs prior to generating sales associated with those costs. For instance, well before you are able to generate any leads or sales, you will need to hire salespeople and invest time and money training them. Even if you are a sole proprietorship, you will incur costs associated with selling your product or service before you receive any cash associated with the sale. For instance, you may have travel expenses like airline tickets or gasoline for your car and infrastructure expenses like a new computer and office furniture. This lag between spending and earning creates a strain on cash flows, whether you are a one-person shop or a growing enterprise, and if your margins are thin to begin with it will be harder to attract the investment needed to launch.

It typically takes three to five years for a firm to reach stability and for operating costs to stabilize. At this point, strong firms hope to achieve net income as a percentage of sales of 10% or better. If the net income margin is lower, it will be hard to generate internal cash for growth or to attract outside investors, to say nothing about generating returns for the founding team.

The exceptions to this rule are businesses that can generate high volumes. During the 1980s and 1990s, many new ventures sought to replicate the Walmart concept. Staples, Office Max, Home Depot, and Lowe's are good examples. Gross margins on these businesses range from 10% to 33% and net income margins from 1.8% to 6.5%. However, the stores do such enormous volumes that they are still able to generate huge profits. For exam-

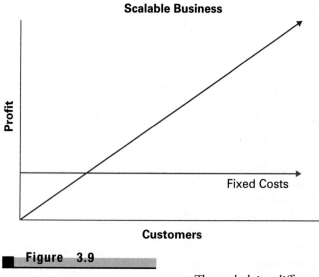

Figure 3.9

Scalability

ple, in the 12-month period ending on January 31, 2014, Walmart had operating income of $26.9 *billion*, which is more in profits than the vast majority of North American companies had in sales, and it was able to do so because it generated $476 billion in sales during the same period. Walmart's gross profit margin of 24.8% is small by most measures, but its sales and profit numbers are clear indicators that its business strategy is working.

The performance of these big companies suggests another kind of industry structure that can be very attractive—fragmented industries. Prior to the launch of Staples and Home Depot, people filled their office supply and hardware needs through "mom and pop" companies. These small enterprises served small geographic regions and rarely expanded beyond them. The big-box stores entered these markets and offered similar goods at much lower prices against which "mom and pop" firms couldn't compete.

The underlying difference that led to the success of the big-box store is due to the fact that it embodied a scalable business model. **Scalability** refers to a company's ability to generate exponential revenue growth while maintaining a stagnant fixed and variable cost.[28] Another example of an extremely scalable business is downloadable software. Once the application is developed, it can be sold and distributed at almost no additional cost, which dramatically increases revenue and streamlines any expenses the company may have. The key to having a scalable business is to maintain a relatively low cost of goods sold while getting demand to drive up revenues. A graph depicting scalability is shown in Figure 3.9.

While entering a fragmented industry and attempting to consolidate it, as big-box stores do, can create huge opportunities, the financial and time investments required are substantial. For instance, Arthur Blank and Bernard Marcus founded Home Depot in 1978 in the Atlanta area. While its individual stores had enormous sales and profit potential, the company needed significant upfront capital for the initial building costs and inventory, and it raised venture capital followed by $7.2 million from its 1981 public offering (which translates to approximately $17.5 million in today's dollars). Almost 10 years later, Thomas Stemberg founded Staples and followed a nearly identical path in office supplies. Here again the startup costs were enormous and the company relied heavily on its founders' experience in retailing. Staples raised $33.83 million in venture capital before it went public in April 1989, raising $51.3 million.[29] The bottom line is that such opportunities are rarer than in emerging markets, and they require a team with extensive industry experience and access to venture capital or other large institutional financing resources.

Reaching the Customer. Reaching the customer can be very difficult, even for the most experienced entrepreneur. Take the example of the founder of Gourmet Stew (the name of the company and the entrepreneur are disguised in this example). After completing her MBA, Emma spent many years with one of the top three food producers in the country where she gained a deeper understanding about the industry. In the 1980s, she joined a small food startup company that developed a new drink concept that became widely successful and was ultimately acquired by Kraft Foods. Still a young woman, she cashed out and started her own venture, Gourmet Stew. Its first product was beef stew in a jar, like Ragú spaghetti sauce. The product tasted better than competitors like Hormel Stew (which came in a can). Despite her extensive entrepreneurial and industry experience and even though her product tasted better, Emma couldn't overcome one obstacle: how to reach the customer.

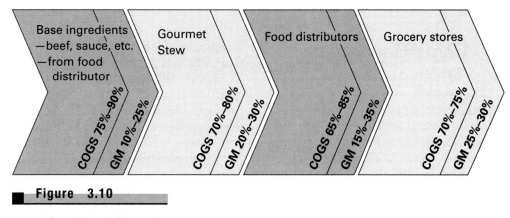

■ Figure 3.10

Value chain of Gourmet Stew

Stew in a jar is usually distributed in grocery stores, but this is a difficult market to enter on a large scale. The industry is consolidated and mature, with only a few chains throughout the entire country. Large product and food companies like Procter & Gamble and General Mills control much of the available shelf space because of their ability to pay the required slotting fees. (Slotting fees are fees that supermarket chains charge suppliers for providing shelf space in their stores.) Grocery stores also have an incentive to deal with fewer rather than more suppliers because it improves their internal efficiency.

Given that, companies that sell only a few products, such as Gourmet Stew, have a more difficult time accessing large chain stores, thereby increasing their cost of client acquisition (CoCA). And even though smaller chains may find a unique product like Gourmet Stew appealing, it costs one-product companies more to distribute through these channels since they have to deal with multiple vendors instead of sealing a few large distribution agreements. Alternatively, Gourmet Stew could work with a large food brokerage company, but that would mean giving a portion of its margins to the brokerage. With all these options, the economics of distribution make it almost impossible to generate a decent margin for this type of company.

One of the most overlooked keys to entrepreneurial success is distribution. How *do* you reach the customer? While Gourmet Stew might have been able to reach the customer through alternative distribution channels like the Internet, these are likely to generate lower sales volume and higher marketing expenses because you have to educate the customer not only about what your product is but also about where to find it.

It is important to understand the entire value chain for the industry you are competing in. You need to lay out the distribution of your product from raw materials all the way to the end consumer. Figure 3.10 captures the value chain for Gourmet Stew.[30] From the figure you can see the respective gross margins of the players—note that their net income margins would be much lower if based on their operating costs. The higher gross margins of the grocery stores indicate their relative power. Consider whether there is a variation on your business idea that would allow you to enter the portion of the value chain where greater margins are available. In sum, you must understand the entire value chain to determine where opportunities to make a profit might exist.

While Gourmet Stew wasn't successful at gaining distribution, the box featuring Stacy's Pita Chips shows how a small food company can slowly gain distribution and build momentum to the point where it achieves a successful harvest for the entrepreneurs.

Stacy's Pita Chips Gaining Widespread Distribution

Stacy's Pita Chips didn't start out as a snack food maker. Instead, Stacy Madison, a social worker by training, and Mark Andrus, a psychologist, wanted to open a restaurant. Their first venture was a small food cart that sold pita bread wraps in downtown Boston. They were instantly successful and soon had long lines of hungry customers waiting for their freshly made wraps. Some of these potential customers tired of waiting in line and would give up before placing an order. To minimize the number of lost customers, Stacy and Mark started serving seasoned pita chips baked from the bread they had left at the end of each day. The pita chips were a hit. In addition to great roll-up sandwiches, customers had a delicious incentive while they waited in line. Eventually, the couple was running two businesses and had to make a choice. They chose the pita chips, figuring they'd be able to gain national growth more rapidly. A new venture was born.

Even though Stacy and Mark had a great product, the question was, "How could they reach the end consumer en masse?" Most people buy chips in the grocery store, but getting space in the snack aisle is nearly impossible. Large distributors sell to grocery stores, and they are interested only in products that their buyers (the grocery stores) want. Recognizing this problem, Stacy decided that there was another way into this channel: Stacy's would place its chips in the natural food aisle and the in-store delis.

Stacy and Mark attended trade shows and made direct contact with grocery stores, sold them on their product, and secured trial placements in the stores. Stacy supplied display racks for her chips to each store and worked hard to increase consumer awareness by giving sample chips to shoppers. Without a distributor, Stacy's Pita Chips often shipped their product via UPS, but once they secured 10 or more stores in a particular geographic region, they went to the stores and asked who distributed snacks to them. The stores often contacted the distributors on Stacy's behalf, asking them to handle the product for them. Stacy noted, "Having customers that the distributor sold to gave us leverage. They wanted to carry our products because we created customer demand for them." Once Stacy's had a few large distributors in line, the company gained momentum and other stores and distributors wanted to carry the product. In 2005, Stacy's hit $60 million[i] in sales, and Frito-Lay, the largest snack food maker in the world, finalized the acquisition of the company in January 2006.

Compiled from a personal interview with Stacy Madison, March 22, 2006.
[i]"Frito-Lay Is Extending Its Healthy Snack Offerings with the Acquisition of Stacy's Pita Chips, Randolph, Mass., for an Undisclosed Sum," *Brandweek*, November 28, 2005.

The Competition

Would-be entrepreneurs often say, "I have a great idea, and the best part is there's *no competition*." If that were true, then as long as you have a customer you have a licence to print money. However, most nascent entrepreneurs turn out to be defining their competition too narrowly. For example, an overly optimistic entrepreneur might suggest that Gourmet Stew has no competition because there are no other companies producing stew in a jar. But that assessment doesn't account for Hormel canned stew (direct competition), and it doesn't account for the multitude of frozen pizzas and other prepared foods that customers can bring home from the grocery store instead of stew (more direct competition). It ignores the customers' options of preparing their own secret recipe for stew (indirect competition) or going out to eat (substitute). In other words, Gourmet Stew's competition isn't just stew in a jar—it is all the other businesses competing for a share of the consumer's stomach. Entrepreneurs ignore these competitors and substitutes at their peril.

To fully identify the competition, start with the customer. How is the customer currently fulfilling the need or want you intend to fill? You must identify direct competitors, indirect competitors, and substitutes. We can use Nike, the athletic sports retail giant, as an example. Nike's direct competitors include Reebok and Adidas; its indirect competitor could be the "knock-off" market. There isn't much Nike can do about the indirect competition, and it only has two options regarding its direct competition: (1) maintain the status quo (Nike can keep a business-as-usual mindset) or (2) it can do something else.

The number and strength of your competitors mirror the market structure. In a mature market, the industry is likely consolidated and the power of existing competitors is likely strong. From the Gourmet Stew example, the industry is highly consolidated. Ten major prepared-food companies—Tyson Foods, Nestlé, Kraft Foods, JBS USA, Dean Foods, General Mills, Smithfield Foods, Mars, Kellogg, and ConAgra Foods—control 45% of the market.[31] Entering this market is difficult, as we saw earlier, because the major competitors control the primary channel of distribution.

Even if you successfully enter the market, the strength of your competitors enables them to retaliate. Competitors, because of their economies of scale and scope, can lower prices to a point that makes it difficult for new ventures to compete. They can spend more on their advertising campaign and other marketing expenditures and increase their visibility because of greater resource reserves or easier access to capital. The good news is that many times strong competitors won't bother with new startups because they're so small that they aren't noticeable or because they don't feel threatened in either the short or the medium term. However, entrepreneurs should plan for contingencies just in case the larger competitors retaliate earlier than expected.

When markets are emerging, like the market for video game consoles, fewer products compete for customers primarily because the demand exceeds the supply. The main struggle within these markets is trying to find and own the dominant design that will become the customer favourite. A recent example of convergence toward a dominant design is the smartphone industry. In the early years, there were a multitude of potential operating systems that used different network providers and different phone manufacturers. In 1993, IBM and Bell South partnered to create the world's first smartphone. Dubbed Simon, the smartphone featured a touchscreen, predictive text, and apps like maps, stock prices, and a camera that could be used by plugging in software cards into the phone. From 1996–2000, Nokia and Ericsson entered the smartphone market with a number of unique phones running on the Symbian operating system. From 2001–2003, Palm and Microsoft both introduced a line of phones running on their own operating systems, Palm OS and Microsoft Windows Mobile. From 2003–2006, BlackBerry dominated the smartphone market with the introduction of the first smartphone optimized for wireless email use. In 2007, Apple changed the smartphone game with its release of the first generation iPhone. In 2008, Taiwanese smartphone manufacturer HTC unveiled the first smartphone powered by Google's Android OS.[32,33]

According to the research firm IDC, Google's Android is the world's most popular smartphone operating system. In 2013, Android accounted for over 162 million units sold and 75% of the smartphone OS market share. Apple's iOS took 17% market share while Symbian, BlackBerry, Linux, and Microsoft accounted for a collective 8% market share.[34]

Figure 3.11 shows some of the competing mobile operating systems and their market shares. It is interesting to note that in 2007 the Symbian OS controlled 64% of the marketplace, Windows Mobile had 12%, BlackBerry 10%, and Linux 10%. Symbian became the dominant operating system primarily because it was included in the most popular smartphones at the time, the Nokia smartphones. With the instant popularity of the open source Android OS in 2008, smartphone manufacturers converged toward the Android OS and existing smartphone manufacturers and new manufacturers alike adopted the Android platform. This example highlights the evolution of most marketplaces. Once a dominant design is in place, the market moves rapidly to maturity.

Emerging markets are characterized by "stealth" competitors. Entrepreneurs often believe their idea is so unique that they will have a significant lead over would-be competitors. But just as your venture will operate "under the radar" as it designs its products, builds its infrastructure, and tests the product with a few early beta customers, there will likely be a number of

Year	Android (Google)	Blackberry (RIM)	iOS (Apple)	Linux	Palm/ WebOS (Palm/HP)	Symbian (Nokia)	Windows Mobile (Microsoft)	Bada (Samsung)	Other
2007	0%	10%	3%	10%	1%	64%	12%	0%	0%
2008	0%	17%	8%	8%	2%	53%	12%	0%	0%
2009	4%	20%	15%	5%	1%	47%	9%	0%	0%
2010	24%	17%	16%	0%	0%	39%	4%	0%	0%
2011	46%	11%	19%	0%	0%	20%	2%	0%	3%
2012-Q1	56%	7%	23%	0%	0%	9%	2%	3%	1%
2012-Q2	68%	5%	17%	2%	0%	4%	4%	0%	0%
2013-Q1	75%	3%	17%	1%	0%	1%	3%	0%	0%

Source: Gartner website, www.gartner.com; "Worldwide market share for smartphones," Yahoo!Finance, September 18, 2012, http://finance.yahoo.com/news/worldwide-market-share-smartphones-220747882--finance.html; and John Koetdier. "Windows Phone Jumps to Third in Global Smartphone Market Share—and Could Be Second Faster Than You Think," VentureBeat, May 16, 2013, http://venturebeat.com/2013/05/16/windows-phone-jumps-to-third-in-global-smartphone-market-share-and-could-be-second-faster-than-you-think.

Figure 3.11

Smartphone operating systems move toward a dominant design

other new ventures at similar stages of development. While it is relatively easy to conduct due diligence on identifiable competition, it is extremely difficult to learn about competition that isn't yet in the marketplace. Thus, it is imperative for new ventures to scan the environment to identify and learn about stealth competition.

There are several sources of intelligence you can tap. It is probable that your competition is using inputs, and thus suppliers, similar to what you are using. As you interview your potential suppliers, make sure to query them about similar companies with whom they are working. While the suppliers may not divulge this information, more often than not they don't see it as a conflict of interest to do so. Outside professional equity capital can also help you determine competitors. Angels and venture capitalists see many deals and have knowledge about how an industry is developing even if they haven't funded one of your stealth competitors. Again, you can talk to professional investors about who they see as strong emerging competitors. Furthermore, a number of widely available databases track and identify companies that receive equity financing. PricewaterhouseCoopers publishes *MoneyTree*,[35] which allows you to screen new investments by industry, region, and venture capitalists making the investment. VentureWire is one of many daily email newsletters published by Dow Jones that tracks current deals.[36] The smart entrepreneur will diligently monitor his or her industry and use these resources, as well as many others, to avoid being surprised by unforeseen competition. In Canada, technology trends and news can be found in the vast database of *TechCrunch*. The online tech reporting website is a leading technology media property dedicated to obsessively profiling startups, reviewing new Internet products, and breaking tech news.[37] *TechCrunch* also offers its subscribers an informative and thorough industry newsletter.

While your direct competition is most relevant to your success, you should also spend some time understanding why your target customer is interested in your indirect competitors and substitutes. As you increase your knowledge of the total marketplace, you will start to understand the **key success factors (KSFs)** that distinguish those firms that win and those that lose. KSFs are the attributes that influence where the customer spends money. If we think once again about Gourmet Stew, customers base their food purchasing decisions on a number of factors, including taste, price, convenience (time to prepare and serve), availability (the distribution channel issue discussed earlier), and healthy attributes of the food, among other factors. As you gather data on these factors, constructing a competitive profile matrix to identify the relative strength of each will help you decide how to position your venture in the marketplace (see Figure 3.12). Gauge

	Gourmet Stew	Hormel	Homemade	DiGiorno Pizza
Taste	Good	Fair	Excellent	Fair
Price	High $3.50	Medium $1.89	Low	Very high $6.50
Convenience	High	High	Low	High
Availability	Low	High	High	High
Healthy	Medium	Low	High	Medium
Revenues		<$135 million*		$500 million*
Gross Margins		23.7%*		34.9%*
Net Income Margins		16.5%*		
Net Profit		$22.3 million*		Loss*

*Financial figures for Hormel and DiGiorno are for the whole company, not just the product.

Figure 3.12

Competitive profile matrix

how well your competitors are doing by tracking their revenues, gross margins, net income margins, and net profits. Note that we don't yet know what the figures are for Gourmet Stew because it has yet to hit the marketplace. Likewise, "homemade stew" in the figure is the creation of the consumer who buys all the ingredients separately at the grocery store.

As you examine the competitive profile matrix, you understand the competitors' strategy and which customers they are targeting. Hormel, for example, is targeting price-sensitive, convenience-minded consumers. Typical customers might include males living on their own, university students, or others who don't have the time or desire to cook but are living on a budget. Homemade stew, on the other hand, falls within the domain of individuals who enjoy cooking and have more time. Stay-at-home parents may have the time to shop for all the ingredients and to cook the stew from scratch, or weekend gourmets might like to have something special for guests or family. Gourmet Stew might appeal to families where both parents work outside the home. They want quality food but don't have the time to cook it from scratch and are not as sensitive to prices. Finally, DiGiorno Pizza (a higher-quality pizza) is targeting families who want something in the freezer for those nights that they just don't have time to cook. While there are many more competitors than we have highlighted in the matrix, it is often best to pick representative competitors rather than to highlight every potential company. The matrix is a tool to help you understand the competitive landscape by drilling down deep on a few key competitors. Although you'll want to be aware of every potential competitor and substitute, focusing on a few in depth will help you devise a successful strategy.

From this information, you can start to get the broad guidelines of the competitors' strategies (e.g., Hormel is pursuing a low-cost strategy) and of what might be an appropriate strategy for Gourmet Stew. It might pursue a differentiation strategy of better quality at a higher price. Moreover, considering the difficulties of entering the distribution channels, it might focus on a niche strategy. Maybe Gourmet Stew could access health-oriented grocery stores like Whole Foods. Understanding the marketplace helps you formulate a strategy that can help you succeed.

Suppliers and Vendors

Understanding the customers and competition is critical to determining whether your idea is indeed an opportunity, but other factors also need consideration. Referring back to the value chain we created for Gourmet Stew (see Figure 3.10), you'll notice that suppliers are providing commodity goods such as beef, vegetables, and other food products. These types of vendors usually have limited power, which means that more of the ultimate gross margin in the chain goes to Gourmet Stew. A sudden rise in the market price of beef, however, could have a negative impact on your margins even though your power over suppliers is strong. A diversified offering that includes vegetarian stew, for example, can guard against such problems.

In other instances, your suppliers can have tremendous power, and that will directly affect your margins. For example, Microsoft, as the dominant operating system and core software provider, and Intel, as the dominant microprocessor supplier, have considerable power over PC manufacturers. Microsoft has gross margins of 74% and Intel has gross margins of 63%,[38,39] whereas average gross margins for PC manufacturers are between 9% and 40%.[40,41] Putting aside the strong competition in the mature PC market for a moment, the fact that suppliers have so much power lessens the opportunity potential for entrepreneurs entering the PC market—unless they find an innovation to supplant the Microsoft operating system or the Intel chip.

The Government

The Canadian government is extremely supportive of entrepreneurship. Taxes are lower for incorporated companies while sole proprietors, or independent business owners, are allowed to offset income tax using expenses incurred to generate their business revenue. Additionally, the Canadian government runs several programs to help aspiring entrepreneurs with financing options, such as the Industrial Research Assistance Program (IRAP) and the Scientific Research and Experimental Development (SR&ED) tax incentive program. The government also funds online information hubs like the Canadian Intellectual Property Office (CIPO) to help entrepreneurs differentiate themselves from competitors by determining existing patents.

Both IRAP and SR&ED, as mentioned in Chapter 1, are government programs that provide aspiring and existing entrepreneurs and fully established corporations with a tax incentive for funds allocated to new and innovative research technologies. IRAP takes its funding one step further by providing financial assistance to innovative small and medium-sized enterprises to hire postsecondary science, engineering, technology, business, and liberal arts graduates.[42]

The Canadian government even created the Business Development Bank of Canada (BDC), the only Canadian bank exclusively dedicated to entrepreneurs. BDC is a financial institution owned by the Canadian government and has been serving Canadian entrepreneurs for over 65 years.[43] The bank also pays special attention to companies in sectors such as exporting, manufacturing, innovation, and knowledge-based industries and to startups in innovative and fast-growth industries attempting to commercialize their research and development efforts.

The Global Environment

As markets become globalized your opportunity is increasingly strengthened by looking overseas. What international customers fit within your PTA, STA, and TTA? (These terms were all defined earlier in this chapter.) How easy is it to reach them? How can the Internet help reach those customers? When might you go international? On the flip side, you also need to be aware of your international competitors. Have they entered your market yet? When might they? It is increasingly common for entrepreneurial firms to use an outsourcing strategy, which means that you may need to evaluate international vendors and their relative power. Additionally, Thomas Friedman, author of the bestselling book *The World Is Flat*, states that the world is now a level playing field.[44] With the mass use of the Internet and powerful search engines like Google, it has never been easier to find information on companies, products, and people. Historically, a startup company would only go global once a state of solid success had been reached in one geographical region. However, with the mass adoption of the World Wide Web, any startup with a cloud-centric or Internet-enabled product can immediately offer their product on a global scale, thereby increasing their chances of success.[45] In Chapter 4 we go into much greater detail on global strategies, but for now let's see whether the global environment makes your idea a stronger or weaker opportunity.

The Opportunity Checklist

Figure 3.13 summarizes the concepts we have covered in this chapter. Use it to evaluate your idea to see whether it is a strong opportunity or to evaluate several ideas simultaneously to see which one has the greatest promise. While your opportunity would ideally fit entirely in the middle column under "Better Opportunities," there will be some aspects

Customer	Better Opportunities	Weaker Opportunities
Identifiable	Clear "core" customer	Several possible customer groups
Demographics	Clearly defined and focused	Fuzzy definition and unfocused
Psychographics	Clearly defined and focused	Fuzzy definition and unfocused
Trends		
Macro market	Multiple and converging	Few and disparate
Target market	Multiple and converging	Few and disparate
Window of opportunity	Opening	Closing
Market structure	Emerging/fragmented	Mature/decline
Market size		
How many	Core customer group is large	Small core customer group and few secondary target groups
Demand	Greater than supply	Less than supply
Market growth		
Rate	20% or greater	Less than 20%
Price/Frequency/Value		
Price	Gross Margin > 40%	Gross Margin < 40%
Frequency	Often and repeated	One time
Value	Fully reflected in price	Penetration pricing
Operating expenses	Low and variable	Large and fixed
Net Income Margin	>10%	<10%
Volume	Very high	Moderate
Distribution		
Where are you in the value chain?	High margin, high power	Low margin, low power
Competition		
Market structure	Emerging	Mature
Number of direct competitors	Few	Many
Number of indirect competitors	Few	Many
Number of substitutes	Few	Many
Stealth competitors	Unlikely	Likely
Strength of Competitors	Weak	Strong
Key success factors		
Relative position	Strong	Weak
Vendors		
Relative power	Weak	Strong
Gross margins they control in the value chain	Low	High
Government		
Regulation	Low	High
Taxes	Low	High
Global environment		
Customers	Interested and accessible	Not interested or accessible
Competition	Nonexistent or weak	Existing and strong
Vendors	Eager	Unavailable

Figure 3.13

Opportunity checklist

where it is weak. Examine the weak aspects and see how you can modify your business model to strengthen them. In the end, of course, the goal is to be strong in more areas than you are weak.

"I Don't Have an Opportunity"

After doing a thorough analysis, some entrepreneurs conclude that the marketplace isn't as large or accessible as they thought or that the competition is much greater than they expected, and they quickly reach the conclusion that they should abandon their dreams. In fact, if you analyze every aspect of the business and if you do your assessment completely, you'll always find a reason for the business to fail. There is no perfect business. There will be areas of weakness in any business model, and it is human nature to amplify those weaknesses until they seem insurmountable. Step back, take a second look, and ask yourself two questions: First, how can you modify your business model so that it isn't as weak in those aspects? Second, what can go right as you launch your business?

The entrepreneurial process is one of continuous adjustment. Many times entrepreneurs stick stubbornly to an idea as it was originally conceived. After a thorough customer and competitive analysis, you need to find ways to modify the business concept so that it better matches the needs of your customer and so that it has advantages over your competitors. The more you learn about the opportunities that exist for your product, the more you must refine your business plan. For instance, as you open your doors and customers come in and provide feedback, you'll find more ways to improve your business model. If you ignore feedback and remain stuck to your initial concept as you originally visualized it (and possibly as you wrote it in your plan), you are more likely to fail. The business planning process is ongoing, and you'll learn more about your opportunity at every step along the way. Therefore, to prematurely abandon your concept after some negative feedback from your analysis is a mistake unless the negatives far outweigh the positives in Figure 3.13. Another beneficial tool to cross-reference your opportunity idea-generation process is the step-by-step stage-gate process, as seen in Figure 3.14, in which opportunity evaluation can be found in stages 2 and 3.

It is also natural to assume the worst possible outcomes, fixating on the weak aspects of the business model and failing to recognize what can go right. For example, Ruth Owades,

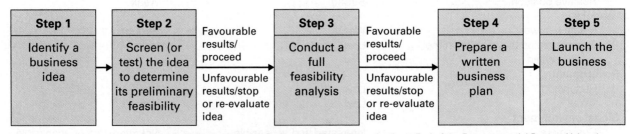

Source: B. B. Barringer and A. R. Gresock, "Formalizing the Front-End of the Entrepreneurial Process Using the Stage-Gate Model as a Guide: An Opportunity to Improve Entrepreneurship Education and Practice," *Journal of Small Business and Enterprise Development* 15 (2008).

Figure 3.14

Opportunity evaluation

who founded Calyx & Corolla (a direct flower-delivery service from the growers to your home), persisted in launching a mail-order catalogue called *Gardener's Eden* for unique gardening tools even though the initial analysis suggested it would be difficult to break even in the first year.[46] While Owades envisioned her business as seasonal—customers would order gardening supplies during the spring planting season—what she found was that she actually had two seasons: People also used the catalogue during the Christmas season for gifts. In addition, the amount people would spend per order was higher than expected, making the dynamics of the business much more robust than she initially imagined.

Your pre-launch analysis is just a starting point. You need to understand the variables in your business model, how they might be greater or less than you initially imagined, and what that might mean for your business. In the next chapter, we will define and examine business models—how you make money and what it costs to generate revenues.

> "Analysis and criticism are of no interest to me unless they are a path to constructive, action-bent thinking. Critical type intelligence is boring and destructive and only satisfactory to those who indulge in it. Most new projects—I can even say every one of them—can be analyzed to destruction."
>
> *—Georges Doriot,*
> *founder of the modern venture*
> *capital industry*

CONCLUSION

All opportunities start with an idea. We find the ideas that most often lead to successful businesses have two key characteristics. First, they are something that the entrepreneur is truly passionate about. Second, the idea is a strong opportunity as measured on the opportunity checklist. To be sure of having a strong opportunity, entrepreneurs need a deep understanding of their customers, preferably knowing the customers by name. Better opportunities will have lots of customers currently (market size) with the potential for even more customers in the future (the market is growing). Furthermore, these customers will buy the product frequently and pay a premium price for it (strong margins). Thus, entrepreneurs need to be students of the marketplace. What trends are converging, and how do these shape customer demand today and into the future?

Savvy entrepreneurs also recognize that competitors, both direct and indirect, are vying for the customers' attention. Understanding competitive dynamics helps entrepreneurs shape their opportunities to reach the customer better than the competition can. As this chapter points out, the entrepreneurial environment is holistic and fluid. In addition to their customers and competitors, entrepreneurs need to understand how they source their raw materials (suppliers) and what government regulation means to their business. If all these elements—customers, competitors, suppliers and government—are favourable, the entrepreneur has identified a strong opportunity. The next step is successfully launching and implementing your vision.

YOUR OPPORTUNITY JOURNAL

Reflection Point	Your Thoughts. . .

1. What do you really enjoy doing? What is your passion? Can your passion be a platform for a viable opportunity?

2. What do your friends and family envision you doing? What strengths and weaknesses do they observe? How do their insights help lead you to an opportunity that is right for you?

3. What ideas do you have for a new business? How can you multiply the stimuli around these ideas to enhance them and identify attractive opportunities?

4. Put several of your ideas through the opportunity checklist in Figure 3.13. Which ideas seem to have the highest potential?

5. How can you shape, reshape, and refine your opportunities so that they have a greater chance to succeed and thrive?

6. Identify some early, low-cost market tests that you can use to refine your opportunity. Create a schedule of escalating market tests to iterate to the strongest opportunity.

WEB EXERCISE

Subscribe to the free listserve VentureWire (www.dowjones.com/privateequityventure capital/product-vw.asp) and TechCrunch Daily (http://techcrunch.com/crunch-daily/). Track the stories on a daily basis. Which companies are receiving venture capital? What trends does this flow of money suggest? How might these trends converge to create new opportunities?

Jim Poss

On his way through Logan Airport, Jim Poss stopped at a newsstand to flip through the June 2004 *National Geographic* cover story that declared "The End of Cheap Oil." Inside was a two-page spread of an American family sitting among a vast array of household possessions that were derived, at least in part, from petroleum-based products: laptops, cellphones, clothing, footwear, sports equipment, cookware, and containers of all shapes and sizes. Without oil, the world would be a very different place. Jim shook his head.

> *. . . and here we are burning this finite, imported, irreplaceable resource to power three-tonne suburban gas-guzzlers with "these colours don't run" bumper stickers!*

Jim's enterprise, Seahorse Power Company (SPC), was an engineering startup that encouraged the adoption of environmentally friendly methods of power generation by designing products that were cheaper and more efficient than twentieth-century technologies. Jim was sure that his first product, a patent-pending solar-powered trash compactor, could make a real difference.

> *In the United States alone, 180,000 garbage trucks consume over a billion gallons of diesel fuel a year.*

By compacting trash onsite and off-grid, the mailbox-sized "BigBelly" could cut pickups by 400%. The prototype—designed on the fly at a cost of $10,000—had been sold to Vail Ski Resorts in Colorado for $5,500. The green technology had been working as promised since February, saving the resort lots of time and money on round trips to a remote lodge accessible only by snow machine.

Jim viewed the $4,500 loss on the sale as an extremely worthwhile marketing and proof-of-concept expense. Now that they were taking the business to the next level with a run of 20 machines, Jim and his SPC team had to find a way to reduce component costs and increase production efficiencies.

Jim returned the magazine to the rack and made his way to the New York Shuttle gate. An investor group in New York City had called another meeting, and Jim felt that it was time for him to start asking the hard questions about the deal they were proposing. These investors in socially responsible businesses had to be given a choice: Either write him the cheque they had been promising—and let him run SPC the way he saw fit—or decline to invest altogether so he could concentrate on locating other sources of funding to close this $250,000 seed round. So far, all Jim had received from this group were voices of concern and requests for better terms—it was time to do the deal or move on.

Green Roots

As a kid, Jim Poss was always playing with motors, batteries, and electronics. He especially enjoyed fashioning new gadgets from components he had amassed by dismantling all manner of appliances and electronic devices. He also spent a lot of time outside cross-country skiing with his father. Jim said that by his senior year in high school, he knew where he was headed:

> *I had read* Silent Spring[47] *and that got me thinking about the damage we are doing to the earth. And once I started learning about the severity of our problems—that was it. By the end of my first semester at Duke University, I had taken enough environmental science to see that helping businesses to go green was going to be a huge growth industry.*

Jim felt that the best way to get businesses to invest in superior energy systems was to make it profitable for them to do so. In order to prepare himself for this path, Jim set up a double major in environmental science and policy and geology—with a minor degree in engineering. He graduated in 1996 and found work as a hydrologist analyzing soil and rock samples for a company that engineered stable parking lots for shopping malls. He didn't stay long:

That certainly wasn't my higher calling. I poked around, and within six months I found a fun job redesigning the production capabilities at a small electronics firm. Soon after that, I started working for this company called Solectria; that was right up my alley.

As a sales engineer at Solectria—a Massachusetts-based designer and manufacturer of sustainable transportation and energy solutions—Jim helped clients configure electric drive systems for a wide range of vehicles. He loved the work and developed an expertise in using spreadsheets to calculate the most efficient layout of motors, controllers, power converters, and other hardware. By 1999, though, he decided that it was once again time to move on:

Solectria had a great group of people, but my boss was a micro-manager and I wasn't going to be able to grow. I found an interesting job in San Francisco as a production manager for a boat manufacturing company—coordinating the flow of parts from seven or eight subcontractors. When the [Internet] bubble burst, the boat company wasn't able to raise capital to expand. My work soon became relatively mundane, so I left.

This time, though, Jim decided to head back to school:

I had now worked for a bunch of different businesses and I had seen some things done well but a lot of things done wrong. I knew that I could run a good company—something in renewable energy, and maybe something with gadgets. I still had a lot to learn, so I applied to the MBA program at Babson College. I figured that I could use the second-year EIT[48] module to incubate something.

Opportunity Exploration

Between his first and second years at Babson, Jim applied for a summer internship through the Kauffman Program. He sent a proposal to the Spire Corporation—a publicly traded manufacturer of highly engineered solar electric equipment—about investigating the market and feasibility of solar-powered trash compactors. Jim had copied his idea to someone he knew on the board, and the same week that the human resources department informed him that there were no openings, he got a call from the president of the company:

Roger Little had talked with the board member I knew and said that while they weren't interested in having me write a case study on some solar whatever-it-was, he said they'd like me to write some business plans for Spire—based on their existing opportunities and existing operations. I said sure, I'll take it.

That summer, Jim worked with the executive team to complete three business plans. When they asked him to stay on, Jim agreed to work 15 hours per week—on top of his full-time MBA classes. Every month or so he would bring up his idea for a solar-powered trash compactor with the Spire executives, but their answer was always the same:

I was trying to get them to invest in my idea or partner with me in some way, and these guys kept saying, "It'll never work." So I just kept working on them. I did the calculations to show them that with solar we could do 10 compactions a day and have plenty [of electric charge] on reserve for a run of cloudy weather. Finally, they just said that they don't get into end-user applications.

Early in his second year, Jim attended a product design fair featuring young engineers from Babson's new sister school, the Franklin W. Olin College of Engineering. He connected with Jeff Satwicz, an engineering student with extensive experience in remote vehicle testing for the U.S. Department of Defense. When Jim got involved with a project that required engineering capabilities, he knew who to call:

> I went up the hill to Olin to ask Jeff if he'd like to help design a folding grill for tailgating—he said sure. It's funny, the two schools are always talking about working together like that, but it doesn't happen until the students sit in the café together and exchange ideas. That's how it works; the faculty wasn't involved—and they didn't really need to be.

Although Jim didn't stay with the grill team, the project had forged a link with an engineer with a penchant for entrepreneurship. Now certain of his trajectory, Jim incorporated the Seahorse Power Company (SPC)—a nod to his ultimate aspiration of developing power systems that could harness the enormous energy of ocean waves and currents.

Understanding that sea-powered generators were a long way off, Jim began to investigate ways to serve well-capitalized ventures that were developing alternative-energy solutions. One idea was to lease abandoned oil wells in California for the purpose of collecting and selling deep-well data to geothermal energy businesses that were prospecting in the area. When Jim sought feedback, he found that even people who liked his concept invariably pointed him in a different direction:

> Everybody kept telling me that wind was where it's at—and they were right; it's the fastest growing energy source in the world. All the venture capitalists are looking at wind power. I realized, though, that if I was going to make wind plants, I'd have to raise $200–$500 million—with no industry experience. Impossible. So instead, I started looking at what these [wind-plant ventures] needed.

The DAQ Buoy

Jim discovered that the Cape Wind Project, a company working to build a wind farm on Nantucket Sound, had erected a $2.5 million, 200-foot monitoring tower to collect wind and weather data in the targeted area. Jim felt that there was a better way:

> Meteorological testing is a critical first step for these wind businesses. I thought, whoa, they've just spent a lot of money to construct a static tower that probably won't accurately portray the wind activity in that 25-square-mile area. And without good data, it's going to be really hard for them to get funding.
>   My idea was to deploy data buoys that could be moved around a site to capture a full range of data points. I spent about six months writing a business plan on my data acquisition buoy—the DAQ. I figured that to get to the prototype stage I'd need between $5–$10 million. This would be a pretty sophisticated piece of equipment, and a lot of people worried that if a storm came up and did what storms typically do to buoys, we'd be all done. I was having a hard time getting much traction with investors.

Finding the Waste

Even while he was casting about for a big-concept opportunity, Jim had never lost sight of his solar compactor idea. With the spring semester upon him, he decided to see if that business would work as an EIT endeavour. Although he was sure that such a device would be feasible—even easy—to produce, he didn't start to get excited about the project until he took a closer look at the industry:

> *I did an independent study to examine the trash industry. I was about a week into that when I looked at the market size and realized that I had been messing around with expensive, sophisticated business models that didn't offer close to the payback as this compactor would.*
>
> *U.S. companies spent $12 billion on trash receptacles in 2000, and $1.2 billion on compaction equipment in 2001. The average trash truck gets less than three miles to the gallon and costs over $100 an hour to operate. There are lots of off-grid sites[49] that have high trash volumes—resorts, amusement parks, and beaches—and many are getting multiple pickups a day. That's a tremendous waste of labour and energy resources.*

Joining him in the EIT module was first-year MBA candidate Alexander Perera. Alex had an undergraduate degree in environmental science from Boston University, as well as industry experience in renewable energy use and energy-efficiency measures. The pair reasoned that if a solar compactor could offer significant savings as a trash collection device, then the market could extend beyond the off-grid adopters to include retail and food establishments, city sidewalks, and hotels (see Exhibit 3.1).

EXHIBIT 3.1 **Target customers**

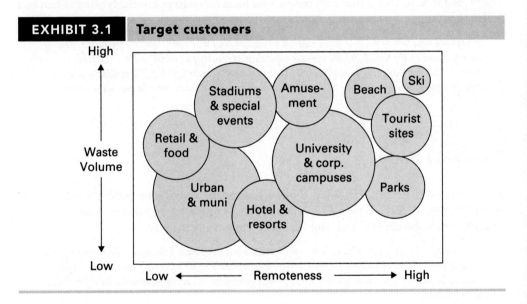

Gearing Up

By the time the spring semester drew to a close, they had a clear sense of the market and the nature of the opportunity—in addition to seed funding of $22,500: $10,000 from Jim's savings and $12,500 through the Hatchery Program at Babson College. Since solar power was widely perceived as a more expensive, more complex, and less-efficient energy source than grid power, it was not surprising to discover that the competition—dumpster and compaction equipment manufacturers—had never introduced a system like this. Nevertheless, Jim and Alex were certain that if they could devise a reliable, solar-powered compactor that could offer end users significant cost savings, established industry players could be counted on to aggressively seek to replicate or acquire that technology.

Understanding that patent protections were often only as good as the legal minds that drafted them, Jim had sought out the best. The challenge was that most of the talented patent attorneys he met with were far outside his meagre budget. In May 2003, Jim got a break when he presented his idea at an investor forum:

> I won $1,500 in patent services from Brown and Rudnick.[50] That might not have taken me too far, but they have a very entrepreneurial mindset. They gave me a flat rate for the patent—which is not something many firms will do. I paid the $7,800 upfront, we filed a provisional patent in June, and they agreed to work with me as I continued to develop and modify the machine.

Jim's efforts had again attracted the interest of Olin engineer Jeff Satwicz, who in turn brought in Bret Richmond, a fellow student with experience in product design, welding, and fabrication. When the team conducted some reverse engineering to see if the vision was even feasible, Jim said they were pleasantly surprised:

> I found a couple of kitchen trash compactors in the Want Ads and bought them both for about 125 bucks. We took them apart, and that's when I realized how easy this was going to be . . . of course, nothing is ever as easy as you think it's going to be.

Pitching without Product

Figuring that it was time to conduct some hard field research, they decided to call on businesses that would be the most likely early adopters of an off-grid compactor. Alex smiled as he described an unexpected turn of events:

> We had a pretty simple client-targeting formula: remoteness, trash volume, financial stability, and an appreciation for the environmental cachet that could come with a product like this. Literally, the first place I called was the ski resort in Vail, Colorado. Some eco-terrorists had recently burned down one of their lodges to protest their expansion on the mountain, and they were also dealing with four environmental lawsuits related to some kind of noncompliance.
> This guy Luke Cartin at the resort just jumped at the solar compactor concept. He said, "Oh, this is cool. We have a lodge at Blue Sky Basin that is an hour and a half round trip on a snow cat. We pick up the trash out there three or four times a week; sometimes every day. We could really use a product like that . . ." That's when you put the phone to your chest and think, Oh my gosh . . .

Jim added that after a couple of conference calls, they were suddenly in business without a product:

> I explained that we were students and that we had not actually built one of these things yet (sort of). Luke asked me to work up a quote for three machines. They had been very open about their costs for trash pickup, and I figured that they'd be willing to pay six grand apiece. I also had a rough idea that our cost of materials would fall somewhat less than that.
> Luke called back and said that they didn't have the budget for three, but they'd take one. I was actually really happy about that because I knew by then that making just one of these was going to be a real challenge.

In September, SPC received a purchase order from Vail Ski Resorts. When Jim called the company to work out a payment plan with 25% upfront, Luke surprised them again:

> He said, "We'll just send you a cheque for the full amount, minus shipping, and you get the machine here by Christmas." That was great, but now we were in real trouble because we had to figure out how to build this thing quickly, from scratch—and on a tight budget.

Learning by Doing

The team set out to design the system and develop the engineering plans for the machine that SPC had now trademarked as the "BigBelly Solar-Powered Trash Compactor." Although his Olin team was not yet versant with computer-aided design (CAD) software, Jim saw that as an opportunity:

> *These guys were doing engineering diagrams on paper with pens and pencils—but now we were going to need professional stuff. I said that we could all learn CAD together, and if they made mistakes, great, that's fine; we'd work through it.*

Concurrent to this effort was the task of crunching the numbers to design a machine that would work as promised. As they began to source out the internal components, they searched for a design, fabrication, and manufacturing subcontractor that could produce the steel cabinet on a tight schedule. Although the team had explained that SPC would be overseeing the entire process from design to assembly, quotes for the first box still ranged from $80,000 to $400,000. Jim noted that SPC had an even bigger problem to deal with:

> *On top of the price, the lead times that they were giving me were not going to cut it; I had to get this thing to Colorado for the ski season!*
>
> *So, we decided to build it ourselves. I went to a local fabricator trade show and discovered that although they all have internal engineering groups, some were willing to take a loss on the research and development side in order to get the manufacturing contract.*
>
> *We chose Boston Engineering since they are very interested in developing a relationship with Olin engineers. They gave me a hard quote of $2,400 for the engineering assistance and $2,400 for the cabinet. By this time, we had sourced all the components we needed, and we began working with their engineer to size everything up. Bob Treiber, the president, was great. He made us do the work ourselves out at his facility in Hudson (Massachusetts), but he also mentored us, and his firm did a tonne of work pro bono.*

Fulfillment and Feedback

As the Christmas season deadline came and went, the days grew longer. By late January 2004, Jim was working through both of the shifts they had set up: from four in the morning to nearly eleven at night. In February, they fired up the device, tested it for three hours, and shipped it off to Colorado (see Exhibit 3.2). Jim met the device at their shipping dock, helped unwrap it, met the staff, and put a few finishing touches on the machine. Although it worked, even at zero degree temperatures, it had never been tested in the field. Jim left after a few days, and for two weeks, he endured a deafening silence.

Jim wrestled with how he could check in with SPC's first customer without betraying his acute inventor's angst about whether the machine was still working, and if it was, what Vail thought about it. Finally, when he could stand it no longer, he placed the call under the guise of soliciting satisfied-customer feedback. The news from Vail nearly stopped his heart:

> *They said that they had dropped the machine off a forklift and it fell on its face. Oh man, I thought; if it had fallen on its back, that would have been okay, but this was bad—real bad. And then Luke tells me that it was a bit scratched—but it worked fine. He told me how happy they were that we had made it so robust. When I asked how heavy the bags were that they were pulling out of the thing, he said, "I don't know; we haven't emptied it yet." I was astounded.*

As it turned out, the Vail crew discovered that the single collection bag was indeed too heavy—a two-bin system would be more user friendly. The resort also suggested that the inside

EXHIBIT 3.2 **The BigBelly arrives in Vail**

a.

b.

cart be on wheels, that the access door be in the back, and that there be some sort of wireless notification when the compactor was full.

As the SPC team got to work incorporating these ideas into their next generation of "SunPack" compactors, they were also engineering a second product that they hoped would expand their market reach to include manufacturers of standard compaction dumpsters. The "SunPack Hippo" would be a solar generator designed to replace the 220-volt AC-power units that were used to run industrial compactors. The waste-hauling industry had estimated that among commercial customers that would benefit from compaction, between 5% and 20% were dissuaded from adopting such systems because of the setup cost of electrical wiring. SPC planned to market the system through manufacturing or distribution partnerships.

Protecting the Property

While the interstate shipment of the BigBelly had given SPC a legal claim to the name and the technology, Jim made sure to keep his able patent attorneys apprised of new developments and modifications. SPC had applied for a provisional patent in June 2003, and it had one year to broaden and strengthen those protections prior to the formal filing. As that date approached, the attorneys worked to craft a document that protected the inventors from infringement, without being so broad that it could be successfully challenged in court.

The SPC patents covered as many aspects of SunPack products as possible, including energy storage, battery charging, energy-draw cycle time, sensor controls, and wireless communication. The filing also specified other off-grid power sources for trash compaction, such as foot pedals, windmills, and waterwheels.

Even without these intellectual property protections, though, Jim felt that they had a good head start in an industry segment that SPC had created. Now they had to prove the business model.

The Next Generation

While the first machine had cost far more to build than the selling price, the unit had proven the concept and had been a conduit for useful feedback. A production run of 20 machines, however, would have to demonstrate that the business opportunity was as robust as the prototype appeared to be. That would mean cutting the cost of materials by more than 75% to around $2,500 per unit. SPC estimated that although the delivered price of $5,000 was far more expensive than the cost of a traditional trash receptacle, the system could pay for itself by trimming the ongoing cost of collection (see Exhibit 3.3).

EXHIBIT 3.3 **Customer economics**

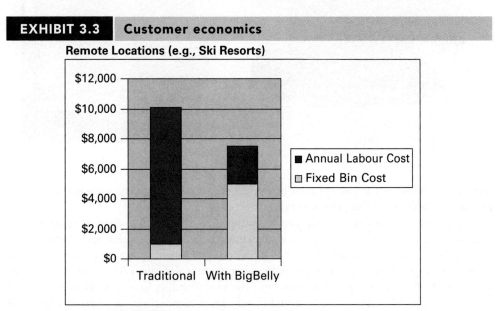

Remote Locations (e.g., Ski Resorts)

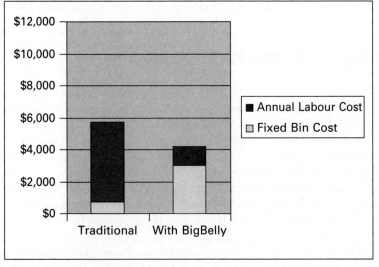

Urban Locations

The team had determined that developing a lease option for the BigBelly would alleviate new-buyer jitters by having SPC retain the risk of machine ownership—a move that could increase margins by 10%. Over the next five years, SPC expected to expand its potential customer pool by reducing the selling price to around $3,000—along with a corresponding drop in materials costs (see Exhibit 3.4).

EXHIBIT 3.4   **BigBelly economics**

Near Term

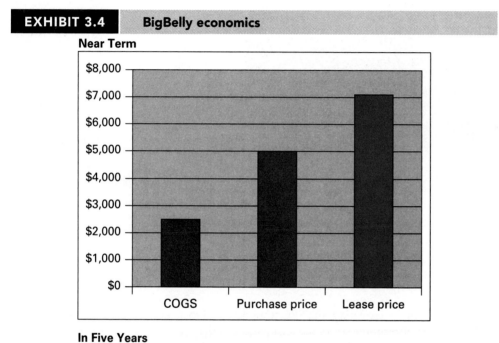

In Five Years

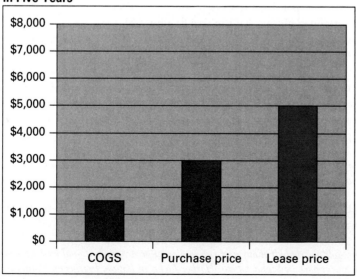

EXHIBIT 3.5   **BigBelly CAD schematic**

a.

b.

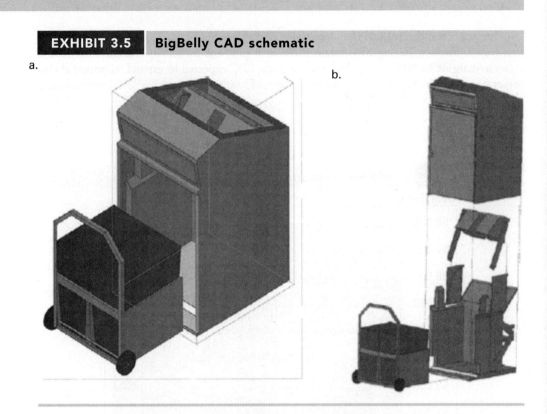

With steel prices escalating, the SPC team designed their new machines with 30% fewer steel parts. They also cut the size of the solar panel and the two-week battery storage capacity in half and replaced the expensive screw system of compaction with a simpler, cheaper, and more efficient sprocket-and-chain mechanism (see Exhibit 3.5).

In order to offer an effective service response capability, the team tried to restrict its selling efforts to the New England area, although "a sale was a sale." One concern that kept cropping up was that this unique device would be a tempting target for vandals.

Team members explained that the solar panel on top was protected by a replaceable sheet of Lexan,[51] that all mechanical parts were entirely out of reach, and that the unit had already proven to be quite solid. The general feeling, Jim noted, was that if the machine could be messed with, people would find a way:

> One state park ranger was worried that it would get tossed into the lake, so I assured him that the units would be very heavy. He said, "So they'll sink really fast . . ."

Jim added that the overall response had been very favourable—so much so that once again, there was a real need for speed:

> We have pre-sold nearly half of our next run to places like Acadia National Park in Maine, Six Flags amusement park in Massachusetts, Harbor Lights in Boston, beaches on Nantucket, and to Harvard University. Fifty percent downpayment deposits should be coming in soon, but that won't cover what we'll need to get this done.

Projections and Funding

During this "early commercialization period," Jim was committed to moderating investor risk by leveraging on-campus and contractor facilities as much as possible. The company was hoping to close on an A-round of $250,000 with a pre-money valuation of $2.5 million by early summer to pay for cost-reduction engineering, sales and marketing, and working capital. The following year the company expected to raise a B-round of between $700,000 and $1 million.

SPC was projecting a positive cash flow in 2006 on total revenues of just over $4.7 million (see Exhibit 3.6). The team members felt that, if their products continued to perform well, their market penetration estimates would be highly achievable (see Exhibit 3.7). Jim estimated that by 2008, SPC would become an attractive merger or acquisition candidate.

EXHIBIT 3.6	SPC financial projections				
	2004	**2005**	**2006**	**2007**	**2008**
BigBelly Unit	50	300	1,200	3,600	9,000
Sales	$225,000	$1,200,000	$4,200,000	$10,800,000	$22,500,000
BigBelly Revenues	0	120,000	525,000	1,620,000	3,937,500
Hippo Royalty Revenues	225,000	1,320,000	4,725,000	12,420,000	26,437,500
Total Income	146,250	660,000	2,100,000	4,860,000	9,000,000
COGS	78,750	660,000	2,625,000	7,560,000	17,437,500
Gross Income	400,000	1,600,000	2,600,000	5,000,000	11,000,000
SG&A	($321,250)	($940,000)	$25,000	$2,560,000	$6,437,500
EBIT					

EXHIBIT 3.7	Market size and penetration				
Top-Down	**2004**	**2005**	**2006**	**2007**	**2008**
SunPack Market* (Billion)	$1.0	$1.0	$1.0	$1.0	$1.0
SunPack % Penetration	0.0%	0.1%	0.5%	1.2%	2.6%
Bottom-Up					
Total Potential Customers**	30,000	30,000	30,000	30,000	30,000
Potential Units/Customer	20	20	20	20	20
Total Potential Units	600,000	600,000	600,000	600,000	600,000
Cumulative Units Sold	50	350	1,550	5,150	14,150
Cumulative % Penetration	0.0%	0.1%	0.3%	0.9%	2.4%

*Assume a $600,000,000 BigBelly market (5% of $12 billion worth of waste receptacles sold to target segments), plus a $400,000,000 power unit market ($1.2 billion worth of compacting dumpsters sold/$12,000 average price × $4,000 per power unit).
**Assume 400 resorts, 600 amusement parks, 2,000 university campuses, 5,000 commercial campuses, 2,200 hotels, 4,000 municipalities, 57 national parks, 2,500 state parks and forests, 3,700 RV parks and campgrounds, and 17,000 fast-food and retail outlets.

In January 2004, as Jim began work on drafting an SBIR[52] grant proposal, his parents helped out by investing $12,500 in the venture. That same month, while attending a wind energy conference sponsored by Brown and Rudnick, Jim overheard an investor saying that he was interested in putting a recent entrepreneurial windfall to work in socially responsible ventures. Jim decided it was worth a try:

I gave him my three-minute spiel on the compactor. He said that it sounded interesting, but that he was into wind power—after all, this was a wind-power conference. "Well then," I said, "have I got a business plan for you!"

That afternoon Jim sent the investor the most recent version of the data acquisition buoy business plan. That led to a three-hour meeting where the investor ended up explaining to Jim why the DAQ was such a good idea. Jim said that the investor also understood how difficult it would be to get the venture fully funded:

[The investor] said, "Well, I sure wish you were doing the Data Acquisition Buoy, but I can also see why you're not." I assured him that my passion was, of course, offshore wind, and that it was something I was planning to do in the future. So he agreed to invest $12,500 in the compactor—but only because he wanted to keep his foot in the door for what SPC was going to do later on.

In February, after the folks at Vail had come back with their favourable review, Jim called on his former internship boss at the Spire Corporation. Roger Little was impressed with Jim's progress, and his company was in for $25,000. In April, the team earned top honours in the 2004 Douglass Foundation Graduate Business Plan Competition at Babson College. The prize—$20,000 cash plus $40,000 worth of services—came with a good deal of favourable press as well. The cash, which Jim distributed evenly among the team members, was their first monetary compensation since they had begun working on the project.

Although SPC could now begin to move ahead on the construction of the next 20 cabinets, Jim was still focused on the search for a rather uncommon breed of investor:

This is not a venture capital deal, and selling this idea to angels can be a challenge because many are not sophisticated enough to understand what we are doing. I had one group, for example, saying that this wouldn't work because most trash receptacles are located in alleys—out of the sun.

Here we have a practical, common sense business, but since it is a new technology many investors are unsure of how to value it. How scalable is it? Will our patent filings hold up? Who will fix them when they break?

Earlier that spring Jim had presented his case in Boston to a gathering of angels interested in socially responsible enterprises. Of the six presenters that day, SPC was the only one offering products that were designed to lower direct costs. During the networking session that followed, Jim said that one group in particular seemed eager to move ahead:

They liked that Spire had invested, and they seemed satisfied with our projections. When I told them that we had a $25,000 minimum, they said not to worry—they were interested in putting in $50K now and $200K later. In fact, they started talking about setting up funding milestones so that they could be our primary backers as we grew. They wanted me to stop fundraising, focus on the business, and depend on them for all my near-term financing needs.

At this point I felt like I needed to play hardball with these guys; show them where the line was. My answer was that I wasn't at all comfortable with that, and that I would be comfortable when I had $200K in the bank—my bank. They backed off that idea, and by the end of the meeting, they agreed to put in the $50,000; but first they said they had to do some more due diligence.

Momentum

By May 2004, the Seahorse Power Company had a total of six team members.[53] All SPC workers had been given an equity stake in exchange for their part-time services. The investor group expressed deep concern with this arrangement, saying that the team could walk away when the going got tough—possibly right when SPC needed them most. Jim explained that it wasn't a negotiable point:

> They wanted my people to have "skin in the game" because they might get cold feet and choose to get regular jobs. I told them that SPC workers are putting in 20 hours a week for free when they could be out charging consulting rates of $200 an hour. They have plenty of skin in this game, and I'm not going to ask them for cash. Besides, if we could put up the cash, we wouldn't need investors, right?

As Jim settled into his seat for the flight to New York, he thought some more about the investors' other primary contention—his pre-money valuation was high by a million:

> These investors—who still haven't given us a dime—are saying they can give me as much early-stage capital as SPC would need, but at a pre-money of $1.5 million and dependent on us hitting our milestones. With an immediate funding gap of about $50,000, it's tempting to move forward with these guys so we can fill current orders on time and maintain our momentum. On the other hand, I have already raised some money on the higher valuation, and maybe we can find the rest before the need becomes really critical.

Discussion Questions

1. Apply the Timmons's entrepreneurship framework (entrepreneur-opportunity-resources) to analyze this case.

2. Discuss Jim Poss's fundraising strategies. What other options might be considered for raising the funds SPC needs? Is this a good investment?

3. Discuss the growth strategy. What additional market(s) should Poss pursue?

Carl Hedberg prepared this case under the supervision of Professor William Bygrave, Babson College, as a basis for class discussion rather than to illustrate either effective or ineffective handling of an administrative situation. Funding provided by the F.W. Olin Graduate School of Business and a gift from the class of 2003. Copyright © by Babson College 2004.

NOTES

1 S. Blank, "Why Lean Start-Up Changes Everything," *Harvard Business Review* (May 2013), www.usric.org/uploads/1/8/4/1/18419537/why_the_lean_start_up_changes_everything.pdf.

2 P. Graham "Bio," http://paulgraham.com/bio.html.

3 P. Graham, "How to Get Startup Ideas," November 2012, http://paulgraham.com/startupideas.html.

4 WorldClassTeams, www.worldclassteams.com.

5 C. Fishman, "Face time with Michael Dell," *Fast Company*, February 28, 2001, www.fastcompany.com/magazine/44/dell.html.

6 J. Boyett and J. Boyett, *The Guru Guide to Entrepreneurship: A Concise Guide to the Best Ideas from the World's Top Entrepreneurs* (New York, NY: Wiley, 2001) 258.

7   S. Wise, "The Double Dip: How to Build Once, Sell Twice, and Make Money Three Times," *Globe and Mail, Report on Business*, December 13, 2005.

8   *ABC Nightline*, "The Deep Dive," aired July 13, 1999.

9   The four-step process outlined in this chapter—gather stimuli, multiply stimuli, create customer concepts, and optimize practicality—comes from a process outlined by Doug Hall: D. Hall, *Jump Start Your Brain 2.0* (Cincinnati, OH: Clerisy Press, 2008).

10 *Pain points* are those aspects of a current product or service that are suboptimal or ineffective from the customer's point of view. Improving on these factors or coming up with an entirely new product or service that eliminates these points of pain can be a source of competitive advantage.

11 For those of you who are interested in learning more about brain writing, visit www.mycoted.com/Brainwriting.

12 W. D. Bygrave and C. Hedberg, "Jim Poss," (case) (Wellesley, MA: Babson College, 2004).

13 S. Wise, "Wise Words," *Globe and Mail, Report on Business*, March 15, 2006, www.theglobeandmail.com/report-on-business/wise-words/article1096483/?page=all.

14 Psychographic information categorizes customers based on their personality and psychological traits, lifestyles, values, and social group membership. It helps you understand what motivates customers to act in the ways they do and is important because members of a specific demographic category can have dramatically different psychographic profiles. Marketing strictly based on demographic information will be ineffective because it ignores these differences. Our use of soccer moms captures both the demographic and the psychographic attributes of a broad customer profile.

15 D. K. Foot and D. Stoffman, *Boom, Bust, and Echo: How to Profit from the Coming Demographic Shift* (Toronto, ON: Macfarlane Walter & Ross, 1996).

16 *The U.S. Baby Boomer Market: From The Beatles to Botox*, 3rd ed. (Rockville, MD: Packaged Facts, November 2002), 7.

17 *The Religious Publishing and Products Market in the U.S.*, 6th ed. (Rockville, MD: Packaged Facts, August 2008), 2.

18 C. L. Grossman, "Starbucks Stirs Things Up with a God Quote on Cups," *USA Today*, October 19, 2005, www.usatoday.com/life/2005-10-19-starbucks-quote_x.htm.

19 D. Tapscott, *Growing Up Digital: The Rise of the Net Generation*," (New York, NY: McGraw-Hill Companies, 1998), 13.

20 Ibid.

21 S. Wise, *Entrepreneurship and the Enterprise*, www.slideshare.net/SeanWise/entrepreneruship-and-the-enterprise, slide 18 of 45.

22 R. Brown, "Managing the 'S' Curves of Innovation," *Journal of Consumer Marketing* 9 (1992): 61-72.

23 *Backlog* is the sales that have been made but not fulfilled because of lack of inventory to finalize the sale.

24 S. Wise, *Hot or Not: How to Know if Your Business Idea will Fly or Fail* (Toronto ON: Ryerson Entrepreneurship Institute, 2012).

25 J. Slaton, "Webvan, Kozmo—RIP. Money Lessons We've Learned from the Last Mile Failures," *SF Gate*, July 21, 2001, http://articles.sfgate.com/2001-07-12/technology/17606161_1_webvankozmo-delivery/2.

26 *Cellular News*, "Amp'd Mobile Subscribers Grew 70% in 1Q to 175,000," April 9, 2007, www.cellular-news.com/story/23071.php.

27 O. Kharif, "Amp'd Mobile Runs out of Juice," *Businessweek*, June 5, 2007, http://www.businessweek.com/stories/2007-06-05/ampd-mobile-runs-out-of-

juicebusinessweek-business-news-stock-market-and-financial-advice.

28 S. Aschaike, "*Dragons' Den*'s Sean Wise on the 5 Best Ways to Evaluate Your Small Business Idea," *Toronto Star*, May 16, 2013, www.thestar.com/business/small_business/exitstrategy/2013/05/16/dragons-den-s-sean-wise-on-the-5-best-ways-to-evaluate-your-sma.html.

29 VentureXpert.

30 Information for this value chain was gathered from financial data on sample industry companies found at http://biz.yahoo.com/ic/340.html and linked pages.

31 General rankings for food sales found at http://biz.yahoo.com/ic/profile/340_1349.html; and Food Processing, "Food Processing's Top 100," www.foodprocessing.com/top100/index.html.

32 R. Darell, "The Evolution of Smartphones (Infographic)," Bit Rebels, 2011, www.bitrebels.com/technology/the-evolution-of-smartphones-infographic/.

33 I. Sager, "Before iPhone and Android Came Simon, the First Smartphone," *Businessweek,* June 29, 2012, www.businessweek.com/articles/2012-06-29/before-iphone-and-android-came-simon-the-first-smartphone#p1.

34 J. Koetdier, "Windows Phone Jumps to Third in Global Smartphone Market Share—and Could Be Second Faster Than You Think," *VentureBeat*, May 16, 2013, http://venturebeat.com/2013/05/16/windows-phone-jumps-to-third-in-global-smartphone-market-share-and-could-be-second-faster-than-you-think.

35 PwC, *MoneyTree*, www.pwcmoneytree.com/.

36 Dow Jones Financial Information Services, "VentureWire Alert," https://www.fis.dowjones.com/Marketing/products/vwirealert3.html.

37 *TechCrunch,* www.techcrunch.com.

38 YCharts, "Microsoft Gross Profit Margin (Quarterly)," http://ycharts.com/companies/MSFT/gross_profit_margin.

39 YCharts, "Intel Gross Profit Margin (Quarterly)," http://ycharts.com/companies/INTC/gross_profit_margin.

40 YCharts, "Apple Gross Profit Margin (Quarterly)," http://ycharts.com/companies/AAPL/gross_profit_margin.

41 J. Tan, "Foreign Brokerages Raise Acer Share Price Target," *Taipei Times,* February 17, 2012, www.taipeitimes.com/News/biz/archives/2012/02/17/2003525647.

42 National Research Council Canada, "Youth Employment Program," www.nrc-cnrc.gc.ca/eng/irap/services/youth_initiatives.html.

43 Business Development Bank of Canada, www.bdc.ca/EN/about/Pages/default.aspx.

44 T. Freidman, *The World Is Flat* (New York, NY: Farrar, Straus and Giroux, 2005).

45 D. Roth, "Today's Startups Are Global Out of the Gate—Are We Ready?" *Forbes*, March 13, 2014, www.forbes.com/sites/davidroth/2014/03/13/todays-startups-are-global-out-of-the-gate-are-we-ready.

46 H. Stevenson, R. Von Werssowetz, and R. Kent, *Ruth Owades,* Case 383051, Cambridge, MA: Harvard Business School Publishing. 1982.

47 *Silent Spring*, written in 1962 by Rachel Carson, exposed the hazards of the pesticide DDT, eloquently questioned humanity's faith in technological progress, and helped set the stage for the environmental movement. Appearing on a CBS documentary shortly before her death from breast cancer in 1964, the author remarked, "Man's attitude toward nature is today critically important simply because we have now acquired a fateful power to alter and destroy nature. But man is a part of nature, and his war against nature is inevitably a war against himself . . . [We are] challenged as mankind has never been challenged before to prove our maturity and our mastery, not of nature, but of ourselves."

atmosphere that encourages people to bond to the company. Yes, your people believe in the mission; yes, they believe in the product; but more importantly the members of your team need to believe in each other and want to continue to be part of the organization. Side effects of a positive and strong work culture include the following:

- Open communication and job satisfaction, which encourages innovation
- Decreases in turnover (lower costs for training new employees)
- Team unity, which fosters cooperation among employees
- Satisfied employees who are more willing to work longer hours to get the job done

Let's break building and maintaining a culture into three main categories: values, selection, and structure.

Values. As the founder, you need to identify what values you want to drive your organization. Values are beliefs shared by all members. For example, JetBlue Airways based its organization building on five core values:[21]

- Safety
- Caring
- Integrity
- Fun
- Passion

Values communicate what kind of work environment founders want to create and what guidelines they use in hiring future employees. For JetBlue, safety is a central value, and without question this is a critical value for the airline industry. The other values communicate that JetBlue treats its employees the way it expects its employees to treat the customers. The values put into place at the company's founding will flow through to formulating and implementing the strategy. More importantly, values create the foundation on which your company will grow.

Selection. It's important to hire the right person the first time. Communicating the values you've identified to new team members goes a long way toward making sure there is a fit between the employee and the company. Every new person added to the company will reinforce the values you've put in place, thereby helping to sustain the company's culture. JetBlue focuses on its five core values when interviewing job candidates and structures its interview questions around these values.[22]

In 1971, when Herb Kelleher founded what is now America's largest domestic air carrier, Southwest Airlines, he was driven to increase the mobility of the common citizen. He sought to do this by offering low-cost fares, and he trimmed costs and services to do so. He knew that underpinning this no-frills approach had to be an enjoyable customer experience. A critical early decision was the hiring of his flight attendant staff that would become the face of Southwest to its customers. Southwest decided to outfit its flight attendants in hot pants and go-go boots (again, this was the 1970s). The only applicants for the job, considering the uniforms, came from the ranks of cheerleading squads and marching band majorettes. Then a funny thing happened. Southwest thought it had hired flight attendants with one key attribute, a figure that was a good fit for the uniform, but quickly realized they had hired people with a much more important attribute, a natural enthusiasm. The cheerleaders were all about spreading enthusiasm, about cheering people on, and convincing the common citizen that they "can win." The cheerleaders were such a perfect fit that Southwest Airlines began only to recruit cheerleaders.[23]

The lesson for an entrepreneur here is simple: You must clearly determine what critical qualities you need in an employee, where you are going to look for it, and how you are going to recognize and measure it.

Structure. The structure of a new venture changes as it matures. Early on it is very informal as the founders and a few early hires do a wide variety of tasks. There are several things to keep in mind as you build your early organization. First, you need to hire people who can "wear many hats"—who can work on a prototype, contact vendors, create budgets, and talk to customers as the need arises. It can often be a mistake to hire a corporate lifer who is used to working in one functional area and having expensive administrative support. Such employees, while talented, may not operate well in the informal startup environment.

Second, as team-building expert Elizabeth Riley[24] says, "over-hire." That is, find team members and early-stage employees who are overqualified for the tasks they will initially be doing. While you might save some money by hiring someone else with fewer skills, as a young and resource-constrained new venture you won't have the time and money to help that person learn on the job.

Finally, you need to create a flexible organizational structure. While you may have an organizational chart, reporting and communications need to be free to flow throughout the organization. That means that any employee during this startup phase can freely talk to any other. This loose structure facilitates learning about your business model, about processes that do and don't work, about customers' needs, and so forth. It fosters and promotes flexibility. The universal truth about strategy formulation and business planning as a whole is that it needs to change and adjust during implementation based on your customers' reactions. If you build a flexible organization, you will be in a better position to adjust your strategy. As the organization matures, the structure will necessarily become more formalized. While it is easy to be informal with 5, 10, or even 20 employees, it is inefficient when you have 150.

In sum, an organization's culture starts at its founding and determines your strategy—and ultimately your success—for the life of the organization. Take time to think about what kind of culture you want and create a plan to make sure it is implemented.

Entry Strategy

Successful launches are iterative. Southwest Airlines didn't start with a nationwide route plan, but instead serviced routes between Dallas, Houston, and San Antonio. After this initial market test in Texas, the company adjusted its processes, improved upon its customer interactions, and then added more routes. Over time, the carrier has continued to add routes and today flies to 96 destinations in 41 states.[25] Since its inception, Southwest has flown one type of airplane—the Boeing 737—which helps streamline its operation. In addition, the company has focused on using less-congested airports and flying point to point rather than using the hub-and-spoke system of traditional airlines. Each new route proved the Southwest business model and created an opportunity to re-evaluate and improve the product. Raising millions in advance of a national route structure and then launching nationwide from day one would have surely led to failure for Southwest, considering the high startup costs of creating an airline. By advancing step by step, the company learned a lot of lessons that it otherwise would have missed. Likewise, you should devise an entry strategy for your firm that allows you to test your concept in the market at a relatively low cost.

Best Practices. Before you raise a dime of outside capital, first learn from others. Benchmark competitors and learn "best practices" from firms that operate inside and outside your industry of interest. Create a simple matrix that identifies the firm and its strategy, core

The Serial Entrepreneur: Can Lightning Strike Twice?

What happens when an entrepreneur is forced from the company he founded? If you're a serial entrepreneur like David Neeleman, you start another airline. On Valentine's Day in 2007, an ice storm blanketed the U.S. east coast. JetBlue had to cancel 1,700 flights and stranded 130,000 passengers. That exposed poor operations and communication. Most airlines responded by cancelling flights prior to the storm and sending passengers home, but JetBlue thought the weather would break and it would be able to fly. Instead, the storm hit with a fury, and there were stories of JetBlue passengers confined to their planes for as long as five hours as they waited on the tarmac for the weather to break. Neeleman was publicly apologetic, even creating a YouTube clip to apologize directly to his customers. JetBlue created a Customer Bill of Rights, which highlighted how they would treat customers affected by future storms. But it wasn't enough. In May 2007, Neeleman was fired as CEO from JetBlue—the company he founded in 2000.

But Neeleman wasn't down for long. In December 2008, Brazilian-born Neeleman launched Azul Airlines, based in Brazil, after securing $200 million from investors—many of them the same investors who previously backed JetBlue. Azul (Portuguese for blue) is trying to replicate JetBlue's low-cost airline success in an emerging economy where flying costs almost 50% more per mile than in the United States. Today, Azul Brazilian Airlines is the third largest airline in Brazil with 10% market share. It has served over 19 million passengers and it has been recognized as the best low-cost airline in Latin America by Skytrax. It looks like lightning can strike twice.[i]

[i] I. Mount, "JetBlue Founder's Revenge: A New Airline," CNN Money.com, March 20, 2009, http://money.cnn.com/2009/03/19/smallbusiness/jetblue_founder_ flies_again.fsb; J. Baily, "JetBlue's C.E.O. Is 'Mortified' After Fliers Are Stranded," *New York Times*, February 19, 2007, www.nytimes.com/2007/02/19/business/19jetblue.html?_r = 1&oref = slogin.

---

customers, sources of competitive advantage, basic revenue model (including margins), and major cost categories—and any other elements that you think might be useful. JetBlue followed much of Southwest's formula during its startup phase. Its founder and former CEO, David Neeleman, worked for six months as an executive vice-president at Southwest Airlines before he was fired. At JetBlue, Neeleman placed a high priority on creating a cooperative company culture and hiring the right people to fit that model. Initially, JetBlue flew only one type of jet. And the flight attendants help clean up the plane for quicker turnarounds at the gate.[26]

Figure 4.6 compares JetBlue to other airlines. It highlights a gap in the marketplace where JetBlue could enter (a geographic opening for a low-cost carrier out of New York) as well as the ways different firms are competing. You can see that a low-cost, point-to-point system focusing on leisure travel makes sense, and it appears that JetBlue should pursue this strategy. Gathering this initial information puts you in a position to do an initial, ideally low-cost, market test.

 Initial Market Test. You can devise your initial market test once you have a strong understanding of the competition. For JetBlue, the initial market test entailed operating one route and then expanding routes based on what it had learned. If you are planning to open a restaurant and believe you will compete based on unique recipes and cuisine, preparing your menu for family and friends would be a simple, low-cost test. Do they like the food? What other items might they like to see on the menu? Note that you can do this test without spending any money on an actual location. Next you might see about catering one or two events. Here, you can test whether people will pay for your cuisine and further refine your menu. The next step might be to offer your food on a mall cart that sells smaller items in common areas at shopping

	JetBlue	Southwest	Porter	Air Canada	WestJet
Strategy	Low cost	Low cost	Regional coverage; easy access for customers	Geographic coverage	Geographic coverage, great customer service
Core Customer	Leisure traveller	Leisure traveller	Business and leisure travellers	Business and leisure travellers	Business and leisure travellers
Competitive Advantage	Cost structure (non-union, no hubs, smaller airports)	Cost structure (no hubs, smaller airports)	Location of airport (downtown Toronto), smaller airport	Size of fleet, geographic coverage	Employees own equity within the business, so they care for their customers
Revenue Model	Airfare, freight	Airfare, freight	Airfare, freight	Airfare, freight	Airfare, freight
Cost Model	Labour, fuel, aircraft, landing fees, and infrastructure	Same	Same plus higher costs associated with "hub" system	Same higher costs associated with "hub" system	Same higher costs associated with "hub" system
Other	Investment in IT, customer focus, employee focus, hands-on CEO	Standardized aircraft, customer and employee focus, hands-on CEO	Easy access location of airport in downtown Toronto; frequent daily flights to popular destinations; expansion to include further flights under discussion	Standardized aircrafts; loyalty program for frequent flyers	Hands-on employees across all platforms; employee and customer focus

■ Figure 4.6

Benchmarking comparison for JetBlue

malls. Are people drawn to your cart? Do they buy? This test helps you determine location. What kind of traffic patterns does the business need? Which demographic group is most drawn to the cuisine? Based on your learning during this market test, you might be ready to open your first restaurant. Figure 4.7 illustrates a market test schedule. Developing this schedule not only guides your learning but also helps you understand when, how, and how much it will cost to achieve the next milestone.

The concept of escalating market tests is powerful. While you can visualize and plan for your business in great detail over a long period of time, you never truly learn whether it is a viable business until you make a sale. Too many entrepreneurs make the mistake of spending $1 million or more to open up that first restaurant only to find that customers don't like the basic concept. Adapting your concept at that point is more costly than it would have been if you had completed some earlier market tests. If you adapt your menu and cuisine at every step in Figure 4.7, you'll be much closer to a winning concept when you open your first restaurant.

It is important to remember that successful new-venture creation is an iterative process. Regardless of how large your company grows, you will continually adapt your business based on what you learn at each market test. At a company like Microsoft, for instance, new software products go through an alpha test, during which the company uses the software internally. After the software is debugged, it goes to a beta test. In beta, a handful of customers use the product and report back problems as well as additional functions that they would

Market Test	What You Expect to Learn	Timing
Prepare dinner for family and friends	Do they like the menu? What else would they add? When would they eat this food? How often?	2–3 events over the next month.
Try to sell a catering event	Can you actually sell the concept? Can you prepare larger quantities in an efficient manner? How does preparing large quantities impact taste?	1–2 events one month after the initial test.
Rent a mall cart	What kind of people (demographics) are attracted to your concept? When do they buy (lunch, dinner)? How much do they buy? How often do they buy? What kind of traffic patterns seem to be most conducive to the business?	Operate for 1–2 months. Do this by month 3 of business.
Open first restaurant	What preparation processes are most effective? What kind of staffing do you need? What hours of operation capture the largest percentage of customers?	6 months after launch.
Open second restaurant	Can the processes be replicated? Do the same types of customers come into this location? What attributes seem to define the best location?	Open 1 year after first restaurant.
Open restaurants 3–5	Can you replicate processes? What processes need to be established at the central level to oversee all the restaurants?	Open in years 2–5.
Franchise the concept	Are potential franchisees interested in your concept? Are your processes sound so that a franchisee can replicate your company-owned restaurants? (CBC's show *Dragons' Den* is known for telling entrepreneurs "If you cannot make a profit with one store, then you definitely can't make a profit with 100 stores," outlining the importance of having all business processes successfully tested.)	Franchise in years 5–8.

■ **Figure 4.7**

Market test schedule

like to see. Based on the feedback, the company might continue with more beta tests. Once they feel that the product is close to their goal, managers release it to the larger market. As any company that has been through a product recall can attest, prematurely releasing a product is an incredibly expensive proposition. The costs include the possibility of having to distribute replacements for defective units, the opportunity costs of disgruntled customers who choose not to buy from you again, and the broader costs of damage to your reputation in the market as customers spread the word that your product is inferior. A controlled launch plan will help you manage the process and avoid these potentially debilitating costs.

Creating a Platform. Figure 4.7 shows the concept of creating a platform on which to grow your business. Opening the first restaurant is the platform, whereas opening successive restaurants is a growth strategy. For many entrepreneurs, opening one restaurant may be the end goal, but others will have larger aspirations. Frank Day grew his restaurant empire to include 144 casual dining restaurants: 44 brewery restaurants (Rock Bottom Restaurant and Brewery, Walnut Brewery, ChopHouse, and Sing Sing) and 100 Old Chicago Pizza and Taprooms. Day is a role model for creating a hugely successful business. He "got into the game" by opening one restaurant he used for experience and learning. To differentiate his Old Chicago in Boulder, Colorado, Day began offering a selection of 110 beers. As he expanded the chain to new locations, Day allowed the restaurants to reflect their local communities and focused on the ambience. Day then replicated his highly successful business model and grew the business into multimillion-dollar chains, with estimated revenues for the private company of over $381.7 million in 2009.[27] In 2010, Centerbridge Capital Partners merged it with Biersch Brewery Restaurant Group to become what is now CraftWorks Restaurants and Breweries. Frank Day moved from CEO to chair of the board and now presides over the combined operations of some 200 restaurants comprising 60 units of Old Chicago Pizza and Taproom, 37 units of Rock Bottom Restaurant & Brewery, and 32 units of the Gordon Biersch Brewery Restaurant Group. Additionally, CraftWorks owns numerous "specialty concept" restaurants consisting of 12 units of the Chophouse, four units of the Big River Grill & Brewing Works, two units of Sing Sing Dueling Pianos, and one unit each of the Blue Water Grille, A1A Ale Works, Ragtime Tavern Seafood & Grill, Seven Bridges Grille & Brewery, and the Walnut Brewery.[28]

This strategy works across industries and marketplaces. P'kolino, for example, entered the children's furniture and toy market with a few designs. As the owners started selling their products and learned what aspects customers liked and didn't like, they continued to add new designs. Over time, they have entered different segments by offering different levels of quality. This type of learning reduces your upfront costs and exposes you to new opportunities that you might not otherwise perceive because you are interacting with customers. Finally, if the worst case should occur and you fail, you will lose less than if you boldly jumped in with multiple restaurants or products all at once.

Opening that first restaurant or selling your first product is your entry into the marketplace. You'll need to have an overriding entry strategy as we discussed earlier—perhaps differentiation. You'll also need to have marketing, operating, and financial plans in place to help achieve your strategy. Much of this is covered in other courses you've taken, and we will explore business planning in depth in Chapters 8 and 9 as well. The key for your entry strategy is to find a pathway into the industry and a way of surviving the first two to three years when most businesses are operating with a negative cash flow. Starting in year three, you need to envision how you will not only grow your firm but also thrive.

Growth Strategy

The first two to three years of any new venture are about survival. The firm has to prove that its customers are interested in its offerings, refine its operations, and increase its visibility. After the first couple of years, many firms will seek growth. In Figure 4.7, we see growth as a function of adding more company-owned restaurants and then ultimately franchising the concept. Managing growth is difficult, and Chapter 14 goes into greater detail on these issues. Our goal here is to think about strategies for growth—what works, when it works, and why it works. Although experience suggests that the first few years of a new venture should focus on testing the market and refining your business model, it is never too early to start thinking about how you will grow. We will explore several common growth strategies.

Franchising. As shown in the example in Figure 4.7, franchising is a strong growth strategy if you have a replicable business model. Most often franchising is used with retail concepts, such as McDonald's or Mail Boxes Etc. We can summarize the keys to success with franchising as follows:

- ◙ Replicability: The business model is well established and proven. As the franchisor, you have worked out the processes of opening and operating a business unit (which is captured in the franchising disclosure document and details the operations, quality controls, policies, procedures, and financial aspects of the business).

◉ Control: The brand is the lifeblood of your business. A poor franchisee can damage your brand, so you need to have monitoring systems in place. Control is also important to ensure that the franchisee is accurately reporting revenues because this controls the revenue you'll receive from your franchising royalty.

Customers have lunch inside a Subway restaurant in Paris. In 2011, Subway became the world's largest fast food chain in terms of restaurants, ahead of McDonald's.

Franchising leads to two types of growth. First, it speeds growth as it brings in new capital to fund that growth. Specifically, the franchisees fund new unit development. Subway is the classic example. In fact, many critics argue that Subway takes advantage of its franchisees (see "The Dark Side of Franchising" box). Subway's growth was phenomenal. Starting with three company stores in 1965, it grew to 134 by 1979 and has exploded to more than 42,000 franchises today. Subway is ubiquitous in the United States and Canada and operates in 105 other countries[29] around the world. It has focused on achieving long-term growth and expanding in countries with high population density, available disposable income, and political and economic stability.[30] Figure 4.8 compares 10 food franchise operations based on current revenue, number of units, and sales per store.[31]

Second, franchising adds new revenues—the royalty fee and the franchising fee. Franchisees owe the franchisor a royalty ranging from 2% to 12.5% on every dollar earned.[32] For this royalty, the franchisor promises to support the franchisee. Often the fee will include royalties the franchisees must pay for advertising, but sometimes this charge is a separate fee. The franchisor pools the advertising royalties and spends it on behalf of the franchisees for regional and national TV, radio, newspaper, magazine, and Internet ads.

The franchisees also pay a fee to secure the rights to the franchise. This ranges from $25,000 for a relatively undeveloped brand to $45,000 for a McDonald's. Moreover, McDonald's

#	Chain	USD Total Franchise Sales	U.S. Franchise Units	Sales per Store
1	McDonald's	$34.2 billion	14,098	$2,425,876
2	Subway	$11.4 billion	24,722	$461,128
3	Starbucks	$9.75 billion	10,787	$903,866
4	Wendy's	$8.5 billion	5,876	$1,446,562
5	Burger King	$8.4 billion	7,231	$1,161,665
6	Taco Bell	$6.8 billion	5,674	$1,198,449
7	Tim Hortons	$5.97 billion[i]	4,304[ii]	$2,265,884[i]
8	Dunkin Donuts	$5.92 billion	7,015	$843,906
9	Pizza Hut	$5.4 billion	7,595	$710,994
10	KFC	$4.5 billion	4,793	$938,869

[i] CAD
[ii] U.S. and Canada
Source: Technomic/Restaurant Finance, compiled by Blue MauMau 2011; Tim Hortons, "2013 Highlights," http://annualreport.timhortons.com/2013-highlights.html.

Figure 4.8

Fast-food franchise operations

The Dark Side of Franchising: Does Subway Take Advantage of Its Franchisees?

Although franchising is an excellent growth strategy for the franchisor, as well as a means for individual franchisees to start their own tried-and-true business, franchising is not without its problems. For example, many critics and franchisees feel that Subway is not a good partner. In 1998, Dean Sagar, the staff economist of the U.S. House of Representatives' Small Business Committee, said, "Subway is the biggest problem in franchising and emerges as one of the key examples of every abuse you can think of."[i]

Today Subway has over 42,000 restaurants,[ii] but that rapid growth has caused some dissension. Many franchisees believe that Subway has violated their agreements by allowing new franchisees to open close to existing restaurants, thereby cannibalizing sales. "In many markets Subway has overbuilt," says International Association of Independent Subway Franchisees (IAISF) executive director Leslee Scott. "There are guys who were doing $8,000 a week three or four years ago who today are doing $4,500."[iii]

Although most Subway franchisees are happy and profitable, the franchise business model is ripe for conflict. "The franchising business is, at its core, antagonistic," says Tom Schmidt, an attorney who is suing the Houston-based Marble Slab Creamery ice cream chain on behalf of nine Marble Slab franchisees. Schmidt continues, "Franchisees must also play by strict rules, and those rules are constantly changing according to the parent company's whims."[iv] Thus, franchisees and franchisors need to be aware of and prepare for likely conflict.

For example, Subway changed how its multimillion-dollar advertising budget is controlled. Jim Hansen, CEO of the North American Association of Subway Franchisees (NAASF), says, "The new franchisee agreement 'threatens' control franchisees have over the advertising funds."[v] So the NAASF, an independent group representing about 67% of all Subway franchisees, along with the Subway Franchisee Advertising Fund Trust, filed lawsuits seeking to bar Subway from instituting these new terms. The groups claimed that "if left intact, the agreement would give Subway the power to redirect franchisee advertising contributions to a separate entity at any time."[vi]

[i] R. Behar, "Why Subway Is the Biggest Problem in Franchising," *Fortune*, 137:126. March 16, 1998.

[ii] Subway, "Explore Our World," www.subway.com/subway-root/exploreourworld.aspx.

[iii] L. Goff, "Encroachment Complaints Hasten Litigation," *Franchise Times* 2 (1996): 3–4.

[iv] J. McCuan, "Six Things to Consider before You Buy a Franchise," Smartmoney.com, April 5, 2005, www.smsmallbiz.com/bestpractices/Six_Things_to_Consider_Before_You_Buy_a_Franchise.html.

[v] A. Johannes, "Franchisees Sue Subway over $400 Million Ad Fund," *Promo*, July 20, 2006, http://promomagazine.com/retail/subway_sued_ad_funds_072006.

[vi] D. MacMillan, "Franchise Owners Go to Court," *Businessweek*, January 29, 2007, www.businessweek.com/stories/2007-01-29/franchise-owners-go-to-courtbusiness-week-business-news-stock-market-and-financial-advice.

requires a down payment that must come from nonborrowed personal resources, exclusive of a personal residence. The initial down payment is 40%[33] of the total cost of a new restaurant, which ranges between $955,708 and $2,290,146, plus McDonald's requires the franchisee to have an additional $750,000 in nonborrowed personal resources after the down payment.[34] For the most part, these fees cover the overhead for managing and monitoring the system, but they are also a source of growth capital.

Some franchisors bring in additional revenue by selling supplies to their franchisees. In fact, the franchising business model can be so lucrative that William Ackman, whose company Pershing Square Capital Management once owned a 4.9% stake in McDonald's, challenged the firm to spin off all its company-owned stores, which, according to his analysis, dragged down the firm's profit. After two years of pressure, Ackman ultimately failed to get the change he wanted and sold all of his shares in McDonald's at the end of 2007.[35] However, it is necessary to have company-owned stores in the launch and early years while the entrepreneur tests and refines the basic operations and market acceptance of the concept. Successful company-owned stores also allow the franchisor to charge larger franchise fees.

Expanding Your Product Mix. Many companies start with one product, but as they gain traction in the marketplace they recognize new opportunities to add to their product mix. Building your product mix should increase your revenue at a rate greater than the associated costs. In other words, you should be able to spread your existing costs across a larger product base. You might use the same vendor to provide raw materials or to produce your product. That would increase your power to secure better terms when negotiating. You also might leverage your existing distribution channels. By selling more products through these channels, you increase your negotiating power.

The key is to leverage your firm's experience as you become more familiar with your core customers and your own operations. Whole Foods, for example, has included lifestyle departments at its stores in Austin and Los Angeles, selling all-natural housewares and clothing. "The development and incorporation of Whole Foods Market Lifestyle reflects the company's founding values into other aspects of life," said Marci Frumkin, a Whole Foods regional marketing director. "The new lifestyle store is another example of how Whole Foods leads by example . . . educating consumers about organic food, natural products and ethical business practices."[36] Like Whole Foods, you should search for ways to extend your product mix that leverage your existing production or customer relationships.

Adding products is a means to grow, but it is not risk free. Eighty percent of new products are failures.[37] The risk is that the company will incur development expenses, the market may not accept the new product, and the unsuccessful product line could reflect unfavourably on the reputation of the existing products. You need a coherent strategy to minimize the risks of new products. Start with your firm's competitive advantage. What do you do better than anybody else? For P'kolino, that advantage is innovative designs. Adding designs increases P'kolino's power by giving it more visibility with its distributors, such as Babies "R" Us. P'kolino also decreases its cost of direct distribution by selling a wider range of products on its website and by having enough products in a catalogue to try a direct-mail strategy. Furthermore, this strategy gives the company more leverage with its vendors. More products ideally result in a larger production volume, which suggests that P'kolino can negotiate better terms.

iRobot was a Massachusetts-based startup focused on building robots on specification for government agencies and industry until it created the Roomba. This innovative self-propelled and self-controlled vacuum cleaner helped iRobot move into the lucrative consumer products market. Rather than partnering with another firm and selling the technology, iRobot decided it could manufacture the Roomba overseas. Although it still builds robots for military and industrial use, iRobot began to focus on branching into other consumer products.[38] Today iRobot is a public company generating over $427 million in sales with several new product innovations such as floor-vacuuming robots (Roomba, over 6 million sold), floor-washing robots (Scooba), shop-sweeping robots (Dirt Dog), pool-cleaning robots (Verro), gutter-cleaning robots (Looj), and programmable robots. iRobot has also sold 3,000 PackBot tactical military robots that have been deployed in support of explosive hazards detection missions in Afghanistan and Iraq.

A product growth strategy identifies synergies within the firm and then leverages those synergies in conjunction with the company's customer knowledge. While sound management imagines what the firm will pursue for product growth during the launch phase, in reality many new opportunities will appear only once you have started selling your first product and gained firsthand market intelligence.

Geographic Expansion. Expanding geographically is another common growth strategy. This natural growth is based on the underlying assumption that customers should like your product or service elsewhere if they like it in the location where you founded the company. All the larger retail companies in existence today had roots in one geographic region before they grew outward. Walmart started in Arkansas, while McDonald's was originally located in Bakersfield, California.

You can plan geographic expansion systematically, or it can happen haphazardly. Oftentimes potential customers will come across your product through the media or the Internet and want it. Founded in Milwaukee in 1844, Pabst Blue Ribbon (PBR) is a beer that is most commonly associated with America's blue-collar Midwest or hipsters who want to (ironically) appear blue collar—which is why anyone could be forgiven for not foreseeing that, in 2010, PBR responded to sudden strong demand in China with exports that are bottled, seductively marketed like champagne, and priced at $44 per bottle.[39] While opportunistic growth can be a smart move, entrepreneurs benefit from developing and following a coherent strategy.

When planning geographic expansion, you'll want to weigh a number of factors:

- Customers: First and foremost, are the customers in the new location similar to those in areas with existing operations? Your initial strategy is predicated on delivering a product or service that satisfies the needs or wants of a core customer group. For your initial expansion, you want to leverage the knowledge you've gained from serving customers in your initial location. For example, Barb Stegemann, founder of social venture 7 Virtues,[40] which makes perfume using ingredients from global conflict zones, such as Afghanistan and Haiti, started out selling fragrances on the east coast of Canada, but soon had a global following. When expanding through retail channels, Stegemann first focused on Canadian retailers (for example, Hudson's Bay) before moving on to international retailers in the U.S., the UK, and Europe. This allowed her to keep her need for language support minimal until demand was justified (for example, moving into South America would have required rebranding into Spanish).

- Vendors: Can you continue to use the same vendors? If not, what costs will you incur to establish new relationships? Remember, the greater your volume, the stronger your negotiating position. If you can continue with the same vendors, you will have greater bargaining power, but that power becomes diluted if you add vendors.

- Distribution: Can you use the same distribution channels? As with vendors, you can increase your leverage and reduce your marginal costs by moving more volume through existing distribution channels.

These factors should guide your decision making as you formulate your growth strategy. If you look at the geographic expansion of retail operations, you'll note that they strive for a critical mass within a region before moving to another region. For example, Dunkin' Donuts is highly concentrated in the northeastern United States. There are approximately 169 Dunkin' Donuts outlets within a five-mile radius of Boston—one outlet for every 3,500 residents. Customers in the Boston area know the company well, and its core customers view stopping at Dunkin' Donuts for their morning coffee as integral to their morning routine. Not only does this high concentration keep the brand at the forefront of the customer's mind, it also gives Dunkin' Donuts considerable operating efficiencies. The key is balancing your company's saturation point—the point when new expansion within the region cannibalizes existing operations—against its opportunities to expand to new regions.

Today with the Internet, it is easier than ever to expand across many regions simultaneously. Potential customers find out about your product and then contact you about buying the product or representing your company in a new region. Before accepting these offers, make sure you understand the tradeoffs. First, most sales and even unsolicited orders require time and effort on your part. This is time and effort that is diverted from establishing your company in its existing regions. Second, your company may not have the infrastructure in place to support the buyer after the sale. Third, consider any additional costs for transporting the product to the customer. While unsolicited orders can be attractive, make sure you understand the hidden costs (mostly in time and effort) that you incur as you fill them.

International Growth. International growth is a special case of geographic expansion. In today's global economy, new entrepreneurial firms often should consider expansion at their inception. Advances in logistics, technology, and manufacturing have allowed smaller and younger firms to compete globally. Firms that look globally from the outset often have tightly managed organizations, innovative products, and strong networks for marketing. They also have more aggressive growth strategies, use more distribution channels, and have more experienced management teams. They don't simply export but instead choose foreign direct investment in the countries in which they seek to operate. With their global reach, these firms can introduce innovative products to new markets, giving them an advantage over startups that operate only in the domestic sphere. They may also operate in industries that are globally integrated from the start.[41]

Statistics Canada reveals that as of January 2014, the total number of Canadian merchandise export value reached $40.6 billion, a 5% change from the previous year; merchandise imports were reported to total $40.8 billion as of January 2014, indicating a 3.5% increase from the previous year.[42] The bottom line is that global business is a competitive but attractive market for entrepreneurs.

In today's market, online ventures are considered global ventures from day one. Websites such as Etsy.com (an ecommerce website focused on unique manufactured products) gives starting entrepreneurs and businesses the ability to reach customers around the world by providing an ecommerce platform to showcase their products. Shopify (Shopify.com), founded in 2004 by Tobias Lutke, Daniel Weinand, and Scott Lake, is an ecommerce platform that enables entrepreneurs and their businesses to easily create their own online stores. The founders were looking to start an online company and could not find an easy-to-use ecommerce website or the software they needed. The three founders decided to create their own software to enable their needs as a new business. Realizing that the extremely easy-to-use tool they had developed would help other companies, they made the decision to share it with others to help people around the world sell their products online. Shopify has since received over US$22 million in funding.[43]

Pat Dickson[44] provides a model that illustrates when and how entrepreneurial ventures go global (see Figure 4.9).

Dickson notes that there are three types of global entrepreneurial firms. Those in the first category, *gradual globals*, enter international markets in stages to reduce their risk. During their initial expansion, gradual globals will enter countries similar to their domestic market and use processes that require lower costs and commitment, such as exporting. Over time, they will enter more, and increasingly dissimilar, countries. Gradual globals will also expand their entry modes, for example moving from exporting to foreign direct investment. The second category of entrepreneurial firms is *born global*. These firms plan to enter international markets right from their outset. Those in the final category, *born-again globals*, have been operating only domestically, but some triggering event, such as an unsolicited order from abroad, causes them to move rapidly into new international markets. Although there is a lot of debate about which type of firm is most likely to succeed globally, entrepreneurs need to think about international business from day one.

Dickson suggests that entrepreneurs pursue enabling strategies, given that new ventures are resource constrained. For instance, they can use intermediaries to reduce needed resources or use low-cost methods like the Internet that enable them to make contact with potential international partners. In many cases, entrepreneurs can tap their existing networks, such as employees, investors, vendors, or customers, to facilitate international entry. One of your vendors, for instance, may have distribution capabilities in another country that you can use on a variable-cost basis. You might also pursue alliances with other companies. The Internet enables entrepreneurs to directly access international markets in a low-cost manner. You can market to firms worldwide by simply putting up a website, and you can proactively manage relationships overseas by using the Internet and email. TOMS Shoes leverages the strong appeal of its one-for-one philanthropic business model to attract many high-profile designers, such as Ferragamo, to produce new designs for its shoes. These designs, produced in high-end design houses in Europe and North America, are then sent via the Web to TOMS production

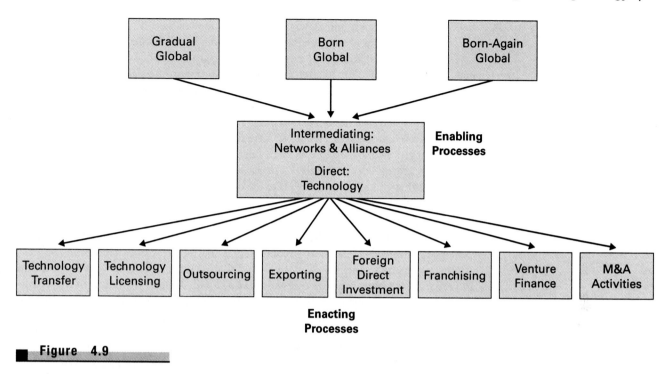

Figure 4.9

The entrepreneurial firm's international expansion process

facilities in China, Ethiopia, Argentina, and Brazil.[45] Companies are also adapting to a growing trend called *telepresence systems*. Telepresence refers to a set of technologies that allow people to feel as if they are physically present at a location other than their true location.[46] Whatever enablers you use, it is easier today to enter global markets than ever before. Dickson's model moves from enabling to enacting processes. There are eight primary means to expand globally:

- Technology transfer (joint venture): When firms choose to enter the global market, they may need to decide whether to sell their technology or produce it abroad themselves. Producing technology overseas can involve significant risk and investment. On the other hand, having a partner firm in the target country or region produce and distribute your product can reduce your entry costs. The costs of technology development and production often lead young firms to build alliances and joint partnerships and to focus on niche markets.[47] However, there is a risk you'll lose control of the technology because the partner firm will gain insight into how you produce the product.

- Technology licensing: Perhaps the most common means to enter a foreign market is to secure an agent to represent the company abroad. Here, the entrepreneur may decide that he or she is better off letting a foreign company produce and sell the product, perhaps rebranded under its own name, with the entrepreneur taking a royalty as compensation. Licensing reduces risk from an operational perspective. While this is an excellent means of generating revenue and conserving resources, it also is a lost opportunity to extend your own brand into new markets.

- Outsourcing: Outsourcing allows businesses to handle key attributes of their products while handing over the responsibility for development and manufacturing to a subcontractor. The outsourced production may be sent back to the company's home country for sale. It is often the first logical step as a firm seeks to expand globally. The primary reason to look at global outsourcing is cost savings.

- Exporting: The cheapest and easiest way to enter new markets is to sell from your head-quarters. However, as always there are tradeoffs. First, it is harder to establish a critical mass in the country if you don't have anyone on the ground, and as mentioned earlier, you may incur additional costs in after-sales support. Your customers also may have difficulty contacting you or providing information about the market and their needs. You incur the transportation costs and risks of getting your products through the target country's customs agency. A second alternative is to hire a sales representative in the target country. The advantages are that sales representatives have deep knowledge of the country and presumably a strong network they can leverage in selling the product. However, agency theory suggests there are risks to consider.[48] First, it is difficult for you to confirm that agents are as skilled as they might claim (which is referred to as *adverse selection*). Second, it is difficult to ensure that the agent is honouring the contract (which is referred to as *moral hazard*).

- Foreign direct investment (FDI): Under this strategy, companies set up a physical presence in the countries of interest, whether that is a sales office, retail outlets, production facilities, or something else. The startup retains control of the assets and facilities, an issue that can prove expensive. The primary means of FDI are acquiring foreign assets and building and expanding current facilities overseas. FDI is usually beyond the means of most early-stage companies. French clothing line Chloé tested the Chinese market by exporting the product first through retail stores. Then, once it learned that Chinese customers liked the product, it started to establish its own retail outlets in Beijing and then Shanghai. Today Asia accounts for over 50% of sales of this high-end fashion house, with 70[49] locations in the Asia-Pacific region.[50] Chloé plans to branch out slowly from those locations.[51] Similarly, Jeff Bernstein started Emerge Logistics[52] by using China's bureaucratic red tape and the unwillingness of American companies to invest in Chinese facilities to his advantage. Bernstein's logistics company has 14 customers, including Harley-Davidson, Mercedes-Benz, and Siemens. For example, Mercedes-Benz needed to ensure effective, reliable after-market parts support for luxury vehicles sold in China. Emerge provided a warehousing facility, customs clearance management, and local delivery to dealers and distributors throughout China.[53]

- Franchising: Some see franchising as a low-risk method of entering a foreign market because it allows the firm to license an operational system. Yet there can be difficulties in monitoring the international franchisee and ensuring that it protects the company's brand (moral hazard).[54] Until recently, the Chinese as a whole had a dim view of franchises.[54] The biggest foreign retailer in China, Carrefour, rapidly closed many of its franchised stores in 2012, which were organized into a loose structure. Franchise owners' profits depended on supplier-paid entrance fees and sales commissions to protect their profit margins. Carrefour attempted to pass price increases onto the consumer. Those attempts were stopped by the Chinese government in November 2012 after seeing a 62% year-over-year inflation in food prices.

- Venture financing: According to Dickson, venture capital is both an enabling and an enacting mechanism. What he means is that the available capital and expertise provided by venture capitalists may enable a firm to go international using any of the previously mentioned means to enter a market. However, research suggests that venture capital often leads to mergers and acquisitions with foreign companies.

- Merger and acquisition (M&A): For some businesses, buying an overseas firm may be the most efficient manner to enter a foreign market. You gain an instant presence in the country with an established infrastructure. M&As also allow an entrepreneurial company to grow and expand quickly. Some research shows that firms that use acquisitions for expansion have a higher survival rate than do those that choose a startup.[55] The capital required means that the firm must secure venture capital or go public; thus, this method is beyond the means of most early-stage entrepreneurs.

As the world becomes increasingly connected, entrepreneurs need to look beyond their home borders to see whether they can expand on their initial opportunity. While it is more difficult to enter and operate in a country that you are not familiar with, technology and increasing trade are reducing the knowledge gap. As research points out, more and more entrepreneurs are becoming global early in their companies' lives. As an entrepreneur, you need to be aware of your options, and the Dickson model provides a solid framework for understanding them.

Many entrepreneurs consider themselves to be involved in global markets from day one. Any company that is online and cloud based enables customers around the world to have access to the product(s) or service(s) the company is offering. Traditionally, an entrepreneur and his or her team would start the business serving local customers, then national, then global once they felt ready. In today's business world, they are in the global business right out of the gate.[56]

CONCLUSION ☐

This chapter moves beyond opportunity recognition to implementation. Once you understand your business model, it is time to think about how you will enter the marketplace and grow your firm. During entry, you are proving that your business model is viable and profitable. Are customers buying your product at the prices you need to be profitable? As you learn more about your customer and business, you'll modify your original vision. Entry into the marketplace provides a platform to identify new opportunities and to reshape your business so that it is best positioned to grow and thrive. Thus, it's wise to think about your growth strategy from the very beginning. Today that growth is more likely than ever to mean you'll consider international expansion.

YOUR OPPORTUNITY JOURNAL ☐

Reflection Point	Your Thoughts. . .
1. Describe your business model. What are your primary sources of revenue? What are your revenue drivers? Your COGS? Your operating expenses?	
2. What is your overall strategy? Why does this strategy help you sell to customers? What tactics can you employ to increase your revenues?	
3. What is your entry strategy? How does this create a platform for your business to grow?	
4. What is your growth strategy? How big do you want your firm to be? How long might it take for it to get there?	

WEB EXERCISE ☐

Pull the income sheets from three companies in the industry that you are interested in entering. Try to find companies that are pursuing different strategies. Examine their business models and see if you can identify the drivers they are influencing to achieve their strategy. What lessons can you learn for your own venture? What new elements can you incorporate into your business model? How do you tie these elements to your strategy?

Zumba Fitness

Alberto Perlman walked out of the old warehouse that served as the offices of Zumba Fitness and into the hot Miami sun. He had just finished meeting with his two partners and the company that they had started with such a bang four years earlier seemed on the ropes. The agreement they had with the marketing company that produced and promoted their exercise videos had broken down, and despite selling millions of dollars' worth of videotapes featuring their unique Latin-based exercise routine called Zumba, the company had not been able to provide enough profitability for it to do more than scrape by. One of his partners, Alberto Aghion, was even looking at starting a medical billing company. With only about $14,000 left in the bank, they needed to figure out how to either make this business profitable or start looking for other opportunities.

Childhood Friends

The Salesman: Alberto Perlman

Alberto Perlman was born and raised in Bogota, Colombia, where his family was very involved in business and entrepreneurship. His great-grandfather had immigrated to Bogota from Jerusalem in the pursuit of business opportunities. Starting out by selling textiles door to door, his grandfather gradually built the second-largest retail store in the country. It was clear that growing up in this environment had a great influence on Perlman.

From the beginning, Perlman seemed destined for business. When he was 6 years old, his father bought him a digital watch with a game on it. The enterprising young Perlman proceeded to loan it to a classmate on weekends in exchange for 750 pesos (approximately $10). When his parents found out, they apologized to the boy's mother and made him return all the money, but a budding entrepreneur was born.

In high school, Perlman noticed a vacant lot near the school that was being occupied by a number of homeless people. At his school, like many others, it was cool to have a car and drive to school. However, Perlman realized that many of the students couldn't drive their cars because they could not find a place to park. He approached the people living in the lot and offered a deal. He would pay them if they would let students park there and keep an eye on the cars. He then charged his classmates 90,000 pesos (about $45 at that time) each month to park. This venture, too, was short-lived.

> Unfortunately, the people found out what I was charging and they started going direct. So, I figured out that being a middle man is not a good deal.

Despite these early setbacks, it was apparent to everyone that he was destined to be an entrepreneur.

> I always knew I was going to do business, but I was a bit rebellious as a teenager and I told my mom I was going to study philosophy. My mom said, "I would never tell any of my kids this, but YOU . . . I'm telling you. You were born to do business. I would never force any of my kids to do anything, but I'm forcing you to do business. So go find a business school."

After graduating from high school, Perlman went backpacking through Europe with his childhood friend, Alberto Aghion, who would figure prominently in a number of his subsequent business ventures. Following the trip, Perlman enrolled in Babson College, a business school located outside of Boston, Massachusetts, known for its entrepreneurship program.

While his official studies were in finance and management information systems, Perlman continued his entrepreneurial ways in the United States. He was fascinated with the Internet and in 1995–1996, while studying at Babson, he got together with two other students and started a Web design company called Cyber Spider Designs.

> We went up and down Newbury Street trying to sell websites at a time when nobody had websites. We did the website for Boston Proper Real Estate. We did a flower site. It was all right. It paid the bills, but nobody was paying good money for that at the time.

It was also at Babson that Perlman made an impression on Professor Prichett, who ended up indirectly playing a key role in the founding of Zumba Fitness. Professor Prichett was impressed with his calculus student and introduced Perlman to his son, who worked at a New York consulting firm called the Mitchell Madison Group and who subsequently offered Perlman a job with the firm.

One of the first projects Perlman was given was working on direct-response television advertising[57] for the First USA division of Bank One. While on this project, he spent considerable time analyzing the business model and operation of successful infomercial companies. Reflecting on his grandfather's retail business and his own experience as a middle man in his short-lived parking venture, he fell in love with the idea of direct marketing to consumers via television.

> I always saw how difficult it was for suppliers to get their products into the stores. The infomercial industry was fascinating because you didn't have to go through a store. You didn't have to go to a big supplier like Walmart. You did it on your own merit. You bought media, created the commercial and it's your product.

By this time Perlman's father was working at a nearby private equity firm, and he was meeting with a Chilean newspaper company that was interested in developing an Internet strategy. Knowing his son's knowledge of the latest technologies, he asked if Alberto would be willing to talk with them. After meeting with them and helping them with their strategy, he realized that his expertise in emerging Internet technologies coupled with his background and connections in Latin American markets provided a unique opportunity for him to once again set out on his own. So, after 10 months he left his job with the Mitchel Madison Group to pursue Internet opportunities in Latin America.

Initially, Perlman, together with his brother and another friend, focused on building an Internet events company in which they would put on conferences for companies, entrepreneurs, and investors who were interested in Internet businesses in Latin America. This provided a way for him to both make money and make connections for future business opportunities.

> We started calling companies like IBM and said, "Hey! Do you want to sponsor an event? It's called Latin Venture. We'll have all the entrepreneurs from Latin America there." And they said, of course . . . how much? Twenty-five thousand dollars. Done. So we sold, and that's when things were going like crazy and we made a couple hundred thousand dollars at our first event.

After the success of the Latin Venture event, Perlman used the money he had made to start an Internet incubator in which he raised money to invest in launching technology companies in Latin America. He was able to raise about $8 million, which they used to eventually fund nine different companies. It was also at this time that he convinced his long-time friend Alberto Aghion to turn down a job offer with Merrill Lynch and join him in one of the incubator's companies.

The Problem Solver: Alberto Aghion

Alberto Aghion grew up with Perlman in Bogota. They attended the same schools, had the same group of friends, and started becoming close friends in their early teens. When Perlman left for Babson following their European adventure together, Aghion decided to continue travelling and eventually ended up at the Hebrew University in Jerusalem, where he took courses in history, studying the Arab–Israeli conflict, and working odd jobs to make ends meet.

> *I had some crazy experiences. I went hiking in Africa. I hiked Kilimanjaro. I mean, I had a really interesting year. When you're 18 years old, you have no real responsibilities and it was an adventure in life. I'm really glad I took that year to do that because if I hadn't done that at that age, at that stage in my life, I couldn't have done that.*

After spending a little more than a year abroad, Aghion returned to Colombia ready for a new challenge. He was always interested in looking at ways to solve problems of all kinds. He excelled in math and physics in high school, so as soon as he returned he applied to study industrial engineering at the Universidad Javeriana in Bogota with the belief that an engineering education would give him a good foundation in problem-solving techniques that he could apply to a number of different situations. However, he soon found out that he did not enjoy the teaching philosophy at the school. As with many engineering programs, there seemed to be a focus on filtering out students early in the program. In addition, it was difficult adjusting to life back at home after more than a year on his own. He felt out of place and restless in Bogota, so he talked to his friend Perlman, who was in his second year at Babson. Perlman seemed to be happy in Boston, so Aghion decided to visit him and look into opportunities in the United States.

> *I went to a few colleges. I mean I checked out Northwestern. Boston College. A few interesting schools. And on the way back, I stopped in Miami and I saw the palm trees, the ocean. So I also went to UM [University of Miami] and FIU [Florida International University] and I checked out those schools and actually I decided, you know what, I think I like Miami better. I'm not a cold weather fan.*

He was accepted at both the UM and FIU, but FIU was less expensive and they agreed to transfer his credits both from Bogota as well as from Israel, allowing him to graduate a year sooner, so he chose FIU where he majored in finance and international business.

> *I wanted to be an entrepreneur. I wanted to do different things. But I had no idea what I wanted to study. Also, I guess I got a little burned out at the university in Colombia. I mean, I like problem solving. I guess maybe if I would have gone to a different school and had a different experience with engineering, I might have stayed with that career. But, because I didn't enjoy that methodology in Colombia, I said, you know what, this is not for me. And at the end of the day, I just wanted to do business. I had picked engineering because I was good at physics and calculus and problem solving, not necessarily because I wanted to be an engineer.*

Aghion excelled in the new environment, getting straight A's for the first two years and graduating with a job offer from Merrill Lynch. He was considering this offer when he got a phone call from Perlman.

> *I spoke with Perlman, he was launching this whole incubator. Really exciting. Internet boom. All this interesting stuff. And he tells me, "Why the hell are you going to go work for a boring bank? Come work with me." So I said OK.*

One of the first ventures Perlman and his partners invested in was FonBox, which was a service for providing a virtual office anywhere in Latin America. Aghion was asked to help develop FonBox, and he did a significant amount of work helping them develop the infrastructure for the business. They eventually sold it to J2 Communications for a loss.

By March 2001, they were working on nine different businesses when the Internet bubble burst. Most of their companies were early-stage companies in their first or second round of funding, and the capital for additional investments in Internet firms quickly dried up. With no funding available, a lack of new businesses to invest in, and $4 million of the original investor's money remaining, they decided to continue to work with the firms they had invested in on the chance that one of them would be successful. They could then return what was left of the money to their investors rather than risk the remaining funds and the relationships with the investors they had worked so hard to establish.

The Third Alberto

Alberto "Beto" Perez grew up in Cali, Colombia, as the son of a young, single, working mother. Always an energetic child, he loved to perform. He would take his mother's hairbrush and use it like a microphone as he would sing and dance. In the same way that Perlman seemed destined for a career as an entrepreneur, Beto seemed born to dance. As his mother recalls,

When he was seven, I took Beto to see the movie Grease. The next day, he was out on the street teaching John Travolta's dance moves to kids who were much bigger than he was.

Growing up in Cali in the 1980s was difficult. Drugs and violence were common on the streets. Beto saw this firsthand when his mother got into an abusive relationship with a drug addict. When he was 14, his mother was hit by a stray bullet, and he had to work multiple jobs to help support the two of them. Despite these hardships, dance was a constant presence in his life.

As a teenager in the 1980s, I was always sneaking out to nightclubs to dance, and my mom was trying to keep me at home, safe.

When Beto was 16 his mother took a job in Miami, but he wanted to stay in Cali to pursue a career in dance. They would keep in touch via telephone and letters, but it would be a long, hard 10 years before they would see each other again.

During this time, Beto continued to try to make it as a dancer. When he was 17, he couldn't afford rent so he slept in the ice cream shop where he worked. He thought he finally had his big breakthrough when he was chosen to represent Colombia at a Latin dance competition in Miami. However, after spending his entire savings on costumes, his U.S. visa request was denied and he was unable to compete.

Because he couldn't afford to attend a dance academy, he worked as a courier in the morning and taught private dance lessons in the evening. The owner of the gym where Beto prepared his dance routines offered him an opportunity to teach a children's class in the summer. Because he was so popular, he was invited to teach more classes. A modeling agent gave him his first job as a choreographer and he gained national attention after winning a lambada competition at the age of 19. Eventually, he saved enough money to attend and graduate from the Maria Sanford Brazilian Dance Academy with a degree in choreography.

While dance was his passion, it was a series of fortuitous events that led to the creation of what is now known as Zumba. One evening a local gym owner telephoned Beto and asked if he could substitute for one of her aerobics instructors who had been injured. Although Beto had never taught aerobics, he needed the money so he accepted the job. He immediately went to a book store and bought a copy of Jane Fonda's *Workout Book* and tried to copy the moves in the book coupled with some of his own dance steps. The class went well, and soon Beto was regularly teaching aerobics classes as well as dance. Then fortune struck again. As Beto recalls,

At one of those sessions, I forgot to bring the music, and all I had were salsa and merengue tapes in my backpack. So I improvised, and that was the beginning of Zumba.

Beto called his new style of aerobics "Rumbacize" as a tribute to the Latin influences behind many of the moves. As Beto's popularity increased, he found himself traveling to Bogota to do television commercials. Eventually, he moved there and began teaching at one of the top gyms in the city where one of his early students was Alberto Perlman's mother.

> *In 1994 Mrs. Perlman was taking my class in Bogota and announced, "This is the best class in the world!" I'll never forget that.*

In addition to his Rumbacize classes, he was gaining attention for his dancing and choreography. He was hired by Sony Music to work with some of their singers, and he helped with the choreography for singer-songwriter Shakira's breakthrough album *Pies Descalzos*. During this time, he began travelling more outside of Colombia and fell in love with the idea of moving to Miami, so he decided to sell everything and move to the United States. However, his lack of English skills made the transition difficult, and he had a hard time finding work.

> *I love Miami, and I knew this is where I wanted to live. At first it was not easy. No one knew who I was, I did not speak English and I ran out money. I even slept on the street one time.*

His big break came one afternoon when one of the gym managers decided to see what Beto could do, so she gave him an impromptu audition. It was the middle of the afternoon and she told Beto to teach a class to one student. Herself.

> *It was 3 p.m., and the gym was empty. Soon a passerby wandered in to watch, then two, three, four. After 20 minutes I had about 15 people. They thought it was a new class and wanted to sign up.*

The manager was impressed and offered Beto a job teaching Saturday mornings. Beto's passion, energy, charisma, and lively exercise programs became increasingly popular, and he soon found himself teaching classes of up to 160 students at gyms throughout the Miami area. Investors were approaching him about opening up his own gym.

The Birth of Zumba Fitness

Following the end of Perlman's incubator venture, Perlman and Aghion found themselves trying to decide what to do with their lives. Reflecting back on his brief time with the Mitchel Madison Group, Perlman was drawn to the idea of an infomercial-based company. Perlman approached Aghion, who was considering going back into the finance world. Aghion was interested, so they began brainstorming potential ideas. As Aghion recalls,

> *I still don't have a family. I still don't have anything. I want to take a risk. Things are happening and I was really interested in the infomercial industry. I thought that it was a good opportunity. And I remember talking to Perlman and saying, why don't we do an infomercial or something? If we make it, we could make a lot of money. And then we can figure something else out.*

During this time, Perlman's family had moved to Miami, and his mother was once again taking Beto's classes. One day his mother suggested that he meet Beto. "Beto has something special," she told him. So Perlman arranged to meet Beto at a Starbucks to learn more. Beto's energy and passion were contagious and Perlman could envision his aerobics routines and personality as a great combination for his infomercial concept. Following their meeting, he immediately called his friend Aghion to see what he thought about the idea.

I remember my stomach saying, I LOVE IT. Ricky Martin was singing "Living La Vida Loca" at the Grammy's. Latin music is crossing over in the U.S. Tae Bo. Fitness. Beto. It clicked in my head immediately.

As Perlman recalls:

It was a gut decision. We were two out-of-work businessmen with no contacts in the fitness industry and a dancer who couldn't speak a word of English, and here we were deciding to launch a fitness business together. But we knew if we could capture the excitement of his class on video, people would go crazy for the music and the moves.

With little money between them, they decided to create their own video, which they would then use as a marketing vehicle for launching the business. They spent the night laying down boards on the beach and the next morning made a video of Beto teaching a class. They then renamed the program "Zumba," which rhymed with "rumba," meaning "party" and Zumba Fitness was born.

Fitness Industry Business Models[58]

The fitness industry consists of a wide range of activities that people engage in for exercise. In general, most forms of exercise have experienced a decline in participation in recent years in the United States (Table C4.1). Notable exceptions are Pilates and yoga, which have seen dramatic increases in participation. Aerobics, while popular in the 1980s and 1990s, has seen a decline in participation since 1998 while other forms of exercising to music have remained relatively steady.

Companies in this industry have used a variety of approaches to enter and compete in this industry. Due to the fact that many of these forms of exercise can be done individually or in groups, companies can target instructors or participants as their primary customers. Revenue models can range from unit sales models to franchising models, each with their own implications. Below are some of the approaches firms in this industry have used.

TABLE C4.1

Fitness Activity	1998	2000	2004	2005	1 yr change (%)	Change from 1998 (%)
Aerobics (High Impact)	7460	5581	5521	5004	−9.36425	−32.9223
Aerobics (Low Impact)	12774	9752	8493	9071	6.805605	−28.9886
Aerobics (Step)	10784	8963	8257	7062	−14.4726	−34.5141
Aerobics (Net)	21017	17326	15767	15811	0.279064	−24.7704
Other Exercise to Music	13846	12337	16365	14428	−11.8362	4.20338
Aquatic Exercise	6685	6367	5812	6237	7.312457	−6.70157
Calisthenics	30982	27790	25562	24854	−2.76974	−19.7792
Cardio Kick Boxing	n.a.	7163	4773	4163	−12.7802	n.a.
Fitness Bicycling	13556	11435	10210	10211	0.009794	−24.6754
Fitness Walking	36395	36207	40299	36348	−9.80421	−0.12914
Running/Jogging	34962	33680	37310	37810	1.340123	8.145987
Fitness Swimming	15258	14060	15636	14553	−6.92632	−4.62053
Pilates Training	n.a.	1739	10541	10355	−1.76454	n.a.
Stretching	35114	36408	40799	42266	3.595676	20.36794
Yoga/Tai Chi	5708	7400	12414	14656	18.06025	156.7624

At the Crossroads

Perlman thought about their predicament. On one hand, there was no doubt about the passion of the Zumba enthusiasts. Once people tried it, they fell in love with it. When they began offering the instructor training, they were amazed to see the same instructors come back again and again, even though they had already been trained. They even began setting up their own cameras and recorders at Beto's classes to capture the new moves and the music. On the other hand, they weren't making much money with their current model and their cash flow was unpredictable. Perlman's thoughts strayed back to the medical billing company Aghion had mentioned. This is ridiculous, he thought. We're not going to let this go. We have to do something. All these instructors keep coming back to Miami, and they are just in love with Zumba. We *have* to be able to come up with something to make this work.

Discussion Questions

1. What business models could Zumba use?
2. Develop a revenue and cost model diagram for each of the options.
3. Which of these models would you recommend that they implement and why?
4. What are the key revenue and cost drivers for your recommended model?
5. What do you feel are the key aspects to implementing this model?

This case was written by Professor Bradley George as a basis for class discussion rather than to illustrate either effective or ineffective handling of an administrative situation. Funding was provided by the Teaching Innovation Fund at Babson College. Copyright by Babson College (2013). No part of this publication may be copied, stored, transmitted, reproduced or distributed in any form or medium whatsoever without the permission of the copyright owner. To order copies or request permission to reproduce materials, contact European Case Clearing House (www.ecch.com/), Harvard Business School Publishing (http://hbsp.harvard.edu/) or Babson College Case Center (cases@babson.edu).

NOTES

1. R. Needleman, "Twitter Still Has No Business Model, and That's OK," *CNET News*, March 27, 2009, http://news.cnet.com/8301-17939_109-10205736-2.html.

2. E. Jackson, "Facebook's MySpace Moment: Why Twitter Is Already Bigger Than Facebook," *Forbes*, September 26, 2012, www.forbes.com/sites/ericjackson/2012/09/26/facebooks-myspace-moment-why-twitter-is-already-bigger-than-facebook/.

3. A. Osterwalder, Y. Pigneur, and T. Clark, *Business Model Generation: A Handbook for Visionaries, Game Changers, and Challengers* (Hoboken, NJ: Wiley, 2010) 214–215.

4. Ibid., 89–90.

5. Toms Shoes, "One for One," http://www.toms.com/one-for-one-en.

6. Blyk, "Blyk Media Grows to 4 Million Opt-in Subscribers Globally," press release, January 19, 2012, http://www.blyk.com/news/news/press-releases/blyk-media-grows-to-4-million-opt-in-subscribers-globally.

7. The accounting definition of COGS is the inventory at the beginning of the period, plus the cost of inventory purchased during the period, minus the inventory remaining at the end of the period.

8. Many software firms amortize research and development and include it in COGS.

9. Toms Shoes, "One for One."

10 D. Mitchell, "Amazon Raises Big Money with Debt Offering," *CNET News*, January 28, 1999.

11 "Happy e-Birthdays, Internet Businesses," *The Economist*, July 23, 2005, 62.

12 A. Osterwalder and Y. Pigneur, *Business Model Generation: A Handbook for Visionaries, Game Changers, and Challengers* (2009): http://businessmodelgeneration.com/book.

13 Ibid.

14 Ibid.

15 A. Maurya, "Why Lean Canvas vs. Business Model Canvas?" *Practice Trumps Theory* (blog), February 2012, http://practicetrumpstheory.com/2012/02/why-lean-canvas.

16 Ibid.

17 *Fast Company*, "A Cautionary Tale," December 19, 2007, www.fastcompany.com/magazine/115/open_features-hacker-dropout-ceo-cautionary-tale.html.

18 Facebook, "Company Info," http://newsroom.fb.com/company-info/; I. Lunden, "Twitter May Have 500M+ Users but only 170M Are Active, 75% on Twitter's Own Clients," *TechCrunch*, July 31, 2012, http://techcrunch.com/2012/07/31/twitter-may-have-500m-users-but-only-170m-are-active-75-on-twitters-own-clients.

19 J. Millot, "Amazon.com Expects to Generate $34 Million from IPO," *Publishers Weekly New York*, 244 (March 31, 1997): 11.

20 C. Anderson, "The Long Tail," *Wired Magazine* (blog), September 8, 2005, www.longtail.com/the_long_tail/faq/.

21 J. Gittell and C. O'Reilly, "JetBlue Airways: Starting from Scratch," Case 9–801–354 (Cambridge, MA: Harvard Business School Publishing, 2001).

22 Ibid.

23 S. Sinek, *Start with Why* (New York, NY: Penguin Books, 2009).

24 Elizabeth Riley is a successful entrepreneur who started Mazza and Riley, Inc., an executive search firm. She has spent much of her career placing people in venture-backed companies.

25 Southwest Airlines, "Southwest Corporate Fact Sheet," http://www.swamedia.com/channels/Corporate-Fact-Sheet/pages/corporate-fact-sheet.

26 C. Salter, "And Now the Hard Part," *Fast Company*, May 1, 2004, 66.

27 A. Wallace, "Rock Bottom Founder Calls Decision to Sell 'Bittersweet,'" *Colorado Daily*, November 9, 2010, www.coloradodaily.com/cu-boulder/ci_16662654#axzz2ANRASvSP.

28 CraftWorks Restaurants & Brewery, www.craftworksrestaurants.com/index.htm.

29 Subway Restaurants, "Why Choose Subway?" http://w.subway.com/en-CA/OwnAFranchise/WhySubway.

30 E. Duecy, "Global Growth, Urban Sites Speed Subway Along Track Toward Overtaking McDonald's," *Nation's Restaurant News*, February 7, 2005, 4.

31 A. McConnell and K. Bhasin, "The Most Popular Fast Food Restaurants in America," July 13, 2012, http://finance.yahoo.com/news/the-most-popular-fast-food-restaurants-in-america.html; Tim Hortons, "2013 Highlights," http://annualreport.timhortons.com/2013-highlights.html.

32 L. Christie, "Franchises: How Much Can You Earn?" CNN Money, July 1, 2004, http://money.cnn.com/2004/04/29/pf/howmuchfranchise.

33 McDonald's, "Acquiring a Franchise," http://www.aboutmcdonalds.com/mcd/franchising/us_franchising/aquiring_a_franchise.html

34 Ibid.

35 C. Burritt and K. Burton, "Bill Ackman Sells McDonald's Stake after Stock Surges," *Bloomberg News*, December 5, 2007, www.bloomberg.com/apps/news?pid=20601103&sid=aZ6kcnn5qqUo&refer=us.

36 D. Desjardins, "Whole Foods Goes Hollywood with Lifestyle Store, *DSN Retailing Today*. November 7, 2005.

37 L. Shanahan, "Designated Shopper," *Brandweek*, January 4, 1999, 38.

[38] L. Buchanan, "Death to Cool," *Inc.* 25 (July 2003): 82–88.

[39] M. Gibson, "Pabst Blue Ribbin Is Classy and Expensive in China," *TIME*, July 21, 2010, http://newsfeed.time.com/2010/07/21/pabst-blue-ribbin-is-classy-and-expensive-in-china/.

[40] 7 Virtues website, www.the7virtues.com.

[41] P. P. McDougall, B. M. Oviatt, and R. C. A. Shrader, "A Comparison of International and Domestic New Ventures," *Journal of International Entrepreneurship* 1 (2003): 59–82.

[42] Statistics Canada, "Latest Statistics (monthly), www.statcan.gc.ca/tables-tableaux/sum-som/l01/cst01/media01-eng.htm.

[43] Shopify, "About Us," www.shopify.ca.

[44] P. Dickson, "Going Global," in *Entrepreneurship*, vol. 2, eds. A. Zacharakis and S. Spinelli (Greenwich, CT: Praeger. 2006), 155–177.

[45] http://traffichoss.com/ferragamo-custom-designer-toms-shoes

[46] Kolabora, "What Is TelePresence?" March 28, 2007, www.kolabora.com/news/2007/03/28/what_is_telepresence.htm.

[47] L. Eden, E. Levitas, and R. J. Martinez, "The Production, Transfer and Spillover of Technology: Comparing Large and Small Multinationals as Technology Producers," *Small Business Economics*, 9 (1997): 53–66.

[48] A. L. Zacharakis, "Entrepreneurial Entry into Foreign Markets: A Transaction Cost Perspective," *Entrepreneurship: Theory and Practice*, 21 (1997): 23–39.

[49] Chloé, "Asia-Pacific," www.chloe.com/#/boutiques/Asia-Pacific-4/en.

[50] S. Fenton, "HK Designer Sees Upside in 'Made in China' Label," Reuters, September 17, 2008, http://uk.reuters.com/article/stageNews/idUKHKG6544920080917.

[51] L. Movius, "Chloé Launches in China," *WWD*, December 29, 2005, www.movius,us/articles/index.html.

[52] Emerge Logistics, "About," www.emerge-3pl.com/page11.php.

[53] R. Flannery, "Red Tape," *Forbes*, March 3, 2003, 97–100.

[54] "China's A&W All-American Restaurants Close," *China Daily*, February 3, 2004. http://www.chinadaily.com.cn/en/doc/2004-02/03/content_302636.htm.

[55] F. Vermeulen and H. Barkema, "Learning through Acquisitions," *Academy of Management Journal* 44 (2001): 457–476.

[56] D. Roth, "Today's Startups Are Global Out of the Gate—Are We Ready?" *Forbes*, March 13, 2014, http://www.forbes.com/sites/davidroth/2014/03/13/todays-start-ups-are-global-out-of-the-gate-are-we-ready/

[57] Direct response television (DRTV) is television advertising that asks consumers to respond directly to the company, typically by either visiting a website or calling a toll-free number.

[58] It should be noted that gyms and fitness clubs account for a major portion of the revenue in the fitness industry. However, these businesses do not specialize in a single form of exercise but rather differentiate themselves on the variety of offerings available.

[59] Funding Universe, "Jazzercise, Inc. History," www.fundinguniverse.com/company-histories/jazzercise-inc-history/.

[60] M. Ogle, "Joseph Pilates: Founder of the Pilates Method of Exercise," About.com, http://pilates.about.com/od/historyofpilates/a/JPilates.htm.

[61] Different types of music licences need to be considered for each song when producing a video or DVD. A mechanical licence allows you to make multiple copies of the recording. This fee is used to pay royalties to the owner of the song's copyright. If you are pairing music with video or other media, this requires a synchronization licence, which would then replace the mechanical licence. If you are using an artist's recording, then a master licence is required, which is paid to the owner of the master recording, typically the record label. If you hire someone to record a cover version of a song, the master licence is no longer needed.

George Pimentel/Getty Images

Arlene Dickinson, star of *Dragons' Den* and *The Big Decision*.

ENTREPRENEURIAL MARKETING

CHAPTER OUTLINE

Why Marketing Is Critical for Entrepreneurs
Learning Objective 5.1 Explain why marketing is critical for entrepreneurs.

Entrepreneurs Face Unique Marketing Challenges
Learning Objective 5.2 Identify the unique marketing challenges entrepreneurs face.

Acquiring Market Information
Learning Objective 5.3 Describe how entrepreneurs acquire market information.

Marketing Strategy for Entrepreneurs
Learning Objective 5.4 Describe the key dimensions and elements of a marketing strategy.

Guerrilla Marketing
Learning Objective 5.5 Describe guerrilla marketing.

Marketing Skills for Managing Growth
Learning Objective 5.6 Describe two key marketing capabilities necessary for strong growth.

> *"You need more than an idea to run a business."*
>
> —*Arlene Dickinson*

MARKETING IS AT the heart of an organization because its task is to identify and serve customers' needs. In essence, marketing spans the boundaries between a company and its customers. It is marketing that delivers a company's products and services to customers and marketing that takes information about those products and services, as well as about the company itself, to the market. In addition, it is marketing's role to bring information about the customers back to the company. Although many people relate the term *marketing* to advertising and promotion, the scope of marketing is much broader. The American Marketing Association defines marketing as

> *Marketing is the activity, set of institutions, and processes for creating, communicating, delivering, and exchanging offerings that have value for customers, clients, partners, and society at large.*[1]

Successful entrepreneurs select and optimize the marketing tools that best fit their unique challenges. Marketing practices vary depending on the type of company and the products and services it sells. Marketers of consumer products, such as carbonated soft drinks, use different tools than marketers of business-to-business products, such as network software. Companies in the services sector, such as banks, market differently from companies that sell durable goods, such as automobile manufacturers.

Why Marketing Is Critical for Entrepreneurs

Marketing is a vital process for entrepreneurs because no venture can become established and grow without a customer market. The process of acquiring and retaining customers is at the core of marketing. Entrepreneurs must create the offer (design the product and set the price), take the offer to the market (through distribution), and at the same time tell the market about the offer (communications). These activities define the famous **Four Ps** of marketing: product, price, place (distribution), and promotion (communication).

Entrepreneurs are often faced with designing the entire "marketing system"—from product and price to distribution and communication. Because it is difficult and expensive to bring new products and services to market—especially for new companies—they need to be more resourceful in their marketing. Many entrepreneurs rely on creativity rather than cash to achieve a compelling image in a noisy marketplace.

An important part of gaining the market's acceptance is building brand awareness, which, depending on the stage of the venture, may be weak or even nonexistent. Entrepreneurs must differentiate their company's product or service so its distinctiveness and value are clear to the customer. This is the job of marketing.

Marketing also plays a central role in a venture's early growth stages when changes to the original business model may be necessary. Companies focused on growth must be able to switch marketing gears quickly and attract new and different customer segments.

Entrepreneurs Face Unique Marketing Challenges

Entrepreneurial marketing is different from marketing done by established companies for a number of reasons. First, entrepreneurial companies typically have limited resources—financial as well as managerial. Just as they rarely have enough money to support marketing activities, they also rarely have proven marketing expertise within the company. Most entrepreneurs do not have the option of hiring experienced marketing managers. Time—as well as money and marketing talent—is also often in short supply. Whereas larger corporations can spend hundreds of thousands or even millions on conducting extensive market research, testing their strategies, and carefully designing marketing campaigns, new ventures find creative and less costly means to validate their ideas and reach customers.

Most entrepreneurs face daunting challenges. Their companies have little or no market share and a confined geographic market presence. As a result, they enjoy few economies of scale; for example, it is difficult for small companies to save money on "media buys" because their range of advertising is so limited. Entrepreneurs usually are restricted in their access to distributors—both wholesalers and retailers. On the customer side, entrepreneurs struggle with low brand awareness and customer loyalty, both of which must be carefully cultivated.

Not only is market information limited, but decision making can also be muddled by strong personal biases and beliefs. Early-stage companies often stumble in their marketing because of a product focus that is excessively narrow. Companies frequently assume that their products will be embraced by enthusiastic consumers when, in reality, consumer inertia prevents most new products from being accepted at all. Research has shown that common marketing-related dangers for entrepreneurs include overestimating demand, underestimating competitor response, and making uninformed distribution decisions.

Top Five Marketing Examples

Some of the top companies today are where they are because of unique marketing techniques that caught the attention of potential customers. Here are the top five examples:

1. Hotmail was a pioneer in viral marketing. In December 1996, Hotmail had 500,000 registered users.[i] Every single email sent by those 500,000 individuals contained a small advertisement promoting their service. Less than a year later, Hotmail had acquired over 12 million users.[ii]

2. PayPal used freebie marketing, which is also known as loss leader marketing, to initially attract customers. They offered every new account $5 to sign up and start using the service. In 2001, PayPal had a monthly growth rate of 18,000 customers and currently has over 10 million registered users.[iii] A plethora of other companies, including Uber (a mobile taxi hailing service) have followed the road paved by PayPal.

3. Lego perfected content marketing and avoided financial difficulty by creating the Lego Club Magazine. To fend off competition, Lego's new magazine was customized for subscribers by local market and age. The magazine allows children of any age to receive content that is relevant to them.

4. GoodLife Fitness approached the fitness and health club industry with the mindset of helping people get in shape as opposed to sneakily binding them into a contract. GoodLife's open and honest marketing campaigns, which embodied the "Everyone is welcome here" mindset, allowed it to dominate the industry. Currently, GoodLife is the fourth-largest gym in the world, with more than 930,000 members and approximately 13,000 employees.[iv]

5. Mountain Dew and Lay's potato chips have ventured into a new territory of marketing called *crowdsourcing*. Both companies have created marketing campaigns allowing their customers to vote for and choose the next flavour of chips or soft drink to be released. Crowdsourcing allows direct consumer involvement in the decision-making process, thereby driving user engagement and increasing brand awareness. This process can dramatically increase sales, as customers will flock to purchase the new flavours.

[i] P. Altoft, "The Top 10 Viral Marketing Campaigns of All Time," *Branded3* (blog), www.branded3.com/blogs/the-top-10-viral-marketing-campaigns-of-all-time/

[ii] Ibid.

[iii] "The PayPal Phenomenon," The NuVantage Group, 2001, www.nuvantage.com/pdfs/NuVantage_PayPal_Phenomenon.pdf.

[iv] J. Daly, "Bulking Up: How GoodLife Became Canada's Dominant Gym," *Globe and Mail*, March 27, 2014, www.theglobeandmail.com/report-on-business/rob-magazine/the-secret-of-goodlifes-success/article17673987/.

Entrepreneurs market to multiple audiences: investors, customers, employees, and business partners. Because none of these bonds is well established for early-stage companies, entrepreneurs must be both customer oriented and relationship oriented. A customer orientation requires understanding the market and where it is going. A relationship orientation is needed to create structural and emotional ties with all stakeholders. *Thus, marketing helps entrepreneurs acquire resources by selling their ideas to potential investors and partners. It also allows entrepreneurs to leverage scarce resources through innovative business approaches.*

In this chapter, we consider entrepreneurial marketing in depth. Building upon the opportunity-defining and -refining discussion in Chapter 3, we provide direction on market research—that is, collecting information that is useful in making marketing and strategy decisions. Next we focus on implementing marketing strategies that make the most of these opportunities. We also look at how certain marketing skills serve to support a new company's growth.

Acquiring Market Information

An entrepreneur needs to do research to identify and assess an opportunity. Intuition, personal expertise, and passion can take you only so far. Some studies show that good pre-venture market analysis could reduce venture failure rates by as much as 60%.[2] However, many entrepreneurs tend to ignore negative market information because of a strong commitment to their idea. Whereas Chapter 2 defined what an opportunity is and Chapter 3 presented a checklist for assessing how attractive your opportunity might be, this chapter provides a drill-down on how you collect data to validate your initial impressions of the opportunity.

We define **marketing research** as the collection and analysis of any reliable information that improves managerial decisions. Questions that marketing research can answer include the following: What product attributes are important to customers? How is customers' willingness to buy influenced by product design, pricing, and communications? Where do customers buy this kind of product? How is the market likely to change in the future?

There are two basic types of market data: **secondary data**, which marketers gather from already published sources like an industry association study or census reports, and **primary data**, which marketers collect specifically for a particular purpose through focus groups, surveys, or experiments. You can find a great deal of market information in secondary resources. Secondary research requires less time and money than primary research, and it should be your first avenue. Entrepreneurs sometimes use databases at college libraries to collect baseline information about product and geographic markets (Figure 8.6 in Chapter 8 lists some common databases).

Some types of primary data are easy to collect, for instance, with personal interviews or focus groups, but keep in mind the limitations of such data, such as observer bias and lack of statistical significance (because the samples are small). To ensure that they obtain high-quality data, some entrepreneurs hire marketing research firms to perform research studies. Lower-cost alternatives do exist. For example, a business school professor might assign the company's project to a student research team. In choosing a research approach, balance your quality and time constraints with the possible cost savings.

The appendix at the end of this chapter provides a list of possible questions to address in a customer research interview. You can structure such an interview as a one-on-one interaction or as a focus group. In focus groups, a discussion leader encourages 5 to 10 people to express their views about the company's products or services. The focus group has distinct stages, and you will need to ask specific questions to get good-quality information from the group participants. Figure 5.1 displays these stages and provides some example questions to use when conducting a focus group.

Stage	Examples of Effective Questions
Introduction	◉ Think of the last time you purchased Product X. What prompted or triggered this activity?
	◉ How often do you use X?
Rapport Building	◉ What are some of the reasons for so many products in this industry?
In-Depth Investigation	◉ Here is a new idea about this market. In what ways is this idea different from what you see in the marketplace?
	◉ What features are missing from this new product?
	◉ What would you need to know about this idea in order to accept it?
Closing	◉ Is this focus group discussion what you expected?

■ **Figure 5.1**

Focus group

Market Research for Revolutionary New Products?

Henry Ford is reputed to have said that if he had asked potential customers for his yet-to-be introduced automobile what they wanted, they would have replied, "a faster horse." Market research may be valuable for existing products and incremental improvements to them, but what is its value for revolutionary new products? By definition, a revolutionary new product has no standard industry classification, so it is virtually impossible to gather meaningful data from secondary sources. And what use are the opinions of primary sources who are unfamiliar with the product because it is different from anything they have ever used? Steve Jobs (along with other Apple executives) had no faith in market research for the radically new products that he introduced. Here is what he had to say on that subject:

> Some people say 'give the customers what they want.' But that is not my approach. Our job is to figure out what they're going to want before they do.[i]

When asked, "Should [Apple] do some market research to see what customers wanted?" [Jobs] replied, "No, because customers don't know what they want until we've shown them."[ii]

On the day he unveiled the Macintosh, a reporter from *Popular Science* asked Jobs what kind of market research he had done. Jobs responded by scoffing, "Did Alexander Graham Bell do any market research before he invented the telephone?"[iii]

Jonathan Ive, Apple's senior vice-president of industrial design, who gave Apple products their sleek, minimalist form, says that Apple has a good reason for not doing focus groups: "They just ensure that you don't offend anyone, and produce bland inoffensive products."[iv]

[i] W. Isaacson, *Steve Jobs* (New York, NY: Simon and Schuster, 2011), 567.

[ii] Ibid., 143.

[iii] Ibid., 170.

[iv] S. Jary, "Apple's Ive Reveals Design Secrets," *Macworld*, July 2, 2009, www.macworld.com/article/1141509/jonathan_ive_london.html.

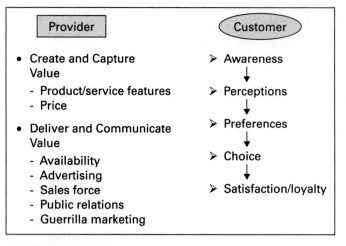

Figure 5.2

Understanding the customer choice process

Customer acceptance of an entrepreneur's idea is proof that the opportunity is worth pursuing. Entrepreneurs must understand the customer decision-making process and how to influence the customer's choice. Such customer understanding enables entrepreneurs to develop the right products at the right prices (create and capture value) and then market these products to the right customers in the right place (communicate and deliver value). Further, such knowledge of customers' behaviour at each stage of the decision-making process helps entrepreneurs be effective and efficient with their communication strategy to reach the target customers. Figure 5.2 provides an illustration of the role that marketing tools play in the customer choice process.

Marketing Strategy for Entrepreneurs

A company's marketing strategy must closely align with its resources and capabilities. Entrepreneurial companies with limited resources have little room for strategic mistakes. Segmentation, targeting, and positioning are key marketing dimensions that set the strategic framework. We begin this section by discussing these three activities and their role in marketing strategy. Then we examine the widely studied marketing elements known as the marketing mix (the Four Ps): product, price, distribution (place), and communications (promotion).

Segmentation, Targeting, and Positioning

Segmentation and *targeting* are the processes marketers use to identify the "right" customers for their company's products and services. In Chapter 3, we talked about the segment your opportunity would initially target, what we call the primary target audience, or PTA. As we move beyond opportunity recognition into implementation of a marketing strategy, we need to revisit our initial conceptions and refine what that PTA segment really means. A **segment** is a group of customers defined by certain common bases or characteristics that may be demographic, psychographic (commonly called *lifestyle characteristics*), or behavioural. Demographic characteristics include age, education, gender, and income; lifestyle characteristics include descriptors like active, individualistic, risk taking, and time pressured. Behavioural characteristics include consumer traits such as brand loyalty and willingness to adopt new products.

Marketers identify the most relevant bases for segmentation and then develop segment profiles. It's common to define a segment using a combination of demographic and lifestyle characteristics—for example, high-income, sophisticated baby boomers. Marketers also segment customers based on where they live (geography), how often they use a product (usage rates), and what they value in a product (product attribute preferences).

Targeting compares the defined segments and then selects the most attractive one, which becomes the PTA. Target market definition is essential because it guides your company's customer selection strategy. The attractiveness of a segment is related to its size, growth rate, and profit potential. Your targeting decisions should also reflect your company's specific capabilities and longer-term goals. Accurate targeting is important for entrepreneurs; however, it is not always clear which customer segment(s) represent the best target market, and finding out may require some research and some trial and error. As we noted in Chapter 3, it is wise to identify secondary target audiences (STAs) in case the PTA doesn't meet expectations. Nevertheless, identifying the appropriate target market early on is critical because pursuing multiple targets or waiting for one to emerge is an expensive strategy.

To illustrate segmentation and targeting, let's look at the example of Nantucket Nectars, the beverage company founded by marketing-savvy entrepreneurs Tom Scott and Tom First. Relevant segment characteristics for this company are age, individualism, and health consciousness. In Nantucket Nectars's early days, its primary target market was young, active, health-oriented consumers who enjoyed breaking with conformity by choosing a noncarbonated soft drink alternative. As Nantucket Nectars gained public awareness, this gave the company power to move beyond its PTA to its STAs and ultimately the broader drink market. Scott and First started the company with an initial investment of $9,000 and a production run of 1,400 cases. In 1997, they sold a majority stake in the business to Ocean Spray for $70 million. Cadbury bought the firm from Ocean Spray in 2002. At the time, Nantucket Nectars had estimated revenues of $80 million.[3] In 2008, Cadbury demerged its beverage business from its confectionary business, creating Dr. Pepper Snapple Group.

While segmentation and targeting profile a company's customers, **positioning** relates to competitors and to customers' *perceptions* of your product. Positioning usually describes a company's offering relative to certain product attributes—the ones customers care about most. Such attributes often include price, quality, and convenience, all of which can be scaled from high to low. For example, if brands of single-serve beverages were shown on a positioning map (see Figure 5.3) with the two dimensions of *price* and *quality*, Nantucket Nectars would be positioned in the high-price, high-quality (upper-right) quadrant, whereas a store-brand juice would likely be positioned in a low-price, low-quality (lower-left) quadrant.

Figure 5.3

Nantucket Nectars's position map

entrepreneurs often outsource their selling efforts to sales brokers who work for a marketing firm rather than investing the time and money to build their own sales force. There are disadvantages to this kind of outsourcing, though: quality is hard to control, the information flow between you and your customer is interrupted, and longer-term cost economies are harder to achieve.

Sometimes channel partners don't do what you want or expect them to do. When Nantucket Nectars's co-founders became frustrated with their distributor's slow progress in getting the brand established, they took over distribution themselves. The company lost millions of dollars trying to change its distribution model, and it went back to contracting with distributors after it found more capable partners. Although distribution mistakes such as those made by Nantucket Nectars extract a price, they also teach early-stage companies what their capabilities are.

Distribution channel strategy includes three types of **channel coverage**: intensive, selective, and exclusive. The appropriate strategy depends on the type of product or service that you will sell. **Intensive distribution** works for consumer goods and other fast-moving products. The carbonated soft drink category is one of the most intensively distributed: Products are sold in supermarkets, drugstores, convenience stores, restaurants, vending machines, sporting event concessions, and fast-food outlets. **Selective distribution** brings the product to specific distributors, often limiting selection geographically by establishing a dealer network. Kate Spade sells her handbags and other fashion accessories to high-end, luxury department stores as well as Kate Spade specialty stores, but not to mainstream retailers or mass merchandisers. Selective distribution can protect dealers and retailers from competition while helping manufacturers maintain prices by thwarting price competition. The third coverage strategy, **exclusive distribution**, is often used for luxury products. For some time, Neiman Marcus had exclusive rights to distribute the Hermès line of fashion accessories.

Channel partnerships (or *relationships*) have important implications for entrepreneurs. Often the channel member with the most power will prevail; for this reason, **channel power** is an important concept in distribution strategy. While channel partnerships can speed a young company's growth, preserve resources, and transfer risk, entrepreneurs must be careful not to sacrifice their direct relationship with customers. Most important, entrepreneurs must carefully manage their relationships with channel partners and monitor them over time.

Another widely applied concept, **channel conflict**, refers to situations where differing objectives and turf overlap, leading to true disharmony in the channel. Channel conflict was a high-profile phenomenon in the early days of the Internet, when many startup companies were using the strategy of **disintermediation**—cutting intermediaries out of traditional distribution channels by selling directly to customers. Amazon created conflict between book publishers and distributors and traditional book retailers. Because Amazon could buy in volume and avoid the high occupancy costs retailers pay, it could offer an enormous assortment of items at deeply discounted prices. Amazon's volume allowed it to negotiate low prices from publishers and wholesalers, who in turn alienated their other customers, the traditional book retailers in the channel.

Entrepreneurs succeed with their distribution strategies when they have a strong understanding of channel economics. Giro, the bicycle helmet company that outfitted both Greg LeMond and Lance Armstrong—famous American winners of the Tour de France and in Armstrong's case subsequently discredited for using performance-enhancing drugs—gained initial access to the retail channel by offering high margins and selective distribution to preferred bike shops. This allowed the company to maintain its premium prices and establish loyalty among experts and cycling enthusiasts.

Current practice reflects a focus on multichannel distribution, which gives a company the ability to reach multiple segments, gain marketing synergies, provide flexibility for customers, save on customer acquisition costs, and build a robust database of purchase information. J.Crew, for instance, has been successful in diversifying its store-based business to include strong catalogue and online channels. But a multichannel strategy adds operating complexity and demands more resources, so entrepreneurs are best to approach these opportunities cautiously and be careful that their timing is in line with their capabilities and resources. For example, TiVo's strategy to push its innovative product through both specialty stores and consumer-electronics superstores created problems for the successful launch of its product. TiVo should have used the specialty store channel exclusively in the beginning rather than both channels. Specialty stores are not willing to provide time and service to develop the market for an innovative product when they have to compete on price with consumer-electronics superstores.

Research shows that many of the most serious obstacles to entrepreneurial success are related to distribution. Specifically, entrepreneurs tend to be overly dependent on channel partners and short on understanding channel behaviour in their industry. It is critical that entrepreneurs take the time to learn about distribution and make fact-based decisions about channel design and channel partnerships to overcome these threats to good distribution strategy.

Marketing Communications Strategy (Promotion). Marketing communications convey messages to the market—messages about the company's products and services as well as about the company itself. The marketing communications element of the marketing mix is a mix within a mix: The **communications mix** is defined as *advertising, sales promotion, public relations, personal selling*, and *direct marketing* (sometimes included with advertising). The marketing communications mix and some of its key elements are shown in Figure 5.9.

The components of the communications mix, like those of the marketing mix, are often referred to as *tools*, and the use of these tools by marketers differs substantially across business and industry contexts. To illustrate, consumer product companies' communications are often aimed at mass markets and include advertising and sales promotions, whereas business-to-business companies use more customized, interactive tools, such as personal selling by a sales force. Of course, the communications a marketer uses are closely aligned with the specific type of product the company is attempting to sell as well as with the company's marketing objectives.

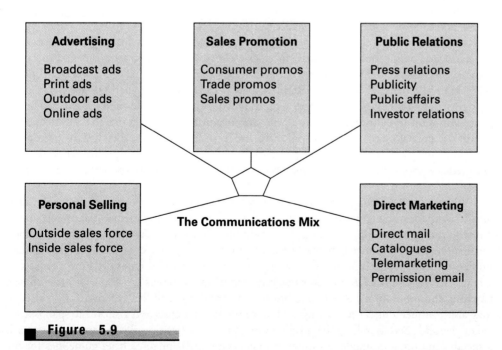

Advertising

Broadcast ads
Print ads
Outdoor ads
Online ads

Sales Promotion

Consumer promos
Trade promos
Sales promos

Public Relations

Press relations
Publicity
Public affairs
Investor relations

Personal Selling

Outside sales force
Inside sales force

The Communications Mix

Direct Marketing

Direct mail
Catalogues
Telemarketing
Permission email

Figure 5.9

Marketing communications

It is common marketing wisdom to use a variety of tools in marketing any product or service. Because of this focus on multiple methods and the need to integrate and coordinate these methods, we often call the process **integrated marketing communications**. A range of factors—including cost, timing, and target market—determines the selection of a company's key communications tools. The question you must answer is, "What is the most effective way to communicate with my customers and influence their actions?" And the sooner you can answer this, the better.

Two communications strategies are *push* and *pull*. A **push strategy** aims to push a product through the channel using tools such as trade promotions, trade shows, and personal selling to distributors or other channel members. A **pull strategy**'s goal, on the other hand, is to create end-user demand and rely on that demand to pull the product through the channel. Pull strategies, which are directly targeted to end users, include advertising and consumer sales promotions, such as in-store specials. These strategies also are relevant for service companies. Fidelity Investments, for example, can push its mutual funds through brokers or advertise them directly to investors who, the company hopes, will then request them.

Marketing communications is a broad and sophisticated field. Many of the most visible tools are primarily accessible to large companies with deep marketing budgets and in-house marketing talent. This is usually the case for large, national television and print advertising and high-penetration direct mail campaigns. Probably the greatest breadth of tools exists within the domain of advertising, which includes everything from billboards to websites to local newspapers to Super Bowl commercials. There also are various direct marketing tools, including catalogues, direct mail and email, telemarketing, and infomercials (vehicles for direct selling).

What *advertising* choices are available to an entrepreneur? Anything that is appropriate, affordable, and measurable, or at least possible to evaluate. Entrepreneurs can use traditional major media by focusing on scaled-back options, such as regional editions of national magazines, locally broadcast commercials on cable television stations, and local newspapers and radio stations. The disadvantage is that it's almost impossible to achieve advertising economies of scale. But you can efficiently conduct tightly targeted campaigns with a focus on cost control.

In addition to regionalized or localized major media, you have a number of minor media options. These include classified ads, the yellow pages and online information services, brochures, flyers, online bulletin boards, local canvassing (for business to business), and educational seminars or demonstrations. As mentioned above, most marketing experts support using multiple methods in combination, in part because different methods have particular strengths and weaknesses. But even though the media are varied, the message and the brand image you want to communicate should be strictly consistent. Two terms that are frequently mentioned in relation to advertising objectives are *reach* and *frequency*. **Reach** is the percentage of a company's target market that is exposed to an ad campaign within a specific period of time. **Frequency** is the number of times a member of your target market is exposed during that time period.

When selecting media, entrepreneurs match their communications goals to media capabilities. Radio is more targeted and intimate than other advertising media; it allows flexibility but requires repetition for the message to get through. Television has a large reach and is good for demonstrating product benefits but is usually expensive and entails substantial production costs. Many magazines with a long shelf life are well targeted (consider how many times a magazine may be read in a doctor's waiting room). Newspapers are good for geographical targeting and promotional advertising but have a very short shelf life. Infomercials, which we may also consider a direct marketing tool, have production costs and a short life span but are persuasive and good for telling the product story. Online advertising allows companies to reach a specific and often desirable customer market. Figure 5.10 presents brief guidelines for the strategic use of advertising media.

Advertising Medium	Key Factors for Entrepreneurs to Consider
Blogs	▣ Affiliated and direct advertisements ▣ Returning user-base ▣ Ability to implement text-linked ads
Brochures and flyers	▣ Allow creative flexibility and focused message ▣ Production quantity and distribution must be well planned
Conferences and trade shows	▣ Allows for integration with industry personnel ▣ Customers are already interested if they are at the conference
Direct mail and email	▣ Permits precise targeting and encourages direct response ▣ Results are measurable and can guide future campaigns
Facebook	▣ User base of over 1 billion people ▣ Web and mobile advertisements ▣ Companies can monitor "likes" ▣ Facebook advertising reached 89% of targeted audience[6] ▣ Mass customization of advertisements
Google AdSense	▣ Content based advertising targeted to specific consumers ▣ Choose-multiple ad formats (i.e., video, text, image)
Google AdWords	▣ Online advertising allowing you to pay for what you can afford ▣ Targeted reach and measurable value for advertiser
Infomercials	▣ Effective for telling a story and communicating or endorsing product benefits ▣ Costly to produce but measurable and good for collecting data
Internet communications	▣ A variety of options, such as banner ads and permission email marketing ▣ Superior for collecting data and measuring responses
Magazines	▣ Can easily be targeted, are involving for readers, and have a long shelf life ▣ Offer budget flexibility but involve a long lead time
Newsletters	▣ Good creative opportunities and maximum control ▣ Cost factors (time and money) should be carefully considered
Newspapers	▣ Best medium for advertising promotions and reaching a geographically based or local market ▣ Shelf life is fairly short and ads are usually not carefully read
Outdoor	▣ Can have strong visual impact and repeat exposure; this medium is believed to offer a high return on investment ▣ Targeting is difficult because ads are location-bound
Radio	▣ Good potential for creativity and connecting with the audience; message can be easily varied ▣ Excellent for targeting, but ads must be repeated to be effective
Telemarketing	▣ Interactive communication with one-on-one selling capabilities ▣ A direct-response method that has faced increased regulation because it is seen by many to be intrusive
Television	▣ High media and production costs but superior reach; most effective way to present and demonstrate a product ▣ Commonly used for brand building
Twitter	▣ Ability to build a community of advocates ▣ Reach extended members of the community through re-tweets ▣ Target consumers through gender, interests or geographical location ▣ Monitor progress through just-in-time analytics
Yellow pages	▣ An important local medium used as a basic reference by consumers; necessary for credibility ▣ Low cost, but standardized format limits creativity

■ **Figure 5.10**

Strategic use of advertising media

Even entrepreneurs often go to marketing experts for advice about how to execute campaigns and how to frame an effective message. While some early-stage companies use established advertising agencies, others contract with freelance marketing professionals, many of whom have experience in the entrepreneurial domain. You'll want to learn the basics of advertising, public relations, and marketing research to be able to select and evaluate agencies or individuals you bring in to assist your company with its early-stage marketing.

The three primary types of sales promotion are *consumer promotions, trade promotions*, and *sales force promotions*. **Consumer promotions** are deals offered directly to consumers to support a pull strategy. **Trade promotions** are deals offered to a company's trade or channel partners—such as distributors or retailers—to support a traditional push strategy. **Sales force promotions** motivate and reward the company's own sales force or its distributors' sales forces.

There are two basic types of sales promotions: price and nonprice. We discussed price promotions earlier in the section on pricing strategy. *Consumer price promotions* include coupons, rebates, and loyalty rewards; *trade price promotions* include discounts, allowances, buyback guarantees, and slotting fees. Types of *consumer nonprice promotions* include product sampling, advertising specialties (such as T-shirts with a brand logo), contests, and sweepstakes. *Trade nonprice promotions* include trade shows and sales contests.

The effects of sales promotions differ from the effects of advertising. In general, sales promotions produce more immediate, sales-driven results, whereas advertising produces a more long-term, brand-building result. Sales promotions have become increasingly popular with companies in the last couple of decades.

Many entrepreneurs derive great value from using **public relations (PR)** as a strategic communications tool. PR has two major dimensions: *publicity* and *corporate communications*. When Google founder Larry Page introduced Google Pack at the 2006 Consumer Electronics Show, it was a corporate communication designed to move users away from Google's competitor Microsoft. When Google joined the O3b (other 3 billion) consortium—a group of companies that support World Wide Web (WWW or Web) access for Africa—it did so to gain positive publicity. Bill Samuels, Jr., the CEO of Maker's Mark Bourbon, used a personal connection and an elaborate plan to gain major-league publicity:

> *Dave Garino covered the Kentucky area for the* Wall Street Journal. *Bill Jr. discovered that he and Dave had a mutual friend, Sam Walker, with whom Dave had gone to journalism school. Bill Jr. knew Dave was going to be in town covering an unrelated story and decided to try a unique approach to persuade him to do a story on Maker's Mark. Bill Jr. staged an event at the distillery and awarded exclusive rights to cover the show to a local news station. He found out which hotel Dave Garino was staying in and had Sam Walker arrange to meet Dave for cocktails in the hotel's bar. Next, Bill Jr. convinced the bartender to turn all the televisions above the bar to the local station that was covering the distillery show. When Dave saw the news footage, he asked Sam what Maker's Mark was and why, if there was so much interest in this distillery, had he never heard of it. When Sam replied that it was the local favourite and offered to introduce him to Bill Jr., he accepted. Subsequently, Dave and Bill Jr. spent three days developing a story that was published on the front page of the* Wall Street Journal *in August of 1980.*
>
> *Bill Jr. recalled: "From that one story we received about 50,000 letters inquiring about our product. The phone lines didn't stop ringing for weeks. We had one salesman at the time and we were trying to figure how to best capitalize from all this publicity."*

And the rest, as they say, is history.[7]

It is often argued that publicity is an entrepreneur's best friend, more valuable than millions of dollars of advertising. The reason is that PR is perceived as more credible and more objective; a reporter's words are more believable than those of an advertising agency. Also, the argument goes, PR is free! This, of course, is not true—it takes a significant amount of time

Maker's Mark Waters Down Image, but Boosts Brand Recognition

In February 2013, Maker's Mark announced that it would be diluting the strength of its bourbon from 45% to 42% by volume and thereby increasing its output, which had fallen short of consumer demand. The announcement outraged some loyal drinkers, who immediately vented their anger via social media; reports of their protests soon spread to conventional media. One week later Bill Samuels, Jr., Maker's Mark founder and chairman emeritus, and Rob Samuels, COO, in a tweet headed "You spoke, we listened" handsomely apologized to their customers for their misstep and reversed their decision by stating that they would make it "just like we've made it since the very beginning."

According to BrandIndex data, Maker's Mark's attention score shot up from 8 on February 9 before the dilution announcement to 24 by February 27, indicating that 24% of the population had heard something good or bad about the brand in the last two weeks. The three-fold increase caused a few skeptics to question whether Maker's Mark's initial announcement was a deliberate marketing move to boost its name recognition rather than a public relations blunder. That was unlikely as it damaged Maker's Mark image. Also the last thing that Maker's Mark needed before it could increase production capacity was more demand that would result from increasing brand recognition. More likely it was following the lead of Tennessee whiskey icon Jack Daniel's, which diluted its strength from 43% to 40% in 2004 with little adverse reaction from drinkers.

The Samuels's swift and effective response is a good illustration of how to handle a public relations disaster in the Internet age when bad news and rumours go viral at lightning speed on the Web.

and effort, sometimes money, and always the ability to leverage connections to generate good PR. If this were not the case, there would not be so many public relations firms charging high fees and battling for the media's attention. Savvy entrepreneurs with fledgling companies are good at managing their own PR. For example, they send out press releases announcing new products, key executive hires, and other significant company events to newspapers, trade magazines, and online media outlets.

For companies operating in a business-to-business environment or those that need to sell into an established distribution channel, *personal selling* is a core component of the communications mix. Although some companies separate sales and marketing, a company's sales force is often its primary marketing tool. Establishing and managing a sales force requires decisions related to sales force size, training, organization, compensation, and selling approaches.

A sales force is often considered to be a company's most valuable asset. Maintaining a strong sales force is an expensive proposition, though, and startup companies often face a difficult decision: whether to absorb the expense and sell directly or hire manufacturers' representatives (*reps*, sometimes called *brokers*) to sell the company's products (along with those of other companies) on commission. Reps are advantageous in that they have existing relationships with customers, but a company has more control—and a closer relationship with its customers—if it invests in its own sales force. A sales force may be organized geographically, by product line, by customer size, or by customer segment or industry. Compensation is usually some mix of base salary and commission, and incentives may be linked to gaining new customers, exceeding sales quotas, or increasing profitability. Current marketing practice places a high value on selecting and retaining customers based on their profit potential to the company. The sales force typically should have access to effective selling materials, credible technical data, and sales automation software that will ensure an effective and efficient selling process.

Personal selling is an important activity for entrepreneurs on an informal, personal level—through professional networking. Leveraging personal and industry connections is a key success factor, especially in the startup or early growth stage of the venture. But this is a time-consuming and often laborious process, which is often neglected and rarely fully optimized. Giro's founder, Jim Gentes, personally attended top triathlons and other high-profile races across the country, demonstrating his helmets and giving them to the best cyclists. He was ahead of his time in understanding the value of endorsements from world-class athletes.

Entrepreneurs can implement *direct marketing* campaigns to be broad based or to be local or limited in scope. Direct marketing methods include direct mail, catalogues, telemarketing, infomercials, and permission email (where consumers "opt in" to receive messages). The effectiveness of direct media is easy to measure, and these media are ideal for building a database that can be used for future marketing and analysis. Direct marketing is an important tool for communicating with new or existing customers, whom you can target for mailings that range from thank-you notes to announcements of future promotions.

With the increased use of technology and databases in marketing, and the growth of the Internet channel, the practice of one-to-one marketing has become pervasive. This type of marketing is interactive and has qualities similar to personal selling: Your company can address a customer on an individual level, factoring in that customer's previous purchasing behaviour and other kinds of information, and then respond accordingly. It is the use of databases that allows marketers to personalize communications and design customer-specific messages.

Customer relationship management (CRM) systems are designed to help companies compile and manage data about their customers. While CRM systems are usually large scale and expensive, an astute entrepreneur can set up a more fundamental system to capture and use customer data to facilitate relationship building. Part of this process is capturing the right metrics—for example, *cost of customer acquisition* or *average lifetime value of a customer*—and knowing how to act on them.

Guerrilla Marketing

Guerrilla marketing is marketing activities that are nontraditional, grassroots, and captivating—that gain consumers' attention and build awareness of the company. Guerrilla marketing is often linked to "creating a buzz" or generating a lot of word of mouth in the marketplace. The terms *buzz, viral,* and *word-of-mouth marketing* aren't interchangeable. According to the Word of Mouth Marketing Association (WOMMA), the three concepts are defined as in the accompanying box.[8]

Entrepreneurs may use all of these nontraditional promotion campaigns to get people's attention, especially younger generations who may not pay attention to TV campaigns and print media. Guerrilla marketing is also attractive to entrepreneurs because often they have to work with a limited or nonexistent promotion budget and traditional media are very expensive. Unfortunately for entrepreneurs, such nontraditional promotional methods are getting the attention of big marketers who want to break through the clutter of existing media. BzzAgent, a Boston-based word-of-mouth marketing agency, has more than 500,000 agents who will try clients' products and then talk about them with their friends, relatives, and acquaintances over the duration of the campaign. It has worked with companies like Anheuser-Busch, General Mills, and Volkswagen. Procter & Gamble's (P&G's) four-year-old Tremor division has a panel of 200,000 teenagers and 350,000 moms who are asked to talk with friends about new products or concepts that P&G sends them. Some experts suggest that traditional marketers underused public relations or used it only as an afterthought, thus opening the door for creative guerrilla marketers.

It is easier to define what guerrilla marketing *does* than what it *is*. Guerrilla marketing is heard above the noise in the marketplace and makes a unique impact—it makes people talk about the product and the company, effectively making them "missionaries" for the brand. It creates drama and interest and positive *affect*, or emotion—all pretty amazing results. But in fact, truly good guerrilla marketing is as difficult as—and maybe more so than—good traditional marketing. Because lots of companies are trying to do it, it's harder to break free of the pack.

Think of guerrilla marketing as guerrilla *tactics* that you can apply to various media or elements of the communications mix rather than as entirely different communications tools. You can use guerrilla tactics in advertising (riveting posters in subways) and in personal selling (creative canvassing at a trade show), but you'll most likely use them as a form of PR—as tactics that garner visibility and positive publicity. The president of Maker's Mark practised guerrilla marketing when he inspired the *Wall Street Journal*'s reporter to learn about and write the story of his bourbon. Nantucket Nectars's Tom and Tom were relentless guerrilla marketers, dressing up like grapes and making a stir on the Cape Cod highway on Memorial Day weekend as thousands of motorists were stuck in traffic, and sending purple vans to outdoor concerts to distribute free juice before it became a common practice.

Much of what we now call *event marketing* is in the realm of guerrilla marketing because it is experiential, interactive, and lighthearted. But as we noted earlier, guerrilla tactics are becoming more and more difficult for entrepreneurs to execute because every corporate marketing executive is trying to succeed at guerrilla marketing, too; and established companies have a much larger budget to employ. Sony Ericsson Mobile executed a guerrilla marketing campaign in New York City in which trained actors and actresses pretended to be tourists and asked passersby to snap a picture with the company's new mobile phone/digital camera product. Deceptive? Yes, but too commonplace a tactic to truly be controversial. Not every guerrilla campaign escapes controversy, though. In 2007, Cartoon Network's Adult Swim launched a guerrilla marketing campaign to promote the show *Aqua Teen Hunger Force*. The campaign used battery-powered electronic light boards of a middle-finger-waving moon man hidden in various areas around 10 cities. People in Boston mistook the packages for bombs, and the police responded. Turner Broadcasting, the owner of Cartoon Network, was forced to pay $2 million to the city of Boston not only to cover the costs of the police and bomb squad responders, but also as a show of goodwill.[9]

An elaborate guerrilla marketing campaign in Toronto, designed to promote an HBO comedy series, featured street teams with TV-equipped backpacks to show pedestrians 30-second promotional clips, chalk drawings promoting the series at major intersections, and ads in the bathrooms of major media agencies that showcased giant quotes from reviews of the show. The attempt by large corporations and advertising agencies to set the standard for guerrilla marketing makes these tactics less accessible to small companies. Still, as long as entrepreneurs are sparked by creativity, guerrilla successes can still be possible, even though they require a continuous stream of ideas and energy.

TYPES OF GUERRILLA MARKETING

- Word-of-mouth marketing: Giving people a reason to talk about your products and services and making it easier for that conversation to take place.

- Buzz marketing: Using high-profile entertainment or news to get people to talk about your brand.

- Viral marketing: Creating entertaining or informative messages that are designed to be passed along in an exponential fashion, often electronically or by email.

ISSUES IN GUERRILLA MARKETING

- Identify challenges and develop creative solutions.

- Find the "inherent drama" in your offerings and translate that into a meaningful benefit.

- Get people's attention and get a "foot in the door" (generating the first sale).

- Create "buzz" once you get in the door (word-of-mouth marketing).

It is also important for an entrepreneur to consciously note the difference between marketing and sales. Both are activities that ultimately strive to increase revenue and are so closely related that entrepreneurs usually forget the difference between the two. Marketing activities mainly include consumer research—identifying the needs of the consumer—and advertising to build a brand and increase product awareness. The goal of marketing and advertising is to generate interest in a product and create prospective consumers. Sales and salespeople are focused on taking those leads and potential consumers generated by marketing and converting them into actual paying consumers. The more leads a marketing campaign creates, the more conversions sales can generate. Thus, marketing focuses on a wide range of people while sales typically focuses on a smaller subset of individuals.

In conclusion, entrepreneurs who create successful marketing strategies must have a clear vision of their goal. They also must understand how one strategic element affects another because, if the marketing mix elements of product, price, distribution, and communications are not perfectly compatible—if the mix is not internally logical—the strategy will not work. Even a good beginning strategy is not enough, however, because the marketplace is dynamic. Entrepreneurial companies, more so than mature businesses, must constantly re-evaluate their strategy and how it is affecting growth.

Marketing Skills for Managing Growth

It is beyond the scope of this chapter to offer a comprehensive discussion of the next step: the marketing processes and capabilities a young company needs in order to pursue strong growth. However, two key areas for you to focus on are *understanding and listening to the customer* and *building a visible and enduring brand*.

Understanding and Listening to the Customer

Although intuition-based decision making can work well initially for some entrepreneurs, intuition has its limitations. Entrepreneurs must be in constant touch with their customers as they grow their companies. When a company decides to introduce its second product or open a new location, for example, it needs to be able to determine whether that product or location will be welcomed in the marketplace. Entrepreneurs with a successful first product or location often overestimate demand for the second, sometimes because their confidence encourages them to rely too heavily on their own intuition.

Entrepreneurs must obtain information that will allow them to understand consumer buying behaviour and customer expectations related to product design, pricing, and distribution. They also need information about the best way to communicate with customers and influence their actions. Finally, they need information about the *effectiveness* of their own marketing activities so they can continue to refine them. Marketers build relationships in part by using information to customize the marketing mix. Good entrepreneurial marketers do whatever it takes to build relationships with customers.

As marketing goes through customization to reach an intended audience, so too does the actual product. As mentioned in Chapter 3, *pivoting* a product's functionality, purpose, or method of use is essential in seeking a product–market fit. Steve Blank, author of *The Four Steps to the Epiphany*, states that products developed with senior management out in front of potential customers early and often win.[10] Blank also mentions that by listening to potential customers—by going out into the field and investigating potential customers' needs and markets before becoming inexorably committed to a specific path—makes all the difference between a product's success and failure.[11]

Entrepreneurs following a high-growth strategy need to continuously find new customer segments to support that growth. Bill Samuels, Jr., recognized that for Maker's Mark to grow significantly, the company would have to reach a new segment—drinkers of other types of alcohol—because the bourbon connoisseur market was near saturation. Rather than relying on his own intuition, Samuels studied the consumer market to understand where he would find his new customers and how he would attract them.

There are a number of ways to listen to customers; some require formal research, and others use informal systems for soliciting information and scanning the market environment. Leonard Berry cites a portfolio of methods that entrepreneurs can use to build a *listening system:*[12]

- *Transactional surveys* to measure customer satisfaction with the company
- *New and lost customer surveys* to see why customers choose or leave the firm
- *Focus group interviews* to gain information on specific topics
- *Customer advisory panels* to get periodic feedback and advice from customers
- *Customer service reviews* to have periodic one-on-one assessments
- *Customer complaint/comment capture* to track and address customer complaints
- *Total market surveys* to assess the total market—customers and noncustomers
- *AB testing* to listen to customers, even when they don't know it
- *Social media monitoring* through Twitter and Facebook via analytical tools
- *Message boards* to monitor customer complaints
- *Post fail* to monitor failures in search and respond by filling the need
- *Shopping cart abandonment* can be monitored by incentivizing the sale

Building the Brand

All entrepreneurs face the need for brand building, which is the dual task of building brand awareness and building brand equity. **Brand awareness** is the customer's ability to recognize and recall the brand when provided a cue. Marketing practices that create brand awareness also help shape **brand image**, which is the way customers perceive the brand. **Brand equity** is the effect of brand awareness and brand image on customer response to the brand. It is brand equity, for example, that spurs consumers to pay a premium price for a brand—a price that exceeds the value of the product's tangible attributes.

Brand equity can be positive or negative. Positive brand equity is the degree of marketing advantage a brand would hold over an unnamed competitor. Negative brand equity is the disadvantage linked to a specific brand. Brand building is closely linked to a company's communications strategy. While brand awareness is created through sheer exposure to a brand—through advertising or publicity—brand image is shaped by how a company projects its identity through its products, communications, and employees. The customer's actual experience with the brand also has a strong effect on brand image.

Maker's Mark used its communications strategy, implemented through humorous, distinctive print advertising in sophisticated national magazines like *Forbes* and *Businessweek,* to create a brand image that would help establish a high-end market for bourbon where none had existed in the past. The company created a likable, genuine brand personality for its bourbon. Because many of the advertisements were in the form of an open letter from Bill Samuels, Jr., to his customers, Samuels was able to represent and personalize the brand.

A new trend to take note of while building a brand is the impact that user-generated content can have. Potential customers will curate marketing material in an effort to focus on brand information provided by other customers. For example, a website for a hotel can promote comfort, affordability, and the best customer service in the city. However, if a potential customer cross-references this information on Trip Advisor and realizes that past guests have nothing good to say, odds are good that the potential customer will go elsewhere. User-generated content through the advent of social media platforms can provide a higher level of authenticity and brand awareness because potential customers will hold the opinion of a current customer higher than that of the company itself. Clay Shirky, a writer and teacher on the social and economic effects of Internet technologies, states that amateurs online are now doing what professionals once did with a passion and drive that will change everything.[13] Internet users are building, creating, and connecting at a surprisingly fast rate, often for the purpose of informing and educating others.[14] For example, Yelp, an online community of restaurant critics, plays a vital role in a restaurant's popularity. Critiquing food and restaurants used to be a paid role, but with the boom of the Internet and social platforms anyone can rate a restaurant and describe their experience, whether good or bad.

Viral Marketing

Viral marketing can play a huge role in building brand awareness. But how exactly does one create content that goes viral? With approximately 5.3 trillion ads shown online each year,[15] it can be tough to cut through all the "noise." But once you do, it can have a significant positive impact on your brand and is a great source of free press. *Harvard Business Review* has published a few pointers to help:

1. Write a compelling title: Research has shown that a clever title can significantly increase an advertisement's penetration rate.

2. Use strong emotional drivers to make people share and care: Hit the target audience hard and fast with emotional triggers, which will create maximum emotional excitement and uphold a viewer's engagement.

3. Create content that strikes the correct emotional chord: Negative emotions are typically not strong viral marketing stimulants, unless coupled with anticipation and the element of surprise. Emotions such as curiosity, amazement, astonishment, and admiration all work well in viral marketing ads.[16]

☐ CONCLUSION

Marketing is often described as a delicate balance of art and science. Certainly developing the expertise to be a master marketer is difficult, especially for entrepreneurs who are constantly pulled in a thousand directions. Nevertheless, the task remains: to have customer knowledge and PR mastery and to recognize effective advertising as well as effective experiential promotion. Entrepreneurial marketers must, first and foremost, be able to sell—sell their ideas, their products, their passion, their company's long-term potential. And they must learn the skill of knowing where the market is going, now and into the future.

Early-stage companies often find it necessary to scale up or change focus. In these scenarios, competition can be a potent driver of marketing decisions, whether you are staying under the radar of giant companies or buying time against a clone invasion. But successful entrepreneurs will have a strong, focused marketing strategy—a consistent strategy—and therefore will not easily be thrown off course.

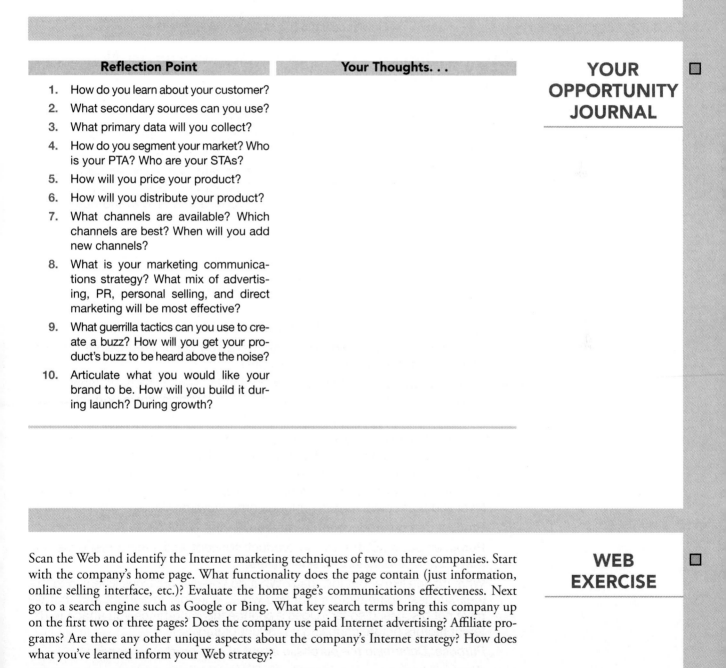

YOUR OPPORTUNITY JOURNAL

Reflection Point	Your Thoughts...
1. How do you learn about your customer?	
2. What secondary sources can you use?	
3. What primary data will you collect?	
4. How do you segment your market? Who is your PTA? Who are your STAs?	
5. How will you price your product?	
6. How will you distribute your product?	
7. What channels are available? Which channels are best? When will you add new channels?	
8. What is your marketing communications strategy? What mix of advertising, PR, personal selling, and direct marketing will be most effective?	
9. What guerrilla tactics can you use to create a buzz? How will you get your product's buzz to be heard above the noise?	
10. Articulate what you would like your brand to be. How will you build it during launch? During growth?	

WEB EXERCISE

Scan the Web and identify the Internet marketing techniques of two to three companies. Start with the company's home page. What functionality does the page contain (just information, online selling interface, etc.)? Evaluate the home page's communications effectiveness. Next go to a search engine such as Google or Bing. What key search terms bring this company up on the first two or three pages? Does the company use paid Internet advertising? Affiliate programs? Are there any other unique aspects about the company's Internet strategy? How does what you've learned inform your Web strategy?

Appendix: Customer Interview

To whom should we ask the questions?
What possible information would we ask about?
Should the questions be open ended or structured?
How should the questions be sequenced?

General Outline: It Needs to Be Tailored to Meet Your Research Needs

1. Opening discussion (introduction and warm-up):

   Briefly describe research purpose, introduce self, ensure confidentiality of response, and state expected duration of the interview session.

   Opening statement: Think of the last time you purchased or used such a product. What prompted or triggered this activity? What specific activities did you perform to get the product or service? What was the outcome of your shopping experience?

2. Current practice:

   How do you currently purchase or use a product/service of interest? How did you go about deciding on what to buy? How frequently do you buy/use this product/service? How much do you buy/use each time? Where do you buy?

3. Familiarity/awareness about product/service:

   What other products/services/stores have you considered before deciding on the final product/service you bought?

4. Important attributes: If you were shopping for such a product, what would you look for? What is important? What characteristic(s) are important to you?

5. Perception of respondents:

   How would you compare different products/services? How well do you think of the product/service you bought compared with those of its competitors with respect to these attributes?

6. Overall satisfaction with or liking of the product/service: Ask satisfaction level and preference ranking among competitive products.

7. Product demo/introduction/description:

   Purpose: Get reactions to the product concept and elicit a response that may identify additional decision drivers.

   What do you like about this idea? What do you dislike? Does listening to this idea suggest some factors that you would consider important and that we have not discussed so far? Does it change the importance you attach to different factors before choosing a product or service?

   Purpose: Determine the purchase intent of new product or service.

   What will be the level of interest or willingness of respondents to buy or use this new product/service? At what price?

We would like to know how likely it is that you would buy such a product or service.

☐ Would definitely buy

☐ Would probably buy

☐ Might or might not buy

☐ Would probably not buy

☐ Would definitely not buy

We would like to know now how much you would be willing to pay for such a product or service:

☐ Would definitely pay $_____.

Please note that comparable products are priced at $_____. Now how much would you be willing to pay for such a product or service?

☐ Would definitely pay $_____.

8. Media habit:

   How do you find out about a product or service?

   What media do you read, listen to, or watch?

9. Demographic information:

   Personal information should be asked at the end of the interview.

   Age, income, occupation, gender, education, etc.

   Size of the firm (revenue, total full-time staff, research and development staff), resources, experience, skills, etc.

10. Wrap-up:

    Any final comments or ideas?

CASE

Eu Yan Sang International, Ltd.

Singapore, 2009. Richard Eu was pleased with the progress of Eu Yan Sang (EYS), the 129-year-old company he served as Group CEO. Revenues had been growing by 10 to 20% annually since 2000, to S$208 million[17] for the fiscal year ending June 30, 2008, and each of the three major markets in which the company operated—Singapore, Hong Kong, and Malaysia—had contributed to that expansion.

As the leading retailer of traditional Chinese medicine (TCM) outside mainland China, the company owned more than 144 attractive retail stores, 21 TCM health clinics, and was experimenting with health spas in both Singapore and Kuala Lumpur, Malaysia.

Equally important, EYS had established indisputable quality leadership in its field. At a time when many herbal products and dietary supplements were found to be contaminated or subject to dosage variations, EYS's customers could be certain of quality, consistency, and safety. The power of its brand had been recognized in many ratings surveys and in 2008 the *Guangzhou Daily* included the company among its "Top 10 Favourite Brands" for the fourth consecutive year.

Mr. Eu could not, however, rest on the company's current success. His board wanted more growth. However, 10 to 20% annual growth would be difficult if not impossible to deliver within the confines of the company's core markets. The total populations of Hong Kong, Singapore, and Malaysia were approximately 38.6 million—7 million, 4.6 million, and 27 million, respectively. EYS had to break into larger markets to achieve its growth goals. Although a foothold has been made in the Taiwan market (population 26 million), China and the United States were seen as likely targets. The company was already shipping products to both countries and had a small retail presence in China, but it had not yet developed strategic plans for exploiting either.

Expansion into China and the United States raised a number of questions. What customer, distribution, and regulatory challenges would have to be overcome in each country? Which of the company's product and marketing strengths, if any, would be applicable to those new markets? Should one market have priority over the other, or should they be attacked simultaneously? These were among the many questions that Richard Eu and his colleagues pondered.

The Company

Company founder Eu Kong left his home in southern China's Guangdong region in the 1870s to work in the small Malaysian tin mining town of Gopeng. Conditions there for labourers were dangerous and unhealthy, and many depended on opium to make their lives bearable. Eu Kong decided to use his knowledge of traditional Chinese remedies to improve the health of these miners. To that end he opened his first Chinese medicine shop in Gopeng in 1879, naming it "Yan Sang." In the Cantonese dialect, *Yan* means humane or kind, while *Sang* connotes birth, life, or livelihood. The company's current motto—"Caring for Mankind"—derives from this name.[18]

In 1890, Eu Kong passed the business on to his eldest son, Eu Tong Sen, who was active in both tin and rubber production. Eu Tong Sen expanded the TCM business in Malaysia and the surrounding region. Today, Eu Yan Sang is the leading provider of high-quality traditional Chinese medicine outside of China and was the first TCM company listed on the Singapore Exchange. Group CEO Richard Eu, who joined the business in 1989 after a successful career in merchant and investment banking, represents the fourth generation of family leadership. Today the company markets over 1,000 Chinese herbs and, under the Eu Yan Sang brand, 280 proprietary Chinese medicines. Beginning in 2007 it became the exclusive worldwide distributor for the Wisconsin (USA) Ginseng Cooperative, producer of what many believe to be the world's finest ginseng.

As described in company literature, EYS's vision is "To be a global consumer healthcare company with a focus in Traditional Chinese Medicine and Integrative Healthcare." Its stated mission is "To care for mankind by helping our consumers realize good life-long health."

Products

Traditional Chinese remedies have for centuries been sold in herb, root, leaf, and powdered form. Many of these take hours to prepare properly for use. Currently, the company offers over 280 product types, from raw herbs to manufactured remedies. In catering to the modern, convenience-oriented market, EYS had developed manufacturing methods for producing and packaging these remedies (and new ones) in ready-to-consume tablets, jellies, tea drinks, and elixirs. Exhibit 5.1 lists the company's best selling products and their revenues.

EXHIBIT 5.1	Key Eu Yan Sang Products	
		2008 Sales (S$millions)
Bo Ying Compound	Infant health	19.6
Bottled Bird's Nest	General health maintenance	19.5
Bak Foong Pills	Women's health	14.1
Lingzhi Cracked Spores Capsules	Immunity improvement	8.8
Essence of Chicken	General health maintenance	6.1
Total		68.1

In FY2008, these five leading products accounted for 33% of all company revenues. Eu Yan Sang's strategy is to diversify its product and revenue mix by launching 9 to 12 new products each year. Typically, only two or three of these new products can be described as radically new. The rest are product line extensions: for example, Essence of Chicken enhanced with ginseng.

Revenue goals for these newly launched products are not specified in advance, and each is given a long time to prove itself in the market. Launches are not accompanied by major promotions, in part because of governmental restrictions on the advertising of health-related products. Instead, newly launched products are integrated into the product mix on store shelves. Store personnel highlight these new items by means of special displays and explain their health benefits to visiting customers. These efforts aim to generate word-of-mouth product awareness.

Products are packaged in a variety of quantities, depending on their intended uses. For example, Bottled Birds Nest represents 25 different SKUs. It is sold in individual 150 mL bottles, six packs, and so forth. Prices range between S$40 and S$200 for these different quantities. Package quantities are also determined by whether the ingredients are in liquid or capsule form.

Traditional Chinese Medicine

The philosophy underlying traditional Chinese medicine (TCM) derives from the same bases that contributed to Taoism. That philosophy reflects the belief that the human body is composed of interlinking systems. Health is seen as dependent on balance within those systems. As described by the University of Minnesota: "Traditional Chinese medicine focuses on achieving health and well-being through the *cultivation of harmony* within our lives. Harmony brings health, well-being, and sustainability. Disharmony leads to illness, disease, and collapse."[19]

TCM includes a number of practices originating in China, including diagnosis and treatments such as herbal medicine, dietary therapy, acupuncture, cupping, massage therapy, relaxation and meditation therapy, and physical exercises such as Tai Chi Chuan.

Next to dietary therapy, herbal medicine of the type supplied by Eu Yan Sang is the most widely used mode of TCM treatment. Herbal medicine, usually formulated from two or more substances, is used both for the treatment and prevention of illness. There are thousands of traditional herbal formulas; TCM practitioners modify them to suit the subtle nuances of a patient's condition or state of health. Many are made in tea or soup form or added to other foods.

Manufacturing

The company's products are processed and packaged in two Good Manufacturing Practice (GMP)–certified plants: one located in Hong Kong and the other in Malaysia. The newly built, 130,000 square foot, state-of-the-art plant in Yuen Long, Hong Kong, was a S$21 million investment. That plant also houses facilities used for academic research and herbalist training.

RGtimeline/iStockphoto

Quality Assurance from Farm Fields to Consumers

Responding to worldwide concern over the quality and safety of food products originating in Asia, the company has taken major steps toward developing the highest product quality standards. In 2007, it began testing its herbs—an industry first. Using advanced analytical techniques, it obtained chromatographic "fingerprints" of over 500 essential TCM herbs. These fingerprints make it possible to eliminate the mistaken use of visually similar but biochemically different ingredients, which is a problem in the industry.

In March 2008 it announced the world's first program for certification of TCM herbs produced through the company's "good agronomic practices" (GAP) (Exhibit 5.2). The program extends through every step of the product cycle, from growing, to formulation and packaging, to shipping, to retailing. The aim is to ensure that high standards for safety and quality are maintained at *all* stages of the cycle. A proprietary software platform—iGates—was built to track all ingredients and all products through every step of the cycle (Exhibit 5.3). Agrifood

Technologies of Singapore acts as a third-party observer in verifying quality compliance. "This is a giant step toward the future of TCM," according to a company press release:

We believe that the EYSGAP-Herbs Certification will help to promote the global acceptance and trust of TCM products . . . As an industry leader, we are creating one recognizable quality standard specifically for TCM herbs. It adopts a scientific approach and uses advanced scientific methods of measurement and accuracy to ensure safety and traceability throughout the whole process. This is a world first and sets the path for how the TCM industry will operate in the future.[20]

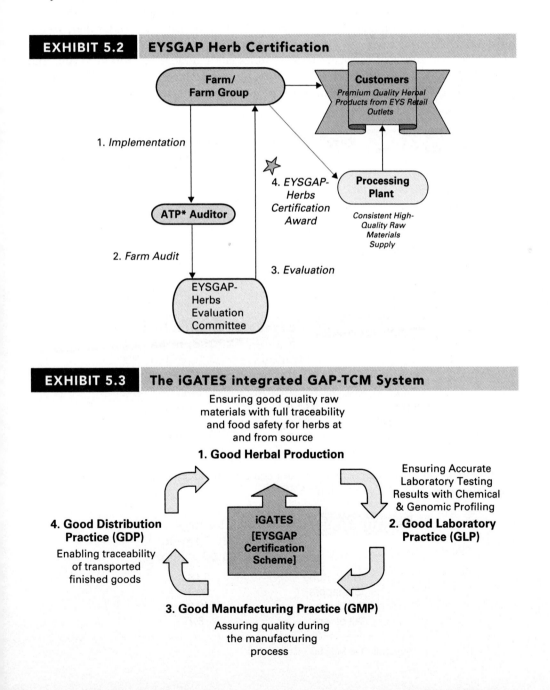

| EXHIBIT 5.2 | EYSGAP Herb Certification |

| EXHIBIT 5.3 | The iGATES integrated GAP-TCM System |

Lingzhi was the first herb to obtain official certification under this quality regimen. The company's popular Wisconsin American Ginseng was the second.

Distribution and Pricing

Eu Yan Sang products are available throughout the world in drugstores, hospitals, convenience stores, health food stores, health clubs, and on the company's ecommerce site. In addition, EYS owns and operates 154 branded retail stores and clinics in Asia; the latter offer products and consultation with licensed TCM doctors (Exhibit 5.4). Of these several distribution channels, retail stores produce the majority of company revenues (Exhibit 5.5). Most individual customer purchases in these stores fall in a range of S$50 to S$100. And since TCM products are for health maintenance, many customers return monthly to renew their supplies. EYS is conducting customer research on the issue of customer loyalty and purchase frequency.

EXHIBIT 5.4	Retail Outlets and Clinics (as of late 2009)	
Country	Retail	Clinics
Singapore	38	17
Malaysia	64	3
Hong Kong	46	1
Macau	2	0
China (Guangzhou)	2	0
Taiwan	2	0

Source: Eu Yan Sang International, Ltd.

EXHIBIT 5.5	Revenue by Distribution Channel, FY2008, in S$ millions	
	Revenues	Change, 2007–2008
Retail	161.0	+16%
Wholesale	33.0	+17%
Clinics	13.7	+ 9%

Essentially all of the company's revenues come from three key geographic areas: Hong Kong, Singapore, and Malaysia (Exhibit 5.6).

EXHIBIT 5.6	Revenues by Key Geographic Region, FY2008, in S$ millions
Hong Kong	93.4
Singapore	60.2
Malaysia	49.2
All others	5.7

Source: Eu Yan Sang International, Ltd.

Owing to the higher quality of its ingredients and processing, EYS herbs and manufactured products have brand power and command a price premium over those offered by competitors. This price premium gives the company a gross margin of about 60%. Ironically, Chinese companies offer little competition for traditional Chinese medicine outside the borders of mainland China, with the result that EYS's competitors in its core markets are other Asian producers. Each of these competitors, however, confines its activities to a single country. Thus, for example, Hockhua is a retailing competitor in Singapore, but has no presence outside that country. It is simply a retailer and has no branded products of its own.

Marketing

EYS's marketing functions are handled by a lean corporate staff and small teams operating within each of three core geographically focused groups: Singapore, Hong Kong, and Malaysia. The corporate staff consists of a handful of people: Joanna Wong, vice-president of brand management and corporate communications, and her direct reports; a media relations specialist; and a brand manager. They routinely collaborate with the company's small product development team, particularly on matters relating to package design. At EYS, all packaging must conform with the brand image. The geographically focused marketing teams are also small, with two to three people (although the Malaysia team has four to six); each team handles advertising and promotion within its region and is accountable for sales results.

Marketing budgets vary year to year but are roughly 6% of annual sales (about S$12 million) and are allocated in roughly equal measures to corporate marketing and to each of the three core region teams. Corporate's focus tends to be on brand issues, whereas the regional teams tend to concentrate on product promotion. The name "Eu Yan Sang" is the corporate name, the retail name, and the name that goes onto each product.

According to VP Joanna Wong, who joined the company in 2000 after a career as an independent advertising and promotion (A&P) consultant, EYS's A&P spending is opportunistically determined: "Marketing allocations to advertising and promotion are not determined by a strict formula, but by whatever is judged best for each product." She attributes the success of EYS's marketing campaigns to this flexible approach, which makes use of television, print media, "buy one, get one free" product promotions, and so forth. Television, however, tends to receive the larger share. Within that medium, the company makes frequent use of 30-minute health programs that highlight the benefits of particular EYS products.

Perhaps because of Joanna Wong's background in public relations and the company's emphasis on marketing efficiency, television and print media promotion is supplemented with extensive publicity, which it generates internally and through an outside consultant. Publicity gives the company and its products low-cost exposure.

China

From its Singapore headquarters, Eu Yan Sang's leadership cannot ignore the revenue potential of its giant neighbour to the north. With that country's rising economic prosperity and population of 1.3 billion, vendors in almost every industry have been looking for ways to do business in China. For EYS, whose existence is based on traditional Chinese medicine, a Chinese presence seems natural. TCM is so much a part of mainland China's food and health culture that marketing efforts there, it believes, should encounter a receptive audience. But breaking into China will not be easy. As Richard Eu puts it, "In China, everything is difficult." Prominent among these difficulties is a paucity of market data on which to make business decisions. According to EYS management, the size of the Chinese TCM market as measured by purchasers, total sales, and every other important parameter is unknown. Even the numbers offered by trade associations are deemed unreliable.

The Regulation Hurdle

For health products manufactured outside China, the regulatory hurdle is challenging. Herbal and other TCM products sourced outside China must deal with the same registration process faced by pharmaceutical manufacturers. Applicants must also demonstrate that their products are *better* than equivalent domestically produced products. The registration process itself can take up to two and a half years and cost millions. Once registered, these foreign-made products are subject to re-registration every few years; re-registration, however, takes only six months and is far less costly. In order to enter the country, EYS's products must go through this slow and expensive registration process.

As of mid-2009, two EYS products had been approved by the regulatory authority: Bo Yung Compound and Bak Foong pills. Owing to their higher quality, these products sell at prices four to six times higher than those of equivalent Chinese products. "Our Bak Foong pills," says CEO Eu, "include 24 ingredients processed in a unique way. We use none of the shortcuts taken by state-run Chinese competitors." A bottle of EYS's Bak Foong pills, enough for three to four doses, generally retails for S$8 versus S$2.25 for a competing product.

Competition

EYS faces many domestic competitors within mainland China. Most are small, have no brand power, and offer products of unverified quality. However, larger vendors exist; chief among them are the following:

- Beijing's Tong Ren Tang Group, China's oldest (1669) and largest TCM producer. Its brand is well known in China. Tong Ren Tang operates a chain of drugstores in China and has a system of worldwide distribution. According to the Economist Intelligence Unit, the company accounted in 2004 for an estimated 30% of Chinese herbal product sold in the UK (total 2004 UK market equals S$405 million). In October 2007, Tong Ren Tang and Greater China Corporation, a U.S. company, announced a partnership under the name Tong Ren Tang Wellness Corporation. According to a company press release, its goal is to "develop spa-like wellness centers that will provide treatments and products based upon China's famous Tong Ren Tang herbal medicines." In addition to a full line of herbal health products, these centres will offer customers acupuncture, massage, acupressure, Tuina, Tai Chi, and other treatments.

- Sanjiu Medical and Pharmaceutical Company, one of China's largest pharmaceutical manufacturers, has many plantations around China where it raises herbs in conformance with government-approved Good Agricultural Practices (GAP). The company has experienced several setbacks in investor confidence, beginning in 2001 when the China Securities Regulatory Commission found evidence of widespread misappropriation of assets. In 2005 it announced the sale of its chain of drugstores, and in 2007 the company was restructured through an investment by a major Chinese conglomerate.

Because of a current lack of transparencies in the Chinese business culture, the revenues and profitability of these and other competitors are undetermined. And, as noted earlier, the size of the Chinese TCM market is not specified with reliable statistics. Even data provided by TCM trade associations is suspect.

Options for Entering the Chinese Market

In 2009 two of EYS's flagship products were being sold through Chinese hospitals, some drugstores, one shopping mall store, and two retail counters. Other products, mostly fine herbs, were being imported as health foods, thus bypassing the regulatory process. Together, however, sales through these channels accounted for less than 4% of company revenues. To achieve meaningful market penetration, the company has concluded that it must pursue the retail channel.

How best to enter the retail channel is an unanswered question. The company's brand enjoys limited awareness in China, and the high price of EYS products means that it must target a relatively small but affluent segment of Chinese society. By its estimates, only 20 million (2%) of the 1,300 million Chinese fit EYS's target demographic profile: affluent individuals 35 years of age or older. The company has considered several market entry strategies:

- *Direct, door-to-door selling:* EYS had some discussions with Mary Kay China, which sells door to door in that country, but regulation has made door-to-store selling risky. The company also worries that its quality brand might be tarnished by door-to-door sales.

- *Corporate gift sales:* The gift-giving tradition is strong in China, both among individuals and corporations. Selling gift baskets of assorted EYS products through prestigious corporations would enhance the quality image of the brand and result in multiproduct sales. This channel would require the hiring and training of corporate sales personnel in cities or regions populated by corporate headquarters.

- *Stand-alone stores:* EYS has extensive experience operating its own retail stores in Singapore, Hong Kong, and Malaysia. This option, however, would require high capital expenditures and an infrastructure of EYS personnel. The company worries that it lacks the brand visibility in China to support EYS branded stores. To test the feasibility, one store was opened in a Guangzhou shopping mall in 2009.

- *Stores within stores:* Following the model of cosmetic sales in the United States and elsewhere, the company envisions arrangements whereby it will have EYS sales counters, staffed by its own employees, located in upscale department stores in major Chinese cities. It estimates that 1,000 such counters would be capable of annually generating a total of S$21 million in five years. Two such counters were opened in 2009.

- *Stocking in leading retail stores:* Placement in leading retail stores seems an easy way to get a foot in the door, and as of spring 2008 EYS products were being carried by several leading retailers in China, including Watsons and Parkson.

- *Integrated health centres:* The company has experienced success in owning and operating integrated health centres in Malaysia and Singapore, and a new facility opened in Hong Kong in 2009. These centres are staffed by certified TCM doctors who consult with patients, and by retail sales personnel who fill prescriptions and conduct transactions for other EYS products. The company acknowledges the difficulty of translating this business model to China, where it would have to compete with free Chinese medical service offered by the state. Also, recruiting certified doctors would be difficult since most TCM doctors pursue life-long careers with the national health service.

In July 2008 the company hired an individual to assess the challenge of entering China; it continued through the year to ponder the potential of each entry option.

Products

Because of the time and cost of product registrations in China, EYS anticipates that only a small number of products would be registered and introduced in the initial stage of any expansion strategy into China. One of these products would likely be Bottled Bird's Nest, one of the company's highest revenue producers. "Bottled Bird's Nest is a much appreciated delicacy in China," says Joanna Wong, "but it is tedious to prepare in the traditional way. Our pre-prepared bottled version would give us a convenience advantage over local competitors."

Manufactured health supplements would also be considered for registration and introduction in China. Although competition is substantial within this product area, EYS's experience is that customers within China do not trust the safety and quality of domestically manufactured versions.

Pricing

EYS branded products are generally sold at premium prices in all markets where the company does business. That price premium is supported by empirical and customer-perceived measures of product quality. Further, EYS maintains price equity across markets. The company anticipates following the same pricing strategy in the China market.

Promotion

Will EYS promote its brand or its individual products? The company believes that it will have to do both upon entry into China, with decisions based on market conditions at the time. Because market entry would be limited initially to a small number of locations, local television, billboards, and public relations would be the favoured avenues of promotion, with costs anticipated to be 10–11% of sales revenues during the early years (in contrast to the company's current 6% of revenues for promotion/advertising spending).

The United States

> For us, S$30 million to S$70 million within five years would represent a successful market entry. Anything less than S$7 million would be a failure.
>
> *CEO Richard Eu*

To EYS, the U.S. market also appears to hold great revenue potential. TCM is a practice that very few U.S. consumers embrace, and awareness of the EYS brand is nonexistent at the broad consumer level. Nevertheless, the number of individuals who fit the company's demographic profile—35 or older, affluent, and health conscious—is much larger in the United States than in China. Also, there are fewer regulatory barriers to overcome.

EYS products are already selling in small volumes in the United States, mostly through retail stores located in the country's many "Chinatowns." Those products are handled through two independent distributors: one on the east coast and one on the west coast. Current revenues from these U.S. distribution arrangements are described as "negligible" by the company.

The U.S. Market

Within the United States, TCM is a small category within the "dietary supplement" industry, which in 2007 was estimated to have annual sales of S$33,230 million (US$23,260 million) and projected growth of 6% each year through 2014, according to the *Nutrition Business Journal's* annual report.[21] Of that amount, approximately S$5,900 million was spent on herbals and botanicals. Chinese medical professionals are quick to point out that their treatments are completely different from dietary supplement herbs. As the American Chinese Medicine Association puts it, "ACMA treatments are professional medicine rather than dietary supplement herbs."[22] However, for regulatory purposes in the United States, they fall into the same category.

As defined by the Dietary Supplement Health and Education Act of 1994 (DSHEA), a dietary supplement is a product (other than tobacco) that is intended to supplement the diet; contains one or more dietary ingredients (including vitamins, minerals, herbs or other botanicals, amino acids, and other substances) or their constituents; is intended to be taken by mouth as a pill, capsule, tablet, or liquid; and is labelled on the front panel as being a dietary supplement.

The Food and Drug Administration (FDA), the U.S. governmental agency charged with regulating dietary supplements, indicates that there are more than 30,000 dietary supplement products on the market. These include (by the FDA's definition) vitamins, minerals, botanicals (i.e., herbals), sports nutrition supplements, weight management products, and specialty supplements. The most rapid growth is in botanicals such as echinacea (for colds and to improve immune system response), gingko biloba (for memory), ginseng (for male sexual performance), garlic (for colds), and St. John's Wort (for depression), with sales of more than S$29 million each.

Estimates vary as to the number of Americans using dietary supplements. The Office of Dietary Supplements (part of the National Institute for Health) put the figure at 52% of the population in 2004 (with men at 47% and women at 56%). The Natural Products Association (NAP), a trade group, estimated in 2006 that 70% of the population used supplements. The NAP describes these consumers as being typically well educated, both in general and about the products they're buying. The reasons for which they take supplements vary. A scientific study involving 2,500 Americans conducted in 2002 gave the reasons cited in Exhibit 5.7.

EXHIBIT 5.7	Why Americans take dietary supplements
Herbals/Supplements	% of Responses
Health/good for you	16
Arthritis	7
Memory improvement	6
Energy	5
Immune booster	5
Joint	4
Supplement diet	4
Sleep aid	3
Prostate	3
Don't know/no reason specified	2
All others	45

Source: D. W. Kaufman, J. P. Kelly, L. Rosenberg, et al., "Recent Patterns of Medication Use in the Ambulatory Adult Population of the United States: The Slone Survey," *Journal of the American Medical Association* 287 (2002): 337–344.

Dietary supplements, per the *Nutrition Business Journal*, are distributed within the United States through many channels: retail health food stores such as GNC and New Chapter, mass-market stores such as Costco and Trader Joe's (many of which have their own brands), mail order, multilevel marketing, and the Internet. One small California drugstore chain, Pharmaca, uses a business model that integrates Western prescription medicines, health foods, and dietary supplements. Each of its stores has as small section dedicated to TCM products.

Expectations for future growth in the U.S. health food/dietary supplements industry are based on several demographic, healthcare, and lifestyle trends:

- *An increased focus on healthy living:* A study reported by *Nutrition Business Journal* found that 85% of Americans were engaged to some degree in health and wellness, up from 70% just a few years earlier.
- *Population aging:* According to the U.S. Census Bureau, the number of Americans 65 and older will increase by 56% between 2000 and 2020.
- *An increasing focus on fitness:* Spending by Americans on health clubs and exercise equipment continues to grow. Actual fitness in America, as measured by body mass (obesity), is bimodal, with the educated and affluent (EYS's target) being more fit and fitness conscious, and the less educated and less affluent being less fit and tending toward obesity.

Product Regulation

Generally, dietary supplement manufacturers do not need to register their products with regulators nor obtain approval before producing or selling their products in the United States. In the United States, the federal government regulates dietary supplements through the FDA. The enabling legislation is the DSHEA. The FDA regulates supplements *as foods* rather than as drugs. It does not require purveyors of dietary supplements to prove the safety of their products in people, as it does with pharmaceuticals. Nor must a manufacturer prove the effectiveness of its product.

While a manufacturer may not make unverified claims of effectiveness, it can say that its product addresses a nutrient deficiency or supports health in some way; for example, "Supports prostate health," or "Omega-3 for heart health." If the manufacturer makes a claim, that claim must be followed by the statement "This statement has not been evaluated by the Food and Drug Administration. This product is not intended to diagnose, treat, cure, or prevent any disease."

Competition in the U.S. Market

The U.S. TCM market, such as it is, has no dominant competitors. There are no established brands (including EYS), nor is there a regime of quality assurance. Dietary supplements in the United States have, in fact, often been found to be of poor quality, and TCM are equally suspect. For example, an NCCAM-funded study of ginseng products found that most contained less than half the amount of ginseng listed on their labels, and some contained contaminants. A similar study by the California Department of Health Services reported that 32% of the Asian patent medicines it tested contained pharmaceuticals or heavy metals not listed on the label.

Contamination and variability in the potency and quantities of active ingredients in dietary supplements has led the FDA to establish rules that require manufacturing, packaging, and labelling practices to ensure that a dietary supplement contains what it is labelled to contain and is not contaminated with harmful or undesirable substances.

TCM and American Consumers

Within urban China and neighbouring regions such as Hong Kong and Singapore, TCM and Western medicine enjoy a collaborative relationship. Consumers see value in both.

They use TCM to *maintain* health, but when health is imperiled—by a broken leg, for example—they are not reluctant to seek out Western medical procedures. The situation is much different in the West, where many if not most medical practitioners view TCM with skepticism—as unscientific, untested folk medicine. That skepticism in the medical community is slowly waning, and many medical schools now include classes on "alternative medicine" (including TCM) in their curricula. Empirical tests are also being conducted to assess the therapeutic efficacy of various herbs, acupuncture, and so forth. Western medicine is beginning to accept some of these practices as complementary or as alternative approaches to health and healing. Eu Yan Sang is encouraging these tests through participation with the Mayo Clinic.

As reported by the Harvard Medical School, the popularity of complementary and integrative medicine in the United States has increased dramatically in recent years. Other studies have documented that 42% of adults in the United States (82 million) routinely use complementary medical therapies to treat their most common medical conditions. In 1997, Americans made an estimated 629 million office visits to complementary therapy providers and spent an estimated S$38,300 million (US$27 billion) out of pocket on complementary care.[23]

Even though this segment of the population may be attracted to traditional Chinese medicine and its health benefits, EYS managers face two nagging questions:

1. Are U.S. consumers willing to pay for TCM products?
2. Given recent revelations about contaminated Chinese product imports, will American consumers be able to differentiate between those and EYS's high-quality products?

Chinese and Asian Americans: A Natural Constituency?

The company recognizes that it cannot expect broad market success in the United States without a substantial investment in consumer education about the benefits of TCM and how to practise it. However, the diverse U.S. population contains a large and growing segment of citizens and immigrants who are already familiar with and potentially friendly to TCM.

Roughly 3.6 million Americans are Chinese immigrants or of Chinese descent—1.2% of the total population. Their numbers are highly concentrated in some states and communities, making access to them through the retail channel practical. For example, the following large cities have Chinese American populations greater than 3%:

- San Francisco, California: 19.6% (152,620)
- Honolulu, Hawaii: 10.7% (39,600)
- Oakland, California: 8.0% (31,834)
- San Jose, California: 5.7% (51,109)
- Sacramento, California: 4.8% (19,425)
- New York, New York: 4.5% (361,531)
- Plano, Texas: 4.3% (10,750)
- Seattle, Washington: 3.4% (19,415)
- Boston, Massachusetts: 3.3% (19,638)

Many smaller communities *within* metro areas have Chinese American populations well over 20%. In California alone, these include

- Monterey Park, California: 41.2% (24,758)
- San Marino, California: 40.6% (5,260)
- Arcadia, California: 34.0% (18,041)
- San Gabriel, California: 33.6% (13,376)
- East San Gabriel, California: 28.2% (4,096)
- Alhambra, California: 33.1% (28,437)
- Rosemead, California: 29.3% (15,678)
- Rowland Heights, California: 29.0% (14,057)
- Hacienda Heights, California: 22.4% (11,921)

Similar concentrations are found in other metro areas. Many of these same towns and cities are home to other Asian Americans. For instance, the city of Honolulu is about 11% Chinese American but 55% Asian American. Those concentrations are useful indicators of where the company's products would most likely enjoy initial success.

An undetermined percentage of the U.S. Chinese and Asian American population practises TCM to some degree. These people are described by the American Chinese Medicine Association as well educated, open minded, knowledgeable, aware of the side effects of pharmaceuticals, and believers in natural medicine.[24]

Options for U.S. Market Entry

The company is considering a number of entry points to the U.S. market, although none have been researched or planned in detail. These entry options include the following:

- *A chain of company-owned stores:* These stores would be patterned on the successful model used by EYS in Hong Kong, Singapore, and Malaysia but modified for the U.S. market. CEO Richard Eu describes this model as the closest to his ideal. "I envision a GNC-style chain, perhaps integrated with Western health foods and supplements."

General Nutrition Centers, Inc. (GNC): An Industry Leader

GNC operates the world's largest nutrition retail store network. In 2009 it had

- 2,614 company-owned stores in the United States and Puerto Rico
- 161 company-owned stores in Canada
- 954 domestic franchised stores
- 1,190 international franchised stores in 449 markets
- 1,712 GNC "store-within-a-store" under its strategic alliance with Rite Aid, a major U.S. drugstore chain

GNC's U.S. revenues from retail operations in FY2008 were US$1,219 million, or S$1,731 million. Slightly over 40% of those revenues came from the sale of vitamins, minerals, and health supplements, which include herbals.

Source: GNC 10K filing, March 14, 2009

- *Stores within stores:* Operate a special TCM section stocked with EYS products within high-quality Western-style health food stores such as GNC or Pharmaca.

- *Distribute through upper-tier food stores:* The company cites the successful model provided by New Chapter, a Vermont producer of premium health supplements. That company's products are distributed through quality-oriented retailers such as Whole Foods and Trader Joe's.

- *Expand current strategy of selling through "Chinatown" stores:* The company is currently selling to stores that cater to Asian Americans through two distributors—one on each coast of the United States. It supports those sales with some TV and print advertising. Promotion decisions, however are controlled by the distributors.

- *Clinical services:* Company-owned clinics would offer acupuncture or an "integrated model" of Western medicine and TCM. The company has substantial experience in managing and marketing this integrated model of TCM-based health service in Asia and Australia.

Products, Pricing, and Promotion

Since each of the market entry options is still in the thinking stage, issues such as pricing, positioning, distribution arrangements, promotion, brand building, and so on remain largely unexplored. However, the company is inclined to follow the same premium pricing regime used in Asian markets. And because of the high cost anticipated in educating mainstream U.S. consumers on the benefits of TCM and EYS products, low-cost public relations would most likely be preferred over traditional advertising media.

Which Way Forward?

As a high-quality producer with a solid distribution base and brand recognition in its home territories, Eu Yan Sang is in a position that many product companies must surely envy. But it cannot rest on its past accomplishments. Management finds itself facing many strategic questions:

- Can it successfully leverage its current strengths to the untested markets of China and the United States?

- Given its limited resources, how should EYS prioritize its growth initiatives?

- What product, branding, pricing, and promotional strategies will make it successful in these different markets?

NOTES

1 American Marketing Association, "About AMA: Definition of Marketing," https://www.ama.org/AboutAMA/Pages/Definition-of-Marketing.aspx.

2 L. M. Lodish, H. L. Morgan, and A. Kallianpur, *Entrepreneurial Marketing* (Hoboken, NJ: Wiley, 2001), xi.

3 "Cadbury Does Yet Another Deal: Nantucket Nectars Will Be Part of Snapple Beverage Group," *Beverage Digest*, March 29, 2002, www.beverage-digest.com/editorial/020329.php.

4 Wharton School, "Marketing: Pricing and Positioning for Entrepreneurial Marketers," Knowledge@Wharton, http://knowledge.wharton.upenn.edu/article/pricing-and-positioning-for-entrepreneurial-marketers.

5 E. M. Rogers, *Diffusion of Innovations* (New York, NY: Simon and Schuster, 2010).

6 Facebook, "Facebook for Business," https://www.facebook.com/business.

7 K. Seiders, "Maker's Mark Bourbon" (case study and teaching note), Arthur M. Blank Center for Entrepreneurial Studies, Babson College, Babson Park, MA, 1999.

8 C. P. Taylor, "Psst! How Do You Measure Buzz?" *AdWeek*, October 24, 2005.

9 CNN, "Turner, Contractor to Pay $2M in Boston Bomb Scare," February 5, 2007, www.cnn.com/2007/US/02/05/boston.turner/index.html.

10 S. G. Blank, *The Four Steps to the Epiphany: Successful Strategies for Products that Win*, 3rd ed., 2006, http://stanford.edu/group/e145/cgi-bin/winter/drupal/upload/handouts/Four_Steps.pdf.

11 Ibid.

12 L. L. Berry, *Discovering the Soul of Service* (New York, NY: Free Press, 1999), 100–101.

13 C. Shirky, *Cognitive Surplus: How Technology Makes Consumers into Collaborators* (New York, NY: Penguin, 2010).

14 Ibid.

15 K. Libert and K. Tynski, "Research: The Emotions that Make Marketing Campaigns Go Viral," *HBR Blog Network*, http://blogs.hbr.org/2013/10/research-the-emotions-that-make-marketing-campaigns-go-viral.

16 Ibid.

17 At the time this case was written, one Singapore dollar (S$) equalled 0.77 Canadian dollars (C$).

18 Eu Yan Sang, "About US: History," www.euyansang.com.sg/our-history/eyscorporate2.html.

19 University of Minnesota, "Traditional Chinese Medicine?" Center for Spirituality and Healing, www.takingcharge.csh.umn.edu/explore-healing-practices/traditional-chinese-medicine.

20 Eu Yan Sang, "Eu Yan Sang and Agrifood Technologies Launch of Eu Yan Sang Good Agronomic Practices for Herbs (EYSGAP-Herbs) Certification Scheme," press release, March 31, 2008.

21 As described in General Nutrition Corporation's 10K filing, March 19, 2009, 2.

22 American Chinese Medicine Association, "Frequently Asked Questions," www.americanchinesemedicineassociation.org/Frequently_asked_questions.htm.

23 Harvard Medical School Office of Public Affairs, news release, July 11, 2000, Boston, MA.

24 American Chinese Medicine Association, "Frequently Asked Questions."

Salesforce chair and CEO Marc Benioff (left) and Salesforce co-founder Parker Harris (right) look on during a keynote address at the 2013 Dreamforce conference in San Francisco, California.

CHAPTER 6

SELLING IN AN ENTREPRENEURIAL CONTEXT

CHAPTER OUTLINE

Why This Chapter Focuses on Selling for Startups

Mindset for Successful Selling: Good Selling versus Bad Selling
Learning Objective 6.1 Describe the mindset an entrepreneur needs for successful selling.

Finding, Assessing, and Preparing to Pursue Sales Opportunities
Learning Objective 6.2 Describe how an entrepreneur finds, assesses, and prepares to pursue sales opportunities.

Developing a Compelling Value Proposition
Learning Objective 6.3 Describe how to develop a value proposition.

Pursuing Sales Opportunities
Learning Objective 6.4 Explain how to pursue sales opportunities.

Developing Sales Skills
Learning Objective 6.5 Explain how to develop sales skills.

Why This Chapter Focuses on Selling for Startups

The topic of selling in an entrepreneurial context requires special attention. Most founders and entrepreneurs are so focused on the design and manufacturing of their product or service that they postpone the work involved with getting ready for market until it's too late.[1] What's more, even if founders do delve into selling strategies early on, but have not yet been exposed to selling through academia or personal experience, they will have to make themselves familiar with selling in an entrepreneurial context. Most of the educational material (i.e., textbooks, videos, tutorials) that focus on selling strategies assume that a product or service has already been established in a marketplace, which is not the case for most startups.[2] This process should not be avoided by hiring an external sales representative, as the founder should become the startup's first salesperson. Only the founder or entrepreneur can communicate the full vision of the company's offering coupled with the commitment and passion needed to entice customers.[3] This chapter will cover the sales mentality and strategy that entrepreneurs need to adopt to successfully market their products.

In every corner of every enterprise—for-profit or nonprofit, business or nonbusiness, large or small—selling is a fact of life. It's going on inside the enterprise and between the enterprise and external entities. An engineer is trying to sell his project idea to his manager, seeking funding, use of facilities and equipment, and other employees to be assigned to his project team. An accountant in the budget office is trying to sell a manager on complying with the reporting guidelines, tracking expenses in a systematic manner, and meeting the quarterly report submission deadline. The finance professional is trying to sell a rating agency on raising the firm's bond rating. A young professional in the marketing department is trying to sell the business unit manager on altering the mix of marketing methodologies and on allocating a larger portion of the marketing budget to search engine optimization. A software engineer in the IT department is trying to sell her boss on abandoning the decades-old legacy software that is consuming the staff with software maintenance and moving to a more productive platform. And, of course, salespeople are meeting with current and potential customers, communicating their value propositions and trying to win orders. Selling gets people talking about the pros and cons of various alternatives as a precursor to making a decision and to agreeing to a path forward. Sales is the human activity that reduces the resistance at every boundary in every value chain and in every value network between supplier and customer.

This chapter explores how selling fits into the portfolio of knowledge, skills, and attitudes necessary for entrepreneurial success. We start by exploring a mindset for success in selling—consultative selling or value selling—and then discuss how to make that mindset operational. We end the chapter with a discussion of the skill sets that can be developed through practice over time.

All too often entrepreneurs fall into the better mousetrap mythology. The statement attributed to Ralph Waldo Emerson goes as follows:

> *If a man can write a better book, preach a better sermon, or make a better mousetrap than his neighbour, though he build his house in the woods, the world will make a beaten path to his door.*

It is commonly accepted business wisdom that this concept misses the importance of sales and marketing. The first author of this chapter served as the director of a technology business incubator for five years and interacted with a significant number of brilliant engineers and scientists who lived the Emerson quote. They were developing innovative technologies with little appreciation for the difficulty of getting customers to write a cheque. The following "Better Mousetrap Case Study" tells one of their sad tales.

Better Mousetrap Case Study

One entrepreneurial team—composed of two mechanical engineers and one software engineer—wrote an excellent business plan for the development of an automated system for circuit board testing and repair. Until that time, all of the elements of the production process for circuit boards had been automated with the exception of test and repair. As a result, circuit boards that failed the testing process piled up in the corner, awaiting human attention. The founders of the new venture had deep experience working in a previous venture involved in computer integrated modular manufacturing, which itself was a spinoff of a world-class automation company.

During the incubator admissions review process, the incubator director commented to the team:

"I believe there is a good chance that you will be able to complete prototype development in three months, as you project in your plan, but I'm more skeptical about the prospects for ramping up sales to $1 million per year by the end of the first year." The company was admitted to the incubator, and sure enough they finished the prototype within three months. At the one-year mark, the company had to shut down—it had not yet made a sale and had run out of cash. In the debrief, a member of the founding team commented to the incubator director: "We heard you when you told us that selling our system might prove to be more difficult than we anticipated in our business plan, but we had no idea what you were talking about. We didn't understand that getting customers to buy our system would be so difficult."

Customer Discovery

Before jumping into the mindset of successful selling, it is important to note that entrepreneurs and their products need to be ready for the market, and similarly, the market needs to be ready for their product. Steve Blank, author of *The Startup Owner's Manual*, has often mentioned that "A business plan never survives first contact with the customer."[4] However, by answering the following four questions, entrepreneurs can help ensure their readiness for first contact with a potential customer:[5]

1. Have we identified a problem a customer wants to see solved?
2. Does our product solve this customer problem?
3. If so, do we have a viable and profitable business model?
4. Have we learned enough to go out and sell?

In paying particular attention to the fourth question, most founders and entrepreneurs immediately respond with "*How do we know when we've learned enough?*" Blank has written about this often overlooked topic and has developed four customer development phases that can help eliminate any doubt in an entrepreneur's mind regarding his or her readiness to go out and sell. Figure 6.1 illustrates the four phases.[6]

Phase 1: State your business model hypothesis: Deconstruct the hypothesis on which the startup was built. This phase directly correlates with the lean canvas discussed in Chapter 8.

Phase 2: Get out of the building to test the problem: Do people care? Testing your hypothesis with potential consumers can help an entrepreneur understand how important the problem is and how big it can become. The goal of phase 2 is to turn the hypothesis in phase 1 into a factual statement.

Phase 3: Get out of the building and test the product solution: Once the hypothesis is confirmed, the validation of the solution or product must also be confirmed. The goal of phase 3 is to build a functional minimum viable product (MVP) that a consumer would pay for.

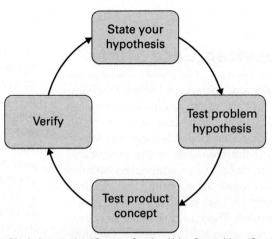

Source: Copyright © Steve Blank. Accessed at "Create a Succinct Value Proposition: 'Customer Discovery' and the Customer Development Model," MaRS, December 16, 2011, www.marsdd.com/mars-library/developing-your-value-proposition-an-overview-of-customer-discovery.

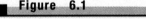 **Figure 6.1**

Customer development phases

Phase 4: Verify the business model and pivot or proceed: After an MVP has been market tested, phase 4 requires that an entrepreneur stop and assess the results and make any necessary changes from the customer feedback. The goal of phase 4 is to validate the consumers' problem and confirm the value proposition that is being offered by the product.

Once a startup's founder has successfully completed all four phases, he or she is ready to adopt a successful mindset focused on selling strategies.

Mindset for Successful Selling: Good Selling versus Bad Selling

When someone is asked what comes to mind when he or she hears the term **salesperson** (or salesman or saleswoman), typical responses include "pressure," "manipulation," "won't take no for an answer," "revulsion," "sleazy," and "slimy." Why do people have these negative reactions? They feel that salespeople have tried to manipulate them into buying something they don't want or need, or that doesn't really fulfill their wants or needs, all for the purpose of meeting the salesperson's need to make quota. The typical consumer has over the years had numerous—and too often negative—interactions with automobile, time-share, appliance, telemarketing, real estate, and insurance salespeople, many of whom are not professionally trained or skillful in relationship or consultative selling. Hence, many consumers have a poor perception of salespeople because they have been repeatedly subjected to bad sales practices.

Bad selling can also take the form of nonselling. If the buyer really needs to buy what the seller has to offer in order to acquire a product or service that is essential for the buyer's success, then the seller has a responsibility to help the buyer through the buying process—ideally professionally, efficiently, and painlessly.

This chapter focuses on **consultative selling**—a concept and philosophy widely espoused in books on the topic of selling. If the right decision for a prospective customer is to buy your product or service, then you have a professional responsibility to help that individual reach that decision. Conversely, if your product or service really isn't a good fit with his or her needs, then you have a responsibility to help the individual recognize that and help him or her pursue an alternative. **Value selling** is a relationship-building process through which the salesperson communicates the potential value of a product or service to prospective customers. The prospective customer returns value to the salesperson by carefully considering the value proposition, engaging with the salesperson in the decision-making process, and ultimately, if the product fits the customer's needs, buying it.

Those who excel in consultative selling will actually serve their customers as **buying consultants**. A highly skillful consultative salesperson will help the customer through the customer's own buying process, helping ensure that the buyer makes a wise decision, even if it's to purchase a competitor's offering. This approach establishes trust—leading the buyer to come back to the consultative salesperson later when there is a good fit between the buyer's needs and the salesperson's offerings, and to refer other buyers to the trustworthy, professional, and skillful consultative salesperson.

Linking the Entrepreneurial Mindset and Selling

An individual who has a well-developed entrepreneurial mindset focuses on two activities: (1) recognizing and assessing opportunity, and (2) a proactive, passionate, persistent, and professional pursuit of the opportunity. In an entrepreneurial context, **opportunity** is defined by the extent to which there is a good fit between a need in the marketplace and the entrepreneur's offering. Typically the need in the marketplace is currently unmet or underserved, or in some cases may be created by a new and innovative offering by the entrepreneur that changes the basis of competition in an industry. Most often the entrepreneur's offering takes the form of a product or service. The concept of opportunity is essentially the same in a sales context. The seller seeks to identify and assess customer needs, and if there is a good fit between the customer's needs and the seller's offerings, then the seller pursues the opportunity for a win-win. The customer wins by making the purchase and the seller wins by making the sale.

The classic nonseller is the typical sales clerk in a store's clothing section of a department store. When the shopper wanders in and starts looking around, the sales clerk will approach and ask, "Can I help you?" The buyer, trying to avoid being bothered by a bad seller, states, "No, I'm just looking." Typically the sales clerk walks away, instead of saying "Perhaps I can help you determine whether we have what you are looking for? If yes, then you can decide whether you are interested in buying it today. Since I know what we have in stock, I've been able to help many other shoppers save time during their search process. If you are willing to share with me what you are looking for, I promise to help you through your search process and, if you prefer, leave you alone in your decision-making process." Most shoppers—whether just browsing or absolutely sure about their purpose in shopping—would be so stunned by this very different and professional approach that they would happily engage the sales clerk in looking for a positive outcome.

Establishing trust is important in entrepreneurial selling. The entrepreneur—particularly during startup and early growth—has no track record (nor established brand) to reduce the perceived risk on the part of the buyer. Any failure to perform in the best interests of the potential customer dramatically decreases the probability that the customer will take on the risk of purchasing an unknown and untried offering and increases the probability that the customer will take the safe route and go with a proven supplier.

Trust is important in all of the relationships the entrepreneur seeks to establish. Entrepreneurs do not always have all the resources they need to pursue their opportunities. Hence entrepreneurs need to be skillful in resource acquisition—which means they are constantly selling someone on their dreams to get access to resources for free, at a discount, or on a temporary, marginal-cost basis. In addition to potential customers, they are selling potential co-founders, key employees, advisors, service providers, landlords, suppliers, investors—and often spouses or significant others. If the entrepreneur is pursuing aggressive growth, the various buyers and the entrepreneur's value proposition are constantly in a state of flux.

Starting with an entrepreneurial mindset, the entrepreneur engages in consultative selling to build trust and to efficiently and effectively determine whether the entrepreneur's offering is a good fit with the buyer's need. However in most cases the first salesperson in an entrepreneurial venture is the founder, who often has deep understanding (and enthusiasm) for a wonderful product, service, or technology. Often the driven entrepreneur will focus 100% on the new product, service, or technology without ever asking prospective customers about their needs. Consultative selling focuses the seller's effort on engaging with the buyer in a process of determining the ideal value proposition (or perhaps a set of alternative and equally acceptable value propositions) from the buyer's perspective. Although the salesperson rarely has the freedom to ignore his or her firm's own selling process, efficiency and effectiveness will improve to the extent that the seller can adapt and align the selling process to the buyer's purchasing process.

Aligning the Buying and Selling Processes

The ultimate role of the salesperson is to help the buyer make a purchase decision. The pathway to that outcome typically does not follow the steps the salesperson has learned to implement in the selling process, but rather the steps the buyer will follow in the buying process. Hence, the salesperson will use whatever is useful in the selling process to engage professionally and proactively in the buyer's buying process. The successful salesperson will do whatever is necessary, appropriate, and useful in assisting customers through the process they use to buy products or services. Figure 6.2 documents the relationship between a typical buying process and a typical selling process.[7] The activities identified in the exhibit are frequently iterative rather than linear, but ultimately must reach closing and post-close follow-up if the selling/buying process is to be successful. If the sales process is truncated quickly and efficiently because it is determined that there is not a good fit between the customer's needs and the seller's offerings, that outcome can be viewed as a success as well.

The seller might execute all the steps in the selling process in outstanding fashion and yet not make the sale. However, if the buyer does everything required in his or her company's

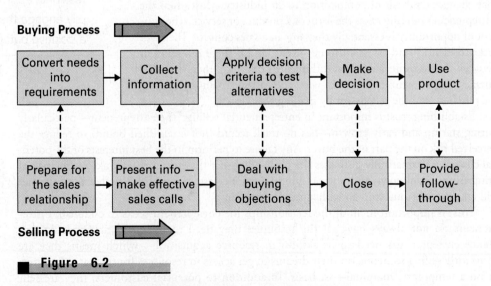

Buying Process

| Convert needs into requirements | Collect information | Apply decision criteria to test alternatives | Make decision | Use product |

| Prepare for the sales relationship | Present info — make effective sales calls | Deal with buying objections | Close | Provide follow-through |

Selling Process

■ **Figure 6.2**

Aligning the selling and buying processes

buying process to make the purchase—even if the seller does not complete all the tasks in the selling process—then the purchase/sale can be closed. Hence, the seller will increase the probability of making a sale by doing everything possible to help the buyer move through the buyer's buying process. This idea goes far beyond addressing the purchase specifications propagated by a buyer's purchasing department. It starts with the idea that the seller will achieve desired sales results only if the seller's product or service enables the buyer to achieve business results, such as increasing market share to grow revenue, increasing profitability, increasing customer satisfaction, and so forth. This requires the seller to engage in a much more comprehensive approach in preparing for the sale.

Finding, Assessing, and Preparing to Pursue Sales Opportunities

The primary reason that companies buy products or services is to improve performance—as measured by increased sales, increased profitability, lower costs, improved utilization of assets, and so forth. The buyer (in the role of seller in the value chain) looks at what its customers need to be successful, and even further to help its customers understand the needs of their customers. This deep understanding of the downstream participant(s) in its value chain, as well as knowledge of what is available from its potential suppliers enables the buyer to develop products or services to meet its customers' needs, and further to define initial requirements and specifications for products or services that it will outsource to suppliers. Meanwhile the seller is studying the needs of the potential buyers for its goods and services—starting with a search for and identification of a set of competitors (an industry) with unmet or underserved needs that the seller might be able to meet. When an attractive industry is identified, then the seller begins identifying and assessing individual potential buyers, a process referred to as **prospecting**.

For a salesperson starting out in an established organization, there already exists a customer base and a sales history. The primary focus of this salesperson may be on doing more of the same and doing it better. However, the salesperson in an entrepreneurial context needs to build the sales pipeline and a customer base, which often means displacing established suppliers. The entrepreneurial firm needs to determine how it can differentiate itself from current suppliers or substitutes—in ways that matter to the buyer. To determine which potential customers may have the greatest motivation to consider the offerings of a new entrant into the marketplace, the entrepreneur needs to develop deep understanding of (1) the overall environment in which the industry operates, (2) the characteristics of the industry, and (3) the characteristics of each individual firm competing in that industry.

Understanding the Environmental Context

Entrepreneurs often pursue opportunities in markets that are dynamic rather than settled with well-established customers and suppliers and well-established routines. These markets may be undergoing rapid change as a result of disruptions in the context in which they operate. The disruptions may be precipitated by (1) government action, such as changing regulations in healthcare or fuel efficiency; (2) rapid change or discontinuities in the economy; (3) environmental changes, such as global warming, hurricanes, or earthquakes; (4) geopolitical crises, like war in the Middle East; (5) decrease in availability of basic inputs, such as energy, water, and raw materials; or (6) breakthrough innovations driven by new scientific discoveries, such as the Internet, mapping the human genome, nanotechnologies, stem cell research, and so forth. Entrepreneurs and entrepreneurial salespeople can get buried in the details of startup and survival and lose sight of the forest while focusing on the trees. In order to understand trends and anticipate change, some percentage of total bandwidth needs to be reserved for maintaining a perspective of the big picture.

In addition to understanding the competitive landscape in the salesperson's own industry, it is important to understand the overall context in which customers operate. The process of identifying and assessing the factors and trends in the external context that may drive decision-making by customers (including buying decisions) is called **environmental analysis**. One commonly used framework for environmental analysis—often referred to as PEST—is based on four components of context:

1. **P**olitical and legal factors and trends
2. **E**conomic factors and trends
3. **S**ocial and cultural factors and trends
4. **T**echnological factors and trends

For the salesperson to keep abreast of changes in the customer's environmental context and industry (as discussed in the next section), it is useful to review industry publications, attend trade shows, subscribe to relevant online newsletters, join industry blogs, view security analysts' reports, and build a professional network. For example, if the salesperson's company has developed a new device to track underground water leakage in pipes, it may be useful to read magazines that target engineers or to attend conferences. Given the large potential investment in provincial and municipal infrastructure, the salesperson may want to contact a provincial representative or city councillor to determine what funding may be available to find and repair water leaks in municipal water systems.

Keeping up to date with the customer's environment will enable the salesperson to identify pressure points that may force an industry to change. For example, if a provincial government introduced a law that required university and college campuses to have a certain type of security device installed on dorm rooms to protect students, this new law may force colleges and universities to replace current door-locking systems, which could present a significant selling opportunity for companies who manufacture advanced security technologies.

Understanding the Customer's Industry

Understanding customers requires the salesperson to develop a deep understanding of the industry in which they operate. The industry view is based on gaining insights from analyzing an entire industry. With this different, more comprehensive, and more coherent view of an entire industry, a rich set of insights can be gained. These insights deal with the dynamics of an industry, eventually leading to an understanding of the basic requirements that must be addressed by all competitors. These basic requirements, called *key success factors* (KSFs), are essential building blocks for developing a sophisticated understanding of competitive strategies being adopted within the set of competitors. This understanding of the KSFs is a prerequisite for figuring out the strategy of each target customer and determining the value that the salesperson can create for each customer.

The basic building block of understanding an industry is the macro business system. It includes all industry participants connected in a successive chain of value-adding units, starting from raw materials and moving downstream to original equipment manufacturer (OEM) customers, wholesalers, retailers, and customers or end users. It may also include complementers that are not directly part of the value chain but who are a part of the overall system. In many situations the value chain also includes a recycling stage.

Just as in macroeconomics, where *macro* denotes the study of the behaviour of the economy as a whole, the term **macro business system** applies to an entire industry with all the relevant participants represented in the value-added stream, both upstream and downstream, from the point of view of any particular participant in the value chain. The number of different stages present in a macro business system depends on the prevalent industry structure and the extent to which one finds freestanding activities among independent firms. For any stage in a macro value chain represented by a significant number of independent entities, a separate stage or participant category needs to be considered for analysis.

A standard (and simplified) model of a business system consists of raw material suppliers, manufacturers, distributors, and customers/end users. Although it is helpful to illustrate the concept of the business system in a simple version, reality is such that most industries are more complex and will require the analyst to think more creatively about the value-creating flow. The standard business system view is appropriate for firms supplying components or raw materials that become part of their global account's own products.

Once the salesperson has assembled the necessary data to lay out the industry macro business system for a potential customer, the next step is to extract the key lessons from the analysis. To be successful in consultative selling, a salesperson needs to learn a client's requirements for success in a given industry. The salesperson needs to crack the code of the industry, which contains the key success factors, or basic competitive requirements to succeed. The **industry code** is the behaviour required from a company participating in the value chain (or network) to assure long-term success. The code must be followed to achieve profitability and success. Implied in this language is the understanding that violating the industry code would endanger the profitability of a business.

To be useful, the code needs to contain an industry's *imperatives,* which are a collection of musts, or things a company must do. They are different from mere *core competencies,* which describe what a company does well. Imperatives are important for a company to know, because they must be observed for long-term success. Also included in the industry code are the key success factors, which are the basic competitive requirements that an industry participant needs to master for long-term success. Typically, KSFs describe basic actions, or industry behaviours, that winning companies must master. We categorize KSFs into **qualifiers**, which determine if a participant is able to play in an industry, and **differentiators**, which are KSFs that can set players apart from others. All industry participants need to comply with the qualifiers, but only some players may perform on the basis of differentiators.

For an industry code to be of value, it must answer some important questions that relate to the competitive behaviour in the industry. Following is a list of some typical imperatives that are part of a code, but each industry is likely to have aspects that may be unique. Here are some of the more frequently cited elements of an industry code:

- *Must segments* are segments in which a competitor needs to be present to be a major player. Must segments are important because of their relative size, their above-average profitability, or their growth and technical development. Once must segments have been identified, every leading player should be in those sectors.

- *Minimum amount of market coverage* to reach strategic goals is also a strategic conclusion that comes from understanding the industry code. For example, a company might need to have access to, say, 60% of the total market opportunity to be a leader. It may be able to achieve its strategic objective with less (or possibly more), but it needs to have determined this factor in the industry code.

- *Critical mass,* a frequently cited notion in many industries, can also be of prime importance. Described as the minimum size required to be competitive or successful, critical mass is difficult to assess because the definition is not apparent. Critical mass may occur around a company's entire volume, or it may be more relevant if assessed by segment, country or geographic unit, key function (such as minimum R&D budget), or another part of a company's business. Again, a deep understanding and appreciation of the industry's relevant critical mass comes from the analysis mentioned earlier.

- *Required level of integration* can be important in some industries. The industry code may require different levels of integration for a firm to be successful. *Forward integration* deals with the ownership or control of the downstream part of the industry. *Backward integration* deals with the upstream aspects of ownership or control. Understanding the relevant amount of integration and its impact on industry profitability is an important part of sizing up the industry.

- *Required focus,* or restrictions on selected activities, is an important part of the industry code in most industries. The important job of the analyst is to figure out where firms should focus. Focus dimensions might include integration levels, range of products, range of segments, geographic spread, range of technologies, and so forth.

- *Strategic dilemmas* can be expressed as critical questions that face company senior executives and cause them to lose sleep at night. One of the most frequently asked questions when dealing with global account teams is how a team can develop a deep understanding of the client's strategic dilemmas. Those dilemmas that are already widely recognized, expressed in a company's annual report, or learned by the seller from discussions with the client are not perceived by the client to be as impressive and as valuable as those obtained independently by the entrepreneur/seller. If an account team wants to do more than read up on an industry, uncovering the answers to a few critical questions that reflect strategic dilemmas will help shape a proprietary view of the client's industry.

Reviewing the industry's development and assessing the strategic dilemmas faced by industry participants could contribute to developing a proprietary view of the client's industry and the challenges facing the client. Dilemmas manifest themselves through choices or decisions to be made—determining which forks in the road to take. Dilemmas could be centred on forward or backward integration, segment focus, bundles of segments, mastering of a single technology or multiple technologies, and so on.

Salespeople need to look beyond the firm or individual normally identified as their *customer* to firms that are one or more steps downstream in the business system. A thorough analysis requires moving all the way downstream, sometimes including multiple stages in the business system to include all downstream industry participants. Equally important, a comprehensive perspective of the business system involves a look at any upstream participants of a firm's industry.

Understanding the Client's Strategy

Building on the foundation of deep understanding of the customer's context and industry, the salesperson also needs to develop a deep understanding of each customer's requirements and strategy to better understand how the salesperson's products or services may be able to create value for the customer.

Assessing the company's competitiveness may start with an understanding of its strategic position compared to that of directly competing firms. Common ways of assessing position are determining industry rankings or market share in either unit volume or sales. While being aware of rankings can be useful, it's also important to be cognizant of the fact that a company may not compete in all sectors of a given industry.

An understanding of the customer's industry and competitive landscape may reveal strategic dilemmas the customer faces. Strategic dilemmas are similar to forks in the road: A decision has to be made as to which fork to take, but it is not always clear which one. In any industry, companies face such choices or dilemmas where a decision appears to be required in the form of a choice, but it is not always apparent how to resolve the dilemma.

The entrepreneurial salesperson should look out for major strategic dilemmas confronting players in an industry. The strategic dilemmas will often drive a firm's strategy to win. Working with many firms, we have found that customers place a premium on salespeople who understand their problems and strategic issues. Demonstrating knowledge of a client firm's strategic dilemmas is a proxy for customer orientation or closeness to a client's business. Such perceived closeness builds credibility and opens the door to more business. Beyond providing credibility with the customer, this kind of close relationship also reveals additional opportunities for the salesperson's firm to deliver value to the customer, and hence to develop additional sales opportunities.

One useful framework for assessing a customer's strategy suggests that a company should seek to be the market leader in operational excellence (enabling lowest cost), should strive for product leadership (requiring a commitment to innovation), or should focus on establishing customer intimacy while being at least average in the remaining two disciplines.[8] Understanding the customer's strategy enables the salesperson to customize the offering and deliver it in a way that maximizes value to the customer.

Data Sources for Developing a Deep Understanding of Context, Industry, and Customer

Naturally, good data sources will be of substantial help. For most consultative salespeople, it is essential to engage in a process of gathering and analyzing data that will create a foundation for deep understanding of the overall environment in which the customer operates, the industry in which the customer competes, and the customer's competitive strategy. This may appear to the salesperson to be a somewhat daunting task and a distraction from getting out there and selling. However, the consultative salesperson cannot provide significant and differentiated value to the customer without this understanding. In today's freewheeling and information-rich environment, an amazing amount of data is openly available at no or low cost—readily accessible to the person who makes an effort.

Throughout the previous sections, we have noted potential sources of data and will provide here only a limited list:

- Investor analyst reports, particularly those sections that cover the industry of a target company, not just the company itself
- Publicly available information on industries through daily newspapers, weekly magazines, industry trade journals, other journals accessible through Web-based search engines, and so forth
- Government-issued information, or reports issued by semipublic agencies
- Reports prepared by independent research organizations, which are usually available for a fee
- Trade shows
- General Web-based information, although the user must be careful to confirm its reliability

Data Sources for Developing a Deep Understanding of the Target Client

- Investor analyst reports, particularly those parts that focus on the target client (we suggest using several analysts, not just one, and being sensitive to potential bias)
- Publicly available information on specific competitors within industries—through daily newspapers, weekly magazines, industry trade journals, other journals accessible through Web-based search engines, and so forth
- Target company publications, including annual reports, SEC filings, websites, and press releases

- General Web-based information, although the user must be careful to confirm its reliability
- Communications with the client via email, mail, telephone, or in-person meetings
- The salesperson's customer service department

Developing a Compelling Value Proposition

Delivering superior value is the essence of a successful selling process. The value offered should be superior to competing alternatives and should create a specific, measurable, and favourable result for the customer. Ultimately, the value the customer seeks is improved business performance. Buying a particular product or service is simply the means to that end. The customer recognizes the current, unsatisfactory state and envisions a future, more satisfactory state. The purchase of the seller's product or service creates value by enabling the customer to move from the current state to the future state.[9] An in-depth understanding of the customer's needs will enhance the potential for discovering and delivering superior value, compared with that achieved by current or other potential suppliers.

A benchmark study of 58 firms determined that clients are willing to pay for four broad categories of value: technology, processes, administrative services that reduce costs, and sales and marketing support.[10] The examples that follow are of established brand-name companies (most often the subjects of business cases), but the principles are equally applicable to entrepreneurial ventures, particularly because they often have to compete against established incumbent suppliers.

Customers highly value technology that is core to their business results but not within their capabilities to produce. For example, Occidental Chemical has developed a portfolio of high-technology, value-added services such as technical support, logistics, product management, and research and development that their customers highly value.

Customers value processes that improve productivity by improving quality, reducing overhead, and producing measurable savings. For example, Marriott has developed a process to train travel agents on their bookings, product knowledge, service knowledge, and consultative skills, which better serves the customers who in turn may opt to stay at a Marriott property. This process improves the individual travel agent's productivity as well as the entire agency's profitability.

Customers value administrative services that reduce costs and improve profit. For example, Boise Cascade Office Products developed an information system that allows customers to review pricing, delivery, service, and remedial action independently at any time.

Sales and marketing support that leads to increased sales is also valued by customers. For example, ACDelco has an advertising campaign that supports a strong brand, which, combined with other retail support boosts sales growth for its customers.

Another useful framework for creating a value proposition is embodied in the concept of a **resulting experience** for the buyer—the events that the customer experiences as a result of using and interacting with the supplying firm's products, services, and actions.[11] A *resulting experience* is

- An event or sequence of events, physical or emotional, that happens in the customer's life because of doing what some supplier business proposes
- The end-result consequence of this event for the customer
- An experience that is superior, equal, or inferior in comparison to a customer's alternative experience

- ◉ The value for the customer of this relative consequence
- ◉ Specific and measurable—one can objectively determine if the customer experienced the events, consequences, and value compared to alternatives

In developing the **value proposition**, it is helpful to have complete understanding of the level of problems the customer is facing and the potential for a superior resulting experience that addresses one or more of those problems. Delivering the value proposition to a customer is a dynamic and continually changing endeavour. For the nature of the relationship between buyer and supplier to change from one focusing on transactions to one that focuses on a strategic relationship, the original value proposition must change—and in fact shift toward creating significantly more value that contributes to the customer's success in ways that can be measured by the customer. Any change in the value proposition will also change its delivery.

The successful delivery of a value proposition is rooted in the supplier company's ability to constantly communicate the value it is creating for the client company and to engage the client company in providing feedback. Effective communication enables a forum in which both companies can improve the value proposition. The value proposition delivery system starts with the strategy of both the supplying company and the client company. The value proposition should include a time frame (for both implementation and delivery), the intended customer (a specific group within the client company or the client's customers), customer alternatives, and the intended resulting experience the client company should receive as a result of the supplier's offering.

Delivery of the value proposition requires putting the understanding of the process of developing the value proposition into action. Delivering the value proposition means turning the abstract concepts behind the value proposition into tangible products, services, and most importantly relationships that are mutually profitable in the long term. Providing a product or a service is the most obvious way the supplier delivers on the value proposition, which starts with engaging with the customer in the buying process, closing on the purchase, and supporting the customer's use of the product or service as a vehicle to achieve an intended business result. The product/service vehicle is tailored to meet the unique intended needs of the client company. Since successful selling is as much about relationships as it is about products and services, the value proposition needs to recognize this, thus making it a product/service/relationship vehicle.

Communication is the means through which a client company understands the value proposition and, if it is superior to competitive offerings, accepts and adopts it. Communications can take the form of advertising, presentations, packaging, or newsletters, but the most compelling communication is carried out through the direct salesperson–buyer relationship. The salesperson should be continuously communicating the value proposition to the client company. The 3M case study in the accompanying box illustrates the process of delivering the value proposition.[12]

3M

A 3M salesperson was assigned to manage the relationship with the IBM Storage business unit, which produces giant magnetic resistive heads (GMR heads) for computer hard drives. After a number of months of interviewing, listening, and planning, the salesperson began to understand how IBM Storage fit into IBM's overall marketing strategy and observed some of the challenges IBM faced in manufacturing GMR heads. Through meetings with IBM's operations and R&D staff, the salesperson learned that one of IBM Storage's major business problems was a manufacturing process that was extremely sensitive to electrostatic discharge (ESD), which causes product loss and increased costs. Knowing that 3M had proprietary technology that could help address IBM Storage's ESD problem, the salesperson worked with his technical group and IBM to solve the problem. Through these efforts, 3M significantly reduced IBM Storage's GMR product loss, which translated into an annual savings of several million dollars for IBM. Because of that success, whenever IBM Storage had a problem, it sought out 3M's salesperson to see if 3M's resources could help. 3M found itself modifying some of its existing products or combining existing technologies to create new products to support IBM's needs.

The process of understanding a customer's environment, industry, and strategy to win in that industry is complex and demanding. However, done well, it provides a foundation for determining how to create value for a customer, which a salesperson must then convert into a compelling value proposition, and finally communicate and deliver to the customer.

Pursuing Sales Opportunities[13]

In the previous sections we discussed how the salesperson can go about building a deep understanding of the environment, the industry, and the target customer(s) and with that understanding can proceed to develop a compelling value proposition. Clearly that understanding and that value proposition can and should be modified and improved based on interactions with the customer. A complement to this process is prospecting for potential clients whose needs profiles align well with the seller's value proposition.

One of the objectives of developing deep understanding of the salesperson's customer is determining who can and will be involved in the buying process—including gatekeepers, decision influencers, decision approvers, and decision makers. The value proposition may very well be different for the different categories and levels of players in the buying process and will likely need to be customized to create maximum value for each player. For example, a design engineer may be most concerned about the match between the features of a component product and the overall design of an assembly or system. A manufacturing manager charged with integrating the component into an assembly may be concerned about ease of installation, training requirements, ability to use existing production equipment, and time of delivery. The vice-president of operations may be interested in the impact of the integration of the new component on manufacturing cycle time, process yields, and reliability of supply. The CFO may be concerned about the impact on profitability. In addition to profitability, the CEO may want to hear about how the new component will enable product or process innovation that will differentiate the company's products from competitors or even enable a new line of business. Whether the salesperson starts with a gatekeeper, a senior decision maker, or anywhere in between, the focus needs to be on the value that matters to that individual.

Cold Calls versus Warm Calls

At some point, the salesperson needs to initiate first contact. Generally, a **cold call**—reaching out via phone or e-mail to a customer contact with whom the salesperson has no prior relationship and no reference to a trusted intermediary—is the least effective method of getting an appointment. Hence, it is typically worth the investment of time and energy to try to identify an individual within the company with whom the salesperson has some connection and who might be willing to serve as an advocate (or at least as a facilitator), increasing the probability that the salesperson will get an audience with a decision maker. Alternatively, the salesperson might reach out to an individual outside the target company who has a potentially useful contact within the target company and who would be willing to serve as an intermediary. Networking and relationship building are an important part of the salesperson's skill set—perhaps even more so in the entrepreneurship context, as the entrepreneur often has little or no track record to stand on. Hence, tapping trust relationships derived from prior experience can be critical for success in making initial sales calls and sales.

In some cases, there is no way for the seller to create a warm call and hence he must resort to a cold call. That often starts with a **gatekeeper**—an individual who stands between the seller and the person with whom the seller would like an appointment—who may be an administrative assistant, an appointments secretary, or a lower-level employee. The professional consultative salesperson treats gatekeepers with professionalism, courtesy, and respect, as they can choose to open doors—or not.

In order to create value for the customer via consultative selling (i.e., serving as a buying consultant), the seller needs to establish a relationship with one or more individuals in the company who are gatekeepers, decision influencers, and decision makers. Generally this is best done person-to-person, although telephone dialogue is often an important part of the communications process, and in some cases is the primary or only medium of communication. Email can support the process, but generally will not create sufficient impact by itself for consultative selling.

Precall Planning

Preparation is a major determinant of sales success. Understanding the context and industry of your customer, as well as the value chain and the customer's strategy to be successful in that environment, establishes the foundation upon which the salesperson and his product or service can create value for the customer. It is also important to research the person the salesperson will be meeting with. Where did the individual go to school? Where was the individual previously employed? What was the individual's hometown? To what organizations do they belong? And what other special interests does the individual have? This research on the person's background can reveal common interests and experiences, and hence can support a natural human-to-human conversation that can start to build common ground and a mutually beneficial relationship.

Before initiating contact, the salesperson should develop a precall planning list, which should include some or all of the following:

- A written sales call objective
- A list of needs analysis questions to ask
- Something tangible to show—a prototype, a chart, a picture of the product or service in use by others
- A list of benefits that could be important to customers. An analysis of the customer's investment return—in other words, quantification of the financial benefits of the benefits of the product or service
- An analysis of points of difference vis-à-vis competitors
- A list of typical or likely concerns and objections that the customer might raise
- Strategies for handling/resolving each potential objection or concern
- Description of possible alternative scenarios for reaching agreement on a sale (closing strategies)
- A list of individuals with whom the salesperson will try to connect, including an assessment of whether each individual is a gatekeeper, influencer, decision approver, or decision maker

Before initiating contact, the salesperson should conduct one or more trial-run practice sessions with a colleague, which will help the salesperson focus on sales call objectives, develop the discipline to use the contact's time wisely, and inspire some alternative approaches for the initial interaction.

Facilitating the Buying Process by Establishing Common Ground

When initial contact is made, the salesperson should engage first in trying to develop a relationship. This practice is called **establishing common ground**. It signals that the salesperson is genuinely interested in the buyer as a human being, rather than just a vehicle through which a transaction is to be made. It doesn't have to take a lot of time, but it gets a conversation started. Generally, finding common ground starts with asking open questions, active listening, and observation—three of the most important skills of a successful salesperson.

In the best-case scenario, the open questions can be derived from the seller's due diligence about the company and the individual being contacted, and hence reflect the seller's understanding of what is personally or professionally important to the buyer. For example, if the buyer is a sports fan, the seller might ask about a local sports team. If the buyer and seller graduated from the same university, the seller might ask about the buyer's perspective on something going on at their shared alma mater. If the seller has been referred to the buyer by a mutual acquaintance, the seller might ask about the history of the buyer's relationship with that individual. If the buyer is engaged in a major new initiative at the company that has received press coverage, the seller might make mention of the story and ask about the progress of the initiative. If the salesperson notices a Six Sigma award plaque or a picture of the buyer at a groundbreaking ceremony, the salesperson might ask questions about them, which in turn may reveal additional insights into the buyer. From the seller's perspective, the exchange should result in a sense of sharing related to something of mutual importance.

Seeking an Exchange of Value

If the seller has done a thorough job of precall due diligence and preparation, it may be possible for the seller to explain to the customer why the seller's product or service is a perfect fit with the needs of the buyer. However, it is much more useful to engage the customer in a discussion of the customer's needs. This approach not only serves to confirm (or adjust) the findings from the seller's due diligence efforts, which are seldom 100% on target, but it also demonstrates to the buyer that the seller values and wants to hear the buyer's perspective.

With this input from the buyer, the seller can begin to explore the extent to which the seller's product or service is actually a good fit with the customer's needs. If there appears to be a good fit, then the outcome of the initial interaction is a shared understanding that the buyer may be able to gain value through the seller's offerings and the seller may be able to gain value through the revenue received, connections to future business, and even connections to other business with other potential customers in the buyer's network. However far the initial conversation progresses, if there appears to be a valid reason to continue the dialogue, the seller should establish the next step. Of course, if it becomes clear that there is not a good fit between the seller's offering and the customer's need, then the seller should acknowledge that and offer information or advice that could help the customer identify an alternative supplier. In addition, the seller should ask for referrals to others in the buyer's network who might value the seller's offering and also for the opportunity to re-engage at some point in the future.

Handling Rejection

No matter how prepared the seller is or how on target is the seller's value proposition is, buyers will have reservations or concerns, which are referred to as **objections**. It is common for new salespeople to view objections as a form of rejection. In fact, as the buyer raises concerns, it shows that he or she is thinking about purchasing the salesperson's product or service and has identified areas of concern where the product or service may not align properly with customer needs. Recognizing and understanding these misalignments gives the salesperson an opportunity to better understand the customer's needs and address their concerns and issues.

There are many possible reasons for the buyer to raise concerns. Maybe there is insufficient motivation for the buyer to consider switching suppliers. Perhaps the buyer is consumed with other more important priorities. Maybe the buyer is just having a bad day—for personal or professional reasons. Although it's possible that there is a personality clash between seller and buyer, usually the rejection by the buyer is not a rejection of the seller, but rather of the seller's offering or request for a meeting. Sometimes the rejection only applies to the present and not to the long term.

The seller should handle the rejection professionally and gracefully and solicit feedback from the buyer regarding the reasons for the rejection. This can provide useful input for determining whether future contact might be welcome and useful, and if so, how the salesperson can be more on target next time. If the seller determines that the probability of fit and a future sale is low, the salesperson should consider this a positive outcome, as it has become clear early in the process that investing additional time and resources in pursuing the sale with this particular buyer has a low probability of providing a good return on investment.

The seller should look at every rejection as an opportunity for continuing education and analyze each rejection for what it can teach about the seller's offering, the marketplace, customer needs, and about the sales approach. In this way, every rejection helps the seller fine tune his or her sales skills and increases the probability of future success.

As mentioned earlier, it is possible that there is a personality clash—or incompatibility of styles—between buyer and seller. Sellers can't change who they are, but skillful sellers are able to assess the buyer's style and adapt their own style appropriately. This can be another sign of respect and professional accommodation that the seller shows the buyer, an appropriate method for establishing a more productive interaction, and a way to ensure that the focus of the interaction can be on the potential for mutual value exchange rather than on the nature of the interaction. Naturally the style may adjust as the relationship between buyer and seller matures over time. If the seller can't sufficiently adapt to the buyer's style and tension remains, it is appropriate to transfer the account to another seller.

Dealing with Objections

An inexperienced or incompetent salesperson fears objections, seeing them as the buyer's rejection of the offering or, worse yet, of the salesperson. No one who is offering something to another likes to hear the word *no*. However, the experienced and competent salesperson recognizes no as a signal, either that it's time to move on and avoid investing additional time and effort in a process that is unlikely to yield the desired outcome—a win-win for both buyer and seller—or that the buyer still has issues that must be resolved before the no becomes a yes. It is common sense generally in sales that the person who gets the most noes also gets the most yeses. Therefore, the competent salesperson welcomes objections. Objections indicate that the customer is considering purchasing from the seller but is not yet ready to reach agreement. Objections reveal what must be resolved before the buyer and seller can close the sale.

An experienced salesperson has engaged in the buying process with many buyers and, chances are, has already heard most or all possible objections. For example, prospective buyers might object to the seller's offering because of its cost, quality, some particular performance feature, the product warranty, the service plan, time lag for delivery, or simply because they are satisfied with their current vendor relationships. The competent salesperson has already worked through typical objections with multiple buyers and has developed alternative approaches to resolving them. In fact, an important asset for the consultative salesperson seeking to serve the buyer as a buying consultant is the experience with other buyers in resolving objections, challenges, problems, and issues that are getting in the way of coming to closure.

The salesperson should be proactive in uncovering objections, as objections can't be resolved until they are identified. However, the salesperson may end up wasting time in addressing objections that are actually smokescreens. It is important to identify real objections—all of them—before investing time and energy in finding solutions. This requires skill in asking probing questions and carefully listening to the buyer's responses. To draw out a buyer's real objections, the salesperson should ask open questions to probe around the edges of a buyer's initial objection and listen attentively, taking notes where helpful. By asking the buyer how the seller can be helpful in resolving the objection, the seller may be handed the best solution.

The skillful, professional consultative salesperson wants the buyer to make the right decision and to succeed. If the consultative salesperson has helped the buyer navigate through the buying process, if all issues and objections have been resolved, and if it's clear that the salesperson's product is the best option for the buyer, then there should be no doubt, uncertainty, or sense of pressure. Instead, the buyer should feel relieved that the decision is clear and feel ready to reach agreement with the salesperson. At this point, it should be easy and comfortable for the salesperson to ask the final closing question—final because it should produce the response from the buyer, "Yes, I'm ready to move ahead with the purchase order."

Structuring the purchase correctly is important for building a long-term relationship. Since the seller may have worked through purchase agreements with multiple buyers, the seller may have a higher level of sophistication than the buyer regarding the variables and the pluses and minuses of various purchase options. Hence the seller should protect the buyer by making sure the purchase is structured in a way that protects the buyer's interests. This is the best approach to building and sustaining trust, which in turn establishes the foundation for future orders and a positive long-term relationship.

As long as the seller is convinced that the buyer is best served by purchasing the seller's product or service, then the appropriate approach by the seller is to be professionally persistent (not *pushy,* but professionally persistent). The seller should approach the end of the buying process—the close—in a spirit of partnership with the buyer, moving forward with confidence and a positive attitude, and assuming that the sale is going to take place. This approach reassures the buyer that it is appropriate to continue moving forward through the buying process to determine whether the purchase makes sense.

In selling in the entrepreneurial context, the offer may be technologically advanced and the buyer may be less knowledgeable than the seller, less confident about executing the buying process effectively, and concerned about making mistakes in the buying process and making the wrong buying decision, and hence being subject to criticism by a superior or even termination for poor performance. The job of the consultative salesperson (buying consultant) is to use professional skills, knowledge, and attitudes to help the buyer through the buying process to the optimal outcome.

Follow-Through and Customer Service

The inexperienced and incompetent salesperson thinks the job is done when the purchase order is signed—failing to remember a cardinal rule of sales: The easiest sale is a repeat sale to a satisfied customer. The skillful and professional consultative salesperson knows that investing time and energy in ensuring follow-through and attentive customer service will generate a highly attractive return on investment, because customer service and support help lay the groundwork for future sales.

Follow-through starts with making sure that the customer receives the product or service in a timely manner, and that the billing is done appropriately. Likewise, if the seller's firm has agreed to provide training or assistance with installation, the salesperson follows up to make sure those services are provided to the satisfaction of the buyer. Naturally, the salesperson needs to be responsive to buyer contacts—answering questions, taking care of requests, and handling issues before they become problems. In addition, periodically the salesperson should follow up with the buyer to ensure continuing satisfaction with the product or service, doing this with the frequency established by the preference of the customer. The salesperson should keep a log of customer service calls as part of tracking and managing the account. With this level of professional attention, the salesperson is also in a good position to stay abreast of needs for additional products and services; to be aware of changing customer needs; to meet new employees in the buyer's company who may be gatekeepers, influencers, and decision makers for future buying processes; to participate in shaping the specifications and timing of future purchase orders; and to ask for references to others in the buyer's network who might value what the seller has to offer.

Typically, others from the seller's company will be involved in providing customer service—trainers, installers, service technicians, the billing department, and so forth. Hence the salesperson needs to be a team player within his or her own company to service accounts successfully, and therefore needs to work diligently to build cordial, professional relationships with the other people in the company who provide sales support.

In some cases the salesperson's product or service will be incorporated into a more comprehensive product or service, which the buyer's firm then sells to another customer downstream in the value chain. The salesperson should be prepared to help the buyer *sell through* to the buyer's customer and to support that sale as well.

Occasionally the salesperson may be caught between the buyer and his or her own customer support network. Perhaps the buyer is being unreasonable in seeking support that goes beyond the purchase contract, or perhaps the buyer has failed to properly install, use, or maintain the seller's product, resulting in a performance problem, and the buyer may attempt to transfer responsibility for dealing with the problem back to the seller's customer support personnel. The salesperson should confront the situation diplomatically and professionally—in a manner that fits the operating style of the client, seeking a mutually satisfactory solution, and thereby enhancing the long-term relationship with the customer.

Sometimes—regardless of whether buyer or seller has responsibility for resolving an issue with the seller's product or service—the salesperson is confronted by an angry customer. Skill in negotiating is a valuable asset for the salesperson in this situation. Rather than being defensive or argumentative, the salesperson should patiently allow the customer to vent the anger and frustration, confirm the complaint and what the customer would like to see happen to resolve the issue, determine what the seller's firm can do to help, communicate that clearly to the customer, and then execute the commitment to resolve the complaint. In reality, effectively dealing with client complaints is an opportunity to build trust, confidence, and customer loyalty.

Developing Sales Skills

It's not enough to have comprehensive knowledge about the selling and buying processes—the salesperson also needs skill that only comes with practice and experience. Naturally there are skills associated with each element of the selling/buying process. Preparing for the sales relationship requires skill in data gathering and analysis to develop a deep understanding of the environmental context, the industry, the strategy of each competitor within a target industry, and the individuals within each target company who may play a role in the buying process. In addition, building a pipeline starts with developing a list of attractive potential targets (in sales parlance, *generating sales leads*). Networking can be a particularly important skill for engaging in this activity. Throughout the segments of the sales process—identified earlier as making sales calls, handling objections, and closing—asking questions and listening are critically important, as are negotiations, creative problem solving, and presentation skills. Throughout the entire engagement with a potential customer, process management, time management, and information management are also important skills.

The value of being skillful at asking questions and listening effectively is often unrecognized or underestimated. Too often salespeople believe that the key is successful presentation of the features and benefits of the product or service. Note that the focus here is on the seller, not on the buyer. There is no doubt that the salesperson has to be prepared to present a compelling value proposition, but it is much easier to do so if the seller first fully understands the buyer's objectives and buying process, and is thereby able to align the value proposition and the selling process to the buyer's objectives and buying process, respectively. Being skillful at asking questions and listening requires that the seller totally owns the knowledge about the buyer and about the seller's offering. That permits the seller to focus on the buyer—with the confidence that the right words (information) will flow out of the seller's mouth at the right time without much thinking on the part of the salesperson. This provides the freedom and the mental bandwidth for the salesperson to do the following:

- Absorb fully what the buyer is communicating—verbally and nonverbally
- Truly hear those messages with all their complexities and subtleties
- Acknowledge those messages, thus affirming the buyer
- Confirm and enhance the seller's understanding of the buyer's needs and objectives
- Explore and document the buying process, including influencers, approvers, and decision makers
- Uncover all the buyer's issues, concerns, and objections that must be addressed
- Offer appropriate responses and follow-up questions to encourage and sustain continuing communication from the buyer
- When appropriate, provide information that addresses the buyer's information needs
- Keep the engagement going forward to closure or until it's clear that the process should be terminated

Highly competent and professional salespeople are able—relatively quickly and easily—to establish trust with the buyer and a shared commitment to achieving a mutually beneficial outcome from the buying process. In a sense, they develop a resonance with their buyers and become partners in achieving a win-win. Naturally, this resonance, a constructive working relationship, and these positive results are easier to achieve with highly competent, professional, and experienced buyers—and may be difficult or even impossible to achieve with inexperienced, distrustful, unskillful, incompetent buyers who lack confidence. Of course, competent and professional salespeople will avoid buyers with whom they have a low probability of establishing a constructive relationship.

How does the salesperson develop these skills? Learning about them and practising them in training programs (whether internally sponsored or provided by an external sales training organization) are important first steps, but it's also important to continue refreshing those skills through periodic retraining. Training programs are important, but on-the-job training is the only way to fully develop the skill set of a highly competent salesperson.

Many people entering sales never achieve competence in selling skills because they have too little success in the early stages of their developmental process; they become discouraged, and they quit before they become skillful—and successful. Hence, in the early going it makes sense for the novice salesperson to ask for support and guidance from sales managers or veteran salespeople to get through the challenging and often frustrating awkward front end of the developmental process. In addition, selecting initial target customers who may be tolerant of a novice salesperson is a good strategy. If the novice salesperson is direct, honest, and focused on helping the buyer (rather than making the sale), it may even be possible to engage buyers as developmental partners.

The good news is that it doesn't take too much experience to become relatively competent and professional, even if a high level of competence and peak performance requires significantly more time and experience.

CONCLUSION

Above all else, consultative selling maximizes the opportunity for buyer and seller to create value for each other and for others in the business ecosystem in which they participate. The highly effective consultative salesperson will likely know as much or more about the customer's environmental context, industry, and competitive strategy as does the customer. Through superior understanding and skill, the consultative salesperson will create and deliver a superior value proposition and product/service/relationship offering. For the entrepreneurial venture, this approach will provide the best opportunity to displace established incumbent suppliers and competing new entrants. Through an effective partnering relationship with the customer as the customer's buying consultant, the entrepreneur can overcome the liability of newness and capture the early adopters, thereby building a foundation for survival, growth, and success.

WEB EXERCISE

Identify three companies that have experienced successful, rapid growth and highlight their product offering in detail. What is the product's value proposition and how does it differ from other products on the market? What customer segment should each product/company target? How would you highlight the value proposition of each product to a potential customer (i.e., what is your pitch)?

YOUR OPPORTUNITY JOURNAL

Reflection Point	Your Thoughts. . .
1. Talk with someone who has excelled at sales. Ask them what skills they think have helped them succeed.	
2. What skills do you possess that would facilitate sales? What skills do you lack that you need to be a good salesperson?	
3. Create a customer persona for your potential customers. What do they look like? What needs do all your customers have in common? What channel could you use to reach your customers?	
4. What questions could you ask your potential customers to begin the sales process?	
5. Create a sales pitch and supporting slide presentation deck.	

CASE	**Susan Niczowski—A Fresh Take on Selling**

Susan Niczowski's love of fresh food began early. "My father tells a story about me picking green tomatoes from our garden when I was four years old and then barbecuing them," said the entrepreneur. "I always had some sort of concoction going on. I love creating and tasting food."[15]

A couple of decades after her barbecued green tomatoes, Niczowski had been experimenting in her parents' kitchen long enough to have developed a couple dozen recipes for salads, appetizers, and dips that she thought could be marketable. In the early 1990s, Canadian consumers didn't have much choice in the grocery store when it came to buying freshly prepared foods. The health kick was just getting into swing, and Niczowski spotted a hole in the market. "I thought there was a need in the marketplace for fresh prepared foods—things that you would find in a white-tablecloth restaurant," she said.[16]

Summer Fresh Salads Inc. now has over 100 full-time employees working in a 63,000-square-foot facility in Vaughan, Ontario.[17] Sales range from $50 to $100 million a year.

The "Salad Days"

In 1991, Niczowski decided to quit her job as a microbiologist at Maple Leaf Foods and launch Summer Fresh. She managed to get a $100,000 bank loan, but only because her mother co-signed. Her father turned her down, not because he didn't believe in her and her idea, but because he wanted to teach her that success doesn't come easily. It's something every entrepreneur learns quickly, and Niczowski was no exception.

Niczowski recalls trying to get financing. "I was young and naive. When the account manager at the bank asked how much collateral I had, I said: 'Collateral? I don't have any collateral.' Everything I'd made up to that time went to shoes, purses, and jewellery."[18]

Niczowski had to "sell" her idea to her family, then to lenders, suppliers, and customers. At first, she sold directly to delicatessens, recognizing that it was more cost efficient for her to make products in larger batches than for the deli owners to make salads themselves or hire chefs to do it. It wasn't a hard sell to her first customers.

Even with a sizable loan, Niczowski started out small, working with her mother chopping ingredients in her parents' kitchen. As the orders piled in, she soon moved to a 3,000-square-foot facility.

While Niczowski's father wouldn't co-sign her initial loan, he's been supportive and active in the business in other ways, as have other family members. Her sister is the vice-president of operations, her mother is involved in processing, and her dad, a retired mechanical engineer, consults on design and workflow issues.

"Food Is Fashion"

Like any business, Summer Fresh has had its share of ups and downs with sales cycles. Its customers are mainly grocery stores, delis, big-box department stores, and restaurants. During a particularly strong growth period, one of the company's biggest customers announced it wouldn't be carrying its products anymore in six months. "If you've got $1 million in sales and you lose 10 per cent of your sales in six months, you're shocked. So you've got to be extremely creative and make up those sales pretty fast," Niczowski said.[19] She keeps a close eye on the environmental context, noting economic cycles and changing customer tastes.

One strategy Summer Fresh has used in an effort to boost sales was by promoting its products as affordable luxuries during the 2008–2009 recession. "People will not be eating out as much, so instead of spending $50 in a restaurant, you're going to treat yourself to that $3.50 dip or tub of salad, so it really is a treat," she said.[20]

But Summer Fresh's key selling strategy is to constantly innovate, just like in the fashion industry. Summer Fresh has actually trademarked the tag line, "Food is fashion." "Trends come and go in food, as they do in fashion. We have to understand that and cater to the constantly changing market," Niczowski said.[21] "The fashionistas have their runway of clothes each season, and we create excitement in the deli."[22]

Summer Fresh has branched out beyond its initial offering of salads and dips with fresh soups and main courses like seafood pasta and even desserts. The recent popularity of kale, for example, showed up in a kale dip. The company works with key customers, like the Metro grocery chain (formerly A&P Canada), to develop new products. Summer Fresh became the private-label maker of fresh salads and soups under Metro's Fresh 2 Go brand. "They continually come to us with new products and concepts, and they are continually refreshing their product with new labels or new recipes," said former A&P spokesperson Tammy Smitham.[23]

Niczowski warns entrepreneurs from being too trendy, urging them to develop and solidify a reputation with reliable, key products. "Maintain your core products while innovating," Niczowski said. "Customers will be more willing to try new products if they believe in your reputation."[24]

Market research is key to innovation, and Summer Fresh does its homework, investigating what various demographics want and need. Niczowski visits grocery stores and restaurants while on holiday to scope out the competition and see what food manufacturers are doing in other regions and countries. "You've really got to know your stuff in terms of your market and whether you're making the next salad or dip that's out there."[25]

Among the company's innovations was a line of SpongeBob SquarePants and Dora the Explorer kids' lunch and snack items licensed from Nickelodeon. "When we took a look at the children's snack food market, we realized there wasn't anything out there that was healthy and appealing to children," said Niczowski. "After extensive market research and countless taste tests, we discovered the most popular flavours and paired that with mini flatbread crackers, perfect for little hands."[26] A few years later, the company realized that adults like packaged fresh lunches, too, and it launched "quadrant" packages with four items—dip, salad, trail mix, and flatbread crackers—that fit inside a briefcase or gym bag.[27]

Summer Fresh's ability to roll with trends gets a thumbs up from marketing experts. "Their 'Food is fashion' strategy—constant innovation, chef-inspired flavours, and discovery-type merchandising—aligns well with the psyche of their core consumer," said Jill Nykoliation of Toronto-based marketing agency Juniper Park.[28]

And just like fashion, not all food trends catch on. Niczowski had no trouble selling retailers on her low-fat gelatin in fruit-shaped moulds. But shoppers weren't convinced. "We had to pull it off the market in six months," she said. "I think it was too far ahead of its time."[29]

While Summer Fresh does not sell directly to consumers, it does reach out to them to help with product innovation. The company lets consumers contact its chefs with feedback and questions, which has helped shape things like packaging.[30] Summer Fresh's own employees provide a handy focus group of consumers to test new recipes and give input on taste, look, and packaging.[31] The company now has thousands of recipes that it can bring back or refresh depending on the seasons and customer tastes and trends.

While many of its products have been gluten free and lactose free from the beginning, Summer Fresh is also doing more to promote this fact as awareness of food allergies grows.[32]

Even the company's manufacturing facility is a sales opportunity, as guests taking a tour get tempted by the smells of roasting vegetables and other fresh ingredients.[33]

Niczowski, as Summer Fresh president, continues to be the company's public spokesperson, making TV and Internet appearances about food and cooking.

Making Sales Calls

When Niczowski launched Summer Fresh, she was (and still is) the chief salesperson—a best practice for any entrepreneur because they are the most passionate person to sell the business and the vision. But it wasn't always easy for her. When she showed up at trade shows, customers would often ask to speak to her boss. She said that still happens a bit today, so she has a way around that. "I [now] make sure that I have a male sales rep beside me. If they want to think that he's the boss, then that's fine," Niczowski said. "We sell to anybody who pays the bills."[34]

Niczowski expresses a sentiment felt by many female entrepreneurs who make sales calls. "People tend to assume that building a family is our primary need, and that our businesses are just a complement. We are not seen as being as career oriented as men," Niczowski said. "I've had to prove time and again that I can be as motivated as a man. It's taught me to work harder and show results year after year."[35]

One benefit of making sales calls is that the feedback she gets directly from customers is invaluable when she goes back to the factory and works with her research and development department, which includes executive chefs, to tweak existing products and develop new ones.

Future Growth

About 80% of Summer Fresh's sales are in Canada and the other 20% are in the United States. While many Canadian manufacturers are exporting their products outside of North America, that's not possible for Summer Fresh, because it can't easily ship refrigerated food overseas.[36] So the company is focusing its growth in North America, particularly south of the border. "There's a huge opportunity for us in the U.S.," Niczowski said.[37]

Niczowski has succeeded not only in a tough industry, but as a small startup in manufacturing. Her determination has won her and Summer Fresh many accolades, including one of the W100 top women entrepreneurs as named by *Chatelaine* and *Profit* magazines, one of Canada's 50 Best Managed Companies by Deloitte, a Star Women in Grocery award from *Canadian Grocer* magazine, one of the 100 Canada's Most Powerful Women Summit from the Women's Executive Network, and a winner of the RBC Canadian Women Entrepreneur Awards.[38]

Selling becomes easier with passion, Niczowski said. "To create a company starting with zero sales and take it to the next level, you've got to be living and breathing it all the time. You have to be extremely passionate about it."[39]

Discussion Questions

1. Among the demographic markets that Susan Niczowski and Summer Fresh identified for new products are children and busy adults. What other types of consumers could Summer Fresh innovate products for?

2. In doing an environmental analysis to assess the competitive landscape for freshly prepared food, Summer Fresh has considered some of the components of the PEST framework. Which ones are they? Which other factors could Niczowski consider and exploit, and how?

3. What do you think Niczowski likely does to demonstrate her products' value proposition to potential customers?

4. Niczowski says that the food industry is similar to the fashion industry, particular in how the industry adapts to trends. If you were an entrepreneur in the fashion industry, what actions might you undertake to better understand your customers' needs and wants?

NOTES

1 J. Schneider and J. Hall, "Why Most Product Launches Fail," *Harvard Business Review,* April 2011, http://hbr.org/2011/04/why-most-product-launches-fail/ar/1.

2 W. Deutsch and C. Wortmann, "Entrepreneurial Selling," www.entrepreneurship.org/~/media/Entrepreneurship/FoundersSchool/PDF/Entrepreneurial%20Selling/EshipSelling_SubTop1_Readings_EntrepreneurialSellingArticle.pdf

3 Ibid.

4 S. G. Blank and B. Dorf, *The Startup Owner's Manual: The Step-by-Step Guide for Building a Great Company* (Pescadero, CA: K&S Ranch, 2012).

5 Ibid.

6 Ibid.

7 The model for the selling process is drawn from *Inc.* magazine's *Real Selling* (1992 videotape series). The videotapes have been used by the authors for the past six years in their course entitled "Business Development through Professional Selling."

8 M. Treacy and F. Wiersema, *The Discipline of Market Leaders* (New York, NY: Perseus Books Group, 1997).

9 B. Stinnett, *Selling Results! The Innovative System for Maximizing Sales by Helping Your Customers Achieve Their Business Goals* (New York, NY: McGraw-Hill Companies, 2006).

10 National Account Management Association (NAMA), *NAM/GAM Benchmark Consortium: National Account Benchmarking* (Chicago, IL: National Account Management Association and HR Chally Group Consortium, 1997).

11 M. J. Lanning, *Delivering Profitable Value* (New York, NY: Perseus Books, 2000).

12 J. P. Sperry, "Giant Companies, Small Details: 3M and IBM Co-creating Value at All Levels," *Velocity* (2000): 16–17.

13 *Inc.* magazine, *Real Selling* videotape series (*Inc.*, 1992). The lessons offered in these videotapes and the teaching materials developed to complement them are the primary source for this section.

14 J. J. Fox, *How to Become a Rainmaker* (New York, NY: St. Martin's Press, 2001).

15 Diane Jermyn, "'Early Crazy Hours' Paid Off for Summer Fresh," The Globe and Mail, August 23, 2012.

16 "Susan Niczowski—Salads Industry Can Make Millions," http://youngandmillionaire.blogspot.ca, November 17, 2007.

17 Summer Fresh corporate website, www. summerfresh.com.

18 Jermyn, "'Early Crazy Hours.'"

19 Ibid.

20 Carey Toane, "Food/Grocery," Strategy, March 1, 2009.

21 "Summer Fresh Salads Announces 4th Consecutive Year as One of Canada's 50 Best Managed Companies," news release, March 2009.

22 "Susan Niczowski—Salads Industry Can Make Millions."

23 "Ibid.

24 Deborah Aarts, "These Are the Women Who Really Mean Business," Profit, September 18, 2014.

25 Jermyn, "'Early Crazy Hours.'"

26 "Summer Fresh Announces an Exciting New Partnership with Nickelodeon," news release, May 2009.

27 "Summer Fresh Launches Fresh, Delicious & Convenient Meal to Go," news release, September 2010.

28 Toane, "Food/Grocery."

29 "Susan Niczowski—Salads Industry Can Make Millions."

30 Toane, "Food/Grocery."

31 "Summer Fresh Salads Announces 4th Consecutive Year as One of Canada's 50 Best Managed Companies."

32 Summer Fresh corporate website, www. summerfresh.com.

33 "Summer Fresh—Healthy, Delicious & Ready Made Food that Doesn't Sacrifice Freshness," Thefoodsisterhod.com, October 30, 2013.

34 "Susan Niczowski—Salads Industry Can Make Millions."

35 Aarts, "These Are the Women Who Really Mean Business."

36 Jermyn, "'Early Crazy Hours.'"

37 Ibid.

38 "Canada's Top Female Entrepreneurs: W100," Chatelaine, September 27, 2012; "Meet Our 2012 Star Women in Grocery Winners," Canadian Grocer, June 26, 2012; "Summer Fresh Salads Announces 4th Consecutive Year as One of Canada's 50 Best Managed Companies"; "Susan Niczowski—Salads Industry Can Make Millions"; "Women Entrepreneur of the Year Awards," Financial Post, November 21, 2006.

39 Jermyn, "'Early Crazy Hours.'"

Getty Images

The Canadian men's hockey team celebrates its gold medal win during the 2014 Olympics in Sochi, Russia.

BUILDING THE FOUNDING TEAM

CHAPTER OUTLINE

DESPITE THE glowing tributes to superstar entrepreneurs that we all read about in the popular press, entrepreneurship is a team sport. Just as in team sports, in entrepreneurship, a team is needed to succeed. The Canadian men's hockey team, which won gold at the 2014 Sochi Olympics, is more than any one player. Even if those players are Jonathan Toews, Sidney Crosby, and Carey Price, the team is more than just a sum of its parts. Similarly, even Bill Gates, one of the richest men in the world, did not start Microsoft by himself. Instead, he and Paul Allen led a hardy team of bright young engineers to the semi-desert of Albuquerque in 1975 to develop the original microcomputer software, BASIC. The group included four programmers, a project manager, a production manager, a lead mathematician, a technical writer, and a bookkeeper. Despite their incredible intelligence and drive, Gates and Allen recognized that the company would never reach its potential with just the two of them.

Today, from its humble beginnings, Microsoft has become the leading software company in the world, with sales of almost $78 billion and 99,000 employees worldwide as of 2013.[1] Indeed, we could look at all the top companies in the world today and identify the team behind the lead entrepreneur, but the point is the same: Successfully launching a business requires support. Even if you are launching a small business, you'll quickly find that your potential to grow beyond a self-employment business requires a team, whether it's your spouse for moral support or a trusted advisor who mentors you through the growing pains you'll inevitably encounter. This chapter will look at the issues entrepreneurs face as they build their initial team and lead this group through the challenging launch process.

The Talent Triangle

In real estate, everyone always preaches "location, location, location" as the ultimate strategy, but when it comes to building a team for a business it is "management, management, management." Many investors agree that they are more willing to back an A-level team with a B-level opportunity over a B-level team with an A-level opportunity.[2]

A study of the top 500 most successful high-growth companies (based on multiple year published lists of Profit 100, Deloitte's Fast 50, and Ernst & Young's Entrepreneur of the Year award program winners) was conducted to determine if there were common management elements within these companies.[3] After issuing surveys to all of the companies, the results indicated that over 80% of them had similar management elements, including three key fundamentals: business acumen, operational experience, and domain knowledge.[4] As mentioned in Chapter 2, these three elements are known as the **talent triangle** (Figure 7.1). Not only did the results reveal that having the right people in place was critical, but how they interacted with each other was even more important.[5]

When building a team, it is vital that a business structures its management to ensure each corner (or element) of the triangle is accounted for. Further, it is important that the people occupying these spaces not only have their own projects and portfolios, but the authority to make decisions within their areas.[6] Let's look at the three elements of the talent triangle in more detail:

- **Business acumen**: A team member with business acumen often has the title of president, chief executive officer (CEO), or chief financial officer (CFO), as he or she has the skills, knowledge, and experience to make business decisions. This person is often responsible for the successful execution of core competencies, human resources management, investor relations, and overall company development and growth. It is likely he or she has previous years of professional experience or experience running a business and are familiar with the leadership role and have the ability to make top-level decisions for the company.

Source: S. Wise, "The Talent Triangle," Report on Business, May 17, 2006, Figure 1, www.ryerson.ca/content/dam/ent/education/articles/2006-05-17-team.pdf.

Figure 7.1

The talent triangle

- **Operational experience:** A team member with expertise in operational experience is focused on logistics, infrastructure, and product development. Management with this experience often has titles such as vice-president of research and development, chief operating officer (COO), or chief technology officer (CTO). Day to day, they make decisions directly related to the business's implementation and execution of the overall business plan. They are responsible for the building, shipping, and support of the product or service the company is selling. Hands-on experience at the product development level or with logistics management, inventory management, or selecting outsourcing partners is critical for this person to succeed.

- **Domain knowledge:** The team member with domain knowledge understands the industry's key value motivators, is aware of any domain impediments, ensures the company's supply chain is not interrupted, as well as focuses on the necessary relationships within the industry to make the desired sales. Management personnel possessing these qualities often have titles such as vice-president of sales, vice-president of business development, or director of corporate development. This person must have direct hands-on experience within the target industry, even if it is from a larger, more corporate perspective.

Fulfilling all elements of the talent triangle provides a balanced management team and a higher success rate for the company, but it isn't necessary to have three individual people represent each corner. The management team could be made up of four or five people, or even two people with a combination of experience that checks all of the corners of the talent triangle. The founders of Microsoft, Dell, and Google occupied multiple corners of the talent triangle simultaneously.

Without all three points of the talent triangle, the company lacks the necessary elements to achieve rapid growth within the industry. For example, a company that lacks domain knowledge but has business acumen and operational experience might develop a well-run venture with a great website and logistics, but will have low client interaction and achieve minimal sales. A business lacking in operational experience could offer investors a great product and infrastructure, but will lack the ability to execute and fulfill sales. Finally, a company lacking business acumen will likely end up with a good product and effective delivery methods, but will have high staff turnover, high burn rates, and a bloated infrastructure.[7]

Let's talk through an example to help illustrate the role of each talent triangle member. If an entrepreneur were looking to open an online grocery store, he or she would have to fill all three points when building the management team. Someone with business acumen would need to have a background in business (not necessarily the grocery industry), understand financial demands, and have experience with ecommerce (since the store is going to be online). Someone with operational experience would have experience in logistics (including delivery concepts, inventory management, and transportation of similar products), as well as knowledge about developing and executing the creation of the digital platforms to sell the products. The team member with domain knowledge has specific experience in the food and grocery industry—perhaps he or she has worked at a physical store or with a brand of physical stores.

Power of the Team

Teams provide multiple benefits. First and foremost, a team enables the entrepreneur to do more than he or she could accomplish alone. No matter how strong the entrepreneur, how many hours she puts into the business, or how many days a week she is willing to work, at some point a team becomes necessary to increase the capacity of the business. Babson College and the London Business School have been studying the impact of entrepreneurship on economies around the globe since 1999. One consistent finding is that businesses with growth aspirations plan on employing more than 20 people within the next five years.[8]

The size of your organization is also directly correlated to the amount of revenue your business can derive. For example, if you are launching a retailing business, your average sales per person will range from $50,600 per employee for a restaurant or bar to $468,800 per employee for a new car dealership.[9] So if you hope to grow a million-dollar business, you'll need to build up an organization capable of generating that kind of revenue. For a restaurant, that means you'll need 20-plus employees. Keep in mind that these figures are revenue and not profits. Thus, if you want $100,000 or more in profits each year, you'll likely need a much larger business. For a full-service restaurant that has generated an annual average net income margin of 2.7%[10] before taxes over the last five years, you'd need sales of $3.7 million per year to pull out $100,000 in profits. Understanding these relationships going into your business will help you set realistic goals and objectives for growing your company.

For growth, it's important to add employees who generate revenue. Too often firms add support staff. While such employees can improve the effectiveness of the people they work for, their impact on revenue is often not large enough to pay for their salary, especially for the early-stage entrepreneurial company. Instead, hire a salesperson who will directly lead to new revenue. In the early years, it is critical to be focused on revenue-generating employees.

The power of the team extends beyond adding sales. Solo entrepreneurs suffer from a number of shortcomings, including a limited perspective, little moral support, and a small network. Research finds that teams have a higher chance of success because of an increased skill set,[11] an improved capacity for innovation,[12] and a higher level of social support,[13] among other factors.

Entrepreneurs benefit by hearing and evaluating suggestions from others about how to better define and shape their business concept. No matter how brilliant your idea is, it can be better. Solo entrepreneurs often fail to get feedback on their idea that could help them better match customer needs and thereby increase product demand. Remember, initially your concept is based on your own perception of a customer need. Just because you are enthralled with the idea doesn't mean that it will generate widespread demand. Your team provides a good initial sounding board for ways to improve your idea. Granted, you can solicit this feedback from people outside your founding team (and you should), but you're likely to find that team members will provide more detailed suggestions because your success directly affects their own

well-being. Moreover, your team members can help you evaluate the feedback you receive from outsiders. As we discussed in Chapter 3, your idea will continue to evolve during the entire entrepreneurial process, from pre-launch all the way through rapid growth. Getting different perspectives on the opportunity will help you come up with a more robust product or service.

Starting a business is hard work. You'll face a roller coaster of emotions as you achieve important milestones (your first sale) and hit unexpected pitfalls (your first unhappy customer). Unfortunately, most new ventures encounter far more pitfalls than milestones in the launch phase. It is all too easy to fold up and find regular employment when you hit a particularly tough problem. Having a team around you provides moral support—you're all in this together. You have a shared responsibility to work hard on each other's behalf because, if the business fails, it is not only you who needs to find alternative employment or opportunities but the rest of the team as well. Furthermore, a team means there are people you can confide in and share your frustrations with because they are facing them as well. The sympathetic ear enables you to let off steam and then refocus your attention on the problem at hand. Finally, it is more fun and rewarding to share the successes with a group of people who have been working toward the same goals. The power of a team is its shared vision of success.

Business is all about relationships. You need to establish relationships with suppliers, distributors, customers, investors, bankers, lawyers, accountants, and countless others. While well-networked individuals make better entrepreneurs, a team dramatically multiplies the size of even a good network. If you build your team wisely, you will gain access to a broader range of contacts that can help your business. This is often most evident in the fundraising phase. Early on, you will likely need to raise equity capital, and the bigger your team, the more contacts you have as you embark on finding that investment. At the very least, your team is a great source for co-investment. In the 2003 edition of the *Inc.* magazine list of the 500 fastest-growing firms, 17% of the entrepreneurs reported that co-founders were a source of seed financing. Even if the co-founders don't invest directly, they can tap their own friends and family for startup capital, as was the case at 10% of the companies on the 2003 *Inc.* listing.[14] Thus, the power of the team greatly enhances your network, which is the lifeblood of any business.

A team also rounds out the skill set needed to launch a business. Most lead entrepreneurs have a vision of the initial product, and many even have the skills necessary to build a prototype—as when a software engineer identifies a new video game opportunity. But it is almost impossible for one individual to possess all the skills necessary in the launch phase. For instance, a person with strong technical skills may lack the business know-how required to successfully introduce a new product to market, or a business guru may see a product need but lack the technical skill to build it. Even a business superstar is unlikely to possess all the business skills needed for long-term success. For example, a financial expert likely will need team members with marketing, sales, operations, and production experience, among others. The key is to understand your own strengths and weaknesses. Know what you know, and more importantly, know what you *don't* know. Once you have a strong sense of who you are, you can create a strategy to construct a powerful team. As you start to build up your team, identify the critical skills for success. Create job descriptions and a timeline of when you need these people. Then work through your network to find the right candidates.

Where Do You Fit?

Just because the business is your idea doesn't mean you must be the CEO. Every entrepreneur needs to take a hard look at himself or herself and decide how to best contribute to the venture's success. Rob Kalin, founder and original CEO of Etsy.com, is a case in point. He took his concept of an online open craft fair that gave sellers personal storefronts to Union

Square Ventures in November 2006. After raising $1 million in Series A funding, Kalin began to scale Etsy by focusing on handmade and vintage items as well as art and photography.[15] In November 2007, buyers spent $4.3 million purchasing over 300,000 items for sale on the marketplace.[16] Etsy's rapid growth created the need for management with senior experience in large organizations. In 2008, Etsy hired former NPR executive Maria Thomas as COO, and Kalin quickly promoted her to CEO. Thomas grew Etsy into a profitable company and increased revenues sevenfold within two years.[17] In 2009, Thomas stepped down as CEO and returned the seat to ex-CEO Rob Kalin. Was Kalin the right person to lead Etsy all along? The future would prove otherwise. In July 2011 Etsy's board of directors asked Chad Dickerson, the company's CTO, to take over the role of CEO.[18] Before joining Etsy, Dickerson served as senior director of Yahoo's in-house startup incubator, Brickhouse & Advanced products team. Although Kalin's innovative nature nurtured and led the company's first few years of growth, Etsy's board of directors and investors felt the company's potential could best be reached by an experienced executive like Dickerson.

Granted, creating a new venture requires most people to develop new skills on the job, but you'll be encountering a plethora of new challenges in the launch process and you need to understand your personal limits. Stubbornly keeping the CEO job could limit the potential of your venture and may even lead to its premature demise. So the question is, "How do you gauge what you already know and what you can comfortably grow into as your business evolves?"

The first thing to do is to update your résumé. This document best captures your skill set to date. The key to revising and reviewing your résumé is to do an *honest* and complete assessment of your demonstrated skills. This is not the time to exaggerate your accomplishments because the only person you're fooling is yourself. You need to understand how your skill set will help you achieve success.

A second thing to keep in mind as you update your résumé is, "What do you really like to do and what do you dislike?" Too many product people fail as CEO because they don't like to sell. These entrepreneurs want to design a product—and then redesign it over and over until it is perfect. While there is definitely a place for this type of founder within a new venture, it's not in the CEO role, which is about selling your company to customers, investors, and vendors.

Even if you're still a student and have limited work experience, building your résumé will help you examine what you have achieved. Do you see patterns in your résumé that suggest some underlying strengths? Can you leverage these strengths as you try to launch a startup? Even if you are relatively young, recognize that many young entrepreneurs built companies large and small starting from their strengths. Mark Zuckerberg, for example, started the social networking site Facebook in 2004 as a sophomore college student at Harvard University. He launched the company on his strengths: a passion for technology and computer programming, which was self-taught. He also started with some partners who added to and complemented his strengths. Co-founder and former vice-president of engineering Dustin Moskovitz was his roommate at Harvard. Former Facebook chief technology officer Adam D'Angelo was Zuckerberg's friend in high school, where they wrote software for the MP3 player Winamp that learned your personal music listening habits and then automatically created a custom playlist to meet your tastes. Other co-founders Chris Hughes and Eduardo Saverin helped promote Facebook in the early years.[19] Although all were young, together they brought an understanding of technology and how young people like to connect and communicate with each other. As of October 2012, Facebook had over 1 billion members.[20]

Likewise, Pete Lescoe created Food Should Taste Good in 2006 with the goal of making a unique new snack with great taste, real ingredients, and sophisticated flavour. Lescoe started from humble beginnings by creating multigrain and jalapeño chips in his tiny apartment kitchen in Waltham, Massachusetts. After months of revising recipes, calling stores, and handing out samples, Lescoe finally made his first sale to a grocery store. Soon after, Food Should Taste Good won the Best New Product award at the Natural Products East Expo.[21]

Sales began to grow, and Lescoe started to create new innovative chip flavours such as olive, chocolate, sweet potato, and cinnamon. Focusing on the growing health concerns in North America, Lescoe ensured that all chip varieties were gluten free, cholesterol free, and had zero grams of trans fats. Plus, many varieties are certified vegan. Food Should Taste Good started to become a household name after being featured in magazines like *Better Homes and Gardens*, *Good Housekeeping*, *Shape*, and *Women's Health*.[22] The brand's increased popularity did not go unnoticed; in February 2012 General Mills acquired Food Should Taste Good for an undisclosed amount.[23] Lescoe's strengths were his ability to bootstrap the business, his persistent never-give-up sales attitude, and his ability to continually innovate new products that stayed true to his vision.

Zuckerberg and Lescoe both started modestly and grew their businesses incrementally (at least in the beginning), which allowed them to develop their own skills in line with the growth of the business. Yet each of them had a key strength he could leverage in the early days, a platform from which he could launch his business. As you examine your résumé, what key strength pops out at you? Is that strength a strong platform from which you can develop the skills necessary to be the company's CEO, or might you be better off taking another role, such as Rob Kalin did, and bring in a more seasoned leader? Can you sell, or are you better suited to another role? You can't build a successful team until you understand your strengths and the best place for you in the company today at its launch and in the future as it progresses through various stages of growth.

While most people are pretty good at identifying their own strengths, they often have trouble understanding their weaknesses. Peter Drucker, the management guru who published over 30 books, suggested that we can all improve our own self-awareness by conducting feedback analysis.[24] His methodology is simple: Every time you make a major decision or take a significant action, record what you expect to happen. For instance, as you decide to take an entrepreneurship class, write down what you expect to learn and what grade you believe you will earn. Several months later, after an outcome has occurred, compare it to what you originally recorded. Are your expectations and your actual results similar? What's different, and why is it different? Drucker's exercise focuses you on performance and results so you can identify your strengths and work to improve them.

Although this exercise and others can help you understand your own strengths, many times people who know you are better judges of you than you are. Talk to those people in your sphere of influence, people who know you well and whom you respect. Talk to your parents, friends, bosses, employers, coaches, professors, and others who can gauge your capabilities. Ask them, "What do you see me doing? What are my strengths and how can these attributes translate into launching a successful venture? What areas do you think I need to work on, and how should I go about it?" It is also important to ask them about your weaknesses: "What characteristics might impede my success? How can I work to rectify them?" Understanding your weaknesses will help you devise a plan to overcome them, whether that be through self-improvement or by hiring the right people to compensate for your weaknesses.

When it comes to self-awareness, there are two types of people. First, there are those who are overly conscious of their own weaknesses; they are their own worst critics. This group may be reluctant to pursue a venture because they fear their own shortcomings will lead to failure. In contrast, the second group seems oblivious to their own weaknesses. While this group may be more likely to launch a business, they are also more likely to fail once they do so because they won't seek help or even recognize that they need help. It is important to strike the right balance between these two extremes. The key to doing so is to develop deep self-awareness.

In addition to self-reflection and feedback from friends and family, there is a wide array of psychological and personality tests available. Some classic examples are the Myers-Briggs Personality Type Indicator, the California Personality Inventory, and the Personal Interests, Attitudes and Values (PIAV) profile. These tests, which vary widely in cost, are designed to help individuals understand things like their underlying interests, motivations, and communication styles.

They can provide valuable insights, but there are several important caveats to keep in mind when using them. First, always remember that no test, no matter how carefully designed and applied, can accurately predict an individual's likelihood for success in an entrepreneurial endeavour. Few things in life are as dynamic and unpredictable as an entrepreneurial environment, so you should expect these tests only to give you a deeper understanding of your own strengths and weaknesses. Second, should you decide to take advantage of these resources, industry newsletter *HR Focus* strongly recommends that you have a trained professional administer and interpret the test for you and that you insist on a test that has been statistically validated. This is a field with little regulation, and as a result it is essential that you use assessments that have a proven track record.[25]

Finally, keep in mind that no single personality or demeanour is best suited for entrepreneurship. In fact, a study by *Inc.* magazine found that many of the most common assumptions about entrepreneurs were misleading or wholly inaccurate. For instance, a classic label applied to entrepreneurs is that of risk taker. In reality, the study found that CEOs of the *Inc.* 500 companies varied widely in their levels of risk tolerance. What many had in common, however, was an ability to work well under highly stressful conditions.[26] The lesson here is that entrepreneurs come in all shapes and sizes, and you need to be careful about letting common myths about entrepreneurs dissuade you from starting a business. Tests can't tell you whether you will be successful, but they can provide you with insights that you can use to help ensure your success.

The key point to remember is that entrepreneurship is hard work. You will not become a millionaire overnight—or in five years. As Walter Kuemmerle notes, entrepreneurship requires patience.[27] As the Internet boom and bust taught us, it can be a mistake to grow too big too fast. It is cheaper to test the business model when a company is small and then shift strategies quickly to better adapt the model to the market reality.[28] This will take years, not months. So you need to ask yourself whether you have the patience to be an entrepreneur—this can be harder for the young and brash.

Once you understand who you are and what skill set you bring to the venture, the next step is to identify what other skills are necessary to successfully launch the business. Create a staffing plan that not only identifies key roles but also tells you when you need to fill those roles. Figure 7.2 provides an example, but staffing plans vary based on the type of company, stage of development, type of industry, and so on. Early on, you likely need only one or two other team members. At this stage, each team member needs to understand that early-stage companies are flat and nonhierarchical. It is more important to know what needs to be done than to worry about who should do it. Nonetheless, the roles for these members should be complementary, and each co-founder should also participate extensively in shaping the vision of the business. An ideal combination might have team members coming from different disciplines such as science and business. Or if they are in the same major field of study, they might have different functional specialties, such as finance and marketing or biology and microbiology. The co-founders will work together on the overall direction of the business, but it is also wise for them to identify and divide primary responsibilities. Many co-founders make the mistake of working on every task and decision together, which often leads to frustration and inefficiency. While everyone's input is valuable, consensus is often a deterrent to success. Someone needs to be in charge.

The sample staffing plan in Figure 7.2 is a working document that grows and evolves as the founding team achieves milestones and moves on to new tasks. The value in creating the staffing plan is that it helps you anticipate where the company is going and plan for those needs. Note that not all the positions are currently filled. It is wise in the launch stage to conserve resources, especially cash. Thus, the founders may take on some of the future roles as their skills permit. If, for example, the team needs a strong finance person with previous experience raising equity capital, it makes sense to start identifying that person early on but to delay bringing him or her onto the team until needed (which might be when the company raises a significant round of financing from angels or through a private placement). While we

Role	Primary Duties	Person Filling Role	When Needed	Talent Triangle
Product Development	Develop prototype	Lead entrepreneur	Now	Operational experience
Market Development	Customer research Channel development	Founder	Now	Domain knowledge
Finance	Raise outside capital	To be determined	Next month	Business acumen
Production	Identify manufacturing partners	To be determined	Three months from now	Operational experience

Figure 7.2

Staffing plan

have found the staffing plan highlighted in Figure 7.2 to be useful, the Management Function Analysis Worksheet[29] is another useful staffing planning device.

Premature Scaling

Startups are classified as temporary organizations that are intended to eventually scale into large companies.[30] The core five dimensions of a startup are customer, product, team, business model, and financials. If a startup isn't able to master the chaos of all five dimensions, and one starts to fall without the others, it is likely it will scale prematurely and fail.[31] Startups focused on consistency are able to keep their customer dimension in line with the product, team, financials and business model, with each dimension progressing evenly. Startups with an inconsistent balance have one of the dimensions either too far ahead or too far behind the customer dimension. Premature scaling is the most predominant form of inconsistency within a startup[32] and it can be caused by many factors:[33]

- Failing to build a management team that covers all three points of the talent triangle
- Hiring too many or too few people to properly serve customers
- Paying high salaries before the startup has a consistent and strong cash flow
- Attempting to increase the startup's revenue while decreasing profit
- Failing to hire people who are sales oriented
- Not paying attention to the difference between users and customers

Scaling prematurely is a direct result of startups focusing on one element within their company and allowing it to advance without the other four elements. Overspending on customer acquisitions, hiring too many employees or not ensuring the management team is driven by a talent triangle causes startups to scale prematurely and, unfortunately, fail.[34] Implementing strategic goals, status meetings and benchmarks will assist startups in avoiding the pitfalls of premature scaling.

How to Build a Powerful Team

Your staffing plan is the first step in building a powerful team. Your next challenge is to identify the individuals needed to fill the gaps. How do you identify the best candidates? The simple answer is to tap your personal network and the network of your advisors, but you'll want to go outside that network to broaden the pool of quality candidates. Work with

Getty Images

Alexis Maybank (left) and Alexandra Wilkis Wilson (right), co-founders of Gilt Groupe

your professors to make contacts with alumni. Search your university's alumni database to find people in the right industry and with the right kind of position. More often than not, alumni are willing to speak with current students. Even if the alumnus isn't willing or able to join your team, he or she may be able to recommend someone from his or her network. You should also check with your investors, accountant, lawyer, or other people affiliated with your efforts (if you have these people lined up already). Oftentimes entrepreneurs will hire a lawyer or accountant earlier than they might need that individual just to tap into his or her network. Moreover, many law firms are willing to work for promising new ventures pro bono, at reduced rates, or for deferred compensation. Thus, it may make sense to hire your lawyer early in your launch process. The key to your success is continually building your network. This will help you meet challenges beyond filling out your team.

A natural place to find co-founders and other team members is your family and friends. A look at the *Inc.* 500 shows that 58% of entrepreneurs teamed up with a business associate, 22% with a personal friend, and 20% with their spouse or other family members.[35] Just remember that working with a close friend or family member can be a double-edged sword. On the plus side, you know these people well, so you have a strong sense of their work ethic and personal chemistry. This was definitely the case for Gilt Groupe co-founders Alexandra Wilkis Wilson and Alexis Maybank. The two met in an undergrad Portuguese class while attending Harvard then decided to go to Harvard Business School together. After graduating, Wilkis Wilson started a career in luxury goods, managing leather goods sales and planning for Louis Vuitton then overseeing operations of 15 BVLGARI North American stores.[36] Maybank started her career as one of the early employees at eBay. After launching and running eBay Canada, she helped found eBay motors, then moved on to become general manager and business development director for AOL's ecommerce businesses.[37] Living in New York, the friends shared a love for high fashion and sample sales. The two reconnected at a Harvard mixer for new students and they found that their skills complemented each other's well and their relationship added a level of trust that can only be found between friends. After securing Double Click co-founders Kevin P. Ryan and Dwight Merriman as early team members, they started Gilt Groupe—an online flash sale website featuring today's top designer labels. Gilt Groupe became wildly popular after being featured on the daytime talk show *The View,* and in May 2011 was valued at $1 billion after it raised $138 million from investors, including Goldman Sachs Group and Softbank Group.[38] In April 2012, the duo released a book titled *By Invitation Only: How We Built Gilt and Changed the Way Millions Shop* documenting their story to inspire entrepreneurship, especially in women.[39]

Another good source is working with family members. It can be difficult, because you are mixing a professional relationship with an already existing personal/familial relationship. John Earle, the founder of the $3.8-million apparel company Johnny Cupcakes, has found a happy medium with his CFO/mom "Momma Cupcakes." Lorraine Earle, a former office manager at a big Boston law firm, encouraged and bankrolled her son's business venture.[40] In the early days of Johnny Cupcakes, she took on bookkeeping duties while John was the creative CEO. As the orders came piling in from the Internet, Lorraine's house became overrun with boxes of shirts.[41] With Johnny Cupcakes literally taking over her life at home, Lorraine decided to quit her job and become CFO of her son's company. First on her agenda was to locate a warehouse. As polar opposites, they operate under a system of checks and balances. Lorraine explains their business relationship: "He doesn't care about the money. He doesn't

care about the bottom line. So I have to be extra diligent. I have to say 'no' more than when he was a kid."[42] Similar dynamics occur when you hire friends. You need to relate to your friends in a different manner—a more professional manner—and this can stress the friendship. Recognizing the consequences of this new dynamic is the first step toward managing it, but there is more that you can do.

Before entering into a team relationship with family or friends (or anyone, for that matter), lay out as much as possible the previous accomplishments, industry profile, and years of experience that person has and the roles and responsibilities that person will fill in your organization going forward. Define decision and reporting responsibilities. We are not saying you need to have a highly formalized structure at an early stage of your venture's development, but you do need to clearly state expectations, tasks, and objectives. More teams self-destruct because of personal conflicts than because of lack of funding. Although the circumstances surrounding the fallout between Facebook co-founders Mark Zuckerberg and Eduardo Saverin remain mysterious, Zuckerberg forced Saverin from the company. Saverin then sued Zuckerberg and Facebook.[43] The moral of the story is that founder conflict occurs and can escalate to the point of endangering the company. Setting expectations and responsibilities in advance of engaging in a relationship can help to mitigate damaging conflict.

It is not at all uncommon for friends to dive into starting a business before they have really considered how it could affect their relationship. An excellent example unfolds in the movie *Startup.com*. This outstanding documentary follows two close friends through the rise and fall of their company during the Internet boom and provides a dramatic example of how working together can affect the relationship of two life-long friends. Although Kaleil Tuzman had to make the difficult and painful decision to fire his friend and co-founder, Tom Herman, the two were ultimately able to piece their friendship back together. This is just one example of the difficulties you may face. Again, the key is to have clear expectations of each other and understand that pitfalls will test your friendship.

Once you have identified the right co-founders or team members, there is still the hurdle of opportunity costs. The best candidates are often already employed in good jobs, frequently in the industry where you will be competing. That means at some point they will need to leave a well-paying job to join your venture, and most new businesses can't afford to pay market rates during the cash-strapped startup phase. In addition, there is much greater risk that a new business will fail, which compounds the personal opportunity costs that co-founders and early team members face. As the lead entrepreneur, you need to convince potential candidates that the job itself is intrinsically rewarding and growth oriented (team members get to do something they like and be part of creating something new and exciting) and that in the long run the financial payoff will be much greater. A young company offers potential team members opportunities to grow into higher management positions (and therefore higher deferred tax–advantaged pay) than might be possible at their current company and to have some ownership in the new venture (through either options or founder stock). These are both powerful tools for convincing talented candidates to take a risk with your company. The more successful the targeted candidate, the harder it will be for you to successfully make these arguments; yet research indicates that many people are willing and eager to jump into the entrepreneurial fray for the right opportunity. Make sure to present your best case. Sell candidates on the vision and back that up by showing them what you've accomplished to date, such as building and testing a prototype or securing outside financing.

Bottom-Up Hiring versus Top-Down Hiring

When growing a business, an entrepreneur can hire in one of two ways: bottom up or top down. Although there are advantages and disadvantages to both methods, it is important that

the entrepreneur focuses on hiring the right people that will contribute to the work culture they are looking to achieve. The first three or four people to be hired at a startup set the tone for the company's culture.

Top-down hiring is a traditional approach to hiring and is often used by large, well-established organizations. This approach is implemented when a company is looking for top executives or people with experience in the industry to join the team to bring in new leadership and management. Startups and new businesses often avoid taking a top-down hiring approach because there is a risk that the new employee will not understand the startup culture and might not be on the same page with the founder's growth and scaling plan(s).

When a company is taking a bottom-up approach to its hiring practices, it hires specific people with specific skills and experience to fill a specific role. It can be considered a grassroots approach to building a company's team, allowing them to find the right people to handle various tasks and responsibilities within the company. A bottom-up approach to hiring can benefit a company that is trying to scale at an appropriate speed, bringing skilled people on for various responsibilities as they arise and the company grows. Employees can learn and adopt the corporate culture and values from the ground up and develop alongside the company and other employees.

Bootstrapping: Building the Team Based on Stage-of-Venture Life

Building your team requires resources, which are scarce in most nascent ventures. Co-founders must often live off their savings or their spouse's income during the early days, as it may be impossible to draw a salary. Recognizing that difficulty, you are likely to find that it is better to bootstrap your team build-out rather than putting everyone in place from day one. It's common for founders of smaller companies to stay at their current jobs and work on the business part-time at night and on weekends. Many companies are able to successfully develop prototypes or raise the first round of outside investment while the founders are still at their current job (although you should not continue working for a firm that you'll directly compete with).

Be careful, though, not to co-mingle activities. When you're at your current job, your attention should be focused on those duties that help your employer succeed. You should *not* use your employer's resources, like computers and copiers, without explicit permission. You should *not* expropriate intellectual property from your current employer to use in your new venture. And you most certainly should *not* solicit your employer's customers while you are still taking a paycheque from that employer. If you handle your startup well, you will often find that your current employer is supportive, especially if the business isn't directly competing with your proposed venture. Thus, you should notify your employer of your intentions as soon as possible.

Another means of earning a salary during the early days is to take a part-time job. While this may mean working as a waiter or for a temp agency, entrepreneurs will often consult in a related field until their main product or service is ready to go to market.

As a lead entrepreneur, you need to prepare for a diminished personal cash flow during the early years of your business, as you will often have to defer drawing a salary. Continuing to work for your current employer, building up a savings war chest, and delaying purchases of new cars or a house all contribute to sustaining you during the beginning. While painful, this frugality is often a small tradeoff to pursue your dream, and if you are successful, you will likely receive a future payoff that will be well worth the initial risk and sacrifice.

Perhaps the most common means to protect your personal cash flow is to continue working in a full-time job during the early phases. The weekend and nighttime entrepreneur is common, but at some point you have to quit and work on your dream full time. For example, Ruthie Davis, founder of DAVIS by Ruthie Davis, an ultra-modern footwear company, continued to consult for Tommy Hilfiger where she had been vice-president of marketing and design for women's footwear. Ruthie's phenomenal success in launching "Tommy Girl Shoes" garnered the attention and support of the entrepreneur and founder Tommy Hilfiger. When Ruthie decided to launch her own firm, Tommy Hilfiger asked her to remain as a consultant for six months. This consulting agreement allowed Ruthie to maintain a salary and contacts while focusing on building her brand.[44]

The tradeoffs of this approach are clear. While you do maintain your personal income, every waking hour is devoted to either your regular job or your new venture. This dual-job strategy usually works only during the planning stages of your new venture—you can write a business plan, build a prototype, and start to make some key vendor and customer contacts, but you likely can't launch the business while working full time elsewhere.

In addition to the time constraints, there are other issues to consider. If you are being paid, that means your time and effort should go toward your current job. Make sure to work on the startup on your own time. There is also the potential for a lawsuit if your new business uses intellectual property developed on the company's time. Once you leave your full-time job, your previous company may feel like a jilted lover. Working to maintain a relationship with your former company is difficult but not impossible. Follow the example of Ruthie Davis. She not only informed Tommy Hilfiger but also got his blessing to work on her business while continuing to consult for his. The risk of informing your current company, of course, is that you might be immediately terminated, but for the long term, it is better to be straight with those affected by your decision.

When you're bringing on team members, many of the same principles apply. Examine your staffing plan to assess when you need that individual on a part-time basis and when you need her on a full-time basis. If the person is critical to building your product, you'll need her sooner. If she will be your primary salesperson, you won't need her until you go to market. Accurately timing when different people join the team conserves company cash and helps the new hire manage her own personal finances. There are tradeoffs, however. First, you need to plan ahead. It often takes four months or more to identify and hire key employees. Second, it is easy for a part-time worker to become disengaged from the startup. If your team member is still at her current job, that will likely take priority over your venture, especially if some special projects come up. Third, people who are already working on the startup full time may resent that the other person isn't as heavily involved in the sweat and tears that characterize the venture. They may feel this person is getting a free ride. As the lead entrepreneur, you need to manage these perceptions and work to keep the part-time and future team members fully apprised of what is happening. Finally, until a person signs up, she is at greater risk of either changing her mind about joining the venture or walking away for another new opportunity. Understanding these risks will help you manage them and still preserve your cash flow. One way to handle these situations is to develop a compensation plan that excites your current and future team members.

Compensation

As resource constrained as new ventures are, you are likely hard-pressed to think about compensation for you and your team. At some point, however, you'll need to pay yourself and others in your organization. The more powerful your team members, the more compensation they will expect, whether that is in salary or in equity (but usually a combination). So how does a startup company determine what to pay its employees? How does it choose among wages, salary, bonuses, equity, or some combination of these options? The answers to these questions depend not only on the nature of your company but also on the nature of your team and employees.

Equity

There are several good reasons why most new ventures distribute equity to at least some of their employees. First, new companies often can't pay market rates for salary and wages. Equity can induce people to work for below-market rates with the expectation that at some point in the future they will be handsomely rewarded. As Lalitha Swart of Silicon Valley Bank put it, "People don't leave large corporations and take on risk without knowing there is an upside in stock."[45] Second, including some equity in the compensation package aligns the employee's interests with those of the company. Basically, the employees become owners, and their stock or options increase in value as the company prospers. Finally, the sense of ownership boosts morale, as employees perceive that everybody is in this together. This added camaraderie helps the team stick together during the inevitable rough times in the early-launch phase. Of course, distributing equity throughout an organization isn't costless; it dilutes the founders' and investors' equity. You need to understand the tradeoffs among motivating employees, conserving cash flow, and preserving your own equity. Understanding the tradeoffs helps you develop a compensation plan.

There are two basic ways of distributing equity: founder shares and an option pool. As the name implies, **founder shares** are equity earned by founders of the company at the time it is officially established or when the first outside equity capital is invested (usually when it is first incorporated, although the shares may vest over time). Founder shares are most often given with no or minimal investment (maybe one cent per share) and are an acknowledgment of the "sweat equity" that the founders have invested in turning their idea into a company or of the track record and value of the founders. There are several considerations to keep in mind when granting founder shares. First, remember that granting shares to new parties dilutes your personal ownership, but this dilution is more than offset if you are granting shares to valuable co-founders who can help the company grow. For example, if you are opening a French restaurant and you have front-room experience as a maître d', it makes sense to co-found the restaurant with an accomplished French chef who can design and run the kitchen. It makes less sense to award founder shares to waiters, dishwashers, busboys, and other staff who are more transient and less central to the restaurant's competitive advantage. Founder shares should be reserved for those team members who are essential to turning the idea into reality.

How many people should get founder shares? It's a serious question. We advise entrepreneurs to keep this group small, usually no more than three people. Again, keep in mind the principle of preserving your equity by avoiding dilution. Once the founding team numbers five or more, dilution can dramatically affect the capital appreciation that each founder receives, especially if the company needs to raise outside equity. Investors like to see founders with a significant stake in the company because "having skin in the game" focuses entrepreneurs on growing the company's future value rather than on maximizing current salaries. If, after a few rounds of outside investment, each of the founders has only 1% to 5% of the equity, they may start to recognize that no matter how big the company becomes, the long-term gain won't be sufficient to compensate them for all the hard work of getting the company to that point. Therefore, the founders might be more inclined to leave the new venture for greener pastures, and disruption in the leadership team is difficult for emerging ventures to survive. The smaller the group of people who receive founder shares, the smaller this dilution problem. This is not to say that other team members should be precluded from equity participation, just that founder shares are not the best way to distribute equity to employees. Options are a better choice, and we'll touch on that topic shortly.

A third consideration regarding founder shares is how to divide them between the founders. Many first-time entrepreneurs fall into the trap of evenly dividing the shares among the founders. So if you have four founders, you might give each person 25% of the founder shares. A number of problems can arise from equal distribution. First and foremost, if each founder has an equal share, it can be hard to make important decisions because the group will want to have consensus. Even if one founder has been designated CEO, the others may perceive that their input needs to be given full consideration. At a minimum, this situation slows the decision-making process, but it can sometimes lead to disaster as the team stalls and becomes incapable of taking action. Another factor is that ambitious people tend to benchmark themselves against their peers. This means that a CEO will benchmark her compensation against that of other CEOs. If the founder shares are equally distributed, it is only a matter of time before the CEO recognizes that she is doing as much work as her peers but has less reward. This discrepancy acts as a disincentive to maintaining the level of commitment required by startups.

While there are no hard-and-fast rules for splitting founder shares, keep in mind these guiding principles centring on past contribution and expected future contribution. First, acknowledge the time and value of past contributions.[46] The entrepreneur who initiated the idea, started doing the leg work, and enticed co-founders to join deserves consideration for all of these efforts and also for her expected contribution going forward—maybe as much as 50% if the founder also continues in a major role as CEO or some other high-level manager. Second, the founder who is CEO should have most of the equity, often as much as 50% of the founder shares. Next, the founder who brings in the intellectual capital—say, a patent or invention—should have 20% to 30% of the founder shares. As you can see, it is difficult to put hard-and-fast rules on founder shares, because founders may assume multiple roles.

While these principles can guide the distribution, the final split comes down to a negotiation. Detail each founder's past and expected future contributions and the role he will assume in the organization and then divide the founders' shares accordingly. It can be useful to engage a lawyer with experience in this area. The lawyer can help you benchmark against other companies and offer outside validation that each founder is getting his or her due share.

Since you will want to minimize the distribution of founder shares, another way to reward other employees and future hires is through an option pool. An **option pool** is equity set aside for future distribution. Options basically give the holder the right to buy a share in the company at a below-market rate. The option price is often determined by the market price of the shares on the day the employee is hired (or in the case of a private company, the price at the last round of financing).

The principles we discussed about founder shares apply to options as well. An option pool will dilute the founders' equity—but to a much lower degree than broadening the number of people who receive founder shares. Granting options also helps align the employees' interests with those of the founders by making the employees partial owners of the company. Additionally, to exercise their options recipients must pay for the shares, which brings money into the company (although the amount is usually too small to be considered as a source of growth capital). During the Internet boom, companies liberally granted options. Unfortunately, as the boom turned to bust, many employees found their options "under water," meaning that the exercise price was greater than the current market price for the share. If options lose their value, they cease to be an incentive and retention tool. When this happens, employees are more likely to leave to seek new opportunities. However, if a company is growing, the value of the options should continue to grow, which increases the incentive and value for the employees.

Since granting options can mean giving up a significant piece of the organization, it is essential that owners know how to use these motivational tools effectively. The worst-case scenario is one in which the entrepreneur gives up equity in the company and receives little or none of the value that equity is supposed to create. Many rank-and-file employees have difficulty understanding exactly how they contribute to the value of the organization. Communicating with employees about the importance of their roles and training everyone about how they can increase shareholder value is essential.

According to the Beyster Institute, a nonprofit organization dedicated to improving the use of employee ownership, entrepreneurs can take several key steps to ensure that options improve organizational performance. First, employees need to fully understand the share ownership program and how they will participate in it. Related to this point, employees should have a solid understanding of how the company is performing. Second, the staff must know how to measure company success and receive training on how to achieve it through their individual roles. Third, as we have mentioned, one of the great benefits of offering options is that it makes employees owners of the company and therefore encourages them to think like owners. However, the key here is that owners are typically more motivated to find solutions to problems or to develop innovations. An entrepreneur who offers options and doesn't harness or listen to this highly motivated workforce is failing to capitalize on the greatest benefit of offering ownership. Fourth, a share ownership plan should offer employees a true opportunity to earn a financial reward. This potential for financial windfall is the key to share ownership plans.[47]

Once the company decides it wants to use options to motivate and reward employees, the question becomes how many options to issue and to whom. Research suggests that issuing options generates increased overall company value through gains in employee productivity and that this increased value offsets the dilution effect.[48] It is common for many technology firms to put aside 15% to 20% of their equity for employee options after a major investment round. From that pool, the company can decide to distribute options to all or just key employees. Don't make the mistake of distributing all the options to existing employees, but anticipate how many new hires you'll make over the coming years. Then you can come up with a distribution plan based on employee level. Higher-level employees—say, vice-presidents and other upper-management employees—will get more options than lower-level employees. Keep in mind that you'll vest shares over an employee's tenure.

Although options are the most commonly used form of equity compensation, the Canadian Institute of Chartered Accountants has adopted regulations that arguably make them more expensive for both private and public companies. Specifically, companies must list options at fair value as an expense on their income statement.[49] While it appears that this rule hasn't dampened the use of options, there are other similar means to reward employees, including restricted shares, share appreciation rights, and phantom shares.[50] **Restricted shares** are actual shares, rather than the option to buy shares, that may be vested over time. Restricted shares have restrictions placed on their disposition by the recipient. Upon grant, the recipient shareholder obtains all of the regular rights of a shareholder, such as entitlement to dividends, the ability to vote on the shares, rights upon dissolution, and continues to enjoy these entitlements throughout the restriction period. The upside to the company is that the expense is the current share price rather than the expected exercise price of an option. The downside is that the recipient gets the shares regardless of company performance, whereas employees exercise options only when the company's share price increases. Tax consequences for the recipient shareholder should also be considered. **Share appreciation rights** accrue to employees only if the share price increases (similar to options). Their advantage over options is that they tend to be lower cost to the company. As with restricted shares, tax consequences for the employee receiving share appreciation rights should also be considered. Finally, **phantom shares** are not really issued equity but a cash bonus paid to employees if the share price appreciates over a set period of time. Phantom shares are expensed over the vesting period, but they have the benefit of lowering dilution. The downside is that you'll need cash once the phantom shares are exercised, and for a resource-constrained startup, cash is at a premium. As with restricted shares and share appreciation rights, tax consequences for the recipient should also be considered.

One of the main reasons to award options, founder shares, or one of the hybrids just mentioned is to keep key employees with the firm. However, what happens if you decide that someone needs to be fired due to poor performance, nonperformance, or any variety of other reasons? If it is a co-founder, that person likely has a sizable chunk of equity and any voting rights associated with it. That may mean the person can interfere with the operations of the business. An important means to protect you from an employee or co-founder who doesn't pan out as expected is to create a vesting schedule. **Vesting** basically means that people earn their shares or options over time, usually over four or more years. For example, if a co-founder is entitled to 25% of the company's shares, you may vest those shares in equal chunks over four years. That way if the person leaves or is fired in the first year, he walks away with only a quarter of the shares he would have been entitled to if he stayed. This maintains the unvested shares for distribution to future hires.

You can also structure an employment contract to permit the company to repurchase the employee's shares at cost or some other predetermined rate when she leaves or is dismissed from the company. You may negotiate a right of first refusal that gives the company or other existing shareholders the right to buy the equity of an ex-employee at the prevailing market rate. It is important for your employment agreement to state that the employee is an at-will employee, regardless of her ownership position in the company, in case you need to fire that employee in the future. Failure to take this step can open your company up to the possibility of a minority shareholder lawsuit. To avoid lawsuits, you should define *fired for cause*, touching on what the company considers to be fraud, negligence, nonperformance, and so forth. Lawsuits aside, having a right of first refusal or the option to repurchase shares when the employee leaves preserves all the shares for redistribution among the remaining founders and employees. To avoid the time and energy of litigation, companies usually buy out fired co-founders after they reach a settlement.

Dilution refers to the change in an entrepreneur's or current shareholder's percentage of ownership when a company issues additional equity.[51] Sometimes entrepreneurs or the founders are concerned with how much ownership they will lose if they decide to offer equity in return for their investments. There are many tools available to help entrepreneurs make the best decisions possible about various equity options or opportunities at hand. OwnYourVenture .com is one of the best tools available, offering entrepreneurs the tools needed to understand the impact of raising money in the early stages of the startup.[52] Entrepreneurs can access OwnYourVenture's equity investment simulator through its website: www.ownyour venture.com/equitySim.html.[53] Another popular tool is the capital calculator offered by Founders Workbench: www.foundersworkbench.com/capital-calculator. Similar to OwnYour-Venture's simulator, this dashboard allows entrepreneurs to manipulate variables, calculating and recalculating the distribution of ownership and equity across investors and founders, thus allowing them to understand the impact and changes that will occur.[54]

Salary

Although equity can compensate for a below-market salary, most of your team will need at least a subsistence salary during the launch phase. The difficulty is trying to set that initial salary. You can start by researching the current market rate for the position you are trying to fill at online resources such as www.salary.com. The website provides general parameters for the position and then allows you to personalize your search by company size, industry, and other factors. For instance, an information technology director might earn anywhere from $155,000 to $208,000 in the Boston metropolitan area.[55] The person's salary would be adjusted by her previous work experience, the industry focus of your company, and other mitigating factors specific to the individual or your company. You can also double check your market figure by looking at some of the Internet job sites like www.linkedin.com, www.monster.com and www.career-builder.com.[56] A scan of these sites found that a chief information technology officer position pays anywhere from $206,000 and $324,000.[57] The market rate is a reference parameter, and you'll adjust it by considering the person's expertise and perceived contribution to the company.

The Dilution Effect: An Example

This hypothetical example shows what happens to an entrepreneur as her firm achieves various milestones/benchmarks of a successful launch and moves on to a harvest/liquidity event. To demonstrate dilution, assume valuations at different rounds (valuation is covered in detail in Chapter 11). The following are some typical milestones that a successful venture might reach.

Milestone Events

1. Entrepreneur entices technology partner to join her firm: gives him **40%** of the equity.

2. Raises **$200,000** in equity from family and friends. The idea is valued post-money at **$1.0 million**.

3. Idea is technically feasible. Needs to hire **software engineers** to build a working prototype. Raises **$1 million** from angels on a **$2.5 million** post-money valuation. Establishes a **15%** option pool to provide equity to current engineers as well as future hires.

4. Prototype looks promising and company successfully raises **$3 million** of venture capital on a **$7 million** post-money valuation to start sales. The venture capitalist imposes the following terms: Company needs to hire an experienced CEO, CFO, and VP of sales, giving the three options worth **10%, 3%,** and **7%**.

5. Sales growth is on plan, and the firm needs to ramp up production to meet increasing demand. Raises **$10 million** of additional venture capital on a **$30 million** post-money valuation.

6. Firm receives acquisition offer from a large company (e.g., Microsoft, Cisco) for **$100 million in the large company's shares**.

Note that while our entrepreneur is being diluted, the increasing value of her firm offsets this dilution.

This example highlights a successful venture. Founders who distribute equity wisely grow the value of their firm, which leads to a higher return for all involved, even as dilution occurs. However, student entrepreneurs often make the mistake of giving too much founder shares to too many different people. If, for example, the firm started with five student founders with equal ownership and still progressed through each step, the final harvest value for each founder would be $1 million. While this sum is attractive, keep in mind that this growth projection likely takes five or more years, and in the early years the founders will be paid below-market salaries (and probably no salaries until the angel round).

Also, if there is any kind of problem that leads to a lower valuation than projected here, the final payoff for the founders is greatly impacted. If, for example, the valuation that the firm receives when the first venture capital comes in is only $5 million versus $7 million, the entrepreneur (as sole initial founder) earns a harvest value of $2.8 million. If there were five initial co-founders who get equal shares, each would earn a bit less than $600,000 for many years of hard work and below-market pay. The lesson is to distribute equity wisely. Make sure that all co-founders will contribute throughout the entire time it takes to build and harvest the company and that each can increase the value of the company.

Event	Entr. Share	Co-Founder	Family/ Friends	Angels	Option Pool	CEO	CFO	VP Sales	VC Rnd1	VC Rnd2	Total	Valuation (000)	Ent's. Value
1	60%	40%									100%		
2	48%	32%	20%								100%	$1,000	$480
3	22%	14%	9%	40%	15%						100%	$2,500	$540
4	8%	5%	3%	15%	6%	10%	3%	7%	43%		100%	$7,000	$562
5	5%	4%	2%	10%	4%	7%	2%	5%	29%	32%	100%	$30,000	$1,605
6	5%	4%	2%	10%	4%	7%	2%	5%	29%	32%	100%	$100,000	$5,349
Harvest Value for All Stakeholders	$5,349	$3,566	$2,229	$9,905	$3,714	$6,667	$2,000	$4,667	$28,571	$33,332			

A younger, less experienced co-founder will earn well below the market rate. A more senior, experienced co-founder with a long record of success might earn close to or above the market rate, but paying the market rate is probably impossible for a startup.

Once you know the market rate, you can negotiate a current salary and expected increases based on your company's improving cash flow. For instance, you might tie an increase to closing the next round of funding. Other increases might be linked to increasing cash flow due to improved sales. Instead of making firm commitments to future salary increases, consider using performance-based bonuses in the early years. This further aligns the team's efforts with the venture's overall goals and preserves cash flow. If team members successfully execute, the venture should have increasing sales, which in turn can lead to rapid growth in bonuses and other profit sharing. The key is to be creative and motivate your team to work toward common goals. That means deferred current income (lower salaries) with the promise of larger returns in the future (bonuses, appreciation of equity, and options).

Although startups should negotiate below-market salaries, it can be helpful to understand the implications of a fully loaded business model. When constructing your pro forma financials, see what happens to your expected profitability if you paid everyone their market rates. All too often entrepreneurs launch into a business expecting attractive profit margins only to realize that these margins are a mirage; once people are paid according to the market rate (say, in the fifth year), the profits disappear. Some entrepreneurs choose to promise market rates but defer payment until cash flow improves. In this case, they are creating a deferred liability that obligates the company to make up for the lower-than-market salary in the future. This means the market-rate salary is reflected in the income statement, the actual pay is shown on the cash flow, and the remainder appears on the balance sheet as a deferred liability.

There are various online tools and resources that entrepreneurs and founders can use to compare startup salaries. A popular website used by startups around the world is Angel-List. Set up as an online community for both startups and investors, the website offers salary information on over 100,000 startups (of which approximately 3,000 are actively seeking employees).[58] Visitors to the website can filter through various job profiles and companies comparing average salaries and roles (sales managers, developers, marketing managers, designers). You can find more information about AngelList through its website: http://angel.co.

However you decide to compensate your team, be cognizant of the full range of possibilities, and keep in mind that you need to preserve cash flow in the early years to fund growth.

Other Compensation Considerations

In addition to equity and salary, as the owner of a company you will need to think through a number of other issues in overall compensation. You will be competing with companies of all shapes and sizes for the most skilled people in the workforce. Putting together a competitive compensation package means thinking beyond just the monetary side of compensation. For instance, while they may not be feasible in the earliest parts of the startup phase, as quickly as possible you will want to consider things like health and dental plans and retirement savings programs. Even from the start, you will need to figure out a holiday and vacation package that makes sense for your company.

Every organization is different, and it's important to align your benefits package with the types of people you intend to hire. If your business will rely on recent university graduates, something like company-sponsored life insurance will probably be unnecessary. However, if your staff will be older, married people who have families, life insurance and a solid family healthcare plan will be essential. The key is that all of these benefits are strategic in nature. Your goal in developing a compensation package is to attract and motivate the best talent in the most cost-effective way possible. You should never underestimate the effect that a thoughtful benefits plan can have on employee satisfaction and loyalty. There are few things as powerful as having a workforce that feels they work for a great company.

External Team Members

Although your core team is critical to your venture's success, you will leverage the team's efforts by building a strong **virtual team**—that is, all those who have a vested interest in your success, including professionals you contract for special needs, such as lawyers, accountants, and consultants. It also includes those who have invested in your business, especially if they have valuable expertise. For instance, you'll be well served if you secure angel investors who are successful entrepreneurs in your industry. You may also be able to gain help from those who haven't financially invested in your firm but are interested in helping new businesses succeed, perhaps by serving on advisory boards for new companies. Finally, at some point you'll likely pull together a board of directors, which is required by law if you are incorporated. Let's examine each of these outside team members in more detail.

Outside Investors

When you are considering bringing on outside investors, whether in the form of angel investors or venture capitalists, never underestimate the value these team members can bring with their experience and wisdom. For many angel investors in particular, the experience of working with a startup is as much about the satisfaction of mentoring a young entrepreneur as it is about financial gain. Take, for example, the story of Norm Brodsky, the long-time entrepreneur and contributor to *Inc.* magazine. In describing his decision to invest in David Schneider's New York City restaurant, he said, "Yes, making money is important. I wouldn't go into a deal unless I thought I could get my capital back and earn a good return. But I don't really do this type of investing for the money anymore. I'm more interested in helping people get started in business. Whatever I make is a bonus on top of the fun I have being a part of it and the satisfaction I get from helping people like David succeed."

For an aspiring entrepreneur, finding an investor with that kind of attitude is invaluable. As David Schneider put it, "I really liked the idea of having somebody I could go to who cared about this place as a business.... It's like he's always pushing people to better themselves. He wants you to move on, to expand, to grow."[59] In business, experience is the greatest competitive advantage, and an investor can bring that asset to a fledgling company. But Schneider's comments also point to another key benefit of having a strong investor on your side: You'll have someone to hold you accountable and keep you focused. Many entrepreneurs underestimate the challenge being your own boss can pose. When the going gets tough or decisions get complicated, it can be incredibly helpful to have someone prodding you forward. For all these reasons, choose carefully if you decide to raise capital through angel investors.

Lawyers

Every new venture will require legal advice. Although you may be able to incorporate on your own, other aspects of your venture will benefit from your attorney's guidance. As discussed earlier, your lawyer can draft an appropriate template for employee contracts. If your business is developing some intellectual property, you may wish to file a patent. The right lawyer can help you search existing patents and decide which elements of your intellectual property are patentable. She or he will devise a suite of patents and then, if you deem it appropriate, help you patent your product in several important countries. Lawyers can also consult on the myriad unforeseen issues that are likely to arise, which is why it is so essential to choose your lawyer carefully.

When making a decision to hire a lawyer, consider several factors. For instance, a smaller firm is likely to offer lower billing rates, a factor that can be important to a startup. However, small firms are often heavily dependent on a small handful of clients who make up the bulk of their business. For this reason, you may find that your company is a low priority for a small firm with several key accounts. In contrast, while a large firm may bill at a higher rate, it will almost always have someone available to answer your questions, and it will also offer the benefit of a large pool of lawyers with diverse areas of expertise to draw from. Since your legal issues may cover everything from employment law to intellectual property, a large firm isn't necessarily a bad choice. While you may pay more, you may also find that a larger firm is more willing or able to set up a flexible payment plan.

In addition, when choosing your lawyer it is essential that you find someone whom you like, who shows an appreciation for and interest in your company, and, most importantly, who has deep knowledge of your industry. The last thing you want is to be paying several hundred dollars an hour to talk with someone who is distant or aloof. And as for hourly rates, yes, you should expect to pay a minimum of $150/hour—and likely much more than that. For this reason, it is critical that you do as much preparation and research as possible before you sit down with your lawyer. Most firms bill in increments of as little as 10 minutes, so you need to use your time with a lawyer as effectively and efficiently as possible. Also keep in mind that, while it is important to have a lawyer from the beginning to ensure that you avoid many of the classic mistakes, there is also a wide variety of free resources available to small businesses. These include everything from online templates for standard agreements and forms to nonprofit- and government-sponsored law centres that can provide low-cost or pro bono advice. While you should always turn to your lawyer for the final word, you can save your company a lot of money by using the available resources to get some of the legwork out of the way. Just remember that, as your company grows, your time will become more valuable, and at some point spending hours doing your own research becomes counterproductive.

When John Earle first started his apparel company, Johnny Cupcakes, intellectual property was the least of his worries, but as his brand grew in popularity, counterfeiting and piracy become rampant. In an effort to bootstrap the company, CFO, John's mother Lorraine, a former law office manager, used her knowledge of the law to write cease-and-desist letters to over 200 counterfeiters. Lorraine used her legal connections to cost-effectively trademark the Johnny Cupcakes logo and copyright designs. Lorraine explained, "People steal our name, our logo, our designs. In some countries, they're actually opening Johnny Cupcakes stores and selling our stuff."[60] Lorraine was able to use her past experience to save thousands of dollars on lawyer fees by doing the work herself and educating her son on legal matters during the process.

Accountants

It's often wise to hire an accountant to handle tax filings in the early years because you're likely to be too busy to do it yourself and too small to have an in-house person, such as a controller or CFO, to manage the process for you. Many of the same caveats about working with lawyers apply to accountants, although you may be well served by an accountant who is a sole proprietor. The nature of accountants' work is somewhat different from that of lawyers, and for this reason you needn't work with a larger firm in your early years. Don't forget that an accountant is a trained business professional; beyond filing tax returns and keeping your filings up to date, an accountant can help you analyze the strengths and weaknesses of your company's financial performance. He or she may be able to help you find ways to improve cash flow, strengthen margins, and identify tax benefits that can save you money down the road. Furthermore, both lawyers and accountants represent another spoke in your network, as both groups frequently have a long list of business and professional contacts. These can include everything from potential partners and customers to angel investor networks and venture capital firms.

Mentors

A popular definition of a *mentor* is "an intense developmental relationship whereby advice, counseling and developmental opportunities are provided to a protégé by a mentor, which, in turn, shapes the protégé's career experiences; this occurs through two types of support to protégés: instrumental or career support and psychological support."[61]

It is commonly believed that mentoring increases the survival of a new venture.[62] When an entrepreneur is starting a new venture it can be extremely difficult on many different levels—financially, socially, intellectually, and personally. Not only does a mentor provide a trusted source of support to the entrepreneur, but he or she influences the survival of the new venture through entrepreneurship accountability, social capital investment, and knowledge transfer from mentor to entrepreneur.[63]

Although having a mentor is important, it is even more important to find the *right* mentor. An entrepreneur would not call a member of his or her board of directors in the middle of the night worried about his financial security or with concerns of failure. A mentor has no direct relationship with the business itself, but rather connects with the person behind the business. A successful mentor–entrepreneur relationship has to have mutual trust, mutual respect, mutual freedom of expression, positive interpersonal chemistry between the parties, and a willingness to listen to each other.[64] A mentor not only provides support for the entrepreneur and the venture, but also advice in achieving the work–life balance needed to achieve the lifestyle the entrepreneur wants.

There are many organizations and businesses built on finding entrepreneurs the right mentor for their new venture. Futurepreneur Canada (formerly the Canadian Youth Business Foundation) is an example of an organization that matches entrepreneurs with mentors based on a number of factors, including needed skills, location of the entrepreneur or venture, background experience, management team, personal skills, and so on. The time commitment for a mentor–entrepreneur relationship can range from a couple of hours a week (four or five) to daily communication (whether it be by phone, email, text, or video messaging).[65]

Board of Advisors

A board of advisors can be extremely beneficial to the early-stage company. Unlike a board of directors, a board of advisors has no fiduciary duty to shareholders. Instead, the goal is to offer a source of expert guidance and feedback to the lead entrepreneur. In choosing a board, you should look to enlist people with expertise in your field and a sincere interest in mentoring an emerging business. Good sources are your professors, current and former entrepreneurs, professional investors such as venture capitalists and angels, suppliers for your firm, and individuals who may have insight into your target customers. Beyond advice, this group can expand your personal network and provide leads to new customers or investors. In fact, board of advisor members will often become investors if your firm goes through a private placement.

One final note on boards of advisors relates to communication. Many first-time entrepreneurs struggle to strike the right balance between too much and too little communication. Keep in mind that, if you have developed a board of powerful advisors, they are busy individuals. Don't email or phone them every time you have a question. Instead, accumulate questions and think about which ones are most critical to your firm and where the advisor can add the most value. Do some preliminary legwork to find alternative answers to these questions and options you might be inclined to pursue. If you are prepared, you will have a more productive conversation with your advisors, and they will be even more supportive of your future efforts.

The flip side to overcommunicating with advisors is touching base with them rarely—or only when you want help raising money. This type of communication suggests that the entrepreneur is interested only in the advisor's network, but the advisor is less inclined to open up that network unless he or she has a strong understanding of the company's progress. Produce a monthly or bimonthly email newsletter that keeps all your important stakeholders, including your board of advisors, informed about the company's progress. This newsletter should be short and concise so that it will get read. More often than not, the newsletter will prompt an advisor to contact you with some useful input or connection to someone in his or her network. Properly managing your board of advisors will pay dividends, so don't neglect it.

Board of Directors

When incorporating a company, entrepreneurs must establish a board of directors whose purpose is to represent the interests of the equity holders. Thus, when you initially incorporate, the only shareholders might be you and your co-founders. Once you seek outside financing, it becomes important to fill out the board beyond the co-founders. Venture capitalists and more sophisticated angels often require representation on the board. A common board structure for the early-stage firm is five board members; these might include two insiders like the CEO and CFO, two members from the lead investors, and one outsider, who most often is selected with strong input from the investors. The outsider is often a person who has significant vertical market expertise and who can add value to the strategic operating decisions.

The board is in charge of governance and represents the shareholders. It meets quarterly to review the company's progress and its strategy going forward. The board will determine compensation for the company's officers and also oversee financial reporting. With the passage of the Sarbanes-Oxley Act in the United States, the responsibilities and potential liability of the board have greatly increased. In response to the passage of the Sarbanes-Oxley Act, the Canadian Securities Administrators (CSA) undertook an extensive consultation process, which eventually led to the introduction of a series of new rules. For the most part, these rules follow Sarbanes-Oxley and the rules and guidelines set by the U.S. Securities and Exchange Commission (SEC) and U.S. stock exchanges, while taking into account the Canadian financial market.[66]

While the legislation applies only to public companies, more and more small businesses are finding it necessary to align with the act if they hope one day to sell to a public company or go public themselves. It's a voluntary choice to do so, but the act's standards are rapidly becoming the "best practices" for accounting and financial control at well-managed companies. This means that developing a clear set of expectations, ethical standards, and procedures for board members is essential. Furthermore, you'll want to ensure that your board has at least one or two members who can be considered independent, which means that they are not susceptible to potential conflicts of interest. Board members should be encouraged to act in the best interest of all the shareholders, not just the principal owner.

The entrepreneurial team should extend beyond the co-founders and early employees to include external individuals who can provide invaluable wisdom and input. Entrepreneurship is truly a team sport—the stronger your team, the more likely you are to not only survive but thrive. The next section looks at some difficulties you might incur once the team is in place.

Keeping the Team Together

We've looked at the value of a well-functioning team. But not every team functions well, even if it's filled with superstars. Consider the Boston Red Sox, which had Major League Baseball's third-highest payroll ($173 million) in 2012.[67] The team finished in last place in the American League East Division despite having all-star David Ortiz and power players such as Adrian Gonzalez, Josh Beckett, John Lackey, Kevin Youkilis, Dustin Pedroia, and Jacoby Ellsbury[68] Why did this happen? Common sense dictates that the team with the best talent should win, but a dysfunctional team often fails. The key here is chemistry: Sometimes the

Family Pressure

If working long hours stresses your team members, it also stresses their families. Spouses and significant others complain to their partners that they are never home or they are too tired to pay attention to their families. Missing a child's hockey games and school performances can create resentment. Stress at home can negatively affect performance at work and increase the risk of turnover. If spouses continually ask why their partners have left good-paying jobs for lower pay and the promise of a future payoff, your team members will question their own motives. So it's imperative that open communication occur on the home front as well.

Counsel your team members to set the expectations of their families even before they join your team. If a spouse is forewarned of the long hours, it minimizes the angst. It's also a good idea to include families in stress-relieving events on a regular basis. Company picnics are a nice way for spouses to connect with other spouses. In this way, they can develop an informal support group with people who are facing the same difficulties. In fact, some new ventures formalize these family support groups by organizing a few events that are spouse specific. It is important to remember and remind all involved that the long hours will subside and that, if the venture is successful, everyone will benefit.

Interpersonal Conflicts

In such a charged environment, interpersonal conflicts among team members are common. Resolve these disputes as quickly as possible, or they may escalate to the point where they become destructive. Lead entrepreneurs typically find that they spend as much time coaching and managing team issues as they do directly working on the business. If you find yourself in this situation, don't worry—this is a valuable and effective use of your time. If you can keep your team working together, you'll have more success than if you try to carry the burden all alone.

As the coach, you may be able to resolve some conflicts only by firing one of the team members. While firing is a necessary part of running a company, you need to be prepared for the inevitable disruption it will cause (although it can be therapeutic to those who remain if it removes some of the stress that the fired individual brought to the company). Depending on the person's agreement with the company, his or her departure may require a buyout of equity and a lump-sum settlement. That's why firing is usually undertaken only if the person is not only prone to interpersonal conflicts but also underperforming in some way (either not skilled enough to do the jobs required or shirking his or her responsibilities). First try to resolve the conflict by mediating between the parties, and be sure not to appear to be favouring either one. It may be prudent to hire an outside expert who is perceived as a neutral party. Whatever resolution you agree upon, make sure that it is implemented as planned.

CONCLUSION

Entrepreneurship is a team sport. The most critical task any lead entrepreneur undertakes is defining who should be on the team and then creating an environment in which that team can flourish. This chapter has identified what type of team members ventures might need, how to entice and compensate them, and how to build a strong, supportive culture. Maintaining a team requires ongoing effort, and many organizations find that team dynamics suffer when the firm experiences rapid growth. Chapter 14 revisits these issues and suggests ways that organizations can keep their entrepreneurial orientation.

Reflection Point	Your Thoughts. . .	YOUR OPPORTUNITY JOURNAL ☐
1. What are your three strongest attributes?		
2. Talk to a close mentor and ask what he or she sees as your strengths. Do these match the attributes you identified above?		
3. What skills do you need to develop prior to launch? What skills can you develop during the launch and early stages of your company? Create a plan to develop those skills.		
4. Create an organization chart for your venture. Show positions to be filled immediately and those to be filled later (along with the dates of filling those positions). Create a staffing plan based on your organization chart.		
5. Think about the types of employees you'd like to hire. What kind of values are you looking for? Remember, this is the point at which you create your company's culture.		

WEB EXERCISE ☐

Scan Monster.com, Salary.com, and other job sites. Look at the postings for CEOs and other key employees of early-stage companies in the industry that you are interested in pursuing. What skills are being sought? What level of previous experience is desired? How much are they offering for these key employees? Use this information to start creating your own staffing plan.

CASE

Zeo, Inc.

The more you know, the better you sleep. ™

Newton, Massachusetts

As students at Brown University in 2003, Eric Shashoua, Jason Donahue, and Ben Rubin shared a problem common to students of every generation—sleep deprivation. Each tried to pack as much as possible into every day with the *least* possible amount of sleep. The result was predictable: They had trouble getting up in the morning and staying alert in class.

One of the three had, through his coursework, become aware of a study commissioned by NASA during the 1960s. That study focused on the human sleep cycle. It identified points in the cycle at which a person would be most alert if awakened. For the three friends, NASA's findings seemed to have practical utility. If they could wake up at the right point in their sleep cycles, they would be less groggy and more effective in the classroom. They could continue cheating the gods of sleep, but with fewer negative consequences. Reasoning that an effective solution would benefit the millions of people who, like them, were burning the candle at both ends, the three set out to build a company around that solution. "We saw ourselves as the target market," recalls Jason. "That market had to be large since companies were pushing caffeine products and special drinks, like Red Bull, to help people stay alert."

Six years on, the college friends were still together, but now as founding executives of Zeo, a business dedicated to a somewhat larger mission—to help people get a better night's sleep. During those years they had raised $14 million, invented a way to track sleep comfortably, and developed and launched a consumer product that was gaining nationwide awareness. And although they were sleeping better than they had in college, they were now dealing with other issues. Zeo was no longer a three guys' college project. It was now a fast-growing enterprise with an increasing number of employees with specialized skills, experiences, and reporting relationships. An older, seasoned CEO was at the helm, and the focus of the enterprise's energy had shifted from developing and launching a product to expanding sales and satisfying customers.

Unsurprisingly, this evolution in the company's life was affecting the founders and their roles in the company. To evolve with the company's needs and contribute as leaders, they had to continue to grow professionally, learn new skills, and step up to new challenges. How would the founders evolve and grow to meet the different needs of the company?

The Sleep Problem/Opportunity

Most people take sleep for granted. Yet 30–50% of the adult U.S. population reports difficulty in sleeping.[77] In a 2005 poll of adult Americans, 24% of respondents reported getting "a good night's sleep" only a few nights *per week*, and 13% reported getting that good night's sleep only a few nights *per month*. Another 13% told pollsters that they *rarely or never* had a good night's sleep.[78]

Sleep problems can have detrimental effects on a person's attentiveness, work and academic performance, and even relationships. Even so, only 8% of people speak with their primary care physicians about their sleep problems. And few doctors bother to ask. By one estimate, less than 20% of doctors ask patients how well they are sleeping as part of their annual physical exams. This "don't ask, don't tell" situation results in millions of people living with their sleep problems for years and years without relief.

For a minority of sleep-deprivation sufferers, the underlying cause can be traced to a medical condition.[79] The medical establishment has responded to these with various forms of clinical diagnoses and therapy. Its primary diagnostic tool is the sleep laboratory, a specially equipped room in which individual patients are observed and monitored by means of polysomnography (PSG)—the gold standard of sleep diagnosis. In the United States, a small number of board-certified sleep specialists (approximately 5,000) attend to the millions who suffer from medical conditions that interfere with normal sleep.

The majority of people with sleep problems, however, have no underlying medical issues. Their difficulties often stem from work or lifestyle choices. These individuals include students, hospital physicians and nurses, shift-workers, people struggling to meet deadlines, long-haul truck drivers, hard-driving professionals, and heavy consumers of caffeinated products and alcohol. Sleep deprivation for them often results in drowsiness and reduced cognitive performance, and a greater susceptibility to accidents at work and on the highway.

It was this market, estimated at 70 million people in the United States alone, that Zeo aimed to serve. From the beginning, the company has made it clear that its product is not intended for the diagnosis or treatment of sleep disorders and warned customers that "If you suspect that you may have a sleep disorder, consult your physician." Zeo did not intend to compete with medical devices, sleep laboratories, or medical practitioners.

Building the Company

When they formed Zeo in December 2003, Eric, Jason, and Ben knew little about sleep science or sleep medicine. Eric, a senior, was studying computer science and French; Jason, then a junior, was majoring in business and Chinese. Ben, a junior majoring in computer engineering, was recruited later through a campus job posting. Brown University, however, was a leading centre for the study of sleep and sleep medicine, so the team worked hard to build relationships with the University's sleep experts and to learn from them and from other campus resources. In time they would expand their relationships and learning to a broader network.

Initially, the business opportunity was narrowly defined around the concept of Smart-Wake™, a technology used to track sleep and identify the optimal times for awakening someone refreshed and alert. To accomplish this, they would have to build a device capable of accurately monitoring and recording a person's sleep stages (wake, light sleep, REM, and deep sleep). They would do this by developing a comfortable, wireless, sensing device that the customer would wear on his or her forehead during the night. The technical breakthrough that made this possible was a dry fabric sensor material developed by the team. The device itself would detect and transmit vital data to a bedside receiver/monitor, which would store and later array the information in a manner that a lay person could easily interpret. Ben initially estimated that he could develop a testable prototype over the school's Christmas break. In fact, the job took over two-and-a-half years.

Sleep Stages

People typically pass through various stages of sleep during the night. These include wake, light sleep, rapid eye movement (REM) sleep, and deep sleep. A person normally experiences repeated cycles of these phases during the night.

Light Sleep: Takes place between the transitions to the other phases of sleep and wakefulness. Usually accounts for the longest phase of the sleep cycle.

REM: Necessary for consolidating memories, learning, creativity, problem solving, and emotional well-being. This is the time when dreams occur.

Deep Sleep: Restorative phase in which the body secretes a growth hormone needed for development and physical repair. People generally feel most groggy when awakened from deep sleep. According to cognitive tests, they may experience impaired mental performance for up to 4 hours when abruptly awakened from deep sleep.

Early Financing

Many people responded affirmatively to the SmartWake™ concept. Eric recalls how he would talk about the project in the campus cafeteria. "Bystanders started to say, 'That's a great idea. Can I invest in your company?'" And many of them did in small amounts. This in turn led Eric to seek out private investors in the community, who invested larger amounts. Ultimately this allowed the group to get more serious efforts underway with a small seed round. In the very beginning, other non-dilutive funds were also sought:

- A $9,000 grant from the Slater Center of Rhode Island
- An $18,000 grant from the National Intercollegiate Inventors and Innovators Alliance
- $10,000 in cash and $10,000 in services from the Brown Entrepreneurship Program Business Plan Competition
- $25,000 in cash and $35,000 in services from winning the State of Rhode Island Business Plan Competition

By mid-2005, all three founders had graduated from Brown and were working full-time in the company, which needed more money. Their fundraising efforts shifted exclusively to angel investors. Responsible for fundraising efforts, Eric pitched to angel groups and individual investors all over southern New England, as well as within the Rhode Island business community and Brown University alumni. "This was hard to do," he says, "given our ages." Each rejection, however, encouraged him to dig for reasons and to refine his presentation. By the end of this 10-month period, with a second oversubscribed round, the company had raised a total of over $1 million from several groups and individuals.

Among Zeo's early investors was Sean Glass. Like the Zeo founding team, Glass had joined with other classmates (in his case, years earlier at Yale) to start a successful business while still an undergraduate. He learned of Zeo through a fellow angel investor, a Brown graduate who had already taken a small stake in new enterprise. Glass thought the company had a strong concept since there were few credible products in the consumer sleep market; as he put it, "People will go to great lengths to solve their sleep problems." Glass also saw a bit of himself and his company's co-founders in the Zeo team. And he liked what he saw. "Eric, Jason, and Ben had different personalities, but they clearly trusted each other in their roles. All were very well organized and open to learning."

Glass invested in 2005 as a member of an angel group. Still, he perceived some difficult hurdles ahead. "They would have to convince people that their product was scientifically valid, and that it really worked. It would also need to be priced right." And from the user's perspective, the headband monitor they were working on had to be comfortable and look good. Otherwise, "how many people will get into bed with their spouses wearing a weird-looking contraption on their heads?"

Advice and Credibility

Sleep science is a relatively new field. Research on the subject only began in the 1950s. As a result, the community of sleep specialists is small, and communication and collaboration is commonplace.

From the outset, the venture team understood the importance of tapping into this scientific community, drawing on its expertise, and gaining credibility by allying with key members. Most of the responsibility for this task fell to Ben Rubin, who, beginning at Brown University, cold-called key people, introduced himself and Zeo, and solicited their advice and support.

To his surprise and relief, these specialists did not automatically show him the door. Most, in fact, expressed genuine interest in the goal Zeo was pursuing. They were intrigued by the potential benefits that an inexpensive, self-administered measuring and monitoring system would bring to the millions of people who suffered from nonmedical-related sleep difficulties.

Each contact produced leads to other notables in the U.S. sleep science community. Before long, Ben and the team had assembled an informal group of sleep health advisors from several of the nation's leading medical institutions. In addition to this group, a key consultant, John Shambroom, joined Ben's development efforts. John brought a unique scientific and engineering background to the team, which included extensive experience in tracking brainwave patterns, critical to ongoing development. This initial group contributed invaluable technical guidance and gave the start-up venture much needed credibility in the eyes of potential investors. John would later join the company and expand this group into a formal board with semiannual meetings. Board members would represent the broad scope of sleep science: a psychologist, a specialist in circadian rhythms, a leading researcher, a clinical practitioner, and so forth (Exhibit 7.1).

| **EXHIBIT 7.1** | **Zeo Advisory Board** |

Chair: **Kenneth P. Wright Jr., PhD**
Director, Sleep & Chronobiology Lab,
University of Colorado, Boulder

Daniel Aeschbach, PhD
Assistant Professor of Medicine,
Harvard Medical School

Michael J. Breus, PhD
"The Sleep Doctor," author, WebMD® sleep
expert and AOL® wellness coach

Charles A. Czeisler, MD, PhD
Director, Division of Sleep Medicine,
Harvard Medical School

Phyllis C. Zee, MD, PhD
Professor of Neurology and Neurobiology and
Physiology Director,
Sleep Disorders Center
Northwestern University Medical School

John W. Winkelman, MD, PhD
Assistant Professor of Psychiatry,
Harvard Medical School and Medical
Director, Sleep Health Center of Brigham
and Women's Hospital

The team also sought business advice. It made a list of pioneers in fields related to Zeo, then approached each in turn. "It usually took a few calls to get through," says Eric, "but once we got past the gatekeepers, most of these people were very approachable."

I'd tell them that we were students who had started a company, that we admired what they had accomplished, and that we would appreciate their advice. I'd then ask, 'Could we meet with you for just a half hour or so?' This is how we met Colin Angle, founder of iRobot, and Sherwin Greenblatt, former president of Bose. Colin had started his company while a graduate student at MIT. We maintained an advisory relationship with these business leaders for over two years, then asked them to join our board, which they did.

A Coach/CEO

The three founders wanted to launch a consumer product company, first nationally and then internationally, and knew that they wouldn't have the best chance of success doing this on their own. Recognizing that they had never done this before, they wanted to find an expert who could help them achieve greater success, and from whom they could learn. So, with the proceeds of the final angel round, which closed in the summer of 2006, they set out to find an experienced person who could guide them through the important stages of final product development, launch, and growth. An executive search firm with an affinity for start-ups was engaged and asked to find qualified candidates for the CEO position. That firm's consultant met with the three founders and interviewed each extensively. What qualities and experiences were they looking for in a candidate? How would they describe their ideal candidate? How did they expect the person to work with them?

Eric, Jason, and Ben were of one mind. They wanted a CEO with an entrepreneurial outlook and a successful record in marketing consumer-health products. More than that, their ideal candidate would be a coach and mentor, helping each of them develop his business and management skills. As they saw it, Zeo was growing from a small start-up into a real business; each founding member wanted to grow quickly into the new roles that operating such a business demanded.

Finding a person with the desired combination of experience and personal qualities was a tall order, but after several months of searching, the recruiter presented the team with several qualified candidates. The candidate they selected was Dave Dickinson, a man roughly twice their ages.

Dickinson's life path had been much different than those of Zeo's founders. As a teenager he had learned something of how entrepreneurial businesses work, and how they differ from bureaucratic organizations. His father had joined with former IBM veterans to develop a small company, and his work experiences were a frequent topic of conversation in the Dickinson household. Dave knew and admired the president of his father's new company.

I remember playing basketball with him when I was a junior in high school. And I still recall how much I wanted to be like him—to know everyone who worked for the company, to know their families, and to enjoy the freedom to get things done without dealing with committees and layers of bureaucracy. How many big company presidents play basketball with their employees' kids?

Despite his youthful attraction to small business life, Dickinson's career path went in the opposite direction. Armed with an MBA in marketing from Northwestern University, he worked for several giant consumer-health product companies: Procter & Gamble, Johnson & Johnson, Arm & Hammer, and Mead Johnson. In 1995, however, his entrepreneurial instincts were given a chance to express themselves. Dickinson's boss at Mead Johnson asked him to create a new product incubation unit, staffed by some 100 employees from market-ing and R&D. "These were disciplines that never spoke to each other," he recalls. "At our Evansville [Indiana] headquarters the marketing people were in a building on one side of a four-lane road, and the R&D people were on the other side. No one ever crossed that road, except to eat lunch."

In accepting the assignment, Dickinson got permission to take over and renovate one floor of unused space in an old industrial building. He hired an architect to implement his vision of an open design in which communication and collaboration between marketing and R&D specialists would naturally occur. There would be no private offices, no cubicles. To further set the incubator apart from the rest of the company, he had the place painted in bright colors. Quotations by famous inventors adorned the walls. White boards and games were set out here and there to encourage interaction. A basketball hoop was mounted on a far wall. A phone booth was installed at the back of the space. "I told people that if they *really* needed to have a private conversation, they could use the phone booth."

The success of this interdisciplinary product incubator changed Dickinson's life in two important ways. First, it made him realize how much he enjoyed breaking free of corporate rules and routines, and building new things from scratch. Second, it led to an important new assignment. In 1998, he was asked to move to Boston and help initiate a novel kind of venture capital firm, jointly funded by Bristol Myers Squibb (parent of Mead Johnson) and General Mills. Consumer health and wellness would be its investment focus. Dickinson recalls how that experience broadened his understanding of innovation, different business models, and the management challenges faced by young and inexperienced entrepreneurs. "I spent a lot of time helping the CEOs of these companies, particularly in the marketing area." He enjoyed sharing his knowledge with these CEOs and helping them with market development. "In many cases, I wished that I was them!" And, in 2001, he became the CEO of his first start-up, a biotechnology company initially incubated within Harvard Medical School.

Dickinson's background brought him into the sights of Zeo's headhunter in late 2006. He offered two unique qualities that Zeo needed: experience in developing, launching, and mar-keting consumer health products, and an open, mentoring personality. For Dickinson's part, Zeo represented an outlet for his entrepreneurial instincts.

Meetings between Dickinson, the founders, and Zeo's key investors were encouraging. The candidate met all of Zeo's expectations, and Dickinson liked what he saw in the venture and its principals. "You could see that these guys were insatiable learners, hungry for experi-ence and knowledge. They were eager to learn from everyone—from people like me, from investors, and from their advisory board. There was no youthful arrogance."

It was a match. After doing due diligence on the venture and its technology, and in return for a reasonable salary and an equity stake vested over time, Dickinson joined the company as CEO in February 2007.

Beyond SmartWake™

By the time Dave Dickinson joined the company, the team had raised over $1 million dollars around its SmartWake™ concept. With Dave now wearing the CEO cap, Eric could turn his full attention to the job of prospecting for additional investment capital and expanding Zeo's strategic connections for business development. Jason's focus would remain on potential cus-tomers: Who were they? What were their needs in a sleep product? How would they connect with Zeo and its evolving technology?

EXHIBIT 7.2   **Product Hardware**

The Zeo Headband, with dry fabric
sensor materials shown.

Zeo Receiver/Display Unit

Source: Zeo, with permission.

Using an SD (secure digital) memory card within the bedside display, the customer can use his or her personal computer to transfer accumulated sleep data to a personal online account, myZeo.com. The website (Exhibit 7.3) has interactive tools for understanding the data. It also provides cause-and-effect information on how individual lifestyle choices—including exercise, diet, drinking, and stress—affect sleep.

Manufacturing of the physical product was outsourced to an Asian contract manufacturer. The price was eventually set at $249 for the product alone, and $349 for the deluxe package, which included the product, a year's supply of headband sensors, and unlimited access to the online 7 Step coaching program. Sales would be made directly to customers via the Internet.

The Launch

As mid-2009 approached, the Zeo crew prepared for the product's official launch. Not having the public company financial resources common to consumer product launches, they needed a high ROI method to gain public exposure. So, working with a Boston-based PR firm, Schneider Associates, they devised an innovative plan to create media buzz. Dozens of reporters were invited to spend the night, courtesy of the company, at a brand-new five-star New York City hotel. Each was given a Zeo device that they would use during the night to record their sleep patterns.

The next morning, the overnight guests were treated to a breakfast in the hotel ballroom, where company personnel were on hand to help them understand their recorded sleep patterns from the previous night. After a brief presentation by Zeo, several scientific experts spoke on the relationship between sleep and human health. Reporters then moved to "break out" tables where specific sleep-related topics such as sleep and human performance, methods for sleeping

EXHIBIT 7.3 Sleep Tools and Coaching Program Information

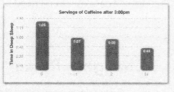

Find out what's stealing your sleep.

Zeo Personal Sleep Coach will help you understand and minimize the factors that negatively affect sleep, so you can take control of your nights. You can use the visual analytical tools in your personal myZeo.com account to see trends and cause & effect patterns.

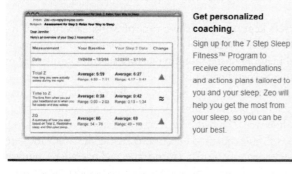

Get personalized coaching.

Sign up for the 7 Step Sleep Fitness™ Program to receive recommendations and actions plans tailored to you and your sleep. Zeo will help you get the most from your sleep, so you can be your best.

better, and so forth, were discussed. At one table, the trainer of the Boston Celtics entertained reporters' questions about sleep and athletic performance. "The idea," says Dave, "was to give reporters opportunities to pick up on many different story lines."

This hotel PR gambit and other launch PR efforts paid huge dividends almost immediately. The first big story about Zeo appeared within days in the *Wall Street Journal*. The *Journal's* health columnist, Melinda Beck, described how Zeo had helped her discover and understand her own sleep problems. "Finding out what's going on in your sleep generally requires spending the night in a professional sleep lab hooked up to lots of wires and monitors," she told millions of readers. "But I've been testing a new home-sleep monitor called the Zeo Personal Sleep Coach that lets people track their sleep patterns nightly in their own bedrooms."[80] She went on to describe her dismal ZQ score, how it responded negatively to tensions surrounding her column deadlines, and how it improved once she switched to decaffeinated coffee and kicked her dog out of the bedroom. In the article, she interviewed members of the company's advisory board and other Zeo users, who shared their positive experiences with the product, its coaching program, and how changes in daily habits affected their ZQ scores.

For the company, Beck's article could not have been more timely or beneficial. Orders began pouring in. Other positive articles quickly followed in the *New York Times*, *Forbes*, *USA Today*, *Popular Science*, *Woman's Day*, and other national periodicals. Ben and Jason soon found themselves interviewed on Fox TV, and America's primo TV pitchman, Regis Philbin, had himself filmed in bed wearing his Zeo headband and talking about his own sleep problems. More orders came in—at a time when consumer product sales in the United States were in the basement!

Over the next six months, the young company continued to score PR coups. One of the most significant of these occurred on December 14, 2009, at the height of the holiday gift-buying season. The nation's most popular morning TV program, *The Today Show*, watched by over six million Americans, ran four short story segments on Zeo's founders and their new product, with testimonials from a user, a leading sleep medical authority, and the TV network's own doctor/journalist. All praised the product. KaBoom! The sky began raining orders and Google identified Zeo as the most searched topic that day, even ahead of a Tiger Woods scandal that was making headlines all over the media.

A Changing Company . . . Changing Roles

The product launch and subsequent media buzz marked a watershed for Zeo. The once-obscure little company was now on the map and receiving enormously positive feedback from reviewers. And the cash register was ringing.

Rather than relax, however, employees kept up a punishing pace of work. Says Eric, "With working many nights and weekends, there hasn't been a lot of time for friends and family, or—ironically—for sleep." The only married member of the founding team, Eric consciously tried to optimize the limited time he had available to spend with his spouse by focusing on communication. Jason Donahue echoed his partner's assessment of the work load. "We don't have a problem with absenteeism around here. Our problem is *presentee-ism*—people not going home."

Even before the June 2009 launch, however, Zeo had been changing. New people with deep and specialized experience had come onboard. Subsequent to Dickinson's joining the company, John Shambroom was hired as the initial vice-president of research, engineering, and operations, but was later asked to focus on the company's scientific and clinical platform as the vice-president of scientific affairs. Later, others were hired to head up e-commerce, finance and manufacturing, and engineering and product development. And as 2009 drew to a close, the team was searching for a specialist in direct-response TV advertising. "These people had technical skills we needed right away," says Dave Dickinson. "We couldn't wait months and years for our own people to develop them. And we'll do more of this as we grow." By late 2009, 19 people were on the payroll. Eight were on the management team, making the company strategically top-heavy in preparation for growth.

The launch and the addition of new people had an impact on the roles of the three founders. "We're now wearing fewer hats," said one. "Each of us is developing new skills and learning a lot

business planning process equates to a $10,
200 hours). However, launching a flawed bu
in spent capital. Most entrepreneurial ventu
if the business will ultimately fail. Assumi
entrepreneur, a two-year investment equate:
cost and the likelihood that other employee
incurred. So do yourself a favour and spend

The business planning *process* helps en
opportunity by raising critical questions, rese:
ing them. For example, one question that eve
tomer's pain?" Conversations with customers
product offering to what customers need anc
money that an entrepreneur might spend try
launched. While all businesses adjust their off
helps the entrepreneur anticipate some of the

As mentioned earlier, the real purpos
entrepreneur writing it then the investor re
answer important questions relating to the
a Canadian organization that helps small l
answered while writing a business plan:[7]

1. What is your primary reason for starti
2. What are some personal objectives yor
3. Write out a vision for your business. \
4. Is the business seasonal? What are you
5. Is the industry growing or declining? I
   five years?
6. What are the past, present and future
7. Have you anticipated technological cl
8. In geographic terms, how large is the
   or services?
9. What percentage of the market do you
   are you going to capture it?
10. Who are your major potential busines
    they buy your product or service?
11. Do you know the strengths and we
    competition?
12. What will be the image of your busin
13. How much will it cost you to acquire
    that one customer? How long will th:

Perhaps the greatest benefit of busi
articulate the business opportunity to \
Business planning provides the backgro
communicate the upside potential to in
to convince potential employees to lea
new venture. Finally, it can also help se
In short, business planning provides th
needs to answer the critical questions th
founded business plan gives the entrepre

2009,www.businessinsider.co
profitable-gets-a-new-ceo-20(

18 N. Bilton, "One on One: C
son, CEO of Etsy," *Bits* (blog)
blogs.nytimes.com/2012/07
one-chad-dickerson-ceo-of-et

19 Facebook, "Founder Bio:
newsroom.fb.com/founder-b

20 B. Stone, "Is Facebook Grov
Fast?" *New York Times,* Marc
www.nytimes.com/2009/03/
ogy/Internet/29face.html.

21 Food Should Taste Good, '
www.foodshouldtastegood.
fstg/our-story/timeline.

22 Food Should Taste Good, "I
2011," www.foodshouldtas
about-fstg/in-the-news/2011

23 Yahoo! News, "General Mills
Maker for Undisclosed Sum,"
2012, http://news.yahoo.c
mills-buys-snack-maker-u
sum-234512789.html.

24 P. Drucker, "Managing Ones
Business Review 83 (2005): 1(

25 *HR Focus,* 82 (September 20(

26 K. McFarland, "The Psycho
cess," *Inc.*, November 15, 20(

27 W. Kuemmerle, "A Test fo
Hearted," *Harvard Business*
(2002): 122–126.

28 Ibid.

29 www.eventuring.org/eShip/:
eVenturing/ShowDoc/:
CacheRepository/Docume
pp276-279.pdf.

30 Startup Genome, "Startup
port Extra on Premature Sca
Dive into Why Most High (
ups Fail," *Startup Genome R*
29, 2011.

31 Ibid.

32 Ibid.

33 Ibid.

34 Ibid.

35 "Brief Profile of 2003 Inc
panies," *Inc.*, October 15,

from Dave." As an obliging mentor, Dave Dickinson made an effort to learn what each founder did innately well and then directed each into areas where he could make the greatest contribution and develop more skills. "To do this I actually used the same profile test for Eric, Jason, and Ben that their recruiter had used on me." Each person's tests results were shared with his colleagues, and this helped each person to better understand his strengths and weaknesses and those of his peers. "That exercise really developed trust, which made the rest of the effort easier."

For Jason Donahue, the post-launch period coincided with a major redirection of attention, from product development, sales, and customers to brand management and assuring high customer satisfaction. With Dave at the helm, Eric Shashoua shifted his primary attention to business development and to relationships that would help the company grow. He was now spending more time with Zeo's directors (Exhibit 7.4), the advisory board, the sleep-health community, and potential channel and product partners. Ben Rubin had once been in charge of technology development, product development, engineering and manufacturing. He was now focused on technology and its application to the company's next generation of sleep-related products.

EXHIBIT 7.4 Zeo Board of Directors

Colin Angle
CEO, iRobot Corporation

Dave Dickinson
CEO, Zeo Inc.

Ronald Chwang
Chairman and President, iD Ventures America

Sherwin Greenblatt
Former President, Bose Corporation

Peter Meekin
Managing Director, Trident Capital

Eric Shashoua
Co-Founder & VP, Zeo Inc.

W. Anthony Vernon
Former Company Group Chairman,
Johnson & Johnson

While all acknowledged the necessity of these changes, they came with some nostalgia. Ben commented that, "As the company has gotten bigger and our roles have become more specialized, we [the founders] have lost something. Each of us probably misses having a larger role." He notes that decision making has also changed. "The three of us can no longer sit down together for five minutes and make a decision. The process is now more complicated. That's good for the business but sometimes frustrating for us." At the same time, Ben accepts the changing roles, seeing them as direct outcomes of choices the three of them made.

If we had decided to be a smaller niche company, our roles would not have had to change nearly as much. Our decision to address a large consumer market had important consequences: It dictated our need for an experienced CEO, for more outside capital, for more employees with specialized know-how, and so forth. We have to recognize and accept the impact of our own decisions.

Any misgivings the founders had about their changing roles appeared to have taken a back seat to conscious efforts to grow into those new roles. Speaking for the group, Eric noted that they had surrounded themselves with experienced employees and routinely interacted with business advisors, investors, sleep-science specialists, and with other entrepreneurs. Jason pointed to books and blogs, and to events and seminars as important sources of learning and growth.[81] For his part, Ben acknowledged the benefit of having experienced and knowledgeable mentors on the board and outside the company.

NOTES

THE MO:
that goe:
petitors,
of all the
ensure a
panies in
business
was sigr
ensure t
Dwight
are usele
academ
Th
story is
student
to beco
isn't jus
that, a
Th
ness pla
the det:
entrepr
of this
10-day
happer
every y
entrepr

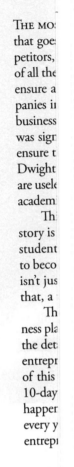

Source: Janvier, Magali (2010, July 30). Our Stor
2014, from *Wajam Blog,* http://blog.wajam.com

Figure 8.1

Back of the napkin design (B

Figure 8.8b

Magazine advertisements

Publication	Circulation	Ad Price for Quarter Page	Total Budget for Year 1
Lexington Minuteman newspaper	7,886	$ 500	$4,000
Boston Magazine	1,400,000	$1,000	$1,000

Sales Strategy. The section on sales strategy provides the backbone that supports all of the subsections described so far. Specifically, it illustrates what kind and level of human capital you will devote to the effort. You should complete a careful analysis of how many salespeople and customer support reps you will need. Will these people be internal to the organization or outsourced? If they are internal, will there be a designated sales force, or will different members of the company serve in a sales capacity at different times? Again, a thoughtful presentation of the company's sales force builds credibility by demonstrating an understanding of how the business should operate.

Sales and Marketing Forecasts. Gauging the impact of sales efforts is difficult. Nonetheless, to build a compelling story, entrepreneurs need to show projections of revenues well into the future. How do you derive these numbers? There are two methods: the *comparable method* and the *build-up method.* After detailed investigation of the industry and the market, entrepreneurs know the competitive players and have a good understanding of their history. The comparable method models the sales forecast after what other companies have achieved and then adjusts these numbers for differences in things like the age of the company and the variances in product attributes. In essence, the entrepreneur monitors a number of comparable competitors and then explains why his or her business varies from those models.

In the build-up method, the entrepreneur identifies all the possible revenue sources of the business and then estimates how much of each type of revenue the company can generate during a given period of time. For example, a bookstore generates revenues from books and artifacts. Thus, a bookstore owner would estimate the average sales price for each product category. Then he or she might estimate the number of people to come through the store on a daily basis and the percentage that would purchase within each revenue source. From these numbers, the bookstore owner could create a sales forecast for a typical day, which could then be aggregated into larger blocks of time (months, quarters, or years). These rough estimates might then be further adjusted based on seasonality in the bookstore industry. In the end, the bookstore owner would have a workable model for sales forecasts.

The build-up technique is an imprecise method for the new startup with limited operating history, but it is critically important to assess the viability of the opportunity. It's so important, in fact, that you might want to use both the comparable and the build-up methods to assess how well they converge. If the two methods are widely divergent, go back and try to determine why. The knowledge you gain about your business model will help you better articulate the opportunity to stakeholders, and it will provide you with invaluable insights as you begin managing the business after its launch. Chapter 9 provides more detail on how to derive these estimates.

While we know for certain that these forecasts will never be 100% accurate, it is essential to minimize the degree of error. Detailed investigation of comparable companies can help you accomplish this goal, as can triangulating your comparable method results with your build-up method results. However you go about building your forecast, always keep in mind that the smaller the error, the less likely your company will run out of cash. Beyond building credibility with your investors, rigorous estimates are also the single best tool for keeping your company out of financial trouble.

Operations Plan

The key in the operations plan section is to address how operations will add value for your customers. Here, you'll detail the production cycle and gauge its impact on working capital. For instance, when does your company pay for inputs? How long does it take to produce the product? When does the customer buy the product and, more importantly, when does the customer pay for the product? From the time you pay for your raw materials until you receive payment from your customers, you will be operating in a negative cash flow. The shorter that cycle, the more cash you have on hand and the less likely you are to need bank financing. It sounds counterintuitive, but many rapidly growing new companies run out of cash even though they have increasing sales and substantial operating profit. The reason is that they fail to properly finance the time their cash is tied up in the procurement, production, sales, and receivables cycle.

Operations Strategy. The first subsection of your operations strategy section provides a strategy overview. How does your business compare on the dimensions of cost, quality, timeliness, and flexibility? Emphasize those aspects that provide your venture with a comparative advantage. It is also appropriate to discuss the geographic location of production facilities and how this enhances your firm's competitive advantage. Your notes should cover such issues as available labour, local regulations, transportation, infrastructure, and proximity to suppliers. In addition, the section should provide a description of the facilities, discuss whether you will buy or lease them, and explain how you will handle future growth (by renting an adjoining building, perhaps). As in all sections detailing strategy, support your plans with actual data.

Scope of Operations. What is the production process for your product or service? Creating a diagram makes it easier for you to see which production aspects to keep in-house and which to outsource (see Figure 8.9a). Considering that cash flow is king and that resource-constrained new ventures typically should minimize fixed expenses on production facilities, the general rule is to outsource as much production as possible. However, there is a major caveat to that rule: Your venture should control aspects of production that are central to your competitive advantage. Thus, if you are producing a new component with hardwired proprietary technology—let's say a voice recognition security door entry—it is wise to internally produce that hardwired component. The locking mechanism, on the other hand, can be outsourced to your specifications. Outsourcing the aspects that aren't proprietary reduces fixed costs for production equipment and facility expenditures, which means you have to raise less money and give up less equity.

The scope of operations section should also discuss partnerships with vendors, suppliers, and partners. Again, the diagram should illustrate the supplier and vendor relationships by category or by name (if the list isn't too long and you have already identified your suppliers). The diagram helps you visualize the various relationships and ways to better manage or eliminate them. The operations diagram also helps identify staffing needs—for example, how many production workers you might need depending on the hours of operation and number of shifts.

Ongoing Operations. This section builds on the scope of operations section by providing details on day-to-day activities. For example, how many units will you produce in a day and what kinds

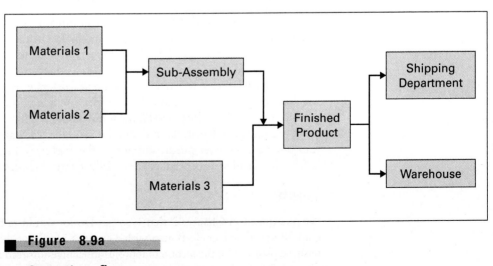

Figure 8.9a

Operations flow

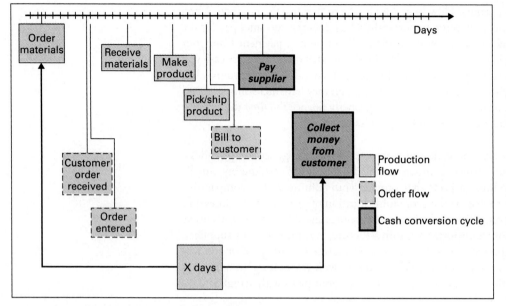

of inputs will you need? An operating cycle overview diagram graphically illustrates the impact of production on cash flow (see Figure 8.9b). As you complete this detail, you can start to establish performance parameters, which will help you to monitor and modify the production process into the future. If this plan is for your use only, you may choose to include such details as the specific job descriptions. However, for a business plan that will be shared with investors, you can get by with a much lower level of detail.

Source: Adapted from Professor Robert Eng, Babson College

Figure 8.9b

Operating cycle

Development Plan

The development plan highlights the development strategy and also provides a detailed development timeline. Many new ventures will require a significant level of effort and time to launch the product or service. This is the prologue of your story. For example, new software or hardware products often require months of development. Discuss what types of features you will develop and tie them to the firm's competitive advantage. This section should also discuss any patent, trademark, or copyright efforts you will undertake.

Development Strategy. What work remains to be completed? What factors need to come together for development to be successful? What risks to development does the firm face? For example, software development is notorious for taking longer and costing more than most companies originally imagined. Detailing the necessary work and what needs to happen for you to consider the work successful helps you understand and manage the risks involved. After you have laid out these details, you can assemble a development timeline.

Development Timeline. A development timeline is a schedule that you use to highlight major milestones and to monitor progress and make changes. It's often useful to illustrate timelines as Gantt charts. Figure 8.10 illustrates a typical Gantt chart for a new business launching a history themed bookstore.

The timeline helps you track major events, delegate responsibilities for project tasks, and schedule activities to best execute those events. In addition to plotting future milestones, it is a good idea to illustrate which development milestones you have already achieved as of the writing of the business plan. Finally, keep in mind that, as the old adage says, "time is money." Every day your product is in development and not on the market, you lose a day's worth of sales. You will have to work hard to meet deadlines, especially in those industries where speed to market is critical.

Team

We mentioned in Chapter 2 that Georges Doriot would rather back a "grade-A man with a grade-B idea than a grade-B man with a grade-A idea." For this reason, the team section of the business plan is often the section that professional investors read right after the executive summary. This section is also critically important to the lead entrepreneur. It identifies the members

Activity	12	11	10	9	8	7	6	5	4	3	2	1	Opening Month
10–12 Months Prior to Opening													
1) Finalize business plan and financials	■												
2) Review plans with local bookstore/ specialty shop owners		■											
3) Fill in skill gaps with advisory board		■											
4) Determine exact location possibilities		■											
7–9 Months Prior to Opening													
5) Register rights to business name			■										
6) Seek funding from appropriate sources				■									
7) Update business plan per feedback from potential financiers				■									
8) Make initial contact with product vendors					■								
9) Contact POS/inventory vendors and store designers						■							
4–6 Months Prior to Opening													
10) Determine exact store design							■						
11) Finalize product vendors								■					
12) Confirm funding								■					
3 Months Prior to Opening													
13) Finalize store design plans									■				
14) Open vendor/bank accounts									■				
15) Place fixture orders										■			
16) Finalize marketing plan and implement to announce store opening events										■			
17) Submit merchandise orders with all vendors										■			
1 Month Prior to Opening													
18) Contact local media re: placement in local newspapers and magazines										■			
19) Code merchandise category data in inventory management system											■		
20) Recruit and train staff											■		
21) Receive merchandise, fixtures, and complete setup of store											■		
Opening Month													
22) "Soft opening" of store to assess customer response, training, and system functioning												■	■
Grand Opening of Store												■	

■ **Figure 8.10**

Gantt chart

responsible for key activities and conveys why they are exceptionally qualified to execute on those responsibilities. The section also helps you consider how well this group of individuals will work together. It is well established that ventures started by strong teams are much more likely to succeed than those led by weak teams.

Team Bios and Roles. Every story needs a cast of characters, and the best place to start is by identifying the key team members and their titles. Often the lead entrepreneur assumes a CEO role. However, if you are young and have limited business experience, it is usually more productive to state that the company will seek a qualified CEO as it grows. In these cases, the lead entrepreneur may assume the role of chief technology officer (if he or she develops the technology) or vice-president of business development. However, don't let these options confine you. The key is to convince your investors that you have assembled the best team possible and that your team can execute on the brilliant concept you are proposing.

Investors looking to inject capital into a startup usually look for three key elements in a management team: business acumen, operational knowledge, and domain knowledge. These elements form the points of what is commonly referred to as the *talent triangle* (refer back to Figure 7.1). As mentioned in Chapter 7, each member of the talent triangle accepts responsibility for his or her own portfolio, which provides investors with added comfort in knowing that each skilled individual will be personally overseeing his or her portion of the enterprise. A person with business acumen[32] is most often seen holding the CEO, president, or CFO position because he or she has the skill, knowledge, and experience to make key business decisions. Operational knowledge[33] is the underlying key to a successful team. This individual will be focused on infrastructure, logistics, and most importantly product development. Finally, the team member with domain knowledge[34] must understand the key motivators within an industry and be aware of the impediments to ensure that product delivery to a consumer is not affected. This individual typically holds the title of vice-president of sales or vice-president of business development.

A simple, relatively flat organization chart is often useful to visualize what roles you have filled and what gaps remain. It also provides a road map for reading the bios that follow. The bios should demonstrate records of success. If you have previously started a business (even if it failed), highlight the company's *accomplishments*. If you have no previous entrepreneurial experience, discuss your achievements in your last job. For example, bios often contain a description of the number of people the entrepreneur previously managed and, more importantly, a measure of economic success, such as "grew division sales by 20-plus percent." The bio should demonstrate your leadership capabilities. Include the team's résumés as an appendix.

Advisory Boards, Board of Directors, Strategic Partners, External Members. Many entrepreneurs find that they are more attractive to investors if they have strong advisory boards. In building an advisory board, you want to create a team with diverse skills and experience. Industry experts provide legitimacy to your new business as well as strong technical advice. Other advisors should bring financial, legal, or management expertise. Thus, it is common to see lawyers, professors, accountants, and others who can assist the venture's growth on advisory boards. Moreover, if your firm has a strategic supplier or key customer, it may make sense to invite them onto your advisory board. Typically, these individuals are remunerated with a small equity stake and compensation for any organized meetings.

By law, most types of organization require a board of directors. While members of the advisory board can also provide needed expertise, a board of directors is different from an advisory board. The directors' primary role is to oversee the company on behalf of the investors, and to that end the board has the power to replace top executives if it feels doing so would be in the best interests of the company. Therefore, the business plan needs to briefly describe the size of the board, its role within the organization, and any current board members. Most major investors, such as venture capitalists, will require one or more board seats. Usually, the lead entrepreneur and one or more inside company members, such as the chief financial officer or a vice-president, will also have board seats.

Strategic partners may not necessarily be on your advisory board or your board of directors, but they still provide credibility to your venture. For this reason, it makes sense to highlight their involvement in your company's success. It is also common to list external team members, such as the law firm and accounting firm that your venture uses. The key in this section is to demonstrate that your firm can successfully execute the concept. A strong team provides the foundation that can ensure your venture will implement the opportunity successfully.

Compensation and Ownership. A capstone to the team section should be a table listing key team members by role, compensation, and ownership equity. A brief description in the text should explain why the compensation is appropriate. Many entrepreneurs choose not to pay themselves in the early months. Although this strategy conserves cash flow, it would misrepresent the individual's worth to the organization. Therefore, the table should contain what salary the employee is due. If necessary, that salary can be deferred until a time when cash flow is strong. Another column that can be powerful shows what the person's current or most recent compensation was and what he or she will be paid in the new company. Highly qualified entrepreneurs taking a smaller salary than at their previous job make an impressive point. While everyone understands that the entrepreneur's salary will increase as the company begins to grow, starting at a reduced salary sends the message that you and your team believe in the upside of your idea. Just be sure the description of the schedule underscores the plan to increase salaries in the future. In addition, it is a good idea to hold stock aside for future key hires and to establish a stock option pool for critical lower-level employees, such as software engineers. The plan should discuss such provisions.

Critical Risks

Every new venture faces a number of risks that may threaten its survival. Although the business plan, to this point, is creating a story of success, readers will identify and recognize a number of threats. The plan needs to acknowledge these potential risks; otherwise, investors will believe that the entrepreneur is naïve or untrustworthy and may possibly withhold investment. How should you present these critical risks without scaring your investor or other stakeholders? Identify the risk and then state your contingency plan. Critical risks are critical assumptions—factors that need to happen if your venture is to succeed as currently planned. The critical assumptions vary from one company to another, but some common categories are market interest and growth potential, competitor actions and retaliation, time and cost of development, operating expenses, and availability and timing of financing.

Market Interest and Growth Potential. The biggest risk any new venture faces is that once the product has been developed no one will buy it. Although you can do a number of things to minimize this risk, such as market research, focus groups, and beta sites, it is difficult to gauge overall demand and the growth of that demand until your product hits the market. State this risk, but counter it with the tactics and contingencies the company will undertake. For example, sales risk can be reduced by mounting an effective advertising and marketing plan or by identifying not only a core customer but also secondary and tertiary target audiences that the company will seek if the core customer proves less interested.

Competitor Actions and Retaliation. Too many entrepreneurs believe either that direct competition doesn't exist or that it is sleepy and slow to react. Don't rely on this belief as a key assumption of your venture's success. Most entrepreneurs passionately believe that they are offering something new and wonderful that is clearly different from what is currently on the market. They go on to state that existing competition won't attack their niche in the near future. Acknowledge the risk that this assessment may be wrong. One counter to this threat is that the venture has room in its gross margins to operate at lower-than-anticipated price levels and the cash available to withstand and fight back against such attacks. You should also identify the strategies you will use to protect and reposition yourself should an attack occur.

Time and Cost of Development. As mentioned in the development plan section, many factors can delay and add to the expense of developing your product. The business plan should identify the factors that may hinder development. For instance, during the extended high-tech boom of the late 1990s and into the new century, there was an acute shortage of skilled software engineers. You need to address how you will overcome the challenge of hiring and retaining the most qualified professionals, perhaps by outsourcing some development to the underemployed engineers in India. Compensation, equity participation, flexible hours, and other benefits that the firm could offer might also minimize the risk. Whatever your strategy, you need to demonstrate an understanding of the difficult task at hand and assure potential investors that you will be able to develop the product on time and on budget.

Operating Expenses. Operating expenses have a way of growing beyond expectations. Sales, administration, marketing, and interest expenses are some of the areas you need to monitor and manage. The business plan should highlight how you forecast your expenses (comparable companies and detailed analysis) and also lay out your contingency plans for unexpected developments. For instance, you may want to slow the hiring of support staff if development or other key tasks take longer than expected. Remember, cash is king, and your plan should illustrate how you will conserve cash when things don't go according to plan.

Availability and Timing of Financing. We can't stress enough how important cash flow is to the survival and flourishing of a new venture. One major risk that most new ventures face is that they will have difficulty obtaining needed financing, both equity and debt. If the current business plan is successful in attracting investors, cash flow will not be a problem in the short term. However, most ventures will need multiple rounds of financing. If the firm fails to make progress or meet key milestones, it may not be able to secure additional rounds of financing. This can put the entrepreneur in the uncomfortable position of having to accept unfavourable financing terms or, in the worst-case scenario, force the company into bankruptcy. Your contingency plans should identify viable alternative sources of capital and strategies to slow the "burn rate."[35]

A number of other risks might apply to your business. Acknowledge them and discuss how you can overcome them. Doing so generates confidence among your investors and helps you anticipate corrective actions that you may need to take.

Offering

Using your vision for the business and your estimates of the capital required to get there, you can develop a "sources and uses" schedule for the offering section of your business plan. The sources section details how much capital you need and the types of financing, such as equity investment and debt infusions. The uses section details how you'll spend the money. Typically, you should secure enough financing to last 12 to 18 months. If you take more capital than you need, you have to give up more equity. If you take less, you may run out of cash before reaching milestones that equate to higher valuations.

Financial Plan

Chapter 9 illustrates how to construct your pro forma financials, but you will also need a verbal description of these financials. We will defer discussion of this section until the next chapter.

Appendices

The appendices can include anything and everything that you think adds further validation to your concept but that doesn't fit or is too large to insert in the main parts of the plan. Common inclusions would be one-page résumés of key team members, articles that feature your venture, and technical specifications. If you already have customers, include a few excerpts of testimonials from them. Likewise, if you have favourable press coverage, include that as well. As a general rule, try to put all exhibits discussed in the written part of the plan on the same page on which you discuss them so the reader doesn't have to keep flipping back to the end of the plan to look at an exhibit. However, it is acceptable to put very large exhibits into an appendix.

Types of Plans

So far in this chapter we have laid out the basic sections or areas you want to address in your business planning process. The earliest drafts should be housed in a three-ring binder so you can add and subtract as you gain a deeper understanding, but at some point you may want to print a more formal-looking plan.

Business plans can take a number of forms depending on their purpose. Each form requires the same level of effort and leads to the same conclusions, but the final document is crafted differently depending on who uses it and when they use it. For instance, when you are introducing your concept to a potential investor, you might send a short, concise summary plan. As the investor's interest grows and he or she wants to more fully investigate the concept, he or she may ask for a more detailed plan.

Even though the equity boom of the late 1990s essentially equated entrepreneurship with venture capital, a business plan serves many more purposes than the needs of potential investors. Employees, strategic partners, financiers, and board members may all find use for a well-developed business plan. Most importantly, the entrepreneur gains immeasurably from the business planning process because it allows him or her not only to run the company better but also to clearly articulate the venture's story to stakeholders, who may never read the plan. In sum, different consumers of the business plan require different presentation of the work.

Your three-ring binder is basically what we would call an *operational plan*. It is primarily for you and your team to guide the development, launch, and initial growth of the venture. There really is no length specification for this type of plan, but it's not unusual to exceed 80 pages. The biggest difference between an operational plan and the one you might present to a potential investor is the level of detail, which tends to be much greater in an operational plan. Remember, the creation of this document is where you really gain the deep understanding that is so important in discerning how to build and run the business.

If you need outside capital, a business plan geared toward equity investors or debt providers should be about 25 to 40 pages long. Recognize that professional equity investors like venture capitalists and professional debt providers like bankers will not read the entire plan from front to back. That being the case, produce the plan in a format that facilitates spot reading. The previous discussion highlighted sections that these readers might find useful. The key is to present a concise version of all the material you have produced in your planning process. Focus on what the investor values the most. Thus, operational details are often less important unless your competitive advantage derives from your operations. Our general guideline is that "less is more." For instance, we've found that 25-page business plans receive venture funding more often than 40-page plans (other things being equal).

You may also want to produce an expanded executive summary. These plans are considerably shorter than an operational plan or the 25- to 40-page plan discussed above—typically no more than 10 pages. The purpose of this plan is to provide an initial conception of the business to test initial reaction to the idea. It allows you to share your idea with confidantes and receive feedback before investing significant time and effort on a longer business plan.

After you've completed the business planning process, rewrite the expanded executive summary. You can use this expanded summary to attract attention. For instance, send it to investors you have recently met to spur interest and a meeting. It is usually better to send an expanded executive summary than a full business plan because the investor will be more apt to read it. If the investor is interested, he or she will call you in for a meeting. If the meeting goes well, the investor often then asks for the full business plan.

Some investors have no interest in a plan at all. Instead, they prefer to see an executive summary and PowerPoint slides, and they often read the PowerPoint slides instead of asking the entrepreneur to personally present those slides. We have already discussed executive summaries, so let's spend a few moments on PowerPoint slides. You should be able to communicate your business opportunity in 10 to 12 slides, possibly along the following lines:

1. Cover page showing product picture, company name, and contact information
2. Opportunity description emphasizing customer problem or need that you hope to solve
3. Illustration of how your product or service solves the customer's problem
4. Some details (as needed) to better describe your product
5. Competition overview
6. Entry and growth strategy showing how you will get into the market and then grow
7. Overview of your business model—how you will make money and how much it will cost to support those sales
8. Team description
9. Current status with timeline
10. Summary including how much money you need and how it will be used

The key to creating a successful presentation is to maximize the use of your slides. For example, graphs, pictures, and other visuals are more powerful and compelling than texts and bulleted lists. Guy Kawasaki, a seasoned venture capitalist, has listened to many pitches throughout his career. He has coined the **10/20/30 rule** for slide decks, which states that a deck should be no more than 10 slides, no more than 20 minutes, and have a font size of at least 30.[44] If a pitch is longer than 10 slides and 20 minutes, odds are that the investor will start to lose interest. Also, if the presentation is full of text and bullet points, you run the risk of having the investor read the slides instead of listening to the pitch. Additionally, entrepreneurs who create bulleted lists often use them as cue cards during an oral presentation and either stare at the screen behind them as they talk or continually look back and forth between the screen and their audience. In either case, this behaviour might prevent you from creating a personal connection with your audience.

This connection is important because it conveys that you have confidence in your plan and that you have a strong command of the concept. A second problem with bulleted lists is that those in your audience will tend to read them, and their attention will be focused on the slide and not on what you are saying. Again, you want to create a strong personal connection with your audience. You should be able to use graphics to communicate the key points. Doing so will better engage your audience and make them more inclined to view your opportunity favourably.

☐ CONCLUSION

The business plan is more than just a document; it is a process, a story. Although the finished product is often a written plan, the deep thinking and fact-based analysis that go into that document provide the entrepreneur with keen insights needed to marshal resources and direct growth. The whole process can be painful, but it almost always maximizes revenue and minimizes costs. The reason is that the process allows the entrepreneur to better anticipate instead of react.

Business planning also provides talking points so that entrepreneurs can get feedback from a number of experts, including investors, vendors, and customers. Think of business planning as one of your first steps on the journey to entrepreneurial success. Also remember that business planning is a process and not a product. It is iterative, and in some sense, it never ends. As your venture grows, you will want to come back and revisit earlier drafts, create new drafts, and so on for the entire life of your business. Keep your three-ring binder close by and continue to add to and revise it often. It is the depository of all the learning that you have achieved as well as your plans for the future. While preparing the first draft of your plan is tough, the rewards are many. Enjoy the journey.

YOUR OPPORTUNITY JOURNAL

Reflection Point	Your Thoughts. . .
1. What data have you gathered about your opportunity?	
a. What do these data suggest as far as reshaping your opportunity?	
b. What new questions do they raise, and who should you talk to to answer these questions?	
2. Who have you shared your vision with?	
a. Who have they referred you to?	
b. What new learning have you gained from these conversations?	
3. What is your "tagline" ?	
4. Does your executive summary have a compelling "hook" ?	
5. Does your business planning process tie together well? Do you have a compelling, articulate story?	

WEB EXERCISE

Scan the Internet for business plan preparation sites. What kinds of templates are available? Do these make it easier to write a plan? What is the downside, if any, of using these templates? What are the benefits? Find some sample plans online. These plans are often advertised as superior to "typical" plans. Are they better? What makes them better?

Additional Exercise: The Elevator Pitch

Practise writing an elevator pitch for the following companies and products:

1. Wikipedia
2. iTunes
3. Netflix
4. The first ever telephone

Answers: (Note: Answers may vary. These are meant as guidelines; they are not definitive answers.)

Wikipedia: Are you tired of carrying a stack of books everywhere you go? Our free, online platform allows you to access million of articles instantly, wherever you are.

iTunes: Do you want to save money by only buying one song instead of an entire album? Our software application allows you to choose from millions of songs and albums. Purchase one digital song and transfer it to all your devices instantly!

Netflix: Do you enjoy paying late fees for movie rentals? Our online platform allows you to stream any of our movie titles to your phone, laptop, or television, anytime you want. Choose from thousands of movie titles for a low monthly fee and never pay late fees again.

The first telephone ever: Are you tired of waiting weeks to deliver a message? With our brand-new invention you can speak to anyone you want, regardless of location by dialling their personal number on our device. Call anyone in the world, anytime you want; connecting has never been easier.

CASE

P'kolino

Pkolino™

Business Plan
May-2005

Prepared by:
J.B. Schneider &
Antonio Turco-Rivas N.

Contact Information:
Phone: (781) 497-0913
Email: jb@pkolino.com
atrn@pkolino.com
Address:
600 West Cummings Park
Suite 5350
Woburn, MA 01801

Executive Summary

P'kolino, LLC

(pee-ko-lee-no)

QUICK FACTS:

Management:
J.B SCHNEIDER: President, Marketing
ANTONIO TURCO-RIVAS: Operations
Sales, Finance
RISD: Design and Development

Industry: Play at Home – Play Furniture

Business: Improving play at home with
products like this:

Patents: Currently filing provisional
patents

Law Firm: Brown Rudnick, and Berlack
Israels LLP

Auditors: N/A

Current Investors: Founders

Financing Sought: $400K

Use of Funds: Manufacturing, Marketing
and Product Development

Employees: Founders (2)

Clients: Conversations with specialty
retailers (e.g. Museum of Modern Arts)

Exit Strategy: Acquisition by toy
manufacturer, furniture retailer or
furniture manufacturer

CONTACT INFORMATION:
600 West Cummings Park, Suite 5350
Woburn, MA 01801
Phone: (781) 497-0913
Email: jb@pkolino.com or
atrn@pkolino.com
Website: www.pkolino.com

Summary:
P'kolino is committed to improving play at home by developing and marketing innovative play products and accessories. P'kolino believes that play should be fun and that play is critical to a child's physical, mental and social development. We hear from parents that they believe this too. Our products,

- are designed for optimal usage by the child,
- grow and adapt to the child's stage of development, and
- integrate with toys and activities to encourage and enhance play.

P'kolino not only improves play at home but its business of "growing" products, toy integration and complementary accessories serves as the foundation for a solid business with recurring, high margin sales.

Strategy:
Our goal is for P'kolino to become synonymous with play at home, and to accomplish this we have designed a progressive growth strategy. Through research we determined that the basis for play, the play space and its furniture, are in need of improvement. We've identified four key areas for improvement:

- Existing play furniture hinders play because it is designed for miniature adults.
- Play furniture rapidly loses its value because children outgrow it.
- The child loses interest in the play furniture quickly because it has few applications.
- Play spaces are cluttered and unorganized

P'kolino addresses these needs by:

- Making play more productive by designing furniture for the ones who use it: children.
- Increasing the useful life of the furniture by designing it to grow with the child
- Maintaining interest in the furniture by increasing its uses. Add-on toy kits integrate with the table for unlimited uses.
- Organizing the play spaces by designing these toys kits to simply fold-up and store away in a child friendly storage unit.

We will build distinctive, high quality products and focus on developing a strong brand. P'kolino will first target the high-end market because it values the brand, its consumers are influencers, and it has the highest margins. We will grow by introducing additional products to the high-end markets and expanding with a different product line into the higher volume mid-market.

Distribution will primarily be direct, however we will partner with key retail showrooms to create familiarity with our products. A strong direct channel will enable us to develop extended relationships with our customers for repeat sales of upgrades, accessories and toy kits.

Market:
Play furniture is a $1.2 billion market. The High-end segment is $51million, growing at 9% and strong margins of 55% gross/20% net. The Mid segment is estimated at $300 million, growing at 8% per year and margins of 48% gross/14% net. The mass segment is estimated at $800 million, growing at 7% and margins of 37% gross and 5% net.

Operations:
Outsourcing manufacturing, and using a collaboration model for product development.

Management Background:

- Antonio Turco-Rivas: co-founder and Sales & Operations Manager is a Babson MBA 2005. Antonio is a proven entrepreneur who successfully launched two ventures. He has managerial and sales experience.

- J.B. Schneider: co-founder and Marketing & Product Development Manager is a Babson MBA 2005 with over 10 years of marketing strategy and communications experience for several Fortune 500 companies.

	Year 1	Year 2	Year 3	Year 4	Year 5
Revenues	612K	1783K	2922K	4168K	5793K
Expenses	643K	1761K	2806K	3786K	5093K
Net Profit	-31K	22K	116K	382K	700K
Head Count	4	7	13	14	14

Confidential Information
Business Plan - Dated May-2005
Woburn, Massachusetts – USA

Confidential Information
Business Plan - Dated May-2005
Woburn, Massachusetts – USA

P'kolino

"P'kolino will develop innovative playroom furniture designed for the child to improve play"

1   Mission Statement

"P'kolino is a product development and marketing company. Our goal is to improve play at home by developing and marketing innovative playroom furniture <u>designed for the child</u>. Our products will grow and adapt to the child's stage of development and integrate with toys and activities to encourage and enhance play."

2   Industry Overview

2.1 Understanding the Playroom Market

Four million children are born in the United States each year.[1] Thus, at any given time, there are 30 million children ages 8 or younger. This large base fuels the $38 billion children's toy and furniture market, currently growing at 13% per year (according to the industry trade publication "Playthings"). The playroom market (meaning the area of the house set aside for children's recreation and play) is part of this pie, and includes elements of both the furniture and the toy industry.

"Children's playroom furniture market is estimated at $1.2 billion, growing at 7% annually for the next five years"

P'kolino will compete in the children's playroom furniture space, estimated to be a $1.2 billion market, growing at 7% annually for the next five years (according to marketresearch.com). However, a playroom is not a playroom without toys. For this reason, P'kolino will develop furniture products and accessories designed to integrate with toys and activities to complete the playroom offering and enhance their play value.

Exhibit 2-A
The Playroom Market
(US$ Billions)

$1.2

$38

☐ Toy + Furniture Market
☐ Playroom Furniture

The dynamics of the playroom market are influenced by both the furniture and toy industry. An overview of each of these industries follows.

2.2 Furniture Industry Highlights

Households in the US spend over $24 billion a year on furniture and this figure is expected to grow at 2% per year according to the American Furniture Manufacturer Association (AFMA). The industry has traditionally been highly segmented, but because of lower margins fueled by intense competition from imports, it has started to consolidate. Last year, for example, products manufactured and imported from other countries (especially China) represented 45%[2] of total purchases.

---

[1] Source: U.S. Census Bureau – www.census.gov
[2] Source: US Department of Commerce – www.commerce.gov

Confidential Information
Business Plan - Dated May-2005
Woburn, Massachusetts – USA

Companies competing in this market are:
- Furniture Brands International, the largest maker of residential furniture and owner of brands like Henredon, Drexel, and Maitland-Smith (the company has over $2.3 billion in revenues).[3]
- Lay Z Boy ($1.9 billion in revenues).
- Ashley Furniture ($1.7 billion in revenues)
- and others; like Ethan Allen and local players.

These companies distribute products through a network of furniture centers, independent dealers (specialty retailers), national and local chains, and department stores.

According to the AFMA, children's furniture generated $4 billion in 2003, 90% related to children's bedroom furniture sales (cribs, changing tables, etc.) and the remaining 10% or $400 million to children's tables, chairs, storage and toys. Niche players have dominated this segment of the industry and according to the American Home Furnishings Alliance (annual publication) it is the fastest growing segment (8% in 2003).

"Children's furniture is the fastest growing segment in the Furniture Industry with 8% growth in 2003"
American Home Furnishing Alliance

We believe the Furniture Industry will continue to face strong competition from foreign manufacturers (selling at lower prices). Local manufacturers will have to invest in technology and compete on quality and speed. In the children's furniture market, the large companies have been traditionally focused on bedroom furniture. Niche players have been taking over the more specialized products - those requiring expertise in other areas - like child development (i.e. the playroom furniture).

Exhibit 2-B
Furniture Industry
(US$ Billions)

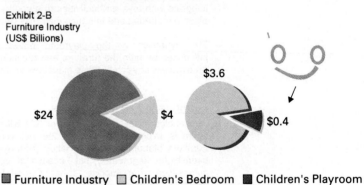

■ Furniture Industry ☐ Children's Bedroom ■ Children's Playroom

---

[3] Source: Hoovers Online – www.hoovers.com

Confidential Information
Business Plan - Dated May-2005
Woburn, Massachusetts – USA

P'kolino

2.3 Toy Industry Highlights

The Toy Industry accounted for $34 billion in 2003.[4] On both the manufacturing and retailing side it is a highly concentrated industry. For the past few years it has been growing at 5-9% per year, with almost 60% of the products being imported from other countries.[5]

According to "Playthings annual report" the Toy industry is highly seasonal with almost 70% of all toy purchases occurring during the Holiday season (Christmas).

The "Playthings annual report" for 2003 also stated the main forces driving the industry as follows:

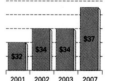

Exhibit 2-C
The Toy Industry
(US$ Billions)

- "Educational toys:" after many ups and downs, it seems like American parents have become more aware of the importance of play and education in the early years. This has resulted in sales growth of 9% per year.
- "Word of mouth and Brand:" proven ways to build sales in this industry.
- "Technology is king:" almost 39% all of toys sales (in terms of US$) are video games or what they like to call "technology related products".
- "Merchant power:" Mass merchandisers, in particular Walmart (sells 25% of the toys sold every year in America), have taken the industry by storm, lowering prices to consumers but also lowering margins to manufacturers.
- "China:" manufacturing has gone overseas.

Retail sales of toys and games are expected to grow 4.3 percent per year to total $37.8 billion in 2007.[6] New video game technologies and the introduction of next generation systems are expected to be the main driver of growth. With respect to toys the leaders in the industry are Mattel ($4.9 billion in sales), Hasbro ($3.1 billion), Lego ($1.6 billion), and Leap Frog ($600 million).[7] Sony takes the lead in video games.

Regarding the playroom furniture market, some companies like Rubbermaid (using the Little Tykes brand) have developed; role-play toys, ride-on toys, sandboxes, activity gyms and climbers, and plastic juvenile furniture. These products are sold in toy stores (not furniture stores) and have been targeting the price sensitive consumer. Our research indicates that these types of

"Parents have become more aware of the importance of play and education in the early years... educational toys sales are up 9% per year"
"Playthings"

---

[4] Source: Industry trade publication "Playthings"
[5] Source: Industry trade publication "Playthings"
[6] Source: Marketreseach.com
[7] Source: revenues for Toy industry leaders from Hoovers Online

Confidential Information
Business Plan - Dated May-2005
Woburn, Massachusetts – USA

"$800 million in playroom furniture products are sold each year by Toy Industry related companies

products carry very low margins (average 5% profit margins).[8] To compete, companies like Brio, another strong player in this niche, sells low price train tables to encourage parents to buy their higher margins trains (they lose money on the furniture to sell the toy).

According to the Marketresearch.com industry report, of the $34 billion, $6 billion accounts for furniture products. However, this number includes car seats, play pens, strollers, etc. For playroom furniture, our research[9] indicates that approximately $800 million is sold each year.

Exhibit 2-D
Toy Industry
(US$ Billions)

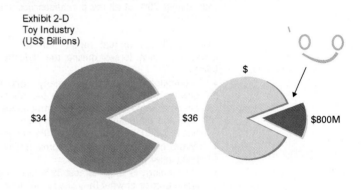

☐ Furniture Industry   ☐ Children's Bedroom   ■ Children's Playroom

Our research concludes that large toy companies dominate the price-sensitive segment of the playroom furniture market. However for mid and high-end play furniture products, niche manufacturers and retailers like Pottery Barn Kids and Land of Nod have taken the lead.

---

[8] Sources: According to 10K fillings for the SEC and/or public financial statements from: Graco, Rubbermaid, Brio and others.
[9] Based on Marketresearch.com Industry Report and Sales of top ten manufactures of playroom furniture products

Confidential Information
Business Plan - Dated May-2005
Woburn, Massachusetts – USA

2.4 How it all Comes Together (Furniture & Toy Industry)

Furniture meets toys in the playroom; both Industries converge and influence the $1.2 billion market.

Exhibit 2-E
The Playroom Furniture Market
(US$ Billions)

"The Furniture and Toy industry converge in the furniture playroom market"

Industry Size	Furniture Industry $24 billion	Toy Industry $34 billion
Portion considered children's furniture	$4 billion	$6 billion
Portion considered children's playroom furniture	$.4 billion	$.8 billion

Playroom Furniture Market $1.2b

The Playroom furniture market (where P'kolino will compete) has inherited many of the competitive dynamics of its parent industries:

- Is growing at an average of 7% annually[10]
- Is highly seasonal (almost 70% of sales during the Holiday season)
- Almost 60% of the products are manufactured abroad[11]
- For highly price sensitive consumers the market is highly concentrated, but at mid and high-end income levels niche players dominate
- Word of mouth and brand are the main drivers of sales

---

[10] Source: Marketresearch.com Industry Report
[11] Based on the Management calculations, supported by AFMA information on Furniture Imports

2.5 Trends Influencing the Playroom Market

More children are being born: According to the latest statistics from the National Center for Health Statistics, women in the United States are having more children now than at any time in almost 30 years. During most of the 1970s and 1980s, the average birthrate was fewer than two children per woman, today that average has increased to 2.1 children. As a result of this trend, the population of children age 5 and under is expected to grow in 2004, and to experience gradually increasing annual percentage gains through 2010.

"...More babies, more disposable income and more spending in children's furniture are also driving the playroom market"

Mom's with more income and spending more: More women are having babies later in life, when their income tends to be higher and more stable. The birth rates for women in their 30s and older are at their highest level in three decades, up 2%-3% since 1990 for women in their 30s, and up more than 7% for women in their 40s.[12] As a result many of them are coming into the toy and furniture markets with higher disposable income than was previously the case.

Grandparents are spending more: According to the U.S. Census Bureau, greater longevity and higher disposable income of a growing U.S. population of grandparents is also boosting average per capita spending on home furnishings and toys for young children. There are about 70 million grandparents in the United States today. As a result of divorces and remarriages, many American children have six to eight adults in the "grandparent" role. According to the research firm Interep (supported by Simmons database), grandparents are spending over $60 billion on grandchildren each year.

More aware/educated parents: Parents these days are being bombarded by advice from experts about developing children's mental, physical, and social skills. Parents understand the value play has on this development and look for products to encourage it. In an interview with the trade publication Playthings (May 2002), Susan Oliver, executive director of the non-profit organization Playing for Keeps, explains:

"Parents with dollars to spend, typically those who have greater amounts of education, are increasingly aware of the connection between play and healthy development. There has been a lot of media coverage about brain development, with an emphasis on the critical role of a stimulating environment during the first three years of a child's life." As long as the market approach is toward kids learning more at a younger age, consumers will pay to get on the higher rung of the educational ladder"

[12] Source: U.S. Census Bureau – www.census.gov

Confidential Information
Business Plan - Dated May-2005
Woburn, Massachusetts – USA

"...The Power of Play program, continues to reach literally millions of people...play has a positive effect on children's overall well-being is instrumental in the child's development"

New laws: New safety legislation has propelled safer product designs as the industry and the media warn consumers not to use older products that do not meet current safety standards.[13]

Home remodeling: With new TV shows encouraging makeovers of home spaces, Americans are likely to spend more on home furnishing in 2005.

The Power of Play Campaign: Children appear to be growing up much faster; they look more mature and they know more about the world at younger and younger ages. Child development experts stress that despite appearances, a child is still a child. This message is a major focus of "The Power of Play" program, which continues to reach literally millions of people throughout our nation as a result of the second phase of broadcast and print public service announcements sponsored by the Toy Manufacturer Association.

The importance of this message was discovered as a result of a national survey conducted in 1999 on behalf of the American Toy Institute, the industry's charitable and educational foundation, recently renamed the Toy Industry Foundation. Ninety-one percent of the survey participants, made up of parents, teachers and child experts, stated that play has a positive effect on children's overall well-being and was instrumental in the development of a child's imagination, self-confidence, self-esteem, creativity, problem-solving and cooperation.

Toys March Up-market: A recent article in the <u>Wall Street Journal</u> (please refer to Appendix 11.1) explained the profit killing price war landscape for toy-making and retailing in the mass market, and highlighted how premium priced toys appear to be outgrowing the simpler less expensive versions.

David Shaw, the new owner of the FAO Schwarz retail stores stated "the admittedly small niche is a vibrant marketplace full of customers looking for something different from what's available at mass retail stores... is a niche that small retailers and catalogs dominate."

A customer commented as she visited one small specialty retailer in New York City "these toys aren't cheap... but they are really good-quality...I know my kids will love them."

---

[13] Source: The U.S. Public Interest Research Group

Confidential Information
Business Plan - Dated May-2005
Woburn, Massachusetts – USA

| 3 | **The Opportunity** |

"Willingness to pay for products that encourage child development is on the rise."

Play is a child's work and education; it is how they learn and grow. Parents are more willing to pay for products that encourage or facilitate play as they become more educated about child development and the importance of play. Evidence of this trend is the growing spending on educational toys (growing at 9% for the last three years)[22], and playroom furnishings (growing at 7% per year[23]). P'kolino has identified a powerful opportunity that leverages this trend.

Through our research we discovered that the basis for play - the play space and its furniture - is in need of improvement. We identified four key areas for improvement:

"The basis for play - the play space and its furniture – is in need of improvement"

- Existing playroom furniture compromises play because it is designed for miniature adults and not children.
- Playroom furniture loses its value fast because children quickly outgrow it. One size fits all in playroom furniture simply doesn't work.
- The child loses interest in the playroom furniture quickly because it has few applications.

"Parents want to know the right toy to buy"

- Lastly, and probably most obviously, play spaces are cluttered and unorganized.

We also discovered that parents are feeling the pressure of wanting to know the right toy to buy, at the right time to effectively support the development of their children.

| 4 | **Company and Product Description** |

4.1 Company and Description:

P'kolino, LLC is based in Woburn, MA and is a product design and marketing company. We believe play is an integral part of a child's healthy development and that current play furniture compromises play. It is our goal to improve the play experience at home. P'kolino currently has 4 product concepts under development through a partnership with the Rhode Island School of Design (RISD).

"P'kolino, improving play at home."

---

[22] According to Parents Magazine and LeapFrog SEC fillings
[23] *According to marketresearch.com*

4.2 The P'kolino Concept

P'kolino will address the opportunity in the play space by designing truly innovative play furniture and child development stage specific toy kits.

These solutions will have the following characteristics:

"P'kolino's playroom furniture is designed for the child and functional for the parent. It grows and adapts to the child's stage of development and integrates with toys/activities to encourage and enhance play"

1. We are making play more productive by designing playroom furniture for the ones who use it, the children. **Functional.**
2. We are increasing the useful life of the furniture by designing it to grow with the child through key stages of development. **Multi-purpose.**
3. We are maintaining interest in the furniture by increasing its uses. The furniture is designed to be a toy and to transform to different activities. This transformation is made possible by add-on toy kits that change the P'kolino table from activity to activity (for example: from a Lego table to a painting table to a train table and so on). **Multi-purpose.**
4. We are organizing the play space by designing the toy kits to simply fold-up and store away in a child friendly storage unit. **Functional.**

In addition to these key differentiators P'kolino's products will be safe, beautiful and fun, as these are necessary attributes to succeed.

These solutions also address the challenges parents have of selecting the right toys for the right stage because our toy kits will be packaged for specific stages of child development.

The "grow with the child" capabilities of our products will reduce our customers' total costs of ownership and provide us with opportunities for follow-on sales. Follow-on products will be in the form of developmentally appropriate toy kits, upgrade packages and accessories.

Confidential Information
Business Plan - Dated May-2005
Woburn, Massachusetts – USA

4.3 Product Description

P'kolino's first product line will include two different table designs, a storage unit, and toy kits. Constant product innovation is part of our strategy, and it will be supported with a product development effort in order to expand our current offering and include accessories and new products every year.

Initial Product line

Table A shows a very contemporary, style driven concept, with plenty of multifunctional (i.e., grow with the child) capabilities resulting from its unique modular design. It is composed of 7 separate pieces and designed to accommodate at least four stages of the child's development. This product will be the hub for the toy kits and the foundation of our playroom offering. The product is made of wood, high-density foam and fabric.

Note: *the following are pictures of prototypes of Table A; the actual product may be different. They are presented here for the purpose of illustrating the concept.*

Confidential Information
Business Plan - Dated May-2005
Woburn, Massachusetts – USA

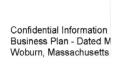

Prototypes designed at risd for P'kolino

Packaging Mode

Toddler Mode

Infant Mode

Two table Mode

Toddler Mode

Toddler 1 Mode

Confidential Information
Business Plan - Dated May-2005
Woburn, Massachusetts – USA

Prototypes designed at risd for P'kolino

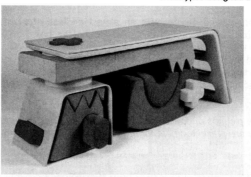

Packaging Mode

Table Mode

Table Mode

Playground Mode

Playground Mode

Table Mode

Confidential Information
Business Plan - Dated May-2005
Woburn, Massachusetts – USA

P'kolino

Children Interacting with Table "B"

The Toy kits: These pieces are the link between the furniture and the toy. They are storage compartments that unfold on top of Table A to change the table top into an activity or toy /play enhancer. The inside of the toy kit will be designed to accommodate the requirements of a specific activity and child stage of development.

For example: if we wanted to convert the table into a toddler "Lego" table, the interior of the toy kit will have stage appropriate Lego plates attached; the unit itself will also hold the Lego blocks. When unfolded, it locks on top of Table A, transforming it into a toddler Lego table. When done, simply fold it up and store it in our storage unit.

Note*: the following are pictures of prototypes of the Toy kits; the actual product may be different. They are presented here for the purpose of illustrating the concept*

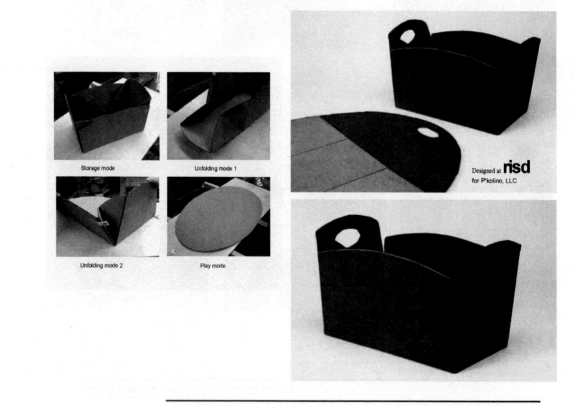

Storage mode

Unfolding mode 1

Unfolding mode 2

Play mode

Designed at **risd** for P'kolino, LLC

Confidential Information
Business Plan - Dated May-2005
Woburn, Massachusetts – USA

The Storage Unit: this unit will hold up to 10 toy kits and is designed to fit the design style of Table A. It allows for ease of use and accommodates a child's height and strength. The unit is made out of wood, but the drawers will be light enough so that children can open them.

Note: *the following are pictures of prototypes of the storage unit; the actual product may be different. They are presented here for the purpose of illustrating the concept*

With capabilities of holding toy kits on top of the piece or in the drawers

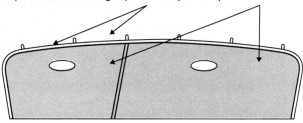

Storage Urti

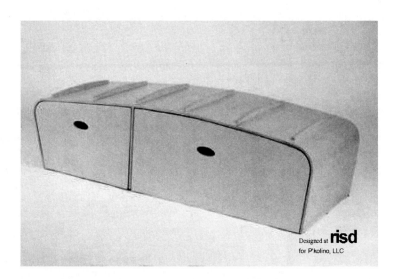

Designed at **risd**
for P'kolino, LLC

Prototypes designed at risd for P'kolino

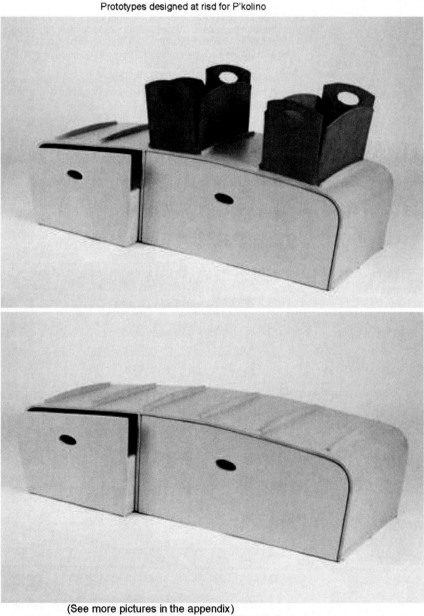

(See more pictures in the appendix)

Confidential Information
Business Plan - Dated May-2005
Woburn, Massachusetts – USA

P'kolino

4.4 Competitive Advantage

P'kolino product attributes can be summed up as follows:

"Our key differentiating benefits will be the increased functionality, the improved educational value and the multi-purpose nature of our products"

- **Multi-purpose:** modifies for changes in activity and grows with children through their stages of development,
- **Functional:** designed to better fit how children use the product (i.e. not miniature adult furniture),
- **Educational**,
- **Fun**,
- **Safe** and
- **Beautiful:** visually appealing.

(Please refer to Appendix 12.2 for details on the product attributes).

Exhibit 4-A
Key Product Attributes

Safety, beauty and fun are absolute necessities in this market. They are the attributes that most competitors have and ones that we will build our differentiating attributes on. Our key differentiating benefits will be the increased functionality, the improved educational value and the multi-purpose nature of our products. By focusing our product development on these key attributes we will have a clear competitive advantage.

Exhibit 4-B
Attribute Comparison Chart – P'kolino's Assessment (rankings: 1 is best in the category, 10 is the worst)

Competitors	Mkt. Segment	Educational	Safe	Multipurpose	Fun	Functional	Beautiful
P'kolino	High / Mid	2	3	1	2	1	3
Brio	Mass	3	5	2	3	7	7
Fischer-Price	Mass	1	2	3	1	6	8
Imaginarium	Mass	4	4	4	4	4	9
Little Tykes	Mass	5	1	6	5	2	10
Pottery Barn Kids	Mid	8	8	5	6	5	1
Land of Nod	Mid	7	7	7	7	3	2
Truck	High	9	10	8	10	8	5
Casa Kids	High	10	9	9	9	9	6
Videl	High	6	6	10	8	10	4

Confidential Information
Business Plan - Dated May-2005
Woburn, Massachusetts – USA

4.5 Our Strategy

Our strategy is designed to accomplish four key objectives:

1. Develop a strong brand → "owning the play-space at home"
2. Develop a solid customer base → " loyalty and recurring revenue"
3. Achieve predictable and sustainable growth → "good margins and repeat purchases"
4. Develop a culture of innovation → "capability of generating champion products"

"P'kolino targets the high-end segment because customers are market influencers, they value brand over price and offers better margins. P'kolino will later expand to the mid segment"

Overview:
To penetrate the children's play market we will need to target influential customers and develop a strong brand. From this position we will expand our product line and extend into new markets expanding our customer base. We will maintain long relationships with our customers by offering them development stage appropriate upgrades, toy kits and accessories. This will provide us with recurring and predictable revenue.

Market Entry:
P'kolino will first target the high-end playroom market because of its favorable characteristics:
• it values innovation and brand over price,
• its consumers are market influencers, and
• it offers the highest margins.

We will focus on establishing and building a reputation for high quality products and target consumers that want the best for their children. Through a mix of public relations and grassroots marketing we will establish our products in the high-end market. Concurrently, we will develop toy-kits and accessories that integrate and complement the furniture to deliver a complete play experience.

Growth Strategy:
Growth in the high-end market is limited due to its size. In order to increase our customer base for sales of additional P'kolino products we will need to expand into the larger mid-market segment. To do this we will leverage our high-end brand reputation and introduce lower cost tables and storage with similar attributes into the larger mid-market. We expect to execute this expansion in our third year of operation.

Confidential Information
Business Plan - Dated May-2005
Woburn, Massachusetts – USA

Exhibit 4-C
Market Penetration Strategy

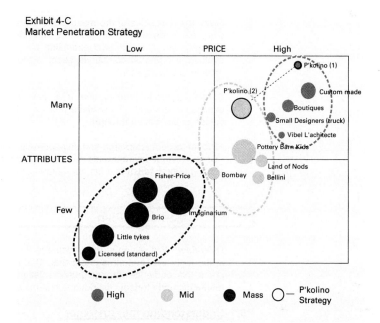

Growth will also be achieved by maintaining long term relationships with our customers to promote repeat purchases of upgrades, accessories and toy kits. Given the targeted age range (0-5 years) of our products and the average of over 2 children per household, a single customer relationship could last over 8 years with multiple sales per year. This will give us a recurring and predictable revenue stream. As we increase our customer base and product line the revenue from these repeat sales will increase dramatically.

Exhibit 4-D
Number of units sold per type of product

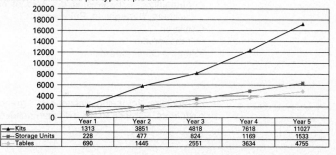

	Year 1	Year 2	Year 3	Year 4	Year 5
Kits	1313	3851	4818	7618	11027
Storage Units	228	477	824	1169	1533
Tables	690	1445	2551	3634	4755

Confidential Information
Business Plan - Dated May-2005
Woburn, Massachusetts – USA

Given the difficulties of the mass market, which include troubled distribution channels, intense price competition, and price sensitive customers, it is not currently part of our market extension plan. However, we will continue to evaluate it. Should conditions become more favorable, we may consider moving to this segment.

Continued product innovation is a key to this market penetration and expansion strategy. To achieve this we will focus internally on creating a culture of innovation through

• Proven product research and development methodologies,
• Creative work environments and employment arrangements, and
• Hiring proven talent that fits our dynamic, innovating culture.

5	Marketing Plan

Overview: We will bring this product to the market by targeting customers in the high-end market segment that want the best for their child. We will reach this audience through public relations, grassroots marketing, direct marketing and strategic distribution channels.

5.1 Understanding the Customer

Our primary customers will be parents who want the best for their children, and are willing and able to pay a premium for a better product.

"Our primary customers will be parents who want the best for their children, and are willing and able to pay a premium for a better product"

According to our research, our initial customers will be educated consumers who possess a strong desire to provide the best environment possible for their children to play at home. They are likely to spend a considerable amount of time researching the web for options, and have a strong bias toward friend and family recommendations (word-of-mouth).

We also see several key influencers in this purchasing decision, they are:
• "Authorities" – Experts in the field of child rearing/development. (e.g., Teachers, Care-givers, Publications).
• Children
• Grandparents
• Peers – Other parents

In addition to being influencers grandparents are also secondary customers. Grandparents are often richer than parents, more involved and

buy large gifts for their grandchildren. The percentage of buyers of relevant children's products that are grandparents.[24]
• Games and toys 26%
• Infant furniture 21%
• Children furniture 16%

There are nearly 60 million grandparents in the U.S. at present and they spend an estimated $30 billion per year on their grandchildren[25]. Although grandparents exercise significant purchasing power, they are likely to ask for parent consent before they buy our products; making the parent our core customer.

5.2 Target Customer Profile

The demographics of our primary target customer are:
• Household Income $150K+ *
• At least one child 0-5 years old.
• Female *
• College educated* (or higher)
• Live in the Northeast*
  *These demographics have the highest indexes for infant, toddler and pre-school purchases.[26]

Additionally these consumers are:
• Not price sensitive.
• More influenced by the product benefits.
• The "concerned" parent, those who genuinely want the best for their child.
• Visionaries; they see the benefits and are going to set the trend for others in this segment to follow

These parents are in parenting groups such as Mothers Forums and Play Groups, and enroll children in early developmental classes (e.g., Creative Movements). They subscribe to parenting magazines, read parenting books or consult with Child Development/Parenting Experts. As a result, they are influenced by "Authorities" either through reading they have done themselves or by first-hand interaction with teachers and caregivers.

Other customer segments in this market are the "competitive" and "compensating" parents. They have the same demographic profile but have different interests. They are the followers. The "concerned" educated parent sets the bar and these others follow.

---

[24] *Source: Simmons data cited by Interep*
[25] *Source: Simmons data cited by Interep*
[26] *Source: Simmons Market Research Bureau, Fall 2002 Study of Media and Markets; Packaged Facts*

Confidential Information
Business Plan - Dated May-2005
Woburn, Massachusetts – USA

As we move down market to the mid-market, the primary customer demographics and behaviors are the same except for the following.
- Household Income drops to $100K+.
- They are influenced by the premium market.
- Due to increased price sensitivity they are more pragmatic in their purchasing decisions.
- They are more likely to do their own research (more shopping around, talking to their friends). Word-of-mouth is very influential in this market.

5.3 Pricing Strategy

Market Entry – High-end pricing strategy will be market-demand pricing to maximize per sale profit. We anticipate the following price ranges per product:

"Market Entry – High-end pricing strategy will be market-demand pricing"

- Table A = $650
- Table B = $1200
- Storage Unit = $450
- Toy Kit = $50 (average)
- Providing contribution margins between 50-60%

Expansion to the mid market will require a different pricing strategy. Lower table prices (around $350) for better market penetration will increase the user/installed base and provide a larger marketing base for the toy kits and accessories.

5.4 Distribution Strategy

P'kolino's distribution goal is to have over 85%[27] of sales come from direct-to-the-customer channels within five years. We expect that we will have to start with a distribution mix of approximately 65% of our sales through retail. Retail channels will enable customer exposure to, and interaction with, the products. As the understanding of our products grows and the brand develops we will shift the distribution mix to direct channels.

"P'kolino's distribution goal is to have over 85% of sales revenue come from channels direct-to-the-customer"

Retail Stores: Retailers will be chosen based on their clientele. We will target non-traditional retailers that give P'kolino a "showroom" for its designs. For example, we will target The Museum of Modern Arts (MoMA) store which features uniquely designed and educationally beneficial products as one of our first outlets. This strategy will help us reach the right

---

[27] Other furniture merchants have proven success in direct channels. Land of Nod estimated at nearly 100% sales are direct; through catalog and web. Pottery Barn Kids – direct sales = 72% of its $392 million in revenue. As stated in the 11/18/04 <u>Wall Street Journal</u> "William Sonoma's, inc Third Quarter 2004 results."

customer and generate some exposure for our products. To encourage customer interaction with us we will offer a free Toy Kit to those who have purchased a table or storage unit through a retail channel. The customer will redeem the free kit through a direct channel (web or mail) so that we may capture relevant customer data. This customer data is critical to our direct marketing to support our migration of customers to the direct sales channels as well as to encourage future purchases.

Direct-to-the-Customer: The goal is to have 85% of our revenue come through direct channels (web, mail and phone). Based on the proven success of other furniture merchants in direct channels (Land of Nod estimated at nearly 100% sales from direct channels like catalogs and the web,[28] and Pottery Barn Kids direct sales equal 72% of its $392MM in revenue)[29] we believe this is achievable.

The primary direct channel will be through the internet as 70% of our target customers have high-speed internet access. We will also offer mail and phone orders.

We will build a website that provides consumers with an easy product review, selection and purchasing experience. Proliferation of high-speed internet access enables us to show the many benefits of our products through the latest multi-media tools (streaming video demonstrations of our products in the form of infomercials through the web).

5.5 Communication Strategy – Year 1

Overview: In the first year our communications strategy will focus on targeted marketing that can be directly attributed to sales. We will try many different tactics to determine what generates the best dollar spent to sales ratio. Additionally, we will build the brand through low cost, guerrilla marketing efforts such as public relations and grassroots marketing.

---

[28] Our estimate based on Land of Nods business model of direct sales and no retail store to date.
[29] As stated in the 11/18/04 WSJ's "William Sonoma's, inc Third Quarter 2004 results.

Confidential Information
Business Plan - Dated May-2005
Woburn, Massachusetts – USA

Exhibit 5-A   Marketing Communications Strategy

Marketing Initiative	Estimated Cost	Estimated Table Sales	Estimated Storage Sales	Estimated Toy Kit Sales	Total Units Sold	Marketing Cost/Sale
Public Relations	$5,000	30	10	57	96	$52
GrassRoots	$5,000	80	26	151	257	$19
Word-of-Mouth	$5,000	50	17	94	161	$31
Online	$25,000	80	26	151	257	$97
Advertising	$15,000	50	17	94	161	$93
Direct Marketing	$20,000	70	23	132	225	$89
Retail Marketing Exp.	$6,000	330	109	622	1061	$6
Total $	81,000	690	228	1300	2218	$37

Public Relations

Public Relations (PR) will be at the center of our communications plan. The first phase of this plan is to utilize the PR potential of cooperation with Babson, the #1 entrepreneurship program in the country, and RISD, the #1 school of design. We have brought together these school's PR departments and have agreements to promote the story at no cost to us. To that end, we are developing a video documentary of the product design process to be used as a PR asset for the schools and P'kolino. From this PR exposure we intend to interest target market publications (e.g. Parenting Magazine) in P'kolino's story.

The PR effort will be a company priority. Management will make constant and persistent efforts to get new and compelling stories to the media. We will become a source of information for key media authorities and eventually seek product placement opportunities. Management will also seek active relationships with key media personalities to support our brand and products.

Grassroots Marketing

Grassroots Marketing will be how we get the customers interacting with the product and start the word-of-mouth engine running. We will start this grassroots effort in Boston targeting Mother's Forums, Play Groups and Day Care Centers (e.g., Bright Horizons). We will expand this effort strategically through major cities in the Northeast. These customers will be driven to the direct channels for purchase.

Word-of-Mouth

"Word-of-mouth is a powerful medium in this market."

As noted, word-of-mouth is a powerful tool is this market. We will encourage word-of-mouth by identifying key influencers in target markets and seeking to make them advocates of P'kolino products. Additionally, we will seek a child development expert endorsement to add additional

Confidential Information
Business Plan - Dated May-2005
Woburn, Massachusetts – USA

Confidential
Business Pl
Woburn, Ma

credibility. Word-of-mouth (viral marketing) tools such as referral benefits and e-mail forwarding will also be used.

Email and Web

The Web (www.pkolino.com) will be a powerful online catalog and direct purchase channel. At pkolino.com we will have product pictures, descriptions and video demonstrations to give customers as near to a physical world shopping experience as possible. The web will also be a means for us to generate awareness through targeted e-mail, keyword search, banner advertising and enhanced web advertising tools (such as rich media and dynamic banners).

Retail Sales Marketing Materials

Collateral materials such as brochures and point of purchase displays will be necessary to support our sales through retailers. Initially we will have a brochure from the RISD product development process that we can use for early discussions. We will also develop a high quality flyer for the two tables and the storage system (Storage unit and Kit). High-quality brochures and catalogs will be developed for use by retailers and distributed through mail and grassroots marketing campaigns.

Advertising

Our advertising goal will be to increase awareness of P'kolino in the high-end market. Our advertising efforts will focus on media that reach a high concentration of our target customer. The advertising will be primarily in print media because of its ability to show our product for a relatively low cost. These ads will drive customers back to pkolino.com for more information or purchase.

Direct Mail

In the first year of operation and in preparation for the 2005 Christmas season we will run a direct mail test. This mailing will target high-end customers in the Northeast to keep resources and expenses to a minimum. A successful test would result in about 1+% purchase rate from mailed brochures. Should this test prove successful we will look to roll-out a larger direct campaign prior to the Christmas season.

5.6 Sales Strategy

The founders will serve as the sales force making direct calls to strategically identified retailers. It will be our strategy to focus on a select number of local retailers so the founders can manage these relationship and still focus on other priorities. When we expand into the mid-market (in year 3) we will hire a dedicated sales manager.

Confidential Information
Business Plan - Dated May-2005
Woburn, Massachusetts – USA

7	Operations

7.1 Operations Strategy

P'kolino's core functions (design and marketing strategy) will be the main operational activities performed in-house. All other operational activities like manufacturing, packaging, shipping and some office/administrative and customer service functions will be outsourced.[30]

For manufacturing, the company has identified several manufacturers in the Bento Goncalves region in Brazil that are currently operating with underutilized (excess) capacity and have the technology and expertise to manufacture our products. We have partnered with one of these companies to manufacture our first line of products. AFECOM, our first manufacturing partner, produces over 140,000 furniture pieces per year and is well known in Europe and Latin America. Late in the 2nd year of operations, P'kolino will reexamine this strategy (when volumes increase) and evaluate alternative manufacturing options in Asia. P'kolino products are built with wood, high-density foam and fabrics. AFECOM's high density foam manufacturing technology, finishing quality, speed, volume requirements and logistic costs are better and more accommodating to P'kolino during this first stage.

The economics of the manufacturing process will be determined by our ability to negotiate with potential manufacturers. For the purpose of this document we will use industry averages.[31] For minimum orders of 150 units, the payment terms are 50% up front and 50% on shipment. For the first year of operations we plan to complete two 150 table orders. Production time is 4 weeks for prototypes and 10 weeks to manufacture and order shipment of the approved prototypes.[32]

Exhibit 7-A
Operations Cycle

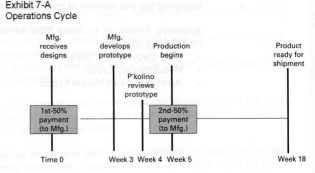

---

[30] Outsourcing cost for manufacturing, packaging, shipping are included in the Cost of goods sold, based on industry average (AFMA)
[31] Sources: AFMA – American Furniture Manufacturing Association
[32] Operations Cycle is a 14 week process for existing products, and an 18 week process for new products

Confidential Information
Business Plan - Dated May-2005
Woburn, Massachusetts – USA

Regarding the product development process for P'kolino, it takes 9 to 12 months to develop a new product (from concept to customer).[33]

Exhibit 7-B
P'kolino Product Development Process

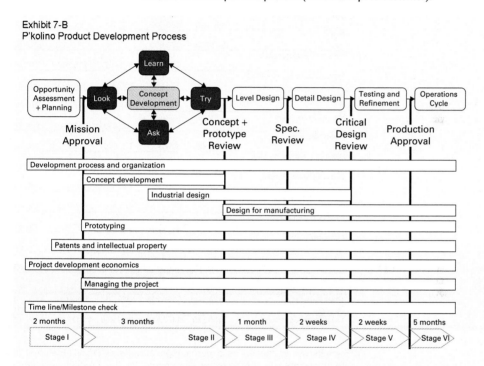

In developing the first product line, the company leveraged its relationship with RISD. For the second generation of products P'kolino will have to assemble a product development team composed of both full-time employees and collaborators. Marketing and sales will also require additional personal, as will in-house administrative and customer service responsibilities. Our staffing plan follows:[34]

---

[33] Based on the current P'kolino product development process.
[34] Salaries are based on Boston average salaries for the respective positions according to the Career Journal (Wall Street Journal online edition) salary search (Salaryexpert.com)

Confidential Information
Business Plan - Dated May-2005
Woburn, Massachusetts – USA

Exhibit 7-C
P'kolino Staffing Plan

Staffing Plan	Year 1	Year 2	Year 3	Year 4	Year 5
CEO	1	1	1	1	1
	$40,000	$70,000	$120,000	$150,000	$220,000
COO	1	1	1	1	1
	$40,000	$70,000	$120,000	$130,000	$130,000
Product Development Mgr.		1	1	1	1
		$69,680	$72,467	$75,366	$78,381
Product Development Staff		1	1	1	1
		$54,080	$56,243	$58,493	$60,833
Operations and Logistics Mgr.			1	1	1
			$64,896	$67,492	$70,192
Marketing Manager			1	1	1
			$80,038	$83,240	$86,570
Sales Manager	1	1	1	1	1
	$35,000	$70,000	$72,800	$75,712	$78,740
Sales and Marketing Staff			1	2	2
			$58,406	$60,743	$63,172
Direct Channel Support			1	1	1
			$64,896	$67,492	$70,192
Customer Service Staff			1	1	1
			$48,672	$50,619	$52,644
Office Administration		1	1	1	1
		$33,280	$34,611	$35,996	$37,435
Accounting				1	1
				$39,370	$40,945
Advisors	1	1	1	1	1
	$20,000	$31,200	$32,448	$33,746	$35,096
Total Headcount	**4**	**7**	**13**	**14**	**14**
Total Salaries	**$135,000**	**$398,240**	**$863,334**	**$989,010**	**$1,087,371**
Benefits	$20,250	$59,736	$129,500	$148,352	$163,106
Total Compensation	**$155,250**	**$457,976**	**$992,835**	**$1,137,362**	**$1,250,476**

Benefits are estimated as a percentage of salaries (15%). Eventual hires are considered in the financial statements for the product development, sales, and marketing efforts.

Confidential Information
Business Plan - Dated May-2005
Woburn, Massachusetts – USA

P'kolino

7.2 <u>Development Timeline</u>

Exhibit 7-D
P'kolino Timeline

Month/Activity	M1	M2	M3	M4	M5	M6	M7	M8	M9	M10	M11	M12	M13	M14	M15	M16	M17	M18	M19	M20	M21	M22	M23
Hire child development expert as advisor	▒																						
Secure funding	█	█	█																				
Launch RISD/BABSON PR campaign	▒	▒	▒																				
Production 150 tables + storage + kits	█	█	█	█	█																		
Website development	▒	▒																					
Develop institutional sales channel			█	█	█	█	█	█	█	█	█	█											
Hire marketing/tech intern			▒																				
Office relocation				█																			
Launch grassroot marketing campaign				▒	▒	▒	▒	▒															
Team focuses on sales					█	█	█																
Production 160 tables + storage + kits (2nd)				▒	▒																		
Collection efforts										█													
Production + 400 tables + storage + kits							▒	▒	▒														
Hire Product Development Manager										█	█												
Hire Marketing Manager												▒	▒										
Website improvements												█											
Marketing campaign															█	█	█	█					
Production 500 tables + storage + kits																▒	▒	▒					
Team focuses on sales																		█	█	█			
Collection efforts																						▒	▒

Confidential Information
Business Plan - Dated May-2005
Woburn, Massachusetts – USA

8	**Critical Risks**

- <u>Highly competitive market</u> – All segments of this market are highly competitive, and this is particularly true in the mid and mass segments. P'kolino will compete with a distinctive product and a different value proposition as a niche player. We will establish our brand in the high-end segment and then moving down to more competitive markets. However, the potential remains that competitors will identify our niche, before our brand has a foothold. We will rely on innovation and speed to compete if competitors attack our niche.

- <u>Copycats</u> – Intellectual property protection can be circumvented to produce competing and possibly cheaper version of our products. P'kolino will base its designs not only on beauty, but on improved usability to the end user (the child). Designing products that are better suited for children to play with, while creating identifiable differences and defining brand attributes that are more difficult to replicate.

- <u>Lawsuits</u> – Although we will take precautions to make our product safe for children it is possible that children may injure themselves while using one of our products. We will carry product liability insurance to protect us financially from such an event but the potential brand damage must be recognized.

- <u>Product defects and/or recall</u> – P'kolino will take precautions to develop durable, reliable and safe products using materials that have proven to stand the test of time. However, it is possible given the expected useful life of these products and the use by children that these products could break creating hazards for children. Should this occur and depending on the situation P'kolino may be obligated or feel it necessary to issue a recall of the defective product. Some manufacturers carry insurance in case the defect is caused by some error during the manufacturing process. We will further explore this possibility.

- <u>Sales lower than expected</u> – In case this happens P'kolino will have the capability of adjusting production volume and shifting strategy fairly quickly because of our size and structure. We will also retain sufficient cash to support an increase in the number of inventory days.

Discussion Questions

P'kolino is a children's furniture company that was launched in 2005. As you read the business plan, keep the following questions in mind:

1. Does the business plan tell a coherent and compelling story?
2. Does the plan capture all of the learning that Antonio and J.B. have accumulated?
3. What three questions do you think Antonio and J.B. need to answer through further planning before they launch the venture?
4. What are the three strongest aspects of the plan?
5. What areas need improvement?

This business plan was prepared by Antonio Turco-Rivas and J.B. Schneider in support of their business. The original drafts were prepared in the Entrepreneur Intensity Track taught by Professor Andrew Zacharakis. © Copyright P'kolino and Babson College, 2005.

NOTES

1. S. Bartlett, "Seat of Your Pants," *Inc.*, October 2002.
2. D. D. Eisenhowser, The Quotations Page, www.quotationspage.com/quote/36892.html.
3. S. Blank, "Why Companies Are Not Startups," March 4, 2014, http://steveblank.com/2014/03/04/why-companies-are-not-startups/.
4. J. Lange, W. Bygrave, and T. Evans, "Do Business Plan Competitions Produce Winning Businesses?" Paper presented at 2004 Babson Kauffman Entrepreneurship Research Conference, Glasgow, Scotland.
5. P. Thomas, P. "Rewriting the Rules: A New Generation of Entrepreneurs Find Themselves in the Perfect Time and Place to Chart Their Own Course," *Wall Street Journal*, May 22, 2004, R4.
6. S. Wise, "Wise Words," *Globe and Mail*, July 18, 2006, http://www.theglobeandmail.com/report-on-business/wise-words/article1106073/?page=all.
7. The Business Link, *Business Planning Workbook: Immigrant Entrepreneur Series*, 2010, www.canadabusiness.ab.ca/docs/Business%20Planning%20Workbook%20Imm%20Entrepreneurs.pdf.
8. S. Wise, *Hot or Not: How to Know if Your Business Idea Will Fly or Fail* (Toronto, ON: Ryerson Entrepreneur Institute, 2011), 80.
9. C. Dixon, "Why You Shouldn't Keep Your Startup Idea Secret," *Chris Dixon's Blog*, August 22, 2009, http://cdixon.org/2009/08/22/why-you-shouldnt-keep-your-startup-idea-secret/.
10. L. Busque, "The Secret to Startup Success? Tell Every Single Person You Meet About Your Ideas," April 8, 2013, www.linkedin.com/today/post/article/20130418021018-6218188-the-secret-to-startup-success-tell-every-single-person-you-meet-about-your-idea.
11. Young Entrepreneur Council, "10 Tips for a Remarkable Tagline," *Inc.*, July 19, 2013. www.inc.com/young-entrepreneur-council/10-tips-for-a-remarkable-tagline.html.
12. D. Gianatasio, "Happy 25th Birthday to Nike's 'Just Do It,' the Last Great Advertising Slogan," *Adweek*, July 2,

2013, www.adweek.com/adfreak/happy-25th-birthday-nikes-just-do-it-last-great-advertising-slogan-150947.

13 J. Pruitt and T. Adlin, *The Persona Life-cycle: Keeping People in Mind Throughout Product Design* (San Francisco, CA: Morgan Kaufmann, 2006).

14 Chetan Sharma Consulting, "Industry Research," www.chetansharma.com/research.htm.

15 J. Makower, R. Pernick, and C. Wilder, *Clean Energy Trends 2008* (San Francisco, CA: Clean Edge, 2008).

16 S. G. Blank and B. Dorf, *The Startup Owner's Manual: The Step-by-Step Guide for Building a Great Company* (Pescadero, CA: K&S Ranch, 2012).

17 T. Serbinski, "The One Competitor Your Startup Forgot About," October 14, 2013, http://tedserbinski.com/the-one-competitor-your-startup-forgot-about/.

18 Ibid.

19 Ibid.

20 R. L. Martin and S. Osberg, "Social Entrepreneurship: The Case for Definition," *Stanford Social Innovation Review* 5 (2007): 28–39.

21 S. Vandermerwe and J. Rada, "Servitization of Business: Adding Value by Adding Services," *European Management Journal* 6 (1989): 314–324.

22 Ibid.

23 Rogers Communications, "Customer Experience," www.rogerscsr.com/EN/customer-experience.html.

24 Ibid.

25 L. Pitt, P. Berthon, and J. P. Berthon, "Changing Channels: The Impact of the Internet on Distribution Strategy," *Business Horizons* 42 (1999): 19–28.

26 Ibid.

27 Ibid.

28 Ibid.

29 O. Sacirbey, "Private Companies Temper IPO Talk," *IPO Reporter*, December 18, 2000.

30 J. Rowley, "Understanding Digital Content Marketing," *Journal of Marketing Management* 24 (2008): 517–540.

31 Ibid.

32 S. Wise, "The Talent Triangle," *Globe and Mail*, April 5, 2009, www.theglobeandmail.com/report-on-business/the-talent-triangle/article1099632/?page=all.

33 Ibid.

34 Ibid.

35 *Burn rate* is how much more cash the company is expending each month than earning in revenue.

36 Wikipedia, "The Waterfall Model," http://en.wikipedia.org/wiki/Waterfall_model.

37 "Agile Methodology," http://agilemethodology.org/.

38 Ibid.

39 Blank and Dorf, *The Startup Owner's Manual.*

40 Ibid.

41 E. Reis, "The Lean Startup Methodology," http://theleanstartup.com/principles.

42 E. Ries, *The Lean Startup: How Today's Entrepreneurs Use Continuous Innovation to Create Radically Successful Businesses* (New York, NY: Random House, 2011).

43 A running sidebar, a visual device positioned on the right side of the page, periodically highlights some of the key points in the plan. Don't overload the sidebar, but one or two items per page can draw attention to highlights that maintain reader interest.

44 G. Kawasaki, "The 10 20 30 Rule of Power Point," *Presentation Magazine,* January 17, 2009, www.presentationmagazine.com/the-10-20-30-rule-of-powerpoint-11710.htm.

Financial stock chart

BUILDING YOUR PRO FORMA FINANCIAL STATEMENTS

CHAPTER OUTLINE

Common Mistakes
Learning Objective 9.1 Identify common mistakes in entrepreneurs' business proposals.

Financial Statement Overview
Learning Objective 9.2 Provide an overview of the three standard financial statements.

Building Your Pro Forma Financial Statements
Learning Objective 9.3 Prepare pro forma financial statements.

Comparable Method
Learning Objective 9.4 Use the comparable method to validate pro forma financial statements.

Building Integrated Financial Statements
Learning Objective 9.5 Prepare integrated financial statements.

Putting It All Together
Learning Objective 9.6 Prepare an overview of completed financial statements.

MANY ENTREPRENEURS are intimidated by numbers, even after they've gone through the business planning process. They understand their concept, and they even have a good sense of the business model, but ask them to put together **pro forma financials** or read an income statement and they have a panic attack.

You might feel that building your financials or understanding them isn't that important because you can always hire an accountant. Although an accountant is a useful advisor, in the pre-launch stage the lead entrepreneur needs to understand the numbers inside and out. After all, the lead entrepreneur is the person who will be articulating his or her vision to potential employees, vendors, customers, and investors. If the entrepreneur is easily stumped by simple questions of profitability or costs, potential employees, customers, and other parties important to the new venture's success will lose confidence in the lead entrepreneur's ability to execute on the concept. Financial statements serve to bridge the entrepreneur's great idea and what that idea really means in terms of dollars and cents. So, although it can be painful, learn the numbers behind your business. The rewards of gaining this deep insight are often the difference between success and failure.

If for no other reason, the lead entrepreneur needs to understand the numbers so he or she can decide whether this business has the potential to provide a good living. It is too easy to get caught in a trap where a new venture is slowly draining away your investment or where you are working, in real terms, for less than the minimum wage.[1] The goal of this chapter is to give you an introduction to entrepreneurial financial planning. Unlike in existing businesses, which have an operating history, entrepreneurs must develop their financials from scratch. There are no previous trends in revenue and costs that you can use as a basis to project future revenues and costs. Yet failing to come up with solid projections may cost you your initial investment as well as that of your investors. This chapter will help you generate sound projections.

Common Mistakes

In preparing this chapter, we sent an email to several acquaintances who are professional equity investors (either angels or venture capitalists). We asked them, "What are the most common mistakes you see when you review an entrepreneur's business proposal?" We wanted to know what "red flags" made them hesitant to believe that the business could survive and succeed. Here are the eight mistakes they consistently cited:

1. *Not understanding the revenue drivers:* Entrepreneurs need to know what the leverage points are that drive revenues. They need to understand how many customers are likely to see the product, how many of those who see it will buy it, and how much, on average, they will buy each time. Although every entrepreneur claims his estimates are "conservative," 99% of the time entrepreneurs are overly optimistic in their projections. So avoid the "conservative" adjective; it strikes most sophisticated investors as naïve.

2. *Underestimating costs:* If you were to graph the revenue and cost projections of entrepreneurs over time, you would often see revenues growing in a "hockey stick" fashion while costs slowly progress upward (see Figure 9.1). We often see revenue projections of $15 million after five years on costs of only $5 million. That is unbelievable. When we dig into those numbers, we often see that the firm has only five employees in year five. That assumes revenues per employee of $3 million, which is nearly impossible. Often entrepreneurs underestimate how much infrastructure they need in the way of employees and

physical assets to achieve that level of sales. Entrepreneurs also underestimate the cost of marketing expenditures to acquire and retain customers. Poor projections lead to cash crunches and ultimately to failure.

3. *Underestimating time to generate revenues:* Pro forma financials often show sales occurring immediately. Typically, a business will incur costs for many months before it can generate revenue. For instance, if you are opening a restaurant, you will incur rent, inventory, and labour costs, among others, before you generate a dime in revenue. Another "red flag" is how quickly revenues will ramp up. Often projections show the business at full capacity within the first year. That is rarely realistic.

4. *Lack of comparables:* Investors typically think about the entrepreneur's concept from their knowledge of similar businesses. They will compare your gross margins, net income margins, and other metrics to industry standards and selected benchmark companies. Yet many entrepreneurs' projections have ratios that far exceed industry standards, and when questioned about this above-average performance they can't explain it. You need to understand your business model in relation to the industry and be able to explain any differences.

5. *Saying there is no competition:* The last thing any investor wants to hear from an entrepreneur is that "they have no competition." There is always competition (either direct or indirect) no matter what industry a company is competing in. If an entrepreneur states that there is no competition, it often indicates that proper market research has not been completed.

There are four types of competition in any industry: pure competition, imperfect competition, oligopoly, and monopoly.[2]

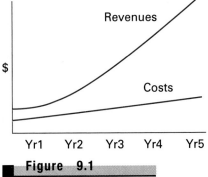

Figure 9.1

Hockey stick sales growth

- *Pure competition:* In an industry with pure competition, no single buyer or seller has total influence over the products and services in the industry. A large number of companies competing for customers offer low barriers of entry for new ventures.

- *Imperfect competition:* In an industry with imperfect competition, there are multiple companies offering variations of the same product or service but with minor differences (price, customer service, location, etc.). There are low barriers to entry within this type of industry. An example of imperfect competition is the restaurant industry: There are a large number of restaurants in a large city, and although they are all offering food and beverages to customers, they vary with regard to type of food, level of service, and price point.

- *Oligopoly:* In an oligopoly industry there are a limited number of companies competing for customers, and the quality of the product and price points between companies is very similar. An example of an oligopoly industry within Canada is telecommunications; Rogers, Bell, and TELUS are the three largest competitors who command most of the market, and they compete for customers across the nation with few differences in their product offerings and price points.

- *Monopoly:* In a monopoly industry the competition is lacking, allowing a single brand or business to dominate the industry and all customers. There are high barriers to entry because of the status of the leading company, its resources, and the relationship it has with customers. An example of this in Canada is VIA Rail. VIA owns and operates all of the passenger rail transportation across Canada. It would be very costly for another company to buy property and build railway tracks across the country to compete.

The *status quo* can also be considered a form of competition within a market. Sometimes a company's biggest competitor is inertia. Consumers are often reluctant to change their behaviour when they are in a routine or are using a product or service that they have already paid for (or have been paying for). One solution to overcoming inertia is to focus on the 10x rule (proving that your product or service is 10x better than the current option or your direct competitor). Is it cheaper? Is it stronger? Is it easier? Is it more readily available? Is it faster? How is it better? It is critical for the company to lay the groundwork to overcome the status quo in their marketing efforts, but it is also important that it is addressed and outlined in the sales process, ensuring customers are aware of your company's 10x solution.

6. *Top-down versus bottom-up forecasting:* Investors often hear entrepreneurs claim that their revenues represent 3% of the market after year three. The implication is that it is easy to get that 3%. Investors know that, although it doesn't sound like much, the trick is how you get to that 3%. They want to see the process—the cost of acquiring, serving, and retaining the customer. Investors won't believe that you can get 3% without causing competitors to take notice and action.

   Top-down financial forecasting takes into consideration the overall market to determine the company demographics and target market and financial goals.[3] Based on the current market activity and forecasted market growth, there is a general assumption that the company will acquire a certain percentage of the market within their first year, increasing year by year.[4] Generally speaking, entrepreneurs tend to be overly optimistic when it comes to their financial forecasting. Investors are more likely to invest in a company that has based their financial forecast(s) on accurate and reasonable assumptions rather than a company that is being overly optimistic.

   Bottom-up financial forecasting is more detailed with budgets and spending plans mapped out by department or area within the company. Revenue projections and financial forecasting is all based on a sales forecast.[5] Bottom-up forecasting is a much more strategic approach taken by entrepreneurs using appropriate and realistic assumptions.

7. *Underestimating time to secure financing:* A major pet peeve of investors is that entrepreneurs assume financing will close quickly. Whether entrepreneurs want to raise $25,000 or $1 million, they project it will happen in the next month. In reality, it often takes as long as six months to close a round of financing. Fred Adler, famed venture capitalist who invested in Data General, used to hand out T-shirts that said, "Happiness is a positive cash flow." Yet if entrepreneurs are too optimistic about how quickly they can close a round of financing, they will quickly have negative cash flow, which often means they are out of business.

8. *Not matching the source of the capital to the stage of the venture:* It is important that an entrepreneur recognize when and where it is appropriate to seek financing or funding. During the initial stages of a startup, an entrepreneur has to look to angel investors or friends and family for what is known as *seed capital*. This will allow the startup to gain traction and break even before looking elsewhere. Once a startup has passed their breakeven stage and are starting to earn revenue and customers, they can seek financing from venture capitalists or make strategic alliances with other firms. It isn't until a startup is in a later stage of their life cycle that they should be considering offering an IPO and going public. An example of a company that followed the financing path in a correct and effective way is Facebook, which went public on May 18, 2012—eight years after Mark Zuckerberg founded the company in 2004.[6] He had gone through the development, early, and later stages of Facebook and was ready to seek funding outside of his venture capitalists, acquisitions and mergers, or strategic alliances.

Understanding these pitfalls will help you generate realistic financials and, more importantly, enable you to convincingly articulate your business model so that you can sell your vision to employees, customers, vendors, and investors. Before we move on, let's do a quick overview of financial statements.

Financial Statement Overview

You'll need to include three standard financial statements in your business plan: the income statement, the statement of cash flows, and the balance sheet. Most people first want to know why there are three statements. The reason is simple: Each one provides a slightly different view of the company. Any one alone is only part of the picture. Together they provide a detailed description of the economics of your company.

The first of these statements, the **income statement**, describes how well a company conducted its business over a recent period of time—typically a quarter (three months) or a year. This indicator of overall performance begins with the company's revenues on the top line. From that accounting of sales, subtract the company's expenses. These include

- Cost of the products that the company actually sold
- Selling, marketing, and administrative costs
- Depreciation—the estimated cost of using your property, plant, and equipment
- Interest on debts
- Taxes on profits

The bottom line of the statement (literally) is the company's profits—called *net income*. It is important to realize that the income statement represents a measurement of business performance. It is *not* a description of actual flows of money.

A company needs cash to conduct business. Without it, there is no business. The second financial statement, the **statement of cash flows**, monitors this crucial account. As the name implies, the statement of cash flows concerns itself exclusively with transactions that involve cash. It is not uncommon to have strong positive earnings on the income statement and a negative statement of cash flows—less cash at the end of the period than at the beginning. Just because you shipped a product does not necessarily mean you received the cash for it yet. Likewise, you might have purchased something like inventory or a piece of equipment that will not show up on your income statement until it is consumed or depreciated. Many noncash transactions are represented in the income statement.

What is curious (and sometimes confusing to those who have never worked with financial statements before) is the way the statement of cash flows is constructed. It starts with the bottom line (profits) of the income statement and works backward, removing all the noncash transactions. For example, since the income statement subtracted depreciation (the value of using your plant and equipment), the statement of cash flows adds it back in because you don't actually pay any depreciation expense to anybody. Similarly, the statement of cash flows needs to include things that you paid for but did not use that period. For example, you might have paid for inventory that has not yet sold, or you might have bought a piece of equipment that will depreciate over time, so you would need to put those items on the statement of cash flows. After all these adjustments, you are left with a representation of transactions that are exclusively cash.

The **balance sheet** enumerates all the company's assets, liabilities, and shareholder equity. **Assets** are all the things the company has that are expected to generate value over time—things like inventory, buildings, and equipment; accounts receivable (money that your customers still owe you); and cash. **Liabilities** represent all the money the company expects to pay eventually. These include accounts payable (money the company owes its suppliers), debt, and unpaid taxes. **Shareholder equity** is the money that shareholders have paid into the company as well as the company's earnings so far. Where the income statement describes a process or flow, the balance sheet is a snapshot of accounts at a specific point in time.

Product/Service Description	Price	Gross Margin	Revenue	COGS
1. Books	$20	40%	$1,687.50	$1,012.50
2. Videos	$30	50%	337.50	168.75
3. Maps	$50	50%	375.00	187.50
4. Ancillary Items	$100	50%	375.00	187.50
5. Other (Postcards, Magazines, etc.)	$5	50%	150.00	75.00
Totals			$2,925.00	$1,631.25

Total Revenue	$2,925.00
COGS	1,631.25
Gross Profit	$1,293.75
Gross Profit Margin	44%

■ **Figure 9.4**

Cost of goods worksheet

As with revenue assumptions, you need to sharpen your COGS assumptions. Use a schedule similar to that in Figure 9.3 to refine COGS by product (see Figure 9.4). After some investigation at Hoovers.com, you find that the gross margin on books is only 27% for the likes of Amazon.com and Barnes & Noble. On other items you might sell, other companies' gross margins are around 24%. Although these margins are lower than first estimated, these companies have a different business model—high volume, lower margins. Where will your bookstore operate? If it is high volume, your margins should be similar to these companies' margins. If you choose to offer a premium shopping experience, meaning a highly knowledgeable sales staff and unique historical artifacts, you would likely achieve higher margins. Remember that your financials need to mirror the story you related in your business plan—be consistent. Figure 9.4 shows the price per item, the gross margin (revenue minus COGS) per item, and the revenue per item (from Figure 9.3) and then calculates COGS in dollar terms [revenue × (1 − COGS)]. Since the gross margins for items differ, the overall gross margin is 44%.

Cost of Client Acquisition (CoCA)

Cost of client acquisition (CoCA) refers to all of the incurred costs associated when a single customer purchases a company's product or service. Examples of some of the costs that are associated with CoCA include product development and research, marketing efforts, retail or shelf space, employee salaries, and so on. A company calculates the CoCA to determine if marketing resources and dollars are being used effectively with the ultimate goal of decreasing the cost to acquire a client. CoCA is also important to an entrepreneur because it is an indicator of whether the venture is strong enough to generate revenue and enable future growth.[14] If the calculated CoCA is too high, there is little chance that the business will generate any revenue because it will be spending all of its resources on acquiring customers; therefore, it is critical that a company's calculated *ARPU is much higher than the CoCA*. Ideally, a company's CoCA will slowly decrease over time once it becomes established within the market and customer referrals or viral marketing effects of the product or service begin.

Scalability

Scalability refers to the ability of a business to grow in a cost-efficient and effective manner.[15] Many technology- and online-driven new companies are scalable because of their lower cost of goods sold (COGS). The Internet provides many resources at a low cost for a new company (especially compared to having to pay rent for a brick-and-mortar retail location), allowing new companies to scale much easier.

A company looking to scale efficiently has to be able to increase its volume (increase sales, revenue, employees, operations, etc.) without negatively impacting its contribution margin, [contribution margin (CM) = revenue (R) – variable costs (VC)].[16] A key ingredient to a company's ability to scale is simplicity.

Everyone in the company's supply chain (employees, management, suppliers, customers, etc.) must be able to explain quickly in simple terms what the company's core business is, otherwise there is limited potential for the company itself to scale. Simplicity in a company's business processes equals a high potential for scalability.

Operating Expenses

In addition to direct expenses, businesses incur operating expenses, such as marketing, salaries and general administration (SG&A), rent, interest expense, and so forth. The build-up method forecasts those expenses on a daily, monthly, or yearly basis as appropriate (see Figure 9.5). For example, you might get rental space for your store at $30 per square foot per year depending on location. You might need about 3,000 square feet, so your yearly rent would be $90,000 (put in the yearly expense column). You'll pay your rent on a monthly basis, so you would show a

Expense	Daily	Monthly	Yearly	Total
Store Rent			90,000	$90,000
Manager Salary			60,000	$60,000
Assistant Manager			40,000	$40,000
Hourly Employees	176			$63,360
Benefits	21		12,000	$19,603
Bank Charges			10,530	$10,530
Marketing/Advertising		1,000		$12,000
Utilities		333		$4,000
Travel			1,000	$1,000
Dues			1,000	$1,000
Depreciation		833		$10,000
Misc.			4,000	$4,000
Totals				$315,493

Assumptions:

Rent—3,000 sq. ft. at $30/sq. ft. = $90,000
Hire 1 manager at $60,000/year
Hire 1 assistant manager at $40,000/year
Store is open from 9 a.m. to 7 p.m. daily, so 10 hours per day
Need 2 clerks when open and 1 clerk an hour before and after open
2 clerks × 10 hours × $8/hour + 1 clerk × 2 hours × $8/hour
Benefits are 12% of wages and salaries
Bank charges about 1% of sales
Advertising—$1,000/month
Travel—$1,000/year to attend trade shows
Dues—$1,000/year for trade association
Depreciation—$100,000 of leasehold improvements and equipment, depreciated over
        10 years using the straight-line method

■ **Figure 9.5**

Operating expenses worksheet

	Mon.	Tues.	Wed.	Thurs.	Fri.	Sat.	Sun.	Total
Store Hours	10:00–9:00	10:00–9:00	10:00–9:00	10:00–9:00	10:00–9:00	10:00–9:00	11:00–5:00	
Hours Open	11	11	11	11	11	11	6	72
Shift 1	9:30–1:30	9:30–1:30	9:30–1:30	9:30–1:30	9:30–1:30	9:30–1:30	10:00–2:00	
Shift 2	1:30–5:30	1:30–5:30	1:30–5:30	1:30–5:30	1:30–5:30	1:30–5:30	1:00–5:00	
Shift 3	5:30–9:30	5:30–9:30	5:30–9:30	5:30–9:30	5:30–9:30	5:30–9:30		
Shift 1 Hrs.	4	4	4	4	4	4	4	
Shift 2 Hrs.	4	4	4	4	4	4	4	
Shift 3 Hrs.	4	4	4	4	4	4	0	
Total Shift Hours	12	12	12	12	12	12	8	80
Staff Headcount								
Shift 1	2	2	1	2	1	4	3	
Shift 2	1	1	0	1	1	4	4	
Shift 3	1	1	1	2	4	4	0	
Total Staff	4	4	2	5	6	12	7	40
Total Hours Worked								
Shift 1	8	8	4	8	4	16	12	
Shift 2	4	4	0	4	4	16	16	
Shift 3	4	4	4	8	16	16	0	
	16	16	8	20	24	48	28	160
Mgr.	0	0	8	8	8	8	8	40
Asst. Mgr.	8	8	8	0	8	8	0	40

Total hourly employee hours/week = 160
Hourly rate $8/hour   8
Total wages per week $1,280
Total wages per year $66,560

Figure 9.6

Headcount table

rent expense of $7,500 in the month-to-month income statement. At this point, however, you are just trying to get a sense of the overall business model and gauge whether this business can be profitable; showing it on a yearly basis is sufficient.

Based on the first cut, your bookstore is projecting operating expenses of approximately $315,000 per year. However, the "devil is in the details," as they say, and one problem area is accurately projecting operating costs, especially labour costs. Constructing a headcount schedule is an important step in refining your labour projections (see Figure 9.6). Although the store is open on average 10 hours per day, you can see from the headcount table that Sunday is a shorter day and that the store is open 11 hours on the other days. The store operates with a minimum of two employees at all times (including either the store manager or the assistant store manager). During busier shifts, the number of employees reaches a peak of six people (afternoon shift on Saturday, including both managers). Looking at the calculation below the table, you see that the new wage expense is about $66,000, a bit higher than the first estimate. This process of examining and re-examining your assumptions over and over is what leads to compelling financials.

Just as you refine the hourly wage expense, you need to also refine other expenses. For example, marketing expenses are projected to be $12,000. Create a detailed schedule of how you plan on spending those advertising dollars. If you refer back to the last chapter, Figure 8.8a has a schedule of detailed expenses. This illustrates another point: *Financial analysis is really just the mathematical expression of your overall business strategy*. Everything you write about in your business plan has revenue or cost implications. As investors read business plans, they build a mental picture of the financial statements, especially the income statement. If the written plan and the financials are tightly correlated, investors have much greater confidence that the entrepreneur knows what she or he is doing.

Preliminary Income Statement

Once you have forecasted revenues and expenses, you put them together in an income statement (Figure 9.7). Figure 9.3 forecasted average daily sales of almost $3,000. You need to annualize that figure. You can expect the store to be open, on average, 360 days per year (assuming that the store might be closed for a few days such as Christmas and Thanksgiving). Note that the first line is called Total Revenues and then shows the detail that creates that total revenues line by itemizing the different revenue categories. COGS is handled in the same manner as revenues; you multiply the typical day by 360 days to get the annual total.

After adjusting the hourly wages per the headcount table (which also means adjusting employee benefits), take the operating expenses worksheet (see Figure 9.5) and put it into the income statement. If you believe that you can secure debt financing, put in an interest expense. However, for the initial forecasts, you may not yet know how much debt financing you'll need or can secure to launch the business, so leave out the interest expense until you derive a reasonable estimate. Next compute taxes. Make sure to account for federal,

Total Revenues	$1,053,000	100%
Historical Books	607,500	
Videos	121,500	
Maps	135,000	
Ancillary Items	135,000	
Other	54,000	
Total COGS	**$587,250**	**55.8%**
Historical Books	364,500	
Videos	60,750	
Maps	67,500	
Ancillary Items	67,500	
Other	27,000	
Gross Profit	**$465,750**	**44.2%**
Operating Expenses		
Store Rent	90,000	
Manager Salary	60,000	
Assistant Manager	40,000	
Hourly Employees	66,560	
Benefits	19,987	
Bank Charges	10,530	
Marketing/Advertising	12,000	
Utilities	4,000	
Travel	1,000	
Dues	1,000	
Depreciation	10,000	
Misc.	4,000	
Total Operating Expenses	**$319,077**	**30.3%**
Earnings from Operations	**$146,673**	**13.9%**
Taxes	**$58,669**	**5.6%**
Net Earnings	**$88,004**	**8.4%**

■ Figure 9.7

Income statement

provincial, and municipal taxes as applicable. Note that the right column calculates the expense percentage of total revenues. This is called a **common-sized income statement**. Although you have been rigorous in building your statement, you can further validate it by comparing your common-sized income statement to the industry standards, which is where you start using the comparable method.

Comparable Method

How can you tell whether your projections are reasonable? In the **comparable method**, you look at how your company compares to industry averages and benchmark companies. The first thing to do is gauge whether your revenue projections make sense and then see whether your cost structure is reasonable. Comparables help you validate your projections. For instance, a good metric for revenue in retail is sales per square foot. The bookstore is projecting sales of $1 million in 3,000 square feet, which equates to $351 per square foot. Secondary research into the average per bookstore[17] and also into what one or two specific bookstores achieve is a good place to start.[18] For example, $351 is in line with independent bookstores ($350/square foot) but higher than a large retailer like Barnes & Noble ($297/square foot).

The projections seem reasonable considering that you will be selling certain items like maps, which have a much higher ticket price than books, but there are a couple of caveats to this estimate. First, it is likely to take a new bookstore some time to achieve this level of sales. In other words, the income statement that has been derived might be more appropriate for the second or third year of operation. At that point, the bookstore will have built up a clientele and achieved some name recognition.

Second, you should run some scenario analyses. Does this business model still work if your bookstore only achieves Barnes & Noble's sales per square foot ($297)? Also run a few other scenarios related to higher foot traffic, recession, outbreak of war (sales of books on Islam increased with September 11 and escalating tensions in the Middle East), and other contingencies. Having some validated metrics, such as sales per square foot, helps you run different scenarios and make sound decisions about whether to launch a venture in the first place and then about how to adjust your business model so that the venture has the greatest potential to succeed.

Other metrics that are easily obtainable for this type of establishment include *sales per customer* or *average ticket price*. Figure 9.3 shows expected sales of $2,925 per day from 75 unique store visitors. That translates into an average transaction per visitor of $39. However, not every visitor will buy; many people will just come in and browse. Figure 9.3 assumed that 75% of visitors would buy a book and a lower percentage would buy other items. If that percentage holds true, 56 people will actually purchase something each day. Thus, the average receipt is $52. This average ticket price is considerably higher than Barnes & Noble's rate of $27.

As with all your assumptions, you have to gauge whether a higher ticket price is reasonable. An entrepreneur might reason that the bookstore isn't discounting its books and is also selling higher-priced ancillary goods. Run scenario analyses again to see whether your bookstore survives if its average ticket price is closer to Barnes & Noble's. In other words, see what happens to the model overall when you change one of the assumptions—in this case, the average selling price.

After you're comfortable with the revenue estimate, you next need to validate the costs. The best way is to compare your common-sized income statement with the industry averages or some benchmark companies. It is unlikely that your income statement will exactly match

	Jan. 3%	Feb. 2%	Mar. 3%	Apr. 4%	May 6%	June 7%	July 9%	Aug. 8%	Sept. 5%	Oct. 3%	Nov. 10%	Dec. 40%	Year 100%
Year 1				$24.0	$36.0	$42.0	$54.0	$48.0	$30.0	$18.0	$60.0	$240.0	$552.0
Year 2	$22.5	$15.0	$22.5	$30.0	$45.0	$52.5	$67.5	$60.0	$37.5	$22.5	$75.0	$300.0	$750.0
Year 3	$31.5	$21.0	$31.5	$42.0	$63.0	$73.5	$94.5	$84.0	$52.5	$31.5	$105.0	$420.0	$1,050.0

Figure 9.10

Seasonality projections

The next consideration in generating your monthly forecasts is seasonality. Revenues in retail are not evenly spread across the 12 months. Figure 9.10 estimates how sales might be spread for a retail operation. The make-or-break time is the holiday season, and you see sales jumping dramatically in November and December. Another important spike might be the tourist season (if you were to locate your store in Niagara-on-the-Lake, demand might jump if you focused on goods related to the War of 1812). Based on these projections, it makes sense to lease and build out the retail space in the January to March time frame when sales levels are expected to be low.

Another consideration is how long it will take your new business to build its clientele and ramp up its revenues. You are projecting sales of $350 per square foot once you hit your optimal operating position. In the first year of operation, that number might be significantly lower—say, $200 per square foot, which is well below the Barnes & Noble average of $297 and the independent bookstore average of $350. In year 2, a reasonable estimate might be that average sales per square foot hit $250, and finally in year 3 you might hit the independent bookstore average of $350. And as you've seen, the business is not generating sales for the first three months of year 1 because of the time it takes to build out the store, so you need to adjust the sales accordingly.

Balance Sheet

The *balance sheet* can be the most difficult to integrate into your other financial statements. For pro forma projections, yearly balance sheets are sufficient. Again, going into great detail is beyond the scope of this chapter, but there are a few items that often cause confusion.

First, will your business sell on credit? If so, it will record accounts receivable. Figure 9.9 shows how your sales from the income statement drive your accounts receivable on the balance sheet (some portion of those sales), which then drive an accounts receivable increase on the statement of cash flows. While you record the sale when the customer takes possession, you may not actually receive payment until some point in the future. Recording the sale has a positive impact on your profitability but does not affect your cash flow until the customer actually pays.

If your business is buying equipment, land, or a plant or is adding leasehold improvements, you will have an asset of plant and equipment. A common error is to show this as a capital expense, meaning that it appears in full on your income statement the moment you contract for the work. This assumes you will fully use that equipment within the year (or whatever length your income statement covers). To accurately reflect the acquisition of the asset, instead show the full outflow of money as it occurs on your statement of cash flows and then depreciate the cost per year of life of the asset on your income statement. You would also have an accumulated depreciation line item on your balance sheet showing how much of the asset has been used up. Referring back to Figure 9.5, you see the bookstore is projecting leasehold improvements of $100,000, which it expects to use up over 10 years ($10,000 per year or $833 per month).

Accounts payable acts in a manner similar to accounts receivable, except that it is a loan to your company from a supplier (see Figure 9.9). Once the new store is able to secure vendor financing on inventory, for example, it will show the COGS as it sells its books, but it may not have to pay the publisher until later (assuming that the book is a fairly fast-moving item). So the expense would show up on your income statement but not on your statement of cash flows—until you pay for it. Until then, it is held in accounts payable on the balance sheet.

The final problem area is retained earnings. Entrepreneurs know that the balance sheet should *balance*. A common error is to use the retained earnings line to make the balance sheet balance. Retained earnings is actually

$$\text{Previous Retained Earnings} + \text{Current Period Net Income}$$
$$- \text{Dividends Paid during the Current Period}$$

If you find that your balance sheet isn't balancing, the problem is often in how you have calculated accounts receivable or accounts payable. Balancing the balance sheet is the most frustrating aspect of building your pro forma financial statements. Yet hardwiring the retained earnings will ultimately lead to other errors, so work through the balancing problem as diligently as possible.

Statement of Cash Flows

If you have constructed your financial statements accurately, the statement of cash flows identifies when and how much financing you need. You might want to leave the financing assumptions empty until after you see how much the statement of cash flows implies you need (see Figure 9.11). One of the many benefits of this process is that it will help you determine exactly how much you need, thus protecting you from giving up too much equity or acquiring too much (or not enough) debt. The bookstore statement of cash flows shows some major outlays as the store is gearing up for operation, such as inventory acquisition and equipment purchases. You can also see from the statement that the business is incurring some expenses prior to generating revenue [($17,000) listed as net earnings]. This net earnings loss is reflected on the company's monthly income statement and is primarily attributable to wage expenses to hire and train staff.

You can see that in the first six months, the cash position hits a low of just over –$316,000. This is how much money you need to raise to launch the business. For a new venture, most of the money will likely be in the form of equity from the entrepreneur, friends, and family. However, the entrepreneur may be able to secure some debt financing against his or her equipment (which would act as collateral if the business should fail). In any event, once you recognize your financing needs, you can devise a strategy to raise the money necessary to start the business. To provide some buffer against poor estimates, you might raise $350,000. This amount would show up on both the statement of cash flows and the balance sheet.

Financial Statements versus Financial Models

Simply stated, *financial models* are based on reasonable assumptions and represent predictions of a company's performance whereas *financial statements* are hard numbers based on the company's past performance.

Before you can have a financial statement, you have to have a financial model. Financial models are malleable and allow an entrepreneur to modify specific numbers to forecast and predict future performance. The model relies on assumptions; investors care more that the assumptions are reasonable (based on multiple factors including industry forecasts, past performance, external factors, etc.) versus right.

	Month 1	Month 2	Month 3	Month 4	Month 5	Month 6
OPERATING ACTIVITIES						
Net Earnings	(17,000)	(12,882)	(2,244)	(7,079)	(1,277)	8,394
Depreciation	1,115	1,115	1,115	1,115	1,115	1,115
Working Capital Changes						
(Increase)/Decrease Accounts Receivable	0	(64)	(88)	40	(48)	(80)
(Increase)/Decrease Inventories	(104,562)	(19,605)	32,676	(39,211)	(65,351)	71,886
(Increase)/Decrease Other Current Assets	0	(230)	(316)	144	(172)	(287)
Increase/(Decrease) Accts Pay & Accrd Expenses	0	3,215	4,421	(2,010)	2,411	4,019
Increase/(Decrease) Other Current Liab	0	3,445	4,737	(2,153)	2,584	4,306
Net Cash Provided/(Used) by Operating Activities	(120,446)	(25,005)	40,301	(49,154)	(60,737)	89,354
INVESTING ACTIVITIES						
Property & Equipment	(101,000)	0	0	0	0	0
Other						
Net Cash Used in Investing Activities	(101,000)	0	0	0	0	0
FINANCING ACTIVITIES						
Increase/(Decrease) Short-Term Debt						0
Increase/(Decrease) Curr. Portion LTD						0
Increase/(Decrease) Long-Term Debt						0
Increase/(Decrease) Common Shares						0
Increase/(Decrease) Preferred Shares						0
Dividends Declared						0
Net Cash Provided/(Used) by Financing	0	0	0	0	0	0
INCREASE/(DECREASE) IN CASH	(221,446)	(25,005)	40,301	(49,154)	(60,737)	89,354
CASH AT BEGINNING OF PERIOD	0	(221,446)	(246,451)	(206,150)	(255,304)	(316,041)
CASH AT END OF PERIOD	(221,446)	(246,451)	(206,150)	(255,304)	(316,041)	(226,687)

Figure 9.11

Statement of cash flows

As mentioned earlier, financial statements are concrete numbers purely derived from the company's performance. It is a reflection of the company's past year, two years, five years, and so on. Financial statements produce financial ratios such as ARPU, CoCA and CLV, which are all valuable to the company. These statements are often reviewed and analyzed on a quarterly basis to ensure a company is on track. If the financial statements indicate numbers that are negatively affecting the company's future, it is important for management to return to the financial model(s) and see what can be adjusted to enhance performance.

Both financial statements and financial models allow entrepreneurs to answer many questions:

- Is there enough business acumen in the management team to move forward with the new or current venture? *Are the numbers reasonable?*

- Is the business sustainable? Do the revenue models come out positive? *Will the company begin generating revenue within a reasonable timeline?*

- Is the business scalable? *Can you grow the business?*

- What is the variability of the business? *Will the company be able to survive?* (*Variability* refers to the company's ability to survive based on the financial ratios and economic factors or threats.)

Putting It All Together

Once you have completed the financial spreadsheets, write a two- to three-page explanation to precede them. Although you understand all the assumptions and comparables that went into building the financial forecast, the reader needs the background spelled out. Describing the financials is also a good exercise in articulation. If your reader understands the financials and believes the assumptions are valid, you have passed an important test. If not, work with the reader to understand his or her concerns. Continual iterations strengthen your financials and should give you further confidence in the viability of your business model.

This section of the business plan should include a description of the key drivers that affect your revenues and costs so that the reader can follow your pro forma financials. This description is typically broken down into four main sections. First, the "overview" paragraph briefly introduces the business model.

The first subsection should discuss the income statement. Talk about the factors that drive revenue, such as store traffic, percentage of store visitors that buy, average ticket price, and so forth. It is also important to talk about seasonality and other factors that might cause uneven sales growth. Then discuss the expense categories, paying attention to the cost of goods sold and major operating expense categories, such as rent, interest expense, and so forth. Based on your description, the reader should be able to look at the actual financials and understand what is going on. The key focus here is to help the reader follow your financials; you don't need to provide the level of detail that an accountant might if he or she were auditing your company.

The next subsection should discuss the statement of cash flows. Here, you focus on major infusions of cash, such as equity investments and loan disbursements. It is also good to describe the nature of your accounts receivable and accounts payable. How long, for instance, before your receivables convert to cash? If you are spending money on leasehold improvements, plant and equipment, and other items that can be depreciated, you should mention them here. Typically, the discussion of the statement of cash flows is quite a bit shorter than the discussion of the income statement.

The final subsection discusses the balance sheet. Here, you would talk about major asset categories, such as the amount of inventory on hand and any liabilities that aren't clear from the previous discussion.

CONCLUSION

Going through these exercises allows you to construct a realistic set of pro forma financials. It's a challenge, but understanding your numbers "cold" enables you to articulate your business to all stakeholders, so you can build momentum toward the ultimate launch of your business. Just as we said in the last chapter that the business plan is a live document, so too are the financial statements—they are obsolete immediately after they come off the printer. As you start your launch process, you can further refine your numbers, putting in actual revenues and expenses as they occur and adjusting projections based on current activity. Once the business is operating, the nature of your financial statements changes. They not only help you assess the viability of your business model, but also help you gauge actual performance and adjust your operations based on that experience.

Although most entrepreneurs tell us that drafting the financials induces some pain, they also concede that going through the process is gratifying and rewarding. They learn to master new management skills, build their business, and protect their investment. So dig in.

Reflection Point	Your Thoughts. . .
1. What are your revenue sources? How can you influence these revenues (what are your drivers)?	
2. Identify some companies that you can benchmark. What are their revenue sources? How do they drive revenue?	
3. Refine your projections. Who can you talk to that is knowledgeable about your business (customers, vendors, competitors)? What secondary sources can you find (Hoovers.com, Robert Morris and Associates database)?	
4. Compare your common-sized financials to those of your benchmark company. Can you validate or explain differences between you and the benchmark company?	
5. Are there other metrics you can use (sales per employee or sales per square foot) to verify your projections?	
6. What happens to the viability of your business when you run some scenario analyses based on the different metrics you've identified?	

Look for some comparison metrics (the *Bizminer* site www.bizminer.com is useful, but see if you can find others). How do your sales-per-employee figures match the benchmark reports? How does your pro forma balance sheet match up to some of the presented ratios? Can you explain any differences?

P'kolino Financials

We revisit the P'kolino business plan in this chapter. Study the financial projections and evaluate how realistic you think they are.

CONFIDENTIAL INFORMATION

Pkolino™

Business Plan
May-2005

Prepared by:
J.B. Schneider &
Antonio Turco-Rivas N.

Contact Information:
Phone: (781) 497-0913
Email: jb@pkolino.com
            atrn@pkolino.com
Address:
600 West Cummings Park
Suite 5350
Woburn, MA 01801

These financials were prepared by Antonio Turco-Rivas and J. B. Schneider in support of their business. The original drafts were prepared in the Entrepreneur Intensity Track taught by Professor Andrew Zacharakis. © Copyright P'kolino and Babson College, 2005.

Confidential Information
Business Plan - Dated May-2005
Woburn, Massachusetts – USA

P'kolino

| 9 | Financial Plan |

9.1 Basis of Presentation

This plan contains five-year projected financial information for our company. While management believes that the assumptions underlying the projections are reasonable, there can be no assurance that these results can be realized or that actual results will meet management expectations. It is important to notice that our first month of operations is expected to be April 2005, causing the holiday season to be reflected in the financial statement as the third quarter in our projections. Monthly financial statements for the first two years are available on request.

9.2 Income Statement Assumptions – Revenues

The number of tables sold each month is the main driver of revenues for P'kolino. This number is estimated based on the expected outcome of the marketing efforts the company has planned for each year. At the beginning the company will sell two different types of tables targeting the high-end segment of the market. However, at the beginning of the third year the company plans to introduce a third table that will target the mid segment.

For the Storage Unit, management assumes that 30% of those customers that purchase tables are likely to buy the Storage Unit as well. The Storage Unit is designed so that it holds up to 10 toy kits (three are offered as a bundled package with the Storage Unit).

Every time a new table is sold, a new customer has been gained. P'kolino projections assume that one out of every two customers will purchase one Toy Kit every 12 months for a period of 3 to 4 years. Gift purchases of the Toy Kits are also estimated as a percentage of the existing customer base. One out of every two existing customers will trigger (influence) one Toy Kit gift purchase every 12 months.

Accessories will enter the revenue stream at the 2nd year of operations. It is estimated that as the product line expands accessories will eventually represent up to 25% of our sales.

The numbers of new customers are expected to increase at an average rate of 35% for years 3,4 & 5 for products targeting the high-end segment and at 45% for those targeting the mid-segment of the market (as a benchmark Pottery Barn Kids sales increased 35% in 2004).

Exhibit 9-A
The Playroom Furniture Market

# Units	Year 1	Year 2	Year 3	Year 4	Year 5
Tables	690	1,445	2,551	3,634	4,755
Table A	449	939	1,268	1,712	2,311
Table B	242	506	683	922	1,244
Table C			600	1,000	1,200
Storage Unit	228	477	824	1,169	1,533
Toy Kits	1,313	3,851	4,814	7,618	11,027
Accessories	0	9,925	15,808	21,068	28,442

P'kolino will remain in the high-end segment of the market for its first 2 years of operations and has priced its products accordingly. All products are priced as a function of both their manufacturing costs and their marketing positioning strategies. At year 3 a $400 table with a 45% contribution margin will be introduced to the mid-segment.

Exhibit 9-B
Prices and Manufacturing Cost

Product	Selling Price	Manufacturing Cost	Contribution in US$	Contribution as % of Price
Table A	$650	$260	$390	60%
Table B	$1,200	$260	$940	78%
Table C	$300	$130	$170	57%
Storage Unit	$450	$140	$310	69%
Toy kit version 1	$30	$10	$20	67%
Toy kit version 2	$55	$26	$29	53%
Accessories	$60	$28	$32	53%

P'kolino will sell its products both online (direct) and through specialty retailers. Retailers are expected to markup our products by 50% (according to our primary research). Thus, our wholesale price will need to account for this markup. Management estimates that even though 80% (30% after year 2) of the units sold will be sold through retailers, only 23% of the revenue will come from this distribution channel. The percentage sold through retailers will drop over time as P'kolino gains brand recognition and further develops its direct distribution channel.

Exhibit 9-C
% of Revenues by Distribution Channel

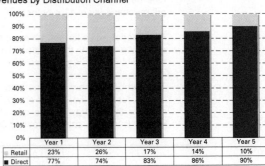

	Year 1	Year 2	Year 3	Year 4	Year 5
Retail	23%	26%	17%	14%	10%
Direct	77%	74%	83%	86%	90%

Confidential Information
Business Plan - Dated May-2005
Woburn, Massachusetts – USA

As stated earlier in this document the Toy kits and accessories are the main vehicles for generating recurrent revenue from existing customers.

Exhibit 9-D
Revenue Mix (% of revenue by type of product)

Revenue Mix	Year 1	Year 2	Year 3	Year 4	Year 5
Tables	79%	57%	54%	55%	54%
Storage	13%	9%	11%	11%	11%
Kits	8%	9%	6%	7%	8%
Accessories	0%	25%	28%	27%	27%

Revenues for P'kolino will increase significantly during the winter holiday season. As is the case in the toy industry, playroom products are seasonal and more than 50% of total revenues will be generated during this period. Summer will be the second best season because children are out of school and spending more time at home.

Exhibit 9-E
Seasonal Sales – Number of tables sold per month Year 1 & 2

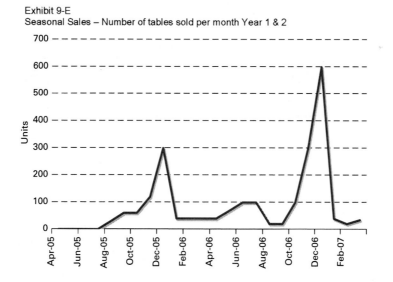

Confidential Information
Business Plan - Dated May-2005
Woburn, Massachusetts – USA

Pkolino

Exhibit 9-F
Revenue Forecast

Revenue per year	Year 1	Year 2	Year 3	Year 4	Year 5
Tables	**$481,501**	**$1,008,361**	**$1,589,988**	**$2,274,038**	**$3,134,920**
Table A	$220,101	$460,937	$711,113	$976,358	$1,354,885
Table B	$261,400	$547,424	$698,876	$997,680	$1,420,035
Table C	$0	$0	$180,000	$300,000	$360,000
Storage Unit	**$79,871**	**$167,267**	**$334,359**	**$474,521**	**$656,146**
Toy Kits	**$50,772**	**$158,621**	**$189,781**	**$310,663**	**$462,848**
Accessories	**$0**	**$449,603**	**$807,891**	**$1,109,235**	**$1,539,278**
Total Revenues	**$612,145**	**$1,783,851**	**$2,922,020**	**$4,168,457**	**$5,793,191**
Revenue Growth		191%	64%	43%	39%

Exhibit 9-G
Revenue Monthly Forecast

Monthly Revenues	Year 1	Year 2	Year 3	Year 4	Year 5
Month 1	$0	$39,182	$64,182	$91,560	$127,247
Month 2	$0	$67,346	$110,316	$157,373	$218,712
Month 3	$0	$101,212	$165,789	$236,510	$328,694
Total 1st Quarter	$0	$207,741	$340,287	$485,443	$674,653
Month 4	$0	$124,420	$203,804	$290,740	$404,062
Month 5	$25,314	$29,350	$48,076	$68,584	$95,316
Month 6	$50,627	$30,775	$50,411	$71,915	$99,945
Total 2nd Quarter	$75,941	$184,545	$302,292	$431,240	$599,323
Month 7	$50,627	$127,270	$208,474	$297,402	$413,320
Month 8	$102,680	$366,132	$599,739	$855,567	$1,189,040
Month 9	$255,986	$729,413	$1,194,808	$1,704,473	$2,368,823
Total 3rd Quarter	$409,293	$1,222,815	$2,003,020	$2,857,442	$3,971,183
Month 10	$36,602	$57,750	$94,596	$134,948	$187,547
Month 11	$39,453	$39,327	$64,420	$91,899	$127,719
Month 12	$50,856	$71,674	$117,405	$167,485	$232,766
Total 4th Quarter	$126,911	$168,751	$276,421	$394,333	$548,032
Total for year	**$612,145**	**$1,783,851**	**$2,922,020**	**$4,168,457**	**$5,793,191**
Average Revenue					
by Month	$51,012	$148,654	$243,502	$347,371	$482,766
by Quarter	$153,036	$445,963	$730,505	$1,042,114	$1,448,298

Note: the Third quarter represents the holiday season.

Confidential Information
Business Plan - Dated May-2005
Woburn, Massachusetts – USA

9.3 Income Statement Assumptions – Cost of Sales

Our business model assumes that manufacturing of all P'kolino products will be outsourced to Brazil and then eventually to an Asian manufacturer. The average cost of sales will be 47% of revenues. Cost of sales is estimated based on manufactured units.

Exhibit 9-H
Cost of Sales

Manufacturing Costs	Year 1	Year 2	Year 3	Year 4	Year 5
Table A	$116,610	$244,205	$329,677	$445,064	$600,836
Table B	$62,790	$131,495	$177,518	$239,650	$323,527
Table C	$0	$0	$84,000	$140,000	$168,000
Storage Unit	$31,878	$66,759	$115,325	$163,668	$214,652
Kits	$25,818	$85,988	$95,251	$157,954	$237,232
Accessories	$0	$277,900	$436,968	$589,907	$796,374
Other	$29,193	$54,504	$200,357	$219,636	$245,602
Total COGS	**$266,289**	**$860,851**	**$1,439,096**	**$1,955,879**	**$2,586,223**

9.4 Income Statement Assumptions – Expenses

Expenses for P'kolino are centered on three main areas: 1) Sales and Marketing, 2) General Administration Expenses and 3) Research and Development.

For the first year, sales and marketing expenses are close to 20% of sales. Developing our website, generating initial marketing materials and a direct mail campaign are the main uses of these funds. Again after year 3, marketing efforts intensify as P'kolino makes an effort to enter the mid-segment of the market with a new product.

Over time, General and Administration expenses converge towards the industry average. However, P'kolino's business model calls for a lean organization that concentrates on sales, product development and marketing. Management will make every effort to outsource all areas of the business not directly related to the core competency of the company. By year 5, the company will have 10 employees. The company will open an office at a business incubator during its first and second year of operations. P'kolino will relocate to a new facility by the end of year 2.

Product development (or R&D) is central to the P'kolino business model. It will require 10% of revenues during the first and second year and 9% on average thereafter (the R&D for the first year has been partially funded and executed prior to starting operations). During years 1&2 the company will

Confidential Information
Business Plan - Dated May-2005
Woburn, Massachusetts – USA

develop a table for the mid-segment of the market as well as new Toy kits and accessories.

Other expenses such as legal expenses, insurance, etc. are estimated based on industry averages.

Exhibit 9-I
Projected Financial Statements

	Year 1	%	Year 2	%	Year 3	%	Year 4	%	Year 5	%
Revenues	$612,145	100%	$1,783,851	100%	$2,922,020	100%	$4,168,457	100%	$5,793,191	100%
Cost of Sales	$266,289	44%	$860,851	48%	$1,439,096	49%	$1,955,879	47%	$2,586,223	45%
Gross Profit	**$345,856**	**56%**	**$923,000**	**52%**	**$1,482,924**	**51%**	**$2,212,578**	**53%**	**$3,206,968**	**55%**
Expenses										
Sales & Marketing	**$121,379**	**20%**	**$354,768**	**20%**	**$559,581**	**19%**	**$861,467**	**21%**	**$1,180,662**	**20%**
Salaries & Benefits	40,250	7%	80,500	5%	242,932	8%	322,503	8%	335,403	6%
Advertising	15,000	2%	50,000	3%	60,000	2%	150,000	4%	300,000	5%
Direct Mail Campaign	20,000	3%	150,000	8%	150,000	5%	250,000	6%	350,000	6%
Free Kit	15,008	2%	31,429	2%	42,429	1%	57,279	1%	77,327	1%
Web Expenses Marketing	25,000	4%	25,000	1%	35,000	1%	40,000	1%	60,000	1%
Other Marketing Expenses	6,121	1%	17,839	1%	29,220	1%	41,685	1%	57,932	1%
General and Administration	**$103,333**	**17%**	**$201,583**	**11%**	**$369,867**	**13%**	**$424,276**	**10%**	**$531,254**	**9%**
Salaries & Benefits	90,000	15%	178,250	10%	319,534	11%	367,276	9%	449,587	8%
Depreciation	1,333	0%	3,333	0%	10,333	0%	17,000	0%	21,667	0%
Rent & Utilities	5,000	1%	10,000	1%	20,000	1%	20,000	0%	35,000	1%
Corporate Office	7,000	1%	10,000	1%	20,000	1%	20,000	0%	25,000	0%
Product Development (R&D)	**$61,000**	**10%**	**$227,324**	**13%**	**$288,017**	**10%**	**$318,938**	**8%**	**$450,095**	**8%**
Salaries & Benefits		0%	142,324	8%	148,017	5%	153,938	4%	160,095	3%
Testing	1,000	0%	5,000	0%	10,000	0%	15,000	0%	20,000	0%
Product Development	60,000	10%	80,000	4%	130,000	4%	150,000	4%	270,000	5%
Other Expenses	**$91,304**	**15%**	**$112,096**	**6%**	**$120,551**	**4%**	**$129,211**	**3%**	**$169,830**	**3%**
Legal	15,000	2%	20,000	1%	25,000	1%	25,000	1%	25,000	0%
Relocation		0%	10,000	1%		0%		0%		0%
Other	1,000	0%		0%		0%		0%		0%
Insurance	15,304	3%	44,596	2%	73,051	3%	104,211	2%	144,830	3%
Interest	60,000	10%	37,500	2%	22,500	1%		0%		
Total Expenses	**$377,016**	**62%**	**$895,771**	**50%**	**$1,338,016**	**46%**	**$1,733,892**	**42%**	**$2,331,841**	**40%**
Profit Before Taxes	**($31,160)**	**-5%**	**$27,229**	**2%**	**$144,908**	**5%**	**$478,686**	**11%**	**$875,127**	**15%**
Taxes		0%	5,446	0%	28,982	1%	95,737	2%	175,025	3%
Net Income	**($31,160)**	**-5%**	**$21,783**	**1%**	**$115,926**	**4%**	**$382,949**	**9%**	**$700,102**	**12%**

Confidential Information
Business Plan - Dated May-2005
Woburn, Massachusetts – USA

9.5 Balance Sheet Assumptions

P'kolino outsources manufacturing of their products allowing it to minimize investment on fixed assets. Inventory is assumed at 45 days (meaning 8 inventory turns per year, equal to the industry average according to Hoover's online database). Management believes it will be able to maintain this level due to its emphasis on direct distribution.

Accounts receivable will average 30 days due to expected receivables from sales to retailers. Direct sales will have limited receivables, occurring mostly by credit card.

Table designs will be considered intangible assets and supported by constant product development efforts.

Accounts payable will be 25 days during the first few years because vendors will require most of our purchases to be paid in advance. Over time, accounts payable will lengthen as we develop a credit history.

Exhibit 9-J
Projected Balance Sheet Statements

	Year 1	Year 2	Year 3	Year 4	Year 5
ASSETS					
Cash	$ 289,628	$ 133,388	$ 106,278	$ 338,241	$ 1,036,185
Accounts Receivable	$ 50,856	$ 71,674	$ 92,140	$ 131,444	$ 182,677
Inventory	$ 70,582	$ 91,338	$ 138,210	$ 197,167	$ 274,016
Total current assets	**$ 411,066**	**$ 296,400**	**$ 336,629**	**$ 666,852**	**$ 1,492,879**
Net fixed assets	$ 6,595	$ 18,476	$ 37,357	$ 44,571	$ 47,119
Fixed Assets	*$ 8,000*	*$ 24,000*	*$ 54,000*	*$ 79,000*	*$ 104,000*
Fixed Assets Acum. Deprec.	*$ 1,405*	*$ 5,524*	*$ 16,643*	*$ 34,429*	*$ 56,881*
Other assets	$ 6,103	$ 8,601	$ 11,057	$ 15,773	$ 21,921
Net Intangibles	$ 50,700	$ 50,700	$ 50,700	$ 50,700	$ 50,700
Patents + Intangibles	$ 50,700	$ 50,700	$ 50,700	$ 50,700	$ 50,700
Total assets	**$ 474,463**	**$ 374,177**	**$ 435,743**	**$ 777,897**	**$ 1,612,619**
LIABILITIES					
Accounts and trade notes payable	$ 42,719	$ 60,206	$ 77,398	$ 110,413	$ 153,449
Income Taxes payable	$ -	$ 5,446	$ 28,982	$ 95,737	$ 175,026
Other	$ 12,205	$ 17,202	$ 22,114	$ 31,547	$ 43,843
Total current liabilities	**$ 54,924**	**$ 82,854**	**$ 128,493**	**$ 237,697**	**$ 372,317**
Convertible LT debt	$ 400,000	$ 250,000	$ 150,000	$ -	$ -
Total liabilities	**$ 454,924**	**$ 332,854**	**$ 278,493**	**$ 237,697**	**$ 372,317**
	$ -	$ -	$ -	$ -	$ -
Paid-in capital	$ 50,700	$ 50,700	$ 50,700	$ 50,700	$ 50,700
Retained earnings	$ (31,161)	$ (9,377)	$ 106,550	$ 489,499	$ 1,189,602
Total liabilities and net worth	**$ 474,463**	**$ 374,177**	**$ 435,743**	**$ 777,897**	**$ 1,612,619**

Confidential Information
Business Plan - Dated May-2005
Woburn, Massachusetts – USA

9.6 <u>Funding Assumptions</u>

The company will fund its operations through equity and convertible long-term debt. Founders have issued $50.7K worth of equity. Proceeds will be used to pay for the product development of the initial product line. Additional funding will come in the form of long-term convertible debt (convertible into equity at the lender's discretion) for up to $400K over the next five years, at a 15% annual interest rate. Friends and family will be the primary investors initially.

Exhibit 9-K
Use of Funds (average)

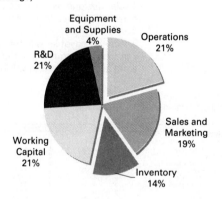

Confidential Information
Business Plan - Dated May-2005
Woburn, Massachusetts – USA

9.7 Cash Flow Assumptions

Investments will maintain positive cash flow the first 2 years. After this period, P'kolino estimates that it will generate enough cash from operations to repay the long-term debt and finance future growth.

Exhibit 9-L
Projected Cash Flow Statements

	Year 1	Year 2	Year 3	Year 4	Year 5
Net Income	$ (31,161)	$ 21,784	$ 115,927	$ 382,950	$ 700,102
Accounts receivable (increase)	$ (50,856)	$ (20,818)	$ (20,467)	$ (39,304)	$ (51,233)
Inventory (increase)	$ (70,582)	$ (20,755)	$ (46,873)	$ (58,956)	$ (76,849)
Depreciation	$ 1,405	$ 4,119	$ 11,119	$ 17,786	$ 22,452
Other Liabilities	$ 12,205	$ 4,996	$ 4,912	$ 9,433	$ 12,296
Accounts Payable	$ 42,719	$ 17,487	$ 17,192	$ 33,015	$ 43,036
Tax payable	$ -	$ 5,446	$ 23,536	$ 66,756	$ 79,288
Operating Cash Flow	**$ (96,270)**	**$ 12,259**	**$ 105,346**	**$ 411,680**	**$ 729,092**
Purchase of PPE	$ (8,000)	$ (16,000)	$ (30,000)	$ (25,000)	$ (25,000)
Other Assets	$ (6,103)	$ (2,498)	$ (2,456)	$ (4,716)	$ (6,148)
Change Intangibles	$ (50,700)	$ -	$ -	$ -	$ -
Cash from Investing	**$ (64,803)**	**$ (18,498)**	**$ (32,456)**	**$ (29,716)**	**$ (31,148)**
Convertible LT debt	$ 400,000	$ (150,000)	$ (100,000)	$ (150,000)	$ -
Issued Stock	$ 50,700	$ -	$ -	$ -	$ -
Cash from Finance	**$ 450,700**	**$ (150,000)**	**$ (100,000)**	**$ (150,000)**	**$ -**
Change in cash	**$ 289,628**	**$ (156,240)**	**$ (27,110)**	**$ 231,963**	**$ 697,944**
Cash Flow:	$ 289,628	$ 133,388	$ 106,278	$ 338,241	$ 1,036,185

9.8 Breakeven Analysis

Exhibit 9-M
Breakeven vs. Revenues

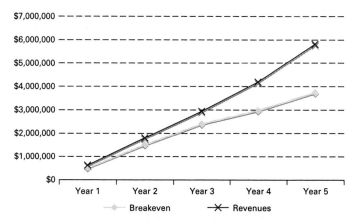

Discussion Questions

1. How do the common-sized income statement ratios compare to industry standards? Can you explain the variances in a way that makes the projections seem sound?

2. How do the revenues per employee compare to industry standards? Again, can you explain the variances?

3. Do the financial projections accurately capture all the expenses that are implied in the written plan (refer back to the previous chapter)?

4. Is the proposed financing sufficient to cover the company's cash-flow needs? What happens if sales are not as high or quick to materialize as expected?

NOTES

[1] By minimum wage, we mean that the money the entrepreneur can take out of the business is less on an hourly basis than the minimum wage.

[2] N. Gilani, "The Four Types of Industry Infrastructures," *Small Business*, http://smallbusiness.chron.com/four-types-industry-infrastructures-24729.html.

[3] D. Ehrenberg, "Bottom-Up vs. Top-Down Forecasting: Realistic Financial Planning," Early Growth Financial Services, August 15 2012, http://earlygrowthfinancialservices.com/bottom-up-vs-top-down-forecasting-realistic-financial-planning/.

[4] Ibid.

[5] Ibid.

[6] Facebook, "Facebook Canada," https://www.facebook.com/facebookcanada?brand_redir=1.

[7] J. Tracy, *How to Read a Financial Report*, 7th ed. (Hoboken, NJ: John Wiley & Sons, Inc. 2009).

[8] SBDC National Information Clearinghouse, "Small Business Research Reports," www.sbdcnet.org/small-business-research-reports/bookstore-2012.

[9] ARPU, "Financial Glossary," http://glossary.reuters.com/index.php?title=ARPU.

[10] Harvard Business School, "Customer Lifetime Value Tool," http://hbsp.harvard.edu/multimedia/flashtools/cltv/

[11] T. Wright, "What Is a TTM Profit Margin?" AZ Central: Business & Entrepreneurship, http://yourbusiness.azcentral.com/ttm-profit-margin-21511.html

[12] Ibid.

[13] MaRS, "Revenue Models, Product Pricing, and Commercializing New Technology," December 6, 2009, http://www.marsdd.com/mars-library/revenue-models-product-pricing-and-commercializing-new-technology/.

[14] A. Elran, "Why You Should Calculate Customer Acquisition Cost before Building a Web Marketing Plan," Page One Power, October 5, 2013, http://pageonepower.com/2013/10/calculating-customer-acquisition-cost/.

[15] M. Savage, "Scalability for Social Enterprises and Non-Profits," *Matthew Savage's Blog*, www.matthewsavage.com/2011/02/scalability-for-social-enterprises-and-non-profits/.

[16] Ibid.

[17] 1999 ABACUS Financial Survey. Annual Survey conducted by the American Booksellers Association. http://bookweb.org.

[18] Look for publicly traded companies on databases such as http://SEC.gov and www.sedar.com.

[19] BizStats, "Other Retailers," http://bizstats.com/otherretail.htm.

Grameen Bank founder and Nobel Peace Prize Laureate Muhammad Yunus speaks during the lecture "A World without Poverty" on February 1, 2010, in Milan, Italy.

FINANCING ENTREPRENEURIAL VENTURES WORLDWIDE

CHAPTER OUTLINE

Entrepreneurial Financing for the World's Poorest
Learning Objective 10.1: Describe the financing available for entrepreneurs in underdeveloped countries.

Entrepreneurs and Informal Investors
Learning Objective 10.2: Describe the relationship between entrepreneurs and informal investors.

Venture Capital
Learning Objective 10.3: Explain what venture capital is and how it is used by entrepreneurs.

Factors Affecting Availability of Financing
Learning Objective 10.4: Identify the factors affecting the availability of financing.

A NEW BUSINESS searching for capital has no track record to present to potential investors and lenders. All it has is a plan—sometimes written, sometimes not—that projects its future performance. This means that it is very difficult to raise debt financing from conventional banks because they require as many as three years of actual—not projected—financial statements and assets that adequately cover the loan. Thus, almost every new business raises its initial money from the founders themselves and what we call *informal investors*: family, friends, neighbours, work colleagues, and strangers; a few raise it from lending institutions, primarily banks; and a minuscule number raise it from venture capitalists, who are sometimes called *formal investors*. This chapter examines funding from entrepreneurs themselves, informal investors, and venture capitalists throughout the world. Chapter 11 will explain how to raise equity capital, and Chapter 12 will look at nonequity sources of financing, including banks.

Before we examine conventional means of financing startups in medium- and higher-income nations, we'll begin by looking at how many would-be entrepreneurs eking out subsistence livings in some of the most impoverished regions of the world are being financed by microcredit organizations.

Entrepreneurial Financing for the World's Poorest

"To 'make poverty history,' leaders in private, public, and civil-society organizations need to embrace entrepreneurship and innovation as antidotes to poverty. Wealth-substitution through aid must give way to wealth-creation through entrepreneurship."[1] But the challenge is this: Where do nascent entrepreneurs living in poverty get any money to start a microbusiness? In Africa, for instance, 600 million people live on less than $3 per day based on purchasing power parity (PPP). For China, the number may be 400 million and for India 500 million.[2]

In the developing world, 1.4 billion people (one in four) were living below US$1.25 a day in 2005, down from 1.9 billion (one in two) in 1981. Poverty has fallen by 500 million since 1981 (from 52% of the developing world's population in 1981 to 26% in 2005), and the world is still on track to halve the 1990 poverty rate by 2015. But at this rate of progress, about a billion people will still live below $1.25 a day in 2015.[3]

Conventional banking is based on the principle that the more you have, the more you can borrow. It relies on collateral, which means that a bank loan must be adequately covered by assets of the business or its owner—or in many cases, both. But half the world's population is very poor, so about 5 billion people are shut out of banks. For example, fewer than 10% of adults in many African countries have bank accounts; even in Mexico the number of families with bank accounts is less than 25%.

Microfinancing

In 1976, in the village of Jobra, Bangladesh, Muhammad Yunus, an economist, started what today is the Grameen Bank. This was the beginning of the microfinance concept, which is best known for its application in rural areas of Bangladesh but has now spread throughout the world. Yunus believes that access to credit is a human right. According to him, "one that does not possess anything gets the highest priority in getting a loan." Even beggars can get loans from the Grameen Bank. They are not required to give up begging but are encouraged to take up an additional income-generating activity, such as selling popular consumer items door to door or at the place of begging.[4] The bank provides larger loans, called *microenterprise loans*, for "fast-moving members." As of June 2009, almost 1.9 million Bangladeshis had taken microenterprise loans at an average loan amount of US$360; the biggest loan was US$23,209 to purchase a truck. The Grameen Bank total loan recovery rate is 97.81%, which is remarkable since the bank relies entirely on personal trust and not collateral.[5]

Microfinancing is now available in many nations. It is generally agreed that it is a powerful tool in the fight to reduce poverty in poorer nations. The following is a microfinance success story from Mexico, excerpted from an article in the *Financial Times*:[6]

> Oscar Javier Rivera Jimenez stands on the corrugated steel roof of his warehouse and surveys the urban wasteland around him. "We constructed all of this with the money from Compartamos," he says. "Before, there was nothing. We built it ourselves. That made it possible. And the help of God as well, which is the secret of everything." Compartamos is Latin America's biggest provider of micro-finance—small loans aimed at budding entrepreneurs, targeted at areas of severe poverty.
>
> Mr. Rivera, who set up his business six years ago in the municipality of Chimalhuacan, one of the poorest slums on the outskirts of Mexico City, is one of Compartamos' most successful clients.
>
> Starting at the age of 21 by delivering parts on a tricycle—much of the area lacks paved roads, while both water and electricity supplies are unreliable—he now controls an impressive warehouse, where builders can buy an array of different girders. He recently opened a second branch about a mile away.
>
> He now has nine employees, four from outside the family—showing that his brand of enthusiastic entrepreneurship might yet rescue the neighborhood.
>
> Compartamos ("Let's share" in Spanish) started life as a non-governmental organisation, and gained its seed capital from multilateral funds. Now with more than 300,000 clients, its next plan is to convert itself into a bank, so that it can take in savings and also start to offer life insurance. Its portfolio grew by 58% last year, and Carlos Danel and Carlos Labarthe, its joint chief executives, intend to keep that growth going.

Compartamos's average loan is for $330,[7] and as is typical of micro-credit elsewhere in the world, only 0.6% of its loans are 30 days or more late.

Microcredit for the Poorest of the Poor

The first Microcredit Summit Campaign was held in 1997. Its aim was "to reach 100 million of the world's poorest families, especially the women of those families, with credit for self-employment and other financial and business services by the year 2005."

In November 2006 the campaign was relaunched to 2015 with two new goals: (1) working to ensure that 175 million of the world's poorest families, especially the women of those families, are receiving credit for self-employment and other financial and business services by the end of 2015, and (2) working to ensure that 100 million families rise above the US$1 a day threshold, adjusted for purchasing power parity (PPP), between 1990 and 2015.[8] The campaign defines the "poorest" people as those who are in the bottom half of those living below their nation's poverty line, or any of the 1.2 billion people (240 million families) in the world who live on less than US$1 per day based on PPP.

In November 2011, to coincide with the release of the *State of the Microcredit Summit Campaign Report 2012* (which will be referred to as SOCR 2012 going forward), the Microcredit Summit Campaign announced that more than 137.5 million of the world's poorest families received a microloan in 2010—an all-time high. Assuming an average of five persons per family, these 137.5 million microloans affected more than 687 million family members, which is greater than the combined populations of the European Union and Russia. SOCR 2012 provides the data shown in Figure 10.1.[9]

Figure 10.2 shows the relationship between the number of families living in absolute poverty in each region (living on under US$1 a day, adjusted for PPP) and the number of poorest

La Maman Mole Motuke lived in a wrecked car in a suburb of Kinshasa, Zaire, with her four children. If she could find something to eat, she would feed two of her children; the next time she found something to eat, her other two children would eat. When organizers from a microcredit lending institution interviewed her, she said that she knew how to make *chikwangue* (manioc paste) and that she needed only a few dollars to start production. After six months of training in marketing and production techniques, Maman Motuke got her first loan of US$100 and bought production materials.

Today Maman Motuke and her family no longer live in a broken-down car; they rent a house with two bedrooms and a living room. Her four children go to school consistently, eat regularly, and dress well. She is currently saving to buy some land in a suburb farther outside the city and hopes to build a house.[i]

[i] www.microcreditsummit.org/about/what_is_microcredit.

Year	Number of Institutions Reporting	Total Number of Clients Reached	Number of "Poorest" Clients Reported
12/31/97	618	13,478,797	7,600,000
12/31/98	925	20,938,899	12,221,918
12/31/99	1,065	23,555,689	13,779,872
12/31/00	1,567	30,681,107	19,327,451
12/31/01	2,186	54,932,235	26,878,332
12/31/02	2,572	67,606,080	41,594,778
12/31/03	2,931	80,868,343	54,785,433
12/31/04	3,164	92,270,289	66,614,871
12/31/05	3,133	113,261,390	81,949,036
12/31/06	3,316	133,030,913	92,922,574
12/31/07	3,552	154,825,825	106,584,679
12/31/09	3,589	190,135,080	126,220,051
12/31/10	3,652	205,314,502	137,547,441

Source: J. P. Maes and L. R. Reed, *State of the Microcredit Summit Campaign Report 2012* (Microcredit Summit Campaign, 2012), 35.

■ **Figure 10.1**

Growth in the implementation of microcredit, 1997–2010

	Asia	Africa/Middle East	Latin America/Caribbean	Eastern Europe & Central Asia
Number of Poorest Families	182.4	79.8	9	3.4
Number Reached by Microfinance	125.5	8.9	2.9	0.13
Percent Coverage	69%	11%	32%	4%

Source: J. P. Maes and L. R. Reed, *State of the Microcredit Summit Campaign Report 2012* (Microcredit Summit Campaign, 2012), 39.

■ **Figure 10.2**

Microfinancing by region, 2010 (in millions)

families reached in each region at the end of 2010. Of the 137.5 million poorest clients reached at the end of 2010, 82.3% (113.1 million) were women. The growth in the number of very poor women reached has increased from 10.3 million at the end of 1999 to 113.1 million at the end of 2010. This is almost a 1,001% increase in the number of poorest women reached from December 31, 1999, to December 31, 2010. The increase represents an additional 102.9 million poorest women receiving microloans in the last 11 years.

In the following sections, we will examine how entrepreneurs in all financial circumstances, from the poor in developing nations to the well-off in developed nations, raise money to start their new businesses.

Entrepreneurs and Informal Investors

Self-funding by entrepreneurs, along with funding from informal investors, is the lifeblood of an entrepreneurial society. Founders and informal investors are sometimes referred to as the **Four Fs**: founders, family, friends, and foolhardy investors. One of the most noteworthy

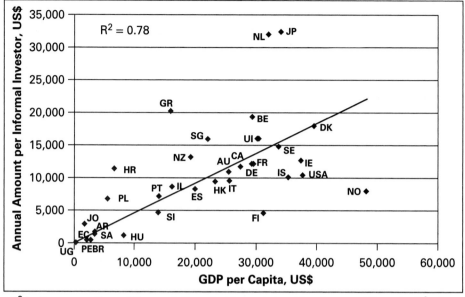

R^2 is the proportion of the variation that is explained by the trend line. An R^2 of 0.78 indicates that 78% of the variation in annual amount per informal investor is explained by GDP per capita.

Figure 10.5

Annual amount per informal investor vs. GDP per capita (US$)

1. **Microfinancing:** As mentioned earlier in this chapter, microfinancing has made it much easier for people who only need a small loan to kick start their business. Kiva.org is an online microfinancing platform that allows people to choose who they want to invest in, thus simplifying the lending process. With a small loan of $25, the lender can monitor the borrower's progress until the lender is paid back. Kiva is currently distributing approximately $2.2 million in loans per week with a total of $420 million since they started in 2005.[10]

2. **Crowdfunding:** This source of financing was created to help bring creative projects to life. Individuals can showcase their ideas, prototypes, or concepts to the entire world (over the Internet) in hopes of receiving a small or large donation in return for future benefits or perks from the company. These small donations eventually add up to the startup capital required. Kickstarter, an online crowdfunding platform, does exactly this. The creators who receive donations must meet a set amount of funding within a certain time frame. It is important to note that equity is not given in exchange for donations; instead, the individuals donating might receive special discounts or the opportunity for first purchase once the project has come to fruition.

3. **Bootstrapping:** When an entrepreneur funds his or her own project using existing resources coupled with careful management of current finances it is referred to as bootstrapping.[11] For example, entrepreneurs might use existing sales, sell their car, or take a second mortgage on their home to fund the company; all would be considered bootstrapping.

4. **Equity crowdfunding:** This refers to a startup's ability to raise seed money through crowd investing. This is currently illegal in Canada, and even though a bill to propose its legality has passed in the United States,[12] the bill has not yet been implemented. We discuss this topic further in Chapter 11.

Amount of Capital Needed to Start a Business

The amount of capital that entrepreneurs need to start their ventures depends, among other things, on the type of business, the ambitions of the entrepreneur, the location of the business, and the country where it is started. Anticipating these figures can be a daunting task for first-time entrepreneurs. However, online tools such as the startup calculator offered by the *Wall Street Journal* can help streamline this process and provide a better understanding of how much will be needed to start a company. The calculator can be found at the following link: http://online.wsj.com/public/page/news-small-business-startupCalculator.html.

In North America, the average amount required to start a business is between $25,000 and $30,000, with entrepreneurs providing 65.8% of the funding. For all the GEM nations combined, the average amount needed to start a business is $53,673; as expected, more is needed for an opportunity-pulled venture ($58,179) than for a necessity-pushed one ($24,467). The amount needed to start a business is highest in the business services sector ($76,263) and lowest in the consumer-oriented sector ($39,594). The businesses that need the most startup capital are those created with the intent to grow and hire employees. For example, nascent businesses that expect to employ 10 or more people five years after they open require an average of $112,943 of startup money. In addition, the data show that businesses started by men typically require more capital than those started by women ($65,010 versus $33,201). A partial explanation is that women are more likely than men to start necessity-pushed businesses, which are more likely to be consumer oriented and less likely to be business services.

To put nations on an approximately equal footing on the basis of wealth, we plot the amount of funding needed to start a business against a nation's GDP per capita, as seen in Figure 10.6. Entrepreneurs in countries falling below the trend line have a comparative advantage over entrepreneurs in countries above the trend line because it costs less to start a business

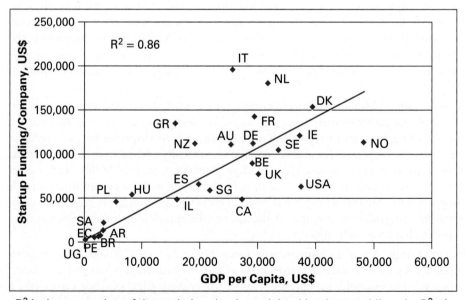

R^2 is the proportion of the variation that is explained by the trend line. An R^2 of 0.86 indicates that 86% of the variation in startup funding per company is explained by the GDP per capita.

■ **Figure 10.6**

Startup funding per company vs. GDP per capita (US$)

relative to the income per capita in those countries, all other things being equal. This finding partially explains why the United States and Canada have the highest total entrepreneurial activity (TEA) rates among the G7 nations and Italy the second-lowest rate. It might also explain to some extent why Norway has a higher TEA rate than its Scandinavian neighbours Sweden and Denmark.

Entrepreneurs seeking funding for their ventures, regardless of the source, can rest assured that the capital required to launch a startup has declined precipitously over the last 15 years. Don Tapscott, author of the international bestseller *Wikinomics* and more recently *Macrowikinomics*, highlighted that the availability of the Internet, open source software, cloud computing, and virtual offices has driven the cost of launching an Internet-based startup from $5,000,000 in 1997 to $500,000 in 2002 to only $50,000 in 2008.[13]

Characteristics of Informal Investors

Entrepreneurs provide 65.8% of their startup capital; this means that others, principally informal investors, provide the remaining 34.2%. But who are these informal investors? We've already seen that they can be categorized as the Four Fs: founders, family, friends, and fools.[14] The amount of funding provided by each is depicted in Figure 10.7. The foolhardy investors among the Four Fs are usually called *business angels*.

Using GEM data for the United States, Bygrave and Reynolds[15] developed a model that predicted whether or not a person was an informal investor. They found that the informal investor prevalence rate among entrepreneurs was 4.3 times the rate among nonentrepreneurs. With just one criterion—whether someone was an entrepreneur—their model correctly classified 86% of the entire population as being or not being informal investors. And with just two criteria—whether a person was an entrepreneur and that person's income—the model correctly identified an informal investor 5% of the time across the entire population, of whom slightly less than 5% were informal investors. Looked at another way, the model was 11 times better than a random choice at singling out an informal investor from the entire adult population. In general, this means that entrepreneurs in search of startup funding should target self-made entrepreneurs with high incomes. More specifically, they should first talk with the entrepreneurs among their close relatives, friends, and neighbours.

Financial Returns on Informal Investment

What financial return do informal investors expect? The median expected payback time, as you can see in Figure 10.7, is two years, and the median amount returned is 1 times the original investment. In other words, there is a negative or zero return on investment for half the informal

Relationship: Investor-Investee	Percent Total	Mean Amount Invested US$	Median Payback Time	Median X Return
Close family	49.4%	23,190	2 years	1 x
Other relative	9.4%	12,345	2 years	1 x
Work colleague	7.9%	39,032	2 years	1 x
Friend, neighbour	26.4%	15,548	2 years	1 x
Stranger	6.9%	67,672	2–5 years	1.5 x
	100.0%	24,202	2 years	1 x

Figure 10.7

Relationship of informal investors to investee

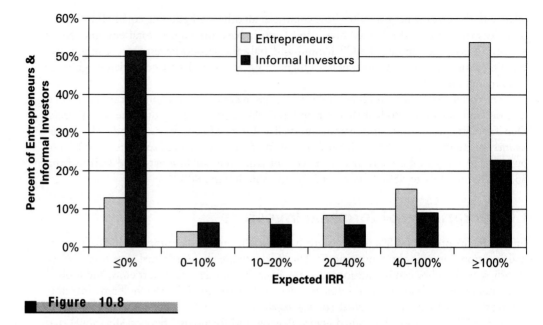

Figure 10.8

Expected IRR for entrepreneurs and informal investors

investments. It seems that altruism is involved to some extent in an informal investment in a relative's or friend's new business.[16] Put differently, investments in close family are often made more for love, not money.

The amount invested by strangers is the highest. What's more, the median return expected by strangers is 1.5 times the original investment, compared with just 1 for relatives and friends. The most likely reason is that investments by strangers are made in a more detached and businesslike manner than are investments by relatives and friends.

There is big variation in the return expected by informal investors: 34% expect that they will not receive any of their investment back, whereas 5% expect to receive 20 or more times the original investment. Likewise, there is big variation in the payback time: 17% expect to get their return in six months, whereas 2% expect to get it back in 20 years or longer.

Entrepreneurs are much more optimistic about the return on the money that they themselves put into their own ventures: 74% expect the payback time to be two years or sooner, and their median expected return is 2 times their original investment, while 15% expect 20 or more times that investment.

The expected **internal rate of return** or **IRR** (compound annual return on investment) is calculated from the expected payback time and the times return for informal investors and entrepreneurs who reported both (see Figure 10.8). The returns expected by entrepreneurs are almost the reverse of those expected by informal investors: 51% of informal investors expect a negative or zero return, and only 22% expect a return of 100% or more; by contrast, only 13% of entrepreneurs expect a negative or zero return, but a whopping 53% expect a return of 100% or more.

Supply and Demand for Startup Financing

Is the amount of funding sufficient to supply the external capital that entrepreneurs need to finance their new ventures? The average amount of an informal investment ($24,202) is more than the average amount of external financing that entrepreneurs need ($18,678). So for those entrepreneurs who are successful in raising money from informal investors, the amount on

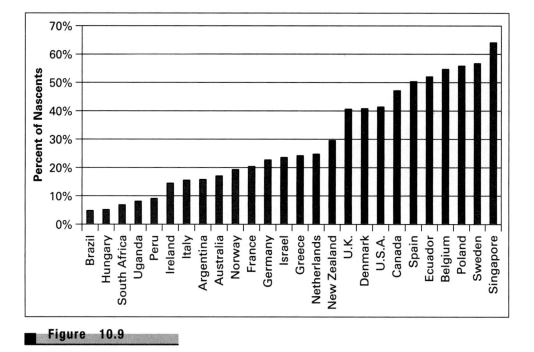

Figure 10.9

Percentage of nascent businesses that could be funded by available informal investment

average more than meets their needs. But is there enough informal investment to supply all the nascent entrepreneurs in a given country?

The percentage of nascent businesses that could be funded with the available informal investment, assuming it all went to nascent businesses, is shown in Figure 10.9. Singapore has the highest percentage of nascent businesses that could be funded and Brazil the lowest. Of course, not all nascent businesses deserve to get funded. Without knowing the merits of each nascent business, and hence whether or not it deserves to be funded, we cannot say if the available informal investment is adequate. But it seems likely that a country with enough informal investment to fund 40% or more of all its nascent entrepreneurs probably has sufficient informal investment because, in the end, the majority of new businesses never become viable in the long term,[17] failing to produce a satisfactory return on investment for either their owners or their investors.

However, just because a country has sufficient startup capital overall does not mean that every deserving nascent business gets funded. An entrepreneur's search for startup capital from informal investors is a haphazard process. If an entrepreneur is unable to raise sufficient money from relatives, friends, and acquaintances, there is no systematic method of searching for potential investors who are strangers. Granted, there are organized groups of informal investors (*business angels*) in many nations, but the number of companies they finance is tiny in proportion to the number of entrepreneurs who seek capital. In addition, most business angel networks in developed nations look for high-potential startups that have prospects of growing into substantial enterprises of the sort that organized venture capitalists would invest in at a subsequent round of funding.

Angels can find high-potential startups in accelerators or incubators, both of which have been on the rise in recent years.[18] Even though both terms are used interchangeably, there is a difference between them. An **incubator** attempts to improve a startup's chance for success by providing office space, professional services, and business advice. An incubator will charge a monthly fee for these services, which usually ranges from a few hundred dollars per month to a few thousand dollars per month. Additionally, an incubator does not have a strict goal-oriented focus for the startups and does not restrict the mount of time a startup can spend in the program.[19] An **accelerator** offers support, funding, and office space for a startup to grow in return for a small percentage of the company (e.g., $50,000 for 5%) and typically gives a startup a fixed start and end date, typically four to six months.[20] A few of the largest Canadian accelerators are the Waterloo Accelerator Centre, the Digital Media Zone (DMZ), and GrowLab. These accelerators will also typically set short-term goals for a startup to achieve and will monitor the achievements closely to help bring those goals to fruition.

Venture Capital

By far the rarest source of capital for nascent entrepreneurs is venture capital.[21] In fact, nascent companies with venture capital in hand before they open their doors for business are so rare that even in the United States—which has almost two-thirds of the total of classic venture capital[22] in the entire world—far fewer than one in 10,000 new ventures gets its initial financing from venture capitalists. In general, venture capital is invested in companies that are already in business rather than in nascent companies with products or services that are still on paper. For example, out of 3,698 U.S. businesses in which $26.5 billion of venture capital was invested in 2012, only 1,163 received venture capital for the first time, and of those relatively few (274) were seed-stage companies. From 1970 through 2012, the venture capital industry invested $556 billion in 41,000 companies at all stages of development.[23] It is estimated that over the same period, informal investors provided more than a trillion dollars to more than 10 million nascent and baby businesses. In every nation, there is far more informal investment from the Four Fs than formal investment from venture capitalists (see Figure 10.10).

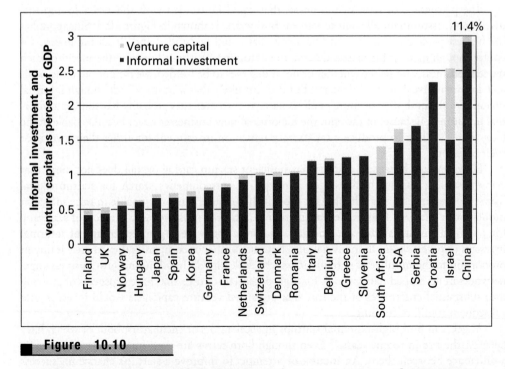

Figure 10.10

Informal investment and venture capital as a percentage of GDP, 2008

Classic Venture Capital

While classic venture capitalists finance very few companies, some of the ones that they do finance play a very important—many say a crucial—role in the development of knowledge-based industries such as biotechnology; medical instruments and devices; computer hardware, software, and services; telecommunications hardware and software; Internet technology and services; electronics; semiconductors; nanotechnology; and clean technology (cleantech). Venture capitalists like to claim that the companies they invest in have the potential to change the way in which people work, live, and play. And indeed an elite few have done just that worldwide; some famous examples are Amazon, Apple, BlackBerry, Cisco, Creo (now part of the Eastman Kodak Company), eBay, Facebook, FedEx, Google, Genentech, Intel, Microsoft, Q9 Networks, Taleo, and Twitter.

It's not by chance that almost all the venture capital–backed companies with global brand names are American; rather, it is because the United States is the predominant nation with respect to classic venture capital investments. In 2008, 74% of all the classic venture capital invested among the G7 nations was invested in the United States. The amount of classic venture capital as a percentage of GDP for the GEM nations is shown in Figure 10.11. Israel, which of all the GEM nations has a venture capital industry most like that in the United States, has the highest amount of venture capital in proportion to its GDP (1.1%), while Italy has the lowest among the G7 nations.

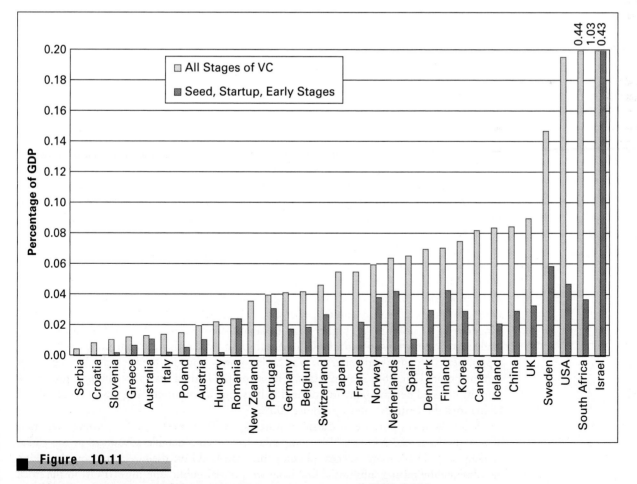

Figure   10.11

Classic venture capital investment as a percentage of GDP, 2008

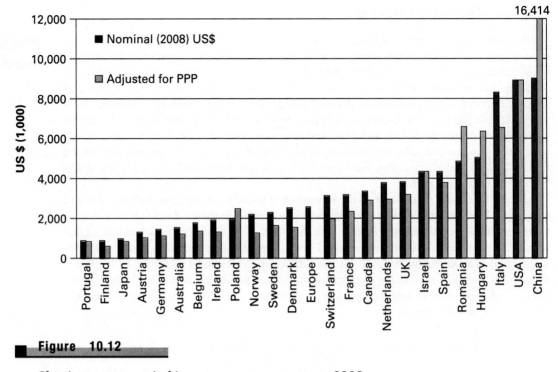

Figure 10.12

Classic venture capital investment per company, 2008

Figure 10.12 shows the amount invested per company for all the GEM nations, including the G7, in 2008. The amount invested per company in Canada was just over $3 million. In 2013, the total amount of venture capital was $2 billion (up 31% from 2012) making the average per company amount in Canada $4.3 million. Looking at Figure 10.12, it is hard to see how companies in Japan, for example, which received on average $972,000 of venture capital, can hope to compete in the global market against companies in the United States that received $8.9 million. It is just as costly to operate a company in Japan as in the United States, if not more so; in fact, entrepreneurs work as many hours in the United States as they do in Japan. Furthermore, the home market where startups initially sell their products and services is more than twice as big in the United States as in Japan. Although the average amounts of venture capital per company in Germany ($1.4 million) and the United Kingdom ($3.2 million) are higher than in Japan, these amounts still appear to be wholly inadequate in comparison with the United States. And when the nominal amount of venture capital per company is adjusted for purchasing power, the gap between the United States and the other G7 nations is even wider. China and the United States are almost equal in the amount invested per company in nominal dollars, but when purchasing power is considered China tops the United States by almost 100%.

Since the main purpose of classic venture capital is to accelerate the commercialization of new products and services, U.S. companies have a considerable advantage in the global marketplace. What's more, successful companies can build on their venture capital backing by subsequently raising substantial financing with initial public offerings (IPOs) in the stock market.

About 80% of the venture capital invested in the United States and 49% of the venture capital invested in Canada finances high-technology companies.[i] By contrast, only 29% of the venture capital invested in the other G7 nations is in high-technology companies. Seventy-three percent of the venture capital invested in high-technology companies at all stages from seed through buyouts in the G7 nations goes to companies in the United States. But when the investment is narrowed down to classic venture capital, the proportion invested in U.S. high-technology companies increases to an estimated 80%, with the U.S. share of classic venture capital invested in biotechnology at 81% and in computer hardware and software at 83%. When it comes to investment in all stages of consumer-related companies, the situation is reversed—only 13% of these companies are in the United States and 87% are in the other G7 nations.

[i]Thomson Reuters for Canada's Venture Capital & Private Equity Association, *Canada's Venture Capital Market in 2012,* www.cvca.ca/files/Downloads/VC_Data_Deck_2012_Final.pdf.

Importance of Venture Capital in the Growing Economy

One way of classifying young ventures is by their degree of innovation and their rate of growth[24] (see Figure 10.13). In the bottom left quadrant of the figure are companies that are not very innovative and grow comparatively slowly. They provide goods and services that are the core of the economy; for the most part, they have lots of competitors and they grow at the same rate as the economy. In the upper left quadrant are companies that are innovative but that are not fast growing because for one reason or another they are constrained—often because they are started and managed by entrepreneurs with limited ability. In the bottom right

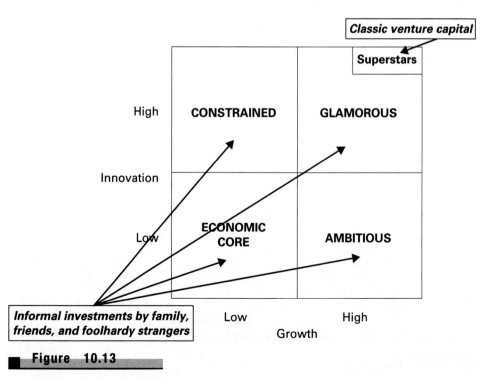

Figure 10.13

Financing entrepreneurial ventures

quadrant are companies that are not particularly innovative but that outpace the growth rate of many of their competitors because they are run by ambitious entrepreneurs with superior management skills. And in the top right quadrant are companies that are innovative and have superior management; among them are the superstar companies that attract media attention.

Informal investment goes to companies in all quadrants. In contrast, classic venture capital goes only to the companies in the uppermost corner of the glamorous quadrant. They are the companies with potential to become the superstars in their industries—and in a few instances, to be central in the creation and development of a new industry segment. By and large, they are led by entrepreneurial teams with excellent management skills. The companies are usually already up and running when the first venture capital is invested, although in a few rare instances venture capital is invested before the company is operational. Looked at another way, classic venture capital accelerates the growth rate of young superstar companies; it seldom finances nascent entrepreneurs who are not yet in business. A relatively sophisticated subset of informal investors, business angels, invests primarily in the glamorous companies, especially those with the potential to become superstars. Business angels are often entrepreneurs themselves, or former entrepreneurs, who invest some of their wealth in seed- and early-stage businesses. Angel investment frequently precedes formal venture capital.

If venture capital dried up there would be no noticeable change in the number of companies being started because so few have venture capital in hand when they open their doors for business, whereas everyone has funding from one or more of the Four Fs. But in the long term the effect on the economy would be catastrophic because venture capital–backed companies generate a disproportionate number of good-paying jobs and create many of the new products and services. Those companies make a major contribution to the economy. For instance, in 2010, venture capital–backed companies accounted for 11% of jobs in the U.S. private sector and 21% of its GDP.[25] Figure 10.14 shows the top 10 venture capital disbursements across North America.

In Canada, venture capital–backed companies have generated nearly 150,000 jobs and generated $18.3 billion toward Canada's GDP, which represent 1.3% of all private sector jobs in Canada.[26] The contributing sectors are ICT (information and communications technology),

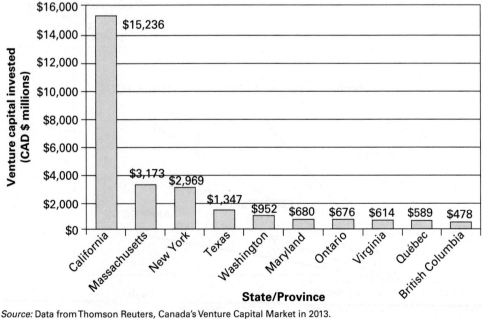

Source: Data from Thomson Reuters, Canada's Venture Capital Market in 2013.

■ **Figure 10.14**

Venture capital disbursement across North America

contributing $15.4 billion; life sciences, contributing $1.9 billion; and other technologies, contributing $1.0 billion.[27]

Venture capital–backed companies employ a high proportion of high-tech workers in the United States. They accounted for 90% of software, 74% of biotechnology, 72% of semiconductor, 54% of computer, and 48% of telecom jobs in 2010.

Venture capital–backed companies, adjusted for size, spend over twice as much on R&D as other companies. In particular, small firms in the venture-dominated information technology and medical-related sectors are big spenders on R&D.

Mechanism of Venture Capital Investing

The formal venture capital industry was born in Massachusetts at the end of World War II when a group of investors inspired by General Georges Doriot, a legendary professor at the Harvard Business School, put together the first venture capital fund, American Research and Development. They did so because they were concerned that the commercial potential of technical advances made by scientists and engineers at the Massachusetts Institute of Technology during World War II would be lost unless funding was available to commercialize them. The fledgling venture capital industry grew and evolved; eventually the most common form of organization for U.S. venture capital funds became the limited partnership.

The mechanism of venture capital investing is shown in Figure 10.15.[28] At the centre of the process are the general partners of venture capital funds, which are limited partnerships

Georges F. Doriot, ca. 1955. HBS Archives Photograph Collection: Faculty and Staff. Baker Library Historical Collections. Harvard Business School (olvworks377916).

Georges Doriot (1899–1987) founded the venture capital industry when he started American Research and Development in Boston in 1946. His venture capital firm made many seed-stage investments, the most famous of which was $70,000 for 77% of the startup equity of Digital Equipment Corporation. (1979 photo)

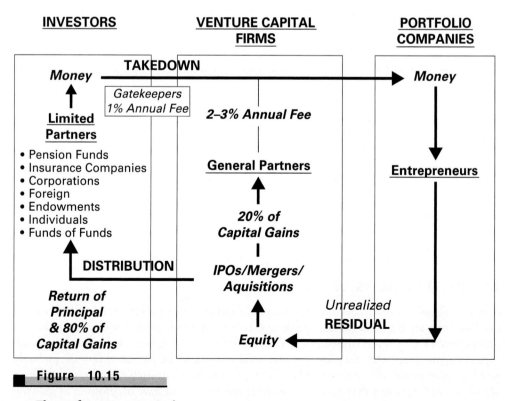

Figure 10.15

Flow of venture capital

Kleiner Perkins Caufield and Byers: A Legendary Venture Capital Firm

Eugene Kleiner and Tom Perkins formed their venture capital firm, then known as Kleiner Perkins, in 1972. Kleiner was one of the founders of Fairchild Semiconductor, and Perkins was a rising star at Hewlett-Packard. It is probably the most successful venture capital firm ever. Today it is known as Kleiner Perkins Caufield and Byers (KPC&B), headquartered on Sand Hill Road in the heart of Silicon Valley. Since 1972 it has invested in more than 400 companies, among them AOL, Amazon, Compaq, Genentech, Google, Intuit, LSI Logic, Netscape, and Sun.

In 2008, KPC&B raised a $700 million fund, Kleiner Perkins Caufield & Byers XIII. The limited partner investors in the 13th fund since 1972 are largely the same ones that have invested in KPC&B funds over the last 25 years or so. This family of funds has been so successful that it is virtually impossible for new limited partners to invest because the general partners can raise all the money they need from the limited partners who invested in previous funds. The $700 million was to be invested by the general partners over three years, mainly in early-stage companies with innovations in greentech, information technology, and life sciences.

with a 10-year life that is sometimes extended. The general partners of venture capital funds raise money from limited partners. In return for managing the partnership, the general partners receive an annual fee of 2% to 3% of the principal that has been paid into the fund. The general partners then invest money in portfolio companies in exchange for equity. If all goes well, the investment in the portfolio companies grows and the equity is eventually harvested, usually with an IPO or a trade sale to a bigger company. The capital gain on the harvest is shared 80%–20% between the limited partners and the general partners once the limited partners have received back all the principal they put into the limited partnership. The general partners' share is called the *carried interest*, which is usually 20%. Sometimes gatekeepers (formally called *investment advisors*) are employed by limited partners to advise them on what venture capital funds they should invest in and to watch over an investment once it has been made. The gatekeeper's fee is approximately 1% of the capital invested.

Historically, the biggest portion of the money invested by limited partners came from pension funds—in both the public and the private sectors—with the balance coming from funds of funds, endowments, foundations, insurance companies, banks, and individuals; however, in 2009 funds of funds overtook pension funds as the top provider.

As we've mentioned, each venture capital partnership (called a *venture capital fund*) has a 10-year life. If a venture capital fund is successful, measured by the financial return to the limited partners, the general partners usually raise another fund four to six years after the first fund. This, in essence, means that successful venture capital firms generally have two to four active funds at a time, since each fund has a life of 10 years.

Financial Returns on Venture Capital

A rule of thumb for a successful venture capital fund is that for every 10 investments in its portfolio, two are big successes that produce excellent financial returns; two are outright failures in which the total investment is written off; three are walking wounded, which in venture capital jargon means that they are not successful enough to be harvested but are probably worth another round of venture capital to try to get them into harvestable condition; and three are living dead, meaning that they may be viable companies but have no prospect of growing big enough to produce a satisfactory return on the venture capital invested in them.

Fund Type	Upper Quartile	Pooled Average Top Quartile IRR	Top Quartile Net Horizon Returns (All periods ending December 31, 2012)		
			3-year	5-year	10-year
Venture capital	5.4	21.6	15.3	11.1	9.8
Buyouts and mezzanine	20.6	31.6	36.9	25.1	42.3
All private equity	12.5	27.0	26.7	19.4	31.4

Source: Data from Thompson Reuters and CVCA

Figure 10.16

U.S. venture capital returns

Approximately 3,000 of the 41,000 or so companies (about 7%) financed with venture capital between 1970 and 2012 have had IPOs.[29] Of the others that were harvested, mergers and acquisitions were the most common exit. In comparatively rare instances, the company's managers bought back the venture capitalist's investment.

The highest return on a venture capital investment is produced when the company has an IPO or is sold to or merged with another company (also called a *trade sale*) for a substantial capital gain. In general, however, trade sales do not produce nearly as big a capital gain as IPOs do because most trade sales involve venture capital–backed companies that aren't successful enough to have an IPO. For instance, one way of harvesting the walking wounded and living dead is to sell them to other companies for a modest capital gain—or in some cases, a loss. The average post-IPO valuation of venture capital–backed companies that went public in the five years through 2011 was $777 million[30] compared with an average valuation of $142 million for those that were exited through mergers and acquisitions.[31]

The overall IRR to limited partners of classic venture capital funds, over the entire period since 1946 when the first fund was formed, has been in the mid-teens. But during those six decades, there have been periods when the returns have been higher or lower. When the IPO market is booming, the returns on venture capital are high, and vice versa. The Canadian returns of venture-backed firms are illustrated in Figure 10.16. Canada's performance data for venture-backed firms indicate a strong growth with a three-year IRR of 15.3%, a five-year IRR of 11.1%, and a 10-year IRR of 9.8%.[32] The returns of U.S. venture capital are shown in Figure 10.17. Over the 20-year horizon, seed- and early-stage funds outperformed balanced and expansion- and later-stage ones. This is what we should expect because the earlier the stage of investment, the greater the risk, so the return should be

Fund Type	Investment Horizon IRR (%) through September 30, 2012				
	1 Year	3 Years	5 Years	10 Years	20 Years
Seed/Early Stage	8.4	12.9	4.5	4.9	39.7
Later/Expansion Stage	5.4	17.1	8.1	10.3	12.5
Multi Stage	7.5	9.4	3.0	6.8	13.9
All Venture Funds	7.7	12.2	4.5	6.1	28.8
NASDAQ	29.0	13.7	2.9	10.3	8.7
S&P 500	30.2	13.2	1.1	8.0	8.5

Source: Cambridge Associates LLC. U.S. Venture Capital Index® and Selected Benchmark Statistics

Figure 10.17

Venture capital IRRs and NASDAQ and S&P 500 Returns

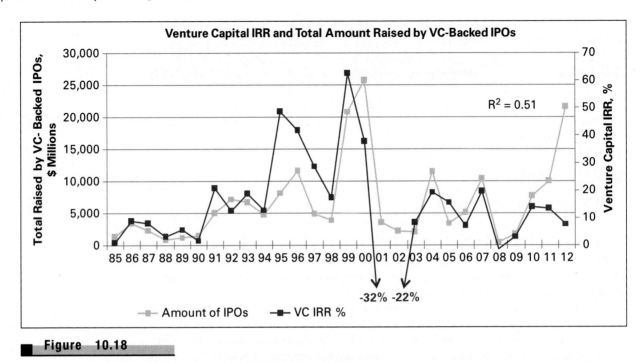

Figure 10.18

Venture capital year-to-year IRR and total raised by venture capital–backed IPOs

higher to compensate for the risk. The seed- and early-stage risk premium was spectacular for the 20-year horizon (39.7% versus 12.5% for expansion- and later-stage funds) because the 20-year horizon includes the years 1999 and 2000, which were the peak of the Internet bubble, when year-to-year returns on all venture capital funds were 62.5% and 37.6%, with returns on seed- and early-stage funds being far higher. However, the 3-, 5-, and 10-year returns on seed- and early-stage funds underperformed expansion- and later-stage funds; but in the most recent year, 2012, seed- and early-stage funds outperformed expansion- and later-stage funds.

The importance of the IPO market for venture capital is demonstrated in Figure 10.18, which shows the year-to-year IRRs of venture capital and the total amount of money raised by IPOs of companies backed with venture capital. This shows a close correlation between the two lines: When the IPO market is thriving, as it was in 1999 and early 2000, the returns on venture capital are high. Not only do lucrative IPOs directly produce spectacular returns on venture capital invested in the companies going public, but they also indirectly raise the returns on acquisitions and mergers because IPO market valuations tend to set the valuations of all private equity deals. For instance, in 2000 during the Internet bubble, the average valuation for a venture capital–backed merger/acquisition was $338.4 million, but by 2002, after the bubble burst, the average valuation fell to $52.2 million.

Google's spectacular IPO in the third quarter of 2004 boosted the confidence of the venture capital industry. Some industry leaders expected that it would herald the start of a new cycle in venture capital investing, with more money being invested in seed- and early-stage businesses. What they were hoping for was another revolutionary innovation that would fire up the enthusiasm of investors such as personal computers did at the beginning of the 1980s and the Internet and the World Wide Web did in the late 1990s. They hoped it would be nanotechnology, but a boom never materialized; next they bet on clean technology; and in 2012 they had high hopes for social media.

Clean technology attracted a lot of venture capital, with the amount invested increasing more than tenfold from $0.4 billion in 2004 to $4.5 billion in 2011. Silicon Valley's preeminent venture capital firm, Kleiner Perkins Caufield & Byers, recruited Al Gore as a partner. According to Gore, who was cited for "informing the world of the dangers posed by climate change" when awarded the 2007 Nobel Peace Prize, clean technology will be "bigger than the Industrial Revolution and significantly faster."[33] But an IPO boom in clean technology stocks didn't occur. What's more in 2012 there were some highly visible failures of venture capital–backed clean technology companies such as Solyndra in solar power and A123 in lithium ion batteries. Returns were dreadful—and in some cases, like A123, there were huge losses—for small investors who had bought stock in the few clean technologies that had gone public. Lack of small investor interest in clean technology stocks meant a paucity of IPOs in that sector, which depressed venture capital returns.

Then in 2012 venture capitalists believed that social media companies would be the next big thing that could rival the Internet boom. After all, Facebook—the most famous social media company—claimed to have about 1 billion users worldwide when it went public in May 2012. Unfortunately, as you will read in the next chapter, Facebook's IPO went awry for investors—especially small ones—who bought the stock at the IPO and lost half the value of their investment four months later. Although those who held on to their stocks recovered most of their investment by July 2012, Facebook's IPO did not turn out to be a get-rich-quick bonanza like the Internet IPO boom, and it made small investors wary of IPOs.

So in 2012 venture capitalists were still waiting for an IPO boom to boost their returns, which had been unsatisfactory for 10 years because limited partners such as pension funds that provided money to venture capital partnerships could have earned as good a return or maybe better by investing in NASDAQ stocks. Limited partners took notice of the inadequate returns from venture capital and cut the money they committed to new venture funds for four consecutive years from 2007 to 2010; the amount increased in 2011, but was 41% less than the amount in 2006. And venture capitalists have become less . . . what else . . . venturesome over the years; for instance, they invested in 38% fewer seed-stage companies in 2012 than in 2011 and the amount they invested in them was the lowest since 2003.

Venture Capital in Europe

Since the mid-1990s, venture capital grew rapidly as most nations strived to emulate the impact that classic venture capital was having on the U.S. economy. It has happened before: at the end of the 1960s, when the United States enjoyed a boom in classic venture capital, and again at the start of the 1980s, when the rest of the world marvelled at the success of the personal computer industry and the emerging biotech sector in the United States. Unfortunately, in both instances it turned out to be a false dawn. Returns on classic venture capital outside the United States were—to say the least—disappointing, and classic venture capital floundered.

One of the principal reasons for the failure of classic venture capital in Europe at the start of the 1990s was the failure of the secondary markets after the general stock market crash of October 1987. The Unlisted Securities Market in London, the Second Marché in Lyon, the Marché Hors-Cote in Paris, the Mercato Restrito in Milan, and the Secondary Market in Brussels had been significant contributors and enabling factors for the introduction of venture capital in those European countries in the early 1980s because they provided ready markets for floating IPOs of venture capital–backed companies. Unfortunately, those European secondary markets, unlike the NASDAQ in the United States, did not recover, and so they faded, which left European venture capitalists without their favourite and most bountiful exit route from their investments: IPOs.[34]

In the late 1990s, markets for IPOs in Europe started to prosper, especially the AIM in the United Kingdom, but just as in the United States after 2001, it again became very difficult to float venture capital–backed IPOs in Europe; consequently, classic venture capital returns fell and investments declined. Once more it demonstrated that classic venture capital cannot do well without a robust IPO market.

Factors Affecting Availability of Financing

The three fundamental elements of an entrepreneurial society are an abundance of would-be entrepreneurs, plenty of market opportunities for new ventures, and sufficient resources—of which financing is a major component—for entrepreneurs to launch their new ventures.[35] Numerous environmental and societal factors affect the three basic elements, and in combination with the basic elements, they determine the degree of entrepreneurial activity in a region. We will now look at how financing correlates with entrepreneurial activity and the factors that affect the availability of financing. Because GEM includes many nations, we can see how informal investment and venture capital are related to environmental, societal, and governmental factors.

Total Entrepreneurial Activity and Informal Investing

The prevalence of informal investors correlates positively with the overall TEA index and three component TEA indices—opportunity, market expansion potential, and high job growth potential. And the amount of informal investment as a percentage of GDP correlates positively with two TEA indices—necessity and high job growth potential. Those correlations are convincing evidence that nations with more informal investing have more entrepreneurial activity, but they do not separate cause from effect. Informal investing and entrepreneurship depend on each other: Informal investment facilitates entrepreneurship, and entrepreneurship brings about a need for informal investment.

Factors Affecting Informal Investing

Money for informal investing comes from a person's after-tax income and savings, which more often than not are accumulated from after-tax income. Thus, it seems reasonable to hypothesize that the higher the rate of taxation, the less likely that a person will have discretionary money to invest, and vice versa. In many nations, especially developed ones, the biggest taxes are social security, income taxes, indirect taxes such as sales tax on goods and services, and taxes on capital and property.

For all the GEM nations, the prevalence rate of informal investors is negatively correlated with social security taxes and with taxes on capital and property. For nations with an income of at least $5,000 per capita, the amount of informal investment per GDP correlates negatively with social security taxes, the highest marginal income tax rate, indirect taxes, and taxes on capital and property. Stated another way, nations with higher taxes on individuals have lower rates of informal investing. High tax rates inhibit informal investing.

Factors Affecting Classic Venture Capital

In contrast to informal investing, the amount of classic venture capital as a percentage of GDP does not correlate with taxes on individuals or corporations. The explanation is that only a small proportion of classic venture capital comes from individuals and corporations. Far more comes from pension funds, which are essentially investing money that has been entrusted to them by others, and hence they are not directly affected by taxes nearly as much as individuals are.

The amount of classic venture capital as a percentage of GDP correlates with the amount of informal investment as a percentage of GDP. This occurs because almost all companies start out with informal investment; then, if they show superstar potential, they attract classic venture capital. Thus, vigorous informal investing paves the way for robust classic venture capital investing. So, although there is no direct link between classic venture capital investment and taxation, there is an indirect link via informal investors, who are influenced by how much they pay in taxes.

As we pointed out earlier, there is a correlation between the returns on venture capital and the IPO market in the United States. In turn, this correlation means that the amount of venture capital provided by limited partners depends on the IPO market because, when the returns on venture capital are good, limited partners put more money into venture capital funds, and vice versa. In 2008, for instance, when the one-year return on venture capital dropped precipitously, commitments of new money by limited partners fell 21%.

A more recent issue affecting venture capital has stemmed from the diminishing costs to launch an IT startup. As mentioned earlier in this chapter, the cost of launching a digital, mobile or software startup has dropped significantly. How does that affect a venture-financing fund with $100 million to invest? They can now invest in many more startup companies since each venture requires less capital to launch their prospective businesses. Don Tapscott reinforces this notion:

> *Lower costs to launch should mean more new companies and more innovation for VCs to fund. But it doesn't. It actually makes it harder for companies to find the money and also the attention they need. Why? More companies receiving investment means more companies to supervise and more demands on the investor's attention. After all, VCs usually add more than just money—they make introductions, assist with strategic sales, and help recruit top talent.*
>
> *So what's the alternative? A form of community-powered venture capital that believes the crowd can both filter the global wealth of opportunities and channel more intellectual horsepower into making each investment successful.*[36]

As venture capitalists adapt to new and emerging ways to manage their vested interest in the startup community, it is no surprise that many startup companies seek the help of angel investors. Angels are often experienced and well-educated professionals who invest their own funds in a business or startup.[37] Organizations such as Canada's National Angel Capital Organization (NACO) make it easier for startups to search and find business angels. More on angel investors will be covered in Chapter 11.

CONCLUSION

Financing is a necessary but not a sufficient ingredient for an entrepreneurial society. It goes hand in hand with entrepreneurs and opportunities in an environment that encourages entrepreneurship.

Grassroots financing from the entrepreneurs themselves and informal investors is a crucial ingredient for an entrepreneurial society. Close family members and friends and neighbors are by far the two biggest sources of informal capital for startups. Hence, entrepreneurs should look to family and friends for their initial seed capital to augment their own investments in their startups. Many entrepreneurs waste a lot of valuable time by prematurely seeking seed capital from business angels and even from formal venture capitalists—searches that come up empty handed almost every time. Entrepreneurs must also understand that they themselves will have to put up about two-thirds of the initial capital needed to launch their ventures.

YOUR OPPORTUNITY JOURNAL

Reflection Point	Your Thoughts. . .
1. How much equity financing do you need to get your business launched? When do you need it?	
2. Where will you get your initial financing? How much money can you invest from your personal resources (savings, second mortgage, etc.)?	
3. Create a strategy for other equity financing. Build a list and rank order Four F funding sources. Estimate how much each of these investors might be able and willing to invest.	
4. Do you think your business has the potential to raise formal venture capital (high-tech, high-innovation, high-growth prospects, first-rate management team, etc.)? If so, when might you be ready for venture capital? How much would you raise?	

WEB EXERCISE

What can you learn about equity financing on the Web? Search for some investor/entrepreneur matching sites (e.g., www.angelonenetwork.ca). Do you think these services are effective? Would they work for your business? What can you learn about venture capital on the Web? Look at www.pwcmoneytree.com. What regions and sectors are receiving the most money? Which venture capital funds are the most active? Are they investing in your sector?

DayOne

In an uncharacteristic show of frustration, Andrew Zenoff nearly tossed the phone into its cradle on his desk when his latest funding lead—number 182—had decided not to invest. With the 2003 winter holiday season in full swing, the 38-year-old seasoned entrepreneur knew that his fundraising efforts would now fall on deaf ears until after the New Year holiday.

Andrew stared out from the open office at a group of young mothers in the retail area—all cradling newborns—chatting with the nursing staff and with each other as they waited for the morning lactation class to begin.

> *Those new moms out there need us; that's why we're doing well despite a terrible location, a recession, and no money for advertising! So why can't I seem to convince investors what a great opportunity this is?! Am I—along with my staff and all of our satisfied customers—suffering from some sort of collective delusion?*

He closed his eyes, breathed deeply, and calmed down. After all, he quickly reminded himself, his San Francisco–based DayOne Center—a one-stop resource for new and expectant parents—was doing just fine as it approached its third year of operations. What Andrew and his team were being told, though, was that, before funds would flow, they would need to provide additional proof of concept—a second centre, sited and scaled to match the DayOne business plan. The chicken–egg challenge, of course, was that they would need about a million dollars to build that proof. Andrew leaned back to consider his best options for moving forward.

My Brest Friend

Andrew was no stranger to entrepreneurial mountain climbing. For three years, he had strived to build a national distribution channel for My Brest Friend, the most popular nursing pillow in a fragmented market. By 1996, he had secured an overseas manufacturer, office space in a San Francisco warehouse, and a few volume accounts that were yielding a decent—but far from satisfying—cash flow. He was still wrestling with the issue of how to educate the buyer about the advantages of his product when suddenly his venture had come under siege:

> *A nursing pillow company that was not doing well somehow thought that I had copied their design. There was no infringement, but they sued us anyway, and I decided to fight. The owner of this company was a woman with kids, and as the suit dragged on, my lawyers convinced me that, if this thing went to trial, a jury might side with her instead of a guy who has no kids and has never been married. If she won, they'd get an injunction against me, and that would be the end of my business.*
>
> *That year I switched law firms three times, spent over $250,000 on legal fees, and ended up paying a settlement in the low six figures. I was emotionally drained, and nearly entirely out of cash, but I had managed to save my business.*

A Question of Distribution

Following that painful settlement in the spring of 1997, Andrew set about to devise a more effective delivery model for his nursing pillow enterprise. He soon came to the realization that the solution he was looking for didn't exist:

> *We definitely had the best product in the category. The problem was that people needed to be educated to that fact—either outright or through trusted word of mouth. The various channels*

I had worked with—big retailers, hospitals, Internet sites, catalogue companies, lactation consultants—each offered only a certain facet of what a new parent needed, and so none of them had been really efficient at delivering my product to the marketplace. What it needed was a combination of education, retailing, and community.

Later that summer, Andrew got a call from one of his customers, Sallie Weld, director of the Perinatal Center at the California Pacific Medical Center. An active promoter of My Brest Friend, Sallie had come to a frustrating juncture in her own career:

During the mid to late 1990s, I had spent a lot of time and energy setting up a new type of perinatal centre. New moms were coming in asking for support and advice on various products— breast pumps in particular. When we started carrying pumps, that sort of opened up a Pandora's Box; now people wanted other products to go with the pumps. Andrew's pillow, for example, was the best on the market, so we started carrying that.

And after a couple of years, this retail aspect of our childbirth and parenting education program began to turn a profit—and the minute it did, the hospital got greedy. They told us that we were not going to be able to hire more trained staff to handle the increased demand for our consults, and they said that all of our retailing profits would be channelled back into the general fund to support other departments. That was incredibly frustrating. I knew I was onto something, though, and I started a consulting business to help other perinatal centres. The problem was, they couldn't pay much for my services. That's when I decided to give Andrew a call.

They agreed to meet at Zim's Restaurant, an aging diner in the upscale Laurel Hill neighbourhood of San Francisco. It was a meeting that would change their lives.

DayOne—Beginnings

In August 1997, Sallie and Andrew met at Zim's for coffee and carrot juice, respectively. Sallie explained that no single service provider had ever been able to adequately serve the various needs of new moms:

A hospital setting would seem to be the natural place to set up an educational support and product centre for these women, but the bureaucracy just won't let that happen. There are also plenty of examples where nurses have tried to offer outside consulting services to new mothers, but while that's a great thought, they never seem to get very far without the business and retail component. And retailing without knowledgeable support is just products on a shelf.

After 90 minutes of brainstorming, the pieces suddenly fell into place. Andrew had found the unique distribution model he'd been searching for:

I said to Sallie, "Let's move these hybrid health-services retailing ideas into a private care centre outside of the hospital—a retail centre that could provide new and expecting parents with everything they needed in one place." We'd be backing up the hospitals and supporting women at a critical and emotionally charged period in their lives.

This was like a lightning bolt of a vision for both of us, and at that moment, we decided that we were going to build a national chain of these centres. That was the beginning of DayOne.

Having already built one business from scratch, Andrew noted that he wasn't surprised that it was months before they were ready to take a material step:

I had told Sallie that, even though this sounded great, she shouldn't think about quitting her job at the hospital until I had a chance to lead us in an exercise to see if this business was a viable idea. I conducted a tonne of focus groups, and every week Sallie and I would get together to talk about what I had learned—and what kind of centre DayOne would be. After about nine months, in the summer of 1998, we decided, yes, this makes sense; let's do it.

Seed Funding

Andrew called investor Mark Anderssen, a shareholder and an active supporter of My Brest Friend. When Mark seemed receptive to the DayOne concept, Andrew paid him a visit:

> *I flew to Norway to meet with him in person. I was sure that after we opened up one of these, we'd be able to attract enough capital to start a chain. I figured that we would need about $300,000 to fund the next year and a half; we would be writing the business plan and working on the build-out requirements so that, when we were ready, we could move through the construction process quickly and get it opened. He said great and put up about half the money to get us started.*

As Sallie focused in on staffing requirements and retail offerings, Andrew began writing the plan, defining the target market (see Exhibit 10.1), designing the space, and looking for the right retail location: upscale, ground floor, easy parking, with excellent signage potential.

That summer, about a year after their momentous meeting of the minds, the Zim's restaurant block fell to the wrecking ball to make way for a brand new office and retail complex. Andrew saw that the location was close to the hospitals, was in a vibrant retail area, had good stroller accessibility, and offered lots of parking. When the developer pointed out the street-level retail availability on the blueprints, Andrew saw that it was precisely where Zim's had been; DayOne would be growing up in the exact spot where Andrew and Sallie had had their first meeting.

Andrew secured the space with a sizable deposit, engaged the architects, and scheduled a contractor to handle the build-out. With their sights now set on an April 2000 grand opening, Sallie left her job to become DayOne's first paid employee. Everything was on schedule and proceeding as planned. Then, suddenly, nothing was.

Scrambling to Survive

In January, Andrew contacted his funding partner for the other half of the seed funding allocation. The investor, who had recently suffered some losses in high tech, explained that he would be unable to extend any more money. Andrew was in shock:

> *Things were already rolling along; I had architects working, Sallie and two assistants on payroll, a huge locked-in lease—and now, suddenly, with the bills mounting up, we were out of capital!*

Andrew had been pitching the DayOne vision to other investors all along, and that same week an individual came forward with a substantial amount of money to invest. Andrew explained that, while the promise of cash got him motivated, he soon concluded that this wasn't just about the money:

> *This investor approached me and said that since I clearly understood the baby industry, he could get me a million and a half bucks for an Internet company. So I spent four weeks trying to figure out how I could do this on the Internet. Then I realized that, even though I probably could come up with something, it wouldn't really provide new parents with what they needed. And so I went back to them and said that I can't do it; it's not in line with my values and my beliefs.*

up $150,000 apiece. $450,000 was about half of what I would need to open, and a lot less than the $1.5 million I was trying to raise as a first round. But it was a start; I pushed the "Go" button again.

I went back to the real estate guy and said, "You know, you're right; even if this is on the second floor, this is my space. I'll keep it." That's when he told me that he had already rented out half of our space to someone else. So, not only were we going to be way in back on the second floor with half the space we needed, but also we were now going to have to pay to completely reconstruct our architectural drawings.

Understanding that he was still a half a million dollars shy of what they would need to open the doors, Andrew continued to dole out just enough money to keep his various service providers on board. In June, the landlord informed him that the building was now ready for occupancy—meaning that the first $10,000 monthly rent payment was due. Andrew made sure to pay that bill on time, and in full.

Grand Opening

The construction business, like many trades, was a close-knit community of craftspeople and professionals. It was not surprising, then, that word was out on the slow-paying, underfunded project up on Laurel Hill that had already gone through three architectural firms and at least that many plan revisions. After a long search, Andrew located a contractor who apparently was not aware of DayOne's precarious financial situation. Along the way, he had signed up another minor investor, so when construction began in August 2000, DayOne had $480,000 on hand. In late November—as the build-out neared completion—the contractor suddenly announced that he would not release the occupancy permits until he and his crew were paid in full for the work they had completed. Andrew recalled that it was another one of those pivotal moments:

I owed these guys something like $200,000, and I didn't have anything left. I just wanted to get to the opening party in January because I felt that, if we got enough people to come and enjoy it and get excited about what we were doing, we'd be able to raise the money we needed. I convinced the contractor to let us open, and at that party, two different guests pulled me aside and said that they wanted to invest. One woman wired me $50,000 the following Monday without so much as glancing at the business plan. I got another $50,000 from a couple who had just had their baby. When we officially opened later that week, the contractor was paid in full, but we were again out of money.

As they had always planned to do, Andrew and Sallie called the area hospitals to let them know that DayOne was open for business and ready to serve. Andrew recalled that the response from the medical community took them completely by surprise:

One reason we thought we could make do with a second-floor location was because our plan had always been to drive traffic by being the type of place that medical professionals would want to send their patients. Instead, hospital directors were telling us that they considered us to be the competition and that they were going to tell all the docs in San Francisco not to support our efforts in any way.

With no help from the hospitals, ineffective signage, cramped facilities (see Exhibit 10.2), and no capital for marketing and advertising, Sallie and Andrew were faced with a harsh reality: Either customers would love the experience enough to spread the word, or their business would quickly wither and die.

EXHIBIT 10.2 Signage and Facility

Delivering a Unique Customer Experience

DayOne immediately began attracting a base of young, mostly affluent new and expectant moms seeking advice on everything from the latest baby carriers to sore nipples. Many signed up for the $99 annual membership on the spot to take advantage of discounts offered on programs and workshops (see Exhibit 10.3). Some dropped by out of curiosity or with

EXHIBIT 10.3 DayOne Membership Flyer

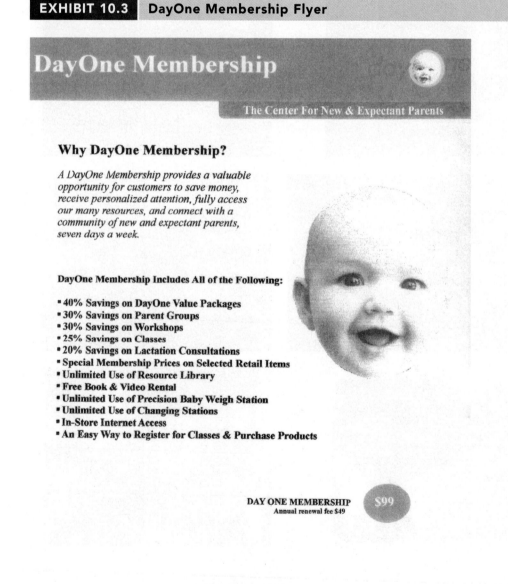

DayOne Membership

The Center For New & Expectant Parents

Why DayOne Membership?

A DayOne Membership provides a valuable opportunity for customers to save money, receive personalized attention, fully access our many resources, and connect with a community of new and expectant parents, seven days a week.

DayOne Membership Includes All of the Following:

- 40% Savings on DayOne Value Packages
- 30% Savings on Parent Groups
- 30% Savings on Workshops
- 25% Savings on Classes
- 20% Savings on Lactation Consultations
- Special Membership Prices on Selected Retail Items
- Unlimited Use of Resource Library
- Free Book & Video Rental
- Unlimited Use of Precision Baby Weigh Station
- Unlimited Use of Changing Stations
- In-Store Internet Access
- An Easy Way to Register for Classes & Purchase Products

DAY ONE MEMBERSHIP
Annual renewal fee $49

$99

Memberships are non-refundable

www.DayOneCenter.com • 3490 California St. San Francisco, CA 94118 • 415.440.DAY1 (3291) specific questions for the professional staff. Sallie quickly established a ground rule that she felt struck a fair balance between the needs of these mothers and the need to advance the business:

> When someone comes in with a question, we have a 10-minute rule. If your question is so involved that one of us cannot answer it in 10 minutes, then you need to make an appointment, and we need to charge you.[38] Ideally, these are people who are members, but many times, if they are not, we can convert them by giving them those 10 minutes and maybe recommending some classes or products right there on the shelves that might be just what they were looking for. And they leave here thinking, wow, where else can I go where I can get that kind of knowledgeable service without having to be a member first?

Sallie noted that, because of their customer-care orientation, she and her nursing staff were always looking out for ways to help—without first trying to calibrate whether a particular act of humanity or assistance would generate profits for the business. Pointing to a basic plastic and metal chair in the corner of her office, Sallie said that she wasn't surprised to see that simple kindness had its rewards:

> Our favourite story is about that chair. We like new moms to be sitting up straight when they first start nursing—versus a rocking chair. I had one mom—not a member—who said every time she came in for a consult that the only way she could breast feed was in that type of chair. Every time she came in she said it, so finally I said, "Hey, why don't you take the chair home with you until you're feeling more comfortable with the whole process?" She looked at me and said, "Really?"
>
> So she took the chair home. The next day she became a member, she bought a breast pump from us instead of the one she was eyeing on eBay, and she went around telling all of her friends that we lent her that chair. She brought it back a few weeks later and has become one of our best customers.
>
> What goes around comes around, and when we give a little bit, it's such a shock to them that they've gotten good service. I have this rule that if there's a mom hanging out in the rocking chair area, one of us goes over and asks if we could get her a glass of cold water. I swear it's like you've just offered them a million dollars! They'll start to ask you questions, and it almost always turns into a sale. It's so funny—and a bit pathetic—that nobody ever thinks about these moms; everybody talks to, and about, the baby.
>
> That's what we do differently. We make them feel good, knowing that if we take care of them, they'll take care of the baby. And all of that is definitely good for business.

Despite an encouraging level of customer interest and loyalty right from the start, the retailing side of the business continued to struggle. Andrew knew what the problem was:

> The thing is, I am not a retailer. So everything we did early on was shooting from the hip. Sallie had some experience selling retail products at the hospital, but she was better on the service side. We had hired one retail buyer who lasted two months; didn't know what she was doing. Then another; same thing. The problem was, these people knew a lot about retailing, but we needed somebody who also understood the baby industry.

DayOne had begun to cover its operating expenses by the end of the summer of 2001, but the business was still in dire need of funding. As the capital markets continued to deteriorate that year, fundraising became an even more arduous task than ever before. While the 9/11 terrorist attacks on the East Coast hurt retail sales and drove potential investors further underground, satisfied clients continued to drive new customers to the centre.

In January 2002, the retail buyer that Andrew and Sallie had been searching for showed up on their doorstep. Ten-year retailing veteran Jennifer Morris had come over from The Right Start, the largest chain of specialty stores for infants and children in the United States. She recounted how she was drawn to the new venture and alluded to why her predecessors might have been overwhelmed by the task:

> *I found out about DayOne through working at The Right Start in San Francisco. I would either see a DayOne tote bag or customers would tell me all about it. I started to investigate and found out that DayOne is not the kind of place you'd stumble onto. I was immediately attracted to the energy in this place; from the customers, the staff, the nurses, to the classes and the workshops, everyone just really seemed to love it.*
>
> *The biggest challenge for us is trying to be a one-stop shop. We have quite a few product categories (see Exhibit 10.4), and I buy from over 100 vendors—sometimes just one item from one vendor. A lot of those decisions are made by listening to our customers. If they come in with a terrific product, we can then go research that item and bring it in. We have no limits on that, really; we carry products from New Zealand, from Australia—from all over the world. If there's a great new product out there, we'll find it.*

EXHIBIT 10.4	Retail Product Offerings
Category	**Approximate Profit Margins**
Maternity Products	40%
Infant Clothing	54%
Nursing Clothes	52%
Breastfeeding Equipment	50%
Gifts	55%
Baby Accessories	47%
Infant Safety & Health	57%
Book Sales	42%
Toys	53%
Preemie Clothing	53%
Skin Care	47%
Hardgoods	44%
Bras	51%
Food & Beverages	10%

Sallie pointed out that in a similar way, she and the nursing staff were always looking for instructors and programs[39] that would distinguish DayOne as a premiere care centre:

> *We search for the best and invite them to teach their classes here. More and more, though, the good ones come looking for us. We have started a lot of fresh and exciting workshops, but almost immediately other places in town copy what we're doing. Sometimes I wonder how long we can keep it fresh and exciting, but then again, that's what we thrive on.*

The DayOne team began its second year of operations finding ways to trim overhead, enhance the customer experience, and refine the retail operations. To further this effort, Andrew tapped New York–based Stephen Cooper—an expert in retailing and finance—to serve as the company's chief operating officer.

By early summer, the company—which in May had been honoured with a "Best of SF" accolade (see Exhibit 10.5)—was signing up a steady stream of new members. Many of those clients were now being referred to the facility by local physicians who were quietly ignoring the sentiments of their hospital administrators. One such referral was Lisa Zoener, a new mom who said that she found out about DayOne from her obstetrician:

I have told lots of people about this place; it's definitely a word-of-mouth type of thing. My husband and I drop a tonne of dough here on baby vitamins and other stuff. DayOne products are definitely higher priced than in other stores, but I'm already here for the classes—and a lot of us feel that buying DayOne products is a way to support what they're trying to do here. I don't find the second floor to be a problem—there is a parking garage right downstairs. It was full today, though.

EXHIBIT 10.5   *SF Weekly* **Best of 2002 Feature**

Best Place to Go After You've Had a Baby

Day One

Your new baby has finally arrived. You're excited, anxious, sleep-deprived, and frankly a little concerned that medical professionals have let you leave the hospital with this newborn. You've forgotten everything you learned in parenting classes, and nothing you were told in childbirth class has happened the way they said it would. In short, you need support, reassurance, help, *something* ... and not from your mother-in-law. Look no more. Strap the little bundle into a carrier and get yourself to the knowledgeable, calm, and compassionate folks at Day One. As a business, the center is an odd mix: a retailer of higher-end baby tools and accessories, a lending library of books and tapes, the home of parenting classes, and a kind of lounge to hang out and nurse, chat, change diapers, or just get the heck out of your living room. As if all of that were not enough, Day One has medical scales to monitor your baby's weight and lactation consultants to help mother and baby get the hang of nursing. An annual membership is only $99, which also gets you a 5 percent discount on merchandise. The center is open seven days a week to fulfill its mission: "to provide new and expectant parents with a single-source, time-efficient solution for the essentials needed during this special and often challenging time of life." A brilliant idea that we're glad has finally arrived.

Details

Address: 3490 California (at Locust), Suite 203, 440-3291,

sfweekly.com | originally published: May 15, 2002

Although he now had actual operating figures, a slew of customer testimonials, and an appropriate town picked out for the second DayOne, Andrew was still unable to raise the money he would need to proceed with those expansion plans. Then, in November, Andrew received a call that he was sure would change everything.

Moving Forward

Andrew checked his cash-on-hand balance. After three years, he had still not taken a dime of salary, and yet he had to smile as he penned this particular company cheque. The cabinetry work at the facility had cost $85,000, and with this disbursement, Andrew would be making good on his promise to pay those guys—not quickly—but in full. There were plenty of others who were still waiting, but in time, they would be paid as well.

The phone rang, and on the other end was a young venture capitalist whose partner's pregnant wife had heard about DayOne from her sister's friend's pediatrician....

Discussion Questions

1. What more can the members of the DayOne team do to build credibility and improve their chances of securing the capital they need to implement the business plan?

2. What other options might be considered for raising the funds needed to move the company ahead?

3. Imagine Andrew has approached you as a potential investor. Has DayOne proven the model yet? What are your concerns? Would you invest?

This case was prepared by Carl Hedberg under the direction of Professor William Bygrave. © Copyright Babson College, 2004. Funding provided by the Frederic C. Hamilton Chair for Free Enterprise. All rights reserved.

NOTES

1. C. K. Prahalad, "Commentary: Aid Is Not the Answer," *Wall Street Journal, August* 31, 2005, A8.

2. Ibid.

3. World Bank, *"New Data Show 1.4 Billion Live on Less Than $1.25 a Day, but Progress Against Poverty Remains Strong,"* August 26, 2008, www.worldbank.org.in/WBSITE/EXTERNAL/COUNTRIES/SOUTHASIAEXT/INDIAEXTN/0,,contentMDK:21880805~pagePK:141137~piPK:141127~theSitePK:295584,00.html.

4. M. Yunus, "Grameen Bank *at a Glance,"* Grameen Bank, 2004, www.grameen-info.org/bank/GBGlance.htm.

5. Microcredit Summit Campaign, www.microcreditsummit.org/involve/page1.htm.

6. John Authers, "Major Victories for Microfinance," *Financial Times, May* 18, 2005, www.ft.com/cms/s/0/44654b98-c739-11d9-a700-00000e2511c8.html#axzz38yLkJg29.

7. Accion International, "Learn More about Microfinance," www.accion.org/moreaboutmicrofinance.

8. Microcredit Summit Campaign, "About the Campaign," www.microcreditsummit.org/about-the-campaign2.html.

9. J. P. Maes L. R. and Reed, *State of the Microcredit Summit Campaign Report 2012,* Microcredit Summit Campaign, www.microcreditsummit.org/resource/46/state-of-the-microcredit-summit.html.

10. R. P. Siegel, "Crowdsourcing Solar is a Bright and Powerful Idea," *Triple Pundit,* April 19, 2013, www.triplepundit.

com/2013/04/crowdsourcing-solar-bright-powerful-idea/.

11 *Entrepreneur,* "Bootstrapping," www.entrepreneur.com/encyclopedia/bootstrapping.

12 D. Misener, "Crowdfunding: The Equity Divide between Borders," *Globe and Mail,* May 17, 2012, www.theglobeandmail.com/report-on-business/small-business/sb-digital/web-strategy/crowdfunding-the-equity-divide-between-borders/article4178757/.

13 D. Tapscott, "The Need to Reinvent Venture Capital," *Huffington Post,* May 10, 2011, www.huffingtonpost.com/don-tapscott/venture-capitalist-investments-_b_860153.html

14 *Businessweek,* "Founders, Family, Friends, and Fools," September 2, 2004, www.businessweek.com/stories/2004-09-02/founders-family-friends-and-fools.

15 W. D. Bygrave and P. D. Reynolds, "Who Finances Startups in the USA? A Comprehensive Study of Informal Investors, 1999–2003," in *Frontiers of Entrepreneurship Research, eds.,* S. Zahra et al. (Wellesley, MA: Babson College, 2004).

16 W. Bygrave and N. Bosma, "Investor Altruism: Financial Returns from Informal Investments in Businesses Owned by Relatives, Friends, and Strangers," in *The Dynamics of Entrepreneurship: Evidence from Global Entrepreneurship Monitor Data, ed. M. Minniti* (London, UK: Oxford University Press, 2011).

17 B. Headd, *"Business Success: Factors Leading to Surviving and Closing Successfully,"* Center for Economic Studies, U.S. Bureau of the Census, Working Paper #CES-WP-01-01, January 2001.

18 V. Kopytoff, "The Number—and Variety—of Business Incubators Is on the Rise," November 6, 2012, www.businessweek.com/articles/2012-11-06/the-number-and-variety-of-business-incubators-is-on-the-rise.

19 D. Mielach, "Business Incubators and Accelerators: Here's the Big Difference," June 19, 2013, www.businessnewsdaily.com/4658-business-incubator-accelerator-difference.html.

20 Ibid.

21 Venture capital data were obtained from the following sources: National Venture Capital Association Yearbooks, European Venture Capital Association Yearbooks, Australian Venture Capital Association, Canadian Venture Capital Association, IVC Research Center (Israel), and South African Venture Capital and Private Equity Association.

22 Classic venture capital is money invested in seed-, early-, startup-, and expansion-stage companies.

23 National Venture Capital Association, *Venture Impact 2009, p. 9;* and PricewaterhouseCoopers, *MoneyTree Report* (based on data from Thomson Reuters). Data updated through 2012.

24 W. D. Bygrave, ed., *The Portable MBA in Entrepreneurship* (New York, NY: Wiley, 1994), 429.

25 National Venture Capital Association, *Venture Impact: The Economic Importance of Venture Capital Backed Companies to the U.S. Economy*, 4th ed., www.nvca.org/index.php?option=com_docman&task=doc_down-load&gid=359&ItemId=93.

26 Canada's Venture Capital & Private Equity Association, *Why Venture Capital Is Essential to the Canadian Economy,* January 2009, https://www.cvca.ca/files/Downloads/CVCA_VC_Impact_Study_Jan_2009_Final_English.pdf.

27 Ibid.

28 W. D. Bygrave, *"Venture Capital Investing: A Resource Exchange Perspective"* (dissertation, Boston University, 1989).

29 National Venture Capital Association, www.nvca.org/def.html.

30 *National Venture Capital Association, Yearbook 2012 (*New York, NY: Thomson Reuters, 2014).

31 Ibid.

32 Canada's Venture Capital & Private Equity Association, "Performance Data—Private Independent Funds," June 18, 2013, www.daicapital.com/media/Q4_12_CVCA_Performance_Private_Release_PI%20%281%29.pdf.

[33] M. Gunther and A. Lashinsky, "Al Gore's Next Act: Planet-Saving VC," *Fortune,* February 12, 2008, http://archive.fortune.com/2007/11/11/news/newsmakers/gore_kleiner.fortune/index.htm?postversion=2007111316.

[34] J. B. Peeters, *"A European Market for Entrepreneurial Companies,"* in *Realizing Investment Value, eds. W. D. Bygrave, M. Hay, and J. B. Peeters* (London, UK: Financial Times/Pitman, 1994).

[35] Excerpted from W. D. Bygrave, "Financing Entrepreneurs and Their Businesses," (speech, Entrepreneurial Advantage of Nations Symposium, New York, April 29, 2003).

[36] D. Tapscott, "The Need to Reinvent Venture Capital," *Huffington Post,* May 10, 2011, www.huffingtonpost.com/don-tapscott/venture-capitalist-investments-_b_860153.html.

[37] National Angel Capital Organization, "Who We Are," http://nacocanada.com/about/who-we-are/.

[38] Personal consulting service was offered at $89/hour, a competitive rate in the Greater Bay area.

[39] In addition to a core of standard classes and support groups dealing with child birth, breastfeeding, and exercise, the centre offered other workshops such as Infant & Child CPR, Infant Massage, Musical Play, First Foods, and Practical First Aid & Safety.

CBC

Canada's Dragons from CBC Television's *Dragons' Den,* a reality show in which aspiring entrepreneurs and their teams pitch their business ideas to the above panel of venture capitalists. From left to right: David Chilton, Michael Werkerle, Arlene Dickinson, Vikram Vij, and Jim Treliving.

RAISING MONEY FOR STARTING AND GROWING BUSINESSES

CHAPTER OUTLINE

Bootstrapping New Ventures
Learning Objective 11.1 Explain how entrepreneurs can bootstrap a new venture.

Valuation
Learning Objective 11.2 Describe the methods of valuing a company.

Financing a New Venture
Learning Objective 11.3 Describe ways to finance a new venture.

Harvesting Investments
Learning Objective 11.4 Describe how investors can harvest or recoup their investment in a venture.

YOU'VE DEVELOPED your business idea and written a business plan in which you have forecast how much money you'll need for your new venture. Now you're wondering where you will get the initial money to start your business and the follow-on capital to grow it. In this chapter, we discuss the mechanics of raising money from investors, including business angels, venture capitalists, and public stock markets. First, we revisit the Jim Poss case, which you studied in Chapter 3, to examine how Jim scraped together the resources to start his business.

Bootstrapping New Ventures

Jim Poss, Bigbelly Solar

During the second year of his MBA studies, Jim enrolled in Babson College's Entrepreneurship Intensity Track, which is for students who want to develop a new venture that they will run full time as soon as they graduate. Jim's first product, the BigBelly®, is an automatic, compacting trash bin powered by solar energy. The innovative BigBelly dramatically cuts emptying frequency and waste handling costs, trash overflow, and litter at outdoor sites with high traffic and high trash volume. The BigBelly's target end users, such as municipalities and outdoor entertainment venues, face massive volumes of daily trash and high collection costs. By the time he graduated in May 2003, Jim had a company, originally named Seahorse Power Company, and a business plan, and he was developing a prototype.

While still in school, Jim won $1,500 worth of legal services at an investors' forum held by Brown Rudnick Berlack Israels, LLP, a leading Boston law firm. Jim used this as part payment for the legal fees associated with his patent application. He invested $10,000 from his savings in BigBelly Solar (BBS) and was awarded $12,500 through the Babson Hatchery Program. He recruited two unpaid Olin College engineering students to help with the design, manufacture, and testing of the prototype. Jim then developed a partnership with Bob Treiber and his firm, Boston Engineering, from which he received a "tonne of work" pro bono and free space in which to assemble and test the prototype. Vail Ski Resort ordered a BigBelly and paid Jim the full purchase price ($5,500) in advance. In fact, he presold nearly half the first production run, and there was a 50% down payment with each order.

Jim's parents invested $12,500. A business angel invested $12,500. Spire Corporation, a 30-year-old publicly traded solar energy company, invested $25,000. Jim won the Babson Business Plan Competition, which brought in $20,000 in cash, which he shared among the team members—the first compensation they had ever received from the project. The award also brought in $40,000 worth of services and lots of publicity. Over the next year, Jim raised $250,000 with an "A" round of private investment from 17 individuals and companies, in amounts ranging from $12,500 to $50,000 with convertible debt. By the fall of 2005, BBS had sold about 100 compactors. In November 2005, Jim closed a round of equity financing.

As of 2012, BigBelly Solar had sold trash compactors to more than 1,000 customers across the United States and 30 other countries. The purchase price of a BigBelly had decreased to $3,900 in 2009 (before any bulk discounts).[1] BBS added wireless SMS text capabilities to its most recent compactors to alert trash collectors when the bins reach capacity. Among BigBelly Solar's most notable customers are the City of Vancouver, the U.S. Forest Service, Harvard University, the Boston Red Sox, the Chicago Transit Authority, and PepsiCo.

Jim Poss is a typical example of how an entrepreneur bootstraps a startup by scraping together resources, including financing, services, material, space, and labour. In Chapter 2, you read about how Steve Jobs and Stephen Wozniak at Apple and Sergey Brin and Larry Page at Google raised their capital. Jobs and Wozniak developed their first computer, Apple I, in a parent's garage and funded it with $1,300 raised by selling Jobs's Volkswagen and Wozniak's calculator. They then found an angel investor, Armas Markkula, Jr., who had recently retired from Intel a wealthy man. Markkula personally invested $91,000 and secured a line of credit from Bank of America. Brin and Page maxed out their credit cards to buy the terabyte of storage that they needed to start Google in Larry's dorm room. Then they raised $100,000 from Andy Bechtolsheim, one of the founders of Sun Microsystems, plus approximately $900,000 from family, friends, and acquaintances. Both Apple and Google subsequently raised venture capital and then went public.

There is a pattern in the initial funding of BigBelly Solar, Apple, and Google that is repeated over and over in almost every startup. The money comes from the Four Fs introduced in Chapter 10: First, the founders themselves dip into their own pockets for the initial capital; next they turn to family, friends, and foolhardy investors (business angels). If their companies grow rapidly and show the potential to be superstars (see Figure 10.13 in Chapter 10), they raise venture capital and have an initial public offering (IPO) or are acquired by a bigger company. The money from family and friends might be a loan or equity or a combination of both, but when it is raised from business angels, from venture capitalists, or with an IPO, it will be equity. Before they raise money in exchange for equity, entrepreneurs must know the value of their companies, so they know how much equity they will have to give up. Before we discuss the mechanics of raising money, let's examine how to value a company.

Valuation

There are four basic ways of valuing a business:

- Earnings capitalization valuation
- Present value of future cash flows
- Market-comparable valuation
- Asset-based valuation

No single method is ideal because the value of a business depends, among other things, on the following:

- Opportunity
- Risk
- Purchaser's financial resources
- Future strategies for the company
- Time horizon of the analysis
- Alternative investments
- Future harvest

The **valuation** of a small, privately held corporation is difficult and uncertain. It is not public, so its equity, unlike that of a public company, has very limited liquidity or probably none at all; hence, there is no way to place a value on its equity based on the price of its shares. What's more, if it is an existing company rather than a startup, its accounting practices may be quirky. For instance, the principals' salaries may be set more by tax considerations than by market value. There may be unusual perquisites for the principals. The assets such as inventory, machinery, equipment, and real estate may be undervalued or overvalued. Goodwill is often worthless. There might be unusual liabilities or even unrecognized liabilities. Perhaps the principals have deferred compensation. Is it a limited liability corporation or a partnership? If so, tax considerations might dominate the accounting.

Just as beauty is in the eyes of the beholder, the value of any startup is in the eyes of the buyer, not in the eyes of the seller. Even though a company's assets may be worth a high

Applying this formula to BFWS:

$$\text{Percentage of Equity} = \frac{4,000,000 \times (1 + 60/100)^5 \times 100}{5,000,000 \times 20} = 42\%$$

There is a lot of uncertainty in this computation: Will BFWS achieve the net income it has forecasted? If so, will it reach it in five years, or longer? Will the price-to-earnings ratio for comparable public companies be 20, or higher? Or will it be lower? Will the window for floating IPOs be open in five years, or will it be shut and delay BFWS's IPO? Any of these contingencies will affect the IRR when the venture capitalists harvest their investment in BFWS. Occasionally, a venture capital–backed company does better than expected. However, more often than not it does not meet its financial forecast; consequently, the actual IRR is usually less than expected.

Asset-Based Valuation Example

Most companies are ordinary rather than glamorous superstars. In this section, we'll examine how to value an ordinary company that does not have the potential to attract venture capital or go public.

Suppose you want to become an entrepreneur by buying out an ordinary business—let's call it XYZ Corporation—that is well established in an industry that is growing about as fast as the overall economy and is an average performer. You will probably hope to buy it for its *modified book value*. The balance sheet for XYZ Corporation is shown in Figure 11.4. It lists the

Assets	As Reported	Adjustments	Restated	Liabilities	As Reported	Adjustments	Restated
Cash	1,500		1,500				
Accounts Receivable (net) (1)	3,300	(100)	3,200	Capitalized Leases	500		500
Inventory (2)	3,419	450	3,869	Long-Term Debt	600		600
TOTAL CURRENT ASSETS	8,219	350	8,569	TOTAL LIABILITIES	4,860	100	4,960
Land and Buildings (3)	1,000	750	1,750				
Machinery & Equipment (4)	750	200	950	SHAREHOLDER EQUITY			
Other Assets (5)	50	(50)	0				
				Capital Shares	500		500
TOTAL ASSETS	10,019	1,250	11,269	Retained Earnings (7)	4,659	1,150	5,809
LIABILITIES							
Accounts Payable	1,700		1,700	TOTAL SHAREHOLDER EQUITY	5,159	1,150	6,309
Short-Term Debt	1,410		1,410				
Accruals (6)	650	100	750				
TOTAL CURRENT				TOTAL LIABILITIES			
LIABILITIES	3,760	100	3,860	& SHAREHOLDER EQUITY	10,019	1,250	11,269

RESTATEMENT NOTES:

(1) Deduct $100 K for uncollectible receivables

(2) LIFO reserve adjustment of inventory to fair market value

(3) MAI appraisal of land & building reflect value of $950 K

(4) Machinery & equipment appraisal reflects current market value of $950 K

(5) Other assets were principally goodwill from expired patents—deduct

(6) Investigation found accurals unrecorded of an additional $100 K

(7) The net pretax effect of change in (1) through (6)

■ **Figure 11.4**

XYZ balance sheet adjusted to reflect fair market value of assets and liabilities ($000s)

assets and liabilities as they are reported on the latest financial statements. The reported book value (total shareholder equity) is $5,159,000. In the second column are the adjustments that the accountants make to bring the assets and liabilities to actual market value; the footnotes explain the adjustments. The third column shows the restated numbers, which are the reported values (column 1) plus the adjustments (column 2). The restated book value is $6,309,000. That is probably what the seller will ask for the company.

Here are the critical questions the buyer should ask before buying an existing business:

- What is the growth rate of the industry?
- By how much is the company's growth rate above or below the industry average?
- What adjustments need to be made to the income statement, statement of cash-flows, and the balance sheet to reflect how the new owners will operate the business?
- How do the adjusted earnings and cash flows compare with industry averages?
- How does the balance sheet compare with industry averages (especially debt to equity)?
- How is the purchase being financed, and how will that change the income statement, statement of cash flows, and balance sheet?
- How will the new owner's strategies affect the company's future performance?

When these questions have been answered, the buyer should make five-year pro forma financial statements and do some **sensitivity analysis** of the critical factors such as sales revenue, cost of sales, and interest and repayment of both the old debt the buyer takes over and any new debt added to help finance the purchase of the business.

As much as valuation is based on financial statements and hard numerical facts, investors themselves, as the buyers of the equity being sold, also heavily influence price. Many factors can influence an investor's valuation of a startup. For instance, previous investments in similar or competing companies could be a deterrent for an investor to put funds toward the new startup. The stage an investor is on in their seven-year investment cycle can also heavily influence their decision. If it is earlier in the cycle, the investor has more available funds and time, which plays in their favour; but if it is later in the cycle they have less time and likely less available funds to offer your company. Finally, how they are personally feeling the day of the meetings or the time during which they need to make the decision can affect the outcome of the investment.

Financing a New Venture

The first financing for your new business will come from you and your partners if you have any. It will be cash from your savings and probably from your credit card. According to the GEM study (see Chapter 10), the average amount of startup financing for a new business is about $60,000, of which about 70% is provided by the entrepreneurs themselves. Perhaps you will also contribute tangible assets such as intellectual capital, like software and patents, and hard assets such as computer equipment. As the company gets under way, you will also be contributing to your company financially by working long hours for substantially less than the salary you could get working for someone else; seven-day work weeks and 12-hour days are not unusual for entrepreneurs starting up businesses.

Before you turn to family and friends for startup money, you should look at all the possibilities of getting funding from other external sources, just as Jim Poss did. Sources might include the following:

- Services at reduced rates (some accounting and laws firms offer reduced fees to startup companies as a way of getting new clients)

- ◙ Vendor financing (getting favourable payment terms from suppliers)
- ◙ Customer financing (getting down payments in advance of delivering goods or services)
- ◙ Reduced rent from a landlord (some landlords, such as Cummings Properties in Massachusetts,[3] offer entrepreneurs reduced rents or deferred rents for the first six months or perhaps a year)
- ◙ An incubator that offers rent and services below market rates
- ◙ Leased instead of purchased equipment
- ◙ Government programs such as the Canada Small Business Financing Program

You should probably also talk to a bank. But keep in mind that banks expect loans to be secured by assets, which include the assets of the business and its owner or of someone else, such as a wealthy parent, who is willing to guarantee the loan with personal assets. In Canada, Futurepreneur Canada and the Business Development Bank of Canada (BDC) can help when you are unable to secure a commercial bank loan through personal or business assets.

Futurepreneur caters to young entrepreneurs between the ages of 18 and 39 with solid business ideas by providing financial support and expert advice.[4] Their programs are built specifically to assist in the entire life cycle of the entrepreneur and the business, including pre-launch support, online business resources, financing, as well as mentoring services.[5] Through a partnership with the BDC, Futurepreneur can provide entrepreneurs with startup financing of $15,000 with the potential to increase to $30,000 depending on the type of business and available funding.[6] Since being established in 1996, Futurepreneur has created more than 23,000 new jobs in Canada through their investments in over 5,600 entrepreneurs across the country.[7]

The Business Development Bank of Canada is a financial institution owned and operated by the Government of Canada.[8] It has helped more than 28,000 businesses reach their full potential by offering financing, venture capital and consulting services to all types of entrepreneurs, with a special focus on businesses in the manufacturing, innovation, exporting, and knowledge-based industries.

An excellent BDC frequently asked questions sheet can be found on their website: www.bdc.ca/EN/about/what-we-do/Pages/faq.aspx#1. Futurepreneur Canada offers more information for interested entrepreneurs at www.futurpreneur.ca/en/about.

Informal Investors

After you have exhausted all the other potential sources of financing, you should turn to **informal investors** for help with the initial funding of your new business. As you read in the preceding chapter, informal investors are by far the biggest source of startup financing after the entrepreneurs themselves. In North America, informal investors provide more than $100 billion per year to startup and young businesses.[9] Approximately 50% of informal investment goes to a relative's business, 28.5% to a friend's or neighbour's, 6.1% to a work colleague's, and 0.4% to a stranger's.[10] In this section, we will look at informal investors who are inexperienced when it comes to funding startup companies; in the next section, we will look at an important subset of informal investors, business angels, who are more sophisticated.

Half of all informal investors expect to get their money back in two years or sooner. This suggests that they regard their money as a short-term loan instead of a long-term equity investment. We are using the term *investment* loosely in this context because it may be more like a loan rather than a formal investment. Whether it is a loan or an equity investment, the downside financial risk in the worst case is the same because if the business fails the informal investors will lose all their money. It is important to make clear to informal investors what the risks are. If you have a business plan, you should give them a copy and ask them to read it. But assume that they probably will not read it thoroughly; hence, you should make sure you have discussed the risks with them. A guiding principle when dealing with family and friends is not to take their money unless they assure you they can afford to lose their entire investment without seriously hurting their standard of living. It may be tempting to borrow from relatives and friends because the interest rate is favourable and the terms of the loan are not as strict as they would be from a bank, but if things go wrong, your relationship might be seriously impaired, perhaps even ended.

How should you treat money that a relative or friend puts into your business in the early days? At the beginning, the business has no operating experience, and it is very uncertain what the outcome will be. Thus, it is extremely difficult—maybe impossible—to place a valuation on the fledgling venture. It is probably better to treat money from friends and family as a loan rather than as an equity investment. As in any loan, you should pay interest, but to conserve cash flow in the first year or two, make the interest payable in a lump sum at the end of the loan rather than in monthly instalments. You should give the loan holders the option of converting the loan into equity during the life of the loan. In that way, they can share in the upside if your company turns out to have star potential, with the possibility of substantial capital gains for the investors.

When you are dealing with relatively small amounts of money from relatives and friends— especially close family such as parents, brothers, and sisters—you may not need a formal loan agreement, particularly if you ask for money when you are under pressure because your business is out of cash. But at a minimum, you should record the loan in writing, with perhaps nothing more than a letter or a note. If you want something more formal, Prosper Marketplace sets up loan agreements for small businesses with informal investors.[11] A documented loan agreement could be important if you subsequently start dealing with professional investors such as sophisticated business angels and venture capitalists.

Crowdfunding. In Canada, in early 2014, six provincial securities regulators announced two proposed exemptions from prospectus requirements that, subject to certain conditions, would allow new companies to raise capital by issuing securities online. The first proposed exemption, the "Start-up Exemption," would allow start-ups and SMEs to raise up to $300,000 every 12 months. They would be allowed to sell securities on crowdfunding portals for up to 90 days. Individual investors can invest up to $1,500 per deal. The Start-up Exemption was adopted in Saskatchewan in 2013 and provincial regulators in British Columbia, Manitoba, Quebec, New Brunswick, and Nova Scotia were seeking public comments until mid-2014. The second proposal, called the "Crowdfunding Exemption," is spearheaded by the Ontario Securities Commission (OSC) and is a collaborative effort between Ontario, Manitoba, Quebec, New Brunswick, and Nova Scotia. The OSC set up a dedicated task force to consult with stakeholders. The Crowdfunding Exemption has higher limits than the Start-up Exemption. It would allow start-ups and SMEs to issue up to $1.5 million in securities through crowdfunding portals every 12 months. Investors could invest up to $2,500 per deal and up to $10,000 per year.[12]

In the United States, the JOBS (Jumpstart Our Business Startups) Act of 2012 and its amendment the Crowdfund Act, enables startups and small and mid-sized businesses to use SEC-approved crowdfunding portals to raise money from anyone online. The crowdfunding provision creates an exemption that will let a company sell up to $1 million in unregistered stock every 12 months to an unlimited number of investors who need not be accredited.

The transaction must go through an intermediary, either a broker or a funding portal. The intermediary must register with the SEC and a self-regulatory organization, make sure investors understand the risks, and conduct a background check on the company's officers, directors, and large shareholders. They are also supposed to make sure investors don't exceed their investing limit. The most one person can invest in all crowdfunded securities combined in one year is the greater of $2,000 or 5% of annual income or net worth (excluding a home) if the person's annual gross income or net worth is less than $100,000, or 10% of annual income or net worth, up to $100,000, if the person's income or net worth is at least $100,000.[13]

Crowdfunding or crowd financing of a business in exchange for equity will be legal as soon as the SEC promulgates its rules, which originally were expected to be announced in January 2013, but were delayed and had not been released by the time of writing.[14]

Crowdfunding has been used to finance not just businesses but a diversity of endeavours including disaster relief, movie production, and political campaigns. An early example was in 1997 when fans underwrote an entire U.S. tour for the British rock group Marillion, raising $60,000 in donations by means of a fan-based Internet campaign. The idea was conceived and managed by fans without any involvement by the band.[15]

Entrepreneurs were using crowdfunding before the JOBS Act but were not allowed to give equity in exchange for cash; instead they usually gave a product or service. For example, Impossible Instant Lab raised $559,232 from 2,509 backers to support the development and production of a device that will "transform your digital iPhone images into real instant photographs that you can touch, caress, and share with friends." In return for their cash, backers were to receive the product at a discounted price or free depending on their level of financing; the estimated delivery date was February 2013. Fundraising commenced on September 10, 2012, and when it closed 28 days later the company had raised more than twice the original goal of $250,000.[16] The shipping date was subsequently rescheduled to August 29, 2013. The company's founder and CEO Doc Florian Kaps "retired" on July 3, 2013.

The Crowdfund Act, when it is put into effect, has the potential to trigger a revolution in the way that entrepreneurs raise funds for their new ventures. Not surprisingly, financial entrepreneurs have already set up crowdfunding platforms in advance of the SEC regulations. Funding platforms will take a percentage of the money that they raise online for a company. Portals such as Crowdfunder.com and WeFunder.com are claiming that they already have millions of dollars committed for investing in startups.[17] But it remains to be seen how many entrepreneurs successfully raise capital through crowdfunding portals. Not all entrepreneurs are enthusiastic about soliciting small investments online. A 2012 survey found that only 9% of *Inc.* 500 CEOs were likely to raise money that way while 72% were not.

In Canada, there are several options available to raise funding through online crowdfunding websites. Websites such as Kickstarter.com, GoFundMe.com, Indiegogo.com, and Kiva.org offer entrepreneurs a platform to raise funds from people around the world who believe in their company, product, or idea.[18] Kickstarter is a popular website used by companies around the world. In 2013 alone, 3 million people pledged US$480 million to fund projects of entrepreneurs.[19] The 3 million people who pledged funding came from 214 different countries and territories, including all seven continents.[20]

Of the many success stories of Kickstarter in 2013, one that made a notable impact on the market was Pebble®, a smart watch developed by the company Pebble Technology.[21] The smart watch is compatible with iPhone and Android smartphones and can receive text messages, emails, calls and social media notifications right on the user's wrist.[22] In April 2012, the Pebble team posted a campaign with an initial goal to raise $100,000 in funding. The company offered backers willing to front $115.00 a discounted watch when they became available. Within a short two hours of the campaign being live on Kickstarter, they had met their initial goal of $100,000, and within six days it became the most funded campaign in Kickstarter history, raising $4.7 million.[23] Serial entrepreneur Mark Cuban (owner of the NBA's Dallas Mavericks, production company Magnolia Pictures, Landmark Theatres, and the AXS TV network) has been known to say that no venture capitalist should invest in a company that isn't on Kickstarter or a similar website.[24] Having a successful campaign on Kickstarter proves to professional investors that there is public interest and faith in the entrepreneur's idea (providing proof of concept).

Business Angels

In the previous chapter, you saw that informal investors are most likely to be entrepreneurs. In the case of the funding of Apple, Google, and many other companies not as famous, such as BigBelly Solar, wealthy entrepreneurs play a key role in the funding of many new ventures. We call those types of informal investors **business angels**.

Business angels fund many more entrepreneurial firms than venture capitalists do.[25] Angels invest in seed-stage and very early-stage companies that are not yet mature enough for formal venture capital or companies that need financing in amounts too small to justify the venture capitalist's costs, including evaluation, due diligence, and legal fees.

We do not know how many wealthy people are business angels, but we do know that securities regulators in Canada define (in part) an "accredited investor" as a person with a net worth in excess of $1 million, or annual income of at least $200,000 in the most recent two years, or combined income with a spouse of $300,000 during those years. Using the United States as an example (given that it has similar definitions regarding accredited investors), it is interesting to note that Forrester Consulting has determined that the number of households in the United States that fit that profile is approximately 630,000.[26] So that is the number of

Angels on Broadway: The Color Purple

The term *angel* was first used in a financial context to describe individual investors who put up money to produce new plays and musicals in the theatre. Putting together a new theatrical production is not unlike starting up a high-potential business. It costs between $10 million and $12 million to produce a Broadway musical. Occasionally, a show is a gigantic success, for example, *Cats*, but more often than not it either fails or is mediocre. Seventy-five percent of Broadway shows fail. It is said that you can make a killing on Broadway, but you can't make a living—in contrast to Wall Street, where you can make a steady living with an occasional killing.

The musical version of *The Color Purple* opened on Broadway in December 2005—eight years after producer, Scott Sanders, first recognized the opportunity of producing a musical stage version of Stephen Spielberg's 1985 movie, in which Oprah Winfrey was one of the stars. Oprah called it one of the greatest experiences of her life. After Sanders persuaded the author, Alice Walker, to allow him to produce a musical based on her 1982 Pulitzer Prize–winning novel, Walker wrote to Oprah in 1997 and asked her "to do a little angel work for the show." But there was no response from Oprah until July 2005.

In the meantime, Sanders had raised almost all the $11 million needed to put the show on Broadway. He put in some of his own money; then in 2002 he raised $2 million from AEG Live—a strategic partner—with a commitment for another $2 million of follow-on investment. With the initial $2 million he produced a month-long trial run of *The Color Purple* in Atlanta to sold-out audiences and standing ovations in 2004. This attracted Roy Furman, a Wall Street financier and frequent Broadway angel, who had worked with Sanders in the past. Furman agreed to raise half of the $11 million that Sanders needed and made a seven-figure investment himself. Furman took an active interest in the production, attending rehearsals and management meetings.

Peter Kramer/Getty Images

Author Alice Walker (L), Producer Scott Sanders, TV personality Oprah Winfrey, and actor LaChanze at the curtain call for *The Color Purple* at the Broadway Theater on December 1, 2005 in New York City.

Then when the show was fully financed, Oprah called. She agreed to allow Sanders to put, "Oprah Winfrey presents *The Color Purple*" on the theatre marquee. To make room for Oprah to invest $1 million, other investors' commitments were trimmed. Oprah also offered to feature a couple of songs from the musical on her hugely successful TV show. A book endorsement by Oprah almost guaranteed a place on the bestsellers list; Sanders and Furman hoped that by featuring *The Color Purple* on her show, Oprah would help to make it a Broadway hit.

Sanders and Furman estimated that if the average audience was 75% of full capacity in the 1,718-seat Broadway Theater, *The Color Purple* would pay back the original investment in 12 months. Five months after its opening, *The Color Purple* was grossing more than $1 million a week, making it one of the top five shows on Broadway. The show recouped its investment within the first year and grossed more than $100 million before it closed on Broadway in 2008.

Sources: "The Making of The Color Purple," Businessweek, November 21, 2005, 105–112.

P. Seitz, "What's a Dream Team's DNA? Businesses Could Learn Some Team Dynamics from Broadway, Scientists," *Investor's Business Daily*, June 6, 2005.

A. Hetrick, "Broadway's *The Color Purple* Will Close Feb. 24," January 24, 2008, www.playbill.com/news/article/114543-Broadways-The-Color-Purple-Will-Close-Feb24.

possible business angels qualified to invest in private offerings governed by American rules. Given that the population of Canada is roughly one-ninth the population of the United States, one could extrapolate that the number of possible business angels qualified to invest in private offerings governed by Canadian rules is approximately 70,000.

 Searching for Business Angels. Most nascent entrepreneurs do not know anyone who is a business angel, so how should they search for one? The good news is that today there are "formal" angel groups, which are angels who have joined together to seek out and invest in young companies. Most of them are wealthy entrepreneurs; some are still running their businesses, while others are retired. Angel investor groups have been around for many years, but they started to proliferate in the late 1990s when it seemed as if everyone was trying to make a fortune by getting in early on investments in Internet-related startups. Although many angels lost a lot of money on their investments when the Internet bubble burst, angel groups continued investing in seed- and early-stage companies, albeit at a much reduced rate.[27]

Angel groups have different ways of selecting potential companies to invest in. A few groups consider only opportunities that are referred to them, but most welcome unsolicited business plans from entrepreneurs. They evaluate the plans and invite the entrepreneurs with the most promising plans to make a presentation to the group at one of their periodic (usually monthly) meetings. A few of those presentations eventually result in investments by some of the angels in the group. Some groups charge the entrepreneurs a fee to make a presentation, and a few even require a fee when an entrepreneur submits a business plan. The size of each investment ranges from less than $100,000 to as much as $2 million—and in a few instances, considerably more.

Important as angel groups have become, they comprise only a few thousand investors compared with hundreds of thousands of business angels who invest on their own. Entrepreneurs are much more likely to raise money from angels who invest individually rather than in packs. Unfortunately, individual business angels are hard to find. Searching for them requires extensive networking. But according to Bill Wetzel, professor emeritus at the University of New Hampshire who pioneered research into angel investing and who started the first angel investment network as the forerunner of ACE-Net

(Angel Capital Investment Network), "Once you find one angel investor, you have probably found another half dozen."[28]

Canada's National Angel Capital Organization (NACO) is a non-profit organization created in 2002 to promote and assist in the creation of the angel community across the country.[29] NACO works with well-educated, high-net-worth individual angels as well as angel groups and has over 2,000 members (angels) in Canada. Country regulations require all angel investors in Canada to be accredited investors. According to the Ontario Securities Commission, there are an estimated 500,000 accredited investors within Canada, but only a small percentage of angels invest in startups. It is estimated that angels invest between $500 million and $1 billion annually in Canadian companies.[30]

Canadian angels are making significant contributions to the rapid growth of the country's startup ecosystem. Some angels choose to invest alone, whereas others have angel groups and make investments together. There are over 30 angel groups (or networks) within Canada, with the majority being NACO members.

Consider how other entrepreneurs found business angels. Steve Jobs and Stephen Wozniak found Armas Markkula through an introduction by a venture capitalist who looked at Apple and decided it was too early for him to invest. Sergey Brin and Larry Page were introduced to Andy Bechtolsheim by a Stanford University faculty member. Jim Poss worked for Spire Corporation and got to know Roger Little, founder and CEO of Spire and a leading expert on solar power; he met another of his angel investors at a wind energy conference sponsored by Brown Rudnick. When a leader in an industry related to the one the new company is entering becomes a business angel, it sends an important signal to other potential investors. For instance, once Andy Bechtolsheim had invested in Google, Brin and Page soon put together $1 million of funding. And Jim Poss's parents said they would invest only if Roger Little invested.

Types of Business Angels. Business angels range from silent investors who sit back and wait patiently for results to others who want to be involved in the operations of the company as a part-time consultant or as a full-time partner. Richard Bendis classifies business angels in the following categories: entrepreneurial, corporate, professional, enthusiast, and micromanagement.[31]

Entrepreneurial angels have started their own businesses and are looking to invest in new businesses. Some have realized substantial capital gains by taking their companies public or merging them with other companies. Others are still running their businesses full time and have sufficient income to be business angels. In general, entrepreneurial angels are the most valuable to the new venture because they are usually knowledgeable about the industry, and just as important, they have built substantial businesses from the ground up and so understand the challenges that entrepreneurs face. They can be invaluable advisors and mentors. Armas "Mike" Markkula is a famous example of a business angel who made his fortune in two entrepreneurial companies, first Fairchild and then Intel. He had "retired" at the age of 38 when Steve Jobs and Stephen Wozniak were introduced to him. He invested in Apple; worked with Steve Jobs to write Apple's first business plan; secured a bank line of credit; helped raise venture capital; recruited Michael Scott, Apple's first president; and then became president himself from 1981 to 1983. According to Stephen Wozniak, "Steve [Jobs] and I get a lot of credit, but Mike Markkula was probably more responsible for our early success, and you never hear about him."[32]

Corporate angels are managers of larger corporations who invest from their savings and current income. Some are looking to invest in a startup and become part of the full-time management team. Corporate angels who have built their careers in big, multinational corporations can be a problem for a neophyte entrepreneur because they know a lot about managing companies with vast resources but have never worked in a small company with limited resources. Here is an example of what might go wrong: A fish-importing wholesaler was started and run by two young men. The company grew fast, but it ran out of working capital. Two angels, one of them a marketing executive with a huge multinational food company, invested $500,000 on condition that the young company hire the marketing executive as its marketing/sales vice-president. Very soon there was a clash of cultures. The founders continued to work 12-hour days, while the new vice-president was travelling first class and staying in fancy hotels when he made sales trips. Within a year, the business angels took control of the company. The two founders left, and a year later it closed its doors.

Professional angels are doctors, dentists, lawyers, accountants, consultants, and even professors who have substantial savings and incomes and invest some of their money in startups. Generally they are silent partners, although a few of them, especially consultants, expect to be retained by the company as paid advisors.

Enthusiast angels are retired or semiretired entrepreneurs and executives who are wealthy enough to invest in startups as a hobby. It is a way for them to stay involved in business without any day-to-day responsibilities. They are usually passive investors who invest relatively small amounts in several companies.

Micromanagement angels are entrepreneurs who have been successful with their own companies and have strong views on how the companies they invest in should be run. They want to be a director or a member of the board of advisors and get regular updates on the operations of the company. They do not hesitate to intervene in the running of the business if it does not perform as expected.

There is no ideal type of business angel. And in general, most entrepreneurs cannot pick and choose because it is so hard to find business angels who are prepared to invest. But just as a wise angel will carefully investigate the entrepreneur before investing, likewise a smart entrepreneur will find out as much as possible about a potential business angel. There is probably no better source of information than other entrepreneurs in whom the angel has previously invested. Ask the business angel whether he or she has invested in other entrepreneurs and whether you may talk with them.

Putting Together a Round of Angel Investment. If you're raising a round of investment from business angels, you'll need a lawyer knowledgeable in this area because there are various government rules that you need to comply with.[33] The first thing you'll want to do is place a value on your startup. Valuation of a seed-stage company is more art than science. It's also very subjective, with entrepreneurs placing a substantially higher value on their company than business angels will. Informed business angels will determine the value based on similar deals made by other angels and venture capital firms. The comparable-market valuation method will provide a back-of-the-envelope estimate to see whether the company has a chance of meeting the business angel's required return.

In general, business angels are satisfied with a lower return than venture capitalists are because, unlike venture capitalists, they have only minimal operating costs and they do not have to pay themselves carried interest on any capital gains. You saw in Chapter 10 that venture capitalists charge as much as 3% per year on the money they invest, and on top of that they deduct carried interest of 20%—sometimes more—from the capital gain they pass on to their investors. So, to produce a return of 25% for their investors, venture capitalists need to get a return of 35% or more from their investment portfolio. According to Fred Wainwright, business angels expect an IRR of 15% to 25%, with a payback time between five and seven years.[34] A Massachusetts Institute of Technology (MIT) study found that business angels expected returns between 3:1 and 10:1 on their investments and that actual returns ranged from losses on 32% of their investments to higher than 10:1 on 23% of investments.[35] The same MIT study found that business angels were evenly split between preferring IPOs and acquisitions as their exit strategy; none preferred a buyback. In practice, 27% of business angel investments ended with an IPO, 35% with an acquisition, 5% with a buyback, and 32% were losses.

While financial returns are important to business angels, they also invest for nonfinancial reasons. These include a desire to give back and mentor budding entrepreneurs, to be involved in startups without total immersion, to have fun, to be part of a network of other business angels, to stay abreast of new commercial developments, to be involved with the development of products and services that benefit society, and to invest in entrepreneurs without the pressure of being a full-time venture capitalist.[36]

Most angel investments are for preferred shares convertible into common shares on a 1-to-1 ratio. Preferred shares give investors priority rights over founders' common shares, which relates to liquidation and voting. The potential problem with convertible preferred shares is that it sets a valuation on the shares at the first round. If that valuation turns out to be higher than the venture capitalist's valuation at the second round, negotiations between the venture capitalist and the entrepreneur will be difficult. The shortfall might even be a deal breaker.

Jim Poss placed a pre-money valuation of $2.5 million on BigBelly Solar when he was raising his first round of funding from business angels. He raised $250,000, so the post-money valuation was $2.75 million. Investors would have owned 9.1% (250,000/2,750,000 × 100%) of the equity if Jim had issued shares. Instead, he issued convertible debt. Some seed-stage companies that expect to get venture capital investment in later rounds of financing use convertible debt rather than convertible preferred shares. **Convertible debt** is a bridge loan that converts to equity at the next round of investment, assuming that it is an equity round. Convertible debt securities allow the next-round investors, who are usually venture capitalists, to set the value of the company and provide the first-round angel investors with a discount. Business angels would like to get a 30% discount, but actual discounts range from 10% to 30%. Convertible debt has an advantage over convertible preferred shares because it reduces or eliminates squabbling over the valuation between venture capitalists and the entrepreneur on behalf of the angels.[37]

The major conditions of a proposed deal are spelled out in a term sheet. Three examples of business angel term sheets are found in *Venture Support Systems Project: Angel Investors*.[38]

Venture Capital

In 2013, Canada's venture capital market experienced significant increases, especially in the amount invested in innovative technology companies.[39] Canadian venture capitalists' investments totalled over $2 billion as of December 31, 2013. This was a 31% increase from the $1.5 billion that was invested in 2012.[40] Ontario showed the most increase in invested dollars per province with venture capitalists investing $676 million in 2013 (35% of the total amount invested in Canada).[41]

Venture capital is almost always invested in companies that are already in business and have demonstrated the potential to become stars or, better yet, superstars in their industry. Nothing excites **venture capitalists** more than a company with a product or service that is already being bought by satisfied customers. Venture capital accelerates the commercialization of new products and services; it seldom pays for the initial development of concepts.

Four Types of Venture Capital. There are four types of venture capital:

- *Seed venture capitalists*: When an entrepreneur is in the setup stage of their business they look for a venture capitalist for seed funding on their new idea or new business plan.

- *Early venture capitalists*: The entrepreneur is beginning to set up the organization and build the management team; a thorough market analysis and business plan has to be analyzed by the venture capitalist to ensure the company has passed the breakeven point and is increasing revenue as time progresses.

◉ *Late venture capitalists*: The company has established itself in the marketplace, built its customer base, and is seeking venture capitalists to invest so that it can expand; this is the last stage before the company considers launching an IPO.

◉ *Venture debt*: Venture debt is financing for companies that lack assets or cash flow, making them unable to get traditional debt financing from a bank; it is a form of risk capital that is often less costly than traditional equity and is normally offered in a three-year term with options of company shares.[42]

Five Biggest Mistakes Made when Pitching to Venture Capitalists. The following are the five biggest mistakes made by entrepreneurs when pitching to venture capitalists:

1. *Lack of nondisclosure agreement (NDA):* Providing a nondisclosure agreement indicates to investors that the entrepreneur and his or her management team is fully prepared and is serious when talking about their business or idea(s).

2. *Top-down versus bottom-up hiring:* To grow the business properly, investors want to know that your management team is willing to grow and progress with the stages of the business.

3. *Saying there is no competition:* Every startup has competition, whether it be direct or indirect; if an entrepreneur says there is no competition it indicates a lack of proper research within the market and industry, effectively indicating that the entrepreneur is not ready to accept funding.

4. *No proof of concept or traction:* Having a launched campaign on Kickstarter provides proof of concept and customer buy-in to any potential investor; if no one around the world is willing to invest in the idea, then why would the investor want to provide funding? Raising funding on Kickstarter (or a similar crowdfunding website) not only proves the concept is valid, it also indicates to the investor that there is a customer base for the business or idea.

5. *Outside of the one-hour fly rule:* A venture capitalist isn't likely to invest in a company that is more than a one-hour flight away from his or her home base; the investor needs to have easy access to the entrepreneur and the company to ensure they are making progress and to be exposed to the company.

Candidates for Venture Capital

Here, in order of importance, are the six top factors venture capitalists look at when evaluating a candidate for investment:[43]

1. Management team
2. Target market
3. Product or service
4. Competitive positioning
5. Financial returns
6. Business plan

Management Team. We've said that the crucial ingredients for entrepreneurial success are a superb entrepreneur with a first-rate management team (that covers all three points of the talent triangle) and an excellent market opportunity.

Not only does the team need to be composed of people with business acumen, operational knowledge, and domain knowledge (the talent triangle), but they also need to have a good working relationship. Personality attributes as well as past work experience can determine how the management team communicates with each other. If the management team members are friends or family outside of the business, it is important for everyone involved to recognize that a *working* relationship is different than a *personal* relationship—that is, you have to adopt a "business isn't personal" approach. Management teams not only have to communicate well, but they also need to be able to challenge each other to achieve decisions that are for the better of the business. It is okay for management team members to butt heads when brainstorming or making decisions, because it forces them to agree on the best possible outcome for the company.

Entrepreneurs should have most of the startup team identified before they approach venture capitalists. If they are sufficiently impressed with the progress a startup company has made, venture capitalists will sometimes help recruit a key member of the team. They will even help recruit a new CEO if they have reservations about the lead entrepreneur's ability to build a rapidly growing company with the potential to go public. The best venture capitalists have extensive contacts with potential candidates for management positions in their portfolio companies.

Target Market. The target market should be fragmented, accessible, and growing rapidly. The Internet triggered a stampede of venture capital investing in the late 1990s because it promised to become a huge market with many different segments; there were no dominant players in the new segments, and the segments were readily accessible to new entrants.

Market traction is considered to be quantitative evidence of market demand, often shown through sales and signed contracts with clients. Market traction can provide proof that there are customers that want your product, convince investors that there is potential for profitability, revenues, further development, and so on.

Product/Service. The product or service should be better than competing products or services, and it should be protected with patents or copyrights, as appropriate. It does not have to be the first product in its market segment. For example, Google was not the first Web search engine; it was simply superior to the existing ones. Again, it is important to stress that a company with a working prototype—or better yet, satisfied customers—has a much better chance of raising venture capital than does an entrepreneur with just an idea and a business plan.

Competitive Positioning. Venture capitalists want to see that there is no dominant competitor in the market niche, distribution channels are open, and the company has an experienced marketing manager with expert knowledge of the market segment. SolidWorks positioned its CAD/CAM software in a niche where it was difficult for well-established competitors, especially Parametric Technology, to move in without cannibalizing their business models.

> "[T]here's plenty of technology, market opportunity, and venture capital, but too few great entrepreneurs and teams [in 2004]."
>
> —*John Doerr, legendary venture capitalist, Kleiner Perkins Caufield & Byers (www.siliconbeat.com/entries/2004/11/13/qa_with_kleiner_perkins_caufield_byers.html)*

Financial Returns. The potential financial return is important, but classic venture capital does not depend on sophisticated financial computations. Venture capitalists have a rule of thumb for early- and expansion-stage companies—they will invest only if the company has the potential to return at least seven times their investment in five years—in venture capital jargon, "seven x" in five years. A 7x return in five years produces an IRR of 47.6%; a 10x return in five years produces an IRR of 58.5%.

Scalability is also important. Scalability refers to the company's potential to earn revenue faster than the growth of their related costs.[44] Facebook is a great example of a scalable business model. Facebook adds thousands of new users each day, but the related costs of each new member does not increase very much because of how they operate their online platform.[45]

Business Plan. Every entrepreneur seeking money from business angels or professional venture capitalists must have a competent written business plan. But no matter how good a business plan may be, it will not impress investors nearly as much as a product or service that is already being sold to customers. Too many entrepreneurs spend too much effort refining and polishing their business plans rather than implementing their businesses. As we discussed in Chapter 8, the process of working your way through a business plan is important. An entrepreneur and his or her team learn so much throughout the process that it becomes much more valuable than the results. It is important that the management team remain focused on the key issues outlined in the business plan to allow for development and growth.

Ideal Candidates for Venture Capital

The *ideal* candidate for a first round of venture capital meets the following criteria:

- CEO/lead entrepreneur has significant management and entrepreneurial experience with demonstrated ability to manage a rapidly growing company in a fast-paced industry segment.
- Vice-president of engineering is recognized as a star in the industry (if it is a technology-based business).
- Vice-president of marketing has a proven track record.
- Some members of the top management team have worked together before.
- The product or service is better than those of its competitors.
- Intellectual capital such as patents and copyrights is protected.
- The market segment is fragmented, growing rapidly, and expected to be big.
- There are no dominant competitors.
- The company has satisfied customers.
- The company projects sales of $50 million in five years.
- The gross income margin is expected to be better than 60%, with a net income margin better than 10%.
- The amount of investment is between $5 million and $10 million.
- The company has the potential to go public in five years.
- Potential return of 7x or higher.
- IRR of 60% or higher.

Actual Venture Capital–Backed Companies

Venture capital–backed companies that have IPOs are the cream of the crop, so by examining profiles of companies at the time they go public, we can see how the best companies measure up to the ideal. Figure 11.5 shows the results of a study of 122 venture-backed companies that went public in the years 1994–1997,[46] when the stock market indices were rising but before the Internet bubble (which ran from the end of 1997 to the beginning of 2001).

The management of those companies came close to the ideal. For instance, half of the top management teams had a combined 114 years of experience or more. Seventy-one percent of the companies had at least one founder with previous startup experience. And in about two-thirds of the companies, two or more founders had worked together before starting their present venture.

Market and operating performance at the time of the IPO was quite different among the industry segments (see Figure 11.5). The industry segments appear in order of their maturity

	Medians			
	Internet	**Software**	**Hardware**	**Semiconductor**
Marketing and Operations				
Market Growth Rate	135.7%	23.5%	37.5%	15.5%
Annual Sales Growth Trend (all years)	87.0%	54.3%	55.7%	24.7%
Sales Growth Trend (12 months)	93.3%	45.9%	54.3%	30.1%
Annualized Sales Revenue	$9,720,000	$23,396,000	$27,268,000	$39,940,000
Gross Margin	72.7%	75.6%	39.1%	42.2%
Profit Margin	−36.7%	3.4%	−0.5%	7.9%
Net Income (last year)	($2,414,530)	$308,000	($639,000)	$1,495,000
Net Income (last quarter annualized)	($3,462,921)	$1,644,000	$2,140,000	$3,226,000
R&D Ratio	27.0%	18.4%	14.5%	14.6%
# of Employees	124	134	92	213
Financial				
IRR	506.9%	124.8%	148.0%	30.5%
Times Return	7.16	6.67	10.71	4.94
Years from 1st VC Investment to IPO	0.96	2.53	4.04	5.00
Time from Incorporation to IPO	5	8	7	11
Price/Share 1st Round of VC	$1.25	$1.50	$1.13	$2.79
IPO Price	$14	$12	$10	$11
P/E Ratio	70	54	32	26
Size of IPO	$34,000,000	$27,600,000	$22,320,000	$29,130,000
Market Capitalization after IPO	$163,488,290	$105,510,812	$89,244,768	$77,468,542

Figure 11.5

Venture capital–backed public companies

from left to right, with the Internet being the least mature and the semiconductor the most mature. Much of the difference between companies in the four industries is explained by the maturity of their industry segment. The Internet market segments were growing much faster than were the semiconductor ones, as was the annual growth rate of sales revenue. There was a big difference between the characteristics of Internet and semiconductor companies.

Internet companies had the least sales revenue at the time of the IPO and semiconductor companies the most. None of the four segments attained the ideal of at least $50 million in annual sales revenue. Not one of the industry segments met the net income margin of at least 10% prescribed for the ideal, but the Internet and software companies exceeded the gross margin requirement of at least 60%, whereas the hardware and semiconductor companies fell short. In all segments except the Internet, the annualized net income improved dramatically in the quarter before the IPO.

However, despite the shortcomings on sales revenue and net income, the venture capitalists met their hoped-for times return on the first round of venture capital in all industries except semiconductors. And their IRR handily topped their expectations. The median IRR for Internet companies was a whopping 507% because they went public only one year after they received their first round of venture capital. In contrast, five years elapsed for semiconductor companies between the first round of venture capital and the IPO. So, although the times return in the semiconductor segment was almost 5 compared with just over 7 in the Internet segment, the IRR in semiconductors was only 30.5% because the longer an investment is held, the lower the IRR. The P/E ratios were 70 for the Internet companies that were profitable, 54 for software, 32 for hardware, and 26 for semiconductors. The differences in the P/E ratios mainly explain the differences in market capitalization among the different industry segments.

In Canada, it is expected that there will be a revival of initial public offerings, especially in the technology industry. Canadian-owned and -operated companies like Hootsuite (based out of Vancouver) and Shopify (based out of Ottawa) have been identified as companies ready to go public within the next two years.[47] IIt is forecasted that more than US$400 million will be raised by Canadian IPOs in 2014, which is the most raised within the industry over the past decade.[48] Many Canadian investors are looking to technology-based companies because of their strong growth within the past three years. HootSuite helps companies manage their social media platforms as well as monitors marketing efforts on websites such as Facebook and Twitter. Shopify has had a goal of going public since day one.[49] Although it is unknown when it will announce that it is going public, it is expected in the near future.

Many Canadian companies have had successful IPOs in the past, such as AlarmForce Industries, Canadian Tire Corporation, Air Canada, Boston Pizza, Indigo Books and Music, Tim Hortons, Rogers Communications, WestJet, and many more.[50] You can find a full list of all the companies traded on the Toronto Stock Exchange at www.tmx.com/HttpController? GetPage=ListedCompaniesViewPage&Language=en&Market=T.

What does this mean for entrepreneurs who are seeking venture capital? First, there is not one set of ideal criteria for a company, but there are tendencies based on the industry sector. Second, the management team must be excellent. Third, the faster the growth of the industry and the growth of the company, the more likely it is to get the attention of venture capitalists. Fourth, entrepreneurs should focus on sales growth rather than profitability in the first few years and then show a profitability spurt in the year before the IPO. Fifth, on average, companies are several years old and have developed products or services before they get their first venture capital investment.

Dealing with Venture Capitalists

The first big challenge for an entrepreneur is reaching a venture capitalist. It is easy to get names and contact information for almost every venture capital firm from the Internet and subscription data sources such as Canada's Venture Capital and Private Equity Association (CVCA).[51] However, venture capital firms pay much more attention to entrepreneurs who are referred to them than to unsolicited business plans that arrive by mail or email. Entrepreneurs are referred to venture capitalists by accountants, lawyers, bankers, other entrepreneurs, consultants, professors, business angels, and anyone else in contact with venture capitalists. But most of them are reluctant to recommend an entrepreneur to a venture capitalist unless they are confident that the entrepreneur is a good candidate for venture capital.

Entrepreneurs should be wary of **finders** who offer to raise venture capital for the entrepreneur. Most venture capitalists do not like dealing with finders because they charge the company a fee based on the amount of money raised—a fee that comes out of the money the venture capitalists invest in the company. What's more, it's the entrepreneur, not the finder, who has to deal with the venture capitalists.

If the entrepreneur is fortunate enough to find a venture capitalist who would like to learn more about the new business, a meeting will take place at either the company's or the venture capital firm's office. The first meeting is usually an informal discussion of the business with one of the partners of the venture capital firm. If the partner decides to pursue the opportunity, he or she will discuss it with more of the partners; if they like the opportunity, they will invite the entrepreneur to make a formal presentation to several partners in the firm. This meeting is the crucial one, so it is important to make as good a presentation as possible. Not only are the venture capital partners assessing the company and its product or service, but they are also carefully scrutinizing the entrepreneur and other team members to see whether they have the right stuff to build a company that can go public.

If the venture capital partners like what they see and hear at this meeting, the firm will pursue the entrepreneur with the intent to invest and will begin its due diligence on the entrepreneur, other team members, and the company. Entrepreneurs who get to this stage will be evaluated as never before in their lives. It is not unusual for a venture capital firm to check dozens of references on the entrepreneur. Any suggestion of dubious conduct by the entrepreneur will be investigated. After all, the entrepreneur is asking the venture capital firm to trust him or her with several million dollars that in most cases is not secured by any collateral. All entrepreneurs should get a copy of their credit reports and be prepared to explain any delinquencies.

Entrepreneurs who get to this stage may be wondering whether the venture capital firm is the right one for them and be tempted to approach other venture capital firms to see what they might offer. But instead, they should conduct due diligence on the venture capital firm. Ask for a list of the entrepreneurs the firm has invested in and permission to speak with them. Here are some things to look for.

Value Added. The best venture capitalists bring more than money to their portfolio companies.[52] They bring what they call **value added**, which includes help with recruiting key members of management, strategic advice, industry contacts, and professional contacts such as accountants, lawyers, entrepreneurs, consultants, other venture capitalists, commercial bankers, and investment bankers.

Patience. Some venture capital firms, especially newer ones with relatively inexperienced partners, are more likely to get impatient when a portfolio company fails to meet expectations. Studies of venture capital–backed companies that have not yet gone public or been acquired find that approximately 50% to 60% of them have changed CEOs at some time after the first round of venture capital;[53] only 18% of those that have had IPOs have changed CEOs.[54] Another indication of lack of patience is a venture capital firm quick to invoke covenants in the investment agreement, which contains a couple of hundred pages. There are all manner of covenants in those agreements, and it is not unusual for a company to violate one or perhaps more. An experienced venture capitalist will usually waive a covenant unless the violation is so severe that it jeopardizes the viability of the company.

VENTURE CAPITAL IS "RELATIONSHIP" CAPITAL

Brook Byers and Ray Lane, talking about how Kleiner Perkins Caufield & Byers helps entrepreneurs:[i]

Brook Byers (referring to Kleiner Perkins Caufield & Byers's network): It's not keiretsu, it's relationship capital.

Ray Lane: Whether you call it a network, a Rolodex, keiretsu, or whatever, it is something that entrepreneurs crave, because they're looking for help. As Brook said, money is not a differentiator in our business, but they're looking for help. Either you have knowledge in their domain, and you can help them get from startup to a company that actually gets something in the market, or you help them scale through relationships. In this world, at least in the enterprise world, it helps to know somebody.

[i] From "Q&A with Kleiner Perkins Caufield & Byers," SiliconBeat, www.siliconbeat.com/entries/2004/11/13/qa_with_kleiner_perkins_caufield_byers.html.

Deep Pockets. Will the firm have enough money to invest in follow-on rounds of venture capital if the company needs it? Venture capital firms that have been in business for a long time have established a reputation of producing good returns for their limited partners, so they are able to raise new funds from time to time. In contrast, a young venture capital firm with only one small fund without a proven track record of producing satisfactory returns for its limited partners will have difficulty raising a second fund.

Dry Powder. Dry powder refers to the money that is held back by a venture capitalist for what could be considered "emergency expenses." It allows the venture capitalist to have available funds on hand to cover any future purchases of assets or equity.[55] Many investors keep dry powder in their pockets to make sure they are not spending their last dollar on a single investment.

Board of Directors. Does the venture capitalist sit on the board and regularly attend meetings? How often does the board meet? And how many boards does the venture capitalist serve on? A rule of thumb is that a venture capitalist should not be on more than half a dozen boards of portfolio companies.

Accessibility. Is the venture capitalist readily available when the entrepreneur needs advice? Conversely, does the venture capitalist interfere too much in the day-to-day running of the company?

Negotiating the Deal

The valuation of the company is probably the biggest issue to be negotiated. Generally, the entrepreneur's valuation is higher than the venture capitalist's. Entrepreneurs can make valuations of the company based on computations like the one earlier in this chapter for BFWS; they can also talk to other entrepreneurs who have recently received venture capital. In general, venture capitalists have more information about pricing than entrepreneurs do because they know the valuations of similar deals that have been recently completed, and those will be the basis for the valuation.

Let's return to BFWS. The entrepreneur's calculations show that the venture capital firm will be looking for 42% of the equity after it has put in its $4 million. Hence, the company will be worth $9.42 million ($4 million/0.42) after the money has been invested—what is called the **post-money valuation**. The **pre-money valuation** is thus $5.42 million ($9.42 million – $4 million).

The venture capitalist knows that comparable deals have been valued at $4 million pre-money. So the venture capitalist needs 50% of the equity post-money. After negotiations, the entrepreneur and the venture capitalist settle on a pre-money valuation of $4.5 million for BFWS, which means that the venture capitalist will get 47.1% of the equity with a post-money valuation of $8.5 million, and the entrepreneurs and any angel investors who have already put money into BFWS will be left with 52.9%. The venture capitalists will expect that a pool of stock, about 15% of the issue, will be reserved for key employees who will be hired in the future.

The next step is for the venture capitalist to provide a **term sheet** listing the main conditions of the deal. (You can find samples on the Web.[56]) The term sheet will specify how much money the venture capital firm is investing, how much equity it is getting, a detailed listing of all the shares issued or reserved for share options both before the venture capital is invested and after. The venture capitalists will in almost every case get convertible preferred shares. The rights of the preferred shares will be spelled out; they will include dividend provisions, liquidation preferences, conversion rights (usually one preferred shares converts to one common share), antidilution provisions, voting rights, and protective provisions.

The term sheet will also have clauses covering information rights, such as a requirement for the company to supply timely unaudited quarterly and audited annual financial statements, board membership, a description of how the venture capital will be used, employment agreements, share registration rights, and terms under which management can sell shares privately. It will also specify the date when the deal will close.

Term sheet provisions are subject to negotiation. But the sheet will contain a date and time when the venture capitalist's offer will expire unless the entrepreneur has accepted the offer in writing.

Follow-On Rounds of Venture Capital

It is quite likely that there will be subsequent rounds of venture capital. In 2012, for instance, 1,163 companies received first-round venture capital financing and 2,535 received follow-on financing in the United States. Let's see what might happen in a second round of financing for BFWS.

Two years after the first round of venture capital, BFWS has met its milestones set out in its business plan, so the venture capitalists are happy. They had expected that the company would go public to raise more money, but the IPO window is closed (as it was in 2002 and 2003, after the Internet bubble burst and investors lost their appetite for IPO stocks not only of Internet-related companies but also of information technology companies in general). BFWS estimates it needs $6 million to stay on its rapid-growth trajectory for the next two years, when it hopes the IPO window will again be open.

When a company has met its milestones, its valuation has increased. It's not unusual for venture capitalists to agree to a valuation three times what it was at the first round. BFWS will be talking both to its present venture capitalists, who will be eager to invest in a second round, and to other venture capitalists so as to get more than one valuation. We'll assume the deal will be struck at a pre-money valuation three times the post-money valuation of the first round, or $25.5 million (3 × $8.5 million). The post-money valuation will be $31.5 million. So the venture capitalist will get an additional 19% of the equity for his $6 million investment at the second round of financing. If all goes well and the IPO window opens up during the next two years, BFWS expects to go public.

Harvesting Investments

When business angels or venture capitalists put money into a business, there has to be a way they can realize their investments at a future date. This is called the exit or **harvest** for the investor. There are three ways to exit an investment: an **initial public offering**, an acquisition, or a buyback of the investor's shares by the company itself. We've mentioned that most investors prefer an IPO because it produces the highest valuation in most cases—but not in every case. An acquisition is the second choice, and a buyback is a distant third because in almost every instance it produces a mediocre return.

One of the questions neophyte entrepreneurs seeking external equity financing most often ask is, "Can I buy back the investors' equity?" The answer is, "In principle yes, but in practice it is extremely unlikely." Buybacks are rare because a successful and rapidly growing company needs all the cash it can get just to keep on its growth trajectory. It has no free cash to buy out its external investors. A firm doing a buyback is more likely to be one of the living dead for which an IPO or acquisition is not feasible, but somehow the company arranges a refinancing in which it buys back the shares owned by the original investors. Sometimes a venture capital agreement includes a redemption (buyback) clause that allows the venture capital firm to exit its investment by selling it back to the company at a premium if an IPO or acquisition does not occur within a specified time period.

Initial Public Offering

Only a miniscule number of companies raise money with a firm commitment IPO.[57] Over the period 2009–2012, 189 venture capital–backed companies went public, which averages out at only 47 IPOs per year.[58] (In 2011, 35% of all IPOs were by venture capital–backed companies.) As we saw in the previous chapter, roughly 7% of companies backed with venture capital have gone public since 1970. Figure 11.6 shows the funding filters that most venture capital–backed companies must pass through to get to an IPO.

Without doubt, IPOs are glamorous and generally yield the biggest returns for the pre-IPO investors, but in the long run they're not always satisfactory for the entrepreneurs and the management team for a variety of reasons. Granted, many entrepreneurs such as Bill Gates (Microsoft), Larry Ellison (Oracle), Robert Noyce and Gordon Moore (Intel), Bernie Marcus

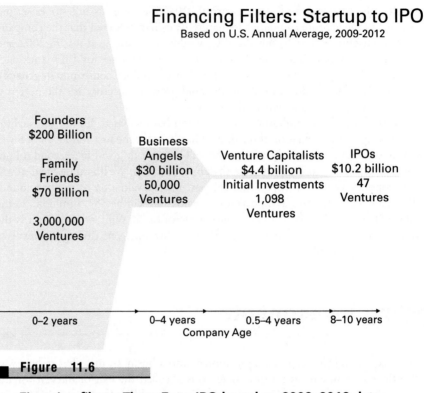

Figure 11.6

Financing filters: Three Fs to IPO based on 2009–2012 data

and Arthur Blank (Home Depot), and Sergey Brin and Larry Page (Google) took their companies public and never looked back, but that is not always the case.

Joey Crugnale took his small chain of brick-oven pizza restaurants, Bertucci's, public in 1991 at $13 per share. But he was unable to satisfy Wall Street's appetite for ever-increasing sales and earnings. By 1998, Bertucci's shares, which at one time peaked at $25, were languishing at $6. Crugnale decided that he wanted to take his company private so that he would be free from the continual scrutiny of investors. He made an offer to buy out the investors for $8 per share. He knew that, once he proposed to buy back the company, there was a possibility other companies might bid for it, but he assumed that was unlikely because he founded the company and he ran it. He soon found out his assumption was wrong. Quite unexpectedly, New England Restaurant Company handily topped his offer with a bid of $10.50 per share. Crugnale agonized over it but decided not to make a counteroffer. He walked away from Bertucci's a wealthy man at 46, but with a feeling of loss because he was no longer running the business he had built from scratch into a chain of 84 restaurants in 11 states and the District of Columbia. He sometimes regrets taking Bertucci's public instead of keeping the company private and building his personal wealth from the cash flow that his restaurants were generating.

Crugnale has subsequently started Cajun-Mexican, Latin-fish, and Italian restaurants— each one with several outlets—hoping to repeat his success with Bertucci's. So far it has eluded him. But he consoles himself with the knowledge that it took several years before Bertucci's was a hit. However, one thing he knows for sure is that his restaurants will not go public. "I have no investors, I own everything myself, so I don't have to answer to anybody . . . There are no restrictions, and I like that freedom."[59]

Pros and Cons of an IPO

The following are the upsides of going public.

Financing. The principal reason for a public offering is to raise a substantial amount of money that does not have to be repaid. For example, the average amount of money raised by the 189 venture capital–backed companies that floated IPOs during the period 2009–2012 was $215 million. The average post-money valuation of the companies that went public in 2010 was $497 million; on average, the companies sold 20.4% of their equity at the IPO.

Canada's IPO market in 2013 ended strong with six new IPOs launched in the fourth quarter, raising a combined $582.6 million.[60] In past years, Canada's IPO market has been driven by the natural resource sector, including mining and energy.[61] More recently, IPOs of real estate investments and technology-based companies have taken over, with expected companies such as HootSuite and Shopify to launch IPOs within the next few years.

Follow-On Financing. A public company can raise more capital by issuing additional shares in a secondary offering.

Realizing Prior Investments. Once a company is public, shareholders prior to the IPO know the value of their investment. What's more, their stock is liquid and can be sold on the stock market after the **lockup period** is over. The lockup period is a length of time after the IPO date (usually 180 days) when the prior shareholders are not permitted to sell any of their shares.

Prestige and Visibility. A public company is more visible and has more prestige. This sometimes helps the company with marketing and selling its products, outsourcing, hiring employees, and banking.

Compensation for Employees. Stock options presently held by employees or granted in the future have a known value.

Acquiring Other Companies. A public company can use its shares to acquire other companies.

And here are the downsides of going public.

High Expenses. Expenses associated with going public are substantial. They include legal and accounting fees, printing costs, and registration fees, which can range from $100,000 to $400,000 or more. Those expenses are not recoverable if the company does not actually go public, which happens to about half the companies that embark on the IPO process and fail to complete it. If the company does go public, the underwriter's commission takes approximately 7% of the money raised.

Public Fishbowl. When a company goes public, regulations require that it disclose a great deal of information about itself that until then has been private and known only to insiders. That information includes compensation of officers and directors, employee share option plans, significant contracts such as lease and consulting agreements, details about operations including business strategies, sales, cost of sales, gross profits, net income, debt, and future plans. The IPO prospectus and other documents that have to be filed are in the public domain, and they are a gold mine for competitors and others that want to pry into the company's affairs. At the peak of the Internet bubble in November 1999, Cobalt Networks went public; its market niche was inexpensive thin servers for small and mid-sized organizations. Before the

IPO, the inexpensive thin-server market hadn't attracted much competition from big companies such as Dell, IBM, Hewlett-Packard, and Sun Microsystems. However, after Cobalt's spectacular IPO, they became aware that the niche was growing rapidly. Ten months later Sun announced it was acquiring Cobalt.

Short-Term Time Horizon. After an IPO, shareholders and financial researchers expect ever-increasing performance quarter by quarter. This expectation forces management to focus on maximizing short-term performance rather than on achieving long-term goals.

Post-IPO Compliance Costs. To meet government regulations, a public company incurs accounting costs it never had when it was private. Those can amount to $100,000 or more annually.

Management's Time. After an IPO, the CEO and the CFO have to spend time on public relations with the research analysts, financial journalists, institutional investors, other shareholders, and market makers—so named because they make a market for the company's shares. This is a distraction from their main job, which is running the company for optimal performance. Some public companies have executives whose main job is dealing with investor relations.

Takeover Target. A public company sometimes becomes the target of an unwelcome takeover by another company.

Employee Disenchantment. A rising share price boosts the morale of employees who own shares or share options, but when it is sinking it can be demoralizing—especially when an employee's options go "underwater" (the share price falls below the options price). Underwater options can make it difficult to motivate and retain key employees.

The Process of Going Public

In Canada, there a number of ways that a company can become a "public company." the most common three are (1) an initial public offering, (2) a reverse takeover (RTO), or (3) through completing a qualifying transaction with a capital pool company (CPC). Becoming a public company means dealing with a number of additional regulations, regulatory bodies, and other service providers, chief among these are the various securities commissions and the exchange on which you are seeking to list your common shares. The securities commissions are primarily concerned with a company's disclosure record. A *disclosure record*, broadly speaking, refers to the information about the company that is made available to the public, which is prescribed in varying pieces of legislation, rules, and regulations. The exchanges are not only concerned about the disclosure record, they will also look at the company's actual business, management skills and experience, governance, and other matters to determine whether the business meets the exchange's basic requirements for being a listed company.

In filing a disclosure document (a final long-form prospectus or similar document) with a securities commission, a company will become a reporting issuer in Canada. Becoming a reporting issuer means that a company becomes subject to all of the disclosure requirements set out in securities laws, including the filing of audited annual financial statements, but it does not mean that a company's securities will be posted and listed for trading on a stock exchange. Listing on a stock exchange is a separate process that typically occurs concurrently since most companies do not want to incur the cost of the public company requirements without securing a listing on a stock exchange.

Entrepreneurs with serious aspirations to take their companies public should plan ahead and consider what information (financial and otherwise) they will need to complete the process. In practice, it will take months to complete the process if your business and records are in good order; if they are not, it could take much longer. Ensuring that you are prepared means, among other things, having your financial statements prepared in a fashion such that an audit could easily be undertaken in a short time frame and having all of your material contracts and records easily accessible and in good order. The company will need to make sure that their accountants are qualified to audit a public company in Canada and that their law firm has experience assisting a private company navigate through the process of going public. Getting the right help may often seem more expensive in the short term, but it will pay off in the long run.

If a company decides that it's time to go public, one of the first steps is for it to speak with a number of investment banks to see if they are willing to support the process and are able to raise any funds that the company may require. Studies have shown that companies backed by leading venture capital firms and taken public by leading **underwriters** have the highest market capitalizations.[62] Investment bankers are not shy and, if they think the company has a good business, they will aggressively pursue the company. The company needs to spend some time and carefully consider whether it believes the investment bank has the ability to follow through on the promises it is making and also ensure that any agreements signed reflect the terms and promises made by the investment bank. The company might consider selecting the underwriter that has had the most success with IPOs in the same industry during the previous few years. If the company selects more than one underwriter, the bank managing the IPO is the **lead underwriter**, and the other banks are part of what is called the **syndicate**.

If a company chooses to go public by way of an IPO, it must prepare and file a preliminary long-form prospectus (**preliminary prospectus**) with the relevant provincial securities regulator and ensure that the preliminary prospectus discloses everything required by the relevant rules and regulations that are aimed at providing the public with all the information it may need to know before deciding whether to buy shares (or other securities) under the offering. In reviewing the preliminary prospectus, the regulators will pay close attention to the company's financial statements. In addition, relatively new rules have been adopted regarding marketing materials: Materials that a company plans on using to market the public offering will need to be disclosed. Given market sensitivities and the fact that any investment bank's ability to raise any required funding can be heavily dependent on market cycles, a delay in the approval process can be problematic for a company and can affect its ability to complete the going public process.

Once the preliminary prospectus is approved, a company can proceed to prepare and file its final long-form prospectus (**prospectus**), which will incorporate any comments received from the regulators and any changes in the business that may have occurred since filing the preliminary prospectus. Once the regulators provide a final receipt for the prospectus, the company is considered a reporting issuer and can proceed to close any concurrent financing. It is important to note that although a prospectus typically deals with financing, it does not necessarily have to and could be a nonoffering prospectus, which would still provide a company with reporting issuer status.

Preparation of the prospectus requires significant participation by the investment bank and their legal counsel because the investment bank will be required to sign the prospectus confirming that the disclosure is accurate and not misleading. As a result, the prospectus will contain details about the offering, what the company plans to do with the proceeds, the company's financial history and its future strategy, information about company management, and the company's industry and will also provide significant disclosure on the risks inherent in the business and market. The preliminary prospectus is colloquially called the **red herring** because the front page is embossed with a notice printed in red stating that some information is subject to change—in particular, the price per share and the number of shares to be offered. As discussed above, there are quite strict marketing rules in relation to any offering by way of prospectus and you should always consult your legal advisors in this respect.

Depending on the market and location of potential purchasers, the investment bank and the company may embark on a tour of financial centres such as Toronto, Vancouver, and Montreal and perhaps non-Canadian centres such as New York, Chicago, London, or Hong Kong to promote the offering and gauge interest on what is called a *road show*. During the road show and immediately after, the investment banker builds a book of investors who say they want to buy the shares. In a nonfixed price offering, the investment bank and the company will price the offering based on the perceived interest and expected orders. The more the offering is oversubscribed, the higher the price the company will be able to negotiate. If the deal is a **firm commitment offering**, then the investment bank or underwriter will commit to deliver the agreed-upon proceeds to the company regardless of whether it sells all the shares at the offering price. This commitment will create tension between the company, which is pushing for a high price, and the underwriter, which wants to set a price that will enable it to sell all the shares at the offering price so that it is not stuck acquiring any "left overs." If the offering is a **best-efforts offering** then the investment bank does not agree to purchase the shares under the offering and the total proceeds will be dependent on the investment bank's ability to sell the shares.

A company can also choose to go public by way of an RTO or CPC transaction. In either case, the company will need to identify an existing public company (in this case called a *shell*) with no active business but with a listing and public distribution. The transaction will be subject to the rules of the exchange on which the shell trades. A CPC is a special program established by the TSX Venture Exchange whereby it permits the creation of a shell with cash and experienced board members whose task it is to go out and find a business that the shell can acquire.[63] Although the rules may be slightly different the concept is much the same as an RTO and will be discussed concurrently.

In an RTO, the disclosure document is typically an information circular prepared by the shell company. The circular needs to contain prospectus-level disclosure regarding all of the same items that would be included in a prospectus, but it will be reviewed by the relevant exchange and not by the securities commissions. All of the same financial reporting, governance, and business requirements continue to exist under this process. The actual transaction will most likely be completed by way of an amalgamation, share exchange, or plan of arrangement, but in any event holders of shares in the private company will end up holding a substantial controlling interest in the public shell company that will have acquired the business. Depending on how much cash the shell company has, a concurrent financing may not be required in an RTO. If it is, it may proceed concurrently either by way of prospectus or private placement pursuant to exemptions from the prospectus requirements under securities laws.

Shares held by the entrepreneurs who started the business and early investors (frequently called *seed shareholders*) will more likely than not be subject to escrow either by operation of securities laws or by virtue of exchange policies. These escrow periods can last up to three years with periodic releases being made over that period. As a result, entrepreneurs may not be able to realize the gains, if any, for some period of time. Even once these seed shares are released from escrow, unless there is sufficient trading in the shares of the company (called liquidity) it may be very difficult for a significant shareholder to sell a large number of shares without completely devaluing the share price.

It is important to remember that even highly visible IPOs can fall short of expectations. A good example of this was Facebook's IPO in May 2012, where what had been described as "the IPO of the century" turned out to be the flop of the decade for investors who bought Facebook shares at the offering price of $38 and subsequently saw them fall below $18 by September 2012.[64]

Governance concerns should also be taken into consideration when taking a company public. The management team and board that you have in place for a growing private company may not be sufficient to meet the governance requirements that are now in place for most listed companies. You will need to make sure that you enough qualified independent directors to meet the requirements and that you also have people with the right skill sets to populate the various committees that will be required. In addition, your CFO, if not CEO, should have significant experience with public companies and reporting requirements, because managing these requirements becomes a key task for a CFO in a listed company. Becoming a public company is just the first step in a new direction and it is always important to make sure that you are ready to comply with the ever-changing rules moving forward.

BFWS Goes Public

Let's return to our example. Two years after raising its second round of venture capital and five years after it was founded, the IPO window for software companies is once again open so BFWS decides to go public. It has exceeded its forecasts and has revenue of $75 million with net income of $8.33 million. Revenue is growing at 50% per year. It wants to raise $50 million gross with an IPO. Based on the prevailing industry P/E ratio of 30, the investment bank values the company post-IPO at $250 million ($8.33 million × 30). To raise $50 million, BFWS will have to sell 20% of its equity (50/250 × 100). That leaves the existing shareholders with 80% of the company.

Everyone should be happy with the return on their investments. At the IPO price, the $4 million of first-round venture capital is worth $64.8 million (16.2 × return and IRR of 100%), and the $6 million of second-round venture capital is worth $38.1 million (6.3 × return and IRR of 152%). The founders and the original investors hold shares worth $72.9 million, and the share option pool is worth $24.3 million. The original founders and shareholders own 9.1% of BFWS, the venture capitalists 41.1%, the share option pool 9.7%, and the public 20%. And the company receives the proceeds of $50 million minus the underwriters' 7% commission—that is, $46.5 million.

Selling the Company

By far the most common way for investors to realize their investment, if a company has done well and chooses not to go public, is to sell the business to another company. A company is usually bought by a bigger company for strategic reasons, such as when a big pharmaceutical company buys out a young biotech company that has developed a promising drug but lacks the resources and experience to take it through the government approval process or to market it once it receives approval.

A Strategic Acquisition: LowerMyBills.com

Sometimes investments are realized through strategic acquisitions. Let's look at an example. Matt Coffin started LowerMyBills.com in 1999. His vision was to provide consumers with a free, one-stop Internet destination to obtain better deals on all their recurring monthly expenses, including mortgages, utilities, automobile loans, insurance, and credit cards. LowerMyBills.com attracts customers for mortgage lenders and others by advertising on a wide variety of websites, including Yahoo, AOL, and MSN. Consumers who click through on mortgage ads, for example, are taken to the LowerMyBills.com website, where they enter information relevant to the mortgage approval process. The website matches this against the lending criteria of the clients of LowerMyBills.com and passes qualifying leads on to several different lenders. The lenders contact the consumer, who can choose the most appropriate offer. LowerMyBills.com is paid for every lead it passes to a lender.

In the last quarter of 2001, LowerMyBills.com posted its first profit. By 2005, it had a leading position in the U.S. market. The company, based in Santa Monica, California, was

Matt Coffin, Founder, LowerMyBills.com

financed with $12 million, first from business angels and then from venture capital firms. Coffin, who still owned 25% of the equity, commented:[65]

By 2004, I knew personally that I was way in the money, but I also knew that I had 99% of my net worth tied up in the business. Back when the Internet crashed, I had a bunch of friends that had started online companies that had gone up and come down fast. One guy who had turned down an offer for $700 million went bankrupt a year later.

Investment banks were calling me like crazy to say it was time for us to go public. We looked at the possibility of raising additional capital from new investors—recapitalize with new shareholders so that current stakeholders could get some liquidity. There was also the option of selling to a corporate buyer, while staying on in some sort of earn-out arrangement.

The team hired an investment bank, gave nine presentations, and within short order had received eight offers from corporate buyers ranging from two to four hundred million dollars. Private equity firms that were interested in a partial buyout were putting forward valuations that averaged half of what the acquirers were offering. This decision was about a lot more than finance. Every employee owns stock in this business, and they have worked really hard to get us to this point. We did need some sort of harvest, but I also knew that we still had a lot of growth ahead of us, and every option has its own set of risks and potential ramifications.

Coffin was in the enviable position of having a business that was growing rapidly in an industry segment that was expanding extremely quickly. LowerMyBills.com had 176 employees. On a pro forma basis, sales in the year ended March 31, 2005, were $120 million with operating profit of $26 million. Clearly, the company could have gone public, but Coffin decided to explore being acquired by a strategic partner. In May 2005, LowerMyBills.com was acquired by Experian, then a member of GUS plc, the British retail and services group. Here are excerpts from a press release by GUS plc:[66]

Acquisition of LowerMyBills.com by Experian

GUS plc, the retail and business services group, today [May 5, 2005] announces that Experian has acquired 100% of the share capital of LowerMyBills.com, a leading online generator of mortgage and other loan application leads in the United States. LowerMyBills.com is complementary to Experian's existing direct-to-consumer activities and operates in large, fast-growing markets. The purchase price is $330 million, plus a maximum performance-related earn-out of $50 million over the next two years. Further strong growth in sales and profit is expected in the current financial year and beyond. The acquisition is being funded from GUS' existing banking facilities. The acquisition is expected comfortably to exceed GUS' financial target of generating a double-digit post-tax return on investment over time.

Experian is establishing leading positions in various markets in connecting consumers with companies via the Internet. Its strategy is to offer a wide range of products that assist consumers in managing the financial aspects of key life events such as moving house or buying a car. Experian enables consumers to find financial products and services that best suit their needs, while helping companies to find new customers quickly and effectively. As well as LowerMyBills.com, the newly formed Experian Interactive operation includes Consumer Direct (selling credit reports, scores, and monitoring products to consumers) and MetaReward and Affiliate Fuel (both of which generate online leads for clients).

This acquisition is attractive because:

LowerMyBills.com operates in large, fast-growing markets. More than 20 million American households take out a new mortgage each year. In 2004, home lenders spent $22 billion on acquiring customers, an amount which has grown by over one-third in the last five years. Of the

$22bn, about $1 billion is currently spent online and this is growing by about 30% a year. For example, Experian estimates that the percentage of mortgages originated online will treble between 2003 and 2008.

LowerMyBills.com has a strong market position. LowerMyBills.com is the most visited home loan service on the Internet. In a highly fragmented market, it is one of only two players of scale with its online leads generating more loans than any individual lending institution. It has strong relationships with more than 400 lenders, including five of the top ten mortgage providers in the United States.

Over time, LowerMyBills.com will benefit from the skills, expertise, and client relationships within Experian:

Consumer Direct, MetaReward, and LowerMyBills.com all work in the same Internet space and can share expertise and traffic. Combined, these businesses have more than 29 million visitors to their websites each month; and there are also benefits of LowerMyBills.com working more closely with Experian's credit business. The introduction of Experian's modelling and analytical capabilities will allow it to improve the quality of leads passed to lenders. Experian will also be able to sell LowerMyBills.com's services to its existing financial services clients, where it has strong relationships.

Don Robert, Chief Executive Officer of Experian, commented:

"This acquisition represents a step-change in building Experian's direct-to-consumer activities. With LowerMyBills.com, we will now assist consumers in making the most cost-effective financial services decisions, while also providing our lender clients with high-quality leads for new borrowers. The strategic fit could not be better and we are delighted to welcome the talented people of LowerMyBills.com to Experian."

Why Be Acquired?

The acquisition of LowerMyBills.com by Experian is a good example of what the seller and the acquirer are seeking from a strategic acquisition. The following are the advantages and disadvantages of an acquisition from the perspective of the seller.

Management. By selling the company rather than going public, the managers can stay focused on what they do best—continuing to build the company—rather than having to spend a lot of time on public relations with the financial community. Also, they probably will not be as driven by quarter-by-quarter results as they would be if the company were public. For example, LowerMyBills.com will have a relatively small effect on Experian's net income; it can probably focus on rapid sales growth rather than optimizing quarterly profits for the next few years.

Founder and CEO. Selling a company the entrepreneur has built from nothing into a thriving enterprise can be traumatic. Edward Marram (co-author of Chapter 14 of this book) sold his company, Geo-Centers, in 2005. He said his head told him that it was the right thing to do, but his heart told him not to do it. After all, he was selling a company he started from nothing in 1975 and built into an organization with 1,100 employees. When a company is private, the CEO reports only to a board of directors, but when it is acquired, he or she has to report to a boss; if the acquirer is a big company, that boss may report to another boss. It can be very frustrating for the CEO/founder who has been making all the important decisions to find that his or her ideas have to be approved by a hierarchy before they can be implemented.

Company. Experian has very deep pockets; it will be able to provide capital to Lower MyBills.com if it needs it.

Investors. Acquisitions are often paid for in cash rather than shares. Thus, investors get cash immediately after the deal is completed, unlike in a public offering, when pre-IPO investors have shares they cannot sell for 180 days, meaning they face the risk that the shares will go down before they can sell them. Of course, if the company is bought with the acquirer's shares instead of cash and if there are restrictions on the sale of the shares, there is still a risk that the share price will go down before the investors can sell it.

Entrepreneur and Employee Shares. If it is a cash transaction, as it was in the LowerMyBills.com acquisition, the entrepreneurs and employees get cash immediately. The potential disadvantage is that they no longer hold shares, so they have no upside potential if the company continues to do well. True, there is usually an **earn-out**, which is additional compensation to be paid in a few years if the company meets targets specified at the time of the acquisition. In the case of LowerMyBills.com, the earn-out is $50 million compared with $330 million paid when the acquisition was completed. It is well worth getting the earn-out, but it is only 15.2% more, so it might not be enough to motivate key employees to stay.

Employment Agreement. Key employees will have an employment agreement that forbids them to compete with the company for a specific number of years—usually no more than two—if they leave. That will probably be the same agreement they had with the company before it was acquired. However, the CEO and top management will almost certainly be required to sign new noncompete agreements as part of their employment contracts with the acquirer.

Culture. Initially, the acquirer will not interfere in the management of the purchased company, but eventually it will probably want to put in its own management system and maybe its own executives in a few key positions. When it does that, there is a risk there will be a clash of cultures.

Expenses and Commissions. The expenses and investment banker's commission are substantially lower for an acquisition than for an IPO.

☐ CONCLUSION

When an entrepreneur accepts money from a financially sophisticated investor such as a business angel or a venture capitalist, there has to be a future harvest when the investment can be realized. Generally, that harvest occurs when the company is acquired; occasionally it happens when the company goes public. The harvest is primarily for the investors rather than the entrepreneurs. If entrepreneurs are not careful, they can give would-be investors the impression that they themselves are planning to exit the company at the harvest. That is not what professional investors like to hear. They want to invest in entrepreneurs whose vision is to build a business and continue building it after the harvest, not in entrepreneurs who are in it to get rich quick. Remember that Bill Gates made almost all his huge fortune by the appreciation of Microsoft's shares after its IPO; so did Microsoft employees and investors who held onto their shares for many years after the IPO.

> "I hate it when people call themselves 'entrepreneurs' when what they are really trying to do is launch a startup and then sell or go public, so they can cash in and move on. They're unwilling to do the work it takes to build a real company, which is the hardest work in business." Steve Jobs[i]
>
> [i] From W. Isaacson, Steve Jobs (New York, NY: Simon & Schuster, 2011), 569.

After a long negotiation between a Boston-area entrepreneur and a venture capitalist for seed-stage financing of a medical device company, the venture capitalist asked the entrepreneur, "Where do you personally want to be in 10 years' time?" The entrepreneur replied that he hoped he would have built a $200 million company that was the leader in its market niche and that he would still be the CEO. The venture capitalist immediately shook the entrepreneur's hand and said, "You have your money." The entrepreneur was surprised because it seemed to him that the venture capitalist already knew about how big the company might become if things went well, so he asked what triggered the spontaneous decision to invest. The venture capitalist replied, "If you had said, 'retired to a house on the beach in Maine,' we would not have invested. We want entrepreneurs who are focused on building businesses for the long haul, rather than short-term personal wealth." The venture capitalist added, "Congratulations, you have just completed the most difficult selling job you will ever do. You have convinced a venture capitalist to invest in a seed-stage company."

Reflection Point	Your Thoughts. . .
1. How can you bootstrap your venture? What services can you get for free or at reduced rates? What equipment can you lease or buy used?	
2. In the last chapter, you created a funding strategy. Now think about how you will gain access to angels and venture capitalists. Who can make introductions on your behalf?	
3. What valuation method makes the most sense for your company? What comparable companies can you refer to as you prepare your valuation?	
4. Imagine your harvest. What companies might likely acquire you? How can you prepare for that future acquisition?	
5. Is there a possibility that your company could go public (high-growth industry)? What do you need to do to prepare for that?	

YOUR OPPORTUNITY JOURNAL ☐

Identify several companies that you can use as comparables in a valuation. What P/E ratios currently prevail across the companies? Can you explain the variance in P/Es? Which comparable company is yours most similar to? Where does its P/E fall in the range? Compute a valuation for your firm. What adjustments should you make?

WEB EXERCISE ☐

Derek Szeto and Red Flag Deals: When to Exit Your Successful Startup

"A bird in the hand is worth two in the bush" is a centuries old proverb that still has relevance to today's entrepreneurs. The proverb means it is preferable to have a small but certain return than a mere potential of a greater one. The proverb helps illustrate why outcome alone isn't sufficient to justify a decision; one must also recognize and account for probability of that outcome.

Founders invest their time, energy, capital, and lifeblood into creating their startup. When it comes time to sell (or "exit") the venture, each founder is faced with a decision: take today's small exit or raise more capital, grow the business and hold out for a better priced exit. This was the issue Derek Szeto, faced when the Yellow Pages Group offered to buy his startup, RedFlagDeals.com.

RedFlagDeals.com (RFD) is a daily virtual destination for over 450,000 Canadian consumers seeking and sharing coupons, promotions, deals. RFD offers access to new customers for online and offline companies.[67] Founder Derek Szeto created the website because he saw an unmet need in the Canadian market and did not hesitate to create something that is ten times better than spending hours a week clipping coupons on his kitchen counter. By no means was Derek's creation of RFD an overnight success; he and his team experienced peaks and valleys, but it was his determination that allowed him to bootstrap his way into creating Canada's largest bargain-hunting community.

Derek's Background

Living in Oakville, Ontario, while in his last year of high school in 1999, Derek was like most other 18-year-old Canadian youths. Derek had lots of friends, lots of parties, and lots of free time. Looking back on that time in his life, Derek describes himself as too lazy to go out and get a summer job at a restaurant, cutting grass, or at the mall. After all, Derek had successfully earned an acceptance to Queen's University in Kingston, Ontario and he was looking forward to starting in the fall. So in the summer of 1999, Derek found himself sitting on his parents' couch in their basement looking at the diminishing balance in his bank account. Derek was determined to find a way to save himself money, especially when he was about to start university in a few months' time.

Even though Derek did not have a job, he enjoyed shopping. With limited income, he was always seeking to find the most optimal deal available on the products and services that suited his interests. At this time there were many deals offered to American consumers online. Derek noticed that there were some amazing deals coming from large companies such as Microsoft and other American software companies, but these deals were not available to him and his fellow Canadians. The Internet was just becoming popular and sitting in his parents' basement using their dial-up Internet access, Derek began searching website after website researching products, prices, and deal availability through many Canadian companies' websites. The more research Derek did, the more he saw a void in the market for Canadian consumers to find such deals.

Derek's passion for sharing great deals with the public continued throughout the creation of RFD. RFD is a free site for consumers. Users can easily access the site and browse the promotions in categories including automotive, entertainment, kids and babies, travel, computer and electronics, small business, and more.

From the beginning, Derek and his team bootstrapped their way to the top. He built the business out of nothing in his parents' basement, with zero outside capital. He and his two employees funded the project themselves, without any external assistance. Derek's domain knowledge was weak in the beginning as his only real knowledge of online retail and couponing came from his own experiences. As a result, it was critical for Derek to build his team by finding others who shared his passion for seeking deals and promotions for the Canadian public. He purposely built his team based on their passion and level of domain, operational and business knowledge.

The value proposition that RFD offers the end consumer is saving money, making it an easy sell to Canadian consumers. Not only was this an unmet need in the Canadian marketplace at the time, but it also assisted RFD to go viral as saving money is usually at the top of consumers' lists and Canadians take pride in how much they save. Word of mouth helped keep RFD user acquisition costs low as their website traffic continued to grow.

Finding the Unique Value Proposition

RFD was not an overnight success. In fact, like most eventual successes there were many times when the RFD accountant was chasing down their account receivables out of fear Derek wouldn't be able to make payroll that week. Late nights and early mornings became part of Derek's daily routine. Not only was Derek launching RedFlagDeals.com, he was also earning his bachelor of commerce from Queen's University. Between classes, projects, and schoolwork, Derek would try and devote as much time as possible to RFD, but the heavy course load was only allowing for 2 to 4 hours a week of "free" time to work on the business. He hired his close friend to join RFD to help out especially during the peak season (Christmas and Boxing Day being the two busiest days of the year).

In November after his graduation from Queen's University, Derek moved to Toronto to open up RFD's first office at the intersection of Yonge and Bloor streets. The office was very small initially, consisting of a couple of desks and a couple of chairs. The team (and office) of three grew as more employees were added monthly as the website began gaining traction. They outgrew their office in the downtown core and moved to Liberty Village to accommodate the 10 employees that had joined the team only.

Derek's "aha moment" came when they had an opportunity to be featured on Toronto's local CityTV channel. Their morning television show had featured RedFlagDeals and it was supposed to be a short mention of the company and what it offered consumers; little did Derek and his team know that this would generate so much traffic that it crashed their servers, resulting in the RFD team saying to each other, "what have we created?" They were pleasantly surprised to learn that there were indeed enough consumers who cared about getting deals as much as they did.

Bumpy Road of Growth

Once RFD established itself in the Canadian marketplace, they began looking to expand. Their initial thought was to introduce similar websites in other English language based communities (e.g., New Zealand). Since Derek and his team were still completely self-funded and had limited resources, they decided not to pursue something at such a great distance. Looking back, had they engaged outside sources of capital, their expansion into other countries could have been a huge moment for RFD and its team.

Derek launched PriceCanada.com in November of 2005—a Canadian shopping comparison service that allowed consumers to compare prices, products, and retailers. Derek swiped (i.e., steal with integrity and pride everywhere) this concept from similar successful business models in the United States. Unfortunately, there was not enough market or enough Canadian retailers selling electronics or similar products, so they were forced to shut down PriceCanada.com as it was only breaking even. This was a pivotal moment for Derek and his team. They knew they had a potential opportunity at their fingertips but needed to focus on strengthening RFD. Derek and his team turned all of their focus to RedFlagDeals.com.

Derek never really considered external funding. It was not until they had reached over two million unique visitors that outside investors approached them to offer them expansion funding.[68] Notwithstanding, Derek declined all offers of investment from outsiders. He and his team were efficiently running the company and had grown from their initial lean team of two people to 15–23 employees.

To Seek Funding or to Not Seek Funding . . .?

Fast forward to January 2010. Derek had spent nearly a decade and an immeasurable number of hours on his passion project: Red Flag Deals. RFD now had offices at a new location on Queen Street in downtown Toronto, and making payroll was no longer a concern for Derek. Derek's life was good. He had met the girl of his dreams, got married, and started a family in what seemed to be a blink of an eye. The RFD team had grown to over 15 employees and companies were now coming to them wanting to advertise their deals on RFD. In 2004, Derek earned the title of CIBC's Student Entrepreneur of the Year for Ontario and was an Ontario Finalist for the 2007 Ernst and Young Emerging Entrepreneur of the Year Award.[69]

To assist with strategy, a Board of Advisors emerged, consisting of industry leaders and experienced entrepreneurs to assist in the growth of RFD. Derek worked very closely with these advisors consulting on decisions regarding future growth and strategy. The Board believed that RFD had not yet reached its maximum potential. They believed that there was still more room to grow.

Between the growth of RFD and the growth of his family, Derek's days were still very busy. As a result, Derek was feeling pressure from all sides of his life to be present and available. From his perspective, he wanted to be spending more time at home with his wife and kids, and the long hours at RFD's offices were beginning to limit the number of breakfasts and dinners he was having at home. That is when Derek received an offer to sell RFD to the Yellow Pages Group. The Yellow Pages Group was facing their own obsolesces, as Google had replaced people's need for their product. The Yellow Pages Group saw RFD as a potential property to sell ads again.

Derek found himself wondering if he had taken RFD as far as he could. What was their next step? He pondered whether he wanted to develop RFD into the next phase. In order to do so, he would have to raise millions in capital and give up part of his equity and control in his own company. Derek wondered if he had the time and energy to take on that challenge. After much consideration and thought, he saw only two options in front of him: take a deep breath and start the challenging process of raising the millions in capital that he needed, or entertain some of the offers that were knocking at the door wanting to acquire RFD.

Raising capital to push RFD forward would allow Derek to continue being the decision maker within his company, but it would be a very challenging and lengthy process resulting in Derek losing equity in RFD, and the long days and nights at the office would continue. If he decided to entertain one of the many external offers to purchase RFD, Derek would have a large financial gain, less day to day pressure on himself, and allow him to spend more mornings and nights at home with his family. Derek did not know what the right answer was, but he knew he could not take this type of decision lightly.

February 2010 marked RFD's most rewarding milestone to date. Derek made the decision that he would sell to Yellow Pages Group Canada. At the time, this seemed to be the best option. Derek felt a sale to Yellow Pages Group was a statement on the success Derek and his team had worked hard creating, and it would allow Derek to spend fewer nights at the office, and more nights at home. But it was a difficult decision to make because RFD still had so much potential.

Life after Exiting

After the transaction, Derek decided to work under the Yellow Pages Group Canada (YPGC) in the position of General Manager: Deals, Coupons, and Shopping. In this role, Derek oversaw business related deals leveraging RFD. It was, however, a hard transition for Derek going from being his own boss to having to report to someone.

In September 2010, Derek helped RFD launch "Deal of the Day" which offers Canadian consumers substantial savings through a group buying service. In a business model similar to Groupon and LivingSocial.com, RedFlagDeals.com sends subscribers emails alerting them of a daily offer. Once a minimum number of consumers agree to purchase the daily deal, the offer is activated and the buyers are able to use the deal. This type of group purchasing offers retailers a very low-risk model for collaborating with RFD, as there are no setup costs and merchants only have to pay for retail sales that are generated. This was a great way for RFD to work with small and medium-sized businesses in Canada.

While in this new role, Derek was successful in doubling RFD's annual top line revenues post acquisition. Derek remained working for YPGC for just over two years before he decided to start working on his next project.

Late in 2011, RFD was one of the 100 most popular websites in the country.[70] To this day, RFD attracts more than 2.5 million monthly readers by providing coupons and promotions across 14 categories.[71]

Discussion Questions

1. Compare Derek's two options, raising external funding or exit and sell:
   a. What were the key points to consider?
   b. How would you decide which option to take?
2. If you were in Derek's position, would you have taken venture capital? Why? Why not?
3. If you were in Derek's position, would you have made the decision to sell, knowing that there was potential to grow with third-party assistance?
4. Post sale, would you have stayed on with Yellow Pages Group to continue working on RFD?

This case is written by Dr. Sean Wise and Madelon Crothers.

NOTES

1 D. Gross, "BigBelly: A Solar Powered Garbage Solution?" *Newsweek,* September 10, 2009, www.newsweek.com/id/215120.

2 *WhatsApp Blog,* May 7, 2014, http://blog.whatsapp.com.

3 Cummings Properties works with local colleges and universities to promote entrepreneurship. Cummings helps sponsor several local business plan competitions and also provides special rate packages for new businesses growing out of college programs. The following site has links to colleges with Cummings Properties sponsorship programs: www.cummings.com/how_to_lease_space.htm#entrep.

4 Futurepreneur Canada, "About," www.futurpreneur.ca/en/about/.

5 Ibid.

6 Ibid.

7 Ibid.

8 Business Development Bank of Canada, "About BDC," www.bdc.ca/EN/about/Pages/default.aspx?ref=hp-ftr.

9 W. D. Bygrave and P. D. Reynolds, "Who Finances Startups in the USA? A Comprehensive Study of Informal Investors, 1999–2003," in *Frontiers of Entrepreneurship Research*, eds. S. Zahra et al. (Wellesley, MA: Babson College, 2004).

10 Ibid.

11 Although borrowing money from relatives, friends, and business associates is common, very little has been written about how to do it well. Prosper Marketplace is a pioneering company that has developed a set of products and services to facilitate these transactions (see www.prosper.com). The company manages loans between relatives, friends, and other private parties and offers information online you can use to get financing quickly. Borrowers:

1. Choose a loan amount and post a loan listing for investors to review and choose a loan that meets their criteria.

2. Formalize the loan with a legally binding document, such as a promissory note.

3. Create a system for repayment that is affordable and reassures the lender that the loan will be repaid.

12 "Canada's National Crowdfunding Association Applauds Regulators for Setting the Stage for Crowdfunding Success," National Crowdfunding Association of Canada news release, March 24, 2014.

13 K. Pender, "Crowdfunding Awaits Key Rules from SEC," *SF Gate,* February 8 2013, www.sfgate.com/business/networth/article/Crowdfunding-awaits-key-rules-from-SEC-4264631.php#ixzz2LNR9Nb4J.

14 R. Empson, "Ready, Set, Crowdfund: President Obama to Sign JOBS Act Tomorrow," *TechCrunch,* April 4, 2012, http://techcrunch.com/2012/04/04/crowdfunding-is-a-go/; Pender, "Crowdfunding."

15 Wikipedia, "Crowdfunding," http://en.wikipedia.org/wiki/Crowd_funding.

16 The Impossible Project, "Impossible Instant Lab: Turn iPhone Images into Real Photos," Kickstarter, www.kickstarter.com/projects/impossible/impossible-instant-lab-turn-iphone-images-into-rea.

17 E. Markowitz, "Inside the New Forces Shaping Crowdfunding's Future," *Inc.,* April 17, 2012.

18 "Top 10 Crowdfunding Sites," http://crowdfunding.org.

19 Kickstarter, "The Year in Kickstarter 2013," www.kickstarter.com/year/2013/?ref=footer#1-people-dollars.

20 Ibid.

21 Pebble Smartwatch, https://getpebble.com

22 Ibid.

23 Kickstarter, "Discover Projects—Most Funded," www.kickstarter.com/discover/most-funded.

24 Mark Cuban Companies, "Mark's Bio," http://markcubancompanies.com/about.html.

25 J. Sohl, "The Angel Investor Market in 2008: A Down Year in Investment

Dollars but Not in Deals," Center for Venture Research, March 26, 2009, www.wsbe.unh.edu/files/2008_Analysis_Report_Final.pdf; National Venture Capital Association/PricewaterhouseCoopers, "MoneyTree Report," October 20, 2009, www.nvca.org/index.php?option=com_docman&task=doc_download&gid=496&ItemId=93.

26 F. Wainwright, "Note on Angel Investing," Case #5001, Hanover, NH: Tuck School of Business at Dartmouth, Center for Private Equity and Entrepreneurship, 2005.

27 As of the writing of this book, a comprehensive list of angel groups can be found at www.inc.com/articles/2001/09/23461.html.

28 http://activecapital.org.

29 National Angel Capital Organization, "Who We Are," http://nacocanada.com/about/who-we-are.

30 Ibid.

31 Cited in D. R. Evanson and A. Berof, "Heaven Sent: Seeking an Angel Investor? Here's How to Find a Match Made in Heaven," *Entrepreneur*, January 1998.

32 J. Zasky, "Steve Wozniak Interview," *Failure Magazine*, July 17, 2000, www.failuremag.com/index.php/site/print/steve_wozniak_interview.

33 The National Angel Capital Organization (NACO) provides information and resources on its website, http://nacocanada.com.

34 Wainwright, "Note on Angel Investing."

35 "Venture Support Systems Project: Angel Investors," Release 1.1, Cambridge, MA: MIT Entrepreneurship Center, February 2000.

36 Ibid.

37 Ibid.

38 Ibid.

39 Thomson Reuters, "Canada's Venture Capital Market in 2013," Canada's Venture Capital and Private Equity Association, www.cvca.ca/files/Downloads/VC_Data_Deck_2013_English.pdf.

40 Ibid.

41 Ibid.

42 R. Gordan, "Venture Debt: A Capital Idea for Startups," Kauffman Fellows, http://kauffmanfellows.org/journal_posts/venture-debt-a-capital-idea-for-startups/.

43 J. Baccher, "Venture Capitalists' Investment Criteria in Technology-Based New Ventures" (dissertation, University of Waterloo, 2000).

44 S. Wise, *Hot or Not: How to Know if Your Business Idea will Fly or Fail* (Toronto ON: Ryerson Entrepreneurship Institute, 2012).

45 Ibid.

46 W. D. Bygrave, G. Johnstone, J. Lewis, and R. Ullman, "Venture Capitalists' Criteria for Selecting High-Tech Investments: Prescriptive Wisdom Compared with Actuality," *Frontiers of Entrepreneurship Research* (Wellesley, MA: Babson College, 1998), www.babson.edu/entrep/fer/papers98/XX/XX_A/XX_A.html.

47 G. D. Vynck, "Canada's Tech Stars Poised to Lead New IPO Boom for Sector as Investors More and More 'Hungry' for Growth," *Financial Post*, March 13, 2014, http://business.financialpost.com/2014/03/13/canadas-tech-stars-poised-to-lead-new-ipo-boom-for-sector-as-investors-more-and-more-hungry-for-growth/?__lsa=276f-6f52.

48 Ibid.

49 Ibid.

50 TSX Group, "Stock Listings," www.tmx.com/TMX/HttpController?GetPage=ListedCompaniesViewPage&Sea.

51 Canadian Venture Capitalist Association, "About CVCA," www.cvca.ca/about/.

52 J. Rosenstein, A. V. Bruno, W. D. Bygrave, and N. T. Taylor, "CEO Appraisal of Their Boards in Venture Capital Portfolios," *Journal of Business Venturing* 8 (1993): 99–113.

53 J. Rosenstein, A. V. Bruno, W. D. Bygrave, and N. T. Taylor, "How Much Do CEOs Value the Advice of Venture Capitalists on Their Boards?" *Frontiers of Entrepreneurship*

ENTREPRENEURS AT SMALL, growing firms, unlike finance treasurers at most *Fortune* 500 companies, do not have easy access to a variety of inexpensive funding sources. In the entire world, only a handful of very large firms have access to funding sources such as asset-backed debt securitizations, A-l commercial paper ratings, and below-prime lending rates. Most financial managers of small- to medium-sized firms are constantly concerned about meeting cash-flow obligations to suppliers and employees and maintaining solid financial relationships with creditors and shareholders. Their problems are exacerbated by issues concerning growth, control, and survival. Moreover, the difficulty of attracting adequate funds exists even when firms are growing rapidly and bringing in profits.

This chapter describes various financing options for entrepreneurs and identifies potential financing pitfalls and solutions. We also discuss how these issues are influenced by the type of industry and the life cycle of the firm and how to plan accordingly.

Getting Access to Funds—Start with Internal Sources

Entrepreneurs requiring initial startup capital, funds used for growth, and working capital generally seek funds from *internal* sources. Managers or owners of large, mature firms, in contrast, have access to profits from operations as well as funds from external sources.

We distinguish internal from external funds because internal funding sources do not require external analysts or investors to independently appraise the worthiness of the capital investments before releasing funds. External investors and lenders also don't share the entrepreneur's vision, so they may view the potential risk/return tradeoff in a different vein and demand a relatively certain return on their investment after the firm has an established financial track record.

Figure 12.1 shows a listing of funding sources and approximately when a firm would use each. In the embryonic stages of a firm's existence, as we've discussed, much of the funding comes from the entrepreneur's own pocket, including personal savings accounts, credit cards, home equity lines, and other assets such as personal computers, fax machines, in-home offices, furniture, and automobiles.

Soon after entrepreneurs begin tapping their personal fund sources they may also solicit funds from relatives, friends, and banks. Entrepreneurs would generally prefer to use other people's money (OPM) rather than their own because, if their personal investment turns sour,

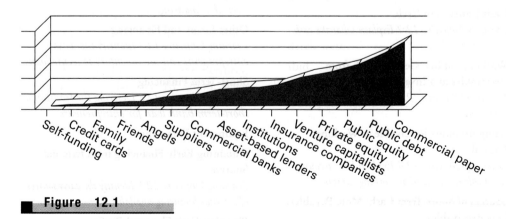

Figure 12.1

Sources of outside funding: Levels of funding and firm maturity

they still have a nest egg to feed themselves and their families. The need to protect a nest egg may be particularly acute if the entrepreneur leaves a viable job to pursue an entrepreneurial dream on a full-time basis. The costs to the entrepreneur in this case include

- ☑ The opportunity cost of income from the prior job
- ☑ The forgone interest on the initial investment
- ☑ The potential difficulty of being rehired by a former employer (or others) if the idea does not succeed

Add to this the embarrassment of having to beg for a new job while paying off old debts, and the prospective entrepreneur quickly realizes that the total cost of engaging in a new venture is very high. Family and friends may volunteer to fund the entrepreneur's project in the early stages and often will do so without a formal repayment schedule or specified interest cost. However, the funds are far from free. Total costs—including nonfinancial indirect costs, such as family pressure, internal monitoring, and strained relations—are probably extremely high. Moreover, family and friends make poor financial intermediaries, since they have limited financial resources, different repayment expectations, and narrow loan diversification. This will contribute to the entrepreneur's desire to get outside funding from a traditional source as soon as possible. Other than family and friends, an entrepreneur may choose the bootstrapping or crowdfunding route. However, the question most entrepreneurs ponder is, "Where can you go before a bank will give you money?"

Credit Cards and Home Equity Lines

Entrepreneurs who require an immediate infusion of cash often don't have the luxury of time to await the decision of a prospective equity investor or credit lender. They're prone to tapping their personal credit cards for business purchases or borrowing against a low-interest-bearing home equity line of credit. According to the Bank of Canada, at the end of 2013 consumers had personal credit outstanding close to $1.36 trillion,[1] with approximately one-third applied to revolving credit (credit cards). Nonrevolving credit includes personal credit associated with loans for automobiles and vacations but does not include home equity lines. This credit, which is derived from commercial banks, finance companies, credit unions, and savings institutions,

Laugh at Your Own Risk

Back in 2000, Adam Lowry and Eric Ryan did not plan on going into the comedy business, but they seemed to make everyone laugh. They both lived in the San Francisco Bay Area, the Internet startup capital of the world. Yet potential investors thought they were crazy for trying to start up their company called Method, a household products company that would sell soap and cleaning supplies from environmentally friendly ingredients in cool packaging. They pooled together $100,000 in personal savings to start. By the spring of 2001, Lowry and Ryan had hired Alastair Dorward as CEO. And they were $300,000 in debt, split among the three partners' credit cards. By this time, the tech bub-ble had burst, and all of a sudden venture capitalists were no longer laughing at their idea. In late 2001, the partners received a term sheet for $1 million. To celebrate, the partners took their investors, lawyers, and accountants out to dinner. The three entrepreneurs' credit cards were all declined. Thank goodness Lowry knew the owner of the restaurant. Lowry said, "We convinced him we were good for it—that the guy over there was about to give us a million bucks." As of 2009 sales were "north of $100 million" and the company had 130 products sold in more than 8,000 stores.

Source: R. McCarthy, N. Heintz, and B. Burlingham, "Starting Up in a Down Economy," Inc., May 1, 2008, www.inc.com/magazine/20080501/starting-up-in-a-down-economy.html.

is for personal consumption. Presumably, entrepreneurs have applied some of it to their businesses. Many banks set up credit cards for either personal or business use. And "points" systems that provide credit toward frequent-flyer miles or future purchases may give consumers an economic incentive to maximize their use of credit cards, whether for personal or business purposes.

Home equity lines of credit (HELOCs) are another important way in which consumers provide funding for their businesses. In mid-2009, there was over $206 billion in outstanding HELOCs according to the Bank of Canada.[2] Several studies have shown that many entrepreneurs use HELOCs to raise capital. For example, in August 2008 a Rasmussen Report found 30% of respondents use home loans for funding. And another study by the Small Business Research Board found that 54% of entrepreneurs use home equity.[3]

Cash Conversion Cycle

One of the most important considerations in setting up a business is deciding when to pay the bills.

The business operating cycle for a traditional manufacturer begins with the purchase of raw materials and ends with collections from the customer. It includes three key components: the inventory cycle, the accounts receivable cycle, and the accounts payable cycle. The **inventory cycle** begins with the purchase of the raw materials, includes the work-in-process period, and ends with the sale of the finished goods. The **accounts receivable cycle** then begins with the sale and concludes with the collection of the receivable. During this operating cycle, the business generally receives some credit from suppliers.

The **accounts payable cycle** begins with the purchase of the raw materials or finished goods, but it ends with the payment to the supplier. The vast majority of organizations, particularly manufacturing operations, experience a gap between the time when they have to pay suppliers and the time when they receive payment from customers. This gap is known as the **cash conversion cycle (CCC)**. For most companies, the credit provided by suppliers ends

Negative Cash Conversion Cycle

In 2000, a second-year college student by the name of Siamak Taghaddos set up a new venture, Grasshopper, that provided emerging growth companies with a professional telephone-answering service. Virtually all Taghaddos's sales were generated through an automated system that he created on the Internet. Customers paid upfront monthly fees ranging from $9.95 to $39.95 that were charged automatically to their credit cards. Taghaddos paid his own expenses a few weeks later. This negative cash conversion cycle enabled him to grow exponentially with little need for

external capital (since he initially leased the equipment required for the service).

By his final year, Taghaddos was generating over $500,000 in revenues and outearned all but a handful of his professors. Two years after his graduation, he had revenues over $5 million and 20 employees and was named, along with his partner David Hauser, by *Businessweek* as one of the top five entrepreneurs in the United States under the age of 25. Although this successful entrepreneur clearly generated the majority of his growth based on unique skill and marketing insight, had he not established a company with a negative cash conversion cycle it's likely that his meteoric growth would have been constrained because of a severe cash crunch.

long before the accounts receivables are paid. This means that, as companies grow sales levels, they need to get external financing to fund working capital needs. One of the primary causes of bankruptcy is the inability to finance operations, shutting down potentially successful ventures.

Some companies generate payments from customers before they need to pay their suppliers. Their cash conversion cycle is negative, although from a cash-flow perspective it is very positive. Your industry's typical cash conversion cycle is one of the most important things you should find out about your overall financing scheme. It makes a big difference to your chances for success and growth—if you are fortunate enough to receive payments before providing the service or paying your supplier.

Working Capital: Getting Cash from Receivables and Inventories

The timing of collection of accounts receivable and payment of accounts payable is a key determinant in whether a firm is cash rich or cash poor. For example, an increase in net working capital (i.e., current assets minus current liabilities) doesn't necessarily translate into an increase in liquidity. One reason is that increases in net working capital often result from increases in operating assets net of increases in operating liabilities. These operating assets, such as accounts receivable or inventory, are usually tied up in operations, and firms don't commonly liquidate them (prematurely) to pay bills; they typically pay bills with liquid financial assets, such as cash and marketable securities, instead. Thus, we can use only liquid financial assets to assess a firm's liquidity.

Further, corporate insolvency usually results when the firm fails to service debt obligations or callable liabilities on time. We can estimate corporate liquidity fairly accurately by taking the difference between liquid financial assets and callable liabilities, referred to as the *net liquid balance*. The net liquid balance is actually a part of net working capital. *Net working capital* is easy to calculate in one of two ways:

- ◉ Take the difference between current assets and current liabilities (as described earlier), or
- ◉ Take the difference between long-term liabilities, including equities, and long-term assets (such as fixed assets).

The first formula is often misinterpreted to be the difference between two liquid components, whereas the second definition suggests that the residual of long-term liabilities minus long-term assets is used to finance current assets, some of which may be liquid. The second definition also enables us to analyze the current assets and liabilities as consisting of both liquid financial/callable components and operating components.

Net working capital is actually the sum of the working capital requirements balance. This suggests that only a part of net working capital is liquid. Clearly, as a small firm grows, current operating assets will increase. If current operating liabilities don't increase at the same rate as the increase in current operating assets (which is true when an entrepreneur pays suppliers before receiving payment from customers), then the entrepreneur will find that the firm's net liquid balance will decrease (assuming the firm does not increase its long-term funding arrangements). This may be true even though the firm is generating paper profits. As long as the increase in working capital requirements *exceeds* the increase in profits, then the firm will find itself reducing its liquidity levels.

This highlights one of the fundamental weaknesses of the traditional liquidity ratios, such as the current ratio or quick ratio. These ratios include both liquid financial assets and operating assets in their formulas. Since operating assets are tied up in operations, including these assets in a liquidity ratio is not very useful from an ongoing-concern perspective. Note the difference between a liquidity perspective and a liquidation perspective. A liquidation perspective assumes that in the event of a crisis, the firm may sell assets off in order to meet financial obligations, while a liquidity perspective assumes that the firm meets its financial obligations without impairing the viability of future operations. From an ongoing perspective, a new ratio—*net liquid balance to total assets*—may be more indicative of liquidity than either the current ratio or the quick ratio.

Using Accounts Receivable as Working Capital

Accounts receivable—that is, the money owed to the company as a result of sales made on credit for which payment has not yet been received—are a major element in working capital for most companies. And they are one of the reasons we can assert that *working capital* is not the same as *available cash* and that the timing of short-term flows is vitally important.

If a company is selling a major part of its output on credit and giving 30 days' credit, its accounts receivable will be about equal to sales of 30 days—that is, to one-twelfth of its annual sales (if sales are reasonably stable over the year). And if the company's collection policies are so liberal or ineffective that in practice customers are paying an average of, say, 45 days after they are billed, accounts receivable are no less than one-eighth of annual sales. Investment in accounts receivable is a use of funds. The company has to finance the credit it is giving to its customers by allowing its money to be tied up in this way instead of being available for investment in productive uses. Therefore, accounts receivable, like cash, have an opportunity cost.

The magnitude of a company's accounts receivable obviously depends on a number of factors:

- The level and the pattern of sales
- The breakdown between cash and credit sales
- The nominal credit terms offered
- The way these credit terms are enforced through a collection policy

We'll discuss each of these factors in detail in the following sections.

The Sales Pattern

The basis of all receivables and collections is clearly *actual net sales*— that is, sales sold minus any returns. From actual sales come the assumptions about receipts from future cash sales and collections of future credit sales. These are the key inputs in forecasting cash flow, as discussed later in this chapter. Techniques for forecasting future sales fall into two broad groups:

- Techniques that use external or economic information
- Techniques that are based on internal or historical data from the company's own past sales

Most managers are more familiar with the techniques in the second group than they are with economic forecasting. The methods for forecasting from historical data range from the very simple (such as a straightforward moving average) to fairly sophisticated models. For instance, variations on exponential smoothing make it possible to take into account both long-term trends in the company's sales and seasonal variations. Simply put, although the more sophisticated techniques are useful, no forecasting method based *only* on historical sales data is completely satisfactory. You cannot be sure that either total industry sales or the company's share of the sales will be the same in the future as they have been in the past; you must consider a variety of external factors.

Methods of forecasting environmental change also fall into two broad groups. One group is primarily concerned with *forecasting the future performance of the economy as a whole*, particularly future levels of the gross national product (GNP) and the national income. These *GNP models*, as they are called, are highly complex, computer-based models. Their construction may be beyond the capabilities of most entrepreneurs, but you can easily purchase their output. The other group is more concerned with *forecasting sales for individual industries and products*. One way to do this is to identify economic time series to use as leading indicators to signal changes in the variable being forecast. Again, this technique is best wielded by an experienced economist with a computer. The important point for the entrepreneur is that forecasting techniques are becoming progressively less of an art and more of a science.

Cash versus Credit Sales

The relative proportions of cash sales and credit sales may make an important difference to expected cash flows. Unfortunately, this is a variable over which most entrepreneurs have little control. For example, a company in retail sales can certainly take steps to increase its cash sales, either by banning credit entirely or by offering a discount on cash sales. But a company selling primarily to other corporate organizations—other manufacturing companies, wholesalers, distributors, or retail chains—has few cash sales. Its best hope is to set its credit terms to encourage prompt payment, but the sales will still be credit sales, not cash sales.

Credit Policies

Credit policies boil down to two general questions:

- ◉ To whom should we give credit?
- ◉ How much credit should we give?

These two questions are closely interconnected. The business needs to evaluate most potential credit sales on their own merits, and this is costly and time consuming. In fact, the salaries and overhead of the credit analysts are likely to be the largest single item in the cost of giving credit to customers.

How much freedom a company has in setting the terms on which it will grant credit depends on its *competitive position*. For example, an organization in a monopolistic position has considerably more flexibility than does one that faces aggressive competition. But real monopolies are rare. Most companies approach such a position only during very short periods, after they have introduced radically new products and before their competitors have had time to introduce similar ones. A company in such a position may be tempted to take advantage of it through product price, but it is likely to tighten up its credit policy as well. The advantage of restricting credit will be fairly short lived, but the damage to customer relations could continue for a long time.

Nevertheless, economic factors do play an important part in credit policy. The key issue is **elasticity of demand** for the entrepreneur's product (we assume that the credit terms are a component of the overall price as the customer sees it and that customers will resist a reduction in credit, just as they will resist a price increase). If demand for a product is *inelastic*— that is, if an increase in price or a restriction in the terms of credit will produce a relatively small drop in demand, with the result that net sales revenues actually increase—then there is some potential flexibility in the terms of sale. Even here, however, it will be the industry as a whole that enjoys this flexibility; individual companies will probably have to accept general industry practice. If demand for a product is *elastic*, on the other hand, there will be little room to change the terms of the sale at either the company or the industry level.

- The bank may require the right to be consulted before any changes are made in the company's top management.

- Some covenants prevent increases in top management salaries or other compensation.

Restrictive covenants are very important in term loans. If any covenant is breached, the bank has the right to take legal action to recover its loan, probably forcing the company into insolvency. On the other hand, covenants may protect the borrowing company as well as the lender, in that their intention is to make it impossible for the borrower to get into serious financial trouble without first infringing one or more restrictions, thus giving the bank a right to step in and apply a guiding hand. A bank is reluctant to force any client into liquidation.

Equipment Financing

Capital equipment is often financed by intermediate-term funds. These may be straightforward term loans, usually secured by the equipment itself. Both banks and finance companies make equipment loans of this type. The nonbank companies charge considerably higher interest rates; they are used primarily by smaller companies that find themselves unable to qualify for bank term loans. As with other types of secured loans, the lender will evaluate the quality of the collateral and advance a percentage of the market value. In determining the repayment schedule, the lender ensures that the value of the equipment exceeds the loan balance. In addition, the loan repayment schedule is often made to coincide with the depreciation schedule of the equipment.

One further form of equipment financing is the *conditional sales contract*, which normally covers between two and five years. The buyer agrees to buy a piece of equipment by instalment payments over a period of years. During this time the buyer has the use of the equipment, but the seller retains title until the payments have been completed. Companies unable to find credit from any other source may be able to buy equipment on these terms. The lender's risk is small because it can repossess the equipment at any time if the borrower misses an instalment. Equipment distributors who sell equipment under conditional sales contracts often sell the contract to a bank or finance company, in which case the transaction becomes an interesting combination of equipment financing for the buyer and receivables financing for the seller.

The credit available under a conditional sales contract is less than the full purchase price of the equipment. Typically, the buyer is expected to make an immediate down payment of 25% to 33% of the full cash price, and only the balance is financed. The cost of the credit given may be quite high. Equipment that is highly specialized or subject to rapid obsolescence represents a greater risk to the lender than widely used standard equipment, and the interest charged on the sale of such specialized equipment to a small company may exceed 15% to 20%.

Obtaining Early Financing from External Sources

It's almost impossible for a brand-new company to get a conventional bank loan because it has no trading history and usually no assets to secure the loan. Even after a young company is up and running, it is still difficult to get a bank loan. Many entrepreneurs overlook the possibility of getting financial help from the Business Development Bank of Canada (BDC) or Futurepreneur Canada.

one of the largest multicategory toy and entertainment companies in the world, employing more than 900 people globally with offices in Toronto, Los Angeles, United Kingdom, France, Italy, Germany, the Netherlands, Central Europe, Hong Kong, China, and Japan.

Spin Master has broken and conquered barriers in food activity (McDonald's Flurry Maker, Hershey S'mores Maker, 7-11 Slurpee Maker, Dairy Queen Blizzard Maker), technology (Zoomer and Flutterbye Fairy), activity (Wackytivities, PixOs, Moon Sand, Aquadoodle, Paperoni, Glodoodle), R/C (Air Hogs), boy's action (Bakugan), dolls (Liv), extreme sports (Tech Deck), and furniture (Marshmallow).

Additionally, Spin Master has begun an aggressive acquisition path, beginning in 2010 by dominating the game aisle with newly acquired game titles that have since moved the portfolio to the top three in games in the United States. The recent acquisition of Spy Gear has been really exciting, taking this classic spy play pattern and launching new and innovative products and turning role play into real play. Spin Master is now a contender in the global construction aisle as well with the acquisition of Meccano/Erector.

But that is not all. Spin Master launched two new entertainment series. Paw Patrol premiered in conjunction with Nickelodeon and Tenkai Knights launched on Cartoon Network. This is just the beginning as Spin Master continues to transform into a true entertainment company.

Since the beginning of this whirlwind adventure, Spin Master has been critically acclaimed, landing 15 of the coveted TOTY awards to date, including outdoor, activity, vehicle, girls, boys, property of the year, innovative, and infant/preschool. Spin Master has also received numerous praise as one of the leading corporations receiving awards such as reaching platinum status of Canada's 50 Best Managed Companies, *Fast Company* 50 Most Innovative Consumer Products Company and Ernst & Young's Entrepreneur of the Year Award.

From the very beginning, Spin Master's roots have been planted in the same core values that have been a critical part of its success: entrepreneurialism, innovation, and fun. Transforming itself from a small toy enterprise into an all-encompassing entertainment company has been difficult, but the company's success comes from adapting to constantly changing times and seeing how spinning one idea can open up a whole new world of opportunities.

Source: Spin Master website, www.spinmaster.com/our-story.php

Planning Cash Flows and Profits

Although there is a relationship between them, cash flows are not the same as profit. **Profit** is an accounting concept designed to measure the overall performance of the company. It is a somewhat nebulous concept, open to variations in measurement techniques and accounting conventions, each of which produces somewhat different results that are then open to different interpretations.

In contrast, **cash flows** are not always a direct measure of a company's performance. For example, take two opposite extremes: a young, profitable company sinking as many funds as it can get into a new venture and an old, unprofitable company heading for bankruptcy. The results in terms of cash flow are likely to be the same: *declining cash balances*. A company can earn a handsome profit and have a net cash outflow in the same month if it pays for new capital equipment in that month. It can equally well show substantial loss and an increased cash balance in one month if the results of new financing or the proceeds from the sale of substantial fixed assets are received in that month.

However, the concept of *cash* is not nebulous: Either the company has a certain amount of cash or it does not. And a lack of cash is critical. A company can sustain losses for a time without suffering, but a company that has no cash is insolvent and in imminent danger of bankruptcy, no matter what its profit picture may be.

Thus, many financial transactions that do not enter into the calculation of profit—such as buying new fixed assets, getting additional financing, and paying dividends—do enter into cash flows. Similarly, some transactions that enter into the determination of profit—notably the deduction of depreciation and the amortization of expenses—do not directly enter into cash flows (although there are cash-flow benefits related to taxes) because they are noncash transactions with no effect on cash balances.

Many entrepreneurs and bankers are becoming increasingly interested in a concept called **free cash flow**. Free cash flow is equal to the firm's cash flow from operations minus investments in capital expenditures that are required to maintain the company's competitiveness. For example, a firm that has $1,500,000 in cash from operations and that spends $2,000,000 in property, plant, and equipment has a *negative* free cash flow of $500,000 ($1,500,000–$2,000,000). This implies that the firm does not have surplus funds from operations because it is, in fact, borrowing to maintain appropriate levels of capital investments.

Another term that is becoming more common is *pretax undedicated cash flow*. Undedicated cash flow is equal to free cash flow plus tax plus interest expense. Undedicated cash flow, or "raider" cash flow, is emerging as an important variable in appraising the investment attraction of engaging in leveraged buyouts, restructuring, and mergers of publicly owned companies. Prospective buyers (raiders) often add back interest and taxes so that they can get the broadest possible picture of the company's available cash. Then the investors determine how they could redirect the cash flows. Since the prospective buyers are going to be owners and not passive shareholders, they are more concerned about having control of the cash than about operating profits. Often much of the operating cash flow is devoted to servicing debt after the transaction. As the firm begins to service the debt arrangement, the equity in the company automatically grows.

CONCLUSION

Working capital is often misinterpreted as being synonymous with *firm liquidity*. In fact, only a part of net working capital is liquid; the balance of net working capital is tied up in firm operations. *Liquidity* is largely a function of a firm's growth and the timing of receipts and payments. In situations where payments are made to suppliers before customers pay, growth in sales generally results in lower liquidity.

Preparing a cash-flow forecast assists entrepreneurs in assessing the timing and maturity of funding needs. With a cash-flow forecast, the entrepreneur can more easily determine the type of funding to procure and the small, growing firm's ability to grow with available funds. This includes efficiencies in accounts receivable, inventories, payables, and accruals. To the extent that entrepreneurs can successfully negotiate with customers and suppliers, they will be able to manage future growth. However, small firms are rarely afforded the benefits associated with growth funded exclusively through internal cash generation. The more common occurrence includes external debt sources, leasing, cash innovations, and governmental programs for small firms. Such is the fate of the small business entrepreneur. Early growth stages result in large funding requirements and huge risks for those who can't meet payroll and supplier demands. However, once an entrepreneur has negotiated for a level of funds from external sources, including bank financing, privately placed debt, leasing options, and other financing innovations, that entrepreneur has a better chance for long-term corporate survival.

Reflection Point	Your Thoughts. . .	YOUR OPPORTUNITY JOURNAL ☐
1. What sources of capital do you have? Are you willing to take on a home equity loan? Use your personal credit cards? How much of a "nest egg" do you need to feel comfortable pursuing a new venture?		
2. What do you expect your cash conversion cycle to be? Is there a way to improve it? What accounts receivable terms are common in your industry? How should you manage accounts receivable?		
3. How much inventory does your business need to carry to avoid stockouts? What terms can you get on inventory (accounts payable)?		
4. Can you finance your accounts receivable? What means (bank loans, factoring, etc.) are most available to you? Can you get loans on your inventory?		
5. What short-term loans are needed for your business (e.g., line of credit)? When will you be bank creditworthy?		

Visit the Business Development Bank of Canada website (www.bdc.ca). The website has useful information on a number of startup issues. Take a look at the BDC loan programs. What steps do you need to undertake to qualify for these programs?

WEB EXERCISE ☐

FEED Resource Recovery

It was the spring of 2006 and Shane Eten had just won a $20,000 sustainability award at the highly competitive Rice University Business Plan Competition. Shane was already thinking about how he would use the $20,000. This wasn't the first time his idea, Feed Resource Recovery (**feed**), had won or placed well in a business plan competition—he'd finished second at the Babson College competition, second at the University of Colorado competition, and second at the UC–Berkeley competition. Although the prize money and services in kind were helpful, Shane knew that he couldn't successfully launch his business on prize money alone. Shane estimated that he would need $150,000–$250,000 to build the anaerobic digester prototype and much more money after that to scale production and sell the system across the country. Where would he get the money?

Based upon his success in the business plan competitions and through strong personal networking, Shane had talked to several venture capitalists and they all expressed strong interest in the business. Potential investors seemed to be coming out of the woodwork, but still Shane was uneasy. How much of the company would he have to give up if he was going to secure their investments? Even from his preliminary conversations with the venture capitalists, he knew that the valuation[11] of the company was only going to be part of the problem. He was discouraged by the grim prospect of having to jump through hoops and answering the venture capitalists endless list of questions. He figured it would take at least six months of battling back and forth over equity and shares during which time the venture capitalists would be looking over his shoulder, and all this before a prototype was ever built. Furthermore, several of the venture capitalists were saying "this is a great idea, come back when you have a prototype built," so Shane wasn't even sure if they were really interested or just talking. But what other choice did he have? How could he raise the substantial amount of funding that he would require to assemble a team and build a working prototype? And how could he accomplish all of this without giving up all rights to his idea? The task was daunting and the answers were scarce.

From Athlete to Entrepreneur: The History of Shane Eten

Shane Eten was born in Philadelphia and lived in a number of places while his father attended medical school. The family eventually settled in Cape Cod, Massachusetts, where his father and mother started a family-owned medical practice. Living near the sea inspired Shane's father.

> *My father built a sailboat in our back yard. He started when I was in sixth grade. He told me he was going to build a sailboat and sail it around the world. He was probably a little crazy, but he actually built a thirty-six foot trimaran.[12]*

For as long as Shane could remember, his father had a dream of building the sailboat. He would wake Shane up early in the morning on weekends and make him help work on the boat, sometimes working 12-hour days. After several years of effort, they successfully launched it and saw it sail.

> *Although at the time I really hated working on that boat, looking back I realize that it was a very important part of my childhood because it taught me the importance of hard work and taking a dream you have and making it reality.*

Like many boys, Shane was more interested in playing sports than school. He always enjoyed the team aspect and the competitive nature that came with athletics. His goal was to play Division I basketball in college. Hampered by knee injuries but still wanting to pursue his dream of playing college basketball, Shane chose to attend Trinity College, a Division III school, and play ball there. Unfortunately, his knees never fully recovered from a series of knee surgeries, so Shane never had a chance to play in college.

At Trinity, Shane majored in psychology and graduated in 2000. Although he enjoyed studying psychology, Shane didn't want to pursue a career in the field, but he didn't know exactly what he wanted.

> I really didn't enjoy school and to continue down the psychology career path would require me going back to school almost immediately. I like getting out there and getting my hands dirty with real work. In the field of psychology, I would have been doing a lot of research and theoretical education-based work. I wasn't ready for that. I wanted to get out in the world and make something happen.

After graduating from Trinity, Shane went to many interviews and eventually found a job working for an up-and-coming computer company, Angstrom Microsystems. Angstrom Microsystems built supercomputers from off-the-shelf components and Linux software. Shane loved working for this fast-growing entrepreneurial company because his job was never the same day to day. He had the opportunity to work with many different aspects of the business. His original job was working with vendors. Then he moved his way up to product development, and finally he settled in customer account management. While Shane was with Angstrom, the company grew from $500,000 to $15 million in sales in his first eight months. With the hands-on experience he gained and the opportunity of being able to see how so many aspects of a company worked, Shane realized:

> Entrepreneurship is fun and, most importantly, competitive. There's a real science to starting a company. It was at this time that I first started thinking about building my own company.

Unfortunately, Angstrom's success was short lived as the market took a turn for the worse when one of Angstrom's largest customers stopped growing. The CFO of Angstrom left for a position at a candle company. He called Shane and convinced him to come along for the ride. The position that Shane had been offered was 180 degrees different from his job at Angstrom and an opportunity to test his abilities in a new way. Although Shane liked the tech industry, he decided to give it a shot. So at age 24 he started as a manager of a candle manufacturing plant.

> It was a drastic change. Laurence Candle Company was a 60-year-old, third-generation company, and I was managing people mostly older than me—some who had been working there for 30 years.

He was forced to get on the floor and get dirty learning the process of making candles.

The Laurence Candle Company was struggling because its product was very similar to another established brand, Yankee Candle. The company needed new ideas so Shane raised his hand and asked if they would give him a shot at designing a new line of candles. After doing market research and going to trade shows to see what was out there, he launched a new line of candles made from a new type of wax made out of soy. Soy wax was environmentally friendly because the wax was made from an all-natural crop; it was considered renewable and therefore sustainable. The soy wax candle line took off. Not only was soy cheaper than traditional paraffin wax, but also it could be sold as all-natural for 30–40% more than traditional candles. Sales jumped instantly. It saved the company.

> There was a new consumer emerging at this time, and if you could say that it was all-natural, then you could say that it was sustainable or noble. This new brand of customer was willing to pay a premium for environmentally friendly products.

Shane put in 60- to 70-hour workweeks developing the line of soy candles. He also started research on adding biodegradable plastic wrappers to the candles. It was at this point that Shane knew if he was going to put in this much time and effort toward an idea, the next time it would be for himself and his own company.

Working for small companies, Shane had learned a lot about how the business world worked, but he knew that he needed a stronger foundation in accounting and working with numbers. If he was going to be successful in starting and managing his own ventures, he was going to have to go back for an MBA. At 28 years of age, he decided it was time to go back to school. Soon after he applied, Shane was accepted to Babson College.

The CleanTech Industry

Shane entered Babson with a goal of finding an idea to launch his own business. He was intrigued with opportunities in the Clean Technology space, especially around combating global warming. Investment and growth in the CleanTech industry exploded in 2007, passing the record set in 2006 in the first three quarters.[13] Exhibit 12.1 shows an explosive upward investment trend.[14]

The increased growth and investment in the CleanTech industry has been brought on not only by the large price increases in gas and other fossil fuels but also by the raised awareness of global warming by prominent figures such as former vice-president Al Gore. Gore's work with the United Nations Intergovernmental Panel on Climate Change, his winning the Nobel Peace Prize, and his involvement in the Academy Award–winning documentary *An Inconvenient Truth* have brought to light the serious issues of climate change and

EXHIBIT 12.1   **Annual CleanTech Investment**

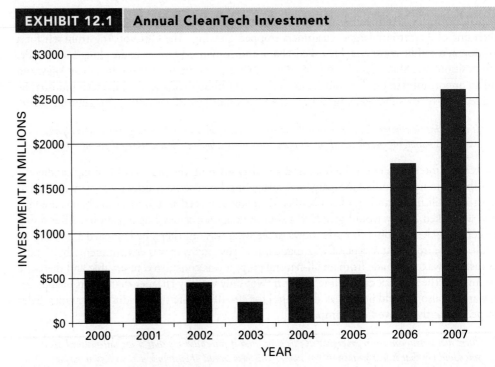

Source: National Venture Capital Association.

global warming. These works have also brought legitimacy and an increased interest in the CleanTech industry.

Taken at face value, the surprisingly entertaining An Inconvenient Truth *provides an idealistic, persuasive, and compelling dissection of the perils of global warming. Frightening and timely, the smartly organized documentary is an urgent plea for responsibility and action as well as an impassioned call to heed the ominous warnings of science.*[15]

Gore's words resonated with Shane. As Gore stated:

But along with the danger we face from global warming, this crisis also brings unprecedented opportunities. What are the opportunities such a crisis also offers? They include not just new jobs and new profits, although there will be plenty of both, we can build clean engines, we can harness the sun and the wind; we can stop wasting energy; we can use our planet's plentiful coal resources without heating the planet.

The procrastinators and deniers would have us believe this will be expensive. But in recent years, dozens of companies have cut emissions of heat-trapping gases while saving money. Some of the world's largest companies are moving aggressively to capture the enormous economic opportunities offered by a clean energy future.

But there's something even more precious to be gained if we do the right thing. The climate crisis also offers us the chance to experience what very few generations in history have had the privilege of knowing: a generational mission; the exhilaration of a compelling moral purpose; a shared and unifying cause; the thrill of being forced by circumstances to put aside the pettiness and conflict that so often stifle the restless human need for transcendence; the opportunity to rise.[16]

Consumers and the public in general are expecting companies to be more eco-friendly; they want to see real efforts made toward carbon reduction and recycling. This has encouraged companies to race toward new technologies in order to capture a piece of this new market. One example of the efforts that mainstream companies are making is Google's recent pledge to become a carbon neutral company.

Google today announced a new strategic initiative to develop electricity from renewable energy sources that will be cheaper than electricity produced from coal. The newly created initiative, known as RE<C, will focus initially on advanced solar thermal power, wind power technologies, enhanced geothermal systems and other potential breakthrough technologies. RE<C is hiring engineers and energy experts to lead its research and development work, which will begin with a significant effort on solar thermal technology, and will also investigate enhanced geothermal systems and other areas. In 2008 Google expects to spend tens of millions on research and development and related investments in renewable energy. As part of its capital planning process, the company also anticipates investing hundreds of millions of dollars in breakthrough renewable energy projects which generate positive returns.[17]

Another example is Walmart. Although Walmart has faced much criticism for its energy consumption and pollution practices, the company has invested large amounts of money in green technologies. For example, Walmart installed solar power in 22 of its super centres, which accounts for roughly 1% of the U.S. super centres. Walmart has also made other green commitments promising to decrease its carbon footprint. It has pledged to eventually use 100% renewable energy sources. In the short run, company officials say they will adapt old stores to be 25% more efficient and new stores to be 30% more efficient.[18]

The increased interest in clean technology has attracted many investors. Exhibit 12.2 shows the distribution of investment in the CleanTech industry by subcategory.[19]

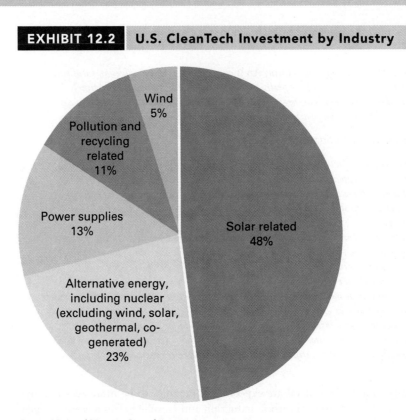

EXHIBIT 12.2 **U.S. CleanTech Investment by Industry**

Source: National Venture Capital Association.

With the wealth of interest by angel investors and venture capitalists alike, many new companies have hit the ground running and have found success. This explains the high interest that Shane received from these investors. The CleanTech Venture Network estimates that over 240 CleanTech companies could be positioned for a liquidity event between 2007 and 2009.[20] A small niche within the CleanTech sector known as waste conversion technologies is beginning to catch on. One such example is Converted Organics Inc. Converted Organics, based in Boston, is a development-stage company dedicated to producing a valuable all-natural, organic soil additive through food waste recycling. Started in 2003, Converted Organics Inc. is a five-employee operation that has just recently gone public raising $9.9 million in an IPO and has a market capitalization of $14.3 million.[21] Other examples of recent transactions involving waste conversion providers are noted in Exhibit 12.3.

Roots of Feed Idea

At Babson, the entrepreneurship professors stress the importance of opportunity and an entrepreneur's fit to that opportunity. So Shane thought he should leverage his past experience and start his own candle line. However, copyright laws and low profit margins discouraged him. Next he looked at biodegradable packaging lines.

When I had an idea, I would do research for maybe three weeks, and see who else was out there, if the product was feasible, and who the customers were. . . . I would usually find a

| EXHIBIT 12.3 | Sample Investments into CleanTech Companies |

- **BlueFire Ethanol, Inc.** is established to deploy the commercially ready, patented, and proven Arkenol Technology Process for the profitable conversion of cellulosic ("Green Waste") waste materials to ethanol. They acquired a $15,000,000 investment from Quercus Trust.[22]
- **Disenco Energy PLC,** a UK-based developer of a revolutionary home power-generating unit known as the Disenco Home Power Plant, closed their initial IPO for $2,750,000.[23]
- **Oakleaf** merged with Greenleaf, which rents stationary compactors, containers, balers, and other waste management and recycling equipment to commercial businesses and haulers.[24]
- Scotts paid $20 million last year for **Rod McLellan Co.,** which focuses on naturally derived fertilizers.[25]
- The Carlyle Group acquired residuals recycler **Synagro Technologies** for about $447.5 million in cash, including the assumption of ~$310 million in debt. Synagro operates at over 1,000 wastewater treatment plants throughout North America, providing operations and residuals management services. Many of these wastewater treatment plants employ anaerobic digestion. The company is using this experience to expand into the agribusiness market with its first operational facility, which was designed and built in Chino, California. This digester is designed for 225 wet tonnes of fresh cow manure per day. It employs dewatering and onsite cogeneration using Capstone Micro turbines.[26]

really big obstacle. Or I just found a company that does this or a big brand that does this or someone that tried to start it and it didn't work. And when I got to biodegradable plastic, I realized there was no way to compost it, so it wasn't as environmentally friendly as I had first imagined. But during this search, I came across composting technology. This seemed like a big idea and a big opportunity. The key with composting that makes it so unique is that someone is getting paid for their raw materials, which is basically trash. Companies paid to have trash hauled away, so that meant composters could get their raw material for free or even be paid to take it away.

Shane started doing research into the composting industry and was intrigued by waste conversion technology. He looked at gasification,[27] plasma arc,[28] aerobic composting,[29] and finally anaerobic digestion.[30] Anaerobic digestion caught his eye. Anaerobic digestion was a relatively proven and cheap technology, and it seemed the most viable option. Next Shane began to look at the waste stream market. He wanted to know who the largest waste producers were, what kind of waste they produced, and what the competition looked like in those industries. He looked at households and small restaurants and found that in most cases they would not generate enough waste to justify an onsite digester and the cost of transporting the waste to a central location would be prohibitive. After further research, Shane found that the food waste produced by processing plants and supermarkets turned out to be the most promising. This was because they both were producing large amounts of food waste and the volume was concentrated in a single location (see Exhibit 12.4).

Babson is great because there are tons of ideas floating around. The professors give us the tools to analyze whether an idea is an opportunity. You start with a problem, and if there's a problem, there's potentially an opportunity. So you have a bunch of students running around with two-page summaries on their ideas, sharing their thoughts, and seeking feedback during breaks from class. The school also has a "Rocket Pitch" event where you get three minutes to convince the audience that your idea has real potential. It takes a lot of work to learn how to pitch your concept in three minutes, but that process really helps you understand the issues around the idea.

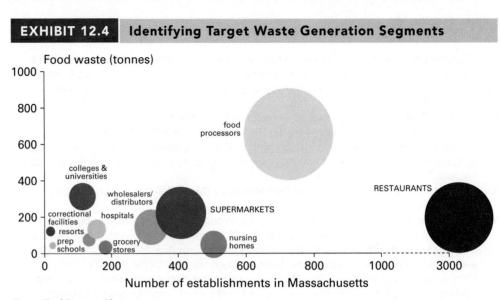

EXHIBIT 12.4 **Identifying Target Waste Generation Segments**

Source: Feed Business Plan.

Shane's two-page opportunity was about the company he wanted to start, which he called Biospan. He would build a large anaerobic digester that would be at a centralized plant, and he would collect food waste from restaurants, grocery stores, and even homes to feed the digester and produce compost and biogas. The basic idea made sense—taking waste and producing a usable byproduct. Shane decided that this idea was worth investing time and effort to really understand it. Shane applied to Babson's Entrepreneur Intensity Track (EIT)[31] program with the idea of launching this business.

Through the EIT program, Shane met with a venture capitalist who asked him tough questions like "How are you going to get six million dollars to build a big plant and how are you going to keep Waste Management from doing it bigger and better than you?" Six million dollars was a lot of money, and Shane didn't like the idea of competing with a company like Waste Management who did $13 billion in revenue each year. By asking the right questions, Shane also realized that a large centralized plant was inefficient. Transporting the waste to the plant and then sending the energy back to users added costs, used energy (gasoline for dump trucks), and wasn't as "Green" as a decentralized unit located where the waste was produced.

Shane then began to look at the industry and who might gain the greatest benefit from a mobile anaerobic system. Food processors, like large pig and chicken farms, were already starting to use anaerobic digestion systems. After more research, Shane found that grocery stores looked like the best option. They were already sorting their waste and sending it to composters, and the volume was low enough to discourage large players from entering. This seemed like a great marketplace for his decentralized systems.

> *You didn't have to ask them to change their habits. They were already sorting their waste, and the system could be implemented on location without disrupting their day-to-day operation.*

Shane wanted to get into the industry as efficiently as possible, so he started to look for existing anaerobic systems that he could adapt to his target. He couldn't find any systems that could handle high-solid content; they were mostly set up for human or animal waste. Furthermore, the companies building these systems were targeting larger scale, centralized plants, not smaller decentralized systems that Shane envisioned. Many people, mainly the business professionals in anaerobic digestion, were saying that decentralized systems would be too small to be effective. In Europe, they were already using anaerobic digestion for food waste but only on a large scale. From the previous business models and the waste industry's frame of mind, the onsite model was not seen as profitable, but with the increases in energy prices and raised awareness in green tech, it started to make more sense. Shane believed that if the technology could be produced, the idea would be easy to market in a food retail industry where the profit margins were razor thin and competition fierce.

The Product

The **feed** system, known as the R2, would use anaerobic digestion (AD)—a clean, safe, and proven technology—to turn biodegradable waste into fuel (biogas) for a distributed electricity generation unit. AD is the breakdown of organic material by microorganisms in the absence of oxygen. Although this process occurs naturally in landfills, AD usually refers to an artificially accelerated operation that processes organic waste to produce biogas and a stable solid residue. People have been turning waste into biogas for hundreds of years, and many developing countries rely on small-scale AD systems for cooking. AD has grown rapidly in Europe, mostly in large centralized plants using advanced technologies. The R2 is a combination of the cheap, compact systems of India and China and the large-scale, expensive, and technologically sophisticated systems of Europe: a fully automated system that enables the customers to process waste and generate energy onsite without changing current waste disposal behaviour.

> *The decentralized nature of our system meant that you could place the R2 (see Exhibit 12.5) at the back of the store right in the same space that the organic waste dumpster currently occupied. It was critical to our potential customers that this system didn't require more space or alter the footprint of the current store (see Exhibit 12.6).*

EXHIBIT 12.5	The R2 System: Compact Onsite Waste Conversion for Supermarkets

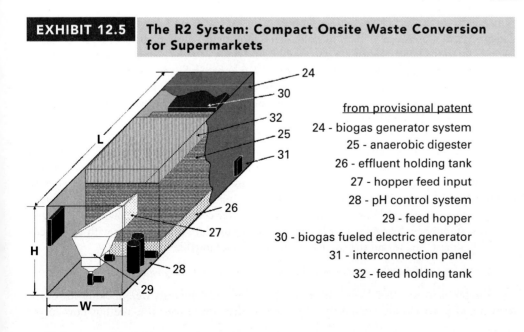

from provisional patent

24 - biogas generator system
25 - anaerobic digester
26 - effluent holding tank
27 - hopper feed input
28 - pH control system
29 - feed hopper
30 - biogas fueled electric generator
31 - interconnection panel
32 - feed holding tank

| EXHIBIT 12.6 | Onsite Waste Conversion |

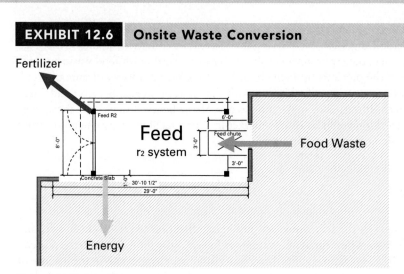

Source: Feed Business Plan.

The automation is made possible by the integrated control technology that operates the patented pH-balancing unit to continually optimize system performance. Other novel and patented ideas that differentiate the system include an integrated biogas generator unit, a gravity-fed system that increases efficiency while reducing cost and complexity, a multitank system for system reliability and flexibility, and pH balancing of the waste stream to handle diverse waste. Other than biogas, the R2 produces nutrient-rich compost that could potentially be sold to farmers. The projected price that the grocery store would pay for its R2 was around $300,000.

Lots of Interest

Craig Benson, a professor at Babson, told Shane that the best way to attract investors was to go and talk to the biggest customer you could find. "*If you can find a customer for your product, investors will be more than willing to get on board,*" Craig noted. Shane started to make as many connections as possible. He called several grocery store chains in the Northeast, including Stop and Shop, Shaw's, Walmart, and Whole Foods, but it was always hard get in front of anyone very high up in the ranks. He was always sent to someone who, even if interested, had no power to do anything about it. How could he get in front of the right person?

The success of **feed** in business plan competitions was also bringing a great deal of interest to his anaerobic digester idea. Many of the venture capitalists and investors that were present at the competitions were serious about its investment possibilities. During the Rice Business Plan Competition in spring 2006 when **feed** won the sustainability award, Dow Chemical Venture Group showed an especially strong interest and said they could introduce Shane to Walmart. The Dow group flew Shane to their headquarters and put him on the phone with top executives at Walmart. Shane said the conversation went something like this:

> *Does it have a 24-month payback time? I said no and they basically hung up.*

The problem was that Dow and most of the venture capitalists were looking for quick returns and proven ready technology. That meant that Shane had to figure out how to get customer payback down to two years. Moreover, once the investors realized that the final product was still in the distant future, they were reluctant to invest the time and resources needed. This meant that Shane needed to build a prototype before the venture capitalists would be interested. Shane started looking elsewhere for the needed capital.

Through the grapevine Shane heard about a Massachusetts Technology Collaborative (MTC) grant for onsite energy providers. To be eligible you needed to meet a set power output and find a buyer for the electricity that would sign on to the project. The MTC grant would then pay a certain amount of money for each kilowatt you could generate from the green energy method. Shane had a connection through a friend of the family at Ring Brothers grocery store, a small local grocery store on Cape Cod. Ring Brothers agreed to sign on as the company sponsor and **feed** won the grant for $195,000.

The grant required that **feed** first run a feasibility study before it could actually start to build the prototype, and the grant provided $20,000 for the research study. So Shane took a look at how much actual food waste Ring Brothers produced and found that they weren't producing enough waste to make the system feasible for the required energy output of 50 kW that was needed for the grant. Without the proper energy production output, they were forced to tell MTC that they were not going to be eligible for the $195,000 grant.

Team Building

Based on his experience with Ring Brothers and the knowledge that he needed to build a prototype, Shane realized that he didn't have the skill set to do this venture on his own. He needed some technical expertise on the founding team. Shane knew that he would need an engineer to run the actual research and production of the first prototype. He needed someone who could take over a large part of the company and have the ability to get things done without supervision. A friend of Shane's who worked at Raytheon told him that he worked with a young engineer who fit the profile that Shane was looking for.

Ryan Begin specialized in product development at Raytheon, where he led a multidisciplinary team of engineers in the integration of advanced missile defense hardware. While Ryan enjoyed the big paycheque, he was looking for something different. Before Raytheon, Ryan had worked on multiple renewable energy and non-energy products through Clarkson University and other private organizations.

> I wanted to get out of the large corporation and saw the **feed** concept as really interesting. It was in the green space, where I had done some work before. But most importantly, I could be on the ground floor of something potentially huge.

When they met, Shane knew that he had found the business partner he was looking for and that Ryan would be a strong addition to the team.

> Ryan has the unique ability to get his hands dirty in putting the prototype together, but at the same time he is also very smart and brings a lot of expertise to the table. He has a great work ethic, and he's the kind of guy that works so hard and is so driven that he makes you feel guilty if you're not working just as hard.

After their initial meeting, Ryan began to run some of the numbers Shane had presented to him regarding the biogas and electricity production of the suggested system. Although he found that many of numbers were on the high end of possibility, they still were within the range of having some real potential.

I could see that some of Shane's projections were off by a lot, but the potential was there. Also the fact that he already had interested customers and investors reaffirmed my feelings that this could be a great opportunity for me.

Ryan was leaving a high-paying job at Raytheon with stability and benefits for a job with a new company and little or no salary.

I had a choice to make: I could continue to take the safe route with Raytheon, or I could put it all on the line to test my skills and have the chance to do something big and exciting. I didn't feel like I was doing any real engineering at Raytheon. Being able to lead product development within the renewable energy field was very appealing to me. I could also see that Shane had real business savvy and really believed strongly in his idea and had what it would take to sell it.

To entice and reward Ryan, Shane agreed to take him on as a co-founder and to give him some founder's shares. After some back and forth on the amount of stock Ryan would receive in the company, they settled on 20% of the founder's shares and the goal of paying a salary once they had raised a significant amount of investment.

EXHIBIT 12.7	**Feed Income Statement Projections**									
Income Statement Years 1 to 5 ($)										
	Year 1		Year 2		Year 3		Year 4		Year 5	
NET REVENUES	320,000	100%	1,880,000	100%	6,555,000	100%	13,985,000	100%	24,345,750	100%
COST OF REVENUE	332,800	104%	1,440,629	77%	4,939,057	75%	8,794,486	63%	15,538,904	64%
GROSS PROFIT	(12,800)	-4%	439,371	23%	1,615,943	25%	5,190,514	37%	8,806,846	36%
OPERATING EXPENSES										
Sales & Marketing	**29,600**	**9%**	**96,400**	**5%**	**315,150**	**5%**	**521,550**	**4%**	**838,373**	**3%**
Salaries & Benefits	0	0%	0	0%	58,500	1%	102,000	1%	108,000	0%
Initial Branding Efforts	20,000	6%	40,000	2%	60,000	1%	0	0%	0	0%
Other	9,600	3%	56,400	3%	196,650	3%	419,550	3%	730,373	3%
Research & Development	**14,600**	**5%**	**190,900**	**10%**	**349,300**	**5%**	**727,550**	**5%**	**1,062,373**	**4%**
Salaries & Benefits	9,600	3%	90,900	5%	249,300	4%	527,550	4%	862,373	4%
Product Development	5,000	2%	100,000	5%	100,000	2%	200,000	1%	200,000	1%
General and Administration	**17,067**	**5%**	**171,100**	**9%**	**485,790**	**7%**	**742,417**	**5%**	**1,048,495**	**4%**
Salaries & Benefits	0	0%	103,500	6%	300,690	5%	405,600	3%	504,000	2%
Depreciation	667	0%	4,000	0%	9,000	0%	11,667	0%	11,667	0%
Rent & Utilities	0	0%	6,000	0%	15,000	0%	15,450	0%	15,914	0%
Legal Feed	10,000	3%	20,000	1%	30,000	0%	30,000	0%	30,000	0%
Other	6,400	2%	37,600	2%	131,100	2%	279,700	2%	486,915	2%
Total Operating Expenses	61,267	19%	458,400	24%	1,150,240	18%	1,991,517	14%	2,949,241	12%
EARNINGS FROM OPERATIONS	(74,067)	-23%	(19,029)	-1%	465,703	7%	3,198,997	23%	5,857,605	24%
TAXES	0	0%	0	0%	(149,043)	-2%	(1,279,599)	-9%	(2,343,042)	-10%
NET EARNINGS	(74,067)	-23%	(19,029)	-1%	316,660	5%	1,919,398	14%	3,514,563	14%

Next Steps

With the start of a team and a strong customer interest, Shane and Ryan knew they had to build a functioning prototype. They had run some preliminary numbers and put together some pro forma financials (see Exhibits 12.7–12.9). They showed that **feed** needed investment now. Where could they get the $250,000 dollars needed to build the prototype? (See Exhibit 12.10.) While most venture capitalists wouldn't invest at this stage, there were a few who might—but at what valuation and how long would it take to close the deal? Shane also could raise the money through family and friends, but this would take time as well. Shane and Ryan were anxious to get started, but they knew if they couldn't build a prototype **feed** would never get off the ground.

EXHIBIT 12.8	Feed Balance Sheet Projections					
	Begin	**Year 1**	**Year 2**	**Year 3**	**Year 4**	**Year 5**
ASSETS						
CURRENT ASSETS						
Cash	250,000	174,926	140,904	866,314	3,127,462	7,174,275
Accounts Receivable		1,200	10,159	40,000	234,000	772,000
Inventories		0	0	60,000	130,000	331,200
Other Current Assets		204	1,224	60,000	130,000	276,000
Total Current Assets	250,000	176,330	152,287	1,026,314	3,621,462	8,553,475
PROPERTY & EQUIPMENT	0	1,500	16,000	29,250	32,500	31,250
TOTAL ASSETS	250,000	177,830	168,287	1,055,564	3,653,962	8,584,725
LIABILITIES & SHAREHOLDERS' EQUITY						
CURRENT LIABILITIES						
Short-Term Debt	0	0	0	0	0	0
Accounts Payable & Accrued Expenses		1,693	10,159	522,000	1,131,000	2,401,200
Other Current Liabilities		204	1,224	60,000	130,000	276,000
Current Portion of Long-Term Debt	0	0	0	0	0	0
Total Current Liabilities	0	1,897	11,383	582,000	1,261,000	2,677,200
LONG-TERM DEBT (less current portion)	0	0	0	0	0	0
SHAREHOLDERS' EQUITY						
Common Shares	250,000	250,000	250,000	250,000	250,000	250,000
Preferred Shares	0	0	0	0	0	0
Retained Earnings		(74,067)	(93,096)	223,564	2,142,962	5,657,525
Total Equity	250,000	175,933	156,904	473,564	2,392,962	5,907,525
TOTAL LIABILITIES & EQUITY	250,000	177,830	168,287	1,055,564	3,653,962	8,584,725

EXHIBIT 12.9 **Feed Cash-Flow Projections**

	Year 1	Year 2	Year 3	Year 4	Year 5
OPERATING ACTIVITIES					
Net Earnings	(74,067)	(19,029)	316,660	1,919,398	3,514,563
Depreciation	500	5,500	11,750	16,750	21,250
Working Capital Changes					
(Increase)/Decrease Accounts Receivable	(1,200)	(8,959)	(29,841)	(194,000)	(538,000)
(Increase)/Decrease Inventories	0	0	(60,000)	(70,000)	(201,200)
(Increase)/Decrease Other Current Assets	(204)	(1,020)	(58,776)	(70,000)	(146,000)
Increase/(Decrease) Accts Pay & Accrd Expenses	1,693	8,466	511,841	609,000	1,270,200
Increase/(Decrease) Other Current Liab	204	1,020	58,776	70,000	146,000
Net Cash Provided/(Used) by Operating Activities	(73,074)	(14,022)	750,410	2,281,148	4,066,813
INVESTING ACTIVITIES					
Property & Equipment Other	(2,000)	(20,000)	(25,000)	(20,000)	(20,000)
Net Cash Used in Investing Activities	(2,000)	(20,000)	(25,000)	(20,000)	(20,000)
FINANCING ACTIVITIES					
Increase/(Decrease) Short-Term Debt	0	0	0	0	0
Increase/(Decrease) Curr. Portion LTD	0	0	0	0	0
Increase/(Decrease) Long-Term Debt	0	0	0	0	0
Increase/(Decrease) Common Shares	0	0	0	0	0
Increase/(Decrease) Preferred Shares	0	0	0	0	0
Dividends Declared	0	0	0	0	0
Net Cash Provided/(Used) by Financing	0	0	0	0	0
INCREASE/(DECREASE) IN CASH	(75,074)	(34,022)	725,410	2,261,148	4,046,813
CASH AT BEGINNING OF YEAR	250,000	174,926	140,904	866,314	3,127,462
CASH AT END OF YEAR	250,000 174,926	140,904	866,314	3,127,462	7,174,275

EXHIBIT 12.10 **Startup Capital Needed to Build Prototype**

Components of Digester	$150,000
Engineering Salaries	75,000
Other/Misc	25,000
Total	**$250,000**

Discussion Questions

1. Is **feed** an opportunity?
2. Where can Shane raise the necessary money to build the prototype?
3. What are the implications on valuation for the different sources?

This case was prepared by Reuben Zacharakis-Jutz under the direction of Professor Andrew Zacharakis. © Copyright Babson College. Funding provided by the John H. Muller Chair in Entrepreneurship. All rights reserved.

NOTES

1. Bank of Canada, "Household Credit," http://credit.bankofcanada.ca/house-holdcredit.

2. B. Rabidoux, "Why Canadian Home-owners Are Likely as Vulnerable as Americans Were," *Maclean's,* August 22, 2012, www.macleans.ca/economy/business/why-canadian-homeowners-are-now-likely-just-as-vulnerable-as-americans-were.

3. *Financial Services for Small Businesses in the United States* (Rockville, MD: Packaged Facts, March 2008), 272.

4. Quote from Dennis Ensing, April 28, 2014.

5. Federal Reserve, "Senior Loan Officer Opinion Survey on Bank Lending Practices," July 2012; V. Williams, "Small Business Lending in the United States, 2010–2011," U.S. Small Business Administration, Office of Advocacy, Office of Economic Research, 2011, www.sba.gov/advocacy/7540/173967.

6. D. Seens, Industry Canada, Biannual Survey of Suppliers of Business Financing Data Analysis, Second Half of 2013, June 2014. Accessed at www.ic.gc.ca/eic/site/061.nsf/eng/02895.html#fnb2.

7. Business Development Bank of Canada, "Financing," www.bdc.ca/EN/solutions/financing/Pages/default.aspx.

8. Business Development Bank of Canada, "Small Business Loan: Get up to $50,000," http://www.bdc.ca/EN/solutions/financing/Pages/financing_request.aspx. Interest rates are subject to change and the indicated 6% is the current rate at the time of writing.

9. Futurepreneur Canada, "Spin Master Innovation Fund: Overview," http://www.futurpreneur.ca/en/programs/innovation/.

10. Business Development Bank of Canada, "Small Business Loan Online Application Checklist," www.bdc.ca/EN/Documents/solutions/small_business_loan_checklist.pdf.

11. The valuation of a company is broken into two parts. The pre-money valuation is how much the company is deemed to be worth prior to the investment. The post-money valuation is the pre-money valuation plus the investment. The percentage of equity that the investor receives is the investment / post-money valuation. The percentage that the entrepreneur retains is the pre-money valuation / post-money valuation.

12. A trimaran is a fast pleasure sailboat with three parallel hulls.

13. National Venture Capital Association, "CleanTech Venture Investments by US Firms Break Record in 2007," Thompson Financial press release, November 28, 2007, http://nvca.org/pdf/CleanTechInterimPR.pdf.

14. Ibid.

15. C. Ogle, "Seeing Entertaining Documentary Makes You Want to Save the World," *Miami Herald,* June 9. 2006, http://ae.miami.com/entertainment/ui/miami/movie.html?id=616935&reviewId=20952.

[16] Excerpt from *An Inconvenient Truth: The Planetary Emergency of Global Warming and What We Can Do About It*, directed by D. Guggenheim, written by A. Gore (2006; Paramount Classics).

[17] J. Fuller, "Google's Goal: Renewable Energy Cheaper than Coal Creates Renewable Energy R&D Group and Supports Breakthrough Technologies," Google press release, November 27, 2007, www.google.com/intl/en/press/pressrel/20071127_green.html.

[18] Walmart, "Environmental Sustainability," http://corporate.walmart.com/global-responsibility/environmental-sustainability.

[19] National Venture Capital Association, "CleanTech Venture Investments."

[20] N. Parker, "CleanTech Is Ripe for Growth," *Israel Venture Capital & Private Equity Journal*, February 14, 2007, www.altassets.com/casefor/sectors/2007/nz9921.php.

[21] L. Van der Pool, "Spurned by VCs, Waste Conversion Startup Goes Public," *Boston Journal*, March 16, 2007, www.bizjournals.com/boston/stories/2007/03/19/story8.html.

[22] "BlueFire Ethanol Closes $15.5 Million in Financing," Business Wire, January 8, 2008, www.businesswire.com/news/home/20080108005535/en/BlueFire-Ethanol-Closes-15.5-Million-Financing#.U-O_yfldWSo.

[23] "Disenco Energy PLC Closes IPO for US$2,750,000 and Lists on the TSX Venture Exchange," PR Newswire, February 26, 2007, www.prnewswire.co.uk/cgi/news/release?id=191571.

[24] "Greenleaf Compaction, Inc. Has Merged with Oakleaf Waste Management," Press Release Headlines, July 27, 2004, http://pressreleaseheadlines.com/greenleaf-compaction-inc-has-merged-with-oak-leaf-waste-management-3865.

[25] E. Lambert, "Organic Miracle Needed," *Forbes,* September 4, 2006, www.forbes.com/forbes/2006/0904/066.html.

[26] "The Carlyle Group to Acquire Synagro Technologies for $5.76 per Share," Carlyle Group press release, January 28, 2007, www.carlyle.com/news-room/news-release-archive/carlyle-group-acquire-synagro-technologies-576-share.

[27] Gasification is a process that converts organic material or biomass into gases or liquid fuels by a combination of high temperatures and reduced oxygen supply. Source: J. Schilli, "Using Gasification to Process Municipal Solid Waste," Environmental and Resource Management Group of HDR, *HDR Innovations*, vol. 12.

[28] Plasma arc gasification is a process in which solid waste is shredded and fed into a furnace where extreme electrical charges bring the temperature above 3,000 degrees. After an hour or so, waste material breaks down into its molecular building blocks, leaving three marketable byproducts: a combustible synthesis gas, or syngas, that can be converted into steam or electricity; metal ingots that can be resold and melted down again; and a glassy solid that can be processed into material for floor tiles or gravel. Source: S. Durst, "Problem No. 3: Waste Disposal," *Fortune*, March 5, 2007, B-4.

[29] Aerobic composting is the process of decomposing organic waste using microorganisms and an aerobic or oxygenated environment. Source: M. Pace, B. Miller, and K. Farrell-Poe, "The Composting Process," Utah State University Extension, AG-WM 01, October 1, 1995.

[30] Anaerobic digestion is a biochemical process in which particular kinds of bacteria digest biomass in an oxygen-free environment. Several different types of bacteria work together to break down complex organic wastes in stages, resulting in the production of "biogas." Source: Oregon.gov, "Bioenergy in Oregon: Biogas Technology," www.oregon.gov/ENERGY/RENEW/Biomass/biogas.aspx.

[31] EIT is a curriculum focused on deep business planning and culminates in the launch of a business during the final year of a student's education.

©iStock.com/filo

LEGAL AND TAX ISSUES, INCLUDING

INTELLECTUAL PROPERTY

CHAPTER OUTLINE

This chapter was written by Margaret Ann Wilkinson, John B.A. Wilkinson, Richard Mandel, Kirk Teska, and Joseph S. Iamdioio.

MANY ENTHUSIASTIC ENTREPRENEURS are so excited about where they're going that they forget to consider where they've been. They're surprised to learn that there may be serious limitations imposed upon their freedom of action arising out of their former employment. Some of these limitations may be the result of agreements signed by the entrepreneur while employed in his or her former position. Others may be imposed as a matter of law, without any agreement or even knowledge on the part of the employee. These considerations are among many that suggest that entrepreneurs consult early with a lawyer.

Unfortunately, many people perceive engaging a lawyer as an unnecessary expense when beginning a new venture. However, the earlier you can consult a professional, the more likely it is that your business will avoid costly mistakes. For example, without having had a lawyer to advise you with regard to the drafting of a partnership or shareholders' agreement (described later in this chapter), if a founder dies the remaining partners or shareholders may have no way of retrieving the share of the business that falls to the estate of the deceased founder. As another example, without legal advice, an entrepreneur may be confronted by a large income tax bill for his receipt of *sweat equity*.

Almost any lawyer called to the Bar of your province or territory is legally entitled to give you advice. In Ontario, it is possible to find lawyers who have received specialist certification from the governing body of the Ontario legal profession, the Law Society of Upper Canada, and this may be helpful to you in selecting a lawyer—but specialist certification is not necessary for a lawyer to provide you with the advice you seek, even in Ontario. Typically many Canadian lawyers concentrate their practices in particular areas: patent lawyers often do very little work in any other area of the law, and most good litigators concentrate on litigating. For some lawyers, representation of startups and small businesses has become an area of concentration.

A lawyer experienced in handling startups will be aware of the myriad issues that should be covered in a shareholders' or partnership agreement and the other unique problems facing entrepreneurs. She or he will be able to advise you about the various choices of legal entities available to entrepreneurial enterprises as well as to advise, for example, if you have any residual obligations owed to a previous employer. In addition, lawyers who practise in the startup world will be familiar with young business's unique cash-flow problems and may be willing to work out instalment payments or other arrangements to ease the strain on tight startup cash flow.

Leaving Your Present Position

Corporate Opportunity

The **corporate opportunity** doctrine is an outgrowth of the traditional obligation of loyalty owed by an agent to a principal. In its most common form, it prohibits an officer or director of a company, a partner in a partnership, or a person in a similar position from identifying a business opportunity that would be valuable to her or his business and using that information for her or his own benefit or the benefit of a competitor.

Generally in the corporate context, to discharge a director's legal obligation to the company of which she or he is a director, the director would be required to disclose the opportunity to the board and allow the board to decide (without her or his participation in the decision) whether the company will like to pursue the opportunity, for instance, to make a purchase. Only after the company has been fully informed and has decided *not* to take advantage of an opportunity may the director use that information for herself or himself. In such a situation, if the information leads the director who first became aware of the opportunity to leave the company of which he or she is a board member and go to work for (or become owner of) a competitor, at minimum she or he would be required to resign her or his director position with the previous business – but there may be situations in which mere resignation will not eliminate the obligation to use the information only for the benefit of the original enterprise: such situations may involve contractual obligations known as **restrictive covenants**, which limit a person's ability to work with a competitor.

While officers of a company, board members, and partners are required to reveal to the business or their fellow officers, board members, or partners knowledge of all matters that may be in any way related to their businesses, there is a sliding scale of obligation for employees of the company. This **duty of loyalty** means that, except if there are contractual obligations, lower-level employees probably have such an obligation only with regard to opportunities that are directly relevant to their positions.

Recruitment of Fellow Employees

Another aspect of the duty of loyalty owed by an employee to a current employer is the legal requirement that the employee not knowingly take action designed to harm the employer's business. This is, perhaps, pure common sense. We would not expect the law to countenance a paid salesperson regularly recommending that customers patronize a competitor, nor would we expect the law to endorse an engineer in one company giving his best ideas to another company. In a similar way, the law frowns upon employees or former employees enticing fellow employees to leave the business. Again, the likelihood that a court will enforce this obligation depends to some extent on the nature of the recruiting employee's activities, his or her position in the company, and contractual agreements. Generally, unless there are relevant restrictive covenants in their respective employment agreements, two budding entrepreneurs need not fear reprisals for having convinced each other to leave a mutual employer; nor would there be much likelihood of liability if the two convinced another employee to leave with them, especially if these conversations took place after working hours. However, if either of them worked in the human resources department, where their job descriptions would have included recruiting and retaining employees, this same activity might well expose them to liability to their former employer. Further, if their plan included the wholesale resignation of a relatively large number of employees, such that the company's ability to continue functioning efficiently might be compromised, a court might be more likely to intervene with an injunction or other relief.

Noncompetition

More general than the obligation not to recruit fellow employees is the obligation not to compete with one's employer. Like most of the obligations we've already discussed, this duty is derived from the fiduciary relationship between employer and employee–specifically, the duty of loyalty. How can we justify accepting a paycheque from our employer while we are simultaneously establishing, working for, or financing a competing business?

The law imposes this duty not to compete on all employees, officers, directors, and partners while their associations with the employer remain in effect. Unless there are relevant restrictive covenants in relevant employment agreements, this noncompete duty only extends until the relationship with the employer is terminated. If the employer wants to extend the obligation, the employer may ask the employee, officer, director, or partner to enter into a contract to that effect (a **noncompetition agreement**).

We can analyze noncompetition agreements along many different dimensions; one is the scope of the obligation. In an extreme case, an employee may have agreed in the contract not to engage in any activity that competes with any aspect of the business his or her former employer engaged in, or planned to engage in, at the time of the termination of the employee's association with the company. At the other end of the spectrum, the employee may have agreed only to refrain from soliciting any of his or her former employer's customers or (somewhat more restrictively) from dealing with any of her former employer's customers, no matter who initiated the contact. We can also compare noncompetitions according to the length of time they extend beyond the termination of employment or their geographic scope.

Such comparisons are important because, in the employment context, the law sometimes takes the position that certain noncompetition agreements contravene basic public policies, such as encouraging competition and allowing each individual to make the best use of her or his talents. Furthermore, although a manufacturer may be able to enforce such an agreement against an officer, salesperson, or engineer who has either direct contact with customers or knowledge of the company's processes and products, it might not be able to enforce the same agreement against a bookkeeper, whose departure would have little effect on the company's goodwill. Even the officer, salesperson, or engineer might be able to resist a noncompetition agreement for a variety of reasons including, for example, that the agreement purports to remain in effect beyond the time that the employer might reasonably need to protect its goodwill and business from the effects of new competition.

Another factor that may affect the enforceability of a noncompetition agreement is whether the employer agrees to continue part or all of the former employee's compensation during the noncompetition period. Similarly, a noncompetition agreement that might be unenforceable against an employee might nonetheless be enforceable against the seller of a business or a major shareholder having his or her shares redeemed. Finally, some courts that find the scope or length of a noncompetition agreement objectionable nonetheless enforce the agreement to the maximum extent it rules acceptable. Other courts take an all-or-nothing approach: If the agreement is objectionable in law in any respect, the court will enforce no part of it.

Intellectual Property

Another potential complication arising out of an entrepreneur's previous employment is whether or not the entrepreneur can use information or technology knowledge acquired while she or he was working for the former employer. Information need not be covered by a patent or copyright to make it unavailable for free use by the entrepreneur. On the other hand, the same law that may prohibit the entrepreneur from using information acquired from a previous employer will be important for the entrepreneur once a viable new business has been created that is generating a body of information the entrepreneur would like to protect as a business asset. Thus, it is important for an entrepreneur to be aware of laws governing intellectual property rights.

Entrepreneurship and **intellectual property (IP)** go hand in hand. Intellectual property refers to creations of the mind, such as inventions; literary, artistic, musical, and dramatic works and other subject matter (such as sound recordings); and symbols, names, images, and designs used in commerce. These creations can be protected as confidential information, patents, trademarks, copyrights, or industrial designs.

Confidential information, including trade secrets, can be protected in one of two ways by Canadian law. **Patents** protect inventions and are important to consider in ensuring that a new business will have freedom to operate (discussed further below). **Trademarks**, which can also be protected in one of two ways in Canadian law, are key in differentiating a business's products and services from those of others and have an important place in franchising arrangements. **Copyrights** protect authors' and creators' original creations, including literary, musical, artistic, software, and other intellectual works. **Industrial design** registration will protect exclusive aesthetic use of artistic works in connection with mass produced useful articles.

Investors need to be assured not only that a business has considered IP but also that it has implemented a plan to protect the company's "crown jewels." And because IP protection costs money, it is necessary to budget for and manage it.

There are few guarantees in the area of IP. Not every patent application is granted; a name you've chosen for your company might not be available or possible to register as a trademark for a variety of reasons. Sometimes entrepreneurs must take risks. To do that wisely, entrepreneurs must understand the IP environment, which is slow to change in its legal underpinnings but is continually being pushed to keep up with technological advances.

Even when a company is successful in protecting its IP, however, that protection is not the end game. A patent, for example, doesn't generate revenue—it's just a document. A patent taken out for a great new idea is nothing unless people are willing to pay for that idea as implemented in a product or service. Timing can play a crucial role in IP, just as it does in exploiting an entrepreneurial opportunity.

Finally, IP is everywhere. Just because a business isn't about technology, don't be misled into thinking it won't ever face IP issues. Patents today cover such nonengineering subject matter as holders for floral bouquets, and even mere users of such products may end up being sued for patent infringement; copyright and trademark law are regularly invoked in the context of Internet search engines, pop-up ads, and websites in general.

The Basics: What Is Protectable and How Should It Be Protected?

When you create a new expression of information or design a new product or method, two of the first questions to arise are (1) Can I uniquely extract value from this idea? and (2) Can I keep competitors from copying this idea?

There are practical reasons for protecting a new idea. Investors are loath to put money into a venture that cannot establish a unique product or service niche. Shareholders will challenge a company's investment of its resources in a program that can be easily copied once it is introduced to the market. All the time, effort, and money you invest in perfecting a product, as well as advertising and promoting it, may be wasted if imitators can enter the market on your heels with a product just like yours. Moreover, the imitators can cut prices because they have not incurred the startup expenses you had to endure to bring the idea from conception to a mass-producible, reliable, and appealing product or service.

The next question to ask is, "Does my new product or service infringe on the IP rights of anyone else?" Only by understanding the basics of IP can that be answered.

Once it is determined that a new idea, product, or method is eligible for one or more forms of IP protection—*protection of confidential information, patent, trademark, copyright, or industrial design*—secure the rights as quickly as the budget allows. A single product or service can qualify for different forms of protection, each obtained in a different manner and providing a different set of rights. For example, a product you produce can involve *patents* in its production, *confidential information* protection in its assembly and marketing strategy, *industrial design* in its appearance, *copyright* in instructions for its use, a *certification mark* from an industry association affixed to it, and *copyright* and *trademark* in symbols affixed to it, its packaging, and the advertising materials developed for it. All of these will be discussed below.

Confidential Information

Confidential information held by your business can be protected by literally keeping it secret (which is sometimes challenging but not impossible), or (more practically) through contracts providing that the information be kept secret by the parties to the contract, or (most usefully) through a combination of both. (In this context, consider the four steps to help protect confidential information set out below.)

One limitation to protection by way of contract is that it only applies to those who are parties to the contract. If the information reaches others that are not party to contracts with you, there will be no ability to sue them under contract law.

However, just such a situation came before the Supreme Court of Canada in 1989—and a landmark court decision resulted.[1] In the case, a small mining company had knowledge about a property (which it did not own) and shared that knowledge with a larger company it hoped to do business with. An agreement was never reached to do business and no contracts were ever signed between them (and therefore the information about the property was not protected contractually). Later the larger company used its acquired knowledge, bought the property, and successfully developed a gold mine. The smaller company sued. The court held that, despite the fact that there was no contractual obligation of confidentiality between the two companies, the larger company (Lac Minerals) was liable to the smaller company (Corona) for breach of confidence because

1. Corona supplied Lac with information having a quality of confidence about it;

2. Corona communicated the information to Lac in circumstances in which an obligation of confidence arose; and

3. Lac, by acquiring the property to the exclusion of Corona, misused or made an unauthorized use of that information.

The noncontractual legal protection for breach of confidence established in this case is available only once a breach has occurred and the facts establish that there was secret, non-public information involved and that any communication of that secret was only made under circumstances where the expectation of confidentiality was clear to the recipient of the information.

It is important to note that this legal protection for breach of confidence does not come from any statute but rather is based on a decision of the courts. There is no government process to "certify" the confidentiality of information. These features make this form of intellectual property (confidential information) different from most of the others we will be discussing: patents, copyrights, industrial designs, and registered trademarks. However, as we shall see, while those other forms of intellectual property are time limited, there is no time limit for legal protection of confidential information: If you can keep the information secret, it will be protected by the courts if and when you need to sue for breach of confidence, assuming you can establish the three criteria that were necessary for success by Corona in the lawsuit described above.

Confidential information also becomes an issue when employees end their employment. For example, when an employee leaves a business, it can be challenging to discern whether the information that leaves with him or her is "know-how" that is part of that employee's own skill set or whether it is confidential information that should not be used or disseminated by that now ex-employee. In *RBC Dominion Securities Inc. v Merrill Lynch Canada Inc.*, "virtually all the investment advisors at [the Cranbrook] RBC, in a move coordinated by the branch manager, Don Delamont, left RBC and went to Merrill Lynch."[2] It was established to the satisfaction of a majority of the Supreme Court that no confidential information from RBC was used by the former RBC employees when they worked at Merrill Lynch and, accordingly, RBC was entitled to no compensation on that ground. However, had the facts established that confidential information belonging to RBC was used at Merrill Lynch, the court was clear that the duty not to misuse confidential information is a duty to which employees are subject post-employment.

In terms of there not being any government process involved in the creation of the intellectual property and having the potential to last forever, confidential information protection is similar to the protection of trademarks through the *passing off* action (which we will discuss below).

A further aspect of similarity between the action for breach of confidential information and the "passing off" protection for trademarks in Canada is that the protection for both is different in Quebec. (Quebec is different from the other nine provinces and three territories in Canada which are "common law" jurisdictions; Quebec is Canada's only "civil law" jurisdiction.) In the *Civil Code of Quebec*, protection of trade secrets is explicit, subject to certain limitations:

> *Article 1472*
> *A person may free himself from his liability for injury caused to another as a result of the disclosure of a trade secret by proving that considerations of general interest prevailed over keeping the secret and, particularly, that its disclosure was justified for reasons of public health or safety.*

In terms of the expansion of this protection to the wider ambit of confidential information, the general doctrine of good faith in Quebec's civil law, combined with other principles of civil liability, would permit roughly the same overall protection of confidences in Quebec as is in place in the common law provinces and territories.

The key characteristic of information that is protectable by the courts through the breach of confidence action is its secrecy, not the subject matter of the secret. Thus legal protection of confidences in Canadian law is considered to extend to a broader category of information than the concept of "trade secrets" implies. When the Canadian government created legislation to protect information that businesses (known for this purpose as "third parties") supply to the federal government from subsequent disclosure by the government to any requestor under the federal Access to Information Act,[3] it provided, among other things, that

> the head of a government institution shall refuse to disclose any record requested under this Act that contains
>
> (a) trade secrets of a third party; [or]
>
> (b) financial, commercial, scientific or technical information that is confidential information supplied to a government institution by a third party and is treated consistently in a confidential manner by the third party.

It must be noted that federal, provincial, and municipal government bodies in Canada are not subject to the action for breach of confidence where they are required to comply with legislated rights of access to information. In addition to the exceptions in provincial and territorial access legislation analogous to the federal Access to Information Act quoted above, there are exceptions to the right of the public to access government-held information found in other legislation. For example, when a patent application is made, it is held in confidence by the Patent Office (located within the Canadian Intellectual Property Office) for the first 18 months because of its obligations under section 10(2) of the Patent Act. As well, the courts have held that information divulged to government by a business because of a regulatory approval process will have to be protected from disclosure.[4]

It is certainly the case that information that could theoretically form the subject matter of a patent application is protectable in Canadian law, even before any patent application is made, through a lawsuit alleging breach of confidence or breach of contract. However, if the information is "leaked" from a business in such a way that the key requirement of novelty for patent protection (discussed further below) can no longer be met, the business will never be able to get a patent. Even if the lawsuit for breach of confidence or contract is successful, the business will only be able to receive other kinds of compensation for the breach. However, if a patent was obtained by a business using information that had been held in confidence by a first business and wrongly acquired by the patent-holding business, courts have ordered that the patent be transferred back to the business that originally held the information in confidence.[5]

Even if a secret is successfully kept within a business, this is no guarantee that another business will not independently acquire the knowledge that was the core of the secret (or acquire it through reverse engineering of the first business's products). If this happens, then both businesses will be legally able to exploit the knowledge. On the other hand, if one business holds a valid patent for an invention, no one else can exploit that invention during the period of the patent protection, no matter how many others gain knowledge of the invention. Holding a valid patent guarantees exclusive exploitation for the period of the patent—maintaining a secret makes it more likely that an idea can be exploited for longer than if a patent is held, but maintaining a secret is not as easy and certain as it may sound.

Don't be misled into thinking that protection of confidential information can only function as an alternative to a patent or, even in those cases where there is a choice between protecting an idea through patent or through protection of confidential information, that protection of confidential information offers "free protection" equivalent to that offered by the more expensive patent process. Consider the feature of the Windows program that allows you to open two files at the same time, display them on the screen, and drag content from one into the other. While this is a nice feature, it cannot be a legally protected as confidential information because it's not a secret: You and everyone else can see the feature in operation every time you use a Windows program. Microsoft even advertises it. Any competitor of Windows can write code that affords the same functionality and not be in violation of any protections.

Businesses often combine protection of confidential information, through contract and through practice, with patent applications. Protection of confidential information is absolutely necessary, as mentioned, to protect the viability of a patent application (in particular, to meet the novelty requirement of a patent). Companies seeking a patent will file a patent application and continue to keep the invention secret until the point approaches where secrecy in the patent process is no longer possible (18 months after the earliest filing date). As that point approaches, some companies will re-evaluate their positions. If the competition, in their estimation, is close to achieving the breakthrough that the patent application represents, they will let the patent issue. If not, they will abandon the patent application (which means the patent process never makes the idea public) and will continue to rely on protection of their confidential information, possibly indefinitely.

Four steps help protect confidential information, including trade secrets:

1. Negotiate confidential nondisclosure agreements with all employees, agents, consultants, suppliers, and anyone else who will be exposed to the secret information. The agreement should bind them not to use or disclose the information without permission.

2. Take security precautions to keep third parties from entering the premises where the confidential information is being used. Sturdy locks, perimeter fences, guards, badges, visitor sign-in books, escorts, and designated off-limits areas are just some of the ways that a business can exercise control over the area containing the secrets.

3. Stamp specific documents containing the secrets with a confidentiality legend and keep them in a secure place with limited access, such as a safe, locked drawer, or cabinet.

4. Make sure all employees, consultants, and others who are concerned with, have access to, or have knowledge about the secrets understand that they are secrets, and make sure they recognize the value to the company of this information and the requirement for secrecy.

Companies rarely take all four steps, but each company must do enough so that a person who misappropriates secrets cannot reasonably use the excuse that she or he didn't know about the secrecy or that the company did not appear to take precautions indicating that something was confidential information.

Despite the weaknesses inherent in the legal protection of confidential information, including trade secrets, some secrets have been appraised at a value of many millions of dollars, and some are virtually priceless. For example, Coca-Cola claims that its formula is one of the best-kept trade secrets in the world. Known as "Merchandise 7X," it has been tightly guarded since it was invented over 100 years ago. It is known by only two people within the Coca-Cola Company and is kept in a security vault at the Trust Company Bank in Atlanta, Georgia, which can be opened only by a resolution from the company's board of directors. The company refuses to allow the identities of those who know the formula to be disclosed or to allow the two to fly on the same airplane. While some of the mystique surrounding the Coca-Cola formula may be marketing hype, it is beyond dispute that the company possesses trade secrets that are carefully safeguarded and extremely valuable.

In other areas of intellectual property (patent, trademark, copyright), in addition to being able to enforce your rights through civil lawsuits, there are also statutory provisions through which criminal charges can be laid. However, the Supreme Court has held that theft of information, in and of itself, cannot be prosecuted in Canada.[6]

Patents

Under Canada's Constitution, patents are governed exclusively by the federal government. In contrast to the nonstatutory, common law protection afforded to confidential information, Canadian patent law derives exclusively from statute: the Patent Act. And, again in contrast to protection of confidential information, gaining patent protection in Canada is a purely formal process: Unless and until a patent is formally issued in Ottawa, you have no patent protection. Only patents issued in Canada have any effect within Canada.

A patent will be issued in Canada for either an invention or an improvement upon an invention. An issued Canadian patent entitles its owner to monopolize making, using, constructing, and selling the patented invention or improvement for what remains of the 20-year period after the patent application was made throughout Canada. This typically results in a 17-year period of protection from the time the patent is issued. However, there are fields, such as pharmaceuticals, in which the periods of actual patent monopoly position in the marketplace turn out to be only a few years counted in single digits.

Many patents are simple combinations of well-known components. Consider the following example. Aerogel is listed in the *Guinness World Records* as the world's lightest substance. A block of aerogel as big as an adult male weighs less than a pound but can support a small car. Recently, numerous companies have been patenting new uses for aerogel—as insulation, in fuel cells, and as building structures, just to give a few examples. Engineers at those companies didn't invent aerogel—a Stanford University researcher discovered it in the early 1930s. Still, patent offices around the world will readily grant patents for new uses of aerogel. In other cases, an improvement patent may be issued to an inventor where the underlying invention upon which it is based is still under patent and owned by someone else. In such a case, despite holding the improvement patent, its holder will not be able to manufacture, use, or sell the improvement without having obtained a licence to manufacture, use, or sell the underlying invention upon which it is based. However, once the patent expires on the original invention, the holder of the improvement patent will monopolize the entire market for the improved product—which the original patent holder will not be able to enter without a licence from the improvement patent holder (while also facing, for the first time, a competitive marketplace for the "old" technology now that the original patent has expired). There is incentive here for both patent holders—the holder of the original patent and the holder of the improvement patent—to consider cross-licensing with each other to create periods of two-way shared markets to their mutual benefit.

Canada is not one of the world's major markets and, for this reason, inventors typically consider patenting in Canada within the context of an overall **global patent strategy**. The

Canadian patent process is not limited to Canadian inventors and, because of international agreements that virtually span the globe, Canadian inventors are perfectly entitled to apply for patents in any other country.

The reason that obtaining a patent in Canada should be considered in the context of a global strategy is that the patent is a centuries-old bargain between the inventor and any given state: in return for the monopolies that the patent gives the inventor, the inventor allows the invention to be published through the country's patent register (typically now a database). This means the idea in the patent will no longer be secret. Since a patent idea will no longer be secret once published in the Canadian Patent Database and since meeting the requirement of novelty for patent requires that the idea be new, a Canadian patent, if not obtained as part of a global patent strategy, can mean that no patent will ever be obtainable on that same idea in any other country. This does not mean that the business holding the Canadian patent will not be able to do business in other countries—it simply means that, while that business will have a monopoly on the Canadian market, it will be facing a competitive marketplace in any other country. The Canadian patent, on the other hand, *will* mean that no other business will be able to obtain monopoly protection in any other country any more than the Canadian patent holder will be able to: All other countries will be in a competitive market situation.

In order to hold patents simultaneously in a number of countries or globally (although that is rare in the business context), it will be necessary to coordinate all the applications from the outset. This is usually done by relying on the international Patent Cooperation Treaty (PCT) that creates a mechanism to coordinate the application dates of patent applications in countries selected by the patent applicant so that no application in any one country invalidates the patent application process in any countries that are members of the PCT. Although such mechanisms have been agreed upon by the world's nations to coordinate aspects of both the substance and process of patenting, there is no "international patent." Since it is expensive to follow through and obtain patents in multiple countries, most businesses strategize and select only those national markets in which they believe they will benefit from a monopoly market presence.

The *timing* of the filing for patent can play an important role in a global patent strategy. In most countries, a patent application must be filed before any disclosure, at all, of the product or process to be patented occurs. If there is public disclosure, the filing will be barred and the opportunity to patent in those jurisdictions will be lost forever. Market testing without confidentiality agreements in place, exhibitions, publication of academic papers, or making presentations anywhere in the world can all constitute public disclosure. Whereas under American law there is an established exception to the concept of public disclosure invalidating a patent application in cases where the public use is for experimental purposes, in Canada there is neither a statutory provision for such an exception nor strong judicial consideration of this concept. On the other hand, if there has been public disclosure of the idea made by the inventor or certain persons connected with the inventor, Canadian law will still permit a patent application to be filed within one year of the disclosure (see section 28(2) of the Patent Act; this one-year period is called the *grace period*). The United States also makes a one-year grace period available, but under slightly different terms and conditions. However, very few other countries have any grace period at all. Thus, if there has been a recent public disclosure in, say, the past three months, while patenting in most other jurisdictions of the world will be ruled out, it may be possible to file for patent in Canada and the United States and thus obtain monopoly protection in the Canadian and American markets while facing a competitive marketplace elsewhere in the world.

Although it is possible to label products as "Patent Pending," the term actually has no legal status: A Canadian patent is either issued and creates a monopoly for the holder or it is not. There is no process in Canada similar to the American "provisional patent" process. Where a product in Canada has been labelled "patent pending," a would-be competitor can't always know exactly what will be patented or when—especially before any relevant patent application is laid open to the public (which happens 18 months after filing). Even once an application has been made public, it is not certain whether or not the patent sought will be granted. Still, others in the field of a product identified as "patent pending" may wish to proceed with caution in making decisions related to offering the same or similar products.

Whether or not an entrepreneur holds or is interested in holding patents, no entrepreneur can ignore the presence of patents in the marketplace. Patents are issued for inventions of "art, process, machine, manufacture or composition of matter."[7] The notion of "art" in the Patent Act is not the same notion as in the copyright context: "art" in a patent sense is the rather old-fashioned sense of "skill in doing something, especially as a result of knowledge or practice."[8]

Section 27(8) of the Patent Act declares that patents cannot be issued for a "mere scientific principle or abstract theorem" and, on that basis, patents for software have sometimes been rejected.[9] In other cases, where the software has been considered part of a computer-implemented invention, it has been included in a patent.[10] As will be discussed below, software, if original, will always receive copyright protection—which is in addition to any patent protection that might be granted for such software. While ways to diagnose medical conditions or injuries, medical instruments, and pharmaceuticals can be patented in Canada, "methods of medical treatment" are considered unpatentable in Canada.

On the other hand, although it was for years thought in Canada that business methods could not be patented in and of themselves (since they cannot be in England), the Federal Court of Appeal in 2011 established clearly that they can.[11] If any part of a business's operations involve, for instance, a process or machine that is under patent, to continue operating either a licence from the patent holder or holders will have to be obtained or another way of operating will have to be found that does not infringe on the patent or patents. Every entrepreneur should perform due diligence to ensure that the business has freedom to operate.

Obtaining a Patent. The Canadian patent process is administered through the Canadian Intellectual Property Office (CIPO), which is where Canada's Patent Office is located. CIPO houses the Canadian Patents Database (http://brevets-patents.ic.gc.ca/opic-cipo/cpd/eng/introduction.html), a record of all patents ever issued in Canada. In addition to other information on patenting, CIPO produces an excellent guide to patents (www.cipo.ic.gc.ca/eic/site/cipointernet-internetopic.nsf/eng/h_wr03652.html).

Although it is possible to complete a patent application in Canada without professional assistance (see the help provided through CIPO at www.cipo.ic.gc.ca/eic/site/cipointernet-internetopic.nsf/eng/h_wr00001.html), it is usually more practical and effective to work with a patent agent registered with CIPO pursuant to the Patent Act. While lawyers can give much helpful patent advice, only patent agents (some of whom are also lawyers) can actually assist in the filing and subsequent communications with the patent office. Many patent agents work in conjunction with law firms.

The patent is a written document consisting of two parts: (1) an abstract and (2) the "specification" of the invention or improvement. The specification is itself in two parts: (1) a description of the invention and its use, which often includes drawings (see Figure 13.1 for patent drawings for a zipper, referred to as a "slide fastener"),[12] and (2) the claim or claims.

The contents of the specification provide written evidence that the claimed invention or improvement is within the proper subject matter of patent and is new ("novel") and useful (has "utility") and is not an obvious development to a person familiar with the field in which it is located. To establish the novelty and "unobvious" aspects of the claimed invention, an applicant will focus on describing the state of the field or art to which the claimed invention is related. The emphasis will be on the point in time just before the application is filed to

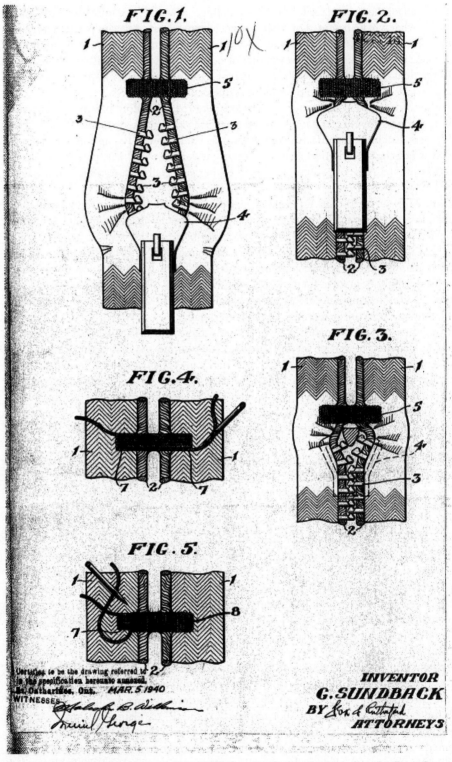

Source: Canadian Intellectual Property Office (CIPO), Canadian Patents Database, Canadian Patent Document 427214, http://brevets-patents.ic.gc.ca/opic-cipo/cpd/eng/patent/427214/summary.html.

Figure 13.1

Slide fastener patent

demonstrate that none of the "prior art" has reached the advance being made by this claimed invention and thus a patent should be issued. One way to show that this claimed invention is new is to demonstrate that no patent has ever been issued before, anywhere in the world, for this claimed invention. Therefore, an inventor or patent agent will have spent time scouring the patent offices of the world looking at all patent registers (which are all publicly available) to find anything that appears related to what is being claimed under the patent application being created for the new invention (or improvement). A claimed invention will also fail to get patent protection if, as discussed above, there is a publication anywhere that already describes it or if there is a product out there that already embodies it. The description of prior art in the application will try to ensure that it deals with both of these concerns. Finally, the description will describe the utility of the claimed invention.

Once a patent is issued, the specification also provides the public with knowledge of the new idea for which patent protection has been given. This is the "bargain" of the patent: The inventor gets a temporary marketplace monopoly, but the public gets immediate knowledge of the advance that the invention represents. Therefore, the specification cannot fail to disclose any part of the inventive idea—it must be possible to understand and replicate the invention simply using the patent document.

The claims describe what it is exactly that the inventor wants to have exclusive monopoly market access over (for the period the issued patent is in force). Most patents have multiple claims. Once a patent is issued, it is the claims that determine the monopoly protection a patent holder has. Usually court cases that arise after a patent is issued do not, in the end, involve all the claims in a given patent but rather turn on certain key claims. For example, at Harvard College in the United States, an advance was made that enabled researchers to manipulate the genes of mice such that mice would be created who were more susceptible to cancers ("oncomice"). Such mice would be very attractive in the marketplace of products supporting medical research because mice with cancer are used to test possible advances in the battle against the disease. Harvard embarked on a global patenting strategy to obtain monopoly protection for its advance. Its Canadian patent application, begun in 1985, described and claimed monopoly protection over both the process for creating the oncomice (delineated in claims 13 to 26 of the patent applied for) and the resulting oncomice themselves (in claims 1 to 12). In 2002, Harvard's efforts to obtain the Canadian patent culminated in an important decision by the Supreme Court, which denied patent protection in Canada to the oncomice because patenting higher life forms in Canada, such as mice, was held not to be contemplated by the Patent Act.[13] However, in subsequent discussions about the case, it is often not understood that Harvard did not lose its patent, only claims 13 to 26—the claims for the process of creating the oncomice (1 to 12) were valid under Canadian law. It is also interesting to note that of the jurisdictions in which Harvard applied for patent protection, it is only in Canada that the entire patent with all its original claims intact was not given protection. Although the mice themselves are not protected by patent in Canada, the oncomouse genes are, so producing the mice will use the patented genes and thus infringe the gene patent claims in Canada.[14]

Once a patent is issued, if the patent holder or a licensee under the patent believes that the patent is being infringed, a lawsuit can be launched. However, a defence to an infringement action that will invariably be raised is the argument that the patent at issue was not properly issued in the first place and is invalid, at least in respect of the claim or claims that are alleged to be infringed in the lawsuit. This raises the point that, under the Patent Act, the issuance of a patent is not an absolute guarantee of its validity or of the validity of any or all of its claims:

s.59 The defendant in any action for infringement of patent may plead as a matter of defence any fact or default which by this Act or by law renders the patent void, and the court shall take cognizance of that pleading and of the relevant facts and decide accordingly.

the works or performers of the performances. The owners of the economic rights will usually not be the owners of the moral rights. Under the Copyright Act, any employed person never owns the economic interests in the works she or he creates because the Copyright Act vests those rights in the employer—but the moral rights are always vested in the author, never in the employer. Even if the author or creator is not employed and therefore, under the Copyright Act, owns the economic rights in the beginning, economic rights are often sold by their original owners. The moral rights, on the other hand, can never be sold, although authors and performers can waive them. The moral rights can become relevant to a planned use of a copyrighted work or performance in a trademark context because of the provision in the Copyright Act that

> *s. 28.2(1) The author's or performer's right to the integrity of a work or performer's performance is infringed only if the work or performance is, to the prejudice of its author's or performer's honour or reputation . . .*
> *(b) used in association with a product, service, cause or institution.*

Industrial Design

There is one other type of intellectual property that can create a monopoly marketplace for an entrepreneur in Canada. However, the monopoly protection created under the Industrial Design Act[26] is very short—five years after registration, which can be renewed once for a second five years. The monopoly created by industrial design registration is for production of more than 50 useful articles that have "features of shape, configuration, pattern or ornament" (Industrial Design Act, section 2) that is visible to the eye. The protection of industrial design does not extend to any aspect of functionality; again, that monopoly protection is left to patent. The protection is extended only to original designs.

The Industrial Design Act is administered by CIPO.[27] The industrial design monopoly allows the registered owner to be the sole business in Canada making, importing for trade or business, selling, or renting any article for which the design is registered or a substantially similar design. As in the cases of patent, copyright, and registered trademark, the registered owner of the design can sue other businesses for infringement to enforce these design monopoly rights.

Even if an entrepreneur does not wish to apply for registration under this statute, it is important to be aware of it because artistic works are often involved in an industrial design and these generally lose their copyright protection (which otherwise would have lasted for the life of the artist plus 50 years) when they are reproduced more than 50 times as part of the useful article, whether or not the industrial design has been registered.[28] However, the relevant legislation also provides that use as a trademark or as a label on a useful article produced in a quantity larger than 50 does *not* take any artistic work that is or is part of that trademark or label out of the protection of the Copyright Act.[29]

The Industrial Design Act can be useful as an aid in developing trademark protection for the shaping or appearance of containers or packaging. To protect such things through passing off or as a distinguishing guise through registration under the Trade-marks Act, as discussed above, a business would have to show that the shape was known in the marketplace in connection with the product. Registration as an industrial design requires no such reputation and its 10-year period of monopoly protection can provide a business with time to create the strength of reputation that will allow trademark to coexist during the latter part of the industrial design monopoly[30] and trademark protection to continue long after the industrial design protection has lapsed.

Figure 13.3 summarizes the various intellectual property devices available in Canada.

	Confidential Information	Patent	Trademark		Copyright
			Passing Off	Registered TM	
Subject Matter	Any information that can be kept secret	Inventions i.e., new products & improvements, (functionality)	Symbols associated with products or services; company names	Symbols associated (or proposed) with products or services	Works of authorship & other subject matter (e.g., software, music, etc.)
Filing Fee (see CIPO)	N/A	Small entity fee (< 50 employees): $200 Standard fee: $400	N/A	Application fee: $250–$300 Registration fee: $200	Filing not necessary but possible: Application fee: $50–$65
Overall Costs, including Filing	Depends on volume of secrets, no. of employees, etc., not "free"	Expensive: $12K–$18K per patent per country	Moderate: $2.5K–$5K per mark	Moderate: $2.5K–$5K per mark	Free without registration; registration inexpensive: less than $500
Government Review	N/A	Yes—extensive and mandatory	N/A	Yes—including publication for public review	Yes—but a "rubber stamp"
Term of Protection	Potentially forever—as long as secret is kept secret	20 years from application, usually about 17 years from issuance	Potentially forever, as long as mark is used and recognized by public	Potentially forever as long as mark is used, renewed every 15 years, and recognized by public	Generally for life of author + 50 years
How Long to Achieve Protection	Immediate	A fairly long time: 3–5 years	As soon as mark is used and recognized by the public	Registration takes about a year, then protected once mark in use	Immediate, upon creation of expression; if sought, registration takes about a month
Pros	No government review; protects ideas and information not protectable by patents as well as that which could become patented (and thus become publicly known)	Strong protection if well drafted—infringer liable even if they didn't know about your patent	No government review; protects things not registrable—such as company names—as well as symbols that could be registered	Cost moderate; proposed marks are often possible; protection nationwide as long as use is shown anywhere in Canada	Free and immediate; non-mandatory registration confers additional enforcement benefits
Cons	Cannot be relied upon if "secret" really isn't kept secret; others have right to discover the secret on their own and then use it	Value is commensurate with the strength and breadth of the claims; high level of government scrutiny; strict time requirements	Only protects symbols in connection with products or services—not function or products or services themselves; only protects where use & reputation actually exist	Only protects symbols in connection with goods or services—not function or products or services themselves	No protection for function; often subject to moral rights of authors where economic rights are held by others; often subject to users' rights

Figure 13.3

Comparative table of select intellectual property devices

Choice of Legal Form

Another important issue all entrepreneurs will confront is what legal form they should use to operate their new venture. Many choices are available.

The most basic business form is the **sole proprietorship**, which is owned and operated by one owner who is in total control. No new legal entity is created; the individual entrepreneur just goes into business, either alone or with employees but without any co-owners.

If there is more than one owner of the business, the default legal position of the business is that it will be considered to be a **partnership**. This is the legal form that results when two or more individuals go into business for profit, as co-owners, sharing profits and losses. It is also possible to deliberately create a *limited partnership (LP),* which, while often used in some sectors, is not appropriate for use by owner-managed businesses. As well, a type of partnership known as a *limited liability partnership (LLP)* is an entity that can only be used in certain circumstances. For example, in Ontario only certain professionals are entitled to operate through this form of business.

The most common choice of business form for entrepreneurs is the **corporation**. A business company may be incorporated in Canada either federally or in any one of the provinces or territories. In any case, with proper registrations in place, a company is generally entitled to do business anywhere in Canada or beyond. Incorporation of a company is a common procedure involving the entrepreneur, with or without legal assistance, filing an application and paying a fee. Once incorporated, the business is a legal entity (a legal "person") with a legal existence apart from its owner or owners (the shareholder or shareholders).

Although a startup may not make a profit, at least initially, it generally cannot be considered a **nonprofit entity**. Nonprofit entities are almost always created as *non-share capital corporations* (better known as *not-for-profit corporations*), which are incorporated in a particular manner[31] and which do not have shares. As well, nonprofit entities do not intend to financially benefit their members, directors, or officers. For example, industry associations are often incorporated either provincially or federally as not-for-profit corporations. Such organizations can assist an entrepreneurial business in many ways, including, as mentioned above, holding and administering a certification mark for which the entrepreneur may apply to be allowed to include that mark on its products or services.

Although we can compare these forms of business on an almost endless list of factors, the most relevant include control issues, exposure to personal liability, tax factors, and administrative costs. We discuss these in detail in the sections below. Figure 13.4 provides an overview of these factors and how they play out in the three most relevant business forms: sole proprietorships, partnerships, and corporations.

Control

Since there is only one principal in the sole proprietorship, she or he wields total control over all issues.

In a partnership, control is divided among the partners in accordance with their partnership agreement (which need not be written but should be, to encourage specificity). The parties may decide that all decisions must be made by unanimous vote, or they may adopt a majority standard. More likely, they may require unanimity for a stated group of significant decisions and allow a majority vote for others.

Regardless of how power is allocated in the partnership agreement, in the eyes of third parties each of the partners will have a free hand to contract with outsiders on behalf of the partnership as a whole, subject only to the internal consequences of the partner's breaching the agreement with the other partners. This is also true for the consequences of torts committed by any partner acting in the course of partnership business.

	Control	Liability	Taxation	Administrative Obligations
Sole proprietorship	Owner has complete control	Unlimited personal liability	Not a separate taxable entity	Only those applicable to all businesses
Partnership	Partners share control	Joint and several unlimited personal liability	Not a separate taxable entity	Only those applicable to all businesses
Corporation	Control distributed among shareholders, directors, and officers	Limited personal liability	Separate taxable entity	Some additional

Figure 13.4

Comparison of various business forms available in Canada

A corporation is controlled by three levels of authority: shareholders, directors, and officers. Broadly speaking, the shareholders vote in proportion to the number of shares each shareholder owns on the election of the board of directors, the sale or dissolution of the business, and amendments to the company's charter (better known as **articles**). In virtually all cases, these decisions are made either by the majority or by two-thirds of the votes cast.

The board of directors, which is elected by the shareholders, in turn makes all the long-term and significant policy decisions for the business as well as appointing the officers of the company. Votes by the board of directors are virtually always decided by majority. The officers, usually consisting of a chair of the board, a president, a treasurer, and a secretary (or a secretary-treasurer), run the day-to-day operations of the company and are the only level of authority that can bind the company by contract.

Personal Liability

Should the business incur current liabilities beyond its ability to pay, must the individual owner or owners risk personal bankruptcy to make up the difference? This unhappy situation does not only occur as a result of poor management or bad business conditions—it could just as easily occur because of an uninsured tort claim from a customer or a victim of a delivery person's careless driving.

In both the sole proprietorship and general partnership structures, the business is not recognized as a legal entity separate from its owners. Thus, the debts of the business are ultimately the debts of the owners if the business cannot pay. This unlimited liability is enough to recommend against these forms for virtually any business, with the exception perhaps of a one-person consulting firm (where liability may be the direct result of its owner's actions in any case).

If this unlimited liability is uncomfortable for the founders of a business, imagine what it would mean to an investor who joins the business as an owner. The investor no doubt has significant assets to lose and will likely have only limited control over the business decisions that may generate liability. This risk is made even worse by the fact that all partnership liabilities are considered joint and several obligations of all partners. Thus, the investor will be responsible for full payment of all partnership liabilities if the founders have no significant assets of their own.

Perhaps the best answer to this problem lies in the corporation, which affords limited liability to all owners. If the business ultimately becomes insolvent, its creditors will be entitled to look only to the assets of the company for payment—any shortfall will be absorbed by the unfortunate creditors. However, this solution is not quite as available as it sounds. To begin with, creditors know these rules as well as entrepreneurs do. Thus, large or sophisticated creditors, such as banks and other financial institutions, will insist on personal guarantees from the owners of the business before extending credit. Second, the law sometimes allows creditors to "pierce the corporate veil" and go after the owners of a failed company under certain conditions. The first situation in which this can occur involves a business that was initially underfunded or "thinly capitalized." A business should start out with a combination of capital and liability insurance adequate to cover the claims it might normally expect to be exposed to. As long as the capital was there at the outset and has not been depleted by dividends or other distributions to owners, the protection of the company, as a separate legal entity, survives even after the capital has been depleted by unsuccessful operation. Another situation that may result in the piercing of the corporate veil is the failure of the owners to treat the company as an entity separate from themselves by

- Failing to use *Inc. or Ltd.* or a similar legal indicator when dealing with third parties or
- Commingling business and personal assets in a personal bank account or allowing unreimbursed personal use of corporate assets or
- Failing to keep business and legal records and hold regular directors' or shareholders' meetings

Taxation

Income taxes, both personal and corporate, that will be paid as a result of starting up and operating a business are an important consideration in the choice of the legal entity for a new venture. The ideal entity from the perspective of income taxes should do the following:

- Minimize or eliminate any personal income tax that might result from receipt of an ownership interest (such as share ownership)
- Maximize the tax shelter for the investors should the business have an annual loss
- Minimize taxes paid by the business, founders, and investors should the business have an annual profit
- Minimize **capital gains** taxes payable by the founders and investors if they sell all or some of their ownership interest (such as shares)

Unfortunately, there is no business form that meets all of these ideals. Accordingly, it must be determined which of the ideals are most important to the owner(s) at the applicable time. For example, it is not uncommon for an entrepreneur to start his or her business as a sole proprietorship during the startup years when losses are expected and then to incorporate the business when profits are anticipated. (It is important to note that a lawyer and an accountant should be consulted when such a transition is undertaken.)

Although sole proprietorships and partnerships allow business losses to be used by the proprietor/partners, operating businesses are commonly set up as a corporation for reasons that we have examined and will examine in the remainder of this and the next section.

Entrepreneurs are often warned about the *double taxation* that arises when a company makes a profit, pays income tax on it, and then distributes part or all of its profit after tax as a dividend to its shareholders, who in turn pay income tax on that dividend. This means that the same money is taxed twice (although potentially at a reduced dividend rate the second time).

In reality, however, double taxation is more a myth than a legitimate threat to the small business. First, corporations are taxed on business income at a much lower rate than the highest marginal tax rate for individuals. Second, dividends are also taxed in the hands of an individual at a much lower rate than business income earned directly by an individual.

Further, most small Canadian-controlled private corporations are entitled to a special rate reduction on a certain amount of profit. These companies often lower or even eliminate the portion of the profit that is not entitled to the reduced rate by increasing deductible salaries and bonuses for the owners. The owners then pay only their own individual income tax on the amounts paid as salaries and bonuses.

It is also important to note that, as a result of the relatively low corporate tax rates, where earnings can be used in the company's business there is also a deferral advantage.

Initial Investment of the Founders

As a general rule, founders normally arrange the issuance of their shares (also known as *equity*) in the venture for very little tangible investment. After all, they intend to look to investors for working capital, and their investment will be the services they intend to perform for the business.

Of practical concern, however, is the fact that any property (including shares) transferred to an employee in exchange for his or her services is generally considered taxable income under the Income Tax Act.[32] Thus, whenever equity is issued to founders in exchange for services (so-called "sweat equity"), they may face an unexpected tax liability as a result.

In the corporate context, at approximately the same time that the founders are receiving their shares for minimal investment, the investors will be putting in the real money. Since the investors will be paying substantially more for their shares than the founders are paying for theirs, the Canada Revenue Agency will likely take the position that the value of the founders' shares is equal to the price paid by the investors.

One way to attempt to solve this problem is to postpone the investor's investment until the founders can argue for an increase in the value of the company's shares. Aside from the essentially fictional nature of this approach, most founders probably cannot wait that long. Instead, the parties must design a vehicle for the investors that is sufficiently different from the founders' interests to justify the higher price. In the corporate context some form of **preference shares** will serve the purpose. How does all this inform the choice of entity? Simply put, only the use of a corporation allows for the flexibility required to implement such a solution.

Administrative Obligations

Newly created startup businesses should obtain business and other numbers from the relevant government office or offices. In some cases, such numbers will be issued automatically when the entity is created. In other cases applications may be necessary. GST or HST numbers should be obtained in most cases. These steps facilitate communication with governments and the reporting and collection of taxes; further, they may qualify the business for statutory exemptions or relevant government programs. In this context, all business entities should budget for a certain amount of accounting expense, specifically for the calculation and reporting of taxable profit and loss.

Incorporating, however, brings some additional administrative burden and expense. In most jurisdictions, companies must file an annual report with the government through whom they were incorporated. This annual reporting usually includes only the business's current address, officers, directors, managers, and similar information, but it may be accompanied by an annual maintenance fee. This paperwork is required in addition to the obligation to file a tax return with, at minimum, the Canada Revenue Agency. Finally, a business may have to file registration documentation in jurisdictions in which it "carries on business" but are not the home jurisdiction of the business.

Shareholders' Agreements

The owners' respective investments in a company will normally be memorialized in a combination of a share purchase agreement, articles of amendment, and a shareholders' agreement. In a partnership, similar provisions allocating ownership interests and rights to distributions of profit and cash flow would appear in a partnership agreement. In all these cases, however, the parties would be well advised to go beyond these subjects and reach written agreement on a number of other potentially thorny issues at the outset of their relationship.

Negotiating Employment Terms

In the event that an entrepreneur finds it appropriate to enter into an employment agreement with the business he or she has created (which may occur when, for example, the business attracts "external" investors), the entrepreneur employee should take great care regarding the drafting and negotiation of that agreement. Assuming that there are such investors, the founder should reach agreement with the investor about his or her commitment to provide services and the level of compensation for doing so. It would be unusual for the founder to forgo compensation solely to share the profits of the business with the investors. For one thing, on what would the founder be living in the interim? For another, the profits of the business are properly conceived of as the amount left over after payment of the expenses of the business—including reasonable compensation to its employees. Thus, in the case of a company, a founder should consider negotiating employment terms into the shareholders' agreement, setting forth his or her responsibilities, title, compensation, and related issues. This is especially important in the case in which any individual founder may hold only a minority interest in the company (depending on the voting rights given to the preference shares). She or he may wish to try to foreclose the possibility that the other owners may ally and use a majority of the shares to remove the founder as a director, officer, or employee of the company.

Transfer to Third Parties

Individual interests in partnerships are usually not transferable. However, in corporations there is often an ability to transfer shares from an owner to another or even to a third party. In the context of a sale to a third party, although such a transfer of shares in a closely held company is made rather difficult by relevant securities regulation and the general lack of any market for the shares, transfers are still possible under the correct circumstances. However, shareholders' agreements frequently restrict such transfers, by requiring, for example, that any owner wishing to transfer equity to a third party must first offer it to the company or the other owner(s), who may purchase the equity, often at the lower of a formula price or the amount being offered by the third party.

Disposition of Ownership Interests upon the Owner's Death

A sole proprietor's business would normally be inherited according to the proprietor's will or, absent a will, as the province or territory has legislated intestacy. A partnership interest usually ends (pursuant to the partnership agreement or the relevant legislation) upon a partner's death, so it is not treated in the same manner (although a partner's liability may continue to be a liability of that partner's estate should the partner die).

Shareholders' agreements should also address the disposition of each owner's equity upon death. Again, it is unlikely that each owner would be comfortable allowing the deceased owner's shares to fall into the hands of the deceased's spouse, children, or other heirs, although this may be more acceptable in the case of a pure investor. Moreover, should the business succeed over time, each owner's equity may well be worth a significant amount upon death. If so, subject to a spousal rollover, capital gains tax will be owing. Under such circumstances, the owner's estate may wish to have the assurance that some or all of such equity will be converted to cash so the tax may be paid. If the agreement forbids free transfer of the equity during the lifetime of the shareholder and requires that the equity be redeemed at death for a reasonable price, the agreement may well be accepted by the Canada Revenue Agency as a persuasive indication of the equity's value, thus avoiding an expensive and time-consuming valuation controversy.

Any redemption provision on the death of the owner of shares, especially one that is mandatory at the insistence of the estate, immediately raises a concern for the business about availability of funds should the provision become operative. Just when the business may be reeling from the effects of the loss of one of its most valuable owners, it may be expected to scrape together enough cash to buy out the deceased's ownership. To avoid this disastrous result, many of these arrangements are funded by life insurance policies on the lives of the owners. These would be in addition to any key person insurance held by the business for the purpose of recovering from the effects of the loss. In structuring such an arrangement, however, the parties should be aware of two quite different models. The first and more tradi-tional model is referred to as a *redemption agreement*. Under it, the business owns the policies and is obliged to purchase the equity upon death. The second model is referred to as a *cross-purchase agreement* and provides for each owner to own insurance on the others and to buy a proportional amount of the deceased's equity. While a cross-purchase is more complicated, especially if there are more than a few shareholders, it has significant benefits compared with a redemption agreement.

Disposition of Ownership upon Termination of Employment

Shareholders' agreements normally also address disposition of equity upon events other than death. Repurchase of equity upon termination of employment can be important for all parties. The former employee whose equity no longer represents an opportunity for employment would like the opportunity to cash in her or his investment. The company and other owners may resent the presence of an inactive owner who can capitalize on their later efforts. Thus, shareholders' agreements will normally provide for repurchase of the interest of a shareholder who is no longer actively employed by the company. This, of course, applies only to shareholders whose efforts on behalf of the company were the basis of their participation in the first place. Such provisions would not apply to a pure investor, for example.

Comparison of Share Redemption Agreement and Share Cross-Purchase Agreement. Provisions in shareholders' agreements that provide for share redemptions and share cross-purchases in the context of the termination of employment present a num-ber of additional problems peculiar to the employee–owner. For example, the company cannot obtain insurance to cover an obligation to purchase equity upon termination of employment. Thus, it may encounter an obligation to purchase the equity of the former employee at a time when its cash position will not support such a purchase. Furthermore, courts uniformly prohibit repurchases that would render the company insolvent. Common solutions to these problems commit the company to an instalment purchase of the affected equity over a period of years (with appropriate interest and security) or commit the remain-ing owners to make the purchase personally if the company is unable to do so for any rea-son. Such provisions, in addition to providing incentive to remain with the company, have complicated tax implications as well.

WHILE ENTREPRENEURSHIP BEGINS with an opportunity, sustainable success comes from creating an organization that can execute on that opportunity. However, as organizations start to gain more sales and customers, managing growth becomes a critical challenge that, if not handled appropriately, can lead to venture failure.

Why do entrepreneurs fail to manage growth? Often they have limited time and resources to spend on organization building. They're constantly fighting fires in the business's day-to-day operations or they're chasing too many opportunities, leaving little time for planning. Entrepreneurs without organizational or business skills may retreat into something they do know and are more comfortable doing, like product development. They may hire salespeople or engineers to handle sales and technical support before bringing in someone with organizational and business skills. But eventually growth overwhelms the operation. To survive and continue to grow, entrepreneurs need to pay attention to the requirements of a firm in its growth phase. They cannot neglect the planning and preparation required for long-term success.

Many believe that entrepreneurial skills and managerial skills are mutually exclusive and operate at different phases of the firm's life. Entrepreneurial skills *are* critical during the venture's launch, while managerial skills become increasingly important thereafter.

> ◉ The objectives of any entrepreneur wishing to create a sustainable enterprise should include building an efficiently operating organization while developing an organization-wide entrepreneurial capability.

Yet the organization will need to retain its entrepreneurial spirit as it grows. It can't function over the long term by simply managing what it has previously created. Customer needs inevitably change. Competitors eventually offer superior products or services. Economic conditions, politics, technology, and a variety of other external shifts will create a constantly changing opportunity set that leads to new possibilities while rendering old opportunities obsolete. Startup Genome is composed of three young entrepreneurs that set out to take a comprehensive and prolific data-driven plunge into what makes a startup successful. A special report released in 2012 called the *Startup Genome Report on Premature Scaling* is based on data from over 3,200 startups and highlights why startups fail. **Premature scaling** refers to growth in anticipation of demand, instead of demand-driven growth.[1] Moreover, startup co-founders need to realize that they are essentially operating on a guess about an unknown opportunity and are hoping that their company will provide the perfect solution for this unknown opportunity. All these unknowns mean that co-founders need to avoid spending money on growing (or scaling) their business before they have really determined what customers want and how to reach them. The *Startup Genome Report on Premature Scaling* found that in 90% of failed startups, 70% failed because they scaled prematurely.[2] Furthermore, the report illustrated that startup founders need two to three times longer to validate their market than most founders expected they would.[3]

Steve Blank, author of *The Startup Owner's Manual*, defines a startup as a temporary organization searching for a sustainable and scalable business model,[4] meaning that a startup should only scale after it has gone through the following stages:

1. The customer validation stage
2. The customer development stage
3. Enough pivots to ensure product/market fit

Once these three stages are complete, a startup can begin making the transition from a startup to a growing and scaling company. This transition is covered in the next section.

It's no wonder that half the businesses started today will not be around in eight years. And far fewer firms will continue to grow and stay profitable—as few as one in seven.[5] What distinguishes those firms that not only survive but also thrive? The answer is entrepreneurs and leaders who build an efficient operating organization while maintaining the organization's entrepreneurial ability.

Making the Transition from Startup to Growth

During startup, the business opportunity is taking shape, but as yet there are no significant sales. The founders are acquiring resources and organizing initial operations—and they do everything. At the other end, in the mature stage and beyond, the business must deal with the problems of a well-established organization. Systems and structures can become entrenched and the culture can impede efforts to grow further, leading to decline. In this chapter, we look at how entrepreneurs operate once they've started and, we assume, their companies have reached a point of initial success with their opportunity. The primary task beyond this startup stage is to create a professional organization capable of managing its current growth, while setting the stage for continued entrepreneurship to ensure the organization can sustain growth as it matures and avoid decline.

The chapter is organized around four driving forces in the growth stages: leadership, the opportunity domain, resources and capabilities, and execution. Before we get to this discussion, let's review a key decision every entrepreneur must consider beyond startup: whether to sell, maintain, or grow the venture.

Looking Forward: The Choice to Grow, or Not . . . or Sell

Figure 14.1 presents post-startup options for an entrepreneurial business. Each option presents at least two alternatives for the founder.

If a new venture is successful in generating sales, entrepreneurs can reap capital gains by finding a suitable buyer. If the entrepreneur decides to sell the business, he or she may stay with the acquiring company or leave and either seek other employment or start another company. The first situation is perhaps the most common; the entrepreneur sells to reap a capital gain but stays on with the organization for several years to help in the transition. When Doug Brenhouse and John Frank, founders of MetaCarta (a geographic intelligence solutions company) sold their company to Nokia in 2010, John remained with the company. Most often the buyer wants the entrepreneur to stay to reduce risk.

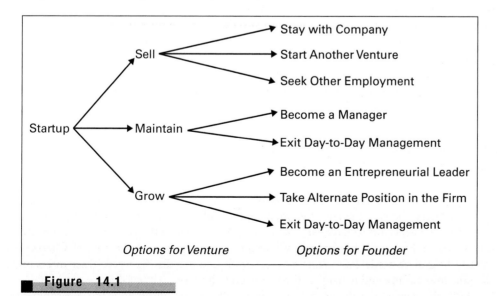

Figure 14.1

Post-startup options

A typical acquisition might give the entrepreneur one-third of the price in cash, one-third in the acquiring company's shares (vested over the term of an employment contract), and one-third in an earn-out that is tied to the performance of the acquired company. If the acquired company meets certain milestones, the entrepreneur earns the full amount of the earn-out. If it falters, the entrepreneur's earn-out is at risk. Thus, the entrepreneur has an incentive to work hard after the acquisition takes place.

If a company is publicly traded, on the other hand, it is easier for the entrepreneur to sell and leave. Jim Clark, who co-founded Silicon Graphics in 1981, sold his remaining interest in the company in 1994 and left. He subsequently went on to co-found Netscape with Marc Andreessen. When selling a business, the founders often have contractual agreements to consider, like restrictions on their activities if they exit; for example, noncompete clauses may place limitations on their next venture. If you sell your business, the acquirer will prohibit you from starting a new, directly competing business.

When maintaining a business, the entrepreneur is faced with two basic choices. He or she can continue to lead the organization or exit day-to-day operations. Google co-founders Sergey Brin and Larry Page started the company in 1998. They both stayed as co-presidents until 2001, when they recruited former Sun Microsystems and Novell executive Eric Schmidt as chair and CEO. They recognized they needed someone with experience and business acumen to grow the company.[6] Having an experienced CEO freed Brin and Page to focus on the aspects of the business they had the most passion for. Brin headed up the technology group at Google while Page ran the products group.[7]

While our focus is on growing a business, it's true that many entrepreneurs choose to operate lifestyle businesses that pay enough salary for them to have a comfortable lifestyle, with less risk and complexity. These firms usually aren't large or successful enough to be sold, and the entrepreneurs don't have the desire to grow the business. One of the authors of this chapter, for example, was working with an ergonomics consulting company that hired her to grow the business. They explored a number of options, but growth would mean hiring more employees and moving out of the founder's basement. The founder decided he preferred the flexibility, lower risk, and greater control associated with staying small. After two engineers who had worked with him part time finished college and moved on to other jobs, he maintained the business as a one-person operation, outsourcing any additional expertise and keeping his commute to "a walk downstairs." What this example illustrates is that the decision to grow (or not) is multifaceted. It should take into account not only the ability to grow (the company could capture more customers if it were larger) but also the desires of the entrepreneur.

We'll now assume the company is currently growing and the owner chooses to sustain a growing organization rather than selling or maintaining a lifestyle business. We'll focus on the founder as CEO, although most of the concepts also apply in the case where the founder is replaced. We next present our model of driving forces in the entrepreneurial firm's growth stages.

A Model of Driving Forces of Growth

Chapter 2 offered a model describing three driving forces that must be in balance during the startup process: the entrepreneur, the opportunity, and resources. In the growth stage, these three driving forces shift to *leadership, the opportunity domain*, and *organizational resources and capabilities*, as Figure 14.2 illustrates. While the business plan is at the core of Chapter 2's model, the growth model has *execution* as its core and fourth driving force. These forces must all come into balance and remain so during the growth phase.

Both the startup and the growth models are affected by uncertainty and environmental conditions. Whether at startup or in its growth phase, an organization is unable to predict

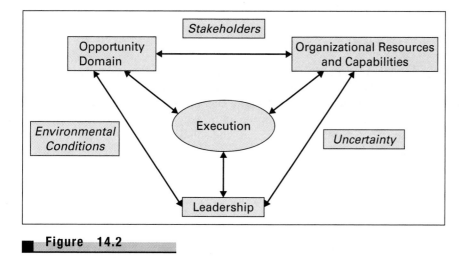

Figure 14.2

Driving forces of growth

many events, such as a competitor introducing a superior product soon after launch or customers adopting a product much more slowly than anticipated. Environmental conditions, such as economic cycles, the regulatory environment, and technological change, can also affect a venture's viability and success. In all phases of its life, the organization will need to balance the driving forces amid conditions it cannot control.

Stakeholders have the largest impact on a firm's growth potential. **Stakeholders** are those who have a stake in the venture's success, including investors, customers, suppliers, and employees. As a new venture grows, it accumulates a range of insiders and outsiders who become increasingly dependent on the firm and exert heavy influence on its decisions. The organization will need to balance the current needs of these stakeholders with its need to think about how to sustain itself over the long term.

The 2009 bankruptcy of General Motors, then the world's largest automobile maker, serves as a clear-eyed example of stakeholder interests running at odds with a company's growth model. GM reported an $8.6 billion loss in 2005. Bankruptcy court filings came four years later, the same year GM lost the title of world's largest automaker to Toyota. Why? Too many stakeholders were vested in maintaining the status quo. GM continued to pay out quarterly dividends to investors at $0.25/share even when its share price was trading below $5.00[8] in what may have been an effort to "keep up appearances."[9] GM's labour force, the United Auto Workers (UAW) union stonewalled GMs innovation and growth initiatives to avoid job elimination and decreased pay and benefits. At one point, GM found itself actually paying its workers not to work. GM retained the car lines Saab and Saturn, even though they had rarely been profitable. Generous pensions and healthcare plans as well as rock-solid job security provided little incentive for GM management to rock the boat and substitute short-term pain for long-term sustainability.[10] In what amounted to a 30-year slow-motion car crash, GM's debts mounted and eventually GM was crushed by the weight of its own complacency, or more appropriately, by the entrenched inertia of GM's own stakeholders.

Today, GM has re-emerged from bankruptcy and again became a publicly traded company, with its stock ticker history wiped clean. What remains to be seen is if new leadership (installed by GM's largest shareholder—the U.S. government) can succeed in changing the stale management culture and renegotiating the labour relations that led to GM's downfall. In 2011, a reborn General Motors reclaimed the title of world's largest automaker, earning $7.6 billion in profits. However Toyota, renowned for its efficiency, surpassed GM again in 2012, calling into question if GM has truly brought its growth model and its stakeholder interests back into alignment.

The Growth Process

Figure 14.3 shows the challenges associated with the four driving forces outlined in Figure 14.2 and the key imperatives the firm needs to address to achieve overall balance among the forces.[11] The table differentiates between a venture's early and later growth stages. This distinction is important because the problems facing a company at an early stage of growth are different from those it faces later, and therefore the decisions and solutions will change. By knowing where the organization stands in the life cycle, an entrepreneur can tell which problems are normal and which require special attention. For example, while an entrepreneur needs to focus his or her firm's strategy during early growth, he or he will need to look toward expansion in later growth stages. The expansion, or scalability of a product should only come at a certain point in the life cycle of a startup. As mentioned in Chapter 5, the Rogers Adoption Curve clearly illustrates that a product should not scale until stage 3 of the growth process, which is when a startup knows its cost per customer acquisition (CoCA), its average revenue per user (ARPU), its product/market fit, and that its revenue is sustainable. Scaling before any of these milestones have been achieved can result in spending money on advertising that is not reaching a specific target market, and even worse, revamping a finished product because of faulty assumptions that are not what consumers actually expected or want.

Execution

The growth model has execution at its core. Execution depends on the other components in the model—leadership, the opportunity domain, and organizational resources and capabilities— but it has the most direct link to profits. The startup is commonly loosely managed, with few controls, very little performance assessment, and a lack of responsibility for outcomes. It often puts an emphasis on sales over profits, with chasing a new customer taking priority over considering the costs of serving that customer, for example. Growth will soon overwhelm operations, however, leaving the company capable only of reacting to inventory outages, overdue collections, diminishing cash flows, and delivery restrictions by suppliers. In addition, uncontrolled growth can lead to poor coordination between activities such as sales and inventory planning.

Without an adequate system of controls, the company can't optimize its decision making and prevent the waste of resources. One example of a startup that failed quickly because it did not understand cost monitoring, and therefore the inherent weaknesses of its own cost structure, was Webvan, one of the first online grocery retailers. Webvan was started by none other than Louis Borders, the successful founder of Borders Books. Borders felt that he could reduce the costs of selling groceries through automated warehousing and online ordering and allow him to offer the convenience of home-delivered groceries to consumers. The low margins (2–3%) of the grocery business required Borders to find customers willing either to pay handsomely for the convenience or to buy in greater volume than they currently did. Neither requirement was likely to be met by cost-conscious consumers who normally shopped once a week, filling their refrigerators each time. Therefore, Borders needed to keep his costs much lower than the competition, and to do this he first needed to monitor them effectively. Webvan's cost control focus was on its warehouse operations, at the expense of its other costs, and it was this blind spot that eventually killed the business.

Webvan had a fast and promising start. In its first six months of business in San Francisco it had over $13 million in sales, and by the end of its first year it had acquired over 47,000 subscribers (customers). However, the average cost of customer acquisition was high at $210, and the average customer order was low at only $81. Compounding this problem was the fatal fact that Webvan was acquiring customers who lived in suburbs, which drove an average delivery cost of $18, which was the heaviest contributor to the total average order handling and fulfillment

	Early Growth		Later Growth	
	Challenges	**Key Imperatives**	**Challenges**	**Key Imperatives**
Execution	Emphasis on sales over profits. Reactive orientation (fighting fires). Rapid growth overwhelms operations. Inadequate systems and planning leads to inefficiency, poor control, and quality problems. Informal communication and processes create confusion and lack of accountability.	Develop basic systems to manage cash, control receivables, inventory, and payables. Develop simple budgets and metrics to track performance and expenditures.	Profit orientation can constrain later growth. Organization outgrows initial systems and planning structure. Difficulties with coordination and control as decentralization increases.	Upgrade and formalize systems for control and planning for the longer term/future—before they are needed. Proactive planning replaces reactive approach. Maintain balance between control and creativity; ensure processes don't constrain innovation.
Opportunity Domain	Tendency to overcommit, pursue many diverse opportunities. Lack of clear strategy for how the venture competes.	Develop a focused strategy that leverages the company's unique value. Maintain the consistency of this strategy with all company activities (such as product development, marketing, operations).	Original opportunity domain may provide fewer opportunities for growth. Competitive pressures and changes in the market may threaten current businesses.	Establish competitive uniqueness and move beyond "one-product" orientation. Expansion into the periphery with products and markets. Also, develop strategy for future that provides new momentum and long-run effectiveness. Anticipate/respond to changes in industry/market environment.
Organizational Resources and Capabilities	Financial and human resources constrained as rapidly expanding sales require more people and financing. Generalized skills increasingly incapable of handling increased complexity.	Get profitability and cash flow in check. Tap early financing sources. Hire people with specialized expertise. Protect intellectual property.	Insufficient resources for growth.	Maintain bootstrap mentality. Manage cash for internal growth resources. Secure growth financing.
Leadership	Company outgrows entrepreneur's abilities. Entrepreneur unable to delegate. Internally promoted managers often lack adequate skills.	Start the process of delegating responsibility to others. Promote/hire functional managers/supervisory-level managers. Invest in management training.	Management lacks the managerial sophistication required for the increasing size and complexity of a growing organization. Inadequate communication throughout organization. Tensions between professional management and entrepreneur, between new and old managers and employees.	Recruit key professional management talent. Build fully functioning board of directors. Ensure leadership team shares in strategic planning and preserves entrepreneurial capability. Create decentralized reporting structure.

■ Figure 14.3

Challenges and key imperatives for managing growth

cost of $27. Webvan was not only spending too much to acquire customers, but it was acquiring customers that were too expensive to serve because they lived in less densely populated areas that required $100,000 trucks driven by drivers earning $25–$35/hour. Making matters worse, after eventually discovering the problem caused by delivery costs, Webvan imposed a $4.50 delivery charge for orders under $50 to offset their costs, which had the negative effect of removing any monetary incentive for customers to order more than $50. This charge did nothing but help hold the average customer order around $81/order, which was far below the $103 average order necessary for Webvan's automated warehouse and ordering system to be cost effective. Webvan eventually applied the $4.50 delivery charge to orders under $75 (still below its required average order size!), but it was too late. Webvan was encumbered by customers that were too expensive to acquire, too expensive to serve, and who were incentivized to order in low volumes that made even its efficient automated warehouse operations too expensive. Webvan eventually shut its doors after only two years, having burned through $1.2 billion of its investors' money.[12]

Even though Webvan was one of the quickest most expensive failures in the history of Silicon Valley, the former Webvan executives are making another run at it. Four key Amazon executives are former Webvan officials. They have spent the last 12 years analyzing the demise of Webvan and decided to relaunch Webvan in 2013 under the AmazonFresh program—a branch of Amazon that delivers groceries to your home. Only time will tell how successful the new venture will be for Amazon, but operating in a $568 billion industry[13] and knowing what not to do might play a significant role in the success of AmazonFresh. The resurrection of Webvan illustrates two key parables of entrepreneurship: Timing is everything, and everything old is new again.

With only so many hours in a day and with only so many days in a week, it is hard to step back, develop and implement new processes, hire and train people, and ensure everything functions adequately. Yet these control tasks are essential to creating an organization that can continue to thrive and grow. Therefore, your most critical first task in transitioning beyond startup is to create an efficient operation. This will eventually overlap with your efforts to sustain an entrepreneurial organization, but the firm will first need to catch up to its burgeoning growth—then it can set the stage for creating new sources of growth in the future. The key objectives for a control system should be to institute controls, track performance, and manage cash.

Other items founders may wish to adopt prior to scaling include Stephen Covey's famous seven habits of highly effective people:[14]

1. Be proactive
2. Begin with the end in mind
3. Put first things first (time management)
4. Think win–win (interpersonal leadership)
5. Seek first to understand, then to be understood
6. Synergize (creative cooperation)
7. Preserve and enhance yourself (balanced self-renewal)

Instituting Controls

Your first control system in early growth should be relatively simple: The organization should quickly and easily be able to get it up and running and train people to use it. With a simple system, there's less that can go wrong, and as employees and managers get accustomed to control practices, you can upgrade the system later to handle a larger and more complex organization. You can also implement the system stepwise—for example, by starting with components having the greatest gap between actual and desired performance or with those that are easiest to put in place and therefore will have immediate impact.

An effective control system includes the following (see Chapter 12 for more details).

- Accounts receivable and collections policies

- ◉ An inventory management system
- ◉ Account payable policies
- ◉ Assessment of performance and expenditures
- ◉ Metrics to track trends in cash, receivables, inventory, payables, expenditures, and performance

One control that is often neglected is to maintain what the company stands for—that is, controlling corporate culture. Adding employees without a focus on culture risks diluting a key advantage of young growth ventures. Clearly indicating a company's framework and work ethic for new and existing hires can help a company maintain its dedication to excellence. Jim Collins, author of *Good to Great*, has completed extensive research on the transition of a good company into a great company. One major component in the journey is a down-to-earth and pragmatic approach where the company's goals are directly instilled and aligned in each of its employees.[15] Furthermore, Collins discusses the *hedgehog concept*,[16] which states that to become a great company, it must do one thing extremely well as opposed to a mediocrity among many smaller things. Three questions that must be asked are (1) What is the company passionate about? (2) What drives the company's economic engine? and (3) What can the company do better than anyone else?[17] Collins mentions that the outputs of the three questions create a company's hedgehog.

Managing costs requires both making decisions about expenditures and instituting controls that monitor spending. A growing firm's selling and administrative costs often expand rapidly with its escalation in sales. This expenditure is often appropriate because you need marketing to generate sales and administrative overhead to support the burgeoning organization. Yet you do need to monitor these areas to determine effectiveness and detect overspending. For example, certain advertising approaches may be more effective than others, or they may work in one region but not another.

As the company begins to sell more and more products in multiple markets, you will want to analyze its performance in different product or market segments, along with how effectively it is spending its resources. You need to understand what each product costs and whether you are truly making a profit. All the costs going into each product are those costs, both variable and fixed, that would disappear if the product were discontinued. What remains after these costs are deducted from the selling price contributes toward company overhead and profit.

You can also develop performance metrics to aid in decisions about investments and expenditures. Performance measures in an early-stage company are designed less for evaluating actual outcomes against a plan (as they would be in a more stable, established organization) than for helping in entrepreneurial decision making. As the company's operations expand, managers can develop metrics to help them answer the following questions:

- ◉ Which products or markets generate the highest revenues and margins?
- ◉ Which customers or customer groups are reliable accounts (make timely payments, are at low risk of default)?
- ◉ How effective are our expenditures in areas such as marketing and sales, and does this differ across markets?

Another popular startup metric for product marketing and product management is Dave McClure's pirate metrics[18]—AARRR—which embodies five key stages:[19]

1. **Acquisition:** The first contact point with a customer as users come to the site from various channels.
2. **Activation:** Customers using your product where they enjoy a happy first visit.
3. **Retention:** Users coming back and visiting the site multiple times.
4. **Referral:** Users liking the product so much that they begin referring others.
5. **Revenue:** Users start spending money through or on the site.

Figure 14.4 illustrates the conversion metrics associated with the five stages of AARRR.

Category	User Status	Conv %	Est. Value
Acquisition	**Visit Site** (or landing page, or external widget)	100%	$.01
Acquisition	**Doesn't Abandon** (views 2+ pages, stays 10+ sec, 2+ clicks)	70%	$.05
Activation	**Happy 1st Visit** (views X pages, stays Y sec, Z clicks)	30%	$.25
Activation	**Email/Blog/RSS/Widget Signup** (anything that could lead to repeat visit)	5%	$1
Activation	**Acc Signup** (includes profile data)	2%	$3
Retention	**Email Open/RSS View – Clickthru**	3%	$2
Retention	**Repeat Visitor** (3+ visits in first 30 days)	2%	$5
Referral	**Refer 1+ users who visit site**	2%	$3
Referral	**Refer 1+ users who activate**	1%	$10
Revenue	**User generates minimum revenue**	2%	$5
Revenue	**User generates break-even revenue**	1%	$25

Source: D. McClure, "Startup Metrics for Pirates," August 7, 2008, www.slideshare.net/dmc500hats/startup-metrics-for-pirates-long-version.

Figure 14.4

Conversion metrics associated with AARRR

Tracking Performance

Tracking performance is integral to one of the core functions of an entrepreneur: decision making. A performance tracking system is what separates decision making under uncertain conditions from merely guessing. Decisions must be sound as well as timely. A performance tracking system is about much more than simply key performance metrics, or KPIs. It is about investing the right dose of organizational effort into a simple, flexible, but deliberate plan to create and sustain a common operating picture that allows everyone in the company to see the critical variables of your business, your market, and your competition. Twenty-first-century entrepreneurship promotes the use of a KPI dashboard, which uses a visual interface to clearly illustrate and consolidate KPIs from several areas of the business.[20] The dashboard would typically be placed at a location that is clearly visible to all employees and would track items such as total funding, total expenses, total revenue generated, cash on hand, number of subscribers, number of downloads, and upcoming milestones. Unlike traditional KPI reports, like Excel documents, business dashboards instantly generate a visual using real-time data.[21] Therefore, instead of manually building a report every month, employees can simply check their dashboard to see the company's current performance. Additionally, modern business dashboards support multidevice systems and allow for multiuser access, creating a universal dashboard that is integrated with information from several departments. An example of a KPI dashboard is illustrated in Figure 14.5.

While tracking systems and the items beings tracked will vary as greatly as companies do, there are basic criteria that the best systems all possess:

- ◉ They identify decisions that require a true "this or that" choice, including those under most likely, best case, and worse-case scenarios.
- ◉ For each decision, they determine the latest point in time at which the decision remains relevant to an outcome (the latest time any performance information would be of value).
- ◉ For each decision, they determine what specific questions must be answered to support a decision. They include what must be answered about the market, your own firm, and your competition.
- ◉ For each question, they determine the specific metrics (both qualitative and quantitative) needed to formulate an answer.
- ◉ They determine where, when, and how to measure each metric, and the name(s) of those responsible for measuring it.
- ◉ They remain simple so that tracking performance does not itself degrade performance.
- ◉ They assign someone responsibility for running the tracking system (using the entrepreneur as the *last choice*).

Startup Name	Total Funding 1,030,000	Funding			Team 👥👥	9 Referrals
Write stuff here... We provide the most innovative blah blah..dashboard solutions More..		family	10,000	12/1/2011	name = title John = Co-founder Tim = Co-founder Jessica = designer Mihir = engineer	❤
		incubator	20,000	3/15/2012		
		series A	1,000,000	6/9/2012		

Launched: 3/1/2012 6 months ago	Total Expenses 53,100	Total Revenue 61,130	Cash on Hand 1,038,030

Buzz			Expenses		Revenue		Monthly Expenses 8,000
Site	Traffic	When	hosting	350	advertising	200	
Allthingsd	2,999	8/9/2012	legal	500	licence	36,000	
Blog1	3,234	6/30/2012	marketing	2,700	oem licence annual	20,000	
Killerstartups	1,000	5/21/2012	outsourcing	3,000	one-time fee	1,000	
LA Times	2,222	5/21/2012	payroll	42,000	subscription	3,930	
Mashable	6,000	4/11/2012	rent	3,500			Runway Months 130
NY Times	1,323	6/30/2012	travel	750			
SF Gate	4,123	6/30/2012	website	300			
TNW	5,000	6/30/2012					
WSJ	3,233	5/21/2012					🙂
Yahoo	1,111	5/21/2012					

Revenue bar chart: Blog 300, Email 100, Twitter 300, Facebook 120, Google + 250

traffic_page_views	1,500	Subscribers 3,403	Downloads 10,000	Dashboards 6,004
traffic_time_onsite	8			
traffic_unique_visits	500			

Source: Infocaptor.com, "Startup Scoreboard Dashboard," www.infocaptor.com/dashboard/startup-scorecard-dashboard.

Figure 14.5

KPI dashboard

Successful entrepreneurs are careful not to invest excessive effort in tracking the activities of their competition too early. They focus on finding and delivering value to their customers and keeping their own business in order. Reliable information about your competition's future actions often takes more time and resources to collect than many startups can spend. Focus on tracking how you are creating value for and relationships with your customers and how you are running your business; track just what is needed to effectively deal with your competition when they get in your way. A simple but deliberate performance tracking system supports a focus on timely action and excellent execution, because when you can efficiently determine where you stand, you will have more time and energy left to apply toward getting to where you want to be.

How do you determine what's good or bad when examining key metrics? For some financial ratios, published sources can provide industry averages for comparison. Entrepreneurial firms, however, often adopt policies that differ from those of more stable, established firms, such as spending on marketing while building brand awareness. Thus, it may be more useful to look at trends in metrics over time; for example, an increase in your collection period for receivables could indicate a relaxing in collection efforts, or a decrease in inventory turns could indicate you are at increasing risk of stockouts. If you see significant changes and they are not the result of policy shifts in your firm, look for causes and consider making adjustments in policy.

One key point is to make performance measures as simple and inexpensive to track as possible while providing information that helps you make better decisions. One very successful consulting firm had simple but useful measures. The entrepreneur tracked performance through his "B-Report." The B-Report was a simple Excel spreadsheet with each consultant occupying a row and columns representing every week of the year. If consultants expected to bill in a given week, they put a "B" in the column. If they did not, they left it blank. If the entrepreneur did not see a lot of B's, he knew he had a problem.

The company can also develop simple budgeting practices to estimate cash and inventory needs, schedule production, determine staffing requirements, and set sales and profitability goals. It should upgrade and formalize these controls, metrics, and budgets as it moves toward later growth. But more importantly, these tools should evolve to provide the best information possible in aiding the company's decision making. The value they provide should more than justify the time and effort spent to develop and maintain them.

There may be times when it's appropriate to slow the pursuit of new growth to give the company room to improve its ability to manage growth. Some indicators that your company is growing at an uncontrollable rate are

- *Your workforce is stretched too thin*, and you and the founding team are allocating too much time to hiring and training new employees at the expense of providing the necessary leadership to existing employees.

- *The percentage of your cash flows from operations is declining against your cash flows from financing*, particularly debt. At this point, your cash conversion cycle, a measure of sustainability, is too long or getting longer. You may need to borrow money to sustain operating activities. Growth under these conditions can exacerbate this problem and leave your business unable to respond to unforeseen costs.

- *Profit margins are shrinking as sales are climbing.* Tight margins equate to a need to run an efficient operation, or have large amounts of cash on hand that are rarely found in a rapidly growing startup. Under these conditions the line between making a profit or incurring losses is very thin, and the overall risk posed by further growth may outweigh the benefits.

- *You are doing other peoples' jobs.* As the tempo of business increases, you are finding it harder to delegate effectively and doing more things yourself instead, which can lead to a breakdown in the organization's structure.

- *Customer complaints, in proportion to increases in sales, are increasing.* This means your company is not learning from your customers. Startups must "learn in order to earn." All companies receive complaints; the best companies embrace this feedback to refine their business to avoid scaling an inefficient business or a business that does not yet understand its customer.

- *Your accountant is nervous.* While accountants in a startup should never be at ease, as the leader you must demonstrate the judgment required to recognize when the accountant's "worry meter" is pegged, slow down, and listen to their counsel.[22]

Joel Kolen, former president of Empress International Ltd., a seafood distributor, emphasizes that

> *By taking a break from growth and putting in controls such as those at a large company, an entrepreneur can ease the growth transition and ensure that the qualities that helped build the company don't get lost in the rush to fill new orders.*[23]

Albercan Drilling Supply	2011	2012	2013	Increase 2011 – 2013
Days sales outstanding	39	45	53	37%
Days in inventory	44	86	98	122%
Days in payables	36	38	53	48%
Cash conversion period	47	92	98	108%

Figure 14.6

Albercan cash conversion analysis

Managing the Cash Cycle

It takes money to make money. Most entrepreneurs know this, and while most pay attention to "how much?" successful entrepreneurs focus on "how fast?" The **cash cycle** shows the amount of time that passes between cash outlays and cash inflows during the company's sales process. It also shows the relationship between three key measures: days in payables, days in inventory, and days sales are outstanding. Let's use Albercan Drilling Supply to illustrate the cash cycle—and how better controls can conserve resources. Albercan's sole business was the sale of drill pipes and collars to drilling contractors in the local area. In 2013, as the company was growing, it seemed to have a constant need for cash. At the same time, its bankers were hesitant to extend more credit. A review of the key measures in Figure 14.6 shows that all have increased substantially in two years, more than doubling the cash conversion period.

As Figure 14.7 illustrates, the cash conversion period extends from the time of cash outlay (to suppliers) to cash inflow (from customers). Looking at this diagram, you can imagine how an increase in sales would actually decrease cash inflows in the short term. The company would need to borrow money to cover the costs associated with this increase in sales until cash comes in 98 days later. In the meantime, as it makes additional sales, the company would need to cover these costs. When cash finally comes in, the company would likely need that cash for more inventory!

Another problem revealed in this analysis is the length of time Albercan takes to pay suppliers. If typical payment terms are 30 days (whereas Albercan is paying in 58 days), the company may be testing its relationship with suppliers. This could lead them to refuse to ship additional product until Albercan pays past invoices, or in the worst case, they might refuse to do business with the company.

The easy solution would be to borrow from a bank or other debt source, preferably using a revolving line of credit that allows the company to draw funds as needed and pay them back when it receives cash. These are short-term loans designed to cover shortfalls such as this. Borrowing can get expensive, though, so why not think about reducing the average cash conversion period? This is much more difficult, but it instills a sense of resource parsimony that boosts a company's efficiency. What if Albercan can reduce its days in inventory to 60 and its days' sales outstanding to 40? We'll also assume Albercan needs to reduce days in payables to 45. This all leaves a cash

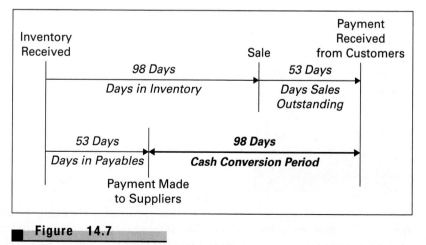

Figure 14.7

Cash conversion period for Albercan: 2013

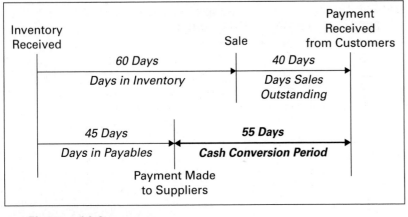

Figure 14.8

Adjusted cash conversion period for Albercan: 2013

conversion period of 55 days, as Figure 14.8 shows. Not only will that reduce the period of time the company would need to borrow, but it would also reduce the average amount needed, because cash comes in more quickly and is therefore available for more inventory.

The cash management practices of Flextronics International Ltd., a Singaporean firm ranked as one of the largest global electronics manufacturing services firms by revenue in 2010 ($24 billion),[24] provides insight into the impact that changes in your cash conversion cycle can have on your company. By the end of 2010, Flextronics had succeeded in cutting its cash conversion cycle in half from 22 days in the previous year to an industry-leading 11 days. This was largely accomplished by reducing its accounts receivable by $121 million and increasing its accounts payable by $413 million as compared to the previous year. During 2010, the company's cash management efforts contributed to a 267% increase in share price, as compared with increases in the Dow Jones, NASDAQ, and S&P 500 indices of 40%, 55%, and 40%, respectively.[25]

Leveraging the Value Chain

> *"Amateurs talk tactics, professionals talk logistics"*

> —Military maxim

We commonly represent a value chain as a series of steps showing the activities and entities that we need to coordinate for the company to execute its product or service. A startup may outsource more than it wants to at first because it does not have the resources or capabilities to do everything in-house. Often it designs a product with as many off-the-shelf parts as possible to minimize design and tooling charges. On the other hand, the firm may need to take on some value chain activities because there is no reliable or ready source for them; this is particularly true for new products or services for which there is little infrastructure. Alternatively, value chain players may not cooperate, leaving the company to sell its product direct, for example, rather than creating channel conflict for distributors who deal with more stable, older companies. As the company grows, you should decide which value chain positions are capable of creating the most value and for which you can establish unique advantage.

For example, when Andrew Kardon founded JoeShopping.com, a social networking site for bargain shoppers, he chose to handle all of the site development in-house. "I don't need someone else to do my job," he wrote. He asked why he should pay someone else to do something that the staff he already had could do. Kardon was trying to develop a comparison-shopping engine from scratch, which would entail combining huge volumes of data feeds of various qualities into an easily searchable product database. This effort cost Kardon many hours and a lot of money, and in the end it worked, but not at the level of quality that he needed. Kardon dismissed outsourcing initially because he wanted to integrate the product search with the social networking across the whole site and the entire shopping experience. He simply wanted to control it all, but he quickly saw that full control came with a price. After his initially disappointing results, he outsourced development to a company that already had

Andrew Kardon, founder of JoeShopping.com

a search engine that was equal or better than what Kardon could have hoped for had he continued for another year trying to develop it himself. The cost of outsourcing this work came in at less than $100 a month. Outsourcing allowed Kardon to cut back on salaries, which at the time was his largest single expense.[26]

Outsourcing can enable a growing company to focus on those activities it can perform particularly well and those underlying its source of competitive advantage. It makes sense to outsource those activities other companies can do more reliably and less expensively, like the shopping networking site just mentioned. But recognize that, while moving activities outside reduces the steps the firm performs in-house, it will also reduce the control you have over those activities—and often consume substantial time just in managing the relationship. The firm will therefore need to weigh some considerations, such as how it will maintain quality and how responsive the value chain partner needs to be in reducing or increasing production in response to fluctuations in sales.

Maintaining the Entrepreneurial Organization

With all this talk about efficiency and controls, it's hard to imagine how anything entrepreneurial can happen. That is sadly the case with many companies. A history of success creates preferences for re-creating the past rather than building toward the future. Efficiency in current operations often does not accommodate new initiatives, like those requiring different sales channels or different value chain partners. Customers want the company to improve the products they know best rather than forcing them to change their behaviour and endure the switching costs of adapting to a new product.

How, then, can a well-run organization maintain the ability to create new businesses? It's primarily a combination of the remaining driving forces of the growth model: how leadership views and manages its opportunity domain and the organization's people and resources.

Opportunity Domain

While a startup is focused on shaping an opportunity and bringing it to life, as the organization grows its leadership needs to define a strategic arena that guides decisions on how it competes in its industry and creates value for its targeted markets. An organization defines this arena through a balance of the unique capabilities it builds and its ability to differentiate itself in its competitive environment. This balance then guides decisions about how the company markets and sells its products and about which opportunities it pursues in expanding its business.

The impact of Stonyfield Farm's strategic focus can be seen in many aspects of its business. Stonyfield positioned itself as producing high-end yogurt products with quality, natural ingredients. It first sold its product through natural food and specialty stores, building a plant to better control its supply of hormone-free milk. The firm's marketing consisted of developing awareness and word of mouth by educating consumers about the quality of the product, promoting the company's social and environmental mission, and building a loyal following through plant tours, newsletters, and other customer relationship–focused programs. Stonyfield introduced new yogurt flavours, low-fat yogurt, and frozen yogurt. Its strategic focus shaped its distribution, manufacturing, marketing, and product development activities.

A focused strategy in early growth helps to guide the firm through the maze of opportunities that materialize once it experiences initial success. All too often, a startup chases diverse opportunities without defining what it can do distinctly well. During early growth, define your firm's core focus and develop capabilities around this, spending your limited resources and time close to this core, just as Stonyfield focused on building awareness of its unique brand and strengthening this brand with new yogurt flavours.

In later growth, your company has established its competitive uniqueness and can now leverage this while training a strategic eye on the future. It may continue to extend its advantage in its current position by, for example, upgrading its products. Over time, however, opportunities will eventually diminish in a particular product space, and you will need to combine incremental extensions with expansion into the periphery. A company may create a next-generation product that includes improvements and new features for existing customers while exploring new products and new markets. A restaurant chain can start offering Sunday brunch to its customers, for example, or it can launch a catering business.

Pay attention, however, to new developments in the industry and market environment. These may determine where you should focus your strategic efforts at specific points in time. For instance, you may emphasize a current product to gain maximum returns before competition comes in. Or you may seek new ground if the market is becoming crowded by large competitors or if a technology foundation is becoming obsolete.

Yankee Candle Company illustrates how a company can expand over time within an existing product/market space and into the periphery. The company traces its origins to young Michael Kittredge's home operation, which soon expanded to an old paper mill. The company grew its sales of candles through gift shops and expanded into the international market through distributors. It started selling online and through catalogues. The company also opened its own retail stores, including a flagship store in South Deerfield, Massachusetts, which serves as a tourist destination, with a candle museum, a restaurant, and sales of toys, gifts, home accessories, and other products, along with candles of all shapes and sizes.

While this expansion continued, the company entered the home fragrance market with products such as electric home fragrancers, room sprays, potpourri, and bath care products. The primary target audience was still women ranging in age from 20 to 60. However, the company started to test new markets through its acquisition of GBI Marketing, a distributor of selected gift products (including Yankee Candle products) to fundraising organizations.

A Cautionary Note on Expanding through Acquisitions: The Channing Bete Setback

Channing Bete enjoyed years of success with its information pamphlets providing advice on a range of topics, from managing diabetes to handling bullies. The company had a broad range of customers that included schools, hospitals, and government agencies. With its acquisition of Developmental Research Programs, Channing Bete set the stage for expanding from its single business of publishing printed information to a consulting operation focused on helping youth steer clear of drug use, delinquency, and pregnancy.

A few years later, revenues from the largest division of the acquired business fell 21.4%, and the division was shut down. A customer commented that Channing Bete's contributions to the business were little more than cosmetic but increased costs substantially. Losses spread to the core business, and the company fired one-fifth of its workforce. Tension mounted within the company as changes were imposed, such as replacing "flextime" with a 9-to-5 workday, even while the company touted its family-friendly culture. One former employee commented that the company got in over its head; it put a great deal of money and energy into the acquisition, neglecting lines of business that had been profitable.

Adapted from S. Dewitt, "Bete Consulting Bet Falls Short: Move Brings Losses, Firings, Retrenchment," Daily Hampshire Gazette, July 18, 2005, A1 and D1. Reprinted with the permission of the Daily Hampshire Gazette. All Rights Reserved.

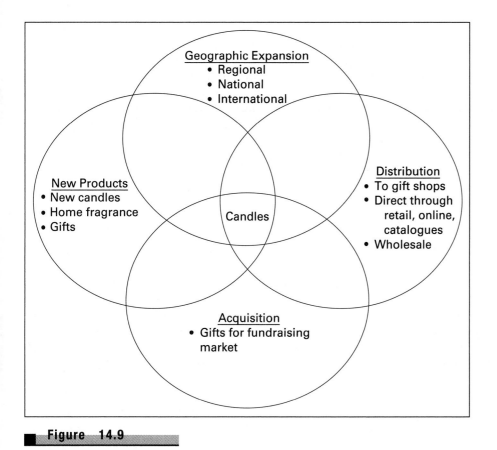

Figure 14.9

Yankee Candle's opportunity domain

As Figure 14.9 shows, Yankee Candle has taken a multipronged approach to expanding its business: geographic expansion, new products, new distribution methods, and acquisition. There is a common logic surrounding all these methods, extending from core elements relating to its original product: candles. You've probably encountered small, single-operation candle shops. The Yankee Candle example[27] shows how a seemingly slow-growth business can become a high-potential venture with sales revenue surpassing $785 million in 2011.

As a company grows, it may experience stagnating growth in its core business but see little opportunity for expansion into the periphery. It may need to make drastic shifts in its business. As Channing Bete's experience illustrates (see the box on expanding through acquisitions), however, the company should make these forays outside the periphery carefully.

Acquisitions can provide inroads into new businesses for a company, but this undertaking requires an underlying logic. While Channing Bete attempted to move from publishing to consulting, Yankee Candle was already in the gift market when it made its acquisition. The central precept is the connection between organizational resources and capabilities and the opportunity domain, as illustrated in Figure 14.2. The growing organization should not consider external opportunities that simply appear attractive unless it has some particular ability to pursue them better than do competitors.

Obviously, a company cannot be driven only by opportunities that leverage current capabilities. Expansion opportunities will stretch these capabilities, and the company may choose to build new ones over time. Think about how this likely happened for Yankee Candle. The company can experiment or partner to reduce risk. It can adopt an options strategy, spreading exploratory resources across multiple business options with the logic that a few, as yet unknown, will warrant more substantial commitments. The company can also stage its investments like venture capitalists do, investing a minimal amount in a new business opportunity and tying further investment to the achievement of milestones or the reduction of uncertainty. These practices minimize impact on the organization until more is known.

The one certainty entrepreneurs can count on, however, is change. You will need to anticipate, respond to, and sometimes even drive change. Professor Richard Osborne examined 26 privately held firms, all of which experienced initial success. Six of these firms were able to sustain growth beyond the entrepreneurial phase while the rest saw their growth stalled. Factors such as inadequate resources, poor managerial capabilities of the entrepreneur, and bureaucracy were minor factors in the growth stall, according to this research. The main factor was the inability to perceive and respond to changing opportunities and conditions in their environment.[28]

The growing company therefore needs to be responsive to impending environmental shifts, maintaining its ability to transform its strategy and establish a new source of uniqueness in a changed environment. For example, exercise physiologist and entrepreneur Brian Cook opened one of the very first personal-training studios in Massachusetts in 1995, called In-Shape Fitness. From 2001 to 2006, Cook developed franchises for a one-on-one studio concept, selling 60 franchises while owning and operating up to five of his own. Cook was able to detect a trend of growing demand among women for a more personalized and customized experience ignored by most large gyms and fitness studios. Seizing the opportunity posed by this trend, Cook sold his franchise-development rights and his personal-training studios in 2006. He redeployed his capital in the same year to found the first Get In Shape For Women studio in Bedford, Massachusetts, as a complete fitness program for women, combining such activities as cardio and weight training for women with nutrition information for a healthy diet and accountability through personal trainers that work with up to four women at time. He hit directly where the untapped demand had been growing, and in less than five years had grown his franchise to over 100 studios in 18 states, producing revenues of $2.4 million in 2011.[29]

As your company grows, its strategic planning efforts will benefit from the input of others inside and outside the company with critical knowledge that can influence the company's direction. Customers, particularly lead users, can provide information about market needs. Specialist employees who are close to markets and technologies can identify future opportunities. The firm can institute a function that gathers and monitors outside information and examines external trends and opportunities.

Organizational Resources and Capabilities

Efforts to finance growth internally go hand in hand with controls. By improving its cash flow, your growing company can better avert a cash crisis and avoid being at the mercy of reluctant or expensive lenders or investors. You may even be able to self-finance some of its future growth, reducing reliance on more expensive sources of funding. The key lesson is this: A bootstrap mentality does not apply just to starting a company; it is a lasting orientation that maximizes returns through resource parsimony.

Obtaining Financial Resources for the Growing Company

Shortening operating cash cycles and increasing margins are vital for conserving cash. They essentially represent costless financing. The rapidly growing organization, however, will likely need to tap additional sources to finance its growth. Not only will you need financing to support accelerating sales, but also new policies, such as granting customer payment terms or taking on bulk orders, as well as investments in new products or services will create a drain on cash.

Despite its success and future prospects, however, a company early in its growth cycle may have only certain options available. For example, a bank would not typically extend credit to a firm with little operating history and fluctuating sales. But as we discussed in Chapter 12, a supplier who is motivated to make a sale and gain a loyal, growing customer might. After a company has been established for a year, a bank might be willing to loan monies against a portion of its receivables, based on the founders' good credit, or with signed guarantees, perhaps requiring loan covenants to maintain certain numbers or ratios.

It's therefore useful to think in terms of stages when financing growth. Sources closed to the firm earlier in its life may open up later. Undertake periodic surveys of the firm's current financing options and consider any changes that may open up new and cheaper financing sources. In this way, you may recognize new opportunities for refinancing at lower rates.

As we covered in chapters 10, 11, and 12, sources of financing for early growth include

- Investment from key management
- Founder loans
- Family and friends
- Angel investors
- Venture capital
- Loans on assets, such as receivables, inventory, and equipment
- Equipment leases
- Credit cards

As the company moves into later growth and undertakes expansion efforts, such as selling internationally or launching new products or services, it will need financing from sources more appropriate for higher-risk and longer-term investment. Banks typically will not loan substantial funds, unsecured, for riskier expansion efforts that won't generate returns for quite some time. The firm will likely need to rely on equity sources.

But there are other ways to finance future growth. Look to strategic partners who may provide more favourable financing terms. You may also decide to expand by franchising. Take the risks of these financing modes into consideration: For example, potential customers who compete with your strategic partner may view a relationship with you as too risky because your partner has some control over your firm or has greater access to information that could unfavourably affect the customer. Determine your resource needs by your firm's range of value chain activities. Reducing activities to those considered core to the business and achieving better coordination throughout the chain can reduce your resource requirements and risk, as we detailed in the execution section.

Intangible Resources and Capabilities

Resources at startup include people, but the focus is on acquiring capital since the key human resource is the founder or founding team. As the company grows, it accumulates capital, to be sure, and fixed assets. But it also builds intangible assets—resources such as the proprietary knowledge underlying its products and services and the skills of the organization's people. You should have addressed intellectual property considerations early on, before early growth—even before starting the business. But this should also be an ongoing process requiring continual legal advice and subsequent actions to protect technologies, processes, and creative work through trade secrets, copyrights, trademarks, and patents (see Chapter 13).

Starting in early growth, you'll need to develop or hire people with specialized skills. Generalist skills are important at startup: Everyone should be able to pitch in and help with shipping, inventory control, marketing, and so forth. As volume increases and the business becomes more complex, it becomes harder to maintain efficiency and effectiveness with generalist skills. Now you will need to hire specialists in areas such as marketing, inventory management, accounting and finance, and logistics.

An organization also develops capabilities that define what it is good at. These are processes that coordinate and integrate the organization's tangible and intangible resources to create unique sources of value. Just like inventory and equipment, they lead to revenues for a company. Think about businesses or organizations that are familiar to you and about what they do best. McDonald's has efficient processes to deliver fast, low-priced meals. Microsoft delivers transformative computer operating systems and software. These transactions translate to capabilities. Now think about whether these organizations would be good at doing something totally different in their industry. Could McDonald's open a high-end restaurant? Will Microsoft's expansion into the tablet PC and smartphone market be a success? Possibly, but not easily. But there are opportunities to expand into the periphery with their capabilities. For example, McDonald's began to offer salads in an attempt to attract more health-conscious, but also convenience-minded and price-conscious, eaters. In 2008, McDonald's rolled out McCafé, which offers specialty coffees such as cappuccino, lattes, and mochas and directly competes with Starbucks.[30] In 2012, in another effort to increase sales from existing customers who are becoming more health conscious, McDonald's rolled out a completely new "Favourites under 400" menu to make it simpler for customers to select items based on their calorie content. In 2012, Microsoft released Surface, its first tablet PC, and the Windows smartphone, both of which were designed to run on the new Windows 8 OS, enabling the first ever-complete integration of Microsoft's Office products into mobile devices.[31]

Your capabilities need to be consistent with your firm's strategic focus. As the opportunity domain section of this chapter reveals, organizations define their strategy both through detecting where the opportunities are for unique advantages in the external competitive environment and through building and leveraging a set of unique capabilities. McDonald's needs to have processes that optimize efficiency and cut costs out of its operations. Microsoft needs to be constantly imagining and developing the next breakthrough operating systems and software applications, then integrating them into seamless ecosystems that help lock customers in. Think again about the capabilities Stonyfield Farm and Yankee Candle needed as they started and expanded their businesses.

Sustained growth in a changing environment requires constant attention to identifying what the company does best and matching that with the potential for unique value in the competitive environment. Your company may be good at user-friendly innovations. If it does this better than rivals and users are willing to pay a premium for that, then leverage it—ensuring the right people and systems are in place to maximize the value you can gain from this capability.

Meanwhile, you need to monitor the uniqueness and value of your company's capabilities over time. If competitors duplicate this ability or customers shift toward more technically complex solutions, reassess what your company does best. Renew key capabilities periodically. A research study of telecommunications and computer startups found that high levels of innovativeness at founding did not translate to higher growth seven, eight, or nine years out. And simply forming alliances didn't help. But those building internal technology capabilities beyond founding were more likely to achieve a higher level of sustained growth.[32]

Leadership

Figure 14.10 summarizes some key differences between entrepreneurs, managers, and entrepreneurial leaders. The entrepreneurial leader plays a distinct role that is critical for sustaining a growing organization. There are three main theories regarding how leaders become leaders. The first is the **traits theory**,[33] which states that people are simply born with innate leadership capabilities. The second theory is the **great events theory**,[34] which states that a crisis brings out the leadership qualities in a person who is not or was not previously considered a leader. The third theory is the **transformational leadership theory**,[35] which states that individuals choose to become leaders and purposely educate themselves to learn the skills involved with being a leader. The third theory is the most widely adopted since entrepreneurs tend to have an internal locus of control. An **internal locus of control** is a concept stating that entrepreneurs believe that their actions, not luck or external sources, are directly correlated with the results they achieve.

Starting the Delegation Process

The entrepreneur typically starts out doing everything. He or she answers phones, ships product, designs advertisements—in essence, performing just about all the activities needed to ensure the organization gets product sold and out the door. But sometime in early growth the organization will outgrow the entrepreneur's ability to keep up. He or she will have neither the time nor the expertise to deal with the range of challenges a burgeoning business presents. The following are symptoms revealing that the organization has outgrown the entrepreneur's capacity:

- The volume of decisions multiplies. The entrepreneur is working harder but accomplishing less.

Entrepreneur	Manager	Entrepreneurial Leader
Locates new ideas	Maintains current operations	Leverages core business while exploring new opportunities
Starts a business	Implements the business	Starts businesses within an ongoing organization
Opportunity driven	Resource driven	Capability and opportunity driven; leverages capabilities and builds new ones to expand opportunity domain
Establishes and implements a vision	Plans, organizes, staffs, controls	Establishes a vision and empowers others to carry it out
Builds an organization around the opportunity	Enhances efficiency of organization	Maintains entrepreneurial ability as organization grows; ensures culture, structure, systems are conducive to entrepreneurship; removes barriers
Leads and inspires others	Supervises and monitors others	Develops and guides entrepreneurial individuals; bridges between individuals and groups with diverse expertise and orientation
Orchestrates change in the competitive environment	Maintains consistency and predictability	Orchestrates change in both the organizational and competitive environment

Figure 14.10

The entrepreneur versus manager versus entrepreneurial leader

- Decisions become more difficult to make: more complex and specialized. The entrepreneur increasingly wonders whether he or she has made the right decision.

- Everyone is still pitching in and doing everything, but something critical slips by or mistakes occur more and more.

- If the entrepreneur is not directly involved in the task, no progress can happen.

Starting in early growth, the entrepreneur must delegate responsibilities to others in the organization. The process of delegation is mapped out in Figure 14.11.

As Figure 14.11 shows, the entrepreneur starts out by assigning specific tasks to others. As delegation proceeds, he or she passes responsibility for achieving objectives to specialists, then managers, without needing to understand or know about the underlying mechanics. Then the setting of objectives moves to others—experienced managers and teams close to the activity. This process enables the entrepreneur to spend less time on the day-to-day details of everything and focus on what he or she does best while those who are most qualified make decisions. At the same time, the entrepreneur needs to oversee execution by providing guidance to managers and using metrics to evaluate progress, but he or she may need to step in when necessary, particularly when initiatives meet with resistance.

Delegation, while necessary for surviving the entrepreneurial growth phase, is typically difficult for the entrepreneur to accomplish. He or she may continue to attempt to do everything but is increasingly unable to do so. Faced with these challenges, the entrepreneur may revert back to what he or she does best, ignoring tasks he or she has neither the comfort level nor the capability to deal with. A technical entrepreneur may retreat to developing new products while ignoring the company's inability to pay bills on time. What's bad is not the entrepreneur doing what he or she does best—it's having no one pay attention to the company's critical problems.

Employees may not have a problem with the lack of delegation because they may prefer that the entrepreneur make decisions that they can then carry out. Then they don't need to take responsibility for outcomes. On the other hand, in allowing employees to take responsibility for decisions, the entrepreneur also needs to let them make mistakes and learn from them, circumstances neither the employees nor the entrepreneur may feel comfortable with. The entrepreneur cannot continue to be the "go-to" person, however, when the volume of decisions mushrooms and he or she becomes increasingly less qualified to provide direction in many areas.

As the entrepreneur delegates, he or she will need to put in place managers who can be responsible for executing in specialized areas. Then, in a leadership role, he or she must develop the ability to inspire people with a range of expertise to organize, communicate, collaborate, and be creative in both running an efficient operation and pursuing entrepreneurial ideas.

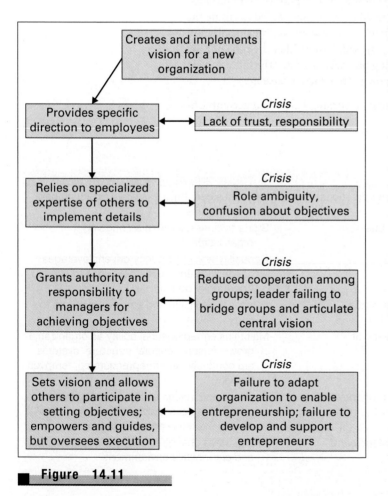

Figure 14.11

Transition from entrepreneur to entrepreneurial leader

First-Level Management

In early growth, the first set of supervisors can come from within. In some sense, they deserve to be promoted because they have been with the company since its early days and have contributed to its success. They were willing to chip in whenever and wherever needed, they have worked closely with you, the entrepreneur, and they therefore understand your vision and the purpose of the organization. They may also have the respect of their peers.

Assess whether these people have the potential to become managers, however, and whether they can develop their abilities through training and experience. There are a few things you should do: (1) set expectations up front, including setting personal performance goals; (2) provide coaching, mentoring, and training; and (3) periodically assess behaviour and performance. But developing managers takes time. If the venture is late forming its management structure and is therefore playing catchup, if internal and external conditions are rapidly changing, or if the learning gap between current employees and needed management is too wide, then allowing managers to learn on the job is too risky. You will need to hire from the outside.

Hiring from the outside has its own hazards because the workers, particularly those who have been there from the beginning, may not respect these outsiders. First, act as a broker between the employees and management during this transition. This includes advising the new manager and recognizing the cooperation and contributions of employees. The latter can mean acknowledging accomplishments through personal contact or making these visible around the organization. In addition, you (and your managers) can ensure employees have a satisfactory career path by promoting them and moving them into jobs in which they increasingly feel engaged and challenged.

Where possible, employ a mix of externally hired managers and internally promoted managers. Again, broker between these internal and external managers during the transition by setting expectations, advising and coaching, and monitoring behaviour. By achieving cooperation among internal and external managers, you're more likely to accomplish broad cooperation across the organization. Also reinforce the authority of your new managers, whether they originate from the inside or the outside. For example, route to them employees who have always gone directly to you.

From Delegation to Decentralization

What starts as a process of delegation in early growth evolves into a decentralized reporting structure as the organization approaches later growth. As functions become more specialized and the product and service offering broadens, responsibility and decision making are best left to those with the expertise and day-to-day involvement in specific areas.

A decentralized structure can also aid communication flow throughout the organization, which increasingly becomes challenged as the organization grows. While closeness to the entrepreneur in early stages helps everyone understand the vision and the organization's objectives, the complexity and changes a growing organization experiences can create confusion about direction and purpose. Communication and understanding need to happen among the members of the management team, who then ensure consistent information flow throughout their areas.

Professional Management and Boards

In later growth, the organization needs to ensure it has a leadership team in place: professional managers who share in the organization's strategic planning process and have the capability to balance the need for efficient operations with the benefits of maintaining its entrepreneurial edge. Once the organization has created control systems, a management structure, and a strategic focus, it needs to look toward its future. This job becomes increasingly complex and requires those with experience and track records. Employees who have been promoted into managerial positions are not likely to be qualified for the organization's top levels. Consequently, professional managers typically come from the outside.

With the introduction of a leadership team, the organization itself becomes more professional. This is a major change, even more so than the shift from startup to early growth. Some employees will leave, but others will make this transition. The practices you put in place to integrate managers and employees and insiders and outsiders during early growth will be critical to your introduction of a professional management team.

By carefully selecting members of the board of directors, you can provide alternative perspectives and depth and breadth of experience. The board should include experts from outside the firm who can become key participants in the strategic planning process. What's important for the firm is a proactive, rather than a reactive, approach to seeking ways to extend and build value. The composition of the company's board of directors will typically undergo changes as the firm emerges from its startup phase. Initially, the board may be informal—occupied by those unlikely to have high-level experience but able to provide support to the entrepreneur in his or her early endeavours. In early growth, boards typically evolve to include those able to provide operational guidance—for example, retired bankers, investors, and lawyers.

As the company professionalizes, the board should be more useful for strategic purposes, with members having a broader and visionary view of the market and industry—for example, other CEOs, industry experts, and senior executives in related businesses. While many investors require representation on the board of directors, avoid stakeholders who can control the firm for their benefit through board positions, such as suppliers, customers, and the company's lenders.

Supplement the skill and experience of the company's leadership and board of directors with the skill and experience of advisory boards and consultants. For example, you may assemble a group of technology experts from universities, government labs, and corporations to examine industry technological trends, or you may bring in a marketing consulting firm to determine tactics for expanding into overseas markets.

Coordinating the Driving Forces

The driving forces model shows a link among the three elements: organizational resources and capabilities, opportunity domain, and leadership. And at the core of this is execution: ensuring the most efficient and effective coordination of these activities in a way that enhances the organization's profitability. Capabilities and the opportunity domain interact: Capabilities define where the company can best play, and opportunities extend capabilities. Leadership maps out a particular opportunity domain with its strategic focus and modifies this focus over time, as the industry and market environment changes and the company seeks future growth. Leadership also ensures its capabilities and opportunity domain are in balance. But as the organization grows, a key concern for its leaders is how to manage its people and maintain its entrepreneurial capabilities, as the next section illustrates.

Leading People; Developing Entrepreneurs

The most common "people mistakes" an entrepreneurial firm makes are preparing people inadequately and maintaining the wrong people as the organization grows. Early in the business's life, organization members do their jobs and pitch in wherever needed. It is more important for the lean team to maintain the flexibility and broad skills needed to accomplish a lot with a little. Early in the game, it is not yet apparent that these employees lack the skills needed to scale up the organization. It is difficult to think about training to develop future skills when growth is consuming everyone's time.

As the need for specialists and managers arises, the tasks you expect of some employees may exceed their abilities, and you may need to place them in other roles—or even fire them if necessary. Other employees may be able to rise up to the challenges presented and assume these new functions and responsibilities. The process of adapting to these new roles takes time, however. The company will often need to do some hiring from the outside. You will have to deal with reduced motivation from setbacks or crises at the same time that employees struggle with adapting to new employees and higher-level managers coming from the outside, both of whom lack the shared experiences gained through the organization's history.

The second tier of employees, beyond the founding group, is often said to be more like 9-to-5ers who tend to view working there as a job. But in most companies, there are entrepreneurs in the mix. While we often think that ideas come from anywhere or that anyone can be creative if given a chance, the reality is that some people don't have the stomach for ambiguity and risk. And in many companies, the entrepreneur remains the sole entrepreneurial engine.

Research on corporate entrepreneurship suggests the organization's leaders need to do the following:

- Identify those exhibiting passion for entrepreneurship.
- Develop their ability to work under conditions of high ambiguity.
- Ensure they have the inclination and credibility to convince others in the organization to contribute and commit to their projects.
- Facilitate, support, and guide their efforts, while also providing them with sufficient freedom and empowerment.
- Recognize their contribution to the company's innovation and growth ambitions.
- View failure as a risk associated with entrepreneurship and an opportunity for learning, therefore ensuring that well-intentioned failures are not punished.

We suspect these practices are also critical in smaller organizations. One study reports that human resource practices like training and development distinguish high-growth firms from more slowly growing ones.[36]

CONCLUSION

Starting a business is a risky endeavour, but staying in business can be just as challenging. As the entrepreneurial firm grows beyond founding, it needs to ensure its organization is capable of managing growth. We have outlined a driving forces model that integrates leadership, opportunity domain, and resources and capabilities—and has execution at the core. The entrepreneur should understand and anticipate the challenges associated with building and managing a growing organization at different stages, prepare the organization to execute effectively at each point, and set the stage for a healthy future.

These efforts, however, must not distance the company from its entrepreneurial roots. Growing companies struggle not just with such concerns as having fewer resources than big companies, but also with coordinating an increasingly bigger and more complex business. The team members must work to prevent the organization from becoming a bureaucracy that inhibits entrepreneurship. They must continually foster entrepreneurial actions even when this is their biggest challenge. They have to consciously work on preserving and maintaining their entrepreneurial spirit, and if they lose it they have to rejuvenate the company and rekindle entrepreneurship before it's too late.

YOUR OPPORTUNITY JOURNAL

Reflection Point	Your Thoughts. . .
1. What are your personal growth objectives for your venture? Is a "lifestyle" business going to meet your personal goals? Or a high-potential venture?	
2. What will your role within the company be at various stages of growth? Do you want to remain the CEO? Are you more interested in another aspect—say, CTO?	
3. What skills will you need to develop as the company grows to satisfactorily fulfill the roles you aspire to? Which of these skills can you learn on the job? Which skills might need further education or other outside development?	
4. What kind of controls can you establish early in your venture's life? How will these help you manage cash and other key components of your business?	
5. Which aspects of your business should you keep in-house and which should you outsource? How do you protect your competitive advantage?	
6. What is your strategic focus for early growth? How do you leverage what you do really well? What are some possible peripheral growth opportunities for later in your venture's life?	
7. What are your organization's key resources and capabilities? What should they be in the future? How do you build toward those resources and capabilities?	
8. What is your leadership plan? When and which responsibilities will you delegate? How will you promote people in your organization? When might you need to go outside to hire?	

WEB EXERCISE

Identify three companies that have experienced successful, rapid growth in your industry. Study their websites and search for articles about the companies. Can you discern their strategic focuses early in their growth cycles? What are the core areas that they are leveraging? How do their growth strategies change later in their lives? What are some peripheral markets/customers they are going for? Have they grown by acquisition? How has that worked out?

Lazybones

Sitting in his Cambridge townhouse, Dan Hermann mulled over the latest performance report for his company, Lazybones, a laundry delivery service for college students. The unit[37] in Boulder, Colorado, was performing well, and he could see the positive results of the company's hiring and training initiatives. The Boston, Massachusetts, store was bringing in decent revenues, but it had just lost its manager. Over the coming weeks, Dan would need to be onsite quite a bit to work with new staff. Meanwhile, the Storrs, Connecticut, location (Lazybones's newest unit) was well below expectations. So in addition to overseeing four other stores and giving extra attention in Boston, Dan needed to spend time in Storrs assessing why that site couldn't get off the ground.

On the surface, the Lazybones store operations were straightforward: collect dirty laundry from college students, clean it, and then deliver it back to their dorm or apartment in less than 24 hours. The process, fine-tuned at their Syracuse, New York, and Madison, Wisconsin, flagship locations, worked flawlessly. Dan and his co-founder Reg Mathelier could monitor each unit remotely via webcam. They also used a barcode tracking system to feed a comprehensive reporting system for each store: the daily dashboard performance monitor. In fact, Dan lived in Boston and Reg lived in Chicago, far from most of the operating units. Yet as the company grew, the workload and processes were becoming more complicated. Dan was rethinking his growth objectives:

I hope I didn't mess up a good thing. I'm making less money, working twice as many hours, and I'm rapidly approaching 40 years old. The hours I put in now have more meaning to me. I've got more at stake today than I had when we were a startup. How should I evaluate that?

Dan's business, prior to adding the new locations, generated a consistent flow of cash and allowed him and Reg to earn a nice living. The business had evolved to the point where it did not require much time or effort to maintain a return. It had become an annuity of sorts, and Dan was free to pursue additional projects, like earning his MBA at Babson College. Dan faced the dilemma that many successful lifestyle entrepreneurs face: Should he keep the business as it is, or should he grow it? Perhaps it was the excitement of his classes at Babson, but Dan felt the itch to grow the Lazybones franchise and the two stores in Boston and Boulder were steps in that direction. Unfortunately, it was proving to be more work than Dan had expected.

The Syracuse, New York, unit

Take It to the Cleaners

It was May 1993 and like many other recent college grads, Dan Hermann and Reg Mathelier needed jobs. But neither saw himself in a corporate position. They both had an urge to start their own company; they just needed an idea. The inspiration came from an unlikely place . . . their own personal negligence. As stereotypical undergraduates, Reg and Dan were not too diligent with cleanliness. A close friend took note and offered to do their laundry in exchange for a small fee. The two friends started to realize that if they had bemoaned doing their laundry, so too would many of the thousands of undergraduate students at their alma mater, the University of Wisconsin at Madison.

The barriers to entry in laundry service were low. With a loan of $12,000 from friends and family, the two newly minted graduates traded in their laid-back academic lifestyle for the sweat and tears needed to launch Lazybones, a laundry delivery service targeted at college students. Their strategy was simple: Appeal to the parents of incoming and returning students and offer a fee-based subscription program. Each subscription covered the weekly pick-up and drop-off of a prepaid amount of laundry. Any overage was billed by the pound.

Dan explained:

The laundry is picked up, separated into lights and darks, washed with top-quality detergent and softeners, dried, meticulously folded, packaged in brown paper, and delivered back to the student within 24 hours of pickup. Parents loved the idea. Now their kids, even if they were hundreds of miles from home, would have clean clothes when they went out in public and, God forbid, be wearing clean underwear if they should be rushed to the emergency room following an accident. Parents willingly prepaid for the semester to bring a little bit of "mom" to college with the kid.

Although they had a rudimentary business plan—Dan laughs when he thinks about how rough and incomplete it was—they mostly learned the business on the job. They started with three home-grade washers and dryers and went out and solicited their first customers. They quickly realized that their service speed was too slow and their prices too low. What they lacked in business experience the two compensated for with diligence. They were literally willing to do whatever it took to get Lazybones off of the ground.

When we first started, we were working day and night, seven days a week. Reg and I knew that our service was going to be based on our quality. We would rewash clothes or hand scrub stains if needed.

The first year was a struggle for survival. Dan and Reg worked around the clock, and they were constantly on the verge of going out of business. They often used credit cards to finance the business over the first few years, especially during the summer, when the business basically came to a halt as students returned home. Fortunately Dan and Reg found a complementary summer business to ease the cash-flow famine. While school was out of session, Lazybones stored student possessions (TVs, furniture, etc.) that the students did not want to lug home and back. Three years passed before either founder took home any money. But by year five, they were turning a profit. The whole process was an exercise in logistics, with a steep learning curve.

We were constantly operating about 30 to 40% over what our actual logical capacity to do laundry was, given our facility, equipment, and staff. Yet we still weren't making money. But we were learning fast and having fun with the challenge of it. The demand for our service exceeded our ability to deliver, and we viewed this as an indicator that, if we hung in there and made adjustments, we would be onto something.

Six years into the business, Reg and Dan decided it was time to expand. After a friend conducted some market research, they identified Syracuse University as an ideal fit; the school charged a high tuition and possessed a large student base with a more-than-adequate amount of disposable income. Dan moved to Syracuse to oversee the opening. They soon received an endorsement from the school, which set up a direct pipeline to acquiring customers. Within a year and a half, the new location was breaking even.

Once a location hit profitability, the unit economics became attractive (see Exhibit 14.1 for the Unit Profit and Loss Statement). Customers loved the service, and many parents

EXHIBIT 14.1 Model Store Five-Year Income Statement

Month	July	Aug	Sept	Oct	Nov	Dec	Semester	Jan	Feb	Mar	Apr	May	Jun	Semester
Laundry Revenue	$—	$2,907	$6,056	$7,994	$6,056	$1,211	$24,225	$36,338	$4,845	$2,423	$2,423	$2,423	$—	$48,450
Storage Revenue	$—	$—	$—	$—	$—	$5,281	$5,281	$—	$—	$—	$1,320	$5,281	$6,601	$13,202
Other Revenue							$—							$—
Total Revenue	$—	$2,907	$6,056	$7,994	$6,056	$6,492	$29,506	$36,338	$4,845	$2,423	$3,743	$7,703	$6,601	$61,652
Cost of Goods Sold	$—	$517	$1,593	$3,014	$4,090	$4,306	$13,519	$3,819	$4,329	$4,583	$4,838	$5,093	$5,093	$27,754
Gross Profit	$—	$2,390	$4,463	$4,980	$1,966	$2,187	$15,986	$32,518	$516	$(2,161)	$(1,095)	$2,611	$1,508	$33,898
Gross Profit %							54%							55%
Selling, General & Administrative	$14,526	$14,526	$12,776	$11,026	$11,026	$11,776	$75,659	$11,776	$11,776	$11,776	$13,526	$15,276	$14,526	$78,659
EBITDA	$(14,526)	$(12,136)	$(8,313)	$(6,046)	$(9,060)	$(9,590)	$(59,672)	$20,742	$(11,260)	$(13,937)	$(14,622)	$(12,666)	$(13,018)	$(44,761)
Interest Expense	$585	$580	$575	$570	$565	$559	$3,434	$554	$549	$544	$538	$533	$528	$3,246
Net Ordinary Income	$(15,111)	$(12,716)	$(8,888)	$(6,616)	$(9,625)	$(10,149)	$(63,106)	$20,187	$(11,809)	$(14,481)	$(15,160)	$(13,199)	$(13,546)	$(48,007)
Net Profit Margin		-437%	-147%	-83%	-159%	-156%	-214%	56%	-244%	-598%	-405%	-171%	-205%	-78%

Year	Year 1	Year 2	Year 3	Year 4	Year 5
Laundry Revenue	$ 72,675	$ 169,575	$ 290,700	$ 387,600	$ 484,500
Storage Revenue	$ 18,483	$ 25,084	$ 46,207	$ 72,611	$ 99,015
Other Revenue	$—	$—			
Total Revenue	$ 91,158	$ 194,659	$ 336,907	$ 460,211	$ 583,515
Cost of Goods Sold	$ 41,274	$ 91,416	$ 158,218	$ 216,124	$ 274,030
Gross Profit	$ 49,884	$ 103,243	$ 178,689	$ 244,087	$ 309,485
Gross Profit %	55%	53%	53%	53%	53%
Selling, General & Administrative	$ 154,317	$ 137,191	$ 142,423	$ 147,716	$ 153,131
EBITDA	$ (104,433)	$ (33,947)	$ 36,265	$ 96,371	$ 156,354
Interest Expense	$ 6,680	$ 5,894	$ 5,034	$ 4,094	$ 3,065
Net Ordinary Income	$ (111,113)	$ (39,841)	$ 31,231	$ 92,277	$ 153,289
Net Profit Margin	-122%	-20%	9%	20%	26%

had approached Dan and Reg about possibly franchising Lazybones to other locations. Dan reflected:

> *Expanding campus to campus meant we would not be able to add a lot of locations in close proximity to one another. Hiring good managers became even more important, as they would potentially need to operate [in] states away from our corporate office location in Massachusetts. Turnover was even more of a stress and an expense. I started to view franchising as the way to go.*

The Industry

In 2009, the non-coin-operated laundry industry represented $9.6 billion in business, with the services sector occupying 21.5% of the total market.[38] Within the services arena, two segments exist: commercial customers, including hotels and hospitals, and noncommercial customers, such as the college-student base that Lazybones targets. This put Lazybones' direct market size at $1.0 billion.

The industry in 2009 was highly fragmented and mature and had reached a sales plateau, with revenues declining by 2.1% from the previous year.[39] This was a market dominated by owner-operated businesses. Just 6% of the industry was composed of companies with 20 or more employees.[40] And from that portion, 5.4% of the market share went to the largest competitors: National Drycleaning Inc.,[41] Dry Clean USA, and Hangers America[42] franchises. Because of its narrow customer segment Lazybones did not compete directly with these three companies.

While sales for the overall market waned, the services segment exhibited increases due to the growing tourism, hospitality, and retail fashion trades.

On the college campuses, Lazybones saw very little competition. Most of its competitors operated at only one school or city—mom-and-pop type players. There were few companies that serviced multiple schools. The most comparable competition, University Laundry in Texas and Soapy Joe's out of Maryland, did not have facilities in close proximity to any current Lazybones location. And while some colleges owned their own internal laundry service for students, enough institutions of higher learning did not offer a comparable service to provide significant competition for Lazybones.

Absentee Owner

> *We grew very quickly in Syracuse, but when we made the transition from me being on hand to me being an absentee owner, we saw many challenges. All of a sudden we realized that we were the glue that held everything together and kept the quality at its highest level. We had to implement systems to sustain the business, or we would be forever tied to the day to day.*

For the first three years, the two founders were tirelessly at work improving the business and evaluating their progress. Efficiency was a priority. Growing the business beyond its existing locations was far from their minds. They focused solely on developing the quality that was needed to sustain Lazybones. Eventually, Dan and Reg were able to get the business to the point where it required only 25 hours per week from each of them. At this stage, Lazybones was teetering between a lifestyle business and a growing business. With time on his hands, Dan decided he needed to figure out how to expand the company.

In September 2003 Dan started in the part-time evening MBA program at Babson College. Through his coursework, Dan's entrepreneurial spirit was sparked again. He started to realize the potential for growth in his business. Dan recalled his first conversation with Reg about growing:

> *Reg, now a family man, wasn't necessarily open to the stress that would come with growing Lazybones. Nonetheless, he was on board. He would have been fine with keeping it a lifestyle business. But he could see my vision. His practicality balanced me, and we both knew we had to have a plan if it was going to work.*

Although Dan and Reg wanted to increase revenues and profits at their existing locations, they recognized that real company growth could be fuelled only by campus-to-campus expansion.

Now living in the Boston area, Dan decided to oversee the opening of a local outlet in August 2008. This new facility would service Boston-area universities, such as Boston University and Babson College. In addition, Dan and Reg decided that it was time to take a risk and test the company's potential to grow. Through careful research, they decided to also open a store in Boulder to service the University of Colorado. Dan pointed out:

> *We needed to push our systems to see how far they could go. Could we really succeed with Lazybones in any location in the United States? It was a gamble, for sure, but we had to know [to what] extent we could take this business. If we couldn't succeed in Boulder, we would have to re-strategize our growth plans.*

In regard to Boulder, Dan and Reg decided to hedge their bets by relocating their seasoned Wisconsin manager to run the new store. He had been very successful at handling the Madison location and had proven that he was trustworthy. Dan and Reg needed to know that the manager for this new store, so far away from where they were located, could be relied on.

During the first year, laundry sales in Boulder were much slower than projected. Dan and Reg came to realize that they had sent an operations specialist into a startup environment. Also, the manager did not know the town or the university. Last, they really needed someone who knew how to sell. Fortunately, revenues from the summer storage rentals came in higher than expected and helped to give the location a financial boost for the close of its first year. Despite the bump in revenue, Dan and Reg knew that they had to make a change if this store was going to succeed. They made the extremely difficult decision to replace their experienced manager, who had been a loyal employee of the company for many years, with someone new.

The problematic management situation in Boulder, in addition to simultaneous manager recruitment activities in three other locations, was the impetus for designing a structured training program. This was a step in the right direction: Lazybones needed more structure and metrics.

Ironing out the Details

Just about a year prior to the Boston and Boulder openings, Dan met Joel Pedlikin during an MBA evening course at Babson. They developed a friendship, but it was not until they learned about franchising, through a finance course, that Joel's interest in joining the company peaked. During their entrepreneurship class in the fall of 2008, Dan and Joel solidified their goal to grow Lazybones, which was now in its fifteenth year of operation. With Reg's full support, Dan and Joel thoroughly explored franchising and the role it could play in growing Lazybones. The possibility of expanding the business to the point at which they could sell it intrigued them. The pair worked on a business plan during their entrepreneurship class to investigate the feasibility of a franchising growth plan.

Dan and Joel identified a few areas of the business that needed to be improved in order to better position the company for growth, franchise development, and eventual acquisition.

Courtesy Dan Hermann

Dan (left) and Joel in front of a Lazybones delivery van

Following a typical franchising growth strategy, Dan and Joel planned on opening several more company stores. They wanted to prove that the process could be replicated and to iron out the unit management and monitoring details. Once they had seven to 10 company stores, the management team would start franchising Lazybones.

By May 2009 Joel had become a partner and full time member of the Lazybones team. It was time to put their diligent research and planning into motion. The first step of the plan was to showcase the successful new company stores. Dan and Joel started by revamping their staffing strategy. Summer 2009 was the first year that the company implemented a hiring strategy. To successfully manage multiple locations, they needed the right people supervising company-owned stores. They realized they had to be thorough. Joel describes the transition:

Our locations were first run by inexperienced managers, who had little more than a high school education. After 16 years, this method had worked for the status quo. To grow, we needed to have different qualifications and the benefits in place to attract the right applicants. So this past year, we put a lot of time and resources into this area.

The new plan included writing formal job descriptions and developing an interview process to screen potential employees. The company would hire only recent alumni of a location's target school for the role of manager. The rationale for this requirement was that an alumnus would understand the market and have potential contacts with university administrators, granting him or her a better chance to receive a university endorsement. Also, college graduates were culturally better suited to market and sell the Lazybones services to the company's target customers. Dan and Joel implemented incentives for the manager to grow the business locally. To minimize the potential for missteps, every candidate would go through both phone and in-person interviews, and at least two executives would thoroughly interview the best managerial candidates.

Eventually, Dan and Joel realized that, although they had been tracking metrics, it did little good unless the store managers had direct access to the same data. Lazybones implemented the Dashboard, which allowed both the executive team and the managers to view performance comparisons, work efficiencies, payrolls, and sales statistics on a daily basis (see Exhibit 14.2).

The University of Connecticut shop in Storrs, Connecticut, was opened in August 2009. That same month they hired new managers for Boulder and Boston based on the new hiring priorities that Dan and Joel had created.

Franchising

Once Dan and Joel proved that they could replicate Lazybones' business model, both managers became certain of the company's future growth through franchising. The primary benefit of this mode of growth is that the franchisees finance each new location, thereby minimizing the need for Lazybones to raise outside capital from investors or banks. In addition, the franchisee would be each new store's manager. Therefore, the head of each new location would have a strong financial incentive to grow the business, which would contribute positively to both the franchisee's and Lazybones' bottom line.

Between 2003 and 2008, U.S. franchise units across all industries grew over 4.5%, compounded annually.[43] This growth totals about 16,000 new units across approximately 3,000 franchised brands.[44] However, access to funding curbed the growth rate significantly starting in the third quarter of 2008.

EXHIBIT 14.2 Performance Dashboard

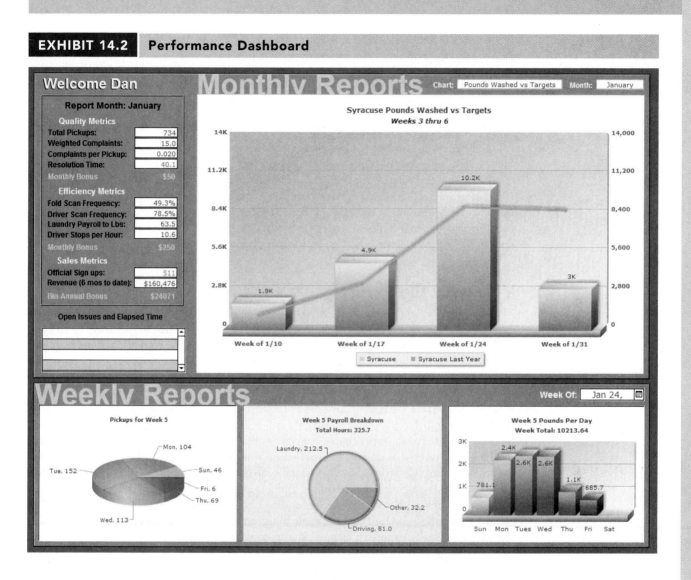

Franchising companies make money through three streams: an initial franchise fee, royalty rates, and advertising contributions. Initial franchise fees typically run from $10,000 to $100,000, with personal service franchises averaging $22,150.[45] This fee covers only the right to use the company name plus training and manuals. The franchisee is responsible for property, equipment, inventory, and staffing. The royalty income is earned either monthly or quarterly and represents a fixed percentage of the franchisee's revenue. The franchisee also pays a fixed ratio, based on revenues, toward any nationwide advertising campaign run by the franchisor.

Dan and Joel identified the benefits to franchising:

> It's [a] faster method for growth and can spread our name nationally. This rapid growth will position us to be an attractive acquisition in the future.

Dan and Joel planned on setting the franchise fee at $35,000. This price was higher than the service industry mean, but the owners believed they could justify the premium with above-average benefits, such as high unit revenues and profits, a proven business model, and location exclusivity.

Lazybones would also receive monthly royalties of 7% on revenue. Again, this was higher than the service industry norm, which was 5.5%. Joel said:

We are confident that our franchisees will make larger net margins with Lazybones than with most franchises. For instance, dry cleaners and laundromats average net margins between 3% and 6%, while Lazybones has historically achieved 15% and 20%. Asking for a 1.5% higher contribution in exchange for a three to five times improvement in net margins is a very fair exchange.

Franchisees will also pay 1% of their monthly revenue to Lazybones' national advertising fund. Corporate executives along with three franchisee representatives will manage the accounts.

Dan and Joel predicted that the company would be ready to franchise once it reached seven to 10 locations, under the condition that a majority of sites made a profit and none operated at a loss. But what challenges would they face in the transition? How could they maintain brand consistency, especially when it comes to service quality? When so much of the business depends upon the skills of the manager, how would Dan and Joel help to ensure the managing franchisees' success?

Vision for the Future

As of December 2009 Lazybones had five locations. They were still shy of their 7–10 store goal—a milestone they felt they should reach before adopting the franchise model. It was imperative that Lazybones provide proof of concept to prospective franchisees.

Before they could worry about where to open next, the Lazybones partners had to get each of their current locations to break even, or even better to operate at a profit. In Boston, for example, they had 155 laundry customers. The first and only urban location, Boston's operating costs were much higher than those of the other sites due to the driving, labour, and marketing expenses needed for functioning in a major city. To increase revenues at this location, the local manager wanted to start servicing residential customers, as opposed to exclusively servicing students. But this process would require some major adjustments to their core operations, including evening pickups and deliveries, and an upgraded company website.

Dan was previously committed to expanding Lazybones and harvesting the value he had created by selling the business. However, growth was proving to be difficult on many levels. Opening additional stores required a tremendous amount of his time, and the new endeavours were draining profits from the successful locations. He worried that perhaps he had talked his partner Reg into going down the wrong road. Maybe they should have stuck with their established successful locations and the nice leisurely life it had been providing for them. That route would mean cutting ties with Joel, who joined the management team only because of the perceived growth potential. Dan had plenty to think about as he prepared for a meeting with Reg and Joel.

Discussion Questions

1. Should Dan grow Lazybones or maintain it as a lifestyle business?
2. If he chooses growth, is franchising the best way forward?
3. What are the advantages and disadvantages of franchising versus other means of growth?
4. Lay out a five-year plan for growth at both the corporate and the individual location levels (that is, show how you can increase revenue per store).

This case was prepared by Sara Gragnolati under the direction of Professor Andrew Zacharakis.

[1] C. Richards, "Are You Growing Fast Enough?" *Compass* (blog), http://blog.startupcompass.co/how-to-avoid-74-percent-of-startup-failures-benchmark-growth.

[2] M. Marmer, B. Herrmann, E. Dogrultan, R. Berman, C. Eesley, and S. Blank, "Startup Genome Report Extra on Premature Scaling," Startup Genome, August 29, 2011, http://gallery.mailchimp.com/8c534f3b5ad611c0ff8aeccd5/files/Startup_Genome_Report_Extra_Premature_Scaling_1.56.pdf.

[3] Ibid.

[4] S. G. Blank and B. Dorf, *The Startup Owner's Manual: The Step-by-Step Guide for Building a Great Company* (Pescadero, CA: K&S Ranch, 2012).

[5] C. Zook and J. Allen, *The Facts about Growth* (New York, NY: Bain Company, 1999).

[6] J. Quinn, "Google Founders Have 'Grown Up' says CEO Eric Schmidt," *The Telegraph*, May 10, 2008, www.telegraph.co.uk/finance/newsbysector/mediatechnologyandtelecoms/2789659/Google-founders-have-grown-up-says-CEO-Eric-Schmidt.html.

[7] More recently, Schmidt has become executive chairman and Page is CEO.

[8] S. O'Brien, "The Biggest Dividend Stock Disasters of All Time," Dividend.com, January 9, 2013, www.dividend.com/news/2012/the-biggest-dividend-stock-disasters-of-all-time.

[9] Ibid.

[10] P. Ingrassia, "The Lessons of the GM Bankruptcy," *Wall Street Journal*, June 1, 2010, http://online.wsj.com/news/articles/SB10001424052748704113504575264641145227612.

[11] Additional resources on growth stages can be found in the following references:

- I. Adizes, *Managing Corporate Lifecycles* (Paramus, NJ: Prentice Hall, 1999).

- N. C. Churchill, "The Six Key Phases of Company Growth," in *Mastering Enterprise*, eds. S. Birley and D. Muzyka (London, UK: Pitman Publishing, 1997).

- E. G. Flamholtz and Y. Randle, *Growing Pains: Transitioning from an Entrepreneurship to a Professionally Managed Firm* (San Francisco, CA: Jossey-Bass, 2000).

- L. E. Greiner, "Evolution and Revolution as Organizations Grow," *Harvard Business Review* 76 (1998): 55–63.

- S. C. Harper, *The McGraw-Hill Guide to Managing Growth in Your Emerging Business* (New York, NY: McGraw-Hill, 1995).

[12] Venture Navigator, "Webvan's Unsustainable Business Model," August 2007, www.venturenavigator.co.uk/content/153.

[13] A. Barr, "From the Ashes of Webvan, Amazon Builds a Grocery Business," Reuters, June 18, 2013, www.reuters.com/article/2013/06/18/net-us-amazon-webvan-idUSBRE95H1CC20130618.

[14] S. Covey, *The 7 Habits of Highly Effective Teens* (New York, NY: Simon and Schuster, 2011).

[15] J. Collins, *Good to great* (New York, NY: HarperCollins, 2001).

[16] Ibid.

[17] Ibid.

[18] L. Gooding, "Growth Hacking Like a Pirate: A Beginner's Guide to Pirate Metrics," *Trak.io* (blog), January 15, 2014, http://blog.trak.io/growth-hacking-like-a-pirate-a-beginners-guide-to-pirate-metrics/.

[19] D. McClure, "Startup Metrics for Pirates," August 7, 2008, www.slideshare.net/dmc500hats/startup-metrics-for-pirates-long-version.

[20] "What Is a Business Dashboard," Klipfolio, www.klipfolio.com/guide-to-business-dashboards.

21 Ibid.

22 Startups, "Is Your Business Growing too Fast?" July 22, 2003, www.startups.co.uk/is-your-business-growing-too-fast.html.

23 J. Kolen and S. B. Jaffe, "Knowing When to Take a Breather: Controlling Company Growth," *Nation's Business* 83 (November 1995): 6.

24 Flextronics International Ltd, *2010 Annual Report,* http://files.shareholder.com/downloads/ABEA-28U2SZ/0x0x675521/8BDA74E8-7BD6-48B1-938B-B387B07CB4C3/FLEXAR2010.pdf.

25 Ibid.

26 Andrew Kardon blog, http://blog.bestvendor.com/2012/08/outsourcing-is-a-startups-best-friend.

27 YCC Holdings Inc., "Item 8. Financial Statements and Supplementary Data," www.secinfo.com/d12Pk6.phtj.htm#_8.

28 R. L. Osborne, "Second Phase Entrepreneurship: Breaking through the Growth Wall," *Business Horizons* 37 (1994): 80–86.

29 "Profile: Get in Shape for Women," *Inc.,* www.inc.com/profile/get-in-shape-for-women.

30 K. O'Brien, "How McDonald's Came Back Bigger than Ever," *New York Times,* May 4, 2012, www.nytimes.com/2012/05/06/magazine/howmcdonalds-came-back-bigger-than-ever.html?pagewanted=all&_r=0; McDonald's, "Nutrition Choices," www.mcdonalds.com/us/en/food/food_quality/nutrition_choices.html; and R. Tepper, "McDonald's Emphasizes Healthy Options with 'Favorites under 400 Calories' Olympics Promotion," *Huffington Post,* July 23, 2012, www.huffingtonpost.com/2012/07/23/mcdonalds-favorites-under-400-calories_n_1695885.html.

31 Microsoft, "The New Windows," http://windows.microsoft.com/en-CA/windows-8/meet.

32 D. Kelley and R. Nakosteen, "Technology Resources, Alliances and Sustained Growth in New, Technology-Based Firms," *IEEE Transactions on Engineering Management* 52 (2005): 292–300.

33 J. Scouller, *The Three Levels of Leadership: How to Develop Your Leadership Presence, Knowhow and Skill* (Gloucestershire, UK: Management Books 2000, 2011).

34 Ibid.

35 Ibid.

36 B. Barringer, F. Jones, and D. A. Neubaum, "Quantitative Content Analysis of the Characteristics of Rapid-Growth Firms and Their Founders," *Journal of Business Venturing* 20 (2005): 663–687.

37 A unit, also called a store, is where Lazybones executes all of its laundry activities.

38 IBISWorld. *IBISWorld Industry Report: Non Coin-Operated Laundromats and Dry Cleaners in the US.* August 2009.

39 Ibid.

40 Ibid.

41 Parent company: DCI Management Group Ltd.

42 Parent company: Cool Clean Technologies.

43 D. M. Johnson, "The State of Franchising," *Franchising World* 41(5): 28–31.

44 Ibid.

45 R. Blair and F. LaFontaine, *The Economics of Franchising* (Cambridge, UK: Cambridge University Press, 2005), 57–71. The 2001 number has been adjusted to 2008 with inflation rates.

Bruce Poon Tip, founder of G Adventures, the world's largest small-group adventure travel company.

SOCIAL ENTREPRENEURSHIP

CHAPTER OUTLINE

The Rise in Social Entrepreneurship
Learning Objective 15.1 Explain the rise in social entrepreneurship.

Social Entrepreneurship Defined
Learning Objective 15.2 Discuss the different definitions of social entrepreneurship.

A Social Entrepreneurship Typology
Learning Objective 15.3 Differentiate among the various types of social entrepreneurial ventures.

Measuring Impact
Learning Objective 15.4 Explain how social entrepreneurs measure their impact or outcomes.

JUST IMAGINE A WORLD where malaria is eradicated, saving 655,000 lives each year,[1] and where entrepreneurs in developing countries have access to 5 billion potential individual investors and lenders through access to the Internet. Imagine car-free cities that dramatically reduce respiratory disease, where food is grown locally in vertical farms, and buildings are made of "green concrete" made by capturing the CO_2 emitted from coal or natural gas power plants. By the year 2020, some of these things will be possible because of dramatic changes in technology, demographics, and sociopolitics. Now, further imagine a world where women in the developing world have equal access to education, resulting in a dramatic slowing of population growth and increasing economic well-being. A world where human potential is no longer ignored or marginalized based on one's race or economic background, but maximized for the benefit of all. Imagine people around the world with the ability to afford to meet their basic needs without the need for government handouts or subsidies.

Many of these social, environmental, and technological changes will be possible because of **social entrepreneurs**. Social entrepreneurs will be essential to creating this new future by solving complex problems, both social problems that have economic consequences and economic problems that have social impact. The intersection of social and economic problems and outcomes is more prevalent today than ever. There is a new world order, characterized by global interconnections and interdependence of business, society, communities, regions, and countries. In particular, technological innovation, decreasing natural resources, shifting demographics, social changes, and political unrest contribute to the complexity of problems as well as the opportunities for solutions (see the "Turning Tragedy into Opportunity" box). These changes in the global environment require solutions that meet the needs of many stakeholders and take into account both social and economic outcomes. This is the world of social entrepreneurship.

Turning Tragedy into Opportunity

The planet has seen an increase in violent weather patterns. The human toll of these events has increased with increasing population. In addition, other factors such as deforestation in Haiti have increased the impact of these events on society. At the same time, global and social media have raised our awareness of these problems and inspired social entrepreneurs to take action.

Realizing that access to clean drinking water is an enormous problem following these events, Tricia Compas-Markman and her professor at California Polytechnic State University, Dr. Tryg Lundquist, invented a personal water treatment bag that can be carried as a backpack and provides individuals with the ability to collect and treat their own water, making it safe to drink. The bags are easy to transport and one pallet of DayOne Waterbags can produce 26 times more drinking water than one pallet of water bottles. Tricia went on to found DayOne Response in order to make their invention commercially available.[i]

[i] DayOne Response Inc., www.dayoneresponse.com.

The Rise in Social Entrepreneurship

With these global changes, it is not surprising that there is a rise in the number of people creating ventures that have both social and economic goals. For example, a 2010 study by the Global Entrepreneurship Monitor found that fewer startup entrepreneurs in the United States focused primarily on economic goals (about 40%, down from almost 50% in 2008). About 7.5% of entrepreneurs indicated that they were pursuing primarily social goals, a slight increase from the 5% in 2008, while those emphasizing both social and economic goals increased from 42% to 46%.[2] And these trends are not limited to new ventures or the United States.

This increased emphasis and awareness of sustainability and social purpose creates opportunities for social entrepreneurs to find new ways to achieve these goals. Why is there a rise in social entrepreneurship? In part, it is because the assumptions upon which new ventures were created have changed. Until the 1990s, energy was relatively inexpensive, labour was widely available (and in some countries very cheap). Access to credit to start businesses was relatively easy, either through credit cards or small loans, and information to start a business only required a computer, cellphone, and Internet hookup. Further, the drivers of opportunities were usually driven by technology or market forces. But more recently, the drivers of entrepreneurial opportunities have shifted, creating new assumptions and conditions for venture creation. In particular, as global social and environmental issues increasingly affect a larger portion of the world, many drivers of entrepreneurial opportunities have shifted from simply market dynamics to more complex environmental and social catalysts. Wicked problems, those that require multiple stakeholders and complex solutions, are more often driving new ventures.[3] For instance, healthcare in a barrio in a Latin American country might be driven by a configuration of the healthcare system, immigration policies, drug importation, and contaminated water. The solution requires social and economic goals and outcomes. In other words, the traditional business model of identifying the opportunity, analyzing the industry, creating the business plan, raising money from investors, and scaling the business may not always work. Furthermore, stakeholders are increasingly active and better equipped to communicate and coordinate with each other, making it necessary to consider a wider variety of goals for any organization. As noted by Lee Scott, CEO of Walmart:

> We thought we could sit in Bentonville, take care of customers, take care of associates—and the world would leave us alone. It doesn't work that way anymore.[4]

With the increasing importance and emphasis on social entrepreneurship, it is important for any aspiring entrepreneur to have a basic understanding of some of the key elements involved. In this chapter, we begin by considering the definition of social entrepreneurship, then provide a typology of different types of ventures to illustrate different options for positioning your venture in the social context. We then show how a venture can move across the typology with different variations of social and economic purpose and impact. Finally, we will discuss ways in which you can measure the success of your venture beyond simply economic success.

Social Entrepreneurship Defined

What exactly is social entrepreneurship? The fact is that almost everyone has his or her own personal definition of social entrepreneurship, what it means, what's included, or where it applies. Further, there are multiple terms used, some of which convey the same thing—for instance, green entrepreneurship, social venture, social enterprise, nonprofit startups, environmental entrepreneurship, social innovation, sustainability, corporate social responsibility, ethics, social justice, and the list can go on and on.

Definitions of social entrepreneurship vary both in content and approach. Some of the most common definitions are shown in the box on definitions of social entrepreneurship. There are *process-based* definitions that focus on actions such as value creation, opportunity recognition, opportunity exploitation, and resource mobilization. Then there are *entrepreneur-centric*

creating a company, they are also committed to breast cancer research. Each year, Vera Bradley sponsors a golf and tennis tournament, which attracts participants from all across the United States to Fort Wayne, Indiana.

"This is a group effort. To break a million dollars for breast cancer research is truly an accomplishment! Every individual, company or foundation, whether they made a $5 or $20,000 donation should be proud to be part of this success," says Catherine Hill, the development director at Vera Bradley Foundation for Breast Cancer. Since 1998, the foundation has raised more than $15 million, and presently endows a chair in oncology, Dr. Linda Malkas, and her 16-member research team at the Indiana University Cancer Center. As a publicly traded company, Vera Bradley has a strong economic mission, but the impact of their business and their philanthropic activities has strong social outcomes. Retail stores sell products supporting breast cancer, several of their designs are in pink and, if purchased, profits go to breast cancer research.

Canadian Barb Stegemann and her team's east coast–based company The 7 Virtues focuses on flexing buying power to empower families in countries that are trying to rebuild.[19] The company sources the essential oils for their fragrances from Haiti, Afghanistan, and the Middle East—all nations that are rebuilding their communities. Sourcing the oils and resources from these nations allow entrepreneurs in those countries to provide seasonal employment for their community or tribe members. The company's goal is to encourage other businesses in Canada and developed countries to increase their trade to help in their rebuilding process. Barb and her team were featured on CBC's *Dragons' Den*, where they were successful with their pitch, adding W. Brett Wilson (long-time philanthropist) to their team. Together they share the mission to harness the company's buying power to encourage and develop positive change in Canada and around the world.[20]

3. Social Purpose Ventures

Similar to traditional ventures, **social purpose ventures** are firms that seek to make profits but that were started with a specific social mission. The opportunity they are addressing has a specific social or environmental aspect to it. Essentially, they are looking for a profitable means of addressing a social issue. Jim Poss, as you recall from the case in Chapter 3, started Big Belly Solar in 2003. He went to college to start a company, specifically an environmental company. While doing an independent study on the trash industry, Jim recognized that trash pickup and hauling represented an enormous waste of fuel and labour and that the burning of that fuel had significant environmental consequences. From there he developed the concept for BigBelly, which is a solar-powered trash compactor for use in rural and urban settings. He founded Big-Belly in 2003 with a mission to reduce fossil fuel consumption through innovative cost-saving approaches to inefficient, everyday problems. Today, BigBelly Solar is changing the concept of waste collection by implementing onsite solar compaction systems. The flagship product, the BigBelly, can be found around the world, reducing pollution by cutting down the frequency of trash collection trips.

BigBelly has an explicit social/environmental mission—"We are committed to improving the environment and economies of the world by utilizing an efficient approach"—but the venture is a for-profit business, seeking to grow and be financially sustainable. The company believes that it cannot solve social problems without economic success: "Our BigBelly product was so successful, we changed our name to BigBelly Solar and refocused the company around a central business proposition: Saving fuel is environmentally and fiscally sound."

Another example is ThinkLite, a lighting company founded by Enrico Palmerino and Dinesh Wadhwani. They got the idea for their company from an ad for an energy-efficient light bulb. They thought they could sell businesses on going green by putting the bottom-line savings up front, rather than the environmental benefit. ThinkLite, founded in 2009, manufactures custom energy-saving light systems. Recognizing that high costs often prevent firms from choosing more environmentally friendly products, ThinkLite uses a unique business model that eliminates the upfront costs by having the customer only pay for the energy it saves. Clients typically pay ThinkLite about 40% of the estimated two- to three-year savings. By eliminating the initial purchase and installation costs, ThinkLite reduces the financial risk to its customers. As ThinkLite describes it,

> *Thinklite is a global lighting efficiency company dedicated to helping businesses and governments go green without having to incur the upfront costs and difficulties associated with the change.*[21]

ThinkLite licenses its technologies from private laboratories in Germany, uses components from Korea, designs them in Boston, and assembles them in China. After ThinkLite installs the lighting system, the client's lighting bill drops on average by 50% to 80%, Wadhwani says. The company has about 100 clients, including AT&T, Kodak, and Babson College, as well as smaller businesses ranging from restaurants to offices. ThinkLite uses different efficient lighting technologies depending on the application, and tailors its design to adapt to the current lighting fixtures and infrastructure already in place, thereby making an effective and efficient retrofit possible for any type of facility.[22] As with BigBelly Solar, ThinkLite has a clear environmental mission but uses a unique business model to drive economic returns.

Bruce Poon Tip's G Adventures is the world's largest small-group adventure travel company, offering travellers socially and environmentally conscious travel opportunities.[23] Bruce launched G Adventures in 1990, believing that travellers around the world would want to share in his responsible and sustainable adventures. G Adventures offers travellers alternative options to resorts or cruises through what is known as *sustainable tourism*.[24] The company and travellers make major efforts to preserve the host country's cultural heritage through conservation and replenishment of the natural environment. You can find out more about G Adventures and Bruce Poon Tip in the case study at the end of this chapter.

4. Enterprising Nonprofits

As mentioned previously, **enterprising nonprofits** are firms offering products or services that generate revenue and income like other entrepreneurial ventures, but in this case that income is put to use to address a social problem rather than returned to investors or the owners. Sometimes social entrepreneurship is equated with nonprofits, but we contend that ventures that rely strictly on donations for their funding operate under entirely different principals than other entrepreneurial ventures and therefore they are not included in our typology. Enterprising nonprofits are driven by a social mission and focus on social outcomes as measures of their performance, but like other ventures they need to find ways to generate revenue and grow their business as a means of increasing their social impact.

One Hen is a nonprofit organization whose mission is to "provide education resources that engage children." The business was built around a book about a young West African boy who received a small loan to buy a hen and then became an entrepreneur. He gradually moved from poverty to economic sustainability. It is the story of how the world can be changed, one person, one family, and one community at a time. The founders, including the author, created a board game based on the book to help students learn about business and finance in a fun, creative way. From there the business has expanded into additional enrichment curriculum that includes One Hen microfinance for kids and the Good Garden: Food Security for Kids. One Hen focuses on microfinance, which is the practice of providing financial services—such as working capital loans, insurance, and savings—to those at the poverty level (see Chapter 10). Such basic financial tools help necessity entrepreneurs build and run their businesses, stabilize consumption, shield them from risk, and find a way out of poverty. The venture generates revenue through the sales of the book and donations, but provides lesson plans, the board game, and other teaching materials free to educators because the primary focus of their venture is to reach as many children as possible. One Hen is an enterprising nonprofit—an entrepreneurial solution to a serious social problem that is focused on social impact.

Another example would be Kiva. Kiva is an organization that provides micro loans around the world. Their mission, "to connect people through lending for the sake of alleviating poverty,"[25] allows individuals to make micro loans to working poor to enable them to have a business and work themselves out of poverty. Kiva is the world's first person-to-person microlending website, empowering individuals to lend directly to unique entrepreneurs around the globe. The organization works this way: Individuals browse entrepreneurs' profiles on the site, choose someone to lend to, and then make a loan, helping a person they have identified to make great strides toward economic independence and improve life for themselves, their family, and their community. The loan period is usually 6 to 12 months, and the lender can receive email journal updates and track repayments. Then, when the loan is repaid, the lender can lend to someone else in need. Kiva partners with existing expert microfinance institutions. Kiva is a nonprofit with a social mission and clear social impact, but the organization is also enterprising in the way that it innovated how microlending was traditionally organized.

Hybrid Ventures

Hybrid ventures are those that pursue social and economic goals equally—for instance, City Fresh Foods, a retail grocery store in Boston, prides itself on being a minority-owned business that employs minorities from the ethnic community. If you ask the founder, he will say that the social and economic missions are equally important. Therefore, the distinction between

Ten Principles of the United Nations Global Compact

Human Rights

- Principle 1: Businesses should support and respect the protection of internationally proclaimed human rights; and
- Principle 2: make sure that they are not complicit in human rights abuses.

Labour

- Principle 3: Businesses should uphold the freedom of association and the effective recognition of the right to collective bargaining;
- Principle 4: the elimination of all forms of forced and compulsory labour;

- Principle 5: the effective abolition of child labour; and
- Principle 6: the elimination of discrimination in respect of employment and occupation.

Environment

- Principle 7: Businesses should support a precautionary approach to environmental challenges;
- Principle 8: undertake initiatives to promote greater environmental responsibility; and
- Principle 9: encourage the development and diffusion of environmentally friendly technologies.

Anticorruption

- Principle 10: Businesses should work against corruption in all its forms, including extortion and bribery.

social/economic goals and social/economic outcomes is not often clear cut because missions and outcomes are more blended.

It is also important to note that customers are increasingly demanding that companies consider human rights, social justice, and environmental issues in their operations. We have seen cases where problems at suppliers for companies like Walmart, Apple, or Nike have led to customer action and damage to their brands. As customers become more aware of companies' global operations through the Internet and social media, companies are increasingly being held accountable to a wider variety of stakeholders. This is a global phenomenon as illustrated by the fact that over 7,000 firms in 145 countries have joined the UN Global Compact since its founding in 2000. Joining the UN Global Compact represents a commitment by firms to align their operations and strategies to ten principles in the areas of human rights, labour, the environment, and corruption.

Being a hybrid venture does not require signing onto the UN Global Compact, but it does involve balancing both the mission and the impacts between social and economic objectives. One example of this type of firm would be Stonyfield Farms, a yogurt company in New Hampshire. The venture was started by Samuel Kaymen and Gary Hirshberg in 1983 as a farming school that taught sustainable agricultural practices with the goal of helping family farms and protecting the environment, clearly a social mission. They made and sold yogurt to fund the school. As the yogurt business grew, they focused on building an economically successful and sustainable business that would not only provide profits, but would have social impact by supporting family farms that used organic practices. This not only gave small family farmers a market for their products, but also encouraged them to use practices that were less harmful to the environment. Stonyfield Farms extended this into its own operations and has clearly stated its economic and social goals in its mission statement:

Our mission: We're committed to healthy food, healthy people, a healthy planet, and healthy business.

- *Healthy food: We will craft and offer the most delicious and nourishing organic yogurts and dairy products.*
- *Healthy people: We will enhance the health and well-being of our consumers and colleagues.*
- *Healthy planet: We will help protect and restore the planet and promote the viability of family farms.*
- *Healthy business: We will prove that healthy profits and a healthy planet are not in conflict and that, in fact, dedication to health and sustainability enhances shareholder value. We believe that business must lead the way to a more sustainable future.*

The company also pursues social impact through the creation of their Profits for the Planet (PFP) fund, which to date has given over $15 million in support to organizations that care for the earth.[26]

Another example of a hybrid venture would be Preserve Products. Preserve Products was founded in 1996 by Eric Hudson, who was concerned about the fact that recyclables were not being turned into new products. This meant that additional resources were being used to make products rather than using recycled materials. He was particularly concerned about plastic because roughly 9% of the world's petroleum usage goes into making plastic products. Preserve Products's mission is "to deliver consumer products that offer great looking design, high performance, and are better for the environment than alternative products."[27] The company uses recycled plastic to make consumer products such as toothbrushes, razors, cutting boards, tableware, and other products which it sells. As Eric puts it:

I saw an opportunity in that 45% percent of people recycled and I thought they would have an interest in products made from their efforts.

While the company's mission is clearly focused on an environmental concern, it is still a for-profit firm that looks for the most profitable and attractive product markets as it develops new lines. At the same time, Preserve also considers environmental and social impacts. It supports the recycling industry through volunteer and community efforts and, in February 2012, it further signalled its commitment to economic and social impacts by joining over 600 other firms in becoming a certified B Corporation™ (see the box on benefit corporations).

Choosing Your Venture Type

It should be clear that each of the different types of ventures requires different resources and strategies. Therefore, it might be helpful to look at how the same firm could choose to operate in the different sectors. Let's take the case of Aravind Eye Hospital in India. India has the highest rate of blindness in the world. The approximately 15 million blind people in India

---

The Rise of Benefit Corporations

While there is increasing interest on both the customer and venture side regarding social missions and social impact, firms in North America have been limited in the extent to which they can pursue social outcomes because of existing legal frameworks. In the United States, the Michigan Supreme Court ruled in 1919 that:

"A business corporation is organized and carried on primarily for the profit of the stockholders. The powers of the directors are to be employed for that end. The discretion of directors is to be exercised in the choice of means to attain that end, and does not extend to a change in the end itself, to the reduction of profits, or to the non-distribution of profits among stockholders in order to devote them to other purposes."

While this ruling is over 100 years old, it has been reaffirmed in other court rulings as well. As a result, the pursuit of social impact can put its directors at risk of legal action for violation of their fiduciary responsibility if the actions cannot be shown to benefit shareholders. Without legal authority, directors may be hesitant to make decisions to pursue both economic and social impacts, even if this is part of the company's stated mission.

In response to this situation, an enterprising non-profit named B Lab was launched in 2007. B Lab created a third-party certification system that allowed companies to become certified Benefit Corporations (or B Corporations). Becoming a B Corporation requires meeting a minimum score on a B Impact Assessment, which looks at the firm's environmental and social impacts. Next, it may be necessary to amend the firm's governing documents to allow directors to consider the impact of its decisions on its employees, customers, suppliers, community, and the environment in addition to its shareholders. However, it is important to note that this may provide some legal protection to directors in states with constituency statutes, those in non-constituency states (including Delaware where the vast majority of U.S. companies are incorporated) are not permitted to consider the interests of stakeholders other than shareholders. Even still, as of 2013 over 600 firms in 60 countries have become certified B Corporations.

The movement is gathering steam, and to date legislation creating a new legal entity, called a Benefit Corporation, has been passed in seven states and introduced in several others. This legislation generally addresses three major provisions: (1) a corporate purpose to create a material positive impact on society and the environment; (2) expanded fiduciary duties of directors that requires consideration of nonfinancial interests; and (3) an obligation to report on its overall social and environmental performance as assessed against a comprehensive, credible, independent, and transparent third-party standard.[i]

[i] W. H. Clark, Jr., "The Need and Rationale for the Benefit Corporation: Why It Is the Legal Form that Best Addresses the Needs of Social Entrepreneurs, Investors, and, Ultimately, the Public," Benefit Corporation White Paper, 2012, www.benefitcorp.net/attorneys/benefit-corp-white-paper.

represent almost one-third of the total number of blind people worldwide, yet up to 80% of these cases are preventable or treatable with cataracts being a major cause of unnecessary blindness.[28] Upon reaching the government's mandatory retirement age, Dr. Govindappa Venkataswamy, or Dr. V. as he is often called, decided to start the Aravind Eye Hospital as a means of addressing this issue.

If we consider the ways in which Dr. V. could have positioned this business, it is easy to see how Dr. V., a highly renowned eye surgeon, recognized that the demand for cataract surgery far exceeded the supply. As such, he could have created a firm whose mission was to maximize profits by providing high-quality eye surgery to patients in India. In this situation, his primary mission would be economic, or profit maximization (quadrant1). For example, he might discover that the wealthier people in India are willing to pay the equivalent of $1000 for the surgery while those in the middle class can only afford $600. His costs per surgery would be $600, a large part of this being the cost of the lenses at $300. The middle class may be a larger market, but would generate less profit per surgery. Alternatively, the upper class is willing and able to pay more, but may represent a smaller number of customers. Each may have different needs or expectations that could further affect operating expenses, so in a purely traditional venture he might determine which market is most profitably served and then acquire the resources to meet the needs of those customers. Since profitability is the main measure of success, he could look at ways to increase his profit margins through operational efficiencies, cost reductions or by offering higher-margin services. While the business may have a social impact by improving eyesight for some individuals, the primary outcome from the business's perspective would be economic and would be measured in net profits to the business, with minimal focus on social benefit.

If Dr. V. wanted to have a social mission, his mission statement might be revised to a primary purpose of "eliminating unnecessary blindness for the largest number of people in India" (quadrant 2). However, he would still be looking at economic impact. The difference would be that instead of simply maximizing profits, he is looking at how he can maximize profits given his social mission. In this case, rather than looking at the most profitable segment, he might consider which is the largest segment he could serve profitably. The largest markets are likely to be people with lower incomes, which makes accomplishing his mission more challenging. In this case he would focus on reducing costs, not to increase his profit margins, but to be able to serve a larger segment of the population at the same margins. By lowering his costs, for example, from $600 to $350, he would be able to charge less than $600, making him able to serve a larger portion of the population while maintaining the same margins. He may even decide that he can increase overall profitability further by decreasing his margins and reaching yet a larger group. He might decide that the best way to do this is to cut the cost of the lenses, so he could start a local lens factory that produces lenses for $50. But because he knows that the wealthy are still willing to pay $1000, he might institute a tiered pricing scale based on ability to pay. This would allow him to maximize profits for the customer segment that can afford to pay, and at the same time serve people in lower income brackets by providing the service at a lower cost. In this case, because Dr. V.'s social mission drives the cost/pricing equation for the business, he establishes a price to achieve acceptable profits while helping the largest number of people.

Alternatively, Dr. V. could decide that he is concerned about other causes of blindness in India, not just eyesight lost due to cataracts that his business is focused on. So while the firm maintains its economic mission, it looks to have greater social impact as well by taking a portion of the profits and donating these to charities that focus on nutritional issues for rural children, another source of blindness in India (quadrant 3). Operationally, the business would still be focused on maximizing profits, but the primary impact he is trying to have may be measured by considering the social outcome—the total number of individuals helped—so the business could be considered a social consequence venture in our typology.

If Dr. V. decided that he wanted to be an enterprising nonprofit (quadrant 4), then he would have a social mission and focus on social rather than economic impact. In some cases, such as in Canada, this may involve an entirely different legal structure for a venture if it is to be a nonprofit. As an enterprising nonprofit, Dr. V. would have a social mission, like the one stated above, but the outcome would be measured in maximum social impact, or people treated, rather than profits or economic returns. Dr. V. might first start by charging only $350 (the cost with the less expensive lenses) to be able to reach the largest number of people. As revenue sources to support his business, he might seek to attract donations or government grants that could pay for some of the operating expenses. In this way, he could lower the price even further and reach a larger number of people.

But, what if the people most in need of eye care cannot afford to pay at all? This is a common situation for enterprising nonprofits. Often those that are not being served by society are those on the fringes, in extreme poverty. In this case, the potential to achieve revenues from the market you want most to serve is zero because the product or service needs to be provided for free. This means that the organization must raise money from government sources or philanthropists to pay for costs. Fundraising becomes a major focus of day-to-day activities because it is the source of operating funds. Reliance on volunteers keeps costs down, but this can make management of the venture more challenging. You will often see these types of companies create large boards of directors because a key function of the board becomes raising money for the venture. While the board still has responsibility for organizational oversight, members are more often chosen for their personal or corporate connections, personal wealth, or enthusiasm for the mission of the organization rather than for their management or industry expertise.

This was the situation facing Dr. V. in India. His mission was to eradicate unnecessary blindness across the entire country. While he had a primary social mission, Dr. V. took an unusual and creative approach, which is an example of a hybrid venture in our typology. He recognized that the poorest in the country could not afford even basic eye care. However, at the same time, he recognized that there was a large population with the ability to pay. As a result, he used a market-based approach similar to a traditional venture to serve the population that was able to pay. He created an assembly-line type process that enabled his doctors to perform 10 times the number of surgeries that doctors in the West performed to increase the revenues and profit from the business. However, because he had a social mission, he used these profits to pay for free surgeries for the poor. In other words, by charging $1000 with a cost of $600, his profits were $400. That meant that for every three paying customers he could use the profits to perform two surgeries for free. So you can see that while his primary mission is social, he also has an economic mission to the extent that it enables him to achieve his social mission. Profit maximization is still important because it allows him to achieve greater social impact. The difference for an enterprising nonprofit is that the increase in revenues is not translated into an increase in profits but rather in operating capital. Another way to think about this is that he is essentially turning his customers into philanthropists by providing a service that they value and are willing to pay for, rather than simply asking them for donations.

So you can see that it is possible to position a venture in different quadrants of Figure 15.1, but that this requires a considerable amount of thought as it will ultimately impact all aspects of the three driving forces necessary for a successful new business (referred to in Chapter 2)—the nature of the opportunity, the resources required, and the team needed to accomplish your mission. However, while you may start in one quadrant, circumstances, strategies, or values can change over time, and you may decide that you are interested in different outcomes or want to change the goals of the organization, so a venture can move between quadrants or, as in the case of Dr. V., occupy a space in more than one quadrant. However, it is important to recognize that movement between quadrants is not simple. Each type of venture has unique characteristics that affect the strategies and resources that the firm needs to succeed.

Measuring Impact

One of the critical things for social entrepreneurs to consider is how they will measure their impact or outcomes. For some ventures it is straightforward. Preserve Products can tell you how much new petroleum was saved by using recycled plastic, BigBelly Solar can determine how many pounds of CO_2 emissions were saved by decreasing the pickup frequency of trash, and Aravind Eye Hospital can determine the number of free cataract surgeries they performed. Each of these represents measures of the social impact related to their mission. Other social issues are more difficult to quantify. You can provide clean water to children in rural Pakistan, but measuring the impact of this is more difficult. Social problems are often quite complex, and there are usually a number of social ventures and other organizations trying to address issues such as infant mortality or AIDS through education, health services, treatment, or other means. In these cases it is difficult to say which approaches are responsible for subsequent outcomes. While it would be nice to think that everyone would be happy if the problem is being diminished, many organizations and companies are fighting for the same resources and often believe very strongly in their particular approach. Further, sometimes reducing the consequences may not solve the problem. For instance, medical problems with dysentery or nutrition in a barrio can be treated with medicine, but it may be that clean water and nutrition education are the causes, therefore the solutions need to be multipronged. It is important for social ventures to determine performance measures that are related to their objectives and that can be directly tied to their particular activities. You remember that Stonyfield Farms's mission revolved around healthy food, healthy people, a healthy planet, and a healthy business. Obviously, it would be difficult to measure the health of people who buy its product and tie that back to its yogurt. Similarly, how would one determine the impact of its business on the health of the planet? However, Stonyfield Farms does realize that any waste from its production has a negative impact on the environment and represents a cost to the business. As such, they measure waste water, plastic, packaging, and other byproducts of their production that do not contribute to the health of the food, people, planet, or business. By decreasing this waste, Stonyfield Farms can show that it is making progress toward social goals and it can be directly attributed to its business.

While it is difficult, more and more companies are realizing that measuring environmental and social impact is increasingly important for their business. As Jeffrey Immelt, CEO of General Electric, puts it:

> "It's up to us to use our platform to be a good citizen. Because not only is it a nice thing to do, it's a business imperative . . . . If this wasn't good for business, we probably wouldn't do it."[29]

The need to consider impacts beyond those of traditional measures of growth and profitability has led to interest in what is known as the **triple bottom line** (TBL). The TBL is a way of measuring success that was originally proposed by John Elkington in his book *Cannibals with Forks*.[30] Elkington argued that businesses need to look at not only the traditional financial bottom line, but also their impact on the environment and society. The key for succeeding is in finding ways to make "doing good" and "doing well" synonymous, thus avoiding the implied conflict between society and shareholders. For entrepreneurs, this will become increasingly important. As we have discussed in this chapter, companies are no longer able to divorce themselves from the communities with which their products and operations interact. And these communities are becoming increasingly informed and able to mobilize. We are also finally acknowledging that we live on a planet of finite resources and that using up or damaging those resources affects our businesses as well as our lives. Companies on the coasts are seeing higher insurance premiums as a result of the increasing volatility of weather events, which most scientists believe is related to global climate change and CO_2 emissions. Climate change may also result in a carbon tax or carbon cap and trade system,

Economic	Environmental	Social
Sales	Air quality	Labour practices
Profits, ROI	Water quality	Community impacts
Taxes paid	Energy usage	Human rights
Jobs created	Waste produced	Product responsibility

Source: A. W. Savitz and K. Weber, *The Triple Bottom* Line (San Francisco, CA: Jossey-Bass, 2006).

■ **Figure 15.2**

Sample impacts

either of which will impact a new venture's costs, which means that even for ventures with a purely economic mission, the need to understand how they interact with society and the environment is important. And as the saying goes, you measure what you care about and you care about what you measure.

So how do you go about deciding what to measure? First, you need to think about the way in which your business touches society and the environment. What communities do your operations affect? In what way? What materials are used in your products? Where do they come from and where do they go? Does your business produce waste products or byproducts? Where do these go and how do they affect the environment? It is important to remember that these not only represent costs or potential areas for improvement, but also potential liabilities if not measured and addressed (just ask Walmart, Nike, or Apple). Figure 15.2 gives some general examples of social and environmental impacts that ventures might consider measuring, but because every venture interacts with the environment and society in a different way and has different objectives based on its mission, it is impossible for us to provide an exhaustive list. Ultimately, it is up to the entrepreneur to determine what measure of performance and impact he or she needs to keep track of to best achieve the organization's mission in the long run.

□ **CONCLUSION**

It should be clear from this chapter that social entrepreneurs have the opportunity to enact enormous change in a variety of ways. In addition to having either a social or economic mission, entrepreneurs need to think about their impacts and how they will measure them. We presented a typology that included what we called "traditional ventures," but one might argue that this type of venture, once the most dominant in entrepreneurship, may become a thing of the past. As we illustrated, firms are increasingly being forced to consider, measure, and report their performance with regard to social impacts as well as economic returns and leading companies are increasingly taking on a hybrid form, illustrating the ability to move between forms. However, the entrepreneur should take the time early on to consider the type of venture he or she wants to have as changing forms can be difficult and costly. It is important to recognize the cost and resource tradeoffs that determine how your venture is positioned in the market.

Entrepreneurship is about doing different things or doing things differently. As Albert Einstein said:

We can't solve problems by using the same kind of thinking we used when we created them.

The world is looking for answers to a wide range of social and environmental issues that have resulted from our current thinking. We believe it is up to social entrepreneurs to find the new way of thinking that will be needed to solve these problems and create a better tomorrow.

Reflection Point	Your Thoughts. . .	**YOUR OPPORTUNITY JOURNAL** ☐
1. What social problems are of particular interest to you?		
2. What are some of the root causes of these problems and in what ways might these be addressed?		
3. What type of venture would you want to create? Do you want to have primarily a social mission or an economic mission? Why?		
4. If you are considering a new venture, how does it interact with the social problems you are concerned with? What are the ways in which your venture could have an impact on these problems?		
5. In what other ways does your venture impact society and the environment?		
6. Think about how you might measure your venture's social impact. What can you directly attribute to your business? How would you measure it and what does this measure mean?		
7. What resources would you need to have or acquire in order to have the type of venture you envision in terms of both mission and impact?		
8. Does it give you information you can act on to improve your impact?		

WEB EXERCISE ☐

Think about companies you admire or aspire to be similar to. Go to two or three websites and look at their missions. Is their mission primarily economic, social, or both? Next, see if you can find out how each one reports its performance. If it is a public company, this can often be found by going to the "Investor" link on the webpage and looking at the annual report. For nonprofits or other companies this can often be found under the "About" link. What is each one reporting? Are these consistent with the mission? If not, why not? What do you think each company should report? Use this information to make a list of possible ways in which you can measure performance for your own venture and describe how this information will tell you whether you are achieving your mission.

Bruce Poon Tip: G Adventures and Social Entrepreneurship

When starting an entrepreneurial venture, how do you know when to quit and when to keep going? At what point does perseverance become a deterrent? Would you give up if critics were putting down your idea, if your team stopped believing in you, or if you ran out of money? As Seth Godin explains in his book *The Dip*, "Persistent people are able to visualize the light at the end of the tunnel when others can't see it."[31]

Creating a new product and tapping into an unmet need often involves an ongoing, uphill climb. Entrepreneurship requires a great deal of perseverance and resistance to adversity to take a business idea from concept to reality.[32] However, knowing when to quit is critical. How do you know when you are chasing a dead end, or simply pushing past "the dip" to make it to the top of the mountain where you will find success?

Introduction

A person born with a strong internal locus of control will often have the ability to see problems happening in the world and visualize a solution.[33] According to research conducted at Nottingham University, entrepreneurs often have an ability to spot opportunities, and they use this skill to try their hand at several different business ventures. Over time, entrepreneurs gain habitual and experienced selection patterns for pursuing opportunities.[34] Recent developments of entrepreneurial processes such as agile development[35] and the lean startup methodology[36] encourage the use of iteration and pivoting between ideas to help evolve a *good* opportunity into a *great* opportunity. These methodologies incorporate scientific trial-and-error experiments into the startup process and embrace pivots as adjustments instead of failures. Bruce Poon Tip, founder of G Adventures, believes that the process of pivoting between ideas is necessary to find a business opportunity that you are extremely passionate about. Today, the lean startup methodology has become a key factor in determining what a desirable match in the current market is. According to Poon Tip, once you finally find this true passion of yours, it's your calling and purpose in life to pursue it.[37]

Poon Tip learned the significance of pursuing your passions and being a market leader all before the age of 15. He was able to spot opportunities that interested him in his very own neighbourhood where he grew up in Calgary. Poon Tip ran three different small businesses during his adolescence, and before his twenty-third birthday he was determined to launch his largest business yet—an innovative travel company called G Adventures.[38]

Adversity Quotients and Delusional Optimism

Adversity quotient (AQ) is defined as a measure of one's perceived capacity to prevail in adverse situations. For example, to pursue a business idea that you are passionate about despite criticism and reluctance of others to adapt the idea, an entrepreneur must have a high tolerance for adverse situations, as well as a high level of self-efficacy. Typically, successful entrepreneurs and innovators score relatively high in certain aspects of measuring one's AQ because of their perceived control over adversity and ownership regarding the outcome of adversity.[39]

On the other end of the spectrum is *delusional optimism*, which is defined as the tendency to expect positive outcomes even when such expectations are not rationally justified.[40]

In entrepreneurship, this means having the confidence to overcome the struggles one is facing in starting a business. Although this may cause entrepreneurs to be overly optimistic in believing that they are on the verge of a breakthrough when in fact they are simply executing on a poor opportunity,[41] delusional optimism can also be beneficial during times of adversity. In the correct circumstances, it provides entrepreneurs with the necessary perseverance to continue building their product despite the concerns and criticism of others.

In entrepreneurship, it is important to distinguish between adversity quotient and delusional optimism. Successful entrepreneurs tend to have the ability to push through adversity as it comes, because they are confident that there is a positive outcome that will result.[42] Those who have high self-efficacy and prominent internal locus of control are able to visualize strategic and timely solutions to overcome tough obstacles.[43] Additionally, those who incorporate delusional optimism to overcome adversity are less likely to be discouraged by the criticism of others because they have a firm belief that there will be positive results.[44] As an entrepreneur, it is also necessary to strike a balance between delusional optimism and having a high tolerance for adversity, as these qualities have the ability to complement each other if used together strategically. In Jim Collins's book *Good to Great,* this balance is described as the Stockdale Paradox, which suggests "You must retain faith that you can prevail to greatness in the end, while retaining the discipline to confront the brutal facts of your current reality."[45]

Entrepreneurs who find themselves in adverse situations need to know how to analyze the environment and situation accurately. By thorough evaluation, one is able to more accurately determine whether to keep going or dissolve the company, realizing that it is just not a viable business opportunity.[46] As CEO and founder of G Adventures (formerly Gap Adventures), Bruce Poon Tip experienced the dilemma of deciding whether he was pursuing a dead end idea or on the verge of a lucrative breakthrough in the market. After all, creative destruction is, by definition, doing something old in a radical new way.

Poon Tip battled with adversity for the first seven years to get his company off the ground. Many people classified this as being overly optimistic in thinking this was a feasible venture. However, Poon Tip had his eye on a bigger prize and was chasing an opportunity to disrupt the market; a goal that, retrospectively, he was confident in and passionate about.

Pursuing a Passion in Business

In his early twenties, Poon Tip discovered that he was passionate about travelling the world. He realized that he genuinely enjoyed exploring new places and learning about other cultures. However, he felt strongly that the travel industry was heading in the wrong direction. For someone who loved authentic, cultural travel experiences so much, Poon Tip was frustrated with the increasing amount of luxury and resort-style vacations that were taking over the market.[47] This fuelled his desire to actually *change the industry* and the way tourism is conducted all over the world. Bruce made up his mind to do this by using a Blue Ocean Strategy,[48] which he hoped would assist him in starting his own company. Using a Blue Ocean Strategy meant he would attempt to implement changes that would increase the value of travel experiences while reducing costs for customers.[49] Specifically, Poon Tip's goal was to add value to the market by creating a new, authentic and culturally sensitive travel experience without the luxurious and lavish prices. He hoped that using this strategy would ultimately displace his competitors and change the direction of the industry, creating a shift in the market that would later be classified as "travel adventures."[50]

The original name for Poon Tip's venture—Gap Adventures—was chosen to emphasize the "gap" in the travel industry. At the time of the company's inception, there was nothing offered to the large market of people who didn't want to go backpacking but also didn't want to partake in luxury vacations.[51] Additionally, there were no travel companies that focused on benefiting the communities being travelled to. Until G Adventures entered the market, travel companies solely focused on making profit. However, Poon Tip was eager to give back to the places he had seen. To him, travelling provided a deep and enlightening perspective of the world, and he felt travellers should sustain that instead of exploit it. Poon Tip decided to launch G Adventures in 1990 with nothing but two credit cards and a dream. Poon Tip didn't have experience working in travel and tourism, nor did he have an experienced CEO to bring on board to the team, but he was passionate enough about this idea to take on the challenge.[52] He was forced to learn as he went along by conducting rigorous market testing, hiring employees, raising money all while paving the way for this new travel experience.

For the first several years, there was heavy criticism of this business model, which focused on empowering local, rural communities that his customers travelled to. However, he was determined to make a change in the industry and create social value through his company. He decided to keep going and pushed the development of G Adventures despite the negative feedback he was receiving. He invested his time, energy, and all of his resources into moving forward and continued to grow the company.[53] Seven years later, in 1997, this growth suddenly came to a halt. Although the Internet and ecommerce websites were booming, the travel industry took a turn for the worse. The introduction of online travel brokers such as Expedia.ca and SellOffVacations.com caused Poon Tip and most other traditional offline travel agencies to lose customers fast. The traditional role of the "travel agent" was becoming obsolete, and the Internet was providing consumers with access to several options, price negotiations, and services that weren't offered to them before.[54] In addition, the decrease in value of the Canadian dollar became a nightmare in securing international sales from a variety of foreign currencies.[55]

Bankruptcy: The End of the Dream

The year 1997 was a critical time for Poon Tip, who was now seven years into what he knew was his undeniable passion, but was struggling just to keep the company afloat. He had worked tirelessly to build a valuable, reputable company and culture with his employees based on the ethics and vision of ecotourism. They had seen a steady growth rate in sales and bookings that allowed the company to continue to operate until it was hit with this shift in the market.[56] What Poon Tip thought would be a small bump in the road turned out to be a huge uphill battle. Despite what was happening with the economy and the company, Poon Tip was determined to continue pushing and fighting to get out of this downturn. However, he was focusing so much energy on staying afloat in the market that he didn't fully realize how much trouble the company was in. He was steadily relying on delusional optimism to get him through the adversity he faced as founder of the company until the day all of his employees' paycheques bounced. This was a wakeup call for Poon Tip, and he was forced to accept the fact that G Adventures was out of money. Suddenly, Poon Tip had an entire team of employees that he was responsible for, who were now in financial trouble. To make matters worse, Poon Tip was unable to deal with the situation right away because he had a group of customers booked for a trip to Tibet, but he couldn't afford to hire a travel guide to accompany the customers. He also couldn't afford to cancel the trip, which would have meant reimbursing $30,000 to his customers. Therefore, a very determined Poon Tip made the decision to guide the tour himself and flew with the group to Tibet.[57]

As he was attempting to put on a brave face for the customers in Tibet, internally a serious consideration of shutting down the company was dwelling inside him. Although he didn't want to admit it, Poon Tip was beginning to think that his dream might be over. Self-doubt began to creep in—maybe he wasn't able to revolutionize the travel industry. Perhaps instead he would be forced to watch tourism go down a path he so distinctively reviled. If Poon Tip decided to let go of his dream, he would be sacrificing years of hard work. However, considering the fact that more than 70% of companies fail within the first ten years, this wouldn't be such a surprising outcome.[58] Poon Tip started to consider the possibility that he had been delusional in his belief that the company could continue to compete with the new players in the market. These doubts were deepened when his business partner and co-founder gave her notice of wanting to exit the company. It seemed nobody was supporting Poon Tip's dream to build an innovative sustainable social travel company. As hopelessness started to set in, he began to come to terms with shutting the company down. Poon Tip pondered this uncomfortable thought over and over until he finally accepted it as being true. He mentally prepared himself to close the company upon his return from Tibet.[59] This would prove to be Poon Tip's biggest lesson in adversity to date.

Turning Adversity into Opportunity

What was originally an unfortunate reason for Poon Tip to make the trip to Tibet would end up being the source of inspiration he needed to pull the company out of bankruptcy. The escape he was able to get from taking this trip, interacting with the Monks who live so peacefully and faithfully in Tibet, and soaking in the majestic traditions of the sacred land had really resonated with Poon Tip. During this trip, he had picked up a copy of *Blue Ocean*, a biography of the fourteenth Dalai Lama, Tenzin Gyatso. *Blue Ocean* (not to be confused with the business book *Blue Ocean Strategy*) shed light on the compelling truths behind the Tibetan Buddhist beliefs. This tome would stir up a storm of inspiration within Poon Tip and provided an unexplainable connection with and admiration of the Dalai Lama.[60]

Blue Ocean amplified the importance of standing up for what you believe in and fighting for what you know to be true in your beliefs, even when others object or criticize. It was becoming evident that to make a stand for his entrepreneurial venture, Poon Tip would need to understand that there is little difference between obstacle and opportunity. Although G Adventures was "failing," if he was able to alter his strategy effectively it just might be possible to turn this obstacle into an advantage. This story encompassed a valuable lesson about acknowledging one's true calling in life when it appears. This trip to Tibet had given Poon Tip a new outlook on life that was significant enough to give him the courage to try one last time to turn the company around. He was sure he had found the right frame of mind this time, and he was ready to try a completely new approach.[61] This new strategy would be used to determine once and for all if G Adventures had a chance at success. As soon as he returned to Canada, the following changes to the company were immediately implemented:

1. *Openness and honesty with G Adventures stakeholders:* Poon Tip broke the news and explained the financial situation to his employees. He admitted that there was not enough money to pay salaries that month, and was prepared for the wave of anger, frustration, and resignations that followed. However, open and honest communication was necessary to build a trusting environment and determine which employees were committed to the bigger purpose of the company. As expected, several employees chose

to resign. Poon Tip then used this opportunity to evaluate the passion and work ethic of the employees that chose to stay. He was living by a "hire slow and fire quickly" approach and wanted to keep only leaders on the team.[62] He would strive for quality and commitment in a select group of employees rather than mediocre performance from many.

2. *Allowing the partner to exit the company:* Poon Tip allowed his partner to exit the company, which meant carrying 100% of the burden himself. Poon Tip had come to the realization that it would continue to be a struggle to reach success if a key partner in the company didn't believe in the business anymore. By taking on the full financial responsibility for G Adventures, Poon Tip would demonstrate his full commitment to the company.

3. *Focusing on changing the world:* He focused significantly more on his promise to use G Adventures to change the world. He began making critical partnerships with the locals he met around the world and brought economic opportunities and growth to their villages. Using a combination of market research, opportunity evaluation, and intuition, Poon Tip began heavily promoting this essential aspect of the business. It became the company's mantra—the goal and mission they lived by. He made the decision to emphasize through the company's branding that they weren't just about "ethical travel adventures" anymore; they were about impact, providing opportunities and microfinancing. Poon Tip set up programs within G Adventures to provide the villagers with the ability to benefit from the business he brought in through developing their *own* entrepreneurial opportunities (e.g., leasing rooms, building boats and lodges, selling local merchandise, working as tour guides). This benefited their economy and helped communities lift themselves out of poverty. This became the heart and soul of the company, and as opportunities to partner with locals increased, so did G Adventures's revenues.[63]

By implementing these changes, G Adventures was now able to make a real, tangible difference in the lives of many people. Poon Tip was able to channel his efforts and drive home the importance of social impact through the power of business. His reinforcement of the socially driven business model also caused customers to feel good about booking trips with G Adventures because they were finally able to get authentic cultural experiences through travelling, as well as make a positive impact on the places they visited. Furthermore, they were paying lower prices than they would have paid traditionally for vacations. This would allow these experiences to become self-sustainable.[64] Poon Tip had cracked the code to building a win-win-win business model where the customers, local communities, and G Adventures's stakeholders all benefited and worked together.

Knowing When Not to Quit

In the case of G Adventures, creating a *higher purpose* for the business was the missing link that was necessary to be successful. Through pivoting, innovation, and iteration, Poon Tip realized that each learning curve brought him closer to the solution, and he was not willing to quit until he got there. By focusing his efforts on creating a strong triple bottom line, which is a corporation's ultimate success measured not just by the traditional financial bottom line but also by its social, ethical, and environmental performance, Poon Tip was able to focus on improvements to people, planet, and profit. This triple bottom line notion, introduced by John Elkington in his book *Cannibals with Forks*, provided the inspiration to harmonize the company's profitable bottom line with environmental quality and social justice.[65] Poon Tip had come to the realization that G Adventures's higher purpose was creating a sustainable, socially impactful business model. This allowed him to finally build a connection with his customers and create an undeniable brand identity. The company's success was completely turned around and they were no longer facing bankruptcy.

However, deciding to continue with the business despite the adversity was a clear demonstration of Poon Tip's high tolerance of risk. It was a risky yet highly calculated act of trusting his intuition after each failure that allowed Poon Tip to make it through the dip. Some entrepreneurs would have quit or given up once the company had reached bankruptcy. However, Poon Tip was so determined and confident in the new purpose of the business that he was willing to make one final attempt at salvaging the company. There was a risk of falling victim to *delusional optimism*—falsely believing in and being unable to accept that your company is failing.[66] However, Poon Tip had gained justifiable confidence in his intuitive understanding of the travel industry for the following reasons:

1. The experiences he gained in his years of running the business, successful or not. He made a point of taking the time to truly understand all stakeholders in the business—employees, customers, partners, and the locals—and what he could do to benefit each of them.

2. By effectively evaluating the market and studying upcoming trends and opportunities, Poon Tip claims he was able to "not skate where the puck currently is, but skate where it is going."[67] This reflects his entrepreneurial alertness and ability to recognize gaps in the market.[68] His continuous market research gave him an understanding of the industry and what he could do to differentiate his company and master his passion as a competitive advantage.

Leveraging Pivots as Learning Opportunities— G Adventures Today

By embracing the limitations and adversity he faced as opportunities to refine and pivot key elements of the company, Poon Tip was able to turn a failing company into the highest ranked travel company in Canada. In fact, today G Adventures earns more than $160 million per year and conducts group travel adventures worldwide for over 100,000 customers.[69]

Most important, he was finally able to build his dream company. He proved that he didn't have to give in to the direction that tourism was heading—that his idea for a better world and creating impactful travel experiences was actually possible. Despite the years of criticism, threats from competitors, lack of support from investors and banks, this change of brand identity and higher purpose provided an opportunity to turn the business around.

Discussion Questions

1. What do you think Poon Tip used to maintain his delusional optimism—why did he keep fighting for this business instead of giving up?

2. If you were Poon Tip and your company had gone bankrupt and the market was evolving with new technologies and processes for booking flights, describe the thought process and market indicators you would use to evaluate whether to continue or exit the company.

3. If you were faced with disapproval and criticism from your company's advisors and other industry professionals, what steps would you take to prove your vision could be successful?

This case was written by Alysha D'Souza (Ryerson University) and Dr. Sean Wise.

NOTES

1 Global Malaria Programme, "World Malaria Report 2011 Fact Sheet," December 13, 2011, World Health Organization, www.who.int/malaria/world_malaria_report_2011/WMR2011_factsheet.pdf.

2 A. Ali et al., *Global Entrepreneurship Monitor 2010 United States Report*, Global Entrepreneurship Research Association, www.gemconsortium.org/docs/download/667.

3 R. Buchanan, "Wicked Problems in Design Thinking," *MIT Press* 8 (1992): 1–25.

4 "The Debate over Doing Good," *Businessweek*, August 14, 2005, 76.

5 "What Is the Difference between Social Entrepreneurship and Corporate Social Responsibility?" SOON, www.discoversoon.nl/EN/2-what-is-the-difference-between-social-entrepreneurship-and-corporate-social-responsibility.

6 Tim Hortons, "Economics: Tim Hortons Coffee Partnership," www.timhortons.com/ca/en/difference/coffee-partnership-partnership-pillars-economic.html.

7 Ibid.

8 M. Schaper, "The Essence of Ecopreneurship," *GMI* 38 (Summer 2002): pp. 26–38.

9 T. J. Dean and J. S. McMullen, "Toward a Theory of Sustainable Entrepreneurship: Reducing Environmental Degradation through Entrepreneurial Action," *Journal of Business Venturing* 22 (2007): 50–76.

10 H. Neck, C. Brush, and E. Allen, "The Landscape of Social Entrepreneurship," *Business Horizons* 52 (2009): 13.

11 Ibid., 13–19.

12 K. Andrews, *The Concept of Strategy* (Homewood, IL: Irwin, 1971).

13 "About CarTrawler," www.cartrawler.com/about/cartrawlergoals.php.

14 Water for People, "About," www.waterforpeople.org/about/mission-and-vision.

15 Ben & Jerry's, "Our Values," www.benjerry.com/activism/mission-statement.

16 J. Mair and I. Marti, "Social Entrepreneurship Research: A Source of Explanation, Prediction, and Delight," *Journal of World Business* 41 (2006): 36–44.

17 C.A.F.E. Practices ensure that Starbucks is sourcing sustainably grown and processed coffee by evaluating the economic, social, and environmental aspects of coffee production. These aspects are measured against a defined set of criteria detailed in the C.A.F.E. Practices Evaluation Guidelines. According to an impact study performed by Conservation International, C.A.F.E. Practices has significantly benefited more than 1 million workers employed by participating farms (SCS Global Services, "Starbucks C.A.F.E. Practices," www.scsglobalservices.com/starbucks-cafe-practices).

18 G. Dees, "The Meaning of 'Social Entrepreneurship,'" October 31, 1998, www.caseatduke.org/documents/dees_SE.pdf, 4; C. W. Massarsky and S. L. Beinhecker, *Enterprising Nonprofits: Revenue Generation in the Nonprofit Sector*, 2002, http://community-wealth.org/sites/clone.community-wealth.org/files/downloads/paper-massarsky.pdf.

19 The 7 Virtues, "The 7 Virtues Story," www.the7virtues.com/about_us.php.

20 Ibid.

21 ThinkLite, "Challenge the Wasteful Practices of Today," www.thinklite.com/index.htm.

22 "Babson Startup ThinkLite Ranked #2 among Bloomberg *Businessweek*'s America's Best Young Entrepreneurs, 2011," Babson College, http://www.babson.edu/news-events/babson-news/pages/10-28-11babson-startup-thinklite-ranked-2-among-bloomberg-businessweek%E2%80%99s-america%E2%80%99s-best-young-entrepreneurs-2011.aspx.

23 G Adventures, "Our Story," www.gadventures.com/about-us.

24 Ibid.

25 Kiva, "About Us," www.kiva.org/about.

26 Stonyfield Farm, Inc., www.stonyfield.com.

27 "Preserve 101," www.preserveproducts.com/explore/preserve-101/mission.

28 Blind Foundation for India, "Key Facts," www.blindfoundation.org/facts.html.

29 Quoted in M. Gunther, "Money and Morals at GE," *Fortune*, November 15, 2004, 176.

30 J. Elkington, *Cannibals with Forks* (North Mankato, MN: Capstone Publishing Ltd., 1997).

31 S. Godin, *The Dip* (New York, NY: Portfolio, 2007).

32 Ibid.

33 M. Dijkstra, "Reducing Conflict-Related Employee Strain; The Benefits of an Internal Locus of Control," *Impact Factor* 3 (2011): 167–184.

34 D. P. W. Ucbasaran, "Does Entrepreneurial Experience Influence Opportunity Identification?" *Journal of Private Equity* 7 (2003): 7–14.

35 J. H. Cockburn, "Agile Software Development: The People Factor," *IEEE Computer Society*, (2001): 131–133.

36 C. Nobel, "Teaching a 'Lean Startup' Strategy," Harvard Business School—Working Knowledge, http://hbswk.hbs.edu/item/6659.html.

37 B. Poon Tip, *Looptail* (Toronto, ON: HarperCollins, 2013).

38 Ibid.

39 G. D. Markman, R. A. Baron, and D. B. Balkin, "Adversity Quotient: Perceived Perserverance and New Venture Formation," Lally-Darden Retreat, Washington, DC.

40 K. Hmieleski, "Entrepreneurs' Optimism and New Venture Performance," *Academy of Management* (2009): 473–488.

41 Ibid.

42 Markman, Baron, and Balkin, "Adversity Quotient."

43 Dijkstra, "Reducing Conflict-Related Employee Strain."

44 Hmieleski, "Entrepreneurs' Optimism and New Venture Performance."

45 J. Collins, *Good to Great* (New York, NY: HarperCollins, 2001).

46 Godin, *The Dip*.

47 S. Wise, "Bruce Poon Tip: The Naked Entrepreneur," www.youtube.com/watch?v=HsycN8ZiQI4.

48 W. Chan Kim and R. Mauborgne, "Blue Ocean Strategy," *Harvard Business Review* (October 2004): 69–80.

49 Ibid.

50 Poon Tip, *Looptail*.

51 Ibid.

52 Ibid.

53 Ibid.

54 Ibid.

55 Wise, "Bruce Poon Tip: The Naked Entrepreneur."

56 Poon Tip, *Looptail*.

57 Ibid.

58 Statistic Brain, "Startup Business Failure Rate by Industry," July 2013, www.statisticbrain.com/startup-failure-by-industry.

59 Wise, "Bruce Poon Tip: The Naked Entrepreneur."

60 Poon Tip, *Looptail*.

61 Ibid.

62 Ibid.

63 Ibid.

64 Ibid.

65 W. Norman and C. MacDonald, "Getting to the Bottom of 'Triple Bottom Line,'" *Business Ethics Quarterly* 14 (April 2004): 243–262.

66 D. Lavallo and D. L. Kahneman, "Delusions of Success: How Optimism Undermines Executives' Decisions," Harvard Business School—Working Knowledge, August 18, 2003, http://hbswk.hbs.edu/archive/3630.html.

67 Poon Tip, *Looptail*.

68 A. Emami, "Entrepreneurial Alertness vs. Framing," *International Journal of Academic Research in Business and Social Sciences* 2 (2012): 66–77.

69 G Adventures, "G Adventures Names Regional Sales Manager," press release, January 27, 2011.

GLOSSARY

10/20/30 rule: A rule for PowerPoint presentations coined by venture capitalist Guy Kawasaki that states a slide deck should be no more than 10 slides, no more than 20 minutes, and have a font size of at least 30.

Accelerator: A resource for startups that offers support, funding, and office space in return for a small percentage of the company. These programs are goal oriented and typically give a startup a fixed start and end date.

Accounts payable cycle: The part of the business operating cycle that begins with the purchase of the raw materials or finished goods and ends with the payment to the supplier.

Accounts receivable cycle: The part of the business operating cycle that begins with the sale and concludes with the collection of the receivable.

Adoption curve: A curve that illustrates the rate at which people accept and use a new technology or product. There are five categories: innovators, early adopters, early majority, late majority, and laggards.

Anglo-Saxon economic system: Largely practised in English-speaking countries such as the United Kingdom and the United States. It is a capitalist macroeconomic model in which levels of regulation and taxes are low. In addition, Anglo-Saxon economies generally are more "liberal" and free-market oriented than other capitalist economies in the world. Another major difference between Anglo-Saxon and non-Anglo-Saxon countries is the legal system, which is based on case law rather than civil code law.

Articles: Amendments to a corporation's charter.

Asset-based valuation: A method to value a company that considers the fair market value of fixed assets and equipment, and inventory. It is most appropriate for asset-intensive businesses such as retail and manufacturing companies.

Assets: All the things the company has that are expected to generate value over time—things like inventory, buildings, and equipment; accounts receivable (money that your customers still owe you); and cash.

Augmented product: The set of attributed related to a core product.

Average revenue per user (ARPU): How much extra a company makes with the addition of each new customer.

Back of the napkin diagram (BoND): Visually explaining a business idea on a sheet of paper without fine detail. The name itself comes from the notion of being able to explain a business idea's key concepts on a napkin, quickly and easily through the use of pictures.

Balance sheet: Summary statement of a company's financial position at a given point in time. It summarizes the accounting value of the assets, liabilities, shareholders' equity. Assets = Liabilities + Shareholder Equity. *(See pro forma financials.)*

Best-efforts offering: The underwriter makes its best efforts to sell as much as it can of the shares at the offering price. Hence, unlike a firm commitment offering, the company offering its shares is not guaranteed a definite amount of money by the underwriter.

Bootstrapping: Building a business out of nothing, with minimal outside capital.

Brand awareness: The customer's ability to recognize and recall the brand when provided a cue.

Brand equity: The effect of brand awareness and brand image on customer response to the brand.

Brand image: The way customers perceive a company's brand.

Bridge financing: Short-term finance that is expected to be repaid relatively quickly. It usually bridges a short-term financing need. For example, it provides cash needed before an expected stock flotation.

Build-up method: Identifying all the possible revenue sources of the business and then estimating how much of each type of revenue the company can generate during a given period of time.

Business acumen: Part of the talent triangle that relates to having the skills, knowledge, and experience to make important business decisions.

Business angel: An individual who invests in private companies. The term is sometimes reserved for sophisticated angel investors who invest sizable sums in private companies. *(See informal investor.)*

Business plan: A document prepared by entrepreneurs, possibly in conjunction with their professional advisors, detailing the past, present, and intended future of the company. It contains a thorough analysis of the managerial, physical, labour, product, and financial resources of the company, plus the background of the company, its previous trading record, and its market position. The business plan contains detailed profit, balance sheet, and cash flow projections for two years ahead, and less detailed information for the following three years. The business plan crystallizes and focuses the management team's ideas. It explains their strategies, sets objectives, and is used to monitor their subsequent performance.

Buying consultants: Salespeople who are extremely skillful at consultative selling who help the customer through their buying process, helping ensure that the buyer makes a wise decision, even if it's to purchase a competitor's offering.

Capital gain: The amount by which the selling price of an asset (e.g., common shares) exceeds the seller's initial purchase price.

Cash conversion cycle (CCC): The gap between the time when a company has to pay suppliers and the time when it receives payment from customers.

Cash cycle: The amount of time that passes between cash outlays and cash inflows during the company's sales process. It also shows the relationship between three key measures: days in payables, days in inventory, and days sales are outstanding.

Cash flow: The difference between the company's cash receipts and its cash payments in a given period.

Certification mark: A mark that is issued through the Canadian Intellectual Property Office that is meant to be used by the organization that holds it to distinguish wares or services that meet a defined standard.

Channel conflict: Situations where differing objectives and turf overlap among the various channel partners, leading to true disharmony in the distribution channel.

Channel coverage: How many channels a company uses to distribute its product. It can be intensive (multiple channels), selective (a subset of channels), or exclusive (one channel).

Channel power: The degree of power each distribution channel member has. It is an important concept in distribution strategy because often the channel member with the most power will prevail.

Chattel mortgage: A loan secured by specific assets.

Churning: The creation of new enterprises and the destruction of obsolete ones.

Cold call: Reaching out via phone or email to a customer contact with whom the salesperson has no prior relationship and no reference to a trusted intermediary; this is the least effective method of getting an appointment.

Collateral: An asset pledged as security for a loan.

Common law mark: A pre-existing mark that can be protected through a passing off action, even if it is not a registered trademark in Canada.

Common-sized income statement: Converting the income statement into percentages with total revenue equalling 100% and all other lines a percentage of total revenue.

Communications mix: The mixture of advertising, sales promotion, public relations, personal selling, and direct marketing that go into conveying messages about the company's products and services as well as the company itself to consumers.

Comparable method: Using existing industry or company financials to forecast your own venture's financials.

Compensating balance: A bank requires a customer to maintain a certain level of demand deposits that do not bear interest. The interest forgone by the customer on the compensating balance recompenses the bank for services provided, credit lines, and loans.

Confidential information: Information that is vital to a company's success, such as trade secrets.

Consultative selling: A concept and philosophy widely espoused in books on the topic of selling where the seller helps prospective customers determine the right product or service to fit their needs and wants; the customers' needs are the basis of the sales dialogue, not product or service attributes.

Consumer promotions: Sales promotions offered directly to end users to create end-user demand and support a pull strategy.

Convertible debt: A loan that can be exchanged for equity.

Copyright: Protect authors' and creators' original creations, including literary, musical, artistic, software, and other intellectual works.

Core product: The essential good or service, without any extras.

Corporate opportunity: A doctrine that prohibits an officer or director of a company, a partner in a partnership, or a person in a similar position from identifying a business opportunity that would be valuable to her or his business and using that information for her or his own benefit or the benefit of a competitor.

Corporation: A business form that is an entity legally separate from its owners. Its important features include limited liability, easy transfer of ownership, and unlimited life.

Cost model: The component of a firm's business model that identifies how it is spending its resources to make money.

Cost of client acquisition (CoCA): The cost for a business to get a single revenue-generating customer.

Cost of goods sold (COGS): The direct cost of the product sold. For a retail business, the cost of all goods sold in a given period equals the inventory at the beginning of the period plus the cost of goods purchased during that period minus the inventory at the end of the period.

Cost-plus pricing: A pricing strategy where firms look at their cost to produce a unit of the product and then add a set percentage on top of that cost to arrive at the price.

Covenant: A restriction on a borrower imposed by a lender. For example, it could be a requirement placed on a company to achieve and maintain specified targets such as levels of cash flow, balance sheet ratios, or specified capital expenditure levels in order to retain financing facilities.

Crowdfunding: Using social media to raise small amounts of capital from a large number of individuals to finance a business venture.

Customer relationship management (CRM): Systems designed to compile and manage data about customers.

Customer value proposition (CVP): The difference between total customer benefits and total customer costs, which are both monetary and nonmonetary. Also known as a positioning statement.

Debt: A source of financing where you don't have to give up any ownership of the business, but you do have to pay current interest and eventually repay the principal you borrowed.

Differentiators: Key success factors that can set players apart from others.

Direct competition: The type of competition that comes from companies that have a similar product offering, are in the same market, and target the same users.

Disintermediation: Cutting intermediaries out of traditional distribution channels by selling directly to customers.

Domain knowledge: Part of the talent triangle that relates to understanding the industry's key value motivators, being aware of any domain impediments, ensuring the supply chain is not interrupted, and focusing on the necessary relationships within the industry to make the desired sales.

Double dipping: A company's ability to generate multiple revenue streams from one product: Build once, sell twice, and make money three times.

Duty of loyalty: The duty that high-level employees (officers, directors, partners, etc.) typically have to reveal to the business all matters that may be related to the business, including if they are planning on leaving the organization to start a new venture. In addition, it states that employees will not knowingly take action designed to harm their current employer's business.

Earnings capitalization valuation: Values a company by capitalizing its earnings. Company value = Net income/Capitalization rate.

Earn-out: A common contract provision when a company is sold or acquired. The founders will earn a portion of the sales price over time based upon continuing performance of the new venture.

Elasticity of demand: The percentage change in the quantity of a good demanded divided by the percentage change in the price of that good. When the elasticity is greater than 1, the demand is said to be elastic, and when it is less than 1, it is inelastic. In the short term, the demand for nonessential goods (e.g., airline travel) is usually elastic, and the demand for essentials (e.g., electricity) is usually inelastic.

Enterprising nonprofits: Firms that offer products or services to generate revenue, but unlike traditional ventures this income is put to use to address a social problem rather than returned to investors or the owners.

Entrepreneur: Someone who perceives an opportunity and creates an organization to pursue it.

Entrepreneurial process: A process that includes all the functions, activities, and actions that are part of perceiving opportunities and creating organizations to pursue them.

Environmental analysis: The process of identifying and assessing the factors and trends in the external context that may drive decision making by customers (including buying decisions).

Equity: A source of financing where you have to give up some of the ownership of the business to get it, but you may never have to repay it or even pay a dividend.

Equity crowdfunding: A startup's ability to raise seed money through crowd investing. This is currently illegal in Canada.

Establishing common ground: When a salesperson tries to develop a relationship with a potential customer upon initial contact.

Exclusive distribution: A distribution strategy where products are sold in only one or very few locations. Often used for luxury goods.

Factoring: A means of enhancing the cash flow of a business. A factoring company pays a certain proportion of the value of the firm's trade debts to the firm and then receives the cash as the trade debtors settle their accounts. Invoice discounting is a similar procedure.

Feedback loop: A method of pivoting and improving on a product or service once feedback from the prospective market has been received. It is a key factor in Eric Ries's lean startup methodology.

Field warehousing: A lien against inventory where the lender physically separates and guards the pledged inventory right on the borrower's premises.

Finder: A person or firm that attempts to raise funding for a private company.

Firm commitment offering: The underwriter guarantees to raise a certain amount of money for the company and other selling shareholders at the IPO.

First-stage financing: Financing to initiate full manufacturing and sales.

Five Cs of credit: The five crucial elements for obtaining credit are character (borrower's integrity), capacity (sufficient cash flow to service the debt), capital (borrower's net worth), collateral (assets to secure the debt), and conditions (of the borrowing company, its industry, and the general economy).

Floating lien: A general lien against a group of assets, such as accounts receivable or inventory, without the assets being specifically identified.

Founder shares: Shares that the founders issue to themselves in exchange for their "sweat equity," meaning that the founders buy their shares for a nominal amount of cash. Founder shares are typically issued prior to the first round of financing.

Four Fs: Founders, family, friends, and foolhardy persons who invest in a person's private business, generally a startup. *(See informal investor.)*

Four Ps: The essential elements of marketing: product, price, place (distribution), and promotion (communication).

Free cash flow: Cash flow in excess of that required to fund all projects that have a positive net present value when discounted at the relevant cost of capital. Conflicts of interest between shareholders and managers may arise when the organization generates free cash flow. Shareholders may desire higher dividends, but managers may wish to invest in projects providing a return below the cost of capital.

Frequency: The number of times a member of your target market is exposed to an ad campaign during a specific time period.

Gatekeeper: An individual who stands between the seller and the person with whom the seller would like an appointment; may be an administrative assistant, an appointments secretary, or a lower-level employee.

Gazelle: A company with an annual growth rate of 20% or more, as measured in sales revenue.

Global patent strategy: A strategy where inventors obtain patents for their ideas in several countries to protect the originality of their idea and to obtain monopoly market presence in multiple countries.

Great events theory: A theory of leadership that states a crisis brings out the leadership qualities in a person who is not or was not previously considered a leader.

Guerilla marketing: Unique, low-cost marketing methods to capture attention in a crowded marketplace.

Harvest: The realization of the value of an investment.

High-growth firm: A firm whose business generates significant positive cash flows or earnings, which increases at significantly faster rates than the overall economy.

Hybrid ventures: Firms that pursue social and economic goals equally.

Income statement: A summary of a company's revenues, expenses, and profits over a specified period of time. *(See pro forma financials.)*

Incubator: A resource for startups that attempts to improve the chance for success by providing office space, professional services, and business advice for a monthly fee.

Indirect competition: The type of competition that comes from companies that are in the same space, target the same users, but offer a different product or service.

Industrial design: A registration that will protect exclusive aesthetic use of artistic works in connection with mass-produced useful articles.

Industry code: The behaviour required from a company participating in the value chain (or network) to assure long-term success. The code must be followed to achieve profitability and success.

Informal investor: An individual who puts money into a private company—usually a startup or a small business. Informal investments range from micro loans from family members to sizable equity purchases by sophisticated business angels.

Initial public offering (IPO): The process by which a company raises money and gets listed on a stock market.

Integrated marketing communications: The integration and coordination of all of the various methods and tools a company will use in its communications mix to market a product or service.

Intellectual property (IP): Knowledge that a company possesses and considers proprietary. IP can be protected through patents, trademarks, etc.

Intensive distribution: A distribution strategy where products are sold in multiple locations. Often used for consumer goods and other fast-moving products.

Internal locus of control: Individuals with an internal locus of control see themselves as responsible for the outcomes of their own actions. These individuals often believe that they control their destiny.

Internal rate of return (IRR): The discount rate that equates the present value of the future net cash flows from an investment with the project's cash outflows. It is a means of expressing the percentage rate of return projected on a proposed investment. For an investment in a company, the calculation takes account of cash invested, cash receipts from dividend payments and redemptions, percentage of equity held, expected date of payments, realization of the investment and capitalization at that point, and possible further financing requirements. The calculation will frequently be quoted in a range depending on sensitivity analysis.

Inventory: Finished goods, work in process of manufacture, and raw materials owned by a company.

Inventory cycle: The part of the business operating cycle that begins with the purchase of the raw materials, includes the work-in-process period, and ends with the sale of the finished goods.

Key person insurance: Additional security provided to financial backers of a company through the purchase of insurance on the lives of key managers who are seen as crucial to the future of the company. Should one or more of those key executives die prematurely, the financial backers would receive the insurance payment.

Key success factors (KSFs): The attributes that customers use to distinguish between competing products or services. KSFs go beyond just product attributes, and may include brand and other intangibles.

Lead underwriter: The head of a syndicate of financial firms that are sponsoring an initial public offering of securities or a secondary offering of securities.

Liabilities: All the money the company expects to pay eventually. These include accounts payable (money the company owes its suppliers), debt, and unpaid taxes.

Line of credit (with a bank): An arrangement between a bank and a customer specifying the maximum amount of unsecured debt the customer can owe the bank at a given point in time.

Liquidation value (of a company): The market value of the assets minus the liabilities that must be paid of a company that is liquidating.

Lockup period: An interval during which an investment may not be sold. In the case of an IPO, employees may not sell their shares for a period of time determined by the underwriter and usually lasting 180 days.

Macro business system: The study of an entire industry with all the relevant participants represented in the value-added stream, both upstream and downstream, from the point of view of any particular participant in the value chain.

Market tests: Tests entrepreneurs need to complete to identify interesting ideas and see whether they are viable opportunities.

Market-comparable valuation: The value of a private company based on the valuation of similar public companies.

Marketing: The activity, set of institutions, and processes for creating, communicating, delivering, and exchanging offerings that have value for customers, clients, partners, and society at large.

Marketing research: The collection and analysis of any reliable information that improves managerial decisions.

Microfinancing: Tiny loans to entrepreneurs too poor to qualify for traditional bank loans. In developing countries especially, microcredit enables very poor people to engage in self-employment projects that generate income.

Minimum viable product (MVP): The minimum feature set a customer is willing to pay for. It is a bare-bones version of the final product and does not contain all the bells and whistles that will aesthetically and functionally enhance the product when it officially goes to market.

Modified book value: Valuation of a business in which all assets and liabilities (including off-balance-sheet, intangible, and contingent) are adjusted to their fair market values.

Noncompetition agreement: A contract that extends the duty of employees not to compete with the company that employs them (by working for the competition) beyond the term of the employee's employment.

Nonprofit entity: Organizations that are incorporated in a particular manner and do not have shares. Unlike for-profit corporations, these organizations do not intend to financially benefit their members, directors, or officers.

Objections: Reservations or concerns that buyers have to a seller's value proposition.

Operational knowledge: Part of the talent triangle that refers to focusing on logistics, infrastructure, and product development. Someone with operational knowledge makes day-to-day decisions that implement and execute the overall business plan.

Opportunity: An idea that has commercial viability and that provides the entrepreneur and company with the potential to earn attractive margins and a return on their investment.

Option pool: Equity that is set aside for future distribution. Options give the holder the right to buy a share in the company at a below-market rate.

Partnership: Legal form of a business in which two or more persons are co-owners, sharing profits and losses.

Patent: Granted by the government to protect unique devices (or combinations of components integrated into a device) and processes.

Penetration pricing: Pricing your product at a relatively lower price to gain high market share, but with lower margins.

Phantom shares: Even though these are called "shares," these are not really issued equity but a cash bonus paid to employees if the share price appreciates over a set period of time.

Pledging: The use of a company's accounts receivable as security (collateral) for a short-term loan.

Positioning: A company's offering on certain product attributes—the ones customers

care about most—relative to competitive offerings.

Post-money valuation: The value of a company immediately after a round of additional money is invested.

Preference shares: A class of shares that incorporate the right to a fixed dividend and usually a prior claim on assets, in preference to ordinary shares, in the event of a liquidation. Cumulative preference shares provide an entitlement to a cumulative dividend if, in any year, the preference dividend is unpaid because of insufficient profits being earned. Preference shares are usually redeemable at specific dates.

Preliminary prospectus: The initial document published by an underwriter of a new issue of shares to be given to prospective investors. It is understood that the document will be modified significantly before the final prospectus is published; also called a red herring.

Premature scaling: Growth in anticipation of demand, instead of demand-driven growth; that is, spending money on growing (or scaling) a business before you have really determined what customers want and how to reach them.

Pre-money valuation: The value of a company's equity before additional money is invested.

Present value of future cash flows (valuation): Present value is today's value of a future payment or stream of payments discounted at some appropriate compound interest or discount rate; also called time value of money.

Price discrimination: A strategy where different customer segments are charged different prices.

Price points: Product pricing in standardized or fixed points.

Price promotion: Discounts from the base price for a short period to attain specific goals such as introducing a product to new customers.

Price skimming: The strategy of pricing your product high to generate high margins, but recognizing that you'll gain limited market share because prices are relatively high.

Primary data: Market research collected specifically for a particular purpose through focus groups, surveys, or experiments.

Primary target audience (PTA): A group of potential customers identified by demographic and psychographic data that will be the focus of the company's early marketing and sales efforts.

Prime rate: Short-term interest rate charged by a bank to its largest, most creditworthy customers.

Product life cycle: A stage model of a product's life, including introduction, growth, maturity, and decline; a similar concept to the S-curve life cycle for an industry.

Profit: An accounting concept designed to measure the overall performance of a company. Synonymous with income and earnings.

Pro forma financials: Projected financial statements: income statement, statement of cash flows, and balance sheets. For a startup company, it is usual to produce pro forma statements monthly for the first two years and annually for the next three years.

Proposed mark: A filing that can be made with the Canadian Intellectual Property Office under the Trade-marks Act to protect a mark that a business is planning on registering as a trademark.

Prospecting: The process of identifying and assessing individual potential buyers.

Prospectus: A document giving a description of a securities issue, including a complete statement of the terms of the issue and a description of the issuer, as well as its historical financial statements. Also referred to as an offering circular.

Public relations (PR): A strategic communications tool that consists of publicity and corporate communications.

Public warehousing: A lien against inventory where the lender transfers the pledged inventory to a separate warehouse.

Pull strategy: When a company creates end-user demand to pull a product through the channel through the use of advertising and consumer sales promotions, such as in-store specials.

Push strategy: When a company aims to push a product through the channel using tools such as trade promotions, trade shows, and personal selling to distributors or other channel members.

Qualifiers: Key success factors within an industry that determine if a company is able to participate in the industry at all. All participants in an industry must comply with qualifiers.

Reach: The percentage of a company's target market that is exposed to an ad campaign within a specific period of time.

Red herring: Preliminary prospectus circulated by underwriters to gauge investor interest in a planned offering. A legend in red ink on its cover indicates that the registration has not yet become effective and is still under review.

Replacement value: Valuation of a company based on what it would cost to replace all of its current assets. It is appropriate when someone is considering whether to set up a similar business from scratch or to buy an existing business.

Restricted shares: A form of equity that can be given to employees. These are actual shares, rather than the option to buy shares, that are vested over time and have restrictions placed on their disposition by the recipient.

Restrictive covenants: Contractual obligations that limit a person's ability to leave a company and go work for or start up a competitor.

Resulting experience: The events that the customer experiences as a result of using and interacting with the supplying firm's products, services, and actions.

Revenue drivers: Elements within a business model that can be influenced to increase revenue, such as price, quantity purchased, awareness of product, availability, and so forth.

Revenue model: The component of a firm's business model that breaks down all sources of revenue that the business will generate, predicting what the financial outcome of the company will be based on many variables and assumptions. There are four types of revenue models: recurring revenue, transactional revenue, project revenue, and services revenue.

Sales force promotions: Sales promotions designed to motivate and reward the company's own sales force or its distributors' sales forces.

Salesperson: A team member who has the responsibility of helping the buyer through the buying process—ideally professionally, efficiently, and painlessly.

Scalability: A company's ability to generate exponential revenue growth while maintaining a stagnant fixed and variable cost.

S-curve: A model of new market product adoption. It illustrates market emergence, rapid growth, stability, and decline.

Secondary data: Market research that is gathered from already published sources, like an industry association study or census report.

Secondary target audience (STA): A group of potential customers identified by demographic and psychographic data that will be a secondary or alternative focus of the company's early marketing and sales efforts.

Second-stage financing: Financing to fuel the growth of an early stage company.

Seed-stage company: A company that doesn't have much more than a concept.

Segment: A group of customers defined by certain common bases or characteristics that may be demographic, psychographic (commonly called lifestyle characteristics), or behavioural.

Selective distribution: A distribution strategy where products are sold in specific locations, often limiting selection geographically by establishing a dealer network.

Sensitivity analysis: An examination of how the projected performance of the business varies with changes in the key assumptions on which the forecasts are based.

Share appreciation rights: A form of equity that can be given to employees where the benefits of the rights accrue to employees only if the share price increases (similar to options).

Shareholder equity: The money that shareholders have paid into the company as well as the company's earnings so far.

Social consequence ventures: Firms that have an economic mission but also have a firm commitment to social impact, sometimes at the expense of economic returns.

Social entrepreneur: Someone who develops social innovation through entrepreneurial solutions. A social entrepreneur recognizes a social problem or need, comes up with a solution, and creates an organization to pursue it. Business entrepreneurs typically measure performance by profit and financial return, whereas social entrepreneurs also take into account a positive return to society.

Social model: This term is often applied to the economic systems of nations where there is high welfare protection, including restrictions on employer's rights to hire and fire employees, generous unemployment benefits, and mandated work weeks (e.g., 35-hour maximum in France). The social models are especially strong in France and Germany.

Social purpose ventures: Firms that seek to make profits by addressing an opportunity that has a specific social or environmental aspect to it. Essentially, they are looking for a profitable means of addressing a social issue.

Sole proprietorship: A business form with one owner who is responsible for all the firm's liabilities.

Stakeholders: Those who have a stake in the venture's success, including investors, customers, suppliers, and employees.

Startup company: A company that is already in business and is developing a prototype but has not sold it in significant commercial quantities.

Statement of cash flows: A summary of a company's cash flow over a period of time. (See *pro forma financials*.)

Status quo competition: The competition that comes from the fact that people don't like to change their habits, so the value proposition offered by a new product or service must be strong enough to overcome an individual's current habits. This is the most often overlooked type of competition.

Sweat equity: Equity acquired by the management team at favourable terms reflecting the value to the business of the managers' past and future efforts.

Syndicate: A group of investors that act together when investing in a company.

Talent triangle: Describes the essential management elements that all businesses must have covered to be successful: business acumen, operational knowledge, and domain knowledge.

Targeting: A process marketers use to identify the "right" customers by comparing the defined segments and then selecting the most attractive one.

TEA (necessity): The percentage of the adult population that is trying to start or has started a baby business because all other options for work are either absent or unsatisfactory.

TEA (overall): The percentage of the adult population that is trying to start or has started a baby business to exploit a perceived opportunity.

TEA (total entrepreneurial activity): The percent of the adult population that is participating in a specific type of entrepreneurship.

Term sheet: Summary of the principal conditions for a proposed investment in a company by a venture capital firm or business angels.

Tertiary target audience (TTA): A group of potential customers identified by demographic and psychographic data that will *not* be the focus of the company's early marketing and sales efforts.

Total addressable market (TAM): The size of your total potential customer base; calculated as the size of the customer's pain point multiplied by the quantity of customers experiencing that pain.

Trademarks: Protection obtainable for any word, symbol, or combination thereof that is used on goods to indicate their source.

Trade promotions: Price promotions offered to retailers to induce them to carry your product.

Traditional ventures: The most common type of company; the primary purpose of these firms is economic gain—maximizing revenues and profits by recognizing and capturing opportunities in the market.

Traits theory: A theory of leadership that states people are simply born with innate leadership capabilities.

Transformational leadership theory: A theory of leadership that states individuals choose to become leaders and purposely educate themselves to learn the skills involved with being a leader.

Trial closes: Closing questions that salespeople should be asking throughout the buying process as a way to check whether the buying process is still on track, what issues the buyer still needs to get resolved before moving ahead, and the comfort level of the buyer.

Triple bottom line: Captures the financial profit the organization earns and also the social and environmental benefit it provides society; associated with social entrepreneurship.

Underwriter: An institution engaged in the business of underwriting securities issues.

Valuation (of a company): The market value of a company.

Value added (by investors): Many venture capital firms claim that they add more than money to investee companies. They call it value added, which includes strategic advice on such matters as hiring key employees, marketing, production, control, and financing.

Value proposition: The value of a business's products and services to its customers.

Value selling: A relationship-building process through which a salesperson communicates the potential value of a product or service to prospective customers. The prospective customer returns value to the salesperson by carefully considering the value proposition, engaging with the salesperson in the decision-making process, and ultimately, if the product fits the customer's needs, buying it.

Venture capitalist: A financial institution specializing in the provision of equity and other forms of long-term capital to enterprises, usually to firms with a limited track record but with the expectation of substantial growth. The venture capitalist may provide both funding and varying degrees of managerial and technical expertise. Venture capital has traditionally been associated with startups; however, venture capitalists have increasingly participated in later-stage projects.

Vesting: The time period before shares are owned unconditionally by an employee who is sold shares with the stipulation that he or she must continue to work for the company. If employment terminates before the end of that period, the company has the right to buy back the shares at the same price at which it originally sold them to the employee.

Virtual team: Outside team members who have a vested interest in your success, including professionals you contract for special needs and those who have invested in your business.

INDEX